Wardens' Accounts and Court Minute Books of the Goldsmiths' Mistery of London

1334–1446

The goldsmiths of London had formed an organised guild, or mistery (in the medieval sense of 'craft' or 'profession') by the twelfth century. Granted their first royal charter in 1327 by Edward III, they are one of the twelve great livery companies, and still oversee the work of goldsmiths, silversmiths and jewellers. Published here for the first time are their two earliest record books, presented in the original languages, French (Anglo-Norman), English and Latin, with a facing-page translation into modern English. From these full records valuable and lively detail emerges: the working practices of goldsmiths and silversmiths, the financial accounts of the wardens, apprentices admitted, participation in civic events such as pageants, and records of offences (both professional and personal) brought before the disciplinary court. The edition is accompanied by a full introduction, a bibliography, a subject and a complete name index.

Lisa Jefferson, M.A., D.Phil., F.S.A., is a medievalist who works both in Oxford and in France.

Wardens' Accounts and Court Minute Books of the Goldsmiths' Mistery of London 1334–1446

edited by
Lisa Jefferson

THE BOYDELL PRESS

First published 2003
The Boydell Press, Woodbridge

ISBN 0 85115 890 0

The Boydell Press is an imprint of Boydell & Brewer Ltd
PO Box 9, Woodbridge, Suffolk IP12 3DF, UK
and of Boydell & Brewer Inc.
PO Box 41026, Rochester, NY 14604–4126, USA
website: www.boydell.co.uk

A catalogue record for this book is available
from the British Library

Library of Congress Cataloging-in-Publication Data
Worshipful Company of Goldsmiths.
Wardens' accounts and court minute books of the Goldsmiths' mistery of London, 1334–1446 / edited by Lisa Jefferson.
p. cm.
English, French, and Latin with parallel translation in modern English.
Includes bibliographical references and index.
ISBN 0–85115–890–0 (alk. paper)
1. Worshipful Company of Goldsmiths – History – Sources. 2. Guilds – England – London – History – Sources. 3. Goldsmiths – England – London – History – Sources. I. Jefferson, Lisa. II. Title.
HD6461.G72 L69 2002
338.6′32–dc21 2002071056

This publication is printed on acid-free paper

Typeset by Joshua Associates Ltd, Oxford
Printed in Great Britain by
St Edmundsbury Press Ltd, Bury St Edmunds, Suffolk

Contents

Foreword

The first two volumes of the Wardens' Accounts and Court Minute books held by the Goldsmiths' Company of London contain a wealth of information and have already been used by historians but have never been published in full before now.

The Goldsmiths' Company has been particularly fortunate that Dr Lisa Jefferson has been able to bring her expertise to the task of editing these records. Her edition presents the records in the original languages in which they were written – Anglo-Norman, Medieval Latin and Middle English – and accompanies the text with a facing-page translation into modern English. For the first time both the contents of these records and the high intrinsic interest and import of the language itself are revealed in full.

The Goldsmiths' Company is delighted to welcome this publication and is glad to have been able to support Dr Jefferson's work which will be of immense value to scholars for years to come.

R. P. T. Came
Prime Warden
May 2003

Acknowledgements

My work on these manuscripts started while I was engaged, under the auspices of the MHRA and the British Academy, on research for the *Anglo-Norman Dictionary*, and it then continued with the full support and help of many others. My first thanks must go to the Wardens and Commonalty of the Mystery of Goldsmiths of the City of London, who gave permission for this work to be undertaken and for it to be published. Mr David Beasley, Librarian of the Goldsmiths' Company, has been an unfailing source of advice, help and encouragement, and I thank both him and also his former assistant, Miss Victoria Lane, and his secretary, Mrs Raakhee Zaman, for the way they have made every visit to the library an enjoyment and a pleasure. For linguistic advice and help I am indebted to Dr Tony Hunt, St Peter's College, Oxford, Dr David Howlett, Editor of the *Dictionary of Medieval Latin from British Sources*, and his assistant editor, Mr Theodore Christchev, and Professor Helen Cooper, University College, Oxford, all of whom have most generously spared time to read through relevant sections of the text. For specialist advice on a number of matters I thank most warmly Miss Lorna Walker, St Andrew's University, whose earlier work on the history of the Goldsmiths' Company has been of invaluable assistance to me and who has always been willing to take time and delve into her deep knowledge of the Company during the Middle Ages in order to help answer my queries. For specialist advice on goldsmiths' work and jewellery my warmest thanks go to Mr John Cherry, Keeper of Medieval and Later Antiquities, British Museum, who has answered my numerous enquiries always with detailed and highly interesting information and comments; and I thank also his colleague, Dr B.J. Cook, Curator of Medieval and Early Modern Coinage at the British Museum, for his advice and help on matters relating to gold and silver and the coinage. My thanks go also to Mrs Philippa Glanville, Director of Waddesdon Manor, for her most helpful information and advice about silver and jewellery. I thank also most warmly Dr Paul Brand, All Souls College, Oxford, who has been of great help to me over a number of medieval legal queries; Dr Christopher Wilson, University College, London, who has helped me with a number of queries relating to Old St Paul's; and Professor Richard Britnell for his support and advice. Mrs Madeline Barber most generously gave time to proofread the whole text, and to her I extend my warmest thanks for all that her eagle eye spotted. All remaining errors are of course my responsibility alone. And lastly, one to whom my thanks go firstly, my husband Giles, for all his constant and continuing advice, support, and encouragement.

Abbreviations

AND	*Anglo Norman Dictionary*, ed. W. Rothwell *et al.* (London: MHRA, 1977–92)
BIHR	Bulletin of the Institute of Historical Research
CCR	*Calendar of the Close Rolls preserved in the Public Record Office*, (London, 1902–63)
CLB	*Calendar of the Letter Books preserved among the Archives of the Corporation of the City of London, A–H*, ed. R.R. Sharpe (London, 1899–1907)
CPMR	*Calendar of the Plea and Memoranda Rolls preserved among the Archives of the Corporation of the City of London at the Guildhall.* I: 1323–1364; II: 1364–81; III: 1381–1412; IV: 1413–37, ed. A.H. Thomas (London, 1926–43); vol. V: 1437–57 and Vol. VI: 1458–82, ed. P.E. Jones (London, 1954–61)
CPR	*Calendar of the Patent Rolls preserved in the Public Record Office* (London, 1901–86)
DEAF	Dictionnaire étymologique de l'ancien français, ed. Kurt Baldinger *et al.* (Tübingen, 1971–)
DMLBS	*Dictionary of Medieval Latin from British Sources*, ed. R.E. Latham *et al.* (Oxford, 1975–)
EHR	*English Historical Review*
FEW	W. von Wartburg, *Französisches Etymologisches Wörterbuch* (Bonn, Leipzig: Klopp, 1928–)
HMSO	Her Majesty's Stationery Office
MED	*Middle English Dictionary*, ed. H. Kurath *et al.* (Ann Arbor: University of Michigan Press, 1956–)
OED	*Oxford English Dictionary*, 2nd edn, ed. J.A. Simpson and E.S.C. Weiner (Oxford, 1989)
PMLA	*Publications of the Modern Language Association of America*
PRO	Public Record Office, Kew, London
MHRA	The Modern Humanities Research Association
TL	Tobler-Lommatzsch, *Altfranzösisches Wörterbuch* (Berlin, 1925–36)

Introduction

THE GOLDSMITHS' MISTERY

The goldsmiths of London had formed themselves into an organised guild or mistery[1] by the twelfth century but only achieved legal status as an official corporate body in 1327 when Edward III granted them their first royal charter. In 1339 they acquired a site on which they then built their communal Hall. The Company is still in existence today, its Hall still stands on the same site in the City of London. It is one of the twelve great livery companies[2] and, unlike many of these, it still operates fully as a working company controlling, overseeing, regulating and encouraging the work of goldsmiths, silversmiths and jewellers, and playing its role in the maintenance of standards through the work of the Assay Office[3] and the annual Trial of the Pyx.[4] Its early history during the Middle Ages has already been researched and written about by T.F. Reddaway and Lorna E.M. Walker,[5] the subsequent centuries have been dealt with in a number of publications,[6] and the history of its activities and work during the twentieth century has recently been splendidly written up by Peter Jenkins.[7]

The intrinsic fascination of gold as well as its central importance to any society's economy and stability because of its link to the coinage have ensured both the survival of the Company and the constant interest in the work it does. Some clear distinctions can be made and, although there is some overlap, a history of the Company is not at all the same as a history of goldsmithry. This is very much true of the surviving medieval records of the Company which concern us here. They contain ordinances relating to the manufacture of gold

1 The word 'mistery' means 'trade' or 'craft' or 'art' or 'profession' and is derived from the Latin word 'ministerium' and is not the same as, though it can be confused with, the word 'mystery' derived from the Latin 'mysterium', Greek 'musterion', 'a secret thing or ceremony'. The spellings with 'i' and 'y' are interchangeable, but I have chosen, in line with many other historians, to use the spelling 'mistery' to denote the meaning of a medieval craft or craft company. See the *OED* and also *The Oxford Dictionary of English Etymology*, ed. C.T. Onions (Oxford, 1966).

2 These have an hierarchic ordering dating in definitive form from 1515, and the Goldsmiths rank fifth. See e.g. J.K. Melling, *Discovering London's Guilds and Liveries*, 5th edn. (Princes Risborough, 1995), p. 25.

3 See J.S. Forbes, *Hallmark: A History of the London Assay Office* (London, 1999).

4 See Forbes, *Hallmark*, pp. 15–16, 53–54, *et passim* (*via* Index).

5 *The Early History of the Goldsmiths' Company, 1327–1509* (London, 1975).

6 See e.g. W. Herbert, *The History of the Twelve Great Livery Companies of London*, 2 vols (London, 1834–36), vol. II; Ambrose Heal, *The London Goldsmiths 1200–1800* (London, 1935); W.S. Prideaux, *Memorials of the Goldsmiths' Company, being gleanings from their records between the years 1335 and 1815*, 2 vols (London, printed for private circulation, 1896); Arthur G. Grimwade, *London Goldsmiths 1697–1837* (London, 1976).

7 *Unravelling the Mystery: The Story of the Goldsmiths' Company in the Twentieth Century*, 2 vols (London, 2000).

and silver jewellery but nothing concerning styles and fashions, and individual pieces of work are only mentioned if something was wrong with them, if the goldsmith who made them was brought before the wardens' court to be charged with false or deceitful workmanship and to be fined for this, and if the record was kept.

Reddaway and Walker used the Goldsmiths' early records as a prime source for their history, but they used many other sources also and their quotations from the records were of necessity both selective and presented in modern English translation only. The present edition therefore both complements and adds to their history, but in no way supplants it. For all background history of the goldsmiths and their mistery in the Middle Ages one cannot do better than to start with Reddaway and Walker's book, but if one wishes to delve deeper and study any aspect in greater detail, then the present edition will provide a very valuable source.

Among a host of other, sometimes important, sometimes minor but always fascinating details, very full information is found here about the rules and regulations governing the organisation and running of the mistery, its ordinances as laid down at various times during this period. The earliest date from 1271, there is a complete copy of the 1327 charter which includes a number of ordinances, and then a very large number of individual ordinances recorded in the register books at the time these were enacted, often with some indication of why a certain ruling was made, what abuse it may have been intended to correct.

Information is recorded about the income of the mistery and how this was spent: income was derived from fees, from fines, from gifts and bequests and later from property; the company as a body spent money on their Hall, on their annual feast, on religious and charitable purposes, on legal fees and on salaries to company officials such as the beadle and to priests and chaplains. Not all such information is recorded unfortunately, and large gaps in our knowledge of the company's income and expenditure exist, but what we do learn builds up into a colourful and fairly full picture. Regular expenditures can be followed, such as that of providing candles to be burnt in a number of churches and chapels, and occasionally extremely detailed infomation is provided so that, for instance, one can relate that 405 bags of lime and 4000 tiles were used in 1382–83 for building works on the Hall, and that a plasterer at this date could charge 7d. per day for his labour (A + a, p. 60).

Full lists are given each year of apprentices admitted, the fees they paid, the names of their masters, and for many of these one can trace a career history; many others, for whatever reason, disappear from the records after the initial mention, and we do not know, except in a few cases, whether they died, ran away, returned to their home town or took up another trade in London. For those who stayed one can derive from these records information about the length of their apprenticeship, the years spent as a serving-man, how many apprentices they in turn took on during their years as a master craftsman, offices held such as renter and warden, any troubles they may have got into, as also any gifts or honours they may have bestowed.

The records of the cases heard in the wardens' court provide some of the most immediately accessible and fascinating information here. Some types of offence are frequent and regularly occur, such as fines for objects made of substandard silver, fines for allowing apprentices to buy out their terms of apprenticeship, or fines for quarrelling and brawling. But other cases are truly *sui generis* and often highly amusing. The three goldsmiths, for instance, who in 1387–88 got together with a pedlar and a Carmelite friar to make and sell objects of fake gold and silver and ended up in prison, while the wardens were left with having to pay compensation out of the company's funds to some of those who had been deceived (A + a, p. 67). Or Walter Prata, who among his numerous crimes 'countr*e*feted the keye of his maystres count*our* chaumbr*e* & of his cheste, of which he confessed hym that his entent was to have take cuppes of gold & of selver gylt & gon awey in to Flaundres w*ith* John Sasse, Flemyng' (A + b, p. 42). Or John Richard, the apprentice of John Hilles, whose threatening words are reported: 'Come on now, for it is hy tyme & I have ordeyned for the, and as I mote be saved thou shalt nev*er* come in to thi chambre' (A + a, p. 140). Or John Trivilias who had been working under the nose of the Prior of St Bartholomew's but unbeknownst to him, and when caught by accident and found to be making objects of latten and copper disguised as silver, evaded the coming punishment by running away: 'while þ*at* þ*is* was avoynge þ*e* seide fals harlot stale awey owt of þe place & ellis he hadde be set in þe stokkis' (A + a, p. 165). Of great interest also when following the fines and punishments imposed for more standard offences is how lenient the wardens could often be, how they could commute or reduce fines, or use sentences that would only come into effect in the case of re-offence, and how imaginative they could be upon occasion.

Other records found here concern the mistery's participation in official events of the City of London: the pageants for instance to celebrate the coronation of Richard II in 1377, to welcome his wife Anne of Bohemia in 1382, and later the welcoming processions to greet Margaret of Anjou, Henry VI's queen, in 1445. Warfare took its toll also, and we hear of the company contributing to the costs of the siege of Calais in 1436. The annual procession of the Mayor riding with the sheriffs and accompanied by men from the various crafts is occasionally mentioned, and we hear too of the Mayor's involvement in some cases of bringing aberrant goldsmiths to book. However, the absence of certain civic matters in the records is also noteworthy, and comparison with other surviving records of the livery companies allows one to see what may be missing. We know, for instance, from other sources, that the Mayor's procession each year was normally accompanied by men from each of the misteries, and that the costs of this could be quite high and were often borne out of the communal funds. The Mercers' accounts regularly show expenses for this event, usually listed as the costs of the livery hoods worn and payments to minstrels, and in 1398–99 for instance these amounted to 33s. 6d. The Merchant Taylors' fifteenth-century accounts regularly list an amount paid for boat-hire to Westminster on these occasions. Only occasional mentions of this annual event are found in the Goldsmiths' accounts. Again, it is known that an obit for Henry V was celebrated each year throughout his son's reign, and that the misteries were officially represented on these anniversaries. Both the Grocers and the Mercers list annual expenses for this, but no mentions occur in the Goldsmiths' records. We should not assume that they did not take part, but rather note that, firstly, these records are not full financial accounts (see below, p. xviii), and secondly that it may be that, at least in some cases, the individuals involved paid their own expenses rather than claiming them from the company.

Many other perhaps unexpected and surprising details can be found here, such as descriptions of the musical instruments belonging to the mistery (e.g. A + a, p. 123), lists of how many altar-cloths they possessed (e.g. A + b, p. 29), or the full document concerning building works at St Paul's precinct paid for by John Hiltoft's bequest (A + a, p. 56). When so many of the records of medieval London have been lost, and so few of the present livery companies hold any records at all going back to the fourteenth century, we must be quite enormously grateful to the medieval goldsmiths who kept these records and to the succeeding generations who have preserved them.

THE MANUSCRIPTS

An unusual point about the manuscripts used for this edition is that the purchase of each one of them is recorded within the manuscripts themselves. The earliest, MS 1518 (Wardens' Accounts and Court Minute Book A + a), was bought in 1358 for 13s. 4d.

> Item, i *gra*unt pap*er*e achaté p*ar* les avantditz iii gardeyns p*ur* regist*r*er totes man*er*es remembrances q*e* sount ou s*er*rount faitez p*ar* la compaignie du dit orfev*er*ie, dount les costages du dit pap*er*e amont – xiii s. iiii d.[8]

For their money the wardens acquired 90 folios of large format paper, 398 x 275mm, which now has foliation in the lower right-hand corners, perhaps done in the sixteenth century, and modern pagination in the centre top of each page (this has been followed in references, to keep in line with other publications, as it is the system used by e.g. Reddaway and Walker); a few quire signatures appear: 'A 1 – A 12, B 1 – B 10, C 1 – C 7, D 1 – D 9, E 1 – E 7, F 1', after which the system stops. The watermark, the same throughout, consists of two circles or large letter 'O's one above the other with the staff of a cross piercing them and the cross above, this sometimes being upside down. Damage from damp, worm, tearing and neglect in general has occurred over the course of years, especially to the early and the later leaves, and the back pages in particular are affected by a number of wormholes. The first leaf has been extensively repaired and tipped on to a modern backing paper, 398 × 280mm, as are also ff. 35, 49, and 50; f. 65, which had clearly been very faded, has been treated with some chemical rendering the whole centre of the page dark brown. An occasional scribble is found on a few pages, and pp. 101, 132, 142 have extensive scribblings, both words and draft sums of money. The sheets are written in a series of different hands, each being that of the then clerk to the Company. Brown ink is usual, but some pages are written in black ink. The text is quite often written out in two columns, especially in the records of the earlier years, but page layout is very variable throughout and was evidently dependent upon subject matter. Most hands are neat and tidy, but there are occasional erasures and emendations, and sometimes a note has been added later (e.g. that a certain fine has been paid). Marginal titles in contemporary hands quite often appear (e.g. each man's name in a series of misconduct cases), and there has been some

[8] 'Item, a large paper register bought by the aforesaid three wardens in order to record all manner of matters worthy of memory that have been or shall be done by the company of the said Goldsmiths' Mistery, of which the costs of the said register amount to – 13s. 4d.'

annotation in Latin, with Latin titles given to important entries such as the Company's ordinances.[9]

In 1371–72 the need for a new and separate register was felt and this was duly bought, for only 2s. 10d. this time, as this was a much smaller record book (now known as MS 1519 – Wardens' Accounts and Court Minute Book A + b). The purchase is recorded twice, first in the older register:

> Item, lez dites gardeyns acomptent avoir paié *pur* i. novel pap*ier* acheté q*e* currera dez gardeyns en gardeyns *et* q*e* ceste *gra*unt papier s*er*ra mys *pur* i. lygg*er*e, a gyser en une cofr*e* ovesq*e* aultr*es* choses: p*ri*s del novelle papier – ii s. x d.[10]

and then on the first page of the new book:

> It*em*, les dites Gardeyns acomptent avoir acheté ceste novelle papier q*e* currera des Gardeyns en gardeyns, et q*e* l'altre *gra*unt papier s*er*ra gysa*n*t en une cofre ovesq*e* aultr*es* choses p*ur* un remembrauncer; p*ri*s de ceste novelle papier – ii s. x d.[11]

The 53 paper sheets that formed this record book are smaller and have a watermark of a large heart from which an arrow issues; the sheets have now been separated and each is tipped on to modern paper of the same size as that of MS 1518; this now means that the size of the fourteenth-century paper leaves varies slightly, from c. 282 × 208 – 290 × 222mm; a foliation system (1–53) runs through in the top right-hand corner and also a pagination system (1–106) placed top central, both being modern additions; some wormholes occur and some discolouration, but these are both minor and the leaves are generally in a better state of preservation than those of MS 1518. The hands are again of a great variety, and the same hands are found here as in the first book (e.g. the first folio here dating from 45 Edw. III can clearly be seen to be that of the same hand for that year in the first accounts book), and for this and the next few years the entries are the same, i.e. these are two separate copies of the accounts. After the first few years however the entries diverge, and although the same hands can often be found at work in both, the function of the two record books has been differentiated. A number of pages remain blank (6, 22, 24, 27–28, 31–32, 35–36, 50, 56, 57, 60, 65, 69–70, 73, 84, 88, 106) and it is clear that the successive scribes also left other pages blank but that these were later used for entries by subsequent writers; the

9 The binding is modern and matches that of other early Court Books held by the Company, and the following description holds for MSS 1519 and 1520 also except that the lettering on each is of course different, as are the additional sheets bound inside the covers. Nineteenth-century binding; 419 x 290 x 40mm; brown leather blind hatched with an overall diamond pattern; covers have three outer blind fillets inside which around all sides is a blind-tooled pattern of interlocking forward and backward facing scrolled Cs; a further inner set of three blind fillets then has a smaller version of this, and on the front cover in the central space gold lettering gives the title: 'Goldsmith's [*sic*] Company / Book A / + / From A.D. 1332 – 1442.'; spine with five bands of sewing; three of the compartments contain a blind-tooled device, and gold lettering in others give the title: 'Warden's [*sic*] Accounts & Court Minutes / 1332 to 1442 / A + a'. Seven modern plain paper flysheets at the front, the last with a cutting from Herbert's account of these books, and eleven plain paper flysheets at the end; glossy brown and pink fake marbled-paper pastedowns with armorial bookplate of Goldsmiths' Hall ('No. 1518: B 39') inside front cover.

10 'Item, the said wardens account for having paid for a new paper register that shall be handed from one set of wardens to the next, and this large register shall be placed as a ledger to be kept in a chest with other things: cost of the new paper register – 2s. 10d.'

11 'Item, the said Wardens account for having bought this new paper register which shall be handed from one set of wardens to the next, and the other large register shall be kept in a chest with other things as a memorandum book, cost of this new paper register – 2s. 10d.'

dating of some of these later additions is clear, but for others dating problems subsist and are indicated at the relevant points in the edition.[12]

The Register of Deeds[13] was a gift to the company, and its price is therefore not recorded, but it must clearly have been far more expensive, for it is both much larger (now bound in two volumes, MSS 1642, 1643) and is of vellum. It was bought in 1418 specifically for the purpose of ensuring that the company's important documents and deeds should be recorded and kept for posterity:

> Fait a remembr*er* q*e* el temps de Will*ia*m Fytzhugh*e*, Joh*a*n Hill*es*, Ric*hard* Wedyall*e* *et* Joh*a*n Walsch*e* est ordeigné *et* escr*i*pt *et* en le tresorye mys un libr*e* de velom conten*a*nt iiiiC foill*es* saunz lez custodyes, c'est assavoir iiii en p*ri*m*er* comencem*ent* *et* iiii en le fyn; le quell*e* libr*e* fuist ordeigné al entent *et* p*ro*fyt de tout la cumpanye; *et* p*ur* ceo q*e* ava*n*t cez heures div*er*cez evydencez ount esté embesylez *et* det*ra*ez, lez av*a*ntdytz gardeins ount lessé entrer toutz lez av*a*ntditz evydencez en l'av*a*ntdit libr*e* p*ur* le pluis record. Et lez av*a*ntditz evydencez chescun p*ar* soy mesmes come as ditz ten*emen*tz app*ar*teignent en div*er*se kofyns *et* boxez mys, *et* issynt lez ditz boxez billez a dir*e* q*e* de tielx ten*emen*tz specefyent, en chescun boxe quantz evydencez escr*i*ptz come en le libr*e* est specefyé, auxi bien copiez come ault*re*s chart*re*s ensealez, les quelx copiez lez av*a*ntditz gardeins en defaut dez evydencez p*er*duz et anientisez ount lez av*a*ntditz copiez hors de Guyldehall*e* ret*ra*ez *et* portez. Que le kalender q*e* ysy est mys . . .[14]

The volumes still contain all 400 leaves, and the original parchment guard-leaves survive. The intended purpose of this book was strictly kept to, and it does indeed contain an invaluable record of all deeds and charters of the time relating to the Company and to all its properties.

Then in 1444–45 it was decided that the Company needed to keep a more permanent record of its official accounts, and William Boston, made warden two years later, donated the very large paper register now known as MS 1520 (Wardens' Accounts and Court Minute Book A),[15] and at its beginning was written in this information:

[12] The problem can be seen not to be one of modern misbinding. The binding is uniform with that of MS 1518, the gold lettering on the front cover bearing the title: 'Goldsmith's [*sic*] Company / A / + [*elongated into a cross*] / Part II / 1372–45 Edw. III – 1446–24 Hen. VI', and the spine lettering: 'Warden's [*sic*] Accounts & Court Minutes / Part II 1372 to 1446 A +'. Bound in with the fourteenth-century sheets are also a series of nineteenth-century manuscript notes and pasted cuttings from Herbert, *The History of the Twelve Great Livery Companies of London.*

[13] This has been used here only for a few relevant excerpts, and a full description of the manuscript and its contents has therefore not been included.

[14] A + a, p. 120. 'Memorandum that in the time of William FitzHugh, John Hilles, Richard Withihale and John Walsh there was ordained and written up and placed in the treasury a book of vellum containing 400 leaves plus the guardleaves, i.e. four at the beginning and four at the end, the which book was ordained for the use and the benefit of all the Company; and because in former times various documents have been embezzled and taken away, the aforesaid wardens have had all the aforesaid documents copied up into the aforesaid book in order to have a better record. And the aforesaid documents have been placed in various chests and boxes each according to which tenement they belong, and the said boxes have been labelled to say that they refer to such tenements, and each box contains as many written documents as are specified in the book, both copies and in other cases sealed charters, the which copies were, in the absence of documents that had been lost and destroyed, retrieved and brought as copies from the Guildhall. That the list of contents which is thus placed . . .'

[15] This book has also only been used for a few relevant excerpts, and no full description of the manuscript and its contents has been included, only the basic details and the points relevant to this edition.

> For as moche as the oolde recordes of acomptis made in time past by the good pollitique rule of oure eldres remayneth not of record but be put in oblivion, because they were writen in smale quayers & in other strowis of no value. Therfor William Walton, William Bismere, William Porter and William Rotheley then beynge wardeins dide so ordeine this booke, to write therynne yeerly the particuler acomptes of the wardeins for the time beyng, to thentent that alle such acomptes as shull be yeerly made may be the moore opynly knowyn, and remayne of recorde withynne the crafte of goldsmythes for evermore, the whiche book was yeven by William Boston, goldsmyth, to the said feleship for the same entent.

The paper for this volume measures 399 × 280mm and consists of 508 pages with modern pagination at the top outside corners (no earlier foliation system is visible). It is in a very good state of preservation and contains the records from 1444 to 1516. It is now bound uniformly with MSS 1518 and 1519 and other early court books of the Company, and at some stage in the past some sheets relating to the mid-fifteenth century have become disordered. Pencil annotations have been added indicating dates applicable to entries, and thus the problem is not serious. Bound in at the front of this volume is a liturgical calendar which records on the relevant days the obits for the following men who were all goldsmiths active during the period covered by the first two record books and who appear in those records: William Boton (11 February); John Pattysle (9 March); Robert Halle (9 March); John Hiltoft (17 May); Simon Le Mazerer (24 May); John Standelf (28 May); John Carler (the Tuesday after Trinity Sunday); Thomas Polle (19 July); William Stameldene (22 July); John Maplesdene (22 July); Thomas Hay (31 August); Nicholas Twyford (7 December); John Fraunceys (13 December); Drew Barantyn (15 December); John Carbonelle (31 December).

Besides these official registers and ledgers, the medieval goldsmiths and their scribes used many 'smale quayers & . . . other strowis of no value' in order to keep their records, and to a very large extent the official books that survive were copied up from other more temporary lists and records. After the first register was purchased in 1358, the first job given to a scribe was that of copying up into it the surviving records from previous years. He started with the wardens' receipts and expenditures for 1334–35 and we must presume either that such records were not kept before this or that they were already lost by 1358. Both suppositions may be true in part, and one needs to remember that, firstly, the goldsmiths of the time had no official residence or offices where records might have been kept, and secondly that responsibility for financial accounting was individual not corporate. The scribe of 1358 must have been given a pile of documents in various hands (some of which he clearly had more difficulty in reading than others) and he chose to copy out first the surviving financial records for each year, including the lists of monies paid for apprentices at the time of their registration and monies paid upon release from their terms of apprenticeship, after which he turned to the longer documents, firstly those that covered the purchase of the site of the mistery's Hall in 1339 and some earlier and later documents relating to this site and establishing the mistery's entitlement to ownership, and secondly documents recording the mistery's first royal charter of 1327 and two subsequent letters conferring further privileges as well as a royal charter regulating the goldsmiths' mistery in Bordeaux and Aquitaine. The next page then records the year's accounts for 1358–59, and from then on these are written up by a series of scribes at the end of each year, other additional records and copies of documents being included as thought fit from year to year, and with the format and the nature of the contents varying, as one would expect, as the years went by.

The monies listed in MSS 1518 and 1519 as received and disbursed by no means form a complete set of financial accounts, and other details must indeed have been kept on other small quires, must have been presented and gone through at the time of each year's audit of accounts, and have now disappeared. Certain set official expenditures are listed for most of the earlier years: the payments for wax for candles and for maintaining a light in various churches, payments for ringing the noonday bell on St Dunstan's day, the expenses of the feast, alms payments; and certain official receipts are listed each year: fees paid for apprentices at registration and fees paid for release from terms of apprenticeship, fines for faulty workmanship or for offensive behaviour. For some years much fuller information is given, extra expenditures for a special feast or other celebration, full details of new building works on the Hall, or just a more detailed than usual listing of standard items. But, with the occasional exception,[16] no totals are given and the knowledge we gain of the company's financial position over these years is incomplete. It is very noticeable also that some items of regular expenditure in the earlier years disappear from the accounts of the later years of our period. Alms payments to the poor, for instance, are listed regularly each year until 1379, and not thereafter except for a specific individual reason. However, it is most improbable that the mistery had stopped these charitable payments, and one must assume that the poor and needy continued to receive support, but that the records of this have not been preserved. Such omissions can be regretted, but, nevertheless, the information and details that do survive build up a most highly interesting and varied picture.

Although these are records of the mistery of goldsmiths as a communal body, and not of the work of any individual craftsman, it is important to realise the role played by certain individuals. In particular, the responsibilities of each year's wardens were, during the early years of our period, individual and not collective. This is why, for instance, the expenses for 1336–37 list:

> It*e*m, en argent doné as pov*er*es encontr*e* la Noel – xxxvi s. viii d.
> q*e* a amountté a chescun gardeyn – ix s. ii d. [17]

and

> L'an dysme la su*m*me de chescun gardeyn amou*n* xxii lib. xi s. v d.[18]

and it is also why an amount is listed each year that the wardens have 'doné al encresse.'[19] During their year of office they have held in their individual hands the monies belonging to the mistery as a communal body. They may either have guarded them intact or may have put them to use, either as straight financial investments or perhaps as loans, or in order to buy the materials of their trade,

[16] e.g. the accounts for 1381–82, Book A + a, p. 58, and those for 1415–16 on p. 113.
[17] 'Item, money given to the poor at Christmas time – 36s. 8d. – which came to 9s. 2d. for each Warden.'
[18] 'In 1336 the total from each Warden amounts to £22 11s. 5d.'
[19] 'given to the increase in funds'

gold, silver and precious stones, from which profit was gained. At the end of each financial year, the outgoing wardens would have handed over to the incoming wardens for the next year all monies in their hands, and would have needed officially to account both for what was and what was not there, i.e. receipts starting with the amount given them the previous year and including all fees paid in, all fines imposed and any other receipts, followed by expenditures on behalf of the mistery as a body. The 'increase' that appears among receipts listed is often stated to be 'horsp*ri*s la q*ui*lete dé app*re*ntiz *et* de m*er*cimentz'[20] and is the amount of profit, calculated by means we have no way of knowing, that the wardens have that year been able to make with the funds at their disposal.

The record books served not only to record financial transactions, but were also used to preserve the full text of all ordinances concerning the mistery, both as an ongoing measure ensuring that these were written in at the time the ordinance was passed, and as a historic measure, recording here for contemporary reference and for posterity ordinances that had been passed in earlier times. The earliest of these date from 1271 and were copied into the register in 1370, specifically as stated in a preface to them 'a durer en remembrance p*er*petuelment'.[21] This particular set of ordinances holds an enormous fascination, for they date from before the official establishment of the mistery as a communal body (by the charter of 1327) and may very probably have been linked to an earlier attempt to gain corporate status.[22] The regulations set out here can be compared to the thirteenth-century ordinances of the goldsmiths of Paris,[23] some of which are similar but others not so much being different as that they appear in one set but not the other. In both, the requirement that gold and silver worked should be of a set high standard is present, the Paris ordinances laying down gold 'a la touche de Paris ou mieudres'; the London ones of this date specifying 'oor de l'asay' (in 1300 this was defined as the same quality as that required in Paris, 19.2 carats);[24] for silver both sets of regulations required the metal to be refined before working to the same standard as that of sterling.[25] Working during the hours of darkness is forbidden except under certain circumstances in both cities, but the exceptions differ greatly: in London it was allowed 'de la Seinte Michel dekes le Nowel et nient pluis',[26] whereas in Paris it was allowed if the work was 'l'euvre lou Roy, la Roïne, leur anfans, leur freres, et l'evesque de Paris'.[27] The Paris regulations

[20] 'excluding the monies collected from apprentices and from amercements'

[21] 'in order to endure in memory for ever'

[22] See for instance George Unwin, *The Gilds and Companies of London*, 4th edn (London, 1963), pp. 64–65; Pamela Nightingale, *A Medieval Mercantile Community: The Grocers' Company and the Politics and Trade of London 1000–1485* (New Haven and London, 1995), pp. 111–12; Elspeth Veale, 'The "Great Twelve": Mistery and Fraternity in Thirteenth-Century London', *BIHR* 64 (1991), 237–63, esp. pp. 242–45.

[23] Etienne Boileau, *Le Livre des Métiers*, ed. René de Lespinasse and François Bonnardot, *Histoire générale de Paris: Les métiers et corporations de la ville de Paris – XIIIe siècle* (Paris: Imprimerie Nationale, 1879); Id., ed. G.-B. Depping, *Reglemens sur les arts et métiers de Paris, rédigés au XIIIe siècle et connus sous le nom du Livre des Métiers d'Etienne Boileau* (Paris, 1837).

[24] Statute of 28 Edward I, c. 20.

[25] The Paris regulation reads 'Nus orfevres ne puet ouvrer a Paris d'argent, que il ne soit ausi bons come esterlins ou mieudres', the London one 'q*e* nul overe . . . pir argent de la moneie'.

[26] 'between Michaelmas and Christmas but at no other time'

[27] 'work for the King, the Queen, their children, their brothers and the bishop of Paris'

are concerned with the number of apprentices (as many as one wants if they were members of one's family, but only one at a time from outside the family), their age when taken on (at least ten years' old), days when working was and was not allowed (not on Apostles' feastdays),[28] responsibility for city dues and duties, and the election of wardens of the mistery (either two or three wardens each year, not to be re-elected until at least three years later). The London ordinances on the other hand are not city regulations but those of a confraternity, and thus the first duties laid down are that all goldsmiths 'soient entreroulee del confrarie de Seint Doneston. Et si nul de la confrarie meurt, toutz viendront a l'enterement . . .'.[29] They also contain a large number of rules for the actual working of gold and silver pieces based upon the highest standards of craft practice, followed by rules about business dealings, buying and selling practices. The wardens' duties are specified in very general terms: 'Et les Wardeyns des toutz cestz choses avanditz loialment fournieront *et* loial acompte rendront p*ar* le s*er*ement q'ils ount fait',[30] apart from the requirement that they conduct an inspection eight times a year to enforce standards of quality.[31]

As the years went by, these regulations were added to, modified or further elaborated, and in the fifteenth century ordinances were drawn up that defined the subsidiary crafts such as those of the finers, the spanglers, the goldbeaters. Not all of these survive, those of the goldbeaters being lost but surmisable from other evidence.[32] By 1478 it was realised that the records scattered through the various registers and surviving on other loose leaves needed to be collected together, and a new record book, now known as MS 2524 (Book of Ordinances, vol. I: 1478–83) was acquired and the ordinances written into it were not in fact just copied, but were where necessary translated into English out of the original French or Latin.[33]

In part, the loss of various records may be attributable to uncertainties over the use of each record book. When MS 1519 was bought in 1371–72 it was stated that its use was to be as the wardens' own record book, as distinct from the earlier register which was now termed 'i. lygg*er*e' and 'un remembrauncer', i.e. a ledger to be kept at the Hall as the official record of the mistery. For the next three years, the contents of the records are the same, and the best supposition would seem to be that the first to be written up was MS 1519 from which MS 1518 was copied, but this must remain a supposition only. Gradually the entries diverge, at first without any apparent plan, so that it

[28] Except that one workshop was allowed to stay open on such days, turns being taken for this among the goldsmiths, and all profits made on that day went into a common alms box.

[29] 'should be enrolled in the fraternity of St Dunstan. And if any of the fraternity should die, all shall come to the burial'.

[30] 'And the wardens shall faithfully see to all these aforesaid things and shall render faithful account on the oath they have sworn.'

[31] 'Et qe les Wardeyns facent serche chescun quarter ii fethe' – 'And that the wardens should make an inspection twice each quarter'.

[32] See for instance the allusion in 1435: 'Also, þat þe wardeynys of þe craft of fyno*ur*is ȝeerly ben sworn in þe Goldsmythis Halle in þe feste of Seynt Dunston as þe wardeynys of þe craft of goldbeteris be wont to be' (A + b, p. 83). See also Reddaway and Walker, pp. 80–81, 213–14.

[33] A very full presentation of this book, with the text of the ordinances translated into modern English, and with cross-references in footnotes to the relevant earlier ordinances, was done by Lorna Walker and is found in Appendix I of Reddaway and Walker, pp. 209–74.

would seem that the scribe was merely using the book that he happened to have at hand and no longer thought he needed to ensure that the record appeared in both books. Thus the records for 1378–79 appear only in MS 1519, those for 1379–80 only in MS 1518, those for 1380–81 only in MS 1519, those for 1381–82 in MS 1518. This alternation may itself be significant, a variety of hypotheses to account for it being imaginable. However, this only lasts for a few years, and in the early years of the fifteenth century a different pattern emerges, and now the lists of apprentices and serving-men are written up in MS 1518 whereas the records of offences against the ordinances and fines imposed for these appear in MS 1519 – but not always, the division of material is not strict. The ordinances for finers and spanglers also appear in this latter manuscript, as do the oaths to be sworn by the wardens and by the 'Dutchmen' – the ordinances of 1434 for these 'Dutchmen' however appear in MS 1518. Overlaps between the record books occur later after the introduction of MS 1520. One of these would appear to have been a simple error: in 1436 the mistery contributed to the costs of the siege of Calais and paid the costs of 2 spearmen and 12 bowmen as their share of the City of London's financial aid for this venture. The monies may have taken some time to come in or perhaps the record of individual contributions, kept on separate sheets, was overlooked and not copied up at the same time as other records for that year. Whatever the explanation, in 1449 or 1450 the scribe entered up these records but in the later and newer record book. He then clearly recognised that perhaps they should have been entered in the older register which contained the other records for 1436, and he thus added a note there to indicate what he had done:

> Be it remembred than in these wardeyns days, that is to sey the xiiii[th] ȝere of Kyng Herry the sexte, was sent by the citee of London to the segge of Calys certeyn sawdio*urs*, that is to sey sper*es* & bowes, of the which sawdio*urs* this craft sonde ii speres & xii bowes which is entred in the grete boke of pap*er*[34] next the counte of Tho*m*as Leget, Barth*olomew* Bremsh*am*, Humfrey Heyford & Herry Bode the xxvii ȝere of the said Kyng.

The list entered into MS 1520 is highly organised, in that it is both divided into three sections, the monies paid by the men of the livery, that paid by the yeomen (those who were of the freedom of the mistery but not of the livery), and that paid by 'Dutchmen', and each list is also ordered by amount paid, so that the men who paid the largest sums are listed first, other subsequent names being placed in descending order of amounts paid.

Again in 1445–46 we find two different books being used to record information about the same events and expenses. The mistery's participation in the city's celebrations to welcome the arrival of Margaret of Anjou, Henry VI's new wife and queen, and the expenses involved in this are in part written up in MS 1519 and in part in MS 1520. And the record of controversy surrounding a portable breviary, William Porter's role in this, and the resolution of the dispute was written up in both manuscripts.

Evidence exists that a very large proportion of the entries in the record books were copied up from other writings. In addition to the obvious copying of the pre-1358 records into MS 1518 and the occurrence of identical entries between

[34] i.e. the register now known as Book A = MS 1520.

the various books, we find for instance that a number of entries are somewhat out of chronological order in a way that suggests that the scribe at the end of an accounting year had a pile of temporary lists and records and from these he compiled his entry for the year, occasionally getting things out of sequence. The entries on pp. 35–36 for instance present matters that relate to 1369 followed by others relating to 1368. Sometimes an entry occurs twice, this sometimes having been later corrected by the scribe, sometimes not, and the way these mistakes occur suggests copying errors.[35] Sometimes, as we saw above over the expenses for the siege of Calais contributions, a record has clearly been made some years after the event to which it refers; the composition of John Hiltoft which is written in after the entries for the year 1379–80 must in fact date from quite considerably earlier, and certainly no later than 1375 since it refers to a bishop of London who was translated to Canterbury in that year. Sometimes also we find phrases in an entry that only make sense if we assume the presence of an exemplar, e.g. occurrences such as that on A + a, p. 169: 'coram infrascriptis Thoma Leget, Thoma Reyner et Ricardo Bradcok', where no such names are found written below, but were no doubt signed on the document being copied up here. Another instance of such mechanical copying is betrayed in the records for 1441: John Blemelle, a goldsmith of Lewes, attempted to deceive the Prior of that place over a nef, but the Prior sent the nef for inspection to the goldsmiths of London who quickly detected the tin and lead stuffing, broke the nef in pieces, and made a full record of what had been done, setting their seals to one half of an indentured document which in itself gave the information that the case was to be recorded for posterity in the mistery's register. The scribe told to copy this document into the register did precisely as he was told, making no allowance for the new site of the record:

> . . . wheche thyng so be us don we have entryd in owr regestre yn þe Halle of owr crafte for mor*e* evydence, recordyng þe untrewthe of John Blemell*e*, other*e*wyse cald Radle or Goldsmyth of Lewes, wheche made þe forseide schyp as we ben enformyd. Into wetenesse wher*e*of we have put our*e* sealles to þat oon p*ar*te of þys enden*ture* þe day & ȝer*e* above sayd. (A + a, p. 180)

Some entries were however perhaps made directly into the registers: names are added at the end of lists that may have been last-minute additions; notes are attached to entries, to explain for instance why a lower fee was paid for a certain apprentice, or for instance to update an entry about an unpaid fine to say it had been paid some years later. Sometimes part of a name is lacking, the scribe clearly having only a first name, or only a surname, and sometimes he had no name, just the fact that it was e.g. the apprentice of a certain master. Gaps are often left in these cases, and sometimes one can see that such gaps have been filled in later, clearly at a point when the scribe obtained the necessary detail from some other source.[36] The entries concerning fines for offences that appear in MS 1519 may certainly, at least at times, be the direct record made either by one of the wardens or by a scribe immediately after the offender was brought to justice. On one page of this manuscript (p. 76) we find a list of fines at the top, each being a very brief one-line record, a large blank space in the middle, and then a much longer paragraph with full details of a

[35] See for instance A + a, p. 130.
[36] See for instance A + a, p. 144.

case placed at the bottom of the page. The best assumption to account for this might be that the space was being left to record later 'everyday' fines as they occurred – but which in the event did not.

The scribes also at times added comments directly to a paragraph that was otherwise being copied from another source. This for instance is no doubt the case for the entries concerning the purchase of MS 1519 cited above. In 1420 John Corby caused the mistery and its wardens enormous trouble, and at the end of his account of what had happened and what measures had been taken the writer says:

> And her*e* uppon in more record & testemonie for he*m* that been to come wardeins & gove*r*nours of this worschipful cumpanye as wel as for he*m* that have been, this ordin*a*nce of his fowle falsnesse & untrowthe is entred in this pape*r* of record for eve*r* to stonde in witnesse. (A + a, p. 128)

It has indeed stood in witness for nearly 600 years already!

DATING AND THE ORGANISATION OF THE RECORDS FOR THIS EDITION

The Goldsmiths' year ran from St Dunstan's Day (19 May), the feastday of their patron saint on which the new wardens took up office each year. Their records are presented each year under a heading with the information of the regnal year and the names of the wardens, and below come their accounts, the court cases they heard, the ordinances they made and other information relating to the period from St Dunstan's Day one year until the same feastday the next year.[37] The vast majority of the entries in the record books are therefore clearly both dated to the time they refer to and datable to the time they were written up, normally within a year, often much less, after the events occurred. Since this is so, it has been decided to present these records chronologically, which has entailed an interweaving of the entries from the two main registers used, with a few intercalations from two other manuscripts containing important relevant and contemporary material. MS 1518 (Book A + a), the earliest register, has been taken as the basis of this edition, thus that when entries in this and MS 1519 (Book A + b) are identical, except perhaps for some minor orthographical variants, Book A + a has been followed. In all cases however a footnote provides the information that such entries are also found in Book A + b, giving the precise page reference. Any variants other than the very minor orthographic ones are given in full. In one case only Book A + b has been followed for this edition, relegating the entry in Book A + a to a footnote reference and footnoting of variants, this being for the list of apprentices admitted in 1403–04, where p. 92 of Book A + a has the usual sort of list giving only the names of both apprentice and master and the fee paid, whereas Book A + b gives a large amount more information about each apprentice. The first entry for John Cokefield, for example, in Book A + a has no more than: 'Joh*a*n Cokefelde app*re*ntys Joh*a*n Hilles – xx s.'; p. 37 of Book A + b however reads:

[37] The precise dates concerned are not mentioned before 1358–59 (i.e. the first year after the purchase of the new register and the start of formal recording for posterity), nor in all subsequent headings to a year's entries, but the vast majority of the headings do give the information and we know it applied throughout.

> Fait a remembr*er* q*e* p*ar* assent *et* bone examinaciou*n* de les gardeyns av*a*ntditz Joh*a*n Standelf, Joh*a*n Halle le eisné, Will*iam* Fraunceys, le xxiii jo*ur* de Maii l'an du r*egne le* r*oi* Henri quarte puys le conqueste quarte, Joh*a*n Cokfelde fitz a Geffrey Cokfelde, jadys groc*er et* citezein de Loundres, fuist resceu p*ur* estr*e* appr*e*ntys a Joh*a*n Hilles p*ur* luy servir en man*ere* d'apr*e*ntys p*ar* t*er*me de x ans, paié – xx s.

How much more interesting it would have been if each year's scribe had included such full information!

Some dating problems occur for both the registers and these are on each occasion indicated in the edition by means of footnotes. Book A + b presents a number of problems arising from scribes using pages earlier left blank in order to record some information. Thus p. 51 contains information about the year 1403–04, p. 53 infomation relating to 1404–05, but p. 52 in between contains the ordinance for spangles of 1441, its date being included within the text (þe xxviij day of March*e* þe xix^{ne} ȝere of Kyng Henry þe vj^{te}), the year being confirmed by the list of wardens following. For this edition we have placed this entry chronologically in correct sequence. Other entries in Book A + b seem clearly out of sequence where they are but more difficult to place exactly, for instance the first entry on p. 58 which was arguably written out a few years later than those on pp. 59ff. and has therefore been incorporated, with due reservation, at a later point than the entries following it; the further entry on p. 58 is clearly dated to 1420–21 and is so placed. Other entries are in sequence but the precise year is difficult to determine because of the lack of entries for a number of years. The undated list on p. 17 of those who made loans to the mistery can be dated to 1376–77 by the later reference made on p. 23 when recording repayments of these loans, but the subsequent lists on pp. 18–19 of those who were rebellious and contrarious and thus put out of the livery and others who were admitted to the livery are undated in themselves, may be presumed to date also from 1376–77 by their position in the book, but might possibly refer to events a year or so earlier – if only other evidence were to turn up! Another example one might pick out is that on p. 71 only one short entry occurs, and is not dated; there are two possible years to which it might be assigned and the choice of where to place it for this edition was determined by the hand of the scribe.

Such problems occasionally arise in Book A + a also, for instance the dating of the lists of apprentices and serving-men on p. 152 which can most probably be assigned to 1431–32 but not with certainty.[38]

The main dating problem in this book concerns the entries between 1360 and 1365. On p. 23 we find the usual heading to a year's entry:

> Ces sount les nouns des gardeyns del orfeve*r*ie de Loundres l'an du regne le Roi Edward tierz apr*és* le conquest xxxiii^{ce} [1359–60]

the regnal year given being that of the year in which the wardens took up office. At the end of this year's usual entries (expenses of the wardens, lists of apprentices and serving-men) an entry occurs on p. 24 that is internally dated to 1360. Below this on the same page we most unusually find a heading phrased in an entirely different manner:

> Ceux sount les nou*n*s d'app*re*ntysez *et* lowys de la orfeve*r*ye entrans et issans en temps dez gardeins, c'est assavoir de William de Burtou*n*, Johan Boton, William

[38] See the note attached to this entry.

> Salusbury, Richard Fraunceys, l'an du regn*e* n*ost*re s*eignur* le Roi Edward lui tierce puis le conquest xxxv[te]

If one assumes here that, despite the unusual phrasing, the regnal year is still that in which the wardens took up office, then the entries below refer to 1361–62, and one year's records, those for 1360–61, are missing. There is nothing intrinsically surprising in this, for the records of a number of other years are missing, and the oddity of phrasing of the heading might suggest some hiatus. On p. 25 the entry for the next year starts, and the usual phrasing for the heading to the year is used:

> Ces sount les nouns de gardeins del orfev*er*ie de Loundres l'an du regne le Roi Edward tierçz puis le conquest xxxvime

Taking the regnal year as the starting point, we must assign the following entries to 1362–63. On p. 26 we find another oddity, a second and separate list of apprentices (one has appeared above on p. 25) followed by a second list of those coming out of their terms of apprenticeship, and it would seem not impossible that the scribe is copying up for reference a list relating to a previous year which he or someone else had realised was missing from the records – could the apprentices listed perhaps have been admitted or released from terms in the missing year 1360–61? One may compare the format and general nature of these extra lists to the similar extra listing on p. 118, where however the scribe indicated that the extra names in a list belonged to another year.

Page 27 contains a standard type of heading for the wardens of 37 Edward III (1363–64) and p. 29 that for 38 Edward III (1364–65), each year's heading being followed by the usual types of lists and entries. On p. 30 we find an entry internally dated to 9 May 1365, and this is followed by a heading giving the names of four wardens for the year, as it says, of 38 Edward III, the same year as given above. The entries following this heading are however far from normal. Firstly is listed the sum of £12 11s. 6d. spent on the feast, then a sum given in alms payments, and this is followed by the announcement:

> Et p*ur* ceo q*e* les bones gentz del mister pristrent dev*er*s eux les p*ro*fitz app*ur*tenantz as dites gardeins, les gardeins ne don*er*ent cest an point d'encrés.[39]

This puzzling statement is followed by an ordinance declaring that the feastday of St Dunstan must be celebrated by all members of the confraternity, that only very good excuses for absence will be accepted and that, even if excused the feast, all members must pay their due contributions to it. The ordinance is prefaced by the explanation that in recent years there had been a vast number of absences on the days when the feast was held, and the ordinance expressly says that the feast should from henceforth be held on St Dunstan's Day itself.

On p. 31 we find the usual type of heading:

> Ces sont les nouns des gardeins del orfev*er*ie de la cité de Loundres l'an du regne le Roi Edward tierçz puis le conquest trent ix[e]

the year 39 Edward III giving the following entries as dating from 1365–66 if we take the regnal year to refer to the date on which the wardens took up office.

[39] 'And since the good men of the mistery took to themselves the profits belonging to the said wardens, the wardens did not in this year give any increase to the funds.'

For the years between 1360 and 1365 we are therefore looking at one year which is apparently missing from the records and one year which apparently had two sets of wardens. Reddaway and Walker when facing the above problems decided to resolve them by assuming that for some years the regnal year given referred to the year in which the wardens demitted office. They therefore assigned the entries on p. 24 onwards to 1360–61, those from p. 25f. to 1361–62, those from p. 27f. to 1362–63, those from p. 29f. to 1363–64 and accepted p. 30's heading as referring to 1364–65, thus eliminating the two sets of wardens for that year and providing for the missing year earlier. But this solution poses problems. Scribes are very much creatures of habit and in records such as these always prefer to keep to a set format (one may note for instance for how many years the heading to each year continued to be written in French long after all subsequent entries were in English and/or Latin). An unsignalled change of practice would therefore be highly surprising. Change does occur, but notably not just when a new scribe takes over but at a period when a new reign has started, and this change is signalled:

> Ceux sont les nou*n*s dez gardeins del orfeverie de Londres l'an du regne le roi Richard sec*on*de puis le conquest primer, finantz lour office en le jour de Seint Dunstan l'an susdit (A + b, p. 21, 1377–78)

This dating system is used until 1382–83 when a new format of phrasing for the heading is brought in:

> Ces sount les nou*n*s des gardeyns de la feste de Seint Dunsto*u*n l'an v tanq*e* a mesme le feste l'an vj^{me} (A + a, p. 59)

It would seem therefore that it would be a very difficult argument to posit that the meaning of the heading for the year changed between 1359–60 when the regnal year signified that for the year when the wardens took up office and 1362–63 when, so the argument would run, it signified the date of demitting office, and then changed back, without this being signalled, for 1365–66. A much more likely explanation for these years is the obvious one that a year's records, those for 1360–61, are missing. That the regnal year given is indeed that of the beginning of the term of office is proved for the year 1362–63, for among the expenses for this year we find listed

> Item, en perte de mesme les gardeins p*er*du mesme l'an sur l'ordinance faite de novel p*ar* le mister – xlii s. p*ur* div*er*ses choses p*ri*s sur Cornhull*e*.[40] (A + a, p. 25)

The reference can only be to Statute 37 Edward III, c. 7. This statute enacted some new measures and amplified and strengthened some existing ordinances.[41] Its dating is certain and the reference in the Goldsmiths' own accounts is entirely logical for this year if we assume the accounts are those for 1362–63. One could easily make out reasons if the entry for these costs had appeared a year late, but to posit that the costs were paid a year early in 1361–62 makes no apparent sense.

We are left therefore with the problem of accounting for two sets of wardens being listed for 1364–65. When one considers the unusual nature of the entries

[40] 'Item, as a loss of the same wardens, lost [i.e. paid out] the same year on the new ordinance made by the mistery – 42s. – for various objects seized on Cornhill.'

[41] See Reddaway and Walker, pp. 31–32 and 53–54, n. 34.

for the second set of wardens listed, the hypothesis that leaps to mind is that something had gone very wrong during the term of office of the previously listed wardens. It would seem that feasts had for some years not been held in a full and proper manner, but on the other hand a large amount of money had been expended by these wardens on entertainment:

> Adeprimes a la feste de Seint Dunstan et altres diverces diners faites par mesme les dictes gardeins aprés, qe amonte outre la quilet – xlii li.[42] (A + a, p. 29)

The £42 spent can be compared with £10 for the previous year, £12 11s. 6d. for the second set of wardens, and £11 11s. for the succeeding year. Extravagance with the communal funds is a charge that might have stuck, and this lends colour to the puzzling and very bare statement that 'the good men of the mistery took to themselves the profits belonging to the said wardens'. This was not normal practice and taken with the other evidence suggests an organised vote of no confidence in the wardens. The following year's wardens, Nicholas Twyford, John Coraunt, Robert Oxenford and John Forster (a notable set), presided over new building works on the Hall and were very punctilious in ensuring that the record stated how much money they had received when they took up office (information not generally given in these accounts), how it had been spent, and that the remainder had been handed over to the goodmen and commonalty of the mistery, the place and date of this being given along with a very full list of witnesses.[43]

From the above arguments I would suggest that the dating of a few lists of wardens given in Reddaway and Walker should be amended, this affecting the career histories of the following men: William de Burton, John Botoun, William Salisbury, Richard Fraunceys, John Maplesdene, John Croydon, John Walsh, Thomas de Worlingworth, John Coraunt, Thomas Piphurst, Thomas Lincoln, Henry Markeby, Thomas Hassay, John Gravelee, Robert Launde and Richard Weston.

In addition one may note here that work on the present edition has perhaps thrown up the names of two possible further wardens for a year for which previously no wardens had been known, 1348–49. John atte Castel and Richard de Felsted are listed among others as witnesses to a document dated 24 June 1349, and each has attached to his name the epithet 'magister'.[44] The word can just mean 'master', but all the others listed as witnesses were also 'masters' in the sense of being fully qualified goldsmiths, and the more specific sense of the word as 'warden' of a city mistery is well attested.[45] The wardens for 1349–50 are known, and thus if these men were wardens they must have been so during the previous year. The word 'magister' is however used in other senses, that of 'schoolmaster' for instance, and one should therefore be cautious since these two men have otherwise no record in these registers (but this is true of several other listed wardens for this period, Ralph Convers of 1346–47 for instance).

[42] 'Firstly, at the feast of St Dunstan and various other dinners given afterwards by the same said wardens, which over and above the collection amounts to – £42.'

[43] A + a, p. 31.

[44] A + a, p. 18: 'Johanne atte Castel, magistro, Ricardo de Felstede, magistro'.

[45] See for instance A + a, p. 56: ' . . . quatuor magistris de artificio aurifabrorum . . .'.

THE LANGUAGE OF THE RECORDS[46]

All three of the languages of medieval England are used in these records, Anglo-Norman (the French used in England from the Conquest until the fifteenth century, also known as Anglo-French), Medieval Latin and Middle English. All the usual features of these languages are found and any particularly noteworthy linguistic usage has been signalled with a footnote. The choice of language used is also in line with that of other comparable contemporary records. From 1334 until about 1420 the official language of record used by the Goldsmiths was Anglo-Norman. During the fourteenth century the use of this French language predominates entirely, only an occasional entry being found in either Latin or English, but gradually as the fifteenth century progressed, first Latin and then English came to be used increasingly, English being finally dominant from 1435 onwards. The same is true of all other comparable records kept by the London craft companies, where these survive, except that the dates at which English takes over varies: the Grocers' accounts for instance were kept in French until 1425 and then after one year of English went back to French for one year in 1427 and then used English again from the next year forward; the Drapers kept their accounts in French until 1435–36; the Merchant Taylors officially changed to use English in 1444–45, and the Mercers, with one brief gap, continued to use French until the very late date of 1459. French, or Anglo-Norman, was equally the official language of record for a very great number of other purposes, as any historian of the period knows. Latin was however the preferred language for many documents, and here in the Goldsmiths' two earliest registers one finds that the legal documents relating to the purchase of the site of their Hall are all in Latin, as are some other legal documents copied up later. The very great majority (though not all) of the legal documents copied into the Register of Deeds are also in Latin.

Throughout the Anglo-Norman sections of the registers is found an admixture of the other two languages, this increasing as the years go by. This occurs in various ways. An individual English word may for instance be inserted into the French text: the 1365–66 expenses on the Hall, for instance, 'p*ur* un sale *et* quezine *et* pantri *et* botylrie *et* ii chaumbris ové dowble gette' (A + a, p. 31) include the words 'pantri' and 'botylrie' which, although they both derive from French, appear here in their English garb. Entirely English words (usually nouns) can be found intercalated also e.g. 'It*em*, p*ur* clowes, ropes *et* tarre pur le chastell*e* - ii s. ii d. ob.' (A + b, p. 21) where 'ropes' and 'tarre' would seem to have been used since the scribe did not know (or could not remember at the time) their French equivalents. One should however be cautious about such an explanation, for the mixing of languages or code-switching is normal in a multilingual society such as that of medieval England.[47]

[46] See also on this subject my article 'The Language and Vocabulary of the Fourteenth- and Early Fifteenth-Century Records of the Goldsmiths' Company', *Multilingualism in Later Medieval Britain* (Proceedings of the Conference held at the University of Wales, Aberystwyth 10–13 September 1997), ed. D.A. Trotter (Cambridge, 2000), pp. 175–211.

[47] For further discussion of these issues one may consult the articles to be found in *Multilingualism in Later Medieval Britain* (see preceding footnote), in particular those of Begoña Crespo García (25–35), Andres M. Kristol (37–52), Paul Brand (63–76), Herbert Schendl (77–92) and Tony Hunt (131–47).

The same type of thing is found also in the sections written up in Latin, e.g. 'Item, Gerard Alfkyn pro defectu operacionis unius cheyne' (A + b, p. 62), but it is unusual to find it in the English sections and such examples as there are can often be seen to be of what might be termed recognised standard importations, e.g. 'Summa' or 'Summa totalis'. Apart from such one-word insertions, one finds also the occasional whole entry in English among a series otherwise in French or Latin e.g. the last entry in the list on A + b, p. 53 and the two entries on p. 54. Marginal notes are used in these texts as in so many others of the Middle Ages to provide quick information to the eye running through a text – nowadays we would use headings and sub-headings above a text. Many, perhaps most of these are in Latin, e.g. 'Qu*o*d nullus fr*atru*m sit absens in [diem] f*est*i S*anc*ti Dunstani' (A + a, p. 30). The emphasis on the use of Latin in a scribe's training will probably account for some particular instances of what nowadays may seem an odd move from one language to another, but which is familiar to those who grow up in a multilingual society, e.g. 'Richard Wareyn, prest in þe chirche of Seint Fasters, singyng for John Mapulsden*e* and Will*ia*m Stamilden*e* & Alic*e* vx*ore* eor*undem* – jur*atus*' (A + a, p. 170). However, at other times one finds a scribe who starts a list in Latin but then goes into French, e.g. the list of fines paid for offences in 1439–40 which is given a heading in Latin, continues with a few entries entirely in Latin form (apart from the word 'girdelbokelles'), but then, for no apparent reason, changes from use of 'pro i defectu' to write 'pur une defaute' (A + b, p. 96).

The use of Latin for the lists of names of apprentices and serving-men is noteworthy in that it would seem that scribes found it more natural, they were habituated to the use of Latin for such lists. The 1369–70 list of apprentices, for instance, is preceded by the heading in French: 'Ceux sont les nouns des app*re*ntiz entrez ceste an' (A + a, p. 38), the first entry below this: 'Joh*a*n Ely app*re*ntiz de Steph*a*n Thorp*e* – ii s.', appears entirely in the same language, but the next few are written with the first name of the apprentice in its Latin form, either in full ('Martinus', 'Robertus') or in abbreviated form ('Ed-us', 'Will-s') although the following phrase uses a French form for the name of the master ('apprentiz de Johan Fairher'). The seventh entry however uses Latin forms for both first names, each being in the correct case, the French word 'de' having disappeared ('Johannes Appelby app-nt- Johannis Walsshe'), this format then continuing down for the rest of the list. The scribe has clearly been trained in both languages and this generally would seem to be true right through the fourteenth and until well into the fifteenth century. Occasionally one may suspect that a certain writer is happier using one language rather than the other, but one cannot of course be sure, since the fact that only French or only Latin is used by a certain scribe does not mean that he did not know the other language. We can be sure at other times of a writer's easy familiarity with the use of both languages of record, as well as that of English also of course, when we find the same hand writing up entries in each language (see e.g. A + a, p. 114 and pp. 124 and 125).

Those who are interested in the languages of medieval England and the ways in which these were used will find a wealth of material in these records of the Goldsmiths of London. The above general points must suffice here, but footnotes to the text sometimes signal some particularly noteworthy usage and readers who study the texts will find many other examples.

EDITORIAL AND TRANSLATION METHODS AND CONVENTIONS

Editorial methods

The pages of Books A + a and A + b have been both foliated and paginated. The pagination system has been followed here in order to allow straight comparisons with other publications which have used this system, e.g. Reddaway and Walker. Many pages at the beginning of Book A + a have been divided into two columns, the text following down the left-hand column and then continuing to the right-hand column. These columns have been indicated. Later in the book, columns may still be found but are more often used as a page layout system placing lists side-by-side. Such columns are not always indicated. The left-hand margin has been used at times to give a heading or title to a paragraph; in the edition these headings have been brought up to be placed above the paragraph in question. Sums of money are not always set off in a separate column, but in the later sections of both books they are more usually found thus; this clarity of presentation has been reproduced, although the exact positionings sometimes differ.

The conventions used for editing are as follows: the text is reproduced exactly except that, in accordance with standard modern editorial practice, 'u' and 'v', 'i' and 'j' have been differentiated according to pronunciation for the text in all three languages used – Anglo-Norman (Anglo-French), Latin, and Middle English. An occasional difficulty can arise, e.g. that it is debatable whether the Anglo-Norman 'ou' = 'with' should be rendered as 'ov' or as 'ou', as it might have been pronounced either way; I have preferred to leave this as 'ou'. In the French text, the acute accent and the cedilla have been used in order to mark pronunciation differences. Occasional difficulties arise over the use of an acute accent, e.g. in such phrases as 'la q*ui*lete de app*re*ntiz *et* de m*er*cimentz': here one might edit 'de' as 'dé' [= de les], or one might leave it as 'de' (= 'from the' or just 'from'). Editorial decisions have been taken on the basis of comparable phrases if such exist, and in cases of doubt the accent has not been used. The use of capital letters at the beginning of words has been largely standardised to modern usage (the fairly frequent use of a capital 'R' and capital 'F' ('ff') in positions not used today may be noted, and are typical of English MSS of this time (whether French, English or Latin)). Punctuation has been added: full stops, commas, colons and the occasional semi-colon, as also the apostrophe, in accordance with modern usage.

In the French text, scribal usage has been followed and no editorial change made for such things as 'al evesque', 'al amoyne'; 'del orfeverie', 'del esglise'. Many modern editors pay heed to medieval grammarians' strictures[48] and

[48] See e.g. *Orthographica gallica*, ed. R.C. Johnston, Anglo-Norman Text Society Plain Texts 5 (London, 1987), p. 13. L30: Item quandocumque hoc [signum] 'the' in anglicis, *le* vel *la* in gallicis ponitur, si *d[e]* vel *a* precedat signum, *e* de *le* debet pretermitti et *l* adjungi cum *a* vel cum *d*, verbi gracia *a le tresredouté seignur, al tresdouté seignur, de le tresnoble seignur, del tresnoble seignur.* L31: Item quando aliqua vocalis inmediate subsequitur post illud signum *le*, tunc debet *e* pretermitti et *l* adjungi cum vocali subsequenti, verbi gracia *a le honorable seignur, a le Evesque* debent scribi *a lonorable seignur, a levesque* etc. L32: Item quandocumque hoc signum *la* in feminino genere scribitur, quamvis consonans inmediate sequatur et *de* vel *a* precedat, *la* stabit in

would edit these to e.g. 'a l'evesque', 'de l'orfeverie', but scribal usage, not only throughout the Goldsmiths' early records but in so many other documents of the period, shows that they thought it as correct to write 'al evesque' as to write 'al chapellein', 'del orfeverie' as 'del mistier'. Other grammarians support these scribes[49] and I have followed both their rules and the scribal usage.

Abbreviations in all three languages are expanded in accordance with the usual spelling of the scribe when the word is found in full; the expansions are indicated by italics; the expansions can differ, since there are over a long period of time a large number of scribes whose verbal practices differ;[50] not infrequently it is impossible to find a full form of a word as written by a particular scribe, and thus general common practice of the time has been the guide followed.[51] In the French and Latin text, the abbreviated 'et' is rendered thus and placed in italics. In the English text, an ampersand ('&') is used. English scribes of the fourteenth and particularly the fifteenth centuries tend to use suspension lines as decoration as well as to indicate a missing letter or letters; some editors tend therefore to ignore such marks. Since the expanded form of almost all such words in question here is very often found in full, I have chosen rather to assume that if an expansion is possible then this was meant, and have thus rendered it, using italics as usual to indicate this (e.g. Shordich*e*, Frenssh*e*, Ewell*e*) . It is often impossible to know whether one should indicate e.g. 'o*u*n' or 'ou*n*' and I have usually chosen the latter, except in cases where the scribe's writing makes it clear that it is the former. For names, one often has a choice between 'ou*n*/o*u*n' and 'on*e*'; general common practice must be the guide in cases where it is always found abbreviated, and I have tried to be consistent (even if the scribes might not have been!). In a few cases a word has been left unexpanded, with an apostrophe to mark a contraction or suspension sign; e.g. 'London'' where it seems impossible to know whether the scribe would have written in full 'Londoniensis', 'Londoniarum' or a variety of other forms, and where it may even be thought uncertain whether the scribe himself would have been sure how to expand the word.

Names are very often written with the abbreviations for the Latin form of a name; lists may contain some names in French or English form, others in Latin form; some names are abbreviated to a form that might be either French or Latin (e.g. Joh') and these have been expanded according to the form of nearby

sua natura sine aliqua divisione, verbi gracia *de la Dame*, *a la tresreverent Dame*. L32a: Item quandocumque illud signum *la* in femino genere scribitur et vocalis inmediate subsequitur, indifferenter potest *l* adjungi cum vocali subsequente vel stare in sua propria natura, ut *a la Abbesse*, *de la Esglise* vel *a labbesse*, *de lesglise*.

49 For example F50: 'Auxint altrefoithe vous escriverez *del*, *de*, *du*, *des*, *al*, *au a as*; [F51] dont qant vous escriveretz l'un ou l'autre, pernés bone garde: qant *de* est devant *le*, *e* del *le* serra oustee et *l* serra joynt al *de*, come *de l[e] Evesqe* serra escript *del Evesqe*, [*de le seignour*] *del seignour*,' *ibid.*, p. 36.

50 For instance, 'gardianos artis aur' may be expanded as either 'artis aurifabrorum' or as 'artis aurifabrie'. Both forms are found in full and when expanding I have chosen to follow the nearest usage in time, preferably of course that of the same scribe.

51 Expansion of abbreviations in Anglo-Norman texts can be tricky with the infinitive of a verb which in continental French would most likely be found with the ending '-ir' and which in Anglo-Norman might have either this or an ending in '-er'. On p. 102 of Book A + a for instance, the word 'garn' has the usual abbreviation sign for an ' -er' ending and this is used since the scribe's writing of e.g. 'tener' and 'server' above supports this, although the word is found elsewhere, in another scribe's hand, as 'garnir'.

names, although at times this is not easy because of the mixture of forms. In the French text, 'John' with a line through the 'h' is rendered as 'Johan', while in English it is rendered as 'John'.[52] In lists where the names are given entirely (or very nearly) in Latin form, the abbreviated form of the word for an apprentice ('app' or 'app-nt') is expanded as the correct form of the Latin 'apprenticius'; although it might be argued that 'app' or 'apprent' could stand for either the French, Latin or English form of the word (and indeed it can), sufficient evidence is provided by the number of full forms of the word in whichever language to show that the scribes were simply abbreviating and not 'fudging the issue'.

Word divisions are, as usual, an occasional problem. When a scribe has either divided a word or combined two together in a way inconsistent with general usage, these occurrences have been corrected silently. For example, the following have been considered to be one word and scribal variation ignored: 'Adeprimes' (may appear as 'A de primes' and 'A deprimes'); 'horspris' (may appear as 'hors pris'); 'acountre' (may appear as 'a countre'); 'desoreenav*a*nt' (may appear as 'des ore en avant' or 'desore enavant' etc.). On the other hand, for instance, 'pur ceo' has been treated as two words rather than one. In the English text, scribal separation into two parts of words such as 'un to', 'be hyght', 'after ward', 'ther for' has been amended.

Translation conventions

The aim has been to keep as closely as possible to the words of the original but without doing damage to modern English word order and phrasing. It has been remembered that the translation is not of a literary text and is not a literary translation. Thus no attempt has been made to improve the style of the original and if the latter says e.g. 'une ordinance fust ordiné', this may well be translated as 'an ordinance was ordained'. Similarly, illogical or ungrammatical sentence structure in the original may be rendered in equally illogical or ungrammatical modern English, if this correctly conveys the sense and phrasing (see e.g. the case of Walter Colney, A + a, p. 108). Some 'tidying-up' has however been done, and if additional words have been added in the translation to make the sense clear, these have been indicated by the use of square brackets.

Certain words and phrases deserve some explanation here in more general and fuller terms than is possible in the text, since they occur repeatedly, and in addition some one-off occurrences of words presenting a particular difficulty have been dealt with by means of a footnote to the text. General points to note are:

allower hors de . . .

This phrase is found several times in the records here, both in the ordinances and in court cases of misconduct against the ordinances. e.g. 'It*e*m, qe nul ne lowast aut*r*e hors de son shope' (A + a, p. 40); 'Fait a remembr*er* q*e* Thomas Davy fust trové en defaute p*ar* les ditz gardeinz *et* aut*r*es bonz gentz de la mest*ier* p*ur* ceo q'il allowast William Tyngewyk hors de son shop*e* encont*r*e les

[52] As an off-the-cuff remark, one may note how very many men who appear in these records bear the name 'John'.

ordenancz faitz d'ancien temps' (A + a, p. 39). The first example would seem to mean that it is forbidden to hire someone to work outside one's workshop (it was indeed forbidden to work in the homes of others, and all work was supposed to be done in the open where it could easily be inspected). In the second example the French word 'allowast' would appear to mean 'hired' 'employed', and the meaning therefore to be that Tingewick was hired by Davy to do some job elsewhere than in his workshop. However, in context this seems very unlikely, as William Tingewick was prime warden this year, and Thomas Davy, later warden, was at this date very young. The true meaning of the phrase can be determined by comparison with other documents, and in particular those in English, and it can be established that the usage arises from a literal translation into French of an idiomatic English expression using the verb 'hiren' in its sense of 'to rent', and that it means 'to hire someone out of his house' = 'to evict someone from rented property' (by whatever means). This does not seem to have been picked up yet by dictionaries, but is found in a number of documents relating to livery companies, and occurs here in an entry for 1439: 'and þat nouther shall sturre nor labour ne durre sturre ne labour to hire auther other oute of house or shoppe' (A + a, p. 173), and unambiguously for instance in the Mercers' accounts.[53]

'Dutchmen'

Both the adjective 'duche' and the noun 'duchman' (spelt in various ways) are used in the Goldsmiths' records here as in many other contemporary documents to refer to men from Germany and the Low Countries. Many of them we should now term 'German' rather than 'Dutch'. It will also be noticed that lists of men headed 'Dutchmen' can be found to include at times Irishmen, Frenchmen and others, the term apparently being seen as a generic term for foreigners. For the translation, it has been decided to use 'Dutch' or 'Dutchman' in inverted commas, thus avoiding too great a departure from the original, keeping in line with the usage of many modern historians, and yet indicating that one should view the word with care.[54]

estranges/estrangers and *forayns.*

Strictly speaking the latter are those who come from outside the City of London, from other parts of England, the former are 'aliens' or 'foreigners' in the modern sense. However, the words can be used somewhat interchangeably

[53] 'The peyne of hem that hire her felawes out of her houses, shoppes or warehous – . . . For as moche as amonge oother good ordynances & constitucions maked and assented of þe compaignye aforseyd, þer is oon good olde ordynance þat no felawe sholde hire other out of his shoppe, warehous ne wonyng hous, but no determynat fyn put ther on in certeyn. . . . . Therfore is it ordeyned thus of þe ful assent of al the compaignye þat noon of hem riche ne pore þat is under þe governance of þe craft, in þe lyveree ne out of þe lyveree, lowys ne apprentice, hire no man þat is in þe lyveree ne out of þe lyveree þat is under þe governance of þe craft out of his wonyng hous, warehous ne shoppe by no manere wey of fraude ne collusion ne by no manere colour agains equitee & good conscience by hym self ne by no mene persone up peyne to paye to þe almesse of þe craft fowre sithes þe value by yere of þe rent of þe hous, shoppe or warehous so hyred' (f. 71v).

[54] These immigrant craftsmen are of great interest and of importance to any study of the history of London of this period. On their role in the Goldsmiths' Mistery, see Reddaway and Walker, pp. 120–25 *et passim* via the Index.

and lists headed by one or the other word may contain the names of those from both categories. The looseness of usage can be seen for example in that Hugh de Everwyk (York) and Henri de Norwiz are both termed 'estrange' (A + a, p. 4), whereas Johan Vandir Hawe is for instance termed a 'forayn' (A + a, p. 10) although his name suggests very much that he is a 'Dutchman' and one might therefore expect him to be labelled an 'estrange'. The translation has sometimes been able to differentiate, dependent on context, but has often used the word 'alien', which may not nowadays be politically correct but has a respectable historical pedigree.

grace

The phrases 'il se myst a lo*ur* g*ra*ce', 'ils les mystront en la g*ra*ce des ditz gardeinz *et* bonz gentz del orfev*er*ie', 'le dite Joh*a*n soy mist a g*ra*ce', 'il paia p*ar* g*ra*ce', 'sur g*ra*ce', 'sur g*ra*ce dé mesmez gardeyns', and others similar are used to refer to judgments made and sentences passed for misdeeds where the penalty paid is not one laid down and fixed by ordinance or statute. 'Grace' has here the meaning of 'favour or goodwill, in contradistinction to right or obligation, as the ground of a concession' (*OED*). Many instances will be found where the warden's judgment is to impose a lighter sentence than that laid down by ordinance, but it is used also where the misdeed committed is not covered by ordinance for a set penalty. The wardens also and very frequently set a penalty and were then appealed to, 'sur grace', to reduce or commute this. The translation for 'il se myst a lo*ur* g*ra*ce' has usually used a phrase such as 'he submitted to their judgment' and although this does not convey the whole flavour of the sense, it is close and the surrounding context often conveys more.[55]

lowys, lowé, allowis, allowé

This word in its various forms refers to a serving-man, a hired man or hired servant. The word is derived from the French verb 'allouer/alouwer' (< Latin 'allocare'), AN 'aluer, alower, allouer', one of whose meanings is 'to hire'. Unfortunately this word was misunderstood by W. Herbert and, following him, by Reddaway and Walker and Susan Hare who all thought that the word derived from the sense of 'to allow' rather than that of 'to hire'.[56] There is however no doubt about the correct meaning, and the word is found in a large variety of other medieval documents concerning hired men and servants. In the sections of the Goldsmiths' registers here which are written in Latin the equivalent word used is 'allocatus'. The confusion over the meaning was perhaps occasioned by the manner in which a number of lists in these registers are headed. In the early years we find lists in which a fee is paid by an apprentice 'p*ur* son dep*ar*tir' or 'pur son aler' – 'for his departure'. In 1344–45 we find the heading 'Ceux sount les app*re*ntiz issauntz de lo*ur* t*er*me de mesme l'an xviiime', and in 1349–50 'Les issauntz de lo*ur* t*er*mes', in 1350–51 'Ceux sunt lé nouns de ceux q*e* sunt venutz hors de lo*ur* terme l'an xxiiiime'. It is not until 1356–57 that the word appears: 'Ces sount les nouns des app*re*ntiz *et*

[55] One may also note the use of the equivalent phrasing in Latin: 'Joh*ann*es Markeby *et* Joh*ann*es Chester posuerunt se in arbitriu*m* Joh*ann*is Pake *et* Johannis Wynne' (A + a, p. 144).

[56] See e.g. Reddaway and Walker, p. 52, n. 21.

lowez entrez en l'an susdit' and the first serving-man listed is Robert Godman: 'Item, de Adam Elsham pur Robert Godman son allowis – ii s.' who has not appeared before as an apprentice, the same being true of others listed afterwards as 'lowys'. They must however of course have been apprentices somewhere and/or have learnt their craft from some master (if from their father or another close relative the same strict rules of registration might not have always been applied at this date). Once an apprenticeship was over, a formal release was necessary and, provided the required standard had been reached, the young man was sworn to abide by all ordinances governing the craft, was registered as a freeman of the city, was perhaps made a member of the fraternity (this sometimes happened only later),[57] and was then qualified to be a serving-man and to be paid for any work done – apprentices of course were not paid for their labour. Thus at the time a young man came out of his terms, he qualified to be a serving-man, and for some years this is indicated in the headings in the Goldsmiths' registers, the matter eventually being abbreviated just to saying that the following list is of 'lowys'.[58]

sonel, sonail

The word 'sonel' and its variants are not otherwise so far attested in Anglo-Norman, and in continental French it is found used only as a small bell attached around the neck of an animal; the word 'soneiz' is found in the sense of 'pealing of bells'.[59] The question has been to decide in examples such as 'Primes, p*ur* soner le g*ra*unt sonel de Seint Dunston al esglise de Seint Poul' (A + a, p. 45) whether one should translate as 'pealing' or 'ringing of bells' or whether one is justified in translating the occurrences here as 'bell', which would lead to the conclusion that one of the great bells at St Paul's at this date was named 'St Dunstan', a fact not otherwise recorded. From the earliest years an amount is regularly found each year in the wardens' expenses for the ringing of a bell or bells at St Paul's on either St Dunstan's Day or its eve. The earliest mention is in 1336–37: 'It*em*, p*ur* soner le noune de Seynt Dunston *et* autr*es* despens faitz – v s.' The other expenses are sometimes defined as for 'beverage' in general terms, sometimes as ale specifically, and bread and cheese are occasionally mentioned also as having been provided for the occasion. St Dunstan is often not mentioned specifically, the phrase used being just either e.g. 'soner le noune' or 'paié p*ur* soner a Seynt Poul'. The first specific mention

[57] See e.g. the career of John Canon, registered as an apprentice in 1357–58, coming out of his terms in 1365–66, and only listed as 'entreez en le fr*a*nchise' in 1369–70.

[58] In 1358–59 and the following year a list was written of 'les nouns de les issantz de lo*ur* appr*e*nticialté', but in 1361–62 we hear of 'les nou*n*s d'appr*e*ntysez *et* lowys de la orfeve*r*ye entrans et issans' and below of 'lowys yssans'. The next year's entry includes a list of 'les issantz hors de lo*ur* te*r*me', the lists of following years are headed similarly, and in 1370–71 there is a return to a previously used phrase: 'Ceux sount lez nounz des lowys ysantz hors de lo*ur* te*r*mes'. The following year this is changed slightly: 'Ceux sount lez nounz des lowys q*e* viegnont hors de lo*ur* te*r*me puis le jo*ur* de Seint Dunston l'a[n] xlv^{te} suisdit' and similar wording is used for the next few years. In 1375–76 a Latin heading is used: 'No*m*i*n*a de novo jur*atorum* indigen*orum*' ('the names of denizens recently sworn') and the phrasing suggests that it may be that the following list is not entirely comparable, but the previous type of phrasing is used for the next few years. Then in 1381–82 one finds the heading: 'Ces sount les nouns des lowys' – the scribe has abbreviated and his usage then becomes standard.

[59] See *AND* sub SONEIZ.

of a bell, 'the great bell of St Paul's' comes in 1366–67: 'It*em*, p*ur* le soner del g*ra*untz seyns de Seint Poul'. In 1371–72 we find the entry given above: 'Primes, p*ur* soner le g*ra*unt sonel de Seint Dunston al esglise de Seint Poul', the following year's entry being similar, while in 1373–74 the bell-tower is mentioned for the first time: 'Primes, p*ur* soner none en le belfray de Seint Poul de div*er*ses costagies – vii s. iii d.' In 1374–75 it is specified that the ringing of the bell was done on the eve of St Dunstan's Day: 'Primes, p*ur* sonere non*e* le veile de Seint Dunstan en la Belfray de Seint Poule p*ur* div*er*s costages – vi s. viii d.' Such entries continue to appear each year, the phrasing of the entries varying over the years as does the amount paid. The last mention of this expense is in the accounts for 1402–03. I consulted Dr Christopher Wilson about these matters, and, in the light of these entries in the Goldsmiths' records, he realised that a curious distich of 1399:

> A. Post Donstanum post somnum meridianum.
> C. Cuculum vixi terrae motum sic tibi dixi.[60]

may very well indicate that London's midday bell was named 'Dunstan'. (St Dunstan had of course been a bishop of London in 959–60 and was a well-respected saint with his own chapel in the cathedral.) The Goldsmiths' records refer several times to 'soner noune' or 'soner le noune de Seynt Dunsto*n*' ('ringing noon', 'ringing the noon of St Dunstan') and putting all these references together it seems that the Goldsmiths, in order to honour their patron saint, undertook each year the expenses of ringing the noonday bell of London on the feastday or its eve. The reasons why no entries occur after 1402–03 may well be, as Dr Wilson has pointed out, that shortly after this all the bells in the bell-tower were taken down and recast, and the break in continuity may have meant that the Goldsmiths chose not to continue with this civic piety.[61]

'yeomen'

A very few examples occur in these early texts of references to e.g. the 'Jeovenes gentz de mesme mestier, (A + a, p. 94) or 'the younge not in the lyv*ery*' (Book A, p. 33). Literally the translation would be 'young men' and we can see from the contexts that they belonged to the freedom but not the livery. In later years the terms 'bachelor' and 'yeoman' (which etymologically means 'young man') came to be applied to junior members of a trade or craft who had not yet been admitted to full membership of the mistery,[62] but at this date no standard term was in use. The term 'bachelor' is found in the Grocers' accounts, the earliest usage being in 1397 but where it does not however have the later full technical meaning.[63] An early instance of the term 'yeoman' is found in the Skinners' records for the year 1402 (the 'yemen companye')[64] and one finds it also in the

[60] See W. Sparrow Simpson, *Documents Illustrating the History of St Paul's Cathedral* (Camden Society, 1880), p. 59.

[61] Further details will be found in Christopher Wilson's forthcoming book, *The Honour and Glory of London: The Architecture of St Paul's Cathedral 1087–1547.*

[62] See e.g. Morris and Valerie Pearl, 'A Revolt in 1529 by Yeomen against the Wardens of the Goldsmiths' Company', *The Review of the Worshipful Company of Goldsmiths*, 1979–80 (London: The Goldsmiths' Company, 1980), 23–27.

[63] See P. Nightingale, *A Medieval Mercantile Comunity: The Grocers' Company and the Politics and Trade of London 1000–1485* (New Haven and London, 1995), p. 341.

[64] See E. Veale, *The English Fur Trade in the Later Middle Ages* (Oxford, 1966), pp. 112–13.

Merchant Taylors' accounts for the year 4 Henry VI (1425–26) ('Item ressu des gardeins del yemon taillours pur soun felawschip – xl s.') By this time these yeomen of the Skinners and Tailors were organised into their own company.[65] I have chosen to use the word 'yeomen' in my translation also, but it should be realised that the Goldsmiths referred to were junior members of the company, but were not at this date a separately organised body – the word matches that of later usage within the Goldsmiths' Mistery, but should not be over-interpreted.

Other standard decisions made about translation are as follows:

The dating by regnal years in usually phrased in the French text by giving the king's designation as e.g. 'E*dward* tierçz puis le conquest' ('Edward the third after the conquest') or 'Henri quarte puys le conqueste' ('Henry the fourth after the conquest'). In the translation, the phrase 'after the conquest' has normally been omitted as redundant in modern English usage.

'pur son departir' and 'pur son aler' have been translated as 'for his release from his terms' or 'on completion of his terms'. Literally the phrases mean 'for his leaving/departure' and 'for his going' but these do not in modern English convey the intended sense: these men have completed their terms of apprenticeship and are paying the regulation fee of 2s. to be released from their apprenticeship.

Fairly regularly I have translated 'orfeverie' as 'goldsmiths' e.g. le mister d'orfeverie – the Goldsmiths' Mistery or Company . . .

The phrase 'en temps de' = 'in the time of', when used to refer to the time during which a set of wardens held office, is normally translated here as 'during the term of office of . . .'.

Names

These are transcribed just as they are in the original text, but in the translation some standardisations have been made. It has been impossible to be entirely consistent in the methodology of this, since so many uncertainties subsist in the text and since modern practice over such matters varies. My aims have been to help readers (not all of whom might recognise e.g. Cologne in 'Coleyne' or realise that e.g. Nichol de Walryngworthe and Nicholas de Wyrlyngworth are the same man) and to make the translation text read in this as in other ways as 'normal English'. The parallel text format allows one at a glance to check any change made, and the name index contains all variant spellings found and other information, and should be used in conjunction with the text.

The following types of standardisation have been used where appropriate: Place names as surnames are given in their modern form, e.g. Salusbery – Salisbury; Teukisbery – Tewkesbury; Bedeford – Bedford; Berkyngge – Barking; Cornhulle – Cornhill. However, Oxenford has been left thus, as has Northwyche, which is very probably Norwich but could also be Northwich (Cheshire) or Northwick (Glos.), and Nichole has also been left thus, although

[65] See Veale, *English Fur Trade*; C.M. Clode, *The Early History of the Guild of Merchant Taylors of the Fraternity of St John the Baptist, London*, 2 vols (London, 1888), I, 60–68.

Thomas de Nichole almost certainly derived his name from Lincoln (the name index allows one to check possible relationships between those with the surname Nichol(e) and those with the surname of Lincoln). Similarly, other names which only occur once and where doubt might subsist (e.g. Bokenham might be either Bockingham, Essex, or Buckingham) have been left unchanged.

The ending -e in Middle English must often be understood as pronounced -ee or -ey, e.g. Bromle, and this applies to a number of place names as surnames. It is not however by any means easy to be sure in many cases since a final -e may also be silent. In cases of doubt, no change has been made.

Many names occur sometimes with and sometimes without a 'de', e.g. Adam (de) Walpole, and the 'de' has always been included in the translation if it appears in the original.

Names derived from a trade or profession have very occasionally been slightly changed to make this clear, e.g. Andrew Selgravere is translated as Andrew Sealgraver. This makes it clear that whereas this may well be his surname, it is possible that the reference is to Andrew, the sealgraver. All such names, particularly in the early years, should be treated with caution: Walter Le Mazerer may well be Walter, the mazerer. As late as 1403–04 Bartholomew Seman appears in the register as Bartholomew Goldbetere.

Contractions of names built from the form 'fitz'/'fis' have all been rendered in the standard modern way as 'Fitz-' e.g. Fithewe – FitzHugh.

For people who appear many times with their names spelt in a variety of ways, the name is standardised to common usage, e.g. Richard Whittington (not Whetyngdoun); or to what appears the most common form, e.g. Coraunt (not Currant). There may well be some inconsistencies in how this has been done, for when a name appears only twice or three times, each with a different spelling, it is often problematic to know how to deal with it, even if (which is not always the case) one is sure it is the same person.

I have resisted the temptation to change Fraunceys to Francis or Frenshe to French, or Morys to Morris, and these have been left in their medieval form. Broun is also left thus, and not changed to Brown (whose pronunciation is different), and Grene has been left unchanged also.

Foster/Faster/Vedast have been rendered as Foster Lane but St Vedast's church.

WARDENS' ACCOUNTS AND COURT MINUTE BOOKS OF THE GOLDSMITHS' MISTERY OF LONDON, 1334–1446

1334–35 . . . ?exarez?[2] a les autres gardeins

A + a

p. 1, col. 1[1]

?De Mathe Vonne? –	xx d.
It*em*, de Richard Henneye –	ii s.
It*em*, de Raulin Counb –	ii s.
It*em*, de rente quite del tenement Rob*er*t le Bret –	i. m*a*rc
It*em*, de Thom*as* de P.. –	i m*a*rc
It*em*, de .. Joh*an* de Hallyngbury –	x li.
It*em*, de Thom*as* le Mazerere –	ii s.

Thom*as* de Oxenford p*ur* son app*re*ntiz Joh*an* Chym*er*ot –	ii s.
It*em*, Joh*an* Makenhened p*ur* son app*re*ntiz Moude de Reynham –	ii s.
It*em*, Nichol de Worlyngworth*e* p*ur* son app*re*ntiz –	ii s.
It*em*, Rob*er*t de Norwich*e* p*ur* son app*re*ntiz –	ii s.
It*em*, Henri Mazere p*ur* son app*re*ntiz William Hamond –	ii s.
It*em*, Joh*an* Kemsyng p*ur* son app*re*ntiz Johan Dedyngtou*n* –	ii s.
It*em*, Andreu Selgraver p*ur* son app*re*ntiz Joh*an* Borforde –	ii s.
Thom*a*s Wariner p*ur* son app*re*ntiz –	ii s.
It*em*, Joh*an* de Kele p*ur* son app*re*ntiz –	ii s.

Les nouns q*e* ne ount paié:

Joh*an* de P*re*stou*n* p*ur* son app*re*ntiz William Pant.. –	ii s.
Ric*hard* Denys p*ur* son app*re*ntiz –	ii s.

Thom*as* de Westmenstr*e* p*ur* son app*re*ntiz –	ii s.
William Mikelh*a*m p*ur* son app*re*ntiz –	ii s.
William de Nortou*n* p*ur* son app*re*ntiz –	ii s.

Les nouns de pov*ere*[s] de mest*ier*:

Joh*an* Croboill*e* –	iii s.
Will*iam* Beauflo*ur* –	iii s.
Ric*hard* Souns*er* –	iii s.
Waut*er* Spaldyng –	ii s.
Joh*an* Blithe –	ii s.
Joh*an* Bonaunt –	ii s.
Joh*an* Maz –	iii s.
Anneys Sayekyn –	ii s.
Joh*an* Kyngestou*n* –	xviii d.
Joh*an* Noel –	iii s.
Will*iam* Hakeneyeman –	xviii d.
Thom*as* Conv*er*s –	ii s.

p. 1, col. 2 Adam Donne . . .

Henr*i* Conventre . . .

Joh*an* Fyngh*a*m . . .

[1] The corners of this and the following few folios have been badly damaged. UV-light has enabled the retrieval of some words or parts of words, others may be guessed at. Uncertain readings are indicated by question marks.

[2] This is very indistinct and is very probably not quite this (not a known word), but something similar: examinez?

1334–35
A + a
p. 1, col. 1

. . . ? to the other Wardens?	
?From Matthew Vonne –	20d.
Item, from Richard Hanneye –	2s.
Item, from Raulin Counb –	2s.
Item, from quitrent of the tenement of Robert le Bret –	1 mark.
Item, from Thomas de P.. –	1 mark.
Item, from .. John de Hallyngbury –	£10.
Item, from Thomas Le Mazerer[1] –	2s.

Thomas de Oxenford for his apprentice John Chymerot –	2s.
Item, John Makenhened for his apprentice Maud de Raynham –	2s.
Item, Nichol de Worlingworth for his apprentice –	2s.
Item, Robert de Norwich for his apprentice –	2s.
Item, Henry Mazere for his apprentice William Hamond –	2s.
Item, John Kemsing for his apprentice John Deddington –	2s.
Item, Andrew Sealgraver for his apprentice John Borforde –	2s.
Thomas Wariner for his apprentice –	2s.
Item, John de Kele for his apprentice –	2s.

The names of those who have not paid:

John de Preston for his apprentice William Pant.. –	2s.
Richard Denys for his apprentice –	2s.

Thomas de Westminster for his apprentice –	2s.
William Mickleham for his apprentice –	2s.
William de Nortoun for his apprentice –	2s.

The names of the poor people [supported by alms] of the mistery:[2]

John Croboille –	3s.
William Beauflour –	3s.
Richard Sounser –	3s.
Walter Spalding –	2s.
John Blithe –	2s.
John Bonaunt –	2s.
John Maz –	3s.
Agnes Sayekyn –	2s.
John Kingston –	18d.
John Noel –	3s.
William Hackneyman –	18d.
Thomas Convers –	2s.

Adam Donne p. 1, col. 2
Henry Coventry
John Fyngham

[1] This might be not a surname but 'Thomas the mazerer'.
[2] The amounts given here should be compared to figures given for the subsequent few years for alms payments.

Will*iam* Bele ..
Joh*an* Sporon . . .

S*umma* – xxxv..

1335–36 Les nouns des gardeins . . . Seint Dunstan . . .
Thom*as* de Porkele, Joh*an* Makenhened,
Ric*hard* Henneye, Simon de Berkyng

Doné al encrés cest an ixe horsp*ri*s la quilette des ap*re*ntiz – xvi m*ar*cs.

La Su*m*me – xli li. xv s. ix d.

Les poys des cirges liv*er*ez as ditz gardeyns de novele sire, c'est a sav*oir* xxxvi ll.

Les am*er*ciamentz q*e* ne sont paiez:

Thom*as* de Westmenstr*e* p*ur* Rob*er*t de Richemond –	.i. ll.
Joh*a*n de Toppesfeld p*ur* mesme celui Rob*er*t de Richemond –	.i. ll.
Joh*a*n de P*re*stou*n* –	.i. ll.

Hugh le Rede *con*tre Joh*a*n Hengestou*n* –	ii s.
Thom*as* de Algate p*ur* verre mys en or –	d*em*i mar*c*.

Argent baillé a William Sporon des am*er*cementz, c'est assav*oir*:
Del argent Bestworth – vi s. viii d.

It*em*, de William Pollin p*ur* trespas fait a Simon Berlyng[3] – iii s.

1336–37
p. 2, col. 1. . . des gardeyns del . . . l'an du r*egne le* R*oi* apr*és* le conquest . . . c'est assavoir:

Joh*a*n de Hengestou*n*
[Joh*a*n] de Toppesfeld
Ric*hard* de Bassyngstoke
Waut*er* le Mazerer

Doné al encress*e* mesme l'an horsp*ri*s la q*ui*lete dé app*re*ntiz *et* de m*er*cimentz – xx m*ar*cz.

Ceux sount lé despeyns de mesme ceux gardeyns faitz l'an avant nomé:
Adep*ri*mes, paié a viii pov*er*es chescun semaigne iii s. iiii d. q*e* amonte l'an viii li. xiii s. iiii d.
It*em*, en argent doné as pov*er*es encontr*e* la Noel – xxxvi s. viii d.

[3] This is very possibly a copying error for 'Berkyng'. This suggested correction is based on the fact that Simon Barking was Warden at the time, and it is offences against the wardens which tend to be prosecuted; also on the lack of any other mention of a Simon Berlyng and on the fact that the register is here being copied up from earlier notes and this sort of error is very possible. However, goldsmiths with the surname Berlyng appear in the fifteenth century and the entry may of course be quite correct as it stands.

William Bele
John Sporon

Total: 35 [s.][3]

The names of the Wardens . . . St Dunstan . . . 1335–36
Thomas de Porkele, John Makenhened,
Richard Hanneye, Simon de Barking

Given to the increase [in funds][4] in this year 9 [Edward III] [1335], excluding monies collected from apprentices – 16 marks.

Total: £41 15s. 9d.

The weight of candles of new wax delivered to the said Wardens, i.e. 36lb.

Amercements unpaid:

Thomas de Westminster for Robert de Richmond –	£1.
John de Toppesfield for the same Robert de Richmond –	£1.
John de Preston –	£1.

Hugh le Rede against John Hingston –	2s.
Thomas de Aldgate for a glass gemstone[5] set in gold –	½ mark.

Money from amercements entrusted to William Sporon, i.e.
From the Bestworth money – 6s. 8d.

Item, from William Pollin for an offence committed against Simon Berlyng[6] – 3s.

. . . of the Wardens of the . . . the year of the reign of King . . . after the Conquest, i.e. 1336–37 p. 2, col. 1
John de Hingston
John de Toppesfield
Richard de Basingstoke
Walter le Mazerer

Given to the increase [of funds] in the same year, excluding the monies collected from apprentices and from amercements – 20 marks.

These are the expenditures of the same Wardens made in the aforesaid year:
Firstly, paid to 8 poor people: 3s. 4d. each week which amounts in the year to £8 13s. 4d.

[3] This total shows that the last few named must have received only small amounts.

[4] An alternative translation of 'encrés' would be 'profit', but this would perhaps convey too modern an impression. On this regular item listed in the records see the Introduction, pp. xviii–xix.

[5] The word 'verre' means 'glass' and must here refer to an artificial gemstone. For the rules about their use, see below, A + a, pp. 40–41.

[6] See note on opposite page.

– q*e* a amountté a chescun gardeyn – ix s. ii d.
It*em*, en ent*er*ement de Thom*as* le Ben – ii s. iii d. ob.
It*em*, p*ur* soner le noune de Seynt Dunsto*n* *et* aut*re*s despens faitz – v s.
It*em*, achatez iii li. de cire plus q*e* le q*uarter* – xviii d. ob.
It*em*, en portag*e* *et* bev*er*ag*e* – iii d.
It*em*, en despens faitz as semblez des bones gentz del orfaverie p*ar* t*r*oiz foiz – xii d.

S*umma* de despences – xi li. ob.[4]

L'an dysme la su*m*me de chescun gardeyn amou*n* xxii lib. xi s. v d.

Ces sount les nouns de app*re*ntiz resceux mesme l'an des gardeyns avauntnomez:
A p*ri*mes:[5]

col. 2 l'ap*re*ntiz Gilb*er*t de Salesbury –	ii s.
It*em*, Rauf Frer*e* l'ap*re*ntiz Joh*a*n de Walepole –	ii s. q*ui*t
Joh*an* Brian l'ap*re*ntiz Will*iam* de Nortou*n* –	ii s. gag*é*
Joh*a*n de Perndou*n* l'app*re*ntiz Joh*an* de Brauncestr*e* –	ii s. q*ui*t
Joh*a*n de Bev*er*le, l'app*re*ntiz Martyn de Dunnesburi –	ii s. gag*é*
Joh*a*n Child, l'apprentiz Joh*an* de Prestou*n* –	ii s. gag*é*
Henr*i* Lap*er*tenhal*e* l'app*re*ntiz Joh*an* de Hyngeston*e* –	ii s. q*ui*t
Ric*hard* de Sandwiz l'app*rentiz* Nichol de Sandwyz –	ii s. gag*é*
Will*iam* atte More l'app*re*ntiz Joh*an* Burdeyn –	ii s. gag*é*
Edmu*n*d de Wyk app*re*ntiz Rob*er*t de [Bes]nes[6] –	ii s. gag*é*
Thom*as* de Brandou*n* app*rentiz* Gilb*er*t de Steyndrop*e* –	ii s.
Joh*a*n Munde app*rentiz* Andrew Brocher*e* –	ii s.
Jon Polbwe app*rentiz* Phelipot Yver –	ii s.
Reynaud de Gerstou*n* app*rentiz* Will*iam* de Mikenh*a*m –	ii s.
Joh*an* Burcestr*e* app*rentiz* Rob*er*t de Norwiz –	ii s.
Will*ia*m de Musch*a*m app*rentiz* Johan de Shaftesbur*i* –	ii s.
Charles de Gerstou*n* app*rentiz* Rob*er*t de Wyk –	ii s.
Joh*an* de Buchesle app*rentiz* Will*iam* de Caustou*n* –	ii s.
Will*iam* Banme app*rentiz* Will*iam* Poleham –	ii s.
l'ap*re*ntiz Thom*as* de Nichol –	ii s.
Will*iam* Soroun apprentiz Waut*er* Ramenh*a*m –	ii s.

S*umma* des app*re*ntiz – xliii s.

Ceux sount les am*er*ciamentz mesme l'an xme:
Adep*ri*mes de Thom*as* de Alegate p*ur* i verre mys en or – v. s.

[4] Here as often elsewhere the sum total figure given does not quite tally with the amounts given for individual expenses; the expenses listed above total £10 19s. 10d. A variety of hypotheses might account for the discrepancy. Such occasions are not generally noted hereafter.

[5] The page is cropped here but in fact nothing may be missing, and the top of the next column may be the straight follow-on (he is not the only anonymous apprentice in this list); however, it is also possible that a line or two may have disappeared.

[6] The first few letters are unclear. This seems the most likely expansion.

Item, money given to the poor at Christmas time – 36s. 8d.
– which came to 9s. 2d. for each Warden.
Item, for the burial of Thomas le Ben – 2s. 3½d.
Item, for bell-ringing at noon[7] on St Dunstan's Day, and other expenditures – 5s.
Item, 3lb. of wax bought more than the quarter[8]–18½d.
Item, in porterage and for drink[9] – 3d.
Item, in expenditures made at three assemblies of the goodmen of the Goldsmiths' Mistery – 12d.

Total expenses: £11 ½d.

In 1336 the total from each Warden amounts to £22 11s. 5d.

These are the names of apprentices admitted in the same year by the aforenamed Wardens:
Firstly:

the apprentice of Gilbert de Salisbury –	2s.		col. 2
Item, Rauf Frere, the apprentice of John de Walpole –	2s.	quit	
John Brian, the apprentice of William de Norton –	2s.	– pledged	
John de Perndoun, the apprentice of John de Brancaster –	2s.	quit	
John de Beverly, the apprentice of Martin de Dunnesbury –	2s.	pledged	
John Child, the apprentice of John de Preston –	2s.	pledged	
Henry Lapertenhale, the apprentice of John de Hingston –	2s.	quit	
Richard de Sandwich, the apprentice of Nicholas de Sandwich –	2s.	pledged	
William atte More, the apprentice of John Burdeyn –	2s.	pledged	
Edmund de Wyk, apprentice of Robert de Besnes –	2s.	pledged	
Thomas de Brandon, apprentice of Gilbert de Staindrop –	2s.		
John Munde, apprentice of Andrew Brochere –	2s.		
John Polbwe, apprentice of Philipot Yver –	2s.		
Reynaud de Garstoun, apprentice of William de Mickleham –	2s.		
John Burcestre, apprentice of Robert de Norwich –	2s.		
William de Muscham, apprentice of John de Shaftesbury –	2s.		
Charles de Garstoun, apprentice of Robert de Wyk –	2s.		
John de Buchesle, apprentice of William de Caustoun –	2s.		
William Bamme, apprentice of William Poleham –	2s.		
the apprentice of Thomas de Nichol[10] –	2s.		
William Soroun, apprentice of Walter Ramenham –	2s.		

Total from apprentices: – 43s.

These are the amercements in the same year 10 [Edward III] [1336]:
Firstly, from Thomas de Aldgate, for a glass gemstone set in gold – 5s.

[7] One could translate here as 'Nones' rather than 'noon', but see Introduction, pp. xxxv–xxxvi.
[8] The meaning of this is obscure: it might mean that they had an annual amount of wax allocated (the quarter-barrel?) and have gone above this by 3lb.
[9] 'Beverage' here and below might refer either to actual drinks supplied or to money given as a 'tip'. From 1384 onwards an amount is listed specifically for ale at the occasion of the tolling of the bell of St Paul's, but for many years previous to that no expense for drink is listed at all.
[10] This is very probably the man named elsewhere as Thomas de Lincoln. See Name Index.

Item, de Piers Conv*er*s p*ur* i trespas fait enver Joh*a*n de Ipeg*ra*ve – iiii s. iiii d.
Item, de Thom*a*s Sporon p*ur* i. t*re*spas fait env*er* Thom*a*s de Porkele – vi s. viii d.
It*em*, de William de Caustou*n* p*ur* la rescette de son app*rentiz* fausement ov*er*eaunt – xii d.
Item, de Joh*a*n de Gauntou*n* p*ur* i t*re*spas fait v*er*s Thom*a*s de Nichole – iii s. iiii d.
It*em*, le valet Joh*a*n de Makenhened p*ur* i t*re*spas fait v*er*s Joh*a*n de Bemesyng – iii s.
It*em*, Wat*er* de Algate *et* de Thomas Bamme p*ur* i fermail oev*eré* de feble or – iii s. iiii d.
Item, Joh*a*n de Gauntou*n* p*ur* un t*re*spas fait a Wat*er* le Mazerer.

S*umma* des am*er*ciamentz – xxvii s. viii d.

1337–38 Ces sount les nouns dé gardeyns del orfaverie de Londou*n* en l'an du regne
p. 3, col. 1 le roi Edward tierçz ap*rés* le conques[t] u[n]szime:
William Sporon
Rob*er*t de Wyke
Nichol de Farndou*n*
Joh*a*n de Walepole

Don*é* al encress horp*ris* lé quylettes des app*re*ntiz *et* d'am*er*ciamentz mesme cel an – viiii li. x s.

Ceux sount lé despenses faites mesme l'an, p*ri*merement p*ur* viii povres – viii li. xiii s. iiii d.
Item, en argent doné contre le Noel – xxxvi s. vi d.
Item, p*ur* l'ent*er*ement William de Hung*ri*e – xvii d.
It*em*, p*ur* le sonner de Noune – v s. vi d.
Item, en costages del lum*er*e outre la q*ui*lette iiii s. vii d.

Les nouns des app*re*ntiz resceux mesme l'an:
P*ri*merement, Thom*a*s de Ippeg*ra*ve l'app*re*ntiz Joh*a*n de Ippeg*ra*ve – ii s.
It*em*, Rog*er* l'app*re*ntiz Thom*a*s de Oxenford – ii s.
Giffr*ei* de Porkele l'app*re*ntiz Thom*a*s de Cleye – ii s.
Will*iam* de Manefeld l'app*re*ntiz Joh*a*n de Gloucestr*e* – ii s.
Item, Rog*er* Bonde l'app*re*ntiz Simon de Eyhsh*a*m – ii s.
Item, Joh*a*n Furneys l'app*re*ntiz Joh*a*n de Goppislond – ii s.
Joh*a*n de Croydou*n* app*re*ntiz Joh*a*n de Bele – ii s.
Ric*hard* app*re*ntiz Thom*a*s Shonke – ii s.
Thom*a*s de Som*er*sete app*re*ntiz Thom*a*s Conv*er*s – ii s.
Will*iam* Soneye app*re*ntiz dame Alice de Besnes – ii s.

Item, from Piers Convers, for an offence committed against John de Ippegrave – 4s. 4d.
Item, from Thomas Sporon, for an offence committed against Thomas de Porkele – 6s. 8d.
Item, from William de Caustoun, for sheltering his apprentice who was doing false work – 12d.
Item, from John de Gauntoun, for an offence committed against Thomas de Nichole – 3s. 4d.
Item, John de Makenhened's boy, for an offence committed against John de Bemesyng – 3s.
Item, from Walter de Aldgate and Thomas Bamme, for a ring-brooch[11] made of sub-standard gold – 3s. 4d.
Item, John de Gauntoun, for an offence committed against Walter Le Mazerer.

Total from amercements – 27s. 8d.

These are the names of the Wardens of the Goldsmiths' Mistery of London in the year 11 Edward III [1337]: 1337–38 p. 3, col. 1
William Sporon
Robert de Wyk
Nicholas de Farndon
John de Walpole

Given to the increase [of funds], excluding the monies collected from apprentices and from amercements in that same year – £9 10s.

These are the expenditures made in the same year, firstly for 8 poor people – £8 13s. 4d.
Item, money distributed at Christmas time – 36s. 6d.
Item, for the burial of William de Hungrie – 17d.
Item, for the bell-ringing at noon – 5s. 6d.
Item, for the costs of the light[12] over and above the collection – 4s. 7d.

The names of apprentices admitted the same year:

Firstly, Thomas de Ippegrave, the apprentice of John de Ippegrave –	2s.
Item, Roger, the apprentice of Thomas de Oxenford –	2s.
Geoffrey de Porkele, the apprentice of Thomas de Claye –	2s.
William de Manfield, the apprentice of John de Gloucester –	2s.
Item, Roger Bonde, the apprentice of Simon de Esham –	2s.
Item, John Furneys, the apprentice of John de Goppislond –	2s.
John de Croydon, apprentice of John de Bele –	2s.
Richard, apprentice of Thomas Shonke –	2s.
Thomas de Somerset, apprentice of Thomas Convers –	2s.
William Soneye, apprentice of the lady Alice de Besnes –	2s.

[11] 'Fermail' is the word used for a ring-brooch, a clasp or fastener on clothes, the morse of a cope.
[12] The light maintained at the Hospital of St James (see below). Later they maintained a light at the church of St John Zachary, and in the chapel of St Dunstan at St Paul's.

Joh*an* Kyle app*r*entiz Rob*er*t de Wyke – ii s.
It*em*, Rob*er*t de Foleh*am* app*r*entiz Waut*er* atte Ferne – ii s.
It*em*, Joh*an* Sauterer app*r*entiz Rob*er*t Shordich*e* – ii s.
It*em*, Will*iam* de Claverynge app*r*entiz Ric*hard* Denys – ii s.
Thom*as* Alard app*r*entiz Rob*er*t puisné[7] – ii s.
It*em*, Will*iam* Bate app*r*entiz Simon *Con*ars – ii s.
It*em*, Ric*hard* de Wykh*am*, brok*er*, app*r*entiz Johan de Shaftesbury – ii s.
Laucas Rauf app*r*entiz Joh*an* Botener – ii s.
Will*iam* Braye app*r*entiz Ric*hard* de Hanneye – ii s.
Rob*er*t atte Stokes app*r*entiz William de Chastre – ii s.
Joh*an* atte Mersshe app*r*entiz William de Caustou*n* – ii s.
Will*iam* Faunt app*r*entiz William de Ippeg*ra*ve – ii s.
Beneyt de Wychelsee app*r*entiz Thom*as* del Algat*e* – ii s.
col. 2 Joh*an* Gerveys app*r*entiz . . .
It*em*, ii aut*r*es app*r*entiz de Will*iam* . . .

S*umma* – liiii s. . . .

p*ur* l'am*er*ciement de Chastre – iii s. iiii d.

1338–39 Ceux sount les nouns des gardeyns del orfaverie de Loundres l'an du regne le roi Edwar tierçz ap*rés* le conquest duszyme:
Nichol de Walryngworth*e*
Rob*er*t de Shordich*e* le puysné
William de Ippeg*ra*ve
Thom*as* de Farndou*n*

Doné al encrés horsp*ri*s les quilettes des app*r*entiz *et* am*er*ciamentz mesme l'an – viii li. xiii s. iiii d.

Ceux sount les despences mesme l'an:
P*ri*merement p*ur* viii pouvres – viii li. xiii s. iiii d.
It*em*, en argent doné countre le Nowel – xxxviii s. viii d.
It*em*, p*ur* le soner de Noune *et* bev*er*ag*e* – vi s. vi d.
It*em*, en despens de lum*ere*, outr*e* la q*ui*lette, al hospital Seynt Jake – v s. x d.
It*em*, p*ur* ii estandard a S*eynt* Pol – ii s. iiii d.

La su*m*me dé despences – xi li. xii s.

Et fait a remenbrer q*e* Ada*m* de Shadewell*e*, bodeler, en despit Seynt

[7] This is almost certainly Rob*er*t de Shordich*e* le puisné.

John Kyle, apprentice of Robert de Wyk – 2s.
Item, Robert de Foleham, apprentice of Walter atte Ferne – 2s.
Item, John Sauterer, apprentice of Robert Shoreditch – 2s.
Item, William de Claverynge, apprentice of Richard Denys – 2s.
Thomas Alard, apprentice of Robert [de Shoreditch] the younger – 2s.
Item, William Bate, apprentice of Simon Conars – 2s.
Item, Richard de Wykham, broker, apprentice of John de Shaftesbury – 2s.
Lucas Rauf apprentice of John Botener – 2s.
William Braye, apprentice of Richard de Hanneye – 2s.
Robert atte Stokes, apprentice of William de Chastre – 2s.
John atte Marsh, apprentice of William de Caustoun – 2s.
William Faunt, apprentice of William de Ippegrave – 2s.
Benedict de Winchelsea, apprentice of Thomas de Aldgate – 2s.
John Gerveys, apprentice . . . col. 2
Item, 2 other apprentices of William . . .

Total: 54s.

for the amercement of Chastre – 3s. 4d.

These are the names of the Wardens of the Goldsmiths' Mistery of London 1338–39
in the year 12 Edward III [1338]:
Nicholas de Worlingworth
Robert de Shoreditch, the younger
William de Ippegrave
Thomas de Farndon

Given to the increase [of funds], excluding the monies collected from apprentices and amercements in the same year – £8 13s. 4d.

These are the expenses of the same year:
Firstly, for 8 poor people – £8 13s. 4d.
Item, money distributed at Christmas time – 38s. 8d.
Item, for the bell-ringing at noon and for drink – 6s. 6d.
Item, for the costs of the light at the Hospital of St James,[13] over and above the collection – 5s. 10d.
Item, for 2 standards[14] at St Paul's – 2s. 4d.

Total expenses: £11 12s.

Memo that Adam de Shadwell, bottler,[15] in despite of St Dunstan and of all

[13] The hospital was for women lepers and was run by nuns.
[14] i.e. wax torches.
[15] Although stated here to be a bottler, he is a goldsmith, who takes apprentices and is later fined – see Name Index. One must presume that A. de S. is already a member of the Bottlemakers' Mistery and is here refusing to join the fraternity of St Dunstan and has been warned that if he falls on hard times he will not be helped from the alms funds of the fraternity.

Dunstan de touz les bones gentz del orfaverie de Loundr*es* ad reneyé *et* refusé l'augmoigne Seynt Dunstan a touz jo*urs*, ceste refuser *et* renier fu fait en temps des gardeyns avauntdit l'an avaunt nomé.

Les nouns de app*re*ntiz mesme l'an resceux:
Will*iam* de Castre app*re*ntiz Joh*a*n de Kelleseye – ii s.
Will*iam* de Wyndesore app*re*ntiz Gilb*er*t de Salisburi – ii s.
Thom*as* app*re*ntiz Hugh fiuz Rog*er* – ii s.
Will*ia*m app*re*ntiz Simon de B*er*kyngg – ii s.
Rob*er*t app*re*ntiz Thom*as* Albold – ii s.
Joh*a*n app*re*ntiz Richard de Hanneye – ii s.
Thom*as* app*re*ntiz Joh*an* de Hyngestou*n* – ii s.
p. 4, col. 1 . . . [app*re*ntiz] Nich*ol* de Sandwiz – ii s.
. . . [app*re*ntiz] Nichol de Wellyngforw – ii s.
. . . ?Forester? app*re*ntiz Joh*a*n de Kele – ii s.
Joh*a*n app*re*ntiz William de Ippeg*ra*ve – ii s.
Rob*er*t app*re*ntiz Gilb*er*t de Steindrop*e* – ii s.
Joh*a*n app*re*ntiz William de Caustou*n* – ii s.
Joh*a*n Grus .p*ur* son dep*ar*tir – ii s.
De Phelemon l'ap*re*ntiz Hugh de Boltou*n* – ii s.
Will*ia*m app*re*ntiz Joh*a*n de Markeby – ii s.
Waut*er* app*re*ntiz Willia*m* de Shordich*e* – ii s.
Joh*a*n app*re*ntiz Thom*as* atte Claye – ii s.
Henr*i* app*re*ntiz Joh*an* de Salesbury – ii s.
Hugh de Ev*er*wyk, est*ra*nge, p*ur* son entré – ii s.
Henr*i* de Norwiz, est*ra*nge, p*ur* son entré – ii s.

Del am*er*ciment Thom*as* de Sporon – iii s. iiii d.

1339–40 Ceux sount les nouns des gardeyns del orfaverie de Londres l'an du regne le Roi Edward tierçz aprés le conquest treszyme:
Richard Denys
Rob*er*t de Shordych l'ysné
Rob*er*t le Mareschal
Joh*a*n de Hyngestou*n*

Doné al encress*e* horsp*ri*s les q*ui*lettes des ap*re*ntiz *et* des mercimentz mesme l'an – ix li.

Ceux sount les despenz faitz mesme l'an:
col. 2 P*ri*merement p[*ur*][8] viii povres – viii li. xiii s. iiii d.
It*em*, en argent doné contre Noel – xxxviii s.
It*em*, en le t*er*eme[nt] Adam Donne – iiii d.

[8] MS: p*ar*.

the good men of the Goldsmiths' Mistery of London, has renounced and refused the alms of St Dunstan for ever, this refusal and renunciation was made in the time of the aforesaid Wardens in the aforesaid year.

The names of apprentices admitted in the same year:
William de Castre, apprentice of John de Kelsey – 2s.
William de Windsor, apprentice of Gilbert de Salisbury – 2s.
Thomas, apprentice of Hugh FitzRoger – 2s.
William, apprentice of Simon de Barking – 2s.
Robert, apprentice of Thomas Albold – 2s.
John, apprentice of Richard de Hanneye – 2s.
Thomas, apprentice of John de Hingston – 2s.
. . . the apprentice of Nicholas de Sandwich – 2s. p. 4, col. 1
. . . the apprentice of Nicholas de Wellyngforw – 2s.
. . . ?Forester?, apprentice of John de Kele – 2s.
John, apprentice of William de Ippegrave – 2s.
Robert, apprentice of Gilbert de Staindrop – 2s.
John apprentice of William de Caustoun – 2s.
John Grus, for his release from his terms[16] – 2s.
from Philemon, the apprentice of Hugh de Bolton – 2s.
William, apprentice of John de Markeby – 2s.
Walter, apprentice of William de Shoreditch – 2s.
John, apprentice of Thomas atte Claye – 2s.
Henry, apprentice of John de Salisbury – 2s.
Hugh de York, alien, for his entry[17] – 2s.
Henry de Norwich, alien, for his entry – 2s.

From the amercement of Thomas de Sporon – 3s. 4d.

These are the names of the Wardens of the Goldsmiths' Mistery of London 1339–40
in the year 13 Edward III [1339]:
Richard Denys
Robert de Shoreditch the elder
Robert le Mareschal
John de Hingston

Given to the increase [of funds], excluding the monies collected from apprentices and from amercements in the same year – £9.

These are the expenditures made in the same year:
Firstly, for 8 poor people – £8 13s. 4d. col. 2
Item, money distributed at Christmas time – 38s.
Item, for the burial of Adam Donne – 4d.

[16] 'Pur son departir' means literally 'for his departure' or 'leaving' or 'coming out', and must refer here and below to the fee payable on completion of an apprentice's terms.
[17] Entry into the fraternity or the Mistery of the Goldsmiths of London.

It*em*, p*ur* la lum*ere* al hospital Seynt Jake outre la quilette q*e* amou*n*te xxxii ll. – *summa* vii s.
Item, p*ur* ii estandard a Seynt Pol – ii s. vi d.
It*em*, p*ur* les cirges des pouvres ové le fazon – iiii s. vi d.
It*em*, p*ur* le souener de noune *et* p*ur* bev*er*age a Seynt Pol – v s. vi d.

Les nouns des app*ren*tiz mesme l'an resceux:

Thom*as* le Renh*am* l'app*ren*tiz Ad*am* le Frenssh*e* –	ii s.
Will*ia*m de Brutou*n* app*ren*tiz William Wyndesore –	ii s.
Ric*hard* de Mich*am* app*ren*tiz Robert de Hatfeld –	ii s.
Joh*an* Dowel app*ren*tiz Joh*an* de Ippeg*ra*ve –	ii s.
Rob*er*t de Meone app*ren*tiz Joh*an* de Chicestr*e* –	ii s.
Joh*an* Broun app*ren*tiz Thom*as* Conv*ers* –	ii s.
Joh*an* de Goldeford p*ur* son app*ren*tiz –	ii s.
Joh*an* de Egentou*n* app*ren*tiz Jakes de Thame –	ii s.
Joh*an* Fairher app*ren*tiz Ric*hard* de Hanneye –	ii s.
Rob*er*t Galle p*ur* son dep*ar*tir –	ii s.
Thom*as* le Mareschal p*ur* son dep*ar*tir –	ii s.
Joh*an* de Birkele p*ur* son dep*ar*tir –	ii s.
Thom*as* de Wilryngworth*e* p*ur* son dep*ar*tir –	ii s.
Rob*er*t Brook p*ur* son dep*ar*ter –	ii s.
Joh*an* de Combirworth*e* p*ur* son dep*ar*tir –	ii s.
Renaud de Bilneye p*ur* son entr*é* –	vi s. viii d.
Laur*ence* de Wynstou*n* p*ur* son entr*é* –	iii s. iiii d.

Les am*er*cimentz mesme l'an:

P*ri*mes Joh*an* Baynard –	vi s. viii d.
Joh*ann*es de Chaftestbury –	ii s.
Reynaud Gargoil –	xiii s. iiii d.
Item, de Ad*am* de Shadewell –	l s.

1340–41 Ceux sount les nouns des gardeyns del orfaverye de Loundr*es* l'an du regne le Roi Edward apr*és* le conquest q*ua*rtoszyme:
William Sporon
Ric*hard* de Basynggestoke
Ad*am* de Walepole
Waut*er* atte Ferne

p. 5, col. 1 Doné al encress*e* horsp*ri*s lé q*ui*lettes des app*ren*tiz *et* de am*er*cimentz mesme l'an:[9]

Ces sount lé despens mesme l'an:
P*ri*merement p*ur* viii povres – viii li. xiii s. iiii d.
Item, en argent doné contre le Noel – xxxvii s.
It*em*, p*ur* la lum*ere* al hospital Seint Jake outre la quilette ové les standars de S*eint* Pol q*e* amou*n*te xxxv ll. – *summa* vi s.

[9] No figure has been entered.

Item, for the light at the Hospital of St James, over and above the collection which amounts to £32 – total 7s.
Item, for 2 standards at St Paul's – 2s. 6d.
Item, for candles for the poor including the making up – 4s. 6d.
Item, for the bell-ringing at noon and for drink at St Paul's – 5s. 6d.

The names of apprentices admitted the same year:
Thomas le Raynham, the apprentice of Adam le Frenshe – 2s.
William de Brutoun, apprentice of William Windsor – 2s.
Richard de Mitcham, apprentice of Robert de Hatfield – 2s.
John Dowel, apprentice of John de Ippegrave – 2s.
Robert de Meone, apprentice of John de Chichester – 2s.
John Broun, apprentice of Thomas Convers – 2s.
John de Guildford, for his apprentice – 2s.
John de Egentoun, apprentice of James de Thame – 2s.
John Fairher, apprentice of Richard de Hanneye – 2s.
Robert Galle, for his release from his terms – 2s.
Thomas le Mareschal, for his release from his terms – 2s.
John de Birkele, for his release from his terms – 2s.
Thomas de Worlingworth, for his release from his terms – 2s.
Robert Brook, for his release from his terms – 2s.
John de Combirworth, for his release from his terms – 2s.

Renaud de Bilneye for his entry – 6s. 8d.
Laurence de Wynstoun for his entry – 3s. 4d.

Amercements in the same year:
Firstly, John Baynard – 6s. 8d.
John de Shaftesbury – 2s.
Reynaud Gargoil – 13s. 4d.
Item, from Adam de Shadwell – 50s.

These are the names of the Wardens of the Goldsmiths' Mistery of London 1340–41
in the year 14 Edward III [1340]:
William Sporon
Richard de Basingstoke
Adam de Walpole
Walter atte Ferne

Given to the increase of funds, excluding the monies collected from p. 5, col. 1
apprentices and from amercements in the same year:

These are the expenses of the same year:
Firstly, for 8 poor people – £8 13s. 4d.
Item, money distributed at Christmas time – 37s.
Item, for the light at the Hospital of St James, over and above the collection, with the standards at St Paul's, which amounts to £35 – total 6s.

It*em*, p*ur* le sonere de Noune *et* p*ur* bev*er*age a Seynt Pol – v s. iii d.

Les nouns des app*re*ntiz mesme l'an resceux:[10]
Joh*an* de Samford app*re*ntiz Joh*an* de Kele – ii s.
Will*iam* de Brutou*n* app*re*ntiz Will*iam* de Wyndesore – ii s.
Ric*hard* de Mich*a*m app*re*ntiz Rob*er*t de Hatfeld – ii s.
Joh*an* Dowel app*re*ntiz Joh*a*n de Ippeg*ra*ve – ii s.
Rob*ert* de Meone app*re*ntiz Joh*an* de Cicest*re* – ii s.
Joh*a*n Broun app*re*ntiz Thom*a*s Conv*er*s – ii s.
Joh*an* de Goldeford p*ur* son p*re*ntiz – ii s.
Walram de Rocheford app*re*ntiz Piers Conv*er*s – ii s.
Will*iam* de Fynchyngfeld app*re*ntiz Will*iam* Salesb*ury* – ii s.
Joh*an* Geraud app*re*ntiz Thom*a*s de Nichole – ii s.
Ric*hard* de Wretele app*re*ntiz Ad*am* atte Ferne – ii s.
Joh*a*n de Wyk app*re*ntiz William de Strethan – ii s.
Joh*an* Columb app*re*ntiz Ad*am* de Walepole – ii s.
Thom*as* de Baldiswell*e* app*rentiz* Will*iam* Flemyng – ii s.

Joh*an* de Grenewyz p*ur* son dep*ar*tir – ii s.
Waut*er* atte Hall*e* p*ur* son dep*artir* – ii s.
Henr*i* de P*ar*tenhal*e* p*ur* son dep*artir* – ii s.
Ric*hard* de Walepole p*ur* son dep*ar*tir – ii s.
Thom*a*s de Renh*a*m p*ur* son dep*ar*tir – ii s.
Will*iam* de Hatfeld p*ur* son dep*ar*tir – ii s.
Henr*i* le Welssh*e* p*ur* son dep*ar*tir – ii s.

Will*ia*m Flemyng p*ur* son entr*é* – iiii s.
Henr*i* de Kent p*ur* son entr*é* – ii s.

Les am*er*ciament[z] mesme l'an de Joh*a*n de Kelleseye *et* Joh*a*n fiz Rog*er* p*ur* le lowerie d'une shope – vi [s.] viii d.

1341–42 Ceux sount les nouns des gardeyns del orfaverie de Londr*e*s l'an du regne le Roi Edward tierce ap*ré*s la conquest quinszyme:
col. 2 Stephen le Frenssh*e*
Joh*a*n Toppesfeld
Simon de Berkynge
Joh*a*n Makenhened

Doné al encress*e* horsp*ri*s les q*ui*lettes des app*re*ntiz *et* de am*er*ciamentz mesme l'an:

Ceo sunt les despens mesme l'an:
P*ri*merement p*ur* viii povres – viii li. xiii s. iiii d.
It*em*, en argent don*é* contre Noel – xxxvii s.
It*em*, p*ur* lum*er*e al hospital Seyn Jak*es* outre la quilette – xviii d.

[10] Several of the names in the following list have already appeared in the previous year's list. A variety of hypotheses might account for this, some sort of copying error being the most likely.

Item, for the bell-ringing at noon and for drink at St Paul's – 5s. 3d.

The names of apprentices admitted the same year:

John de Samford, apprentice of John de Kele –	2s.
William de Brutoun, apprentice of William de Windsor –	2s.
Richard de Mitcham, apprentice of Robert de Hatfield –	2s.
John Dowel, apprentice of John de Ippegrave –	2s.
Robert de Meone, apprentice of John de Chichester –	2s.
John Broun, apprentice of Thomas Convers –	2s.
John de Guildford, for his apprentice –	2s.
Walram de Rochford, apprentice of Piers Convers –	2s.
William de Finchingfield, apprentice of William Salisbury –	2s.
John Geraud, apprentice of Thomas de Nichole –	2s.
Richard de Wretele, apprentice of Adam atte Ferne –	2s.
John de Wyk, apprentice of William de Streatham –	2s.
John Columb, apprentice of Adam de Walpole –	2s.
Thomas de Baldeswelle, apprentice of William Flemyng –	2s.

John de Greenwich for his release from his terms –	2s.
Walter atte Halle for his release from his terms –	2s.
Henry de Pertenhall for his release from his terms –	2s.
Richard de Walpole for his release from his terms –	2s.
Thomas de Raynham for his release from his terms –	2s.
William de Hatfield for his release from his terms –	2s.
Henry le Welsshe for his release from his terms –	2s.

William Flemyng for his entry –	4s.
Henry de Kent for his entry –	2s.

The amercements of the same year – from John de Kelsey and John FitzRoger for the hire of a shop – 6s. 8d.

These are the names of the Wardens of the Goldsmiths' Mistery of London 1341–42
in the year 15 Edward III [1341]:
Stephen le Frenshe col. 2
John Toppesfield
Simon de Barking
John Makenhened

Given to the increase of funds, excluding the monies collected from apprentices and from amercements in the same year:

These are the expenses of the same year:
Firstly, for 8 poor people – £8 13s. 4d.
Item, money distributed at Christmas time – 37s.
Item, for the light at the Hospital of St James, over and above the collection – 18d.

It*em*, p*ur* le sonner *et* p*ur* bev*er*age a Seynt Poul – v s. iii d.

Les nouns des app*re*ntiz messme l'an resceux:

Joh*a*n de Salesbur*i* app*re*ntiz Will*iam* de Salesbur*i* –	ii s.
Jon de Fynchyngfeld app*re*ntiz Will*iam* de F*ynchyngfeld* –	ii s.
Joh*an* app*re*ntiz Simon Cosyn –	ii s.
Salaman app*re*ntiz Joh*a*n Makenhened –	ii s.
Rob*er*t T*ra*ier app*re*ntiz Nichole de Lythyngtou*n* –	ii s.
Thom*a*s Brook app*re*ntiz Rob*er*t Brook –	ii s.
Ph*ilip* de Yslep app*re*ntiz Gybon de Steyndrop*e* –	ii s.
Ric*hard* Chaundeler app*rentiz* Joh*an* de Hyngeston*e* –	ii s.
Ric*hard* de Ewell*e* app*rentiz* Joh*a*n atte Rye –	ii s.
Henr*i* de Carstou*n* app*rentiz* Rob*er*t de Shordich*e* –	ii s.
Huchon de Ware app*rentiz* Will*iam* de Caustou*n* –	ii s.
Rob*er*t Hardbene app*rentiz* Ric*hard* atte Haye –	ii s.
Will*ia*m Holdwych*e* app*rentiz* Henr*i* Wein*er* de Norwicz –	ii s.

Will*ia*m de Salesbury junior p*ur* so*n* dep*artir* –	ii s.
Simon de Porkele p*ur* son dep*ar*tir –	ii s.
Will*ia*m Bat*e* p*ur* son dep*ar*tir –	ii s.
Joh*a*n de Combirworþe p*ur* son dep*ar*tir –	ii s.

Les am*er*cimentz mesme l'an:

Wauter de Algate –	vi d.
Huchon de York –	ii s.
Rob*er*t de Stoke –	v s.
Will*iam* le Brabant –	xx d.

1342–43 Ces sount les nouns des gardeyns del orfaverie de Loundr*e*s l'an du regne le Roi Edwardti[11] tierce xvj^{me}:

p. 6, col. 1 [Nicholas de] Wyrlyngworth
Will[iam de] St*r*ath*a*m
Rob*er*t de Wyk
Gilbert de Steyndrop*e*

Ces sount les despens mesme l'an:
P*ri*merement p*ur* viii povres – viii li. xiii s. iiii d.
It*em*, en argent don*é* contre Noel – xxxvii s.
It*em*, en lum*er*e a Seint Pol pri en puis qi le quiliere – [12]
It*em*, p*ur* le sounre Noune *et* p*ur* le bev*er*age a Seynt Pol – v s. iii d.
It*em*, en sepult*ur*e de iii povres – iiii s. viii d.
It*em*, p*ur* fere novelement la cire as povres – vii d.

[11] *Sic.*
[12] No figure is entered for this expense.

Item, for the bell-ringing and for drink at St Paul's – 5s. 3d.

The names of apprentices admitted in the same year:

John de Salisbury, apprentice of William de Salisbury –	2s.
John de Finchingfield, apprentice of William de Finchingfield –	2s.
John, apprentice of Simon Cosyn –	2s.
Solomon, apprentice of John Makenhened –	2s.
Robert Traier, apprentice of Nicholas de Lythyngtoun –	2s.
Thomas Brook, apprentice of Robert Brook –	2s.
Philip de Islip, apprentice of Gybon de Staindrop –	2s.
Richard Chaundeler, apprentice of John de Hingston –	2s.
Richard de Ewelle, apprentice of John atte Rye –	2s.
Henry de Carstoun, apprentice of Robert de Shoreditch –	2s.
Huchon de Ware, apprentice of William de Caustoun –	2s.
Robert Hardbene, apprentice of Richard atte Haye –	2s.
William Holdwyche, apprentice of Henry Weiner of Norwich –	2s.

William de Salisbury the younger, for his release from his terms –	2s.
Simon de Porkele for his release from his terms –	2s.
William Bate for his release from his terms –	2s.
John de Combirworth for his release from his terms –	2s.

The amercements in the same year:

Walter de Aldgate –	6d.
Huchon de York –	2s.
Robert de Stoke –	5s.
William le Brabant –	20d.

These are the names of the Wardens of the Goldsmiths' Mistery of London 1342–43
in the year 16 Edward III [1342]:
Nicholas de Worlingworth p. 6, col. 1
William de Streatham
Robert de Wyk
Gilbert de Staindrop

These are the expenses of the same year:
Firstly, for 8 poor people – £8 13s. 4d.
Item, money distributed at Christmas time – 37s.
Item, for the light at St Paul's, over and above the collection –
Item, for the bell-ringing at noon and for drink at St Paul's – 5s. 3d.
Item, for the burial of 3 poor people – 4s. 8d.
Item, for the making up of new wax candles for the poor – 7d.

Les nouns de les app*r*entiz mesme l'an xvj^{me}:

Joh*an* Rolf app*r*entiz Will*iam* de Cartou*n* –	ii s.
Joh*an* le Walssh*e* app*rentiz* Henr*i* Walssh*e* –	ii s.
Thom*as* Tydy app*r*entiz Joh*an* de Keleseye –	ii s.
Thom*as* de Braxhing app*rentiz* Waut*er* de Algat*e* –	ii s.
Ric*hard* Gerlaund app*r*entiz Ad*am* Walepol –	sol'[13]
Joh*an* Hervy app*r*entiz Will*iam* de Paryz –	sol'
Thom*as* Hauteyn app*r*entiz Joh*an* de Gravele –	sol'
Will*elmus* Carles app*rentiz* Thom*as* Carles –	sol'
Joh*an* Corxim app*r*entiz Thom*as* Shordich*e* –	sol'
Galfr*ei* Clement app*r*entiz Ric*hard* Walepol*e* –	sol'
Joh*an* atte Grene app*r*entiz Rob*er*t de Hatfeld –	sol'
Joh*an* le P*e*rer app*r*entiz Will*iam* de Salesbur*i* –	sol'
Ric*hard* Sprot app*rentiz* Joh*an* de Lyncolle –	sol'
Thom*as* Sochyn app*r*entiz Gylot Shordich*e* –	sol'
Thom*as* Red app*r*entiz Thom*as* Wirlyngworth –	sol'
Ric*hard* de Burdeux app*r*entiz Thom*as* de Farndou*n* –	sol'
Ad*am* Warener app*r*entiz Joh*an* Bliklyng –	sol'
Joh*an* Saleman app*rentiz* Joh*an* Licheler –	sol'
Ric*hard* de Thorneye app*rentiz* Andr*eu* de Essex –	sol'
Joh*an* Cheseman app*r*ent*iz* Joh*an* Gildesford –	sol'
Ric*hard* Bryd*e* app*rentiz* Reynaud Gargoil –	sol'
Thom*as* atte Croux app*rentiz* Th*omas* de Algate –	sol'

Ric*hard* Gylemyn p[*ur*][14] son dep*ar*tir – sol'	
Rog*er* de Dillesham p*ur* son dep*ar*tir –	sol'
Esmon de Wyk p*ur* son dep*ar*tir –	sol'
William atte Candewyk p*ur* son dep*ar*tir –	sol'
Nichol de Sellyng p*ur* son dep*ar*tir –	sol'
Rauf q*e* fust l'app*rentiz* Johan de Make[n]hen[e]d –	sol'
Joh*an* de Coraunt p*ur* son dep*ar*tir –	sol'
Lucas Rauf p*ur* son dep*ar*tir –	sol'
Nichol Elyoth*e* p*ur* son dep*ar*tir –	sol'
Thom*as* de Banhened, estraunge dem*ur*rant ou Ad*am*	
col. 2 de Wallop p*ur* son entré[15]	
William Cristemasse p*ur* son entré – est*r*ange, payé –	ii s.
It*em*, estr*a*unges fr*a*unceys dem*ur*aunt ou Reynaud Gargoil[16]	
Joh*an* de Henlee p*ur* son entré –	ii s.

[13] It is unclear why the scribe writes not the amount but the abbreviation 'sol' against the rest of the names in this list, but it is probable that it was thus on the list from which he is copying. I have not expanded the abbreviation, since there are at least three alternative ways this could be done. 'Sol' can be used as an abbreviation for 'solidus' – 'shilling', but it is most improbable that these men were paying only 1 s.

[14] MS: p*ar*.

[15] No sum visible but page is damaged at that point.

[16] No sum given.

The names of the apprentices this same year [1342]:

John Rolf, apprentice of William de Cartoun –	2s.
John le Walsshe, apprentice of Henry Walsshe –	2s.
Thomas Tydy, apprentice of John de Kelsey –	2s.
Thomas de Braxhing, apprentice of Walter de Aldgate –	2s.
Richard Gerlaund, apprentice of Adam Walpole –	paid.
John Hervy, apprentice of William de Paris –	paid.
Thomas Hauteyn, apprentice of John de Gravele –	paid.
William Carles, apprentice of Thomas Carles –	paid.
John Corxim, apprentice of Thomas Shoreditch –	paid.
Geoffrey Clement, apprentice of Richard Walpole –	paid.
John atte Grene, apprentice of Robert de Hatfield –	paid.
John le Perer, apprentice of William de Salisbury –	paid.
Richard Sprot, apprentice of John de Lincoln –	paid.
Thomas Sochyn, apprentice of Gylot Shoreditch –	paid.
Thomas Red, apprentice of Thomas Worlingworth –	paid.
Richard de Bordeaux, apprentice of Thomas de Farndon –	paid.
Adam Warener, apprentice of John Blickling –	paid.
John Salemon, apprentice of John Licheler –	paid.
Richard de Thorneye, apprentice of Andrew de Essex –	paid.
John Cheseman, apprentice of John Guildford –	paid.
Richard Bride, apprentice of Reynaud Gargoil –	paid.
Thomas atte Croux, apprentice of Thomas de Aldgate –	paid.

Richard Gilmyn, for his release from his terms –	paid.
Roger de Dillesham for his release from his terms –	paid.
Edmund de Wyk for his release from his terms –	paid.
William atte Candewyk for his release from his terms –	paid.
Nicholas de Sellyng for his release from his terms –	paid.
Ralph, who was the apprentice of John de Makenhened –	paid.
John de Coraunt for his release from his terms –	paid.
Lucas Rauf for his release from his terms –	paid.
Nicholas Elyothe for his release from his terms –	paid.
Thomas de Banhened, alien living with Adam de Wallop, for his entry –	col. 2
William Cristemasse for his entry – alien, paid –	2s.
Item, the alien Frenchmen living with Reynaud Gargoil	
John de Henley for his entry –	2s.

1343–44 Ceo sunt les nouns des gardeyns de orfaverie de Loundres l'an du regne le Roi Edward tierce apr*é*s le conquest xviime:
Rob*er*t de Shordich*e* l'eisné
Johan de Hyngeston*e*
Johan de Cicestr*e*
Rob*er*t de Hatfeld

Don*é* al encress*e* mesme l'an horsp*ris* les quilettes des app*rentiz* *et* am*er*ciamentz:[17]

Et sount ceux les despences mesme l'an:
Adep*ri*mes, don*é* a viii povres – vii li. xvi s.
It*em*, don*é* contr*e* Noel as povres – xxxvii s. iiii d.
It*em*, p*ur* le lum*er*e a Seynt Poul outre le quilette – ii s. vi d.
It*em*, p*ur* le sonner de Noune *et* p*ur* le beverage a Seynt Pol – vi s. viii d.

L'entré des est*ra*unges mesme l'an: Adep*ri*mes:

p*ur* une orfevre[18] de Coventre –	vi s. viii d.
p*ur* Andrew de Sandwiz –	xiii s. iiii d.
p*ur* un est*ra*unge ou William Antra –	vi s. viii d.

Ces sount les nouns des app*re*ntiz mesme l'an:

Thom*as* de Sale[s]bur*y* p*ur* son app*rentiz* Thom*as* Reyn*er* –	ii s.
Joh*a*n de Castelacre p*ur* son app*rentiz* Will*iam* atte Conduyt –	ii s.
Joh*a*n de Hych*a*m p*ur* son app*rentiz* Thom*as* fitz Waut*er* –	ii s.
Waut*er* atte Halle p*ur* son app*rentiz* Will*iam* de Gyndewik –	ii s.
Will*iam* de Streth*a*m p*ur* son app*rentiz* Thom*as* de Abyndou*n* –	ii s.
Joh*an* de Makenhen[e]d p*ur* son app*rentiz* Ric*hard* de Copptou*n* –	ii s.
Ric*hard* de Hanneye p*ur* son app*rentiz* Elis Spay –	ii s.
Joh*an* de Salesb*ury*[19] p*ur* son app*rentiz* Thom*as* de Hanneye –	ii s.
Rob*er*t Brok p*ur* son app*rentiz* Ric*hard* de Acton –	ii s.
Thom*as* de Shordissch*e* p*ur* son app*rentiz* Thom*as* le Frenss –	ii s.
Will*iam* Bat p*ur* son app*rentiz* Joh*an* de Norfolch*e* –	ii s.
Joh*an* de Henle p*ur* son app*rentiz* Ric*hard* de Thame –	ii s.
Estiphene Lichiere p*ur* son app*rentiz* Joh*an* Gerners –	ii s.
Will*iam* de Nortou*n* p*ur* son app*rentiz* Rob*er*t Hugh*e* –	ii s.
Rauf Souns*er* p*ur* Ric*hard* Fraunceys –	ii s.
p. 7, col. 1 Joh*a*n de Lylu*m* p*ur* son app*rentiz* Ric*hard* Mirorer –	ii s.
Will*iam* Humfrey p*ur* son app*rentiz* Thom*as* Chanprom –	ii s.
Thom*as* Cantebrigge p*ur* son app*rentiz* Steph*ene* Crise –	ii s.
Will*iam* de Caustou*n* p*ur* son app*rentiz* Rob*er*t Broseyerd –	ii s.
Rob*er*t Mareschal p*ur* son app*rentiz* Will*iam* de York –	ii s.
Simon Maas p*ur* son app*rentiz* Renaund Rope –	ii s.
Simon de Kele p*ur* son app*rentiz* Simon de Suttflete –	ii s.
Rob*er*t de Norwiz p*ur* son app*rentiz* Nicho[l] Skynner*e* –	ii s.

[17] No sum given.
[18] It is improbable that this was a female goldsmith, the use of 'une' instead of 'un' being not uncommon in Anglo-Norman documents.
[19] MS: 'Salesbrs', a common Latin abbreviation.

These are the names of the Wardens of the Goldsmiths' Mistery of London in the year 17 Edward III [1343]: 1343–44
Robert de Shoreditch the elder
John de Hingston
John de Chichester
Robert de Hatfield

Given to the increase of funds in the same year, excluding the monies collected from apprentices and amercements:

And these are the expenses of the same year:
Firstly, given to 8 poor people – £7 16s.
Item, given to the poor at Christmas time – 37s. 4d.
Item, for the light at St Paul's over and above the collection – 2s. 6d.
Item, for the bell-ringing at noon and for drink at St Paul's – 6s. 8d.

Entries of aliens this same year. Firstly:

for a goldsmith of Coventry –	6s. 8d.
for Andrew de Sandwich –	13s. 4d.
for an alien [working/living] with William Antra –	6s. 8d.

These are the names of apprentices the same year:

Thomas de Salisbury for his apprentice Thomas Reyner –	2s.	
John de Castelacre for his apprentice William atte Conduyt –	2s.	
John de Hitcham for his apprentice Thomas FitzWalter –	2s.	
Walter atte Halle for his apprentice William de Gyndewik –	2s.	
William de Streatham for his apprentice Thomas de Abingdon –	2s.	
John de Makenhened for his apprentice Richard de Copptoun –	2s.	
Richard de Hanneye for his apprentice Ellis Spay –	2s.	
John de Salisbury for his apprentice Thomas de Hanneye –	2s.	
Robert Brook for his apprentice Richard de Acton –	2s.	
Thomas de Shoreditch for his apprentice Thomas le Frensshe –	2s.	
William Bate for his apprentice John de Norfolk –	2s.	
John de Henley for his apprentice Richard de Thame –	2s.	
Stephen Lichiere for his apprentice John Gerners –	2s.	
William de Nortoun for his apprentice Robert Hughe –	2s.	
Ralph Sounser for Richard Frauncеys –	2s.	
John de Lylum for his apprentice Richard Mirorer –	2s.	p. 7, col. 1
William Humfrey for his apprentice Thomas Chanprom –	2s.	
Thomas Cambridge for his apprentice Stephen Crise –	2s.	
William de Caustoun for his apprentice Robert Broseyerd –	2s.	
Robert Mareschal for his apprentice William de York –	2s.	
Simon Maas for his apprentice Renaud Rope –	2s.	
Simon de Kele for his apprentice Simon de Southfleet –	2s.	
Robert de Norwich for his apprentice Nicholas Skynnere –	2s.	

Joh*an* Galle p*ur* son app*rentiz* Joh*an* de Excestre – ii s.
Hugh*e* de York p*ur* son app*rentiz* Joh*a*n de Schrovesbury – ii s.
Aleyn Wynstou*n* p*ur* son app*rentiz* Nich*ol* Weynflet – ii s.
Will*iam* de Salesbur*y* p*ur* son app*rentiz* Will*iam* Issebourn*e* – ii s.
Will*iam* de S.[20] p*ur* son app*rentiz* Johan Vyncent – ii s.
Ad*am* de Shadewell*e* p*ur* son app*rentiz* – ii s.

Will*iam* apprentiz Will*ia*m de Gartou*n* p*ur* son dep*artir* – ii s.
Laurenche Bon Marché p*ur* son dep*ar*tir – ii s.
Ric*hard* de Ewell*e* p*ur* son dep*ar*tir – ii s.
Thom*as* de Bristowe p*ur* son dep*ar*tir – ii s.
Esmon de Reynh*a*m p*ur* son dep*ar*tir
Gilb*er*t Barentyn p*ur* son dep*ar*tir

Le frere Rob*er*t de Norwich*e* p*ur* son entr*é*

1344–45 Ceux sount les nouns des gardeyns del orfaverie de Loundres l'an du regne le Roi Edward tierce puis le conquest xviiime:
Adam de Walpol
Thom*as* de Farndou*n*
Adam le Frenssh*e*
Rob*er*t de Shordich*e* puisné

Ceux sount les despens mesme l'an:
Adep*ri*mes don*é* a vii povres – vii li. xvi s.
It*em*, don*é* contre le Noel as povres – xxxvii s. iiii d.
It*em*, p*ur* le lum*er*e a Seynt Poul – ii s. vi d.
It*em*, p*ur* sonner noune a Seynt Paul *et* p*ur* lour beverage – v s. iiii d.

L'entr*é* des est*ra*unges mesme l'an:
Nichol Egreth*e*
Gelemyn Godefray
Hudinet Banche
Peryn le Loung
Hanekyn de Wautetoup*e*
Hanekyn Amaillo*ur*
Hanekyn de Almayne

col. 2 Ceux sount les nouns dé app*re*ntiz mesme l'an:
Johan Spenc*er* app*re*nt*iz* Ricard Tylemyn – ii s.
Will*ia*m de Mikelh*a*m app*re*ntiz Joh*ann*i Baynard – ii s.
Joh*an* Lencryk*e* app*re*ntiz Will*iam* But – ii s.
Symond de Evesh*a*m app*re*ntiz Simon so*n* frere – ii s.
Thom*as* Westou*n* app*rentiz* Thomas Wyrlyngworth*e* – ii s.

[20] *Sic.*

John Galle for his apprentice John de Exeter – 2s.
Hugh de York for his apprentice John de Shrewsbury – 2s.
Alan Wynstoun for his apprentice Nicholas Wainfleet – 2s.
William de Salisbury for his apprentice William Issebourne – 2s.
William de S.[18] for his apprentice John Vyncent – 2s.
Adam de Shadwell for his apprentice – 2s.

William, apprentice of William de Gartoun, for his release from his terms – 2s.
Laurence Bon Marché for his release from his terms – 2s.
Richard de Ewelle for his release from his terms – 2s.
Thomas de Bristowe for his release from his terms – 2s.
Edmund de Raynham for his release from his terms –
Gilbert Barantyn for his release from his terms –

The brother of Robert de Norwich for his entry

These are the names of the Wardens of the Goldsmiths' Mistery of London 1344–45
in the year 18 Edward III [1344]:
Adam de Walpole
Thomas de Farndon
Adam le Frenshe
Robert de Shoreditch the younger

These are the expenses of the same year:
Firstly, given to 7 poor people – £7 16s.
Item, given to the poor at Christmas time – 37s. 4d.
Item, for the light at St Paul's – 2s. 6d.
Item, for bell-ringing at noon at St Paul's and for their[19] drink – 5s. 4d.

The entries of aliens in the same year:
Nichol Egrethe
Gelemyn Godefray
Hudinet Banche
Peryn le Long
Hanekyn de Wautetoupe
Hanekyn the enameller
Hanekyn de Almayne

These are the names of apprentices in the same year: col. 2
John Spencer, apprentice of Richard Tylemyn – 2s.
William de Mickleham, apprentice of John Baynard – 2s.
John Lencryke, apprentice of William But – 2s.
Simon de Evesham, apprentice of Simon, his brother – 2s.
Thomas Weston, apprentice of Thomas Worlingworth – 2s.

[18] The abbreviated 'S.' may well indicate that this is William de Salisbury, as above, but other possible candidates are Wm Shoreditch, Wm Sporoun and Wm Streatham.
[19] i.e. of the bell-ringers.
[20] One is tempted to wonder whether the few in this list who are given as 'ové' ('with') someone are not apprentices but serving-men.

Will*iam* Beauchamp*e* app*rentiz* Rob*er*t Horner*e* – ii s.
Hugh*e* Beauchamp*e* ové Gilb*er*t Stayndrop*e* – ii s.
Will*iam* Cornewaill*e* app*rentiz* Adam Frenssh*e* – ii s.
Joh*an* Hakeneye app*re*ntiz Joh*an* Hingestou*n* – ii s.
Joh*an* Shirborn*e* app*rentiz* Nichol Wyrlyngworth*e* – ii s.
Ric*hard* Sook ové Thom*as* Bregeford – ii s.
Will*iam* Bryd app*rentiz* Joh*a*n Heylof – ii s.
Philip Noel app*rentiz* Rob*er*t de Wyke – ii s.
Joh*a*n Chikewell*e* app*rentiz* Thom*as* Mareschal – ii s.
Joh*a*n Pounchardou*n* ové Joh*an* Ippeg*ra*ve – ii s.
Rob*er*t Berman app*rentiz* Rob*er*t de Louthe – ii s.
Will*iam* Poche ové Joh*a*n Pypeshull*e* – ii s.
Will*iam* de Belyngtou*n* *et* Adam Elsham les app*re*ntiz
Gilb*er*t de Salesburi – iiii s.
Thom*as* de Badewe ové Joh*an* de Bliclyngg – ii s.
Nich*olas* de Parys app*rentiz* Joh*a*n Shaftesburi – ii s.
Joh*a*n Mappelden*e* app*rentiz* Joh*an* son frere – ii s.
Joh*an* Welssh*e* app*rentiz* Henr*i* Welssh*e* – ii s.
Rob*er*t app*rentiz* Joh*a*n Mynot – ii s.
Joh*a*n Bantre app*rentiz* Joh*a*n Botoner – ii s.

Ceux sount les app*re*ntiz issauntz de lo*ur* t*er*me de mesme l'an xviii[me]: . . .
Hugh*e* de Walcote – ii s.
Joh*an* de Croydou*n* – ii s.
Giffr*ey* de Porkele – ii s.
Will*ia*m atte More – ii s.
Joh*a*n Rolf – ii s.
Eydmu[n]d de Reynh*a*m – ii s.
Gilb*er*t Barentyn – ii s.
Joh*a*n Brian – ii s.

1345–46 Ceux sount les nouns des gardeyns del orfaverie de Loundres l'an du regne le Roi Edward tierçz puis le conquest xix[me]:
William Sporoun
Johan Makenhened
Joh*a*n Hiltoft
Thom*as* Wyrlyngford

Don*é* al encress*e* mesme l'an horsp*ri*s quilettes des app*re*ntiz *et* am*er*ciamentz – iiii li.

Et sount les despenc*es* mesme l'an:
A de p*ri*mer a vi povres – iiii li. vi s. viii d.
It*e*m, don*é* a pov*re*s countr*e* le Noel – xxxvii s. vi d.
p. 8, col. 1 It*e*m, p*ur* lum*er*e a Seynt Paul outre la q*ui*lette – iii s.
It*e*m, p*ur* le sonner de noune a Seynt Paul *et* lou*r* beverage – v s. vi d.

William Beauchamp, apprentice of Robert Horner –	2s.
Hugh Beauchamp, with[20] Gilbert Staindrop –	2s.
William Cornwall, apprentice of Adam Frenshe –	2s.
John Hackney, apprentice of John Hingston –	2s.
John Sherborne, apprentice of Nicholas Worlingworth –	2s.
Ricahrd Sook, with Thomas Bregeford –	2s.
William Brid, apprentice of John Heylof –	2s.
Philip Noel, apprentice of Robert de Wyk –	2s.
John Chigwell, apprentice of Thomas Mareschal –	2s.
John Pounchardoun, with John Ippegrave –	2s.
Robert Berman, apprentice of Robert de Louth –	2s.
William Poche, with John Pypeshulle –	2s.
William de Billington and Adam Elsham, the apprentices of Gilbert de Salisbury –	4s.
Thomas de Badewe, with John de Blickling –	2s.
Nicholas de Paris, apprentice of John Shaftesbury –	2s.
John Maplesdene, apprentice of John his brother –	2s.
John Walsh, apprentice of Henry Walsh –	2s.
Robert, apprentice of John Mynot –	2s.
John Bantry, apprentice of John Botoner –	2s.

These are the apprentices coming out of their terms [of apprenticeship] in the same year [1344]:

Hugh de Walcote –	2s.
John de Croydon –	2s.
Geoffrey de Porkele –	2s.
William atte More –	2s.
John Rolf –	2s.
Edmund de Raynham –	2s.
Gilbert Barantyn –	2s.
John Brian –	2s.

These are the names of the Wardens of the Goldsmiths' Mistery of London in the year 19 Edward III [1345]: 1345–46

William Sporon
John Makenhened
John Hiltoft
Thomas Worlingford

Given to the increase of funds the same year, excluding monies collected from apprentices and amercements – £4

And these are the expenses of the same year:
Firstly, to 6 poor people – £4 6s. 8d.
Item, distributed to the poor at Christmas time – 37s. 6d.
Item, for the light at St Paul's over and above the collection – 3s. p. 8, col. 1
Item, for the bell-ringing at noon at St Paul's and their drink – 5s. 6d.

L'entré des est*ra*unges mesme l'an:

Melys de Dourdreyght }
Hanekyn Dourdreyght } xx s.

Gerarde de Coloyne – d*emi* m*a*rc
Nich*olas* Polayn – d*emi* m*a*rc
Hanekyn de Flo*ur*delys – d*emi* m*a*rc
Henr*i* de Reynbaugh – d*emi* m*a*rc

1346–47 Ceux sount les nouns des gardeyns del orfaverie de Loundres en l'an du regne le Roi Edward tierçz puis le conquest vyntisme:
Rob*e*rt de Shordich*e*, l'eisné
Adam de Walpol
Joh*a*n de Lyncoln*e*
Rauf Conv*er*s

Don*é* al encress*e* mesmes l'an horsp*ri*s q*ui*lettes des app*re*ntiz *et* am*er*ciamentz p*ar* les ditz gardeyns – x m*a*rcs.

Ceux sount les nouns des app*re*ntiz paiez en l'an susdite:

Joh*a*n Brian p*ur* s'app*re*ntiz Henr*i* de Hoclee –	ii s.
William Aqura p*ur* s'app*re*ntiz Rob*e*rt Ward –	ii s.
Joh*a*n Marschal p*ur* s'apprentiz Thom*as* Beal –	ii s.
Rob*e*rt de Norwich*e* p*ur* s'app*re*ntiz Edmu[n]d Betoigne –	ii s.
Will*iam* de Norwich*e* p*ur* s'app*re*ntiz Rob*e*rt de Oxeborogh*e* –	ii s.
William de Fynchingfeld p*ur* ses deux app*re*ntiz Nichol Waryn, Ric*hard* atte Fen –	iiii s.
Thom*as* Salesburi fitz William Salesbur*i* p*ur* sa app*re*ntiz Nichol Dunmowe –	ii s.
Nichol Farndou*n* p*ur* sa app*re*ntiz Th*omas* Burdeux –	ii s.
Laurence Wynstou*n* p*ur* s'app*re*ntiz Johan de Leye –	ii s.
col. 2 Raulyng Sporoun p*ur* s'app*re*ntiz Joh*a*n Hallyng*e* –	ii s.
Joh*an* Stortwich*e* p*ur* sa apprentiz Joh*an* de Westou*n* –	ii s.
Rob*e*rt Honor*e* p*ur* sa apprentiz William Hakeney –	ii s.
Will*ia*m Bate p*ur* s'apprentiz Will*ia*m Hortwell*e* –	ii s.
Ric*hard* de Walpol p*ur* s'app*re*ntiz Joh*a*n Berouth*e* –	ii s.
Joh*a*n Boton p*ur* s'app*re*ntiz Joh*a*n Forester –	ii s.
Thom*as* Porche p*ur* s'app*re*ntiz Johan Foleh*a*m –	ii s.
Ad*am* Frenssh*e* p*ur* s'app*re*ntiz Joh*a*n Rokyngh*a*m –	ii s.
Simond de Berkyngge p*ur* s'app*re*ntiz Joh*a*n Wroth*a*n –	ii s.
Gilb*e*rt Barantyn p*ur* son app*rentiz* Joh*a*n de Gretou*n* –	ii s.
Thom*as* de Halfard p*ur* son app*rentiz* Will*ia*m Saleman –	ii s.
Joh*a*n Castelacre p*ur* sa app*re*ntiz Philipot Gentil –	ii s.
Waut*er* Algate p*ur* son app*rentiz* Joh*a*n de Kyngestou*n* –	ii s.
Piers Herdwyk pur son[21] p*re*ntiz Ric*hard* atte Wode –	ii s.
Th*omas* Hamptou*n* q'est ou Will*iam* Selouth*e* –	ii s.
Cecilie Boton*er*, wif, p*ur* s'app*re*ntiz Jon Hatfeld –	ii s.

21 MS: san.

Entries of aliens in the same year:
Melys de Durdrecht }
Hanekyn Durdrecht } 20s.

Gerard de Cologne – ½ mark
Nicholas Polayn – ½ mark
Hanekyn Fleurdelys – ½ mark
Henry de Reynbaugh – ½ mark

These are the names of the Wardens of the Goldsmiths' Mistery of London 1346–47
in the year 20 Edward III [1346]:
Robert de Shoreditch, the elder
Adam de Walpole
John de Lincoln
Ralph Convers

Given to the increase of funds the same year, excluding monies collected from apprentices and amercements by the said Wardens – 10 marks

These are the names of apprentices paid for in the aforesaid year:

John Brian for his apprentice Henry de Hoclee –	2s.
William Aqura for his apprentice Robert Ward –	2s.
John Marshal for his apprentice Thomas Beal –	2s.
Robert de Norwich for his apprentice Edmund Beteigne –	2s.
William de Norwich for his apprentice Robert de Oxeborough –	2s.
William de Finchingfield for his two apprentices Nicholas Waryn, Richard atte Fen –	4s.
Thomas Salisbury, son of William Salisbury, for his apprentice Nicholas Dunmow –	2s.
Nicholas Farndon for his apprentice Thomas Bordeaux –	2s.
Laurence Wynstoun for his apprentice John de Leye –	2s.
Raulyn Sporon for his apprentice John Hallyng –	2s. col. 2
John Stortwich for his apprentice John de Weston –	2s.
Robert Honore for his apprentice William Hackney –	2s.
William Bate for his apprentice William Hortwelle –	2s.
Richard de Walpole for his apprentice John Berouthe –	2s.
John Boton for his apprentice John Forester –	2s.
Thomas Porche for his apprentice John Foleham –	2s.
Adam Frenshe for his apprentice John Rockingham –	2s.
Simon de Barking for his apprentice John Wrothan –	2s.
Gilbert Barantyn for his apprentice John de Gretoun –	2s.
Thomas de Halfard for his apprentice William Saleman –	2s.
John Castelacre for his apprentice Philipot Gentil –	2s.
Walter Aldgate for his apprentice John de Kingston –	2s.
Piers Herdwyk for his apprentice Richard atte Wood –	2s.
Thomas Hamptoun who is with William Selouthe –	2s.
Cecilie Botoner, wife, for her apprentice John Hatfield –	2s.

Aleyn Wynston p*ur* s'app*re*ntiz Aleyn Kem –	ii s.
John Salema[n], licher, p*ur* Simond Barantyn –	ii s.
Rob*er*t Galle p*ur* sa app*rentiz* Rob*er*t Tankard –	ii s.
Joh*an* Gildeford p*ur* sa app*rentiz* Andreu Warwyk –	ii s.
Ric*hard* Galle p*ur* sa app*rentiz* Aleyn Hardbene –	ii s.
Joh*an* Mertelane p*ur* sa app*rentiz* Ric*hard* Henh*a*m –	ii s.
Rob*er*t Hatfeld p*ur* sa app*rentiz* Thom*as* Okere –	ii s.
Joh*a*n Combirworth*e* p*ur* sa app*re*ntiz –	ii s.
Simon Edward q'est ové Raulyn Fazard –	ii s.
Gilb*er*t de Salesbur*y* p*ur* s'app*rentiz* Elemo*n*t de Grenewich*e* –	ii s.
Swafh*a*m q*e* fust ové Piers Conv*er*s –	ii s.
Martyn Anmesbury p*ur* s'app*re*ntiz –	ii s.
Joh*an* Bartou*n* p*ur* s'app*re*ntiz Rob*er*t Haleng –	ii s.
Raulyn Sporoun p*ur* s'app*re*ntiz Joh*a*n Morys –	ii s.

Ceux sount les nouns des app*re*ntiz issantz de lour t*er*me en mesme l'an xxme:

Thom*as* Andreu p*ur* son dep*ar*tir –	ii s.
Janyn Shordich*e* p*ur* son dep*ar*tir –	ii s.
Joh*an* Bassyngbourn*e* p*ur* son aler –	ii s.
Cok Sy*m*me, amayll*our*, p*ur* son aler –	ii s.
un q*e* fust ou William Fynchyngfeld –	ii s.
Ric*hard* Mich*a*m q*e* fust ové Rob*er*t Hatfeld p*ur* son aler –	ii s.
William Lissebourn*e*, amayl*our*, p[*ur*][22] son aler –	ii s.
Henr*i* de Garstou*n* le frere a Charles p*ur* so[n] aler –	ii s.

Ceux sount les nouns dé gentz est*ra*unges du dit mest*er* entrés en mesme l'an xxme:

William Friskeneye –	xx s.
Ric*hard* Stalworth*e* –	xx s.
Janin M*er*cer q'est ové Joh*a*n de Chicestre –	x s.
William Lirpol q*e* est ové Rob*er*t Marcesch*e* de xx. [s.] resc*eux* –	x s.
It*e*m, de . . .[23] qe [est] ové Rob*er*t de Chelthet de xx s. resc*eux* –	xvii s.
Bertandr*e* Mounstre resceux –	xx s.

1349–50 Ceux sount les nouns des gardeyns del orfaverie de Loundr*es* en l'an du
p. 9, col. 1[24] regne le Roi Edward tierce puis la conquest xxiiime:

Joh*an* Hiltoft – Joh*a*n de Chicestre
Joh*a*n Boton – William de Berkyng

22 MS: p*ar*.

23 A blank space is left for the name.

24 Two years' records are missing, because of the Black Death. See Reddaway and Walker, pp. 27–28. However, the names of two wardens can probably be supplied from the document entered on p. 18 of Book A + a, since among the witnesses to the charter are listed John atte Castel and Richard de Felsted, both of whom are termed 'magister'. Both this Latin term and the equivalent French word 'mestre' are not uncommonly at this date used to designate a warden of a City mistery.

Alan Wynston for his apprentice Alan Kem –	2s.
John Saleman, 'licher'[21] . . . for Simon Barantyn –	2s.
Robert Galle for his apprentice Robert Tankard –	2s.
John Guildford for his apprentice Andrew Warwick –	2s.
Richard Galle for his apprentice Alan Hardbene –	2s.
John Mertelane for his apprentice Richard Henham –	2s.
Robert Hatfield for his apprentice Thomas Okere –	2s.
John Combirworth for his apprentice –	2s.
Simon Edward who is with Raulyn Fazard –	2s.
Gilbert de Salisbury for his apprentice Elemont de Greenwich –	2s.
Swafham who was with Piers Convers –	2s.
Martin Amesbury for his apprentice –	2s.
John Barton for his apprentice Robert Haleng –	2s.
Raulyn Sporon for his apprentice John Morys –	2s.

These are the names of apprentices coming out of their terms in the same year [1346]:

Thomas Andrew, for his release from his terms –	2s.
Janyn Shoreditch, for his release from his terms –	2s.
John Bassingbourne, for his release from his terms[22] –	2s.
Cok Symme, enameller, for his release from his terms –	2s.
one who was with William Finchingfield –	2s.
Richard Mitcham who was with Robert Hatfield, for his release from his terms –	2s.
William Lissebourne, enameller, for his release from his terms –	2s.
Henry de Garstoun, the brother of Charles, for his release from his terms –	2s.

These are the names of aliens of the said mistery who entered in the same year [1346]:

William Friskney –	20s.
Richard Stalworthe –	20s.
Janin Mercer who is with John de Chichester –	10s.
William Liverpool who is with Robert Marcesche, of 20s. – received	10s.
Item, from .. . who is with Robert de Chelthet, of 20s, – received	17s.
Bertandre Mounstre – received –	20s.

These are the names of the Wardens of the Goldsmiths' Mistery of London in the year 23 Edward III [1349]: 1349–50 p. 9, col. 1

John Hiltoft
John de Chichester
John Boton
William de Barking

[21] This appears to be a trade not a name, and might possibly be read as a physician (leech). However, J.S. is named as the apprentice of John Licheler in 1342–43, and it might be that he has adopted his master's surname.

[22] The French phrase has changed slightly here and for the next entries: 'pur son aler' literally means 'for his going', but the meaning of release from apprenticeship terms must be the same.

Don*é* al encress*e* du dit almoyne clerment en or *et* en argent contaunt totes choses countés – xl m*a*rcz.

Ceux sount lu*r* despens du dit an:
Adep*ri*mes, p*ur* ceo q*e* touz les gardeyns avaunt an furunt mortz, despendu
fuit p*ri*mes p*ur* soner a Seynt Poul }
It*em*, p*ur* beire au dit soner } – iiii s. viii d.
It*em*, p*ur* la lum*er*e al hospital – iiii s. vi d.
It*em*, puis en argent don*é* countre Noel, c'est a dire a les povres – vi s. viii d.
It*em*, puis soner a Seynt Poul – iiii s. x d.
It*em*, en lum*er*e outre la quilette *et* pur la fason – vi s. iii d.

Ceux sount les nouns des app*re*ntiz mesme le dit an xxiiime:

Joh*an* Bildwas app*rentiz* Will*iam* atte Stokke –	ii s.
Thom*as* de Pantou*n* app*rentiz* Andreu Essex –	ii s.
Joh*an* Wirhal*e* app*rentiz* William Tygtwell*e* –	ii s.
Rob*er*t Harri app*rentiz* William F*ra*unceys –	ii s.
Joh*a*n Bradeselt app*rentiz* William atte Stowe –	ii s.
Ric*hard* Hervy app*rentiz* Thom*as* de Bassyngstok –	ii s.
Henr*i* Aurenle app*rentiz* Will*iam* Fraunceys –	ii s.
Adam Walpol, Ric*hard* Brinchisle, Nichole Gone – app*rentiz* Joh*an* Brynchisle –	vi s.
Thom*as* Chilerin app*rentiz* Will*iam* de Burtou*n* –	ii s.
Joh*an* Wiltchire app*rentiz* Thom*as* de Lyncoln*e* –	ii s.
Rob*er*t Stevene app*rentiz* Giffrey Walpol –	ii s.
Joh*a*n de Shengh*a*m app*rentiz* Joh*an* de Bartou*n* –	ii s.
Thom*as* de Farndou*n* app*rentiz* Will*iam* Hatfeld –	ii s.
Joh*an* Scherengg*e* app*rentiz* Janyn Shordich*e* –	ii s.
Joh*an* Wirhale app*rentiz* Will*iam* Tyngewyk –	ii s.
Thom*as* Brise app*rentiz* Will*iam* Salesburi –	ii s.
Hamond Chose app*rentiz* Joh*a*n Chose –	ii s.
Thom*a*s Daventre app*rentiz* William Daventre –	ii s.
Will*ia*m Croos app*rentiz* Joh*a*n Hiltoft –	ii s.
Will*ia*m Glasene, Joh*an* Lyndeseye, app*rentiz* Joh*an* de Croydou*n* –	iiii s.
Thom*as* Munden*e* app*rentiz* la fe*m*me Ric*hard* P*a*rgate –	ii s.
Will*ia*m Berkwey app*rentiz* Joh*an* Lont –	ii s.
Thom*a*s Shonk app*rentiz* Ad*a*m de Esh*a*m –	ii s.
Will*ia*m March*a*m app*rentiz* Rob*er*t Selg*ra*vere –	ii s.
Joh*an* de Cauntirbery, Joh*an* Bonyng, app*rentiz* Joh*an* de Chichestr*e* –	iiii s.
Will*ia*m Thom*a*s app*rentiz* Will*ia*m March*a*m –	ii s.
Joh*an* Pixle app*rentiz* Colard de Coloyne –	ii s.
col. 2 Rob*er*t P*er*le app*rentiz* Adam de Shadewell*e* –	ii s.
Rob*er*t Waryn app*rentiz* Will*iam* Philip –	ii s.
Ric*hard* Munde app*rentiz* Thom*a*s Munden*e* –	ii s.
Ric*hard* Westwode app*rentiz* Gibon Steyndrop*e* –	ii s.

Given to the increase of the said alms funds, net in gold and in silver coins, all told – 40 marks.

These are their expenses of the said year:
Firstly, since all the Wardens of the previous year had died, the first expense was to have the bells tolled at St Paul's
Item, for drink at the said tolling of the bells } – 4s. 8d.
Item, for the light at the Hospital – 4s. 6d.
Item, later, for money distributed at Christmas time, i.e. to the poor – 6s. 8d.
Item, later, for bell-ringing at St Paul's – 4s. 10d.
Item, for the light, over and above the collection, and for the making up [of candles] – 6s. 3d.

These are the names of apprentices in the same said year [1349]:

John Buildwas, apprentice of William atte Stokke –	2s.
Thomas de Panton, apprentice of Andrew Essex –	2s.
John Wirral, apprentice of William Tygtwelle –	2s.
Robert Harry, apprentice of William Fraunceys –	2s.
John Bradeselt, apprentice of William atte Stowe –	2s.
Richard Hervy, apprentice of Thomas de Basingstoke –	2s.
Henry Aurenle, apprentice of William Fraunceys –	2s.
Adam Walpole, Richard Brinchisle, Nicholas Gone, apprentices of John Brinchisle –	6s.
Thomas Chilerin, apprentice of William de Burtoun –	2s.
John Wiltshire, apprentice of Thomas de Lincoln –	2s.
Robert Stevene, apprentice of Geoffrey Walpole –	2s.
John de Shengham, apprentice of John de Barton –	2s.
Thomas de Farndon, apprentice of William Hatfield –	2s.
John Scherengge, apprentice of Janin Shoreditch –	2s.
John Wirral, apprentice of William Tingewick –	2s.
Thomas Brise, apprentice of William Salisbury –	2s.
Hamond Chose, apprentice of John Chose –	2s.
Thomas Daventry, apprentice of William Daventry –	2s.
William Croos, apprentice of John Hiltoft –	2s.
William Glasen, John Lindsey, apprentices of John de Croydon –	4s.
Thomas Mundene, apprentice of the wife of Richard Pargate –	2s.
William Barkway, apprentice of John Lont –	2s.
Thomas Shonk, apprentice of Adam de Esham –	2s.
William Marcham, apprentice of Robert Sealgraver[23] –	2s.
John de Canterbury, John Bonyng, apprentices of John de Chichester –	4s.
William Thomas, apprentice of William Marcham –	2s.
John Pixle, apprentice of Colard de Cologne –	2s.
Robert Perle, apprentice of Adam de Shadwell –	2s. col. 2
Robert Waryn, apprentice of William Philip –	2s.
Richard Munde, apprentice of Thomas Mundene –	2s.
Richard Westwood, apprentice of Gibon Staindrop –	2s.

[23] Or possibly 'Robert the seal engraver'?

Rob*er*t Chapman, Joh*an* Payn, app*rentiz* Joh*an* Coraunt – iiii s.
Joh*an* Newerk app*rentiz* Joh*an* Hiltoft – ii s.
Ric*hard* Bartou*n* app*rentiz* Thom*as* Hyngestou*n* – ii s.

Les issauntz de lo*ur* t*er*mes:
Peris Walpol – ii s.
Joh*an* Brynchisle – ii s.
Adam Merefeld – ii s.
Rog*er* Femenhale – ii s.
Joh*an* Chose – ii s.
Giffrey Walpol – ii s.
Thom*as* de Brandou*n* – ii s.
Ric*hard* Fraunceys – ii s.
Ric*hard* Arnold – ii s.
Thom*as* de Pantou*n* – ii s.
Joh*an* Walche – ii s.
Joh*an* Hallyng – ii s.
Will*iam* Tyngewyk – ii s.
Thom*as* Mundene – ii s.
Will*ia*m Philip – ii s.
Henr*i* Alsle – ii s.
Will*ia*m March*a*m – ii s.
Joh*a*n Walden*e* – ii s.
Simond Antra – ii s.
Edmond Tyngewyk – ii s.
Nichol Lovel – ii s.
Rog*er* Blod – ii s.
Perys Dunstal – ii s.

L'entr*é* de est*ra*unges mesme l'an du Roi E*dward* xxiiime:
Matheu Langres – xx s.
Hanekyn Corbitre – xx s.
Solemyn l'amailo*ur* – xx s.
Hanekyn Wandirhale – xx s.
Joh*a*n de Huntyngdou*n* – xx s.
Thom*a*s Belkh*a*m – xx s.
Rob*er*t de Geldeford – lx s.
Selemyn Neufle – xx s.
Will*iam* Derby – xl s.
Hanekyn de Coloyne – x s.
Hanekyn Valenciens – xx s.

1350–51 Seux sount les nouns des gardeyns q*e* furunt l'an xxiiiime, s'est assavoir:
Gilb*er*t Steyndrop*e*
Will*ia*m Ippeg*ra*ve
Gemys de Thame
Will*ia*m de Bourton*e*

Robert Chapman, John Payn, apprentices of John Coraunt –	4s.
John Newark, apprentice of John Hiltoft –	2s.
Richard Barton, apprentice of Thomas Hingston –	2s.

Those coming out of their terms:

Piers Walpole –	2s.
John Brinchisle –	2s.
Adam Mirfield –	2s.
Roger Femenhale –	2s.
John Chose –	2s.
Geoffrey Walpole –	2s.
Thomas de Brandon –	2s.
Richard Frauncey s –	2s.
Richard Arnold –	2s.
Thomas de Panton –	2s.
John Walsh –	2s.
John Hallyng –	2s.
William Tingewick –	2s.
Thomas Mundene –	2s.
William Philip –	2s.
Henry Alsle –	2s.
William Marcham –	2s.
John Waldene –	2s.
Simon Antra –	2s.
Edmund Tingewick –	2s.
Nicholas Lovel –	2s.
Roger Blod –	2s.
Piers Dunstall –	2s.

Entries of aliens in the same year [1349]:

Matthew Langres –	20s.
Hanekyn Corbitre –	20s.
Solomon, the enameller –	20s.
Hanekyn Wandirhale –	20s.
John de Huntingdon –	20s.
Thomas Belkham –	20s.
Robert de Guildford –	60s.
Solomon Neufle –	20s.
William Derby –	40s.
Hanekyn de Cologne –	10s.
Hanekyn Valenciennes –	20s.

These are the names of the Wardens who were in the year 24 [Edward III] [1350], i.e.: 1350–51

Gilbert Staindrop
William Ippegrave
James de Thame
William de Burtoun

p. 10, col. 1 Ces sount les nouns des app*re*ntiz queux[25] furunt entrez en l'an avauntdit:

Thomas Ixasse –	ii s.
Henr*i* Chekessond –	ii s.
Joh*a*n Broun –	ii s.
Will*elmu*s Gartou*n* –	ii s.
Joh*anne*s Canteburi –	ii s.
Joh*anne*s Naybrok –	ii s.
Ric*hard* atte Watere –	ii s.
Joh*anne*s Onphanerynge –	ii s.
Will*elmu*s Sulbury –	ii s.
Joh*anne*s Dallynge –	ii s.
Will*elmu*s Caperoun –	ii s.
Rob*ert* Liv*er*ing –	ii s.
Petrus Lu*m*bard –	ii s.
Henr*i* Lirepol –	ii s.
Joh*an* Godman –	ii s.
Henr*i* Crips –	ii s.
Henr*i* Arnald –	ii s.
Henr*i* Croydou*n* –	ii s.
Simon Wilseby –	ii s.

Ceux sunt lé nouns de ceux q*e* sunt venutz hors de lo*ur* terme l'an xxiiiime:
Andreas Grauntcourt
Ric*hard* Herrin

Les nouns de forayns se est assavoir:
Johan Vandir Hawe – iii s. viii d.

1351–52 Ceux sount les nouns des gardeyns del orfaverie de Loundres l'an du regne le Roi [Edward] tierce puis le conquest xxvme:
Nichol de Farndou*n*
Will*ia*m de Berkyng
Joh*a*n Gravele
Joh*a*n Brinchisle

Ceux sount lo*ur* despenses en l'an avauntdit:
Adep*ri*mes paier a un p*re*stre p*ur* chaunt*er* pur la comune del orfaverie – iiii li. xiii s. iiii d.
It*e*m, paié a les ii. povr*e*s hommes a Niwel – vi s. viii d.

[25] MS: q*ue*uex.

These are the names of apprentices who were admitted in the aforesaid year: p. 10, col. 1

Thomas Ixasse –	2s.
Henry Chicksands –	2s.
John Broun –	2s.
William Gartoun –	2s.
John Canterbury –	2s.
John Naybrok –	2s.
Richard atte Water –	2s.
John Onphanerynge –	2s.
William Sulbury –	2s.
John Dallyng –	2s.
William Caperoun –	2s.
Robert Livering –	2s.
Peter Lumbard –	2s.
Henry Liverpool –	2s.
John Godman –	2s.
Henry Crips –	2s.
Henry Arnald –	2s.
Henry Croydon –	2s.
Simon Wilseby –	2s.

These are the names of those who came out of their terms in the year [1350]:
Andrew Grauntcourt
Richard Herrin

Names of aliens,[24] i.e.
John Vandir Hawe – 3s. 8d.

These are the names of the Wardens of the Goldsmiths' Mistery of London 1351–52
in the year 25 [Edward] III [1351]:
Nicholas de Farndon
William de Barking
John Gravele
John Brinchisle

These are their expenses in the aforesaid year:
Firstly, paid to a priest to sing [masses] for the commonalty[25] of the Goldsmiths' Mistery – £4 13s. 4d.
Item, paid to the 2 poor men at Christmas – 6s. 8d.

[24] The French word used here is 'forayns', whereas above 'estranges' had been used. These two words are sometimes differentiated, 'forains' being used for those coming from outside the City of London, from other parts of England, and 'estranges' being used for those we now term 'foreigners'. However, at this date, the two words were clearly interchangeable for the Goldsmiths. See Introduction, pp. xxxiii–xxxiv.

[25] 'la comune' at this date and in this context probably means the whole community, although it can also be used to refer to 'the commons' = the ordinary members excluding the wardens etc. The English word 'commonalty' can also historically bear both these meanings.

col. 2 It*em*, paié p*ur* lum*er*e outre la quilette[26] – v s. i d.
It*em*, paié p*ur* soner a Seynt Poul – v s. iiii d.

S*um*m*a*: Cx s. v d.
La quele su*m*me d'argent est paié *et* l'argent rendu ent*er*ement sus.

Ces sount les nouns des app*r*entiz entrés ou le papir mesme l'an:

Will*ia*m Fortune apprentiz Joh*a*n Brynchele –	ii s.
Huchon Betonie app*rentiz* Peris Walpol –	ii s.
Ric*hard* Lacer app*rentiz* Will*ia*m Stour –	ii s.
Will*ia*m Ferour app*rentiz* Thom*a*s Hassay –	ii s.
Waut*er* Eriswell*e*, Will*ia*m Gerveys app*rentiz* Rog*er* Femeshal –	iiii s.
Ric*hard* Sherrene apprentiz Nichol Guiford –	ii s.
Thom*a*s Forest*er* app*rentiz* Sim[on][27] Mazerer –	ii s.
Peris Cook app*rentiz* Will*iam* Antra –	ii s.
Betonie q*e* fui app*rentiz* Will*iam* Ippegr*a*ve p*ur* son aler –	ii s.
Johan Dory p*ur* son entré *et* aler –	iiii s.

1352–53 Ceux sount les nouns des gardeins del orfaverie de Loundres l'an du regne le Roi Edward tierçz puis le conq*uest* xxvj[me]:
William de Burtou*n*
Joh*ann*es Botou*n*
Thom*a*s Baldiswell*e*
Joh*ann*es Coraunt

Ceux sount lur despences en l'an avauntdit:
Adep*r*imes payer a une p*r*estrer p*ur* chaunter p*ur* la comune del orfaverie p*ur* demy an *et* un q*ua*rter – iiii li.
It*em*, paié p*ur* lum*er* outre la quilett*e* – iii s.
It*em*, paié p*ur* soner a Seynt Pool – v s. v d.
It*em*, paié a le crest de Seynt Dunstan – iiii li.

S*um*m*a* – xii li. viii s. *et* v. d.

It*em*, payé a lé deux powres ho*m*mes – vi s. viii d.

Ceux sount les nouns des prentiz entrez en le papir mesme l'an xxvj[me]:

p. 11, col. 1 Ric*hard* de Childrin apprentiz William Fr*a*unceys –	ii s.
Thom*a*s Bughod apprentiz Thom*a*s Regh*a*m –	ii s.
Rob*er*t Canteneys app*rentiz* William Berkyngge –	ii s.
Joh*a*n Cok app*rentiz* Adam Aynish*a*m –	ii s.
Steph*an*us Mertou*n* app*r*entis Harri Markisby –	ii s.
Thom*a*s atte Melle app*rentiz* Richard Burnam –	ii s.

[26] MS: quilettes.
[27] MS: Simine/Sumne.

Item, paid for the light over and above the collection – 5s. 1d. col. 2
Item, paid for bell-ringing at St Paul's – 5s. 4d.

Total: 110s. 5d.
The which sum of money is paid and the money has been handed over in full.

These are the names of apprentices enrolled in the register in the same year:

William Fortune, apprentice of John Brinchisle –	2s.
Huchon Betonie, apprentice of Piers Walpole –	2s.
Richard Lacer, apprentice of William Stour –	2s.
William Ferour, apprentice of Thomas Hassay –	2s.
Walter Eriswelle, William Gerveys, apprentices of Roger Femeshal –	4s.
Richard Sherrene, apprentice of Nicholas Guiford –	2s.
Thomas Forester, apprentice of Simon Mazerer –	2s.
Piers Cook, apprentice of William Antra –	2s.

Betonie who was the apprentice of William Ippegrave for his release from his terms –	2s.
John Dory, for his admission and on release –	4s.

These are the names of the Wardens of the Goldsmiths' Mistery of London 1352–53
in the year 26 Edward III [1352] :
William de Burtoun
John Botoun
Thomas Baldeswelle
John Coraunt

These are their expenses in the aforesaid year:
First, paid to a priest to sing [masses] for the commonalty of the Goldsmiths' Mistery, for three-quarters of a year[26] – £4
Item, paid for the light over and above the collection – 3s.
Item, paid for bell-ringing at St Paul's – 5s. 5d.
Item, paid to the increase of St Dunstan['s funds] – £4

Total: £12 8s. 5d.

Item, paid to the 2 poor men – 6s. 8d.

These are the names of the apprentices entered in the register in the same year 1352:

Richard de Childrin, apprentice of William Fraunceys –	2s.	p. 11, col. 1
Thomas Bughod, apprentice of Thomas Raynham –	2s.	
Robert Canteneys, apprentice of William Barking –	2s.	
John Cok, apprentice of Adam Eynsham –	2s.	
Stephen Mertoun, apprentice of Harry Markeby –	2s.	
Thomas atte Melle, apprentice of Richard Burnham –	2s.	

[26] The French text says 'for half a year and a quarter', this being the way the salary due has been calculated.

William Hanneye app*rentiz* Joh*a*n Buteyng – ii s.
William Wirhale apprentiz William Lerepol – ii s.
William Pech*a*m apprentiz William Stok*e* – ii s.
Ric*hard* Brandou*n* app*r*entiz Thom*a*s Hessay – ii s.
app*r*entiz Roberd Norwich*e* – ii s.
Rob*er*tus atte Launde app*rentiz* Joh*a*n Coraunt – ii s.
Joh*a*n Pipeherst app*rentiz* Thom*a*s Lyncoln*e* – ii s.

Henr*i* Bronle p*ur* son aler – ii s.
Janyn Pixle p*ur* son aler – ii s.
Ric*hard* Brinchisle p*ur* son aler – ii s.
William Mertou*n* p*ur* son aler – ii s.
Joh*a*n Morgon p*ur* son aler – ii s.
Joh*a*n Craneb*our*ne p*ur* son aler – ii s.

Waut*er* Dorem p*ur* gré fait acountre les gardeyns – x s.
Edmu*n*d Cokyn p*ur* gré fait acount*re* les gardeyns – vi [s.] viii d.

Les p*ar*celes am*er*ciamentz en le tienz de les ditz gardeyns del companie del orfaverie:
Adep*ri*me William Ippeg*ra*ve p*ur* son cotel tr*err*é acountre William Derby – x s.
Edmu*n*d Ippeg*ra*ve p*ur* son cotel treré acountr*e* William Hatfeld – x s.
Petrus le Mazerer p*ur* son cotel treré a Joh*a*n Herwy *et* sanc gouté – xx s.
William Berkynge p*ur* son cotel t*re*ré a Thom*a*s Pipeherst – x s.

Et de ceux rien payé.

1353–54 Ceux sount les nouns des gardeyns del orfaverie de Loundres l'an du regne le Roi Edward puis le conquest xxviime:
Joh*a*n Hiltoft
William Ippeg*ra*ve
Thom*a*s Hyngeston*e*
Thom*a*s Hassay

Ceux sount lo*ur* despenses l'an avauntdit:
Adep*ri*mes paié p*ur* lum*er*e outre la quilette – v s.
It*e*m, paié p*ur* la son*er* a Seynt Poul – v s. ii d.
It*e*m, paié a ii povr*e*s contr*e* Noel – vi s. viii d.
It*e*m paié a un prestr*e* p*ur* chaunt*er* p*ur* la comun*e* a la glise de Seynt Matheu – iiii li. xiii s. iiii d.
It*e*m, payé al encress – iiii li.

Ces sount les nouns des app*r*entiz mesme l'an xxviime:
William Wirhal*e* app*rentiz* Will*iam* Letherpol – ii s.
Ric*hard* Brinchisle app*rentiz* Rog*er* Hemeshal – ii s.

William Hanneye, apprentice of John Buteyng –	2s.
William Wirral, apprentice of William Liverpool –	2s.
William Pecham, apprentice of William Stoke –	2s.
Richard Brandoun, apprentice of Thomas Hassay –	2s.
– the apprentice of Robert Norwich –	2s.
Robert atte Launde, apprentice of John Coraunt –	2s.
John Piphurst, apprentice of Thomas Lincoln –	2s.

Henry Brenle, for his release –	2s.
Janyn Pixley, for his release –	2s.
Richard Brinchisle, for his release –	2s.
William Mertoun, for his release –	2s.
John Morgon, for his release –	2s.
John Cranebourne, for his release –	2s.

Walter Dorem, in settlement with the Wardens – 10s.
Edmund Cokyn, in settlement with the Wardens – 6s. 8d.

Details of amercements in the time of the said Wardens of the Goldsmiths' Mistery:
Firstly, William Ippegrave, for having drawn his knife against William Derby – 10s.
Edmund Ippegrave, for having drawn his knife against William Hatfield – 10s.
Peter le Mazerer,[27] for having drawn his knife against John Herwy and having drawn blood – 20s.
William Barking, for having drawn his knife against Thomas Piphurst – 10s.

And none of these have paid.

These are the names of the Wardens of the Goldsmiths' Mistery of London in the year 27 Edward III [1353]: 1353–54
John Hiltoft
William Ippegrave
Thomas Hingston
Thomas Hassay

These are their expenses for the aforesaid year:
Firstly, paid for the light over and above the collection – 5s.
Item, paid for the bell-ringing at St Paul's – 5s. 2d.
Item, paid to 2 poor people at Christmas time – 6s. 8d.
Item, paid to a priest, to sing for the commonalty at the church of St Matthew – £4 13s. 4d.
Item, paid to the increase [of funds] – £4.

These are the names of apprentices in the same year 1353:

William Wirral, apprentice of William Liverpool –	2s.
Richard Brinchisle, apprentice of Roger Hemeshal –	2s.

27 Or 'Peter the mazerer'?

col. 2 William Portesmoth*e* app*rentiz* William Hassay – ii s.
Joh*a*n Lodelowe app*rentiz* Johan Boton – ii s.
Joh*a*n de Thidenham app*rentiz* William Tyngewyk – ii s.
Rob*er*t de Tyngewynk[28] app*rentiz* William Tyngewyk – ii s.
Thom*as* de Hyngeston*e* p*ur* son app*rentiz* William Hult – ii s.

William de Salesburi p*ur* son aler – ii s.
Joh*a*n Forester p*ur* son aler – ii s.

It*em*, Johan Litleg*ra*ve, orbat*ur*, dona p*ur* son entré en orfaverie – Lx s.
It*em*, p*ur* Will*ia*m Hap*er* sou*n* apprentys – ii s.

1354–55 Ceux sount les nouns des gardeyns del orfaverie de Loundres l'an du regne le Roi Edward tierce puis le conquest xxviiime:
Will*ia*m de Burtou*n*
Will*ia*m de Berkyng
Joh*a*n Croidou*n*
Will*ia*m F*ra*unceys

Ceux sount lur despenses:
Adep*ri*mes paié p*ur* lum*er*e outre la q*ui*lette – v s.
It*e*m, paié p*ur* sonner a Seynt Poul – v s. iii d.
It*e*m, paié countr*e* le Nowel – vi [s.] viii d.

Ceux sount les nouns des app*re*ntiz mesme l'an – xxviiime:
Joh*a*n Peryntou*n* app*rentiz* Joh*a*n Chichestre – ii s.
Joh*a*n de Leicestr*e* app*rentiz* Will*ia*m de Burtou*n* – ii s.
It*e*m, Capeler app*rentiz* de Will*iam* Tynggewyk – ii s.

Raulyn de Lynne p*ur* son entré – vi [s.] viii d.

1355–56 Ceux sount les nouns des gardeyns del orfaverie de Loundres l'an du regne le Roi E*dward* ter*c*e puis le conquest xxixme:
p. 12, col. 1 Joh*a*n Botou*n*
William Tyngewyk
Joh*a*n Mapelesden*e*
Joh*a*n de Brinchislee

Ceux sount lo*ur* despences:
Adep*ri*mes paier p*ur* le soner a Seynt Poul – iii s. ii d.
It*e*m, paié a le chapelein – iiii li.
It*e*m, paié a les povres trovés del almoigne countre Noel – vi s. viii d.

[28] *Sic.*

William Portsmouth, apprentice of William Hassay – 2s. col. 2
John Ludlow, apprentice of John Boton – 2s.
John de Thidenham, apprentice of William Tingewick – 2s.
Robert de Tingewick, apprentice of William Tingewick – 2s.
Thomas de Hingston, for his apprentice William Hult – 2s.

William de Salisbury, for his release – 2s.
John Forester, for his release – 2s.

Item, John Litlegrave, goldbeater, gave for his entry into the Goldsmiths' Mistery – 60s.
Item, for William Haper, his apprentice – 2s.

These are the names of the Wardens of the Goldsmiths' Mistery of London 1354–55
in the year 28 Edward III [1354]:
William de Burtoun
William de Barking
John Croydon
William Fraunceys

These are their expenses:
Firstly, paid for the light over and above the collection – 5s.
Item, paid for bell-ringing at St Paul's – 5s. 3d.
Item, paid out at Christmas time – 6s. 8d.

These are the names of apprentices in the same year 1354:
John Peryntoun, apprentice of John Chichester – 2s.
John de Leicester, apprentice of William de Burtoun – 2s.
Item, Capeler, apprentice of William Tingewick – 2s.

Raulyn de Lynne for his entry – 6s. 8d.

These are the names of the Wardens of the Goldsmiths' Mistery of London 1355–56
in the year 29 Edward III [1355]:
John Botoun p. 12, col. 1
William Tingewick
John Maplesdene
John de Brinchisle

These are their expenses:
Firstly, paid for the bell-ringing at St Paul's – 3s. 2d.
Item, paid to the chaplain – £4
Item, paid to the poor people supported out of the alms funds at Christmas time – 6s. 8d.

It*em*, doné p*ar* le comune assent al ov*er*aign*e* del eglise de Seint Pere en Chepe – xx li.
It*em*, don*é* al eglise Seint Jon Zakar*ie* – x li.
It*em*, don*é* a la eglise de Seint Math*e*u en Friday Strete – vi li. xiii s. iiii d.
It*em*, don*é* a la eglise de Seint Faster – xxvi s. viii d.

It*em*, outre ceo entrerent deux pov*er*es [al] almoign*e*, c'est assavoir: Pieres Hung*ere* *et* Henr*i* Toteberd.

It*em*, don*é* al encrese – xl s.

Ceux sount les nouns des app*re*ntiz entrez en l'an susdit:
Adep*ri*mes rec*eu* de Joh*an*ne Fairheir p*ur* son app*re*ntiz William Som*er*vill*e* – ii s.
It*em*, de Thom*as* de Salisbur*i* p*ur* William Brens, William atte More, ses app*re*ntiz – iiii s.
It*em*, de Joh*an* Beteign*e* p*ur* sou*n* app*re*ntiz Ric*hard* Frendisburi – ii s.
It*em*, de Joh*an* Croydou*n* p*ur* so[n] app*re*ntiz Andrew atte Halle – ii s.
It*em*, de Will*ia*m de Derby p*ur* son app*re*ntiz Joh*an* Mapiltou*n* – ii s.
It*em*, de Will*ia*m Ficher p*ur* son app*re*ntiz Johan May – ii s.
It*em*, de Joh*an* Chose p*ur* son app*re*ntiz Johan Barb*er* – ii s.
It*em*, de Rog*er* Blod p*ur* son app*rentiz* David Blod – ii s.
It*em*, de Rauf de Lynne p*ur* son app*rentiz* Dominik de Dunstou*n* – ii s.
col. 2 It*em*, de Waut*er* Mazerer p*ur* son app*rentiz* – ii s.
It*em*, de Joh*an* Mapelesden*e* p*ur* son app*rentiz* Will*iam* Makenhened – ii s.

Ceux sount les entrés:
Joh*an* Cappe – xxvi s.
Ric*hard* Pain – xiii s. iiii d.
Joh*an* Rollyng – v s.
Ric*hard* Tastard – v. s
Joh*an* Wirhale – ii s.
Joh*an* Godesou*n* – ii s.
Hamond Chose – ii s.
Joh*an* de Lyndeseye – ii s.
Ric*hard* de Petresburgh*e* – ii s.
Hugh*e* de Bylyngden*e* – ii s.
William Stameden*e* – ii s.
Joh*an* atte Thorne – iii s. iiii d.
It*em*, de Ric*hard* Brid*e* – iii s. iiii d.

1356–57 Ceux sount les nouns des gardeyns del orfaverie de Loundres l'an du regne le Roi Edward tierce puis le conquest xxxme:
Thomas Hassay
Joh*an* Fairheir
Thom*as* Hyngston*e*
Thom*as* de Reinham

Item, given by common consent to the works of the church of St Peter in Cheap – £20
Item, given to the church of St John Zachary – £10
Item, given to the church of St Matthew in Friday Street – £6 13s. 4d.
Item, given to the church of St Vedast – 26s. 8d.

Item, besides this, two poor people were granted alms, i.e.
Piers Hungry and Henry Toteberd

Item, given to the increase [of funds] – 40s.

These are the names of apprentices entered in the aforesaid year:

Firstly, received from John Fairher for his apprentice William Somerville –	2s.
Item, from Thomas de Salisbury for William Brens, William atte More, his apprentices –	4s.
Item, from John Beteigne for his apprentice Richard Frindsbury –	2s.
Item, from John Croydon for his apprentice Andrew atte Halle –	2s.
Item, from William de Derby for his apprentice John Mapiltoun –	2s.
Item, from William Ficher for his apprentice John May –	2s.
Item, from John Chose for his apprentice John Barber –	2s.
Item, from Roger Blod for his apprentice David Blod –	2s.
Item, from Ralph de Lynne for his apprentice Dominic de Dunston –	2s.
Item, from Walter Mazerer for his apprentice –	2s. col. 2
Item, from John Maplesdene for his apprentice William Makenhened –	2s.

These are the entries:

John Cappe –	26s.
Richard Payn –	13s. 4d.
John Rollyng –	5s.
Richard Tastard –	5s.
John Wirral –	2s.
John Godesoun –	2s.
Hamond Chose –	2s.
John de Lindsey –	2s.
Richard de Peterborough –	2s.
Hugh de Billington –	2s.
William Stameldene –	2s.
John atte Thorne –	3s. 4d.
Item, from Richard Bride –	3s. 4d.

These are the names of the Wardens of the Goldsmiths' Mistery of London 1356–57
in the year 30 Edward III [1356]:
Thomas Hassay
John Fairher
Thomas Hingston
Thomas de Raynham

Ces sount les despens*es* faites p*ar* les gardeyns en lo*ur* temps come en lo*ur* feste, les povres, lum*ere*, *et* le soner – xx li.

Ces sount les nouns des app*re*ntiz *et* lowez entrez en l'an susdit:
Adep*ri*mes rec*eu* de Will*iam* de Berkyngge p*ur* Joh*a*n Colman son app*re*ntiz – ii s.
It*e*m, resc*eu* de William Liv*er*pol p*ur* Johan Liv*er*pol son app*re*ntiz – ii s.
It*e*m, resc*eu* de Joh*a*n de Bartou*n* p[*ur*][29] Ric*hard* Peyver son apprentiz *et* Joh*a*n de Norwich*e* son app*rentiz* – iiii s.
It*e*m de Joh*a*n de Croydou*n* p[*ur*][30] Henri Chamb*er*leyn *et* Aben Astou*n* ses app*rentiz* – iiii s.
It*em* de Joh*an* de Huntyngdou*n* p*ur* Joh*an* Bruges son app*re*ntiz – ii s.
It*e*m, de Ad*am* Elsh*am* p*ur* Rob*ert* Godma*n* son allowis – ii s.
p. 13, col. 1 It*e*m, de Joh*a*n Craneb*ur*ne p*ur* William Pye son app*re*ntiz – ii s.
It*e*m, de Thom*as* de Lincoln*e* p*ur* Joh*a*n de Lincoln*e* son allowys – ii s.
It*e*m, de Thom*as* Hyngeston*e* p*ur* Simond Hyngeston*e* – ii s.
It*e*m, de Herv*é* Markeby p*ur* Joh*a*n Vele son app*re*ntiz – ii s.
It*e*m, de Thom*a*s Hassay p*ur* Joh*a*n Russh*a*m son app*rentiz* – ii s.
It*e*m, de Thom*a*s de Reynham p*ur* Thom*as* Wygo, lowys – ii s.
It*em*, de Joh*an* Broun p*ur* Ric*hard* Broun son app*re*ntiz – ii s.
It*e*m, de Joh*an* Fairher p*ur* Will*iam* Burden*e* son app*rentiz* – ii s.
It*em*, de Rob*er*t Gardenir p*ur* son app*re*ntiz Joh*an* Pixle – ii s.
It*em*, de Thom*as* Reynh*a*m p*ur* Joh*an* Sellyng son app*rentiz* – ii s.
It*em*, de Rob*er*t de Norwich*e* p*ur* Will*iam* Mersh*a*m, lowis – ii s.

1357–58 Ces sount les nouns des gardeyns del orfaverie de Loundres l'an du regne le Roi Edward tierce puis le conquest xxxj^{me}:

William de Burtone
Joh*a*n de Gravele
Thom*a*s Pipphurst
Thom*a*s Ba*m*me'
} l'an xxxj^{me}

Don*é* al encrés del almoigne Seynt Dunston outre totes maner costages, messes ou povres del mestir *et* autre nieuwe[31] costages de clerc – viii li.

Ceux sount les nouns des app*re*ntiz *et* de lowis de l'an susdit:
Will*ia*m Kebbul, lowys – ii s.
Thom*a*s Rokyngh*a*m – ii s.
Ric*hard* Mayn, app*re*ntiz – ii s.
Berthelemeu Ostoune, lowys – ii s.
Simond atte Wode, lowys – ii s.
Richard de Bartou*n*, lowys – ii s.

[29] MS: p*ro*.
[30] MS: p*ro*.
[31] This might alternately be read as 'menwe'.

These are the expenditures made by the Wardens during their time [term of office], such as at their feast, on poor people, on the light, and the bell-ringing – £20.

These are the names of apprentices and serving-men entered in the aforesaid year:

Firstly, received from William de Barking for John Colman, his apprentice –	2s.
Item, received from William Liverpool for John Liverpool, his apprentice –	2s.
Item, received from John de Bartoun for Richard Peyver, his apprentice and John de Norwich, his apprentice –	4s.
Item, from John de Croydon for Henry Chamberlayn and Aben Astoun, his apprentices –	4s.
Item, from John de Huntingdon for John Bruges, his apprentice –	2s.
Item, from Adam Elsham for Robert Godman, his serving-man –	2s.
Item, from John Cranebourne for William Pye, his apprentice –	2s. p. 13, col. 1
Item, from Thomas de Lincoln for John de Lincoln, his serving-man –	2s.
Item, from Thomas Hingston for Simon Hingston –	2s.
Item, from Harvey Markeby for John Vele, his apprentice –	2s.
Item, from Thomas Hassay for John Russham, his apprentice –	2s.
Item, from Thomas de Raynham for Thomas Wygo, serving-man –	2s.
Item, from John Broun for Richard Broun, his apprentice –	2s.
Item, from John Fairher for William Burdeyn, his apprentice –	2s.
Item, from Robert Gardenir for his apprentice John Pixley –	2s.
Item, from Thomas Raynham for John Sellyng, his apprentice –	2s.
Item, from Robert de Norwich for William Mersham, serving-man –	2s.

These are the names of the Wardens of the Goldsmiths' Mistery of London in the year 31 Edward III [1357]: 1357–58
William de Burtoun
John de Gravele
Thomas Piphurst
Thomas Bamme

Given to the increase of the alms funds of St Dunstan, excluding [once having paid out] all manner of expenses, masses, and for the poor of the Mistery, and other new[28] expenses of the clerk – £8

These are the names of apprentices and serving-men of the aforesaid year:

William Kebbul, serving-man –	2s.
Thomas Rockingham –	2s.
Richard Mayn, apprentice –	2s.
Bartholomew Ostoune, serving-man –	2s.
Simon atte Wood, serving-man –	2s.
Richard de Barton, serving-man –	2s.

[28] Or 'small, minor' – see opposite page.

Joh*a*n Saybrok, lowis –	ii s.
Joh*a*n Pit, lowys –	ii s.
Joh*a*n de Brugis, lowis –	ii s.
Joh*a*n Godman, lowis –	ii s.
Rob*er*t Freman, app*re*ntiz –	ii s.
Edmund Forest*er* –	ii s.
Will*iam* Aulmare, app*re*ntiz –	ii s.
col. 2 (Butmet)[32] Richard, app*re*ntiz –	ii s.
Joh*a*n Whitchirche, app*re*ntiz –	ii s.
Andrew Pycok, app*re*ntiz –	ii s.
Joh*a*n Sour, app*re*ntiz –	ii s.
Nicholas Mirfeld, app*re*ntiz –	ii s.
William de Wottou*n*, app*re*ntiz –	ii s.
Joh*a*n de Burtou*n*, app*re*ntiz –	ii s.
Joh*a*n Kampenade, app*re*ntiz –	ii s.
William Samekyn, app*re*ntiz –	ii s.
Giliu, app*re*ntiz Rob*er*t Bilindou*n* –	ii s.
William Trigh*a*m, app*re*ntiz –	ii s.
Joh*an* Swofh*a*m, app*re*ntiz –	ii s.
Joh*a*n Trentemas, app*re*ntiz –	ii s.
Joh*an* Hauf, app*re*ntiz –	ii s.
Joh*an* Canoun, app*re*ntiz –	ii s.
Thom*as* Clire, app*re*ntiz –	ii s.
Joh*a*n Ymeworthe, app*re*ntiz –	ii s.
Joh*a*n Lache, app*re*ntiz –	ii s.
Waut*er* Gildhalle, app*re*ntiz –	ii s.
Thom*as* Fyndou*n*, app*re*ntiz –	ii s.
Joh*a*n Langring, app*re*ntiz –	ii s.
Joh*an* Aschebourne, app*re*ntiz –	ii s.
Thom*as* Davy, app*re*ntiz –	ii s.
Edward Wyn, app*re*ntiz –	ii s.
Steph*anus* Dennys, app*re*ntiz –	ii s.[33]
Rob*ertus* Oxinford payer p*ur* entr*er*[34] –	v. m*a*rcs

Les nouns des est*ra*unges gentz entrez mesme l'an:
Roberd d'Oxenford
Thom*as* Wilby
Joh*a*n Palyng
Hanekyn Undirlilie
Hanekyn Lindowe
William Hamond de Coventre.

[32] This word would appear to have been scored out.
[33] This entry and the next are slightly later additions, in the same hand.
[34] The word 'tant' has been inserted above the last 2 words.

John Seybrook, serving-man –	2s.
John Pit, serving-man –	2s.
John de Bruges, serving-man –	2s.
John Godman, serving-man –	2s.
Robert Freman, apprentice –	2s.
Edmund Forester –	2s.
William Aulmare, apprentice –	2s.
Richard ?Butmet?, apprentice –	2s. col. 2
John Whitchurch, apprentice –	2s.
Andrew Pycok, apprentice –	2s.
John Sour, apprentice –	2s.
Nicholas Mirfield, apprentice –	2s.
William de Wootton, apprentice –	2s.
John de Burtoun, apprentice –	2s.
John Kampenade, apprentice –	2s.
William Samekyn, apprentice –	2s.
Giliu, apprentice of Robert Billington –	2s.
William Trigham, apprentice –	2s.
John Swaffham, apprentice –	2s.
John Trentemas, apprentice –	2s.
John Hauf, apprentice –	2s.
John Canoun, apprentice –	2s.
Thomas Clire, apprentice –	2s.
John Ymeworthe, apprentice –	2s.
John Lache, apprentice –	2s.
Walter Gildhalle, apprentice –	2s.
Thomas Findon, apprentice –	2s.
John Langring, apprentice –	2s.
John Ashbourne, apprentice –	2s.
Thomas Davy, apprentice –	2s.
Edward Wyn, apprentice –	2s.
Stephen Dennys, apprentice –	2s.
Robert Oxenford – has paid to enter[29] –	5 marks

The names of aliens entered in the same year:
Robert d'Oxenford
Thomas Wilby
John Palyng
Hanekyn Undirlilie
Hanekyn Lindowe
William Hamond of Coventry

[29] Interlinear note = 'so much'?

1323 Sciant presentes et futuri quod nos, Johannes de Insula Senior, miles de comitatu p. 14, col. 1[35] Essex', frater Georgius de Wakerle et Thomas de Flore, rector ecclesie de Kyslingbury, Lincolniensis Diocesii, executores testamenti bone memorie domini Nicholai de Segrave, militis, iam defuncti,[36] dedimus, concessimus, vendidimus et hac presenti carta nostra confirmavimus domino Willelmo de Clif, clerico, totum tenementum cum domibus superedificatis, libertatibus et omnibus aliis pertinenciis suis ad dictum tenementum spectantibus quod quondam fuit dicti domini Nicholai in vico vocato Sancti Vedasti in parochia Sancti Johannis Zacharie London', quod eciam jacet inter tenementa Thome de Lincolnia, aurifabri London', et tenementum quondam Walteri de Hendoun et tenementum Abbatis de Wardoun ex parte orientali et dictum vicum sancti Vedasti ex parte occidentali, et jacet in latitudine inter venellam vocatam Inglane ex parte aquilonari et tenementum dicti domini Abbatis de Wardoun ex parte australi videlicet quicquid prefatus dominus Nicholas unquam ibidem habuit vel heredes sui aliquo modo seu jure habere poterunt ut in terris, edificiis, lignis, lapidibus, longitudine, latitudine, altitudine, profunditate, et rebus cunctis absque aliquo inde retenemento [seu] diminucione, habendum et tenendum totum predictum tenementum cum domibus superedificatis, libertatibus et omnibus aliis suis pertinenciis predicto domino Waltero de Clif, heredibus et assignatis suis quibuscumque libere, quiete, integre, bene et in pace, in feodo, et in hereditate imperpetuum de capitalibus dominis feodi illius pro |
col. 2 servicia inde debita et de jure consueta pro omnibus aliis servic[iis] secular[ibus][37] demandis et rebus cunctis. Et nos predicti[38] Johannes, frater Georgius et Thomas de Flore totum predictum tenementum cum domibus superedificatis, libertatibus et aliis omnibus pertinenciis suis predicto domino Willelmo de Clif, heredibus et assignatis suis quibuscumque contra omnes gentes warantizabimus imperpetuum. Pro hac autem donacione, concessione, vendicione, warancia et presentis carte nostre confirmacione dedit nobis predictus dominus Willelmus quandam summam pecunie premanibus ad ultimam voluntatem dicti testatoris complendum. In cuius rei testimonium presenti carte sigilla nostra apposuimus, hiis testibus. Nicholao de Farndoun tunc maiore civitatis London',. Johanne de Grantham et Rogero de Ely tunc vicecomitibus eiusdem civitatis, Henrico de Secheford tunc Aldermanno illius warde, Ricardo de Wirhale, Roberto Box, Thoma de Lyncolnia, aurifabro, Roberto Burdeyn, Hugone de Lemenstre, Willelmo Poterel, Willelmo de Wyndesore, Johanne Michel et aliis. Datum London' decimo nono die mensis Maii anno domini millesimo tricentesimo vicesimo tercio et regni regis Edwardi filii regis Edwardi sexto decimo.

Sciant presentes et futuri quod nos Frater Georgius de Wakerle et Thomas de Flore, rector ecclesie de Kyslingbury Lincolniensis diocesii, executores testamenti bone memorie domini Nicholai de Segrave, militis iam defuncti, dedimus concessimus vendidimus et hac presenti carta nostra confirmavimus

[35] The following documents concerning the Hall are also copied into the Register of Deeds, vol I, ff. 17–20.

[36] He died in 1322. See his entry in the *DNB*.

[37] MS: servicibus secularibus.

[38] MS: predictis.

Be it known to those present and future, that we, John de Insula the elder, knight of the county of Essex, Friar George of Wakerley, and Thomas de Flore, rector of the church of Kyslingbury in the Diocese of Lincoln, executors of the will of Sir Nicholas de Segrave of good memory, knight, now deceased, have given, conceded, sold and by this present charter of ours we have confirmed to Sir William de Clif, cleric, the whole tenement with its superstructures, its liberties, and all its other appurtenances which pertain to the said tenement which formerly belonged to the said Sir Nicholas in the street called St Vedast's [Foster Lane] in the parish of St John Zachary, London, which lies between the tenements of Thomas de Lincoln, goldsmith of London, and the tenement previously of Walter de Hendon and the tenement of the Abbot of Warden on the eastern side, and the said Foster Lane on the western side, and which lies laterally between the lane called Inglane[30] on the northern side and the tenement of the said Lord Abbot of Warden on the southern side, that is to say whatever the aforesaid Sir Nicholas ever owned there or his heirs in any manner or by any right may be able to own, that is in lands, buildings, wood, stones, in length, breadth, height, depth and everything, without any retention or diminution, to the aforesaid Sir W[illiam][31] de Clif, his heirs and assigns whoever they may be, to have and to hold the whole of the aforesaid tenement with its superstructures, its liberties and all its other appurtenances, freely, quit, wholly, in well-being and in peace, in fee, and with hereditary rights in perpetuity from the lords in chief of that fee for service owed for it and customary by law, for all other secular services, requests and all things. And we, the aforesaid John, Friar George and Thomas de Flore guarantee in perpetuity the whole of the aforesaid tenement with its superstructures, liberties and all its other appurtenances to the aforesaid Sir William de Clif, his heirs and his assigns whoever they may be, against all people. And for this donation, concession, sale, guarantee and our confirmation in these present letters the aforesaid Sir William gave us a certain sum of money, [paid] into our hands, in order to fulfil the last wishes of the said testator. In testimony of which we have affixed our seals to the present charter, these being the witnesses, Nicholas de Farndon, then Mayor of the City of London, John de Grantham and Roger de Ely then sheriffs of the same City, Henry de Secheford, then alderman of that ward, Richard de Wirral, Robert Box, Thomas de Lincoln, goldsmith, Robert Burdeyn, Hugh de Leominster, William Poterel, William de Windsor, John Michel and others. Given in London on the nineteenth day of the month of May in the year of Our Lord 1323 and of the reign of King Edward son of King Edward[32] the sixteenth.

1323
p. 14, col. 1

Be it known to those present and future, that we, Friar George of Wakerley, and Thomas de Flore, rector of the church of Kyslingbury in the Diocese of Lincoln, executors of the will of Sir Nicholas de Segrave of good memory, knight, now deceased, have given, conceded, sold and by this present charter of ours we have confirmed to Sir William de Clif, cleric, the whole tenement with

30 Also called Maiden Lane; and now Gresham Street.
31 Here and elsewhere the scribe has mistakenly copied 'Walter' instead of 'William'; the Register of Deeds copies show the same errors.
32 i.e. Edward II.

domino Willelmo de Clif, clerico, totum tenementum cum domibus superedificatis, libertatibus et omnibus aliis pertinenciis suis ad dictum tenementum spectantibus, quod quondam fuit dicti domini Nicholai in vico vocato Sancti Vedasti in parochia Sancti Johannis Zakarie London', quod eciam jacet inter tenementa Thome de Lincolnia, aurifabri London' et tenementum quondam Walteri de Hendoun et tenementum Abbatis de Wardoun ex parte orientali et dictum vicum Sancti Vedasti ex parte occidentali, et jacet in latitudine inter venellam vocatam Inglane ex parte aquilonari et tenementum dicti domini Abbatis de Wardoun ex
p. 15, col. 1 parte australi, videlicet quicquid prefatus dominus Nicholas unquam | habuit vel heredes sui aliquo modo habere poterunt ut in terris, edificiis, lignis, lapidibus, longitudine, latitudine, altitudine, profunditate, et rebus cunctis absque aliquo inde retenemento seu diminucione habendum et tenendum totum predictum tenementum cum domibus superedificatis, libertatibus et omnibus aliis suis pertinenciis prefato domino Willelmo de Clif heredibus et assignatis suis quibuscumque libere, quiete, integre, bene et in pace, in feodo et in hereditate imperpetuum de capitalibus dominis feodi illius pro servicia inde debita et de jure consueta pro omnibus aliis servic[iis] secular[ibus][39] demandis et rebus cunctis. Et nos predicti frater Georgius et Thomas de Flore totum predictum tenementum cum domibus superedificatis, libertatibus et omnibus aliis suis pertinenciis prefato domino Willelmo de Clif heredibus et assignatis suis quibuscumque contra omnes gentes warantizabimus imperpetuum. Pro hace autem donacione, concessione, vendicione, warantiza et presentis carte nostre confirmacione dedit nobis predictus dominus Willelmus quandam summam pecunie premanibus ad ultimam voluntatem dicti testatoris inde complendum. In cuius rei testimonium huic presenti carte sigilla nostra apposuimus, hiis testibus Nicholao de Farndoun tunc maiore civitatis London', Johanne de Grantham, Rogero de Ely tunc vicecomitibus eiusdem civitatis, Henrico de Secheford tunc Aldermanno illius Warde, Ricardo de Wirhale, Roberto de Box, Thoma de Lincolnia, aurifabro, Roberto Burdeyn, Hugone de Lemenstre, Willelmo Poterel, Willelmo de Wyndessore, Johanne Michel et aliis.

Sciant presentes et futuri quod ego Frater Georgius de Wakerle, executor testamenti bone memorie domini Nicholai de Segrave, militis iam defuncti, dedi, concessi, vendidi et hac presenti carta mea confirmavi domino Willelmo de Clif, clerico, totum tenementum cum domibus sup[er]edificatis, libertatibus et omnibus aliis pertinenciis suis ad dictum tenementum spectantibus, quod quondam fuit dicti domini Nicholai in vico vocato Sancti Vedasti in parochia Sancti Johannis Zacharie London', quod eciam jacet inter tenementa Thome de Lincolnia, aurifabri London', et tenementum quondam Walteri de Hendoun et tenementum Abbatis de Wardoun ex parte orientali et dictum vicum Sancti Vedasti ex parte occidentali, et jacet in latitudine inter venellam vocatam Inglane ex parte aquilonari et tenementum dicti domini Abbatis de Wardoun
col. 2 ex parte australi, videlicet quicquid prefatus dominus Nicholas | unquam ibidem habuit vel heredes sui aliquo modo seu jure habere poterunt ut in terris, edificiis, lignis, lapidibus, longitudine, latitudine, altitudine, profunditate et rebus cunctis absque aliquo inde retenemento seu diminucione, habendum et tenendum totum predictum tenementum cum domibus superedificatis,

[39] MS: servicibus secularis.

its superstructures, its liberties, and all its other appurtenances which pertain to the said tenement which formerly belonged to the said Sir Nicholas in the street called St Vedast's [Foster Lane] in the parish of St John Zachary, London, which lies between the tenements of Thomas de Lincoln, goldsmith of London, and the tenement previously of Walter de Hendon and the tenement of the Abbot of Warden on the eastern side, and the said Foster Lane on the western side, and which lies laterally between the lane called Inglane on the northern side and the tenement of the said Lord Abbot of Warden on the southern side, that is to say whatever the aforesaid Sir Nicholas ever | owned there or his heirs p. 15, col. 1
in any manner or by any right may be able to own, that is in lands, buildings, wood, stones, in length, breadth, height, depth and everything, without any retention or diminution, to the aforesaid Sir William de Clif, his heirs and assigns whoever they may be, to have and to hold the whole of the aforesaid tenement with its superstructures, its liberties and all its other appurtenances, freely, quit, wholly, in well-being and in peace, in fee, and with hereditary rights in perpetuity from the lords in chief of that fee for service owed for it and customary by law, for all other secular services, requests and all things. And we, the aforesaid Friar George and Thomas de Flore guarantee in perpetuity the whole of the aforesaid tenement with its superstructures, liberties and all its other appurtenances to the aforesaid Sir William de Clif, his heirs and his assigns whoever they may be against all people. And for this donation, concession, sale, guarantee and our confirmation in these present letters the aforesaid Sir William gave us a certain sum of money, [paid] into our hands, in order to fulfil the last wishes of the said testator. In testimony of which we have affixed our seals to the present charter, these being the witnesses, Nicholas de Farndon, then Mayor of the City of London, John de Grantham and Roger de Ely then sheriffs of the same City, Henry de Secheford, then alderman of that ward, Richard de Wirral, Robert de Box, Thomas de Lincoln, goldsmith, Robert Burdeyn, Hugh de Leominster, William Poterel, William de Windsor, John Michel and others.

Be it known to those present and future, that I, Friar George of Wakerley, executor of the will of Sir Nicholas de Segrave of good memory, knight, now deceased, have given, conceded, sold and by this present charter of mine have confirmed to Sir William de Clif, cleric, the whole tenement with its superstructures, its liberties, and all its other appurtenances which pertain to the said tenement which formerly belonged to the said Sir Nicholas in the street called St Vedast's [Foster Lane] in the parish of St John Zachary, London, which lies between the tenements of Thomas de Lincoln, goldsmith of London, and the tenement previously of Walter de Hendon and the tenement of the Abbot of Warden on the eastern side, and the said Foster Lane on the western side, and which lies laterally between the lane called Inglane on the northern side and the tenement of the said Lord Abbot of Warden on the southern side, that is to say whatever the aforesaid Sir Nicholas | ever owned there or his heirs in any manner or by any right may col. 2
be able to own, that is in lands, buildings, wood, stones, in length, breadth, height, depth and everything, without any retention or diminution, to the aforesaid Sir William de Clif, his heirs and assigns whoever they may be, to have and to hold the whole of the aforesaid tenement with its superstructures,

lib*er*tatib*us* et om*n*ib*us* aliis suis p*er*tin*enciis* p*re*d*ict*o d*om*ino Will*elm*o de Clif, hered*ibus* et assign*atis* suis quibuscu*m*q*ue* libere, quiete, integre, bene *et* in pace, in feodo *et* hereditate imp*er*petuu*m* de capitalib*us* d*om*inis feodi illius p*ro* s*er*vicia inde debita *et* de jure consueta pro om*n*ib*us* aliis s*er*viciis secularib*us* demandis *et* rebus cunctis. Et ego, p*re*d*ict*us frat*er* Georgius totu*m* p*re*d*ict*u*m* ten*ementum* cu*m* domib*us* sup*er*edificatis lib*er*tatib*us* et om*n*ib*us* aliis p*er*tin*enciis* p*re*fato d*om*ino Will*elm*o de Clif, heredib*us* et assign*atis* suis q*ui*buscu*m*q*ue* cont*ra* om*n*es gentes warantizabo imp*er*petuu*m*. Pro hac aute*m* concess*ione*, vendic*ione*, warantiza *et* p*re*sentis carte mee confirmac*ion*e dedit m*ihi* p*re*d*ict*us d*omin*us Will*elmu*s q*ua*ndam su*m*mam pecunie p*re*manib*us* ad ulti*m*am voluntatem d*icti* testatoris inde complendu*m*. In cuius rei testimoniu*m* huic p*re*senti carte sigillu*m* meu*m* apposui. Hiis testib*us* Nich*ola*o de Farndou*n*, tunc Maiore civitatis London', Joh*ann*e de Granth*a*m *et* Rog*er*o de Ely tunc vicecomitib*us* London', Henr*ico* de Secheford, tunc Aldermanno illius warde, Ric*ard*o de Wirhale, Rob*er*to Box, Thoma de Lincoln*ia*, aurifabro, Rob*er*to Burdeyn, Hugone de Lemenstr*e*, Will*elm*o Pot*er*el, Will*elm*o de Wyndessore, Joh*ann*e Michel *et* aliis *et*c.

1339 Pl*ac*ita t*er*re tent*a* die lune p*roxima* post f*estu*m S*anct*i Barnabe ap*osto*li anno r*egni* E*dwardi* t*er*cii post conquestu*m* t*er*ciodecimo.

P*ro*batu*m* fuit testamentu*m* Will*elm*i de Clif, cl*er*ici, in hec v*er*ba. It*em*, lego Will*elm*o de Clif, fil*io* meo, om*n*ia ten*ementa* mea cu*m* domib*us* sup*er*edificatis in vico vocato Silverstrete. It*em*, lego p*re*d*ict*is executorib*us* meis totu*m* ten*ementum* meu*m* in vico S*anct*i Vedasti *et* Ingenelane, London', ad vendendu*m* p*ro* quadraginta marc*is*, et si plus recip*er*int q*uo*d Will*elm*o fil*io* meo reddant, faciendu*m* p*ro* anima mea et ut isti sunt administ*ra*tores bona legat*a* sicut viderint se post morte*m* mea*m* melius p*ro* anima mea expedire. Et si quid residuu*m* fu*er*it *et*c. Conditu*m* fuit istud test*amentu*m die Mart*ii* p*roxima* ante festu*m* S*anct*i Dunstani E*pisco*pi a*nno* d*om*ini mill*esim*o CCC^{mo} tricesimo nono.

p. 16, col. 1 Executores testamenti p*re*d*ict*i:
Laur*encius* de Clif
D*omin*us Joh*ann*es de Bokeden*e*

Testes eiusdem ad p*ro*bandu*m*
Nich*ola*s de Totenhale
Will*elmu*s de Shirwode

Sciant p*re*sentes et fut*uri* q*uo*d nos Laurencius de Clif de com*itatu* Ebor', Joh*ann*es de Buckeden*e*, capell*an*us, executores testamenti d*om*ini Will*elm*i de Clif, cl*er*ici iam defuncti, ulti*m*am voluntatem eiusdem defuncti juxta posse n*ost*r*a*m exequi *et* adimplere cupientes ut tenem*us* virtute *et* autoritate testamenti p*re*d*ict*i p*ro*bati *et* irrotulati in hustengo London' de pl*ac*itis t*er*re tent*is* die lune p*roxima* post f*estu*m S*anct*i Barnabe ap*osto*li anno regni regis Edwardi t*er*cii post conquestu*m* t*er*cio decimo, vendidim*us*, concessim*us* et hac p*re*senti carta n*ost*ra confirmavim*us* Hugoni de Brandou*n*, Simoni de Berkyng, Ric*ard*o Denys, Will*elm*o Sporoun, Ric*ard*o de Basynggestok*e*, Steph*an*o le Frenssh*e*, Rob*er*to de Wyke, Joh*ann*i de

its liberties and all its other appurtenances, freely, quit, wholly, in well-being and in peace, in fee, and with hereditary rights in perpetuity from the lords in chief of that fee for service owed for it and customary by law, for all other secular services, requests and all things. And I, the aforesaid Friar George guarantee in perpetuity the whole of the aforesaid tenement with its superstructures, liberties and all its other appurtenances to the aforesaid Sir William de Clif, his heirs and his assigns whoever they may be against all people. And for this donation, concession, sale, guarantee and my confirmation in these present letters the aforesaid Sir William gave me a certain sum of money, [paid] into my hands, in order to fulfil the last wishes of the said testator. In testimony of which I have affixed my seal to the present charter, these being the witnesses, Nicholas de Farndon, then Mayor of the City of London, John de Grantham and Roger de Ely then sheriffs of the same City, Henry de Secheford, then alderman of that ward, Richard de Wirral, Robert Box, Thomas de Lincoln, goldsmith, Robert Burdeyn, Hugh de Leominster, William Poterel, William de Windsor, John Michel and others, etc.

Land pleas held on the Monday following the Feast of St Barnabas the apostle 1339
in the year 13 Edward III [14 June 1339]
The will of William de Clif, cleric, was proved in these words: Item, I bequeath to William de Clif, my son, all my tenements with their superstructures in the street called Silver Street. Item, I bequeath to my aforesaid executors the whole of my tenement in Foster Lane and Ingenlane, London, to be sold for 40 marks, and if they should receive more, they should hand this over to my son William, to do for the good of my soul and as they as administrators think fit with these bequests if they after my death can achieve more for my soul. And if there be any residue etc . . . This will was drawn up on the Tuesday before the Feast of St Dunstan, bishop, [18 May] in the year of Our Lord 1339.

Executors of the aforesaid will: p. 16, col. 1
Laurence de Clif
Sir John de Buckedene

Witnesses of the same at the probate:
Nicholas de Totenhale
William de Sherwood

Be it known to those present and future that we Laurence de Clif of the County of York, John de Buckedene, chaplain, executors of the will of Sir William de Clif, cleric now deceased, wishing to carry out and fulfil the last will of the same deceased man in so far as we are able, as we are obliged to by the virtue and authority of the aforesaid testament proved and enrolled in the Husting Court of London at the land pleas held on the Monday following the Feast of St Barnabas the Apostle in the year 13 Edward III [14 June 1339], have sold, conceded and by this our present charter we have confirmed to Hugh de Brandon, Simon de Barking, Richard Denys, William Sporoun, Richard de Basingstoke, Stephen le Frensshe, Robert de Wyke, John de Toppesfield, Robert de Shoreditch the

Toppesfeld, Ro*ber*to de Shordich*e*, seniori, Nich*ola*o de Farndou*n*, Thome de Porkele, Joh*anne* de Makenhened, Will*elm*o de Ippegr*a*ve, Ro*ber*to de Shordich*e* juniori, Joh*ann*i de Hynggeston*e*, Joh*ann*i de Walepole, Ade de Walepol*e*, Thome de Far[n]done[40] et Walt*er*o atte Ferne, civib*us* et aurifabris London', totu*m* illud ten*ementum* cu*m* domib*us* sup*er*edificatis, lib*er*tatib*us* et om*n*ib*us* aliis p*er*tin*enciis* suis ad d*ictu*m ten*ementum* qualit*er*cu*m*q*ue* spectantib*us* quod quondam fuit d*omi*ni Nich*ola*i de Segr*a*ve, militis, in vico vocat*o* S*anc*ti Vedasti in p*a*rochia S*anc*ti Joh*ann*is Zakarie *et* in varda de Aldresgate London', quod *et* jacet int*er* tenementa Thome de Lincoln*ia*, aurifabri London', *et* ten*ementum* quond*am* Will*elm*i de Hendou*n* *et* ten*ementum* Abb*at*is de Wardone ex p*ar*te orientali *et* d*ictu*m vicu*m* S*anc*ti Vedasti ex p*ar*te occidentali, et jacet in latitudine int*er* venellam vocat*am* Inglane ex p*ar*te aquilon*ari* *et* ten*ementum* d*ic*ti d*omi*ni Abb*at*is de Wardon*e* ex p*ar*te aust*r*ali, videl*ice*t quicquid p*re*fatus d*omi*nus Will*elmu*s de Clif unq*ua*m h*ab*uit v*e*l hered*es* sui aliquo modo seu jure h*ab*ere pot*er*unt ut in t*er*ris, edificiis, lignis, lapidib*us*, longitudine, latitudine, altitudine, p*ro*funditate et rebus cunctis a[bs]que[41] aliquo inde retenemento seu diminuc*io*ne quacu*m*q*ue*. Et quod quid*am* col. 2 ten*ementum* idem d*omi*nus | Will*elmu*s de Clif h*ab*uit *et* adquisivit ex concessione et vendic*io*ne executor*um* d*omi*ni Nich*ola*i de Segr*a*ve, militis sup*ra*d*ic*ti, habend*um* et tenend*um* totu*m* p*redictu*m ten*ementum* cu*m* domib*us* sup*er*edificatis, lib*er*tatib*us* *et* om*n*ib*us* aliis suis p*er*tin*enciis* p*re*fatis Hugoni de Brandon*e*, Simoni de Berkyngg*e*, Ric*ard*o Denys, Will*elm*o Sporoun, Ric*ard*o de Basynggestok*e*, Steph*an*o le Frenssh*e*, Ro*ber*to de Wyke, Joh*ann*i de Toppesfeld, Ro*ber*to de Shordich*e* seniori, Nich*ola*o de Farndou*n*, Thome de Porkele, Johanne de Makenhened, Will*elmu*s de Ippegr*a*ve, Ro*ber*to de Shordich*e* junior, Joh*ann*i de Hyngeston*e*, Joh*ann*i de Walepole, Ade de Walepole, Thome de Farndou*n*, et Walt*er*i atte Ferne, eor*um* heredib*us* et assign*atis* q*ui*buscu*m*q*ue* libere, quiete, integre, bene *et* in pace, in feodo *et* hereditate imp*er*petuu*m* de capitalib*us* d*omi*nis illius feodi p*ro* s*er*vicia inde debita *et* de jure consueta pro om*n*ib*us* aliis s*er*viciis secularib*us* demandis *et* reb*us* cunctis. Pro hac autem vendic*io*ne, concessione *et* p*re*sentis carte n*ost*re confirmac*io*ne dederunt nobis p*redic*ti Hugo, Simon, Ric*ardu*s Denys, Will*elmu*s Sporoun, Ric*ardu*s de Basynggestok*e*, Steph*anu*s, Ro*ber*tus de Wyke, Joh*anne*s de Topesfeld, Ro*ber*tus de Shordich*e* senior, Nich*ola*s, Thom*a*s de Porkele, Joh*ann*e Mankanhened, Will*elmu*s de Ippegr*a*ve, Ro*ber*tus de Shordich*e* junior, Joh*anne*s de Hyngeston*e*, Joh*ann*e de Walepole, Adam, Thom*a*s de Farndou*n* *et* Walt*er*us atte Ferne q*u*and*am* su*m*ma*m* pecunie p*re*manib*us* in g*er*suma*m* ad ulti[*m*]am voluntate*m* d*ic*ti testatoris inde complend*um*. In cuius rei testimoniu*m* huic p*re*senti carte sigilla n*ost*ra apposuim*us*, Henr*ico* Darcy tunc maiore civitatis London', Hugon*e* le Marberer *et* Will*elm*o de Pontefracto tunc eiusdem civitatis vicecomitib*us*, Nich*ola*o Crane tunc aldermanno illius warde. Hiis testib*us* Thoma de Cantebrigge, Joh*anne* atte Loke, Rog*er*o de Woxebrigge, Thoma de Lincoln*ia*, Gilb*er*to de Steyndrop*e*, Joh*ann*e Smart, Joh*ann*e de Stebenheth*e*, cl*er*ico, *et* mu*lti*s aliis. Dat*um* apud London' die Jovis p*roxima* post f*es*tu*m* S*anc*ti Barnabe ap*osto*li anno regni regis Edwardi t*er*cii post conquestu*m* t*er*ciodecimo *et*c.

[40] MS: Fardone.
[41] MS: asbque.

elder, Nicholas de Farndoun, Thomas de Porkele, John de Makenhened, William de Ippegrave, Robert de Shoreditch the younger, John de Hingston, John de Walpole, Adam de Walpole, Thomas de Farndon, and Walter atte Ferne, citizens and goldsmiths of London, all that tenement with its superstructures, liberties and all its other appurtenances which in any way whatsoever regard the said tenement which was formerly that of Sir Nicholas de Segrave, knight, in the street called St Vedast's [Foster Lane] in the parish of St John Zachary and in the ward of Aldersgate, London, and which lies between the tenements of Thomas de Lincoln, goldsmith of London, and the tenement formerly of Walter de Hendon and the tenement of the Abbot of Warden on the eastern side and the said Foster Lane on the western side, and which lies laterally between the lane called Inglane on the northern side and the tenement of the said Abbot of Warden on the southern side, that is to say, whatever the aforesaid Sir William de Clif ever owned or his heirs are able to own in any manner or by any right as in lands, buildings, wood, stones, in length, breadth, height or depth and in all things without any retention or diminution whatsoever. And that the same Sir William de Clif had and acquired that tenement by the concession and sale of the executors of Sir Nicholas de Segrave, the aforesaid knight, to have and to hold the whole of the aforesaid tenement with its superstructures, liberties and with all its other appurtenances by the aforesaid Hugh de Brandon, Simon de Barking, Richard Denys, William Sporoun, Richard de Basingstoke, Stephen le Frensshe, Robert de Wyke, John de Toppesfield, Robert de Shoreditch the elder, Nicholas de Farndon, Thomas de Porkele, John de Makenhened, William de Ippegrave, Robert de Shoreditch the younger, John de Hingston, John de Walpole, Adam de Walpole, Thomas de Farndon, and Walter atte Ferne, and by their heirs and assigns whoever they may be, freely, quit, wholly, in well-being and in peace, in fee and in inheritance, in perpetuity from the lords in chief of that fee for service owed for it and accustomed by law, for all other secular services requested and all other things. And for this sale, concession and confirmation in this our present charter the aforesaid Hugh, Simon, Richard Denys, William Sporoun, Richard de Basingstoke, Stephen, Robert de Wyke, John de Toppesfield, Robert de Shoreditch the elder, Nicholas, Thomas de Porkele, John Makenhened, William de Ippegrave, Robert de Shoreditch the younger, John de Hingston, John de Walpole, Adam, Thomas de Farndon and Walter atte Ferne have given to us a certain sum of money into our hands as a payment in order to fulfil the last will of the said testator. In witness of which we have affixed our seals to this present charter, Henry Darcy then Mayor of the City of London, Hugh le Marberer and William de Pontefract then sheriffs of the same City, Nicholas Crane then alderman of that ward. With these witnesses: Thomas de Cambridge, John atte Loke, Roger de Woxebrigge, Thomas de Lincoln, Gilbert de Staindrop, John Smart, John de Stebenhethe, cleric, and many others. Given in London on the Thursday following the Feast of St Barnabas the Apostle in the year 13 Edward III [17 June 1339]. etc

1323 p. 17, col. 1 Universis Sancte Matris Ecclesie fili[i]s[42] ad quos presens scriptum pervenerit, Johannes de Everdoun, decanus ecclesie[43] Sancti Pauli London' et capitulum eiusdem, salutem in domino. Noveritis quod cum bone memorie dominus Nicholas de Segrave, miles iam defunctus, in ultima voluntate sua in testamento suo nobis et prefate ecclesie nostre legasset omnes domos et tenementa sua in civitate London' pro uno sacerdote inveniendo pro anima eiusdem domini Nicholai singulis diebus imperpetuum celebraturo in forma que subsequitur. Videlicet: Item, lego domos meas in London' ecclesie Sancti Pauli pro uno sacerdote perpetuo celebrante pro anima mea sic, videlicet quod illi de ecclesia Sancti Pauli satisfaciant monachis de Woubourne in omnibus demandis racionabilibus quod si illi de Sancto Paulo talem condicionem voluerint admittere, volo et ordino per presentes quod predicte domus vendantur et de precio satisficit monachis predictis pro omnia secundem racionem et residuum pecunie distribuatur pro anima mea. Nos in pleno loci capitulo personaliter constituta viso et plenius intelecto ac diligenter examinato testamento predicto, consideratisque oneribus eisdem dominibus et tenementis incombentibus advertentes legatum illud nobis et ecclesie nostre predicte nimis onerosum et ultra modum dampnosum esse tali condicione admittendum quia pretextu omni juri exactioni, demande aut calumpnie nobis vel successoribus nostris nomine dicte ecclesie nostre virtute legati et testamenti predictorum competenti quovismodo renunciamus et eadem domos et tenementa admittere omnino recusamus, consedentes insuper unanimi assensu remittentes et imperpetuum quietum clamantes pro nobis et succesoribus nostris prefatis executoribus et eorum cuilibet aut aliis seu illi quibus vel cui iidem executores seu eorum aliquis assignare vel vendere voluerunt vel voluerit totum jus vel clamen quod virtute legati et testamenti predictorum in eisdem domibus et tenementis habuimus vel aliqualiter habere poterimus. Ita quod nec nos seu successores nostri predicti quicquam in eisdem domibus seu tenementis exigere vel vendicare poterimus in futurum quovismodo seu titulo qualicumque In cuius rei testimonium sigillum nostrum commune huic scripto est appensum. Datum in capitulo nostro septimo decimo die mensis Maii anno domini millesimo tricentesimo vicesimo tercio et regni regis Edwardi filii regis Edwardi sexto decimo.

1349 col. 2 Sciant presentes et futuri quod nos Nicholas de Farndoun et Willelmus de Ippegrave, cives et aurifabri London', unanimi assensu et voluntate dedimus, concessimus et hac presenti carta nostra confirmavimus domino Roberto de Shene, rectore ecclesie Sancti Johannis Zakaria London' et Thome Spray, bladario et civi dicte civitatis totum illud tenementum cum domibus superedificatis, libertatibus et aliis omnibus suis pertinenciis ad dictum tenementum qualitercumque spectantibus quod quondam habuimus simul cum Hugone de Brandoun, Simone de Berkyng, Ricardo Denys, Willelmo Sporoun, Ricardo de Bassyngstoke, Stephano Frenche, Roberto de Wyke, Johanne de Toppesfeld, Roberto de Shordiche seniore, Thoma de Porkele, Johanne Mankenhened, Roberto de Shordiche juniore, Johanne de Hyngestone, Johanne de Walepole, Adam de Walepole, Thoma de Farndoun et Waltero

42 MS: filius.
43 MS: ecclesie ecclesie.

To all sons of Holy Mother Church whom the present letter may reach, John de 1323
Everdoun, dean of the church of St Paul in London and of its chapter, greetings p. 17, col. 1
in the Lord. Know that whereas Sir Nicholas de Segrave of good memory, knight now deceased, in his last will and testament left to us and to our aforesaid church all his houses and tenements in the City of London in order to provide for a priest to celebrate [masses] for the soul of the same Sir Nicholas every day in perpetuity in the form which follows: i.e. Item, I leave my houses in London to the church of St Paul for a priest to celebrate [masses] perpetually for my soul thus, i.e. that those of the church of St Paul may satisfy the monks of Woburn in all reasonable requests and that if those of St Paul's shall wish to accept such a condition, I will and ordain by these present letters that they should sell the aforesaid houses and from the price obtained they should satisfy the aforesaid monks in everything reasonable, and the residue of the money should be distributed for [the good of] my soul. We in full chapter of the place personally constituted, having seen and more fully understood and having diligently examined the aforesaid testament, and having considered the charges incumbent upon the same houses and tenements, we reject that bequest to us and our aforesaid church as it would be too burdensome and excessively injurious to accept such a condition, because it could be the pretext of any lawful exaction, demand or calumny to us or our successors. In the name of our said church by the competent power of the legacy and testament aforesaid, we in every way renounce and entirely refuse to accept those same houses and tenements, conceding besides by unanimous assent, remitting and quit-claiming in perpetuity for us and our successors, the aforesaid executors and any one of them or others, whether they, the same executors, or any one of them may wish to assign or sell to them or any one of them, the whole right or claim which we have or in any way might have by virtue of the aforesaid legacy and testament in those same houses and tenements. Thus that neither we nor our aforesaid successors shall be able to demand or claim anything in those same houses or tenements in the future by any means or by any title whatsoever. In testimony of which our communal seal is affixed to this document. Given in our chapter on the seventeenth day of May in the year of Our Lord 1323 and in the sixteenth year of the reign of King Edward son of King Edward.[33]

Be it known to those present and future that we Nicholas de Farndon and 1349
William de Ippegrave, citizens and goldsmiths of London, have by unanimous col. 2
assent and by our wish given, conceded and by this our present charter we have confirmed to lord Robert de Sheen, rector of the church of St John Zachary in London, and to Thomas Spray, corn-dealer and citizen of the said City, the whole of that tenement with its superstructures, its liberties and all all its other appurtenances which in any way whatsoever regard the said tenement which we formerly owned together with Hugh de Brandon, Simon de Barking, Richard Denys, William Sporoun, Richard de Basingstoke, Stephen Frenshe, Robert de Wyke, John de Toppesfield, Robert de Shoreditch the elder, Thomas de Porkele, John Makenhened, Robert de Shoreditch the younger, John de Hingston, John de Walpole, Adam de Walpole, Thomas de Farndon and

[33] i.e. Edward II.

atte Ferne, civibus et aurifabris London' ex dono et feoffomento Laurencii de Clif de comitatu Ebor' et Johannis de Buckedoun capellani, executorum testamenti domini Willelmi de Clif, clerici, in vico vocato Sancti Vedasti in parochia Sancti Johannis Zakarie in warda de Aldresgate London'. Quod quidem tenementum antedictum cum suis pertinenciis jacet inter tenementa Johannis de Chichestre, aurifabri, et tenementum quondam Willelmi de Hendoun ac tenementum Abbatis de Wardone ex parte orientali et dictum vicum Sancti Vedasti ex parte occidentali, et jacet in latitudine inter venellam vocatam Inglane ex parte aquilonari et tenementum dicti Abbatis de Wardone ex parte australi. Et quod tenementum quondam fuit domini Nicholai de Segrave videlicet quicquid ibidem habuimus, habemus seu aliquo [modo] habere poterimus ut in terris, domibus, edificiis, lignis, lapidibus, longitudine, latitudine, altitudine, et profunditate ac rebus cunctis sine ulla inde retenemento seu diminucione quacumque, habendum et tenendum totum predictum tenementum cum domibus superedificatis, libertatibus et omnibus aliis suis pertinenciis ad dictum tenementum qualitercumque spectantibus prefatis domino Roberto de Shene et Thome Spray heredibus et assignatis suis quibuscumque libere, quiete, integre, bene et in pace de capitalibus dominis feodi illius pro servicia inde eis debita et de jure consueta in feodo et hereditate imperpetuum. Et nos predicti Nicholas de Farndoun et Willelmus de Ippegrave ac heredes nostri totum predictum tenementum cum domibus superedificatis libertatibus et omnibus aliis suis pertinenciis ad dictum tenementum qualitercumque spectantibus prefatis domino Roberto de Shene et Thome Spray heredibus et assignatis suis quibuscumque contra omnes gentes warantizabimus imperpetuum. In cuius rei testimonium huic presenti carte sigilla nostra apposuimus, Johanne Lovekyn tunc Maiore London', Simone Dolsali et Henrico Pycard tunc vicecomitibus dicte civitatis, hiis testibus Thome de Cantebrigge, Johanne de Chichestre, Johanne atte Castel, Ricardo de Felstede, Willelmo de Rameseye, Johanne de Tame, Willelmo de Tame et multis aliis. Datum London' die Martis proxima post festum Ascencionis domini anno regni regis Edwardi tercii post conquestum Anglie vicesimo tercio regni vero sui Francie decimo.

p. 18, col. 1 Sciant presentes et futuri quod nos Robertus de Shene, rector ecclesie Sancti Johannis Zakarie London' et Thomas Spray, bladarius et civis dicte civitate, unanimi assensu et voluntate dedimus, concessimus, et hac presenti carta nostra confirmavimus Nicholao de Farndoun, Willelmo Ippegrave, Johanni Hiltoft, Gilberto de Steyndrope, Johanni Bret, Martino de Ambresburi, Johanni de Chichestre, Roberto de Norwiche, Willelmo de Hatfeld, Johanni Botoun, Willelmo de Berkyng, Thome de Basingstoke, Thome de Baldeswelle, Johanni de Bartoun, Johanni Coraunt, Johanni Gravele, Johanni de Bassingbourne, Johanni de Maplesdene, Willelmo Antra, Willelmo Bate, Thome Piphirste, Johanni de Ippegrave, Thome de Lincolnia, Willelmo Tyngewyke, Johanni Lont, Thome de Hyngestone, Roberto Broke, Thome Bamme, Johanni de Brichesle et Thome de Renham, civibus et aurifabris London' totum illud tenementum cum domibus superedificatis, libertatibus et omnibus aliis suis pertinenciis ad dictum tenementum qualitercumque spectantibus quod nuper habuimus ex dono et feoffamento Nicholai de

Walter atte Ferne, citizens and goldsmiths of London, which tenement we had by the gift and enfeoffment of Laurence de Clif of the county of Yorkshire and John de Buckedene, chaplain, the executors of the will of lord William de Clif, cleric, and which is in the street called Saint Vedast's [Foster Lane] in the parish of St John Zachary in the ward of Aldersgate in London. The which aforesaid tenement with its appurtenances lies between the tenements of John de Chichester, goldsmith, and the tenement formerly of William de Hendon and the tenement of the Abbot of Warden on the eastern side and the said Foster Lane on the western side, and it lies laterally between the lane called Inglane on the northern side and the tenement of the said Abbot of Warden on the southern side. And that tenement which was formerly that of lord Nicholas de Segrave, i.e. whatever we have owned there, own or in any manner may own whether in lands, houses, buildings, wood, stones, in length, in breadth, in height or in depth, and in all things without any retention or diminution whatsoever from these, to have and to hold the whole of the aforesaid tenement with its superstructures, its liberties, and with all its other appurtenances which in any way whatsoever regard the said tenement, to the aforesaid lord Robert de Sheen and Thomas Spray, and to their heirs and assigns whomsoever they may be, freely, quit, wholly, in well-being and in peace from the lords in chief of that fee for service owed for it to them and accustomed by law, in fee and in inheritance in perpetuity. And we the aforesaid Nicholas de Farndon and William de Ippegrave and our heirs guarantee against all men to the aforesaid lord Robert de Sheen and Thomas Spray and their heirs and assigns whomsoever they may be the whole of the aforesaid tenement with its superstructures, liberties and all its other appurtenances which in any way whatsoever regard the said tenement in perpetuity. In witness of which we have affixed our seals to this present charter, John Lovekyn then Mayor of London, Simon Dolseley and Henry Picard then sheriffs of the said City, with these witnesses: Thomas de Cambridge, John de Chichester, John atte Castel, Richard de Felsted, William de Ramsey, John de Thame, William de Thame and many others. Given in London on the Tuesday following the feast of the Ascension of the Lord in the twenty third year of the reign in England of King Edward III after the Conquest and the tenth year of his reign of France [26 May 1349].

Be it known to those present and future that we Robert de Sheen, rector of the p. 18, col. 1
church of St John Zachary in London, and Thomas Spray, corn-dealer and citizen of the said City, have by unanimous assent and by our wish given, conceded and by this our present charter we have confirmed to Nicholas de Farndon, William Ippegrave, John Hiltoft, Gilbert de Staindrop, John Bret, Martin de Amesbury, John de Chichester, Robert de Norwich, William de Hatfield, John Botoun, William de Barking, Thomas de Basingstoke, Thomas de Baldeswelle, John de Barton, John Coraunt, John Gravele, John de Bassingbourne, John de Maplesdene, William Antra, William Bate, Thomas Piphurst, John de Ippegrave, Thomas de Lincoln, William Tingewick, John Lont, Thomas de Hingston, Robert Broke, Thomas Bamme, John de Brinchisle and Thomas de Raynham, citizens and goldsmiths of London, the whole of that tenement with its superstructures, its liberties and all all its other appurtenances which in any way whatsoever regard the said tenement which we recently had by the gift and enfeoffment of Nicholas de Farndon and William

Farndou*n* *et* Will*elm*i de Ippeg*ra*ve civu*m* *et* aurifabru*m* London' in vico vocato S*anct*i Vedasti in d*ict*a p*a*roch*ia* S*anct*i Joh*ann*is Zakar*ie* *et* in warda de Aldresgate London'. Quod quidem ten*ementum* anted*ict*um cu*m* suis p*er*tin*enciis* jacet int*er* ten*ementa* Joh*ann*is de Chichestre, aurifabr*i*, *et* ten*ementum* quond*am* Will*elm*i de Hendou*n* *et* ten*ementum* Abb*at*is de Wardon*e* ex p*ar*te orientali *et* d*ict*um vicu*m* S*anct*i Vedasti ex p*ar*te occidentali, et jacet in latitudine int*er* venella*m* vocat*am* Inglane ex p*ar*te aquilon*ari* *et* ten*ementum* Abb*at*is de Wardon*e* ex p*ar*te aust*ra*li. Et quod tenementu*m* quond*am* fuit d*omi*ni Nich*ola*i de Seg*ra*ve, militis, videl*ice*t quicquid ibidem unq*ua*m h*ab*uim*us,* h*ab*emus seu aliquo modo h*ab*ere pot*erim*us in fut*ur*um ut in domib*us*, edificiis, lignis, lapidib*us*, longitudine, latitudine, altitudine *et* p*ro*funditate ac reb*us* cunctis sine ullo inde retenemento seu diminuc*io*ne quacu*m*q*ue*, h*ab*end*um* et tenend*um* totu*m* p*re*d*ict*um ten*ementum* cu*m* domib*us* sup*er*edificat*is*, lib*er*tatib*us* et om*n*ib*us* aliis suis p*er*tin*enciis* ad d*ict*um ten*ementum* qualit*er*cu*m*q*ue* spectantib*us* p*re*fatis Nich*ola*o, Will*elm*o, Joh*ann*i, Gilb*er*to, Joh*ann*i, Martino, Joh*ann*i, Rob*er*to, Will*elm*o, Joh*ann*i, Will*elm*o, Thome, Thome, Joh*ann*i, Joh*ann*i, Joh*ann*i, Joh*ann*i, Joh*ann*i, Will*elm*o, Will*elm*o, Thome, Joh*ann*i, Thome, Will*elm*o, Joh*ann*i, Thome, Rob*er*to, Thom*e,* Joh*ann*i *et* Thome, heredib*us* *et* assign*atis* suis quibuscu*m*q*ue* lib*er*e, quiete, integre, bene *et* in pace, de capitalib*us* d*omi*nis feodi illius p*ro* s*er*vicia inde eis debita *et* de jure consueta in feodo *et* h*e*redit*ate* imp*er*petuu*m*. Et nos p*re*d*ict*is Rob*er*tus de Shene *et* Thomas Spray ac heredes n*ost*ri totu*m* p*re*d*ictum* ten*ementum* cu*m* domib*us* sup*er*edificat*is*, lib*er*tatib*us* *et* om*n*ib*us* aliis suis p*er*tin*enciis* ad d*ict*um ten*ementum* qualit*er*cu*m*q*ue* spectantib*us* p*re*fatis Nich*ola*o, Will*elm*o, Joh*ann*i, Gilb*er*to, Joh*ann*i, Martino, Joh*ann*i, Rob*er*to, Will*elm*o, Will*elm*o, Joh*ann*i, Will*elm*o, Thome, Thome,
col. 2 Joh*ann*i, Joh*ann*i, Joh*ann*i, Joh*ann*i, Joh*ann*i, | Will*elm*o, Will*elm*o, Thome, Joh*ann*i, Thome,Will*elm*o, Joh*ann*i, Thome, Rob*er*to, Thome, Joh*ann*i et Thome, heredib*us* et assign*atis* suis quibuscu*m*q*ue* cont*ra* om*n*es gentes warantizabim*us* imp*er*petuu*m*. In cui*us* rei testimoniu*m* huic p*re*senti carte sigilla n*ost*ra apposuim*us*, Joh*ann*e Lovekyn tunc Maiore London', Simone Dolsali *et* Henr*ico* Picard tunc vicecomitib*us* London', hiis testib*us* Thoma de Cant*ebrigge*, Joh*ann*e de Chichestre, Joh*ann*e atte Castel, mag*ist*ro, Ric*ard*o de Felstede, mag*ist*ro,[44] Will*elm*o de Ramneseye, Joh*ann*e de Thame, Will*elm*o de Thame et multis aliis. Dat*um* London' in festo Nativitatis b*ea*ti Joh*ann*is Bapt*ist*e anno regni reg*is* Edwardi t*er*cii post conquestu*m* Angl*ie* vicesimo t*er*cio r*egni* veroq*ue* Franc*ie* decimo.

1327 Anno primo E*dwardi* t*er*cii / Prima Carta Au*rifabrorum* Auctoritate
p. 19, col. 1 p*ar*liamenti[45]

Edward p*ar* la g*ra*ce de Dieu roi d'Englet*er*re, S*eignur* d'Irlond *et* Ducs d'Aquitaigne, as touz ceux as queux cestes p*re*sentes l*ett*res vendrount,

[44] The 'magistro' attached to these two names very possibly indicates that they were the wardens for that year. The names of the wardens for the year 1348–49 are otherwise unknown, the Minute Book merely giving the information the next year that the previous year's wardens had all died (in the Black Death). See above, A + a, p. 9.

[45] Various other copies of the charter below exist; see Reddaway and Walker, pp. xxv, 1–2, 7, 8, 222–24.

de Ippegrave, citizens and goldsmiths of London, in the street called Saint Vedast's [Foster Lane] in the said parish of St John Zachary in the ward of Aldersgate in London. The which aforesaid tenement with its appurtenances lies between the tenements of John de Chichester, goldsmith, and the tenement formerly of William de Hendon and the tenement of the Abbot of Warden on the eastern side and the said Foster Lane on the western side, and it lies laterally between the lane called Inglane on the northern side and the tenement of the said Abbot of Warden on the southern side. And that tenement which was formerly that of lord Nicholas de Segrave, knight, i.e. whatever we have ever owned there, own or in any manner may own in the future, whether in houses, buildings, wood, stones, in length, in breadth, in height or in depth, and in all things without any retention or diminution whatsoever from these, to have and to hold the whole of the aforesaid tenement with its superstructures, its liberties, and with all its other appurtenances which in any way whatsoever regard the said tenement, to the aforesaid Nicholas, William, John, Gilbert, John, Martin, John, Robert, William, John, William, Thomas, Thomas, John, John, John, John, John, William, William, Thomas, John, Thomas, William, John, Thomas, Robert, Thomas, John and Thomas, and their heirs and assigns whomsoever they may be, freely, quit, wholly, in well-being and in peace from the lords in chief of that fee for service owed for it to them and accustomed by law, in fee and in inheritance in perpetuity. And we the aforesaid Robert de Sheen and Thomas Spray and our heirs guarantee against all men to the aforesaid Nicholas, William, John, Gilbert, John, Martin, John, Robert, William, William, John, William, Thomas, Thomas, John, John, John, John, John, William, William, Thomas, John, Thomas, William, John, Thomas, Robert, Thomas, John and Thomas and their heirs and assigns whomsoever they may be the whole of the aforesaid tenement with its superstructures, liberties and all its other appurtenances which in any way whatsoever regard the said tenement in perpetuity. In witness of which we have affixed our seals to this present charter, John Lovekyn then Mayor of London, Simon Dolseley and Henry Picard then sheriffs of London, with these witnesses: Thomas de Cambridge, John de Chichester, John atte Castel, master, Richard de Felsted, master, William de Ramsey, John de Thame, William de Thame and many others. Given in London on the feast of the Nativity of the blessed John the Baptist in the twenty third year of the reign in England of King Edward III after the Conquest and the tenth year of his reign of France [24 June 1349].

1 Edward III [1327] – First Charter of the Goldsmiths by the authority of Parliament 1327 p. 19, col. 1

Edward by the grace of God King of England, Lord of Ireland and Duke of Aquitaine, to all those whom these present letters may reach – Greetings.

Salutz. Moustrez no*us* ount noz biens amez les orfev*er*es de n*ostr*e citee de Loundres p*ar* lo*ur* petitiou*n* mys devant no*us* *et* n*ostr*e conseil en n*ostr*e p*ar*lement tenuz a Westm*oustier* apr*é*s la feste de la Purificaciou*n* N*ostr*e Dame pr*o*schein passé, q*e* come avant ces hures nul marchaunt privé ne estrange ne soloit amesner en ceste t*er*re nulle monoye forgé mesq*ue* plate de argent pur faire eschaunge a n*ostr*e Coigne. Et auxint feust ordeiné q*e* touz ceux qi feurent del mestier des orfev*er*es soloient seer en lo*ur* shopes en la haut rue de Chepe, et q*e* nul argent en plate ne vessel d'or ne d'argent ne deveroit estre venduz en la cité de Loundres si noun a n*ostr*e eschaunge ou en Chepe en l'orfaverie, *et* ceo ov*er*tement q*e* les gentz del dit mestier poaient avoir avisement del vendour s'il feust loialment avenuz a tiel vessel ou ne mye. Ore novelement les marchantz susditz, auxibien privés come est*ra*unges, amesnent de estraunges t*er*res en ceste t*er*re esterling contrefait, dount la liv*er*e ne vaut forsq*e* sesze sold*es* del droit esterling, et de cele monoye ne poet ho*m*me avoir conissance s'il ne soit p*ar* fieu. Et auxint pluso*ur*s q*e* se fount del dit mestier des orfev*er*es tignent lo*ur* shopes en veneles oscures *et* rues foreines, *et* achatent vessells d'or *et* d'argent en musset *et* ne mye en querant si le vessel soit emblé ou de loial p*ur*chaz, *et* meintenant le mettent al fieu *et* fount t*ra*nslater en plate *et* le vendent as marchauntz passajours p*ur* le porter hors de ceste t*er*re, *et* ensement fount fauces ov*er*aignes d'or *et* d'argent come de coronaux, fermeux, aneux *et* altres jueux es q*ue*ux ils mettent veirres de div*er*ses colo*ur*s contrefaitz a perrie, et mettent plus de lai en l'argent q*e* faire ne deussent, les queux ils vendent as m*er*cers *et* as autres qi de ceo ne ount conissance. Et les cotelers en la cotellerie coverent l'esteym d'argent si tenuement q*e* l'argent ne purra jamés estre severi del esteym et ensi vendent l'esteym covert d'argent pur argent fyn, a g*ra*unt damage et decette de no*us* *et* de n*ostr*e poeple. Sur queux choses lé ditz orfevres
col. 2 no*us* ount requiz q*e* no*us* y voilloms mettre | covenable remedie. Nous, tieux damages *et* decettes voillantz eschivre, del assent prelatz, countes, barouns *et* autres g*ra*untz, *et* de la co*mun*alté de n*ostr*e roialme p*ur* co*mun*e pr*o*fit de no*us* *et* de n*ostr*e poeple voloms *et* g*ra*untoms p*ur* no*us* *et* p*ur* noz heirs q*e* desore nul marchaunt privé ne estrange ne porte en ceste t*er*re nulle man*er*e de moneie forgee mesq*e* plate d'argent fyn, ne q*e* nul or ne argent overez d'orfaverie ne plate d'argent soient venduz as marchauntz pur revendre de porter hors del roialme mes soient venduz a n*ostr*e dit eschaunge ou ov*er*tement en la dite orfaverie p*ur* depescer *et* ne mye p*ur* revendre. Et q*e* nul qi cleyme estre du dit mestier ne tigne shope forsq*e* en Chepe, q*e* ho*m*me peusse veer q*e* lo*ur* ov*er*aignes soient bons *et* covenables. Et q*e* ceux del dit mestier puissent p*ar* v*er*tue de cestes l*ettr*es eslire bones gentz loialx *et* sufficiantz qi meutz se conissent el dit mestier d'enquere des choses susdites; et q*e* mesmes ceux issinc esluz peussent les defaltes trovez el dit mestier amender p*ar* droite consideraciou*n* del dit mestier, et sur ceo mettre due punissement as cont*ra*riantz les pointz susditz, par eide del meire *et* des viscountes q*ua*nt mestier s*er*ra. Et q*e* en totes les citees *et* villes d'Englet*er*re ou orfev*er*es sount *et* repeir de marchantz facent *et* tignent mesmes les ordinances q*e* ceux de Loundres fount. Et q*e* un [ou] deux de chescune citee ou ville avandites

Our well-beloved goldsmiths of our City of London have demonstrated to us by their petition placed before us and our Council in our Parliament held at Westminster after the Feast of the Purification of Our Lady just gone by,[34] that whereas in previous times no merchant whether native or alien was accustomed to bring into this country any coined money, but only plate of silver to be exchanged in our mint; and it was also ordained that all those who were of the mistery of goldsmiths used to sit in their shops in the high street of Cheap, and that no silver in plate and no vessel of gold or silver should be sold in the City of London except at our Exchange or in Cheap in the Goldsmiths' quarter, and this in the open, so that those of the mistery were able to judge of the vendor whether he had come by such a vessel legally or not; now recently the said merchants both native and alien have been bringing from foreign countries into this country counterfeit sterling of which the pound is worth only sixteen shillings of the rightful sterling, and one cannot recognise this money except by fire;[35] and also many who claim to be of the said mistery of goldsmiths keep their shops in dark alleyways and in streets outside the City's jurisdiction, and they buy gold and silver vessels in secret and without enquiring whether the vessel may be stolen or whether it has been legally acquired, and they at once melt it down and make it into plate and sell it to itinerant merchants to take out of this country; and they also make false works of gold and silver such as coronals, ring-brooches, rings and other jewellery in which they set glass-stones of various colours counterfeiting precious stones, and they put more alloy in the silver than they should, and they sell these pieces to mercers and others who are ignorant of these matters; and the cutlers in the cutlery-quarter cover tin with a layer of silver so thin that the silver cannot be separated from the tin, and they sell this silver-plated tin for fine silver to the great loss and deceit both of us and of our people. About these matters the said goldsmiths have requested us that we should wish to provide a suitable remedy. We, wishing to eschew such losses and deceits, with the assent of prelates, earls, barons and other magnates, and that of the commons of our kingdom, for the common weal of ourselves and of our people, wish and grant for ourselves and for our heirs that from henceforth no merchant whether native or alien shall bring into this country any kind of coined money but only plate of fine silver, and that no worked gold or silver pieces nor silver plate should be sold to merchants for resale to be taken out of the kingdom, but they should be sold at our said exchange or openly in the said goldsmiths' quarter to be broken up and not for resale. And that no one who claims to be of the said mistery should keep a shop anywhere except in Cheap, so that one may see that their works are good and up to standard. And that those who are of the said mistery may by virtue of these letters elect good, loyal and competent men who are the most knowledgeable about the said mistery who shall enquire into the above matters, and that these men thus elected may correct faults found in the same mistery by means of rightful consideration of the said mistery and that they may inflict due punishment on those who go against the above points, with the aid of the Mayor and Sheriffs when the need arises. And that in all the cities and towns of England where goldsmiths are [found] or to which merchants resort, the same ordinances should be made and held to as those in London. And that one or two [men] from each aforesaid city or town should come

[34] This parliament was held from 2 February 1327 n.s.

[35] Assaying by fire or cupellation. See Forbes, *Hallmark*, pp. 20–24.

veignent a Loundres pur le dit mestier de quere lour certeine touche d'or et ensement le pounceoun ové la teste de leopard pur mercher lour overaignes come auncienement feust ordeiné. En tesmoignance de quele chose nous avoms fait faire cestes noz lettres overtes. Doné a Westmoustier le treszisme jour de Marcz l'an de nostre regne primer.

1341 Edwardus dei gracia Rex Anglie et Francie et dominus Hibernie, omnibus ad quos presentes littere pervenerint, salutem. Sciatis quod cum dilecti nobis aurifabri civitatis nostri London' nobis supplicaverunt ut cum quamplures homines de mistero illo igne et fumo argenti vivi cecati, et quidam eorum opere manuali adeo consternati et diversis infirmitatibus opressi et debilitati existant, quod ipsi se ipsos juvare et sustinere non poterunt nisi eis aliunde subveniatur, ac diversi homines civitatis predicte statu dictorum cecorum, consternatorum et oppressorum compacientes diversa tenementa et redditus in eadem civitate usque ad valorem viginti librarum per annum hominibus et
p. 20, col. 1 comunitati misteri predicti | in auxilium sustentacionis dictorum cecorum, consternatorum et infirmorum, necnon cuiusdam capellani missam eisdem infirmis singulis diebus pro animabus omnium defunctorum juxta ordinacionem inde faciendam celebraturi, dare et concedere disposuerint imperpetuum habendum. Dum tamen iidem homines de dicta comunitate licenciam a nobis habuerint competentem, voluimus eis huiusmodi licenciam concedere graciose. Nos piam intencionem dictorum hominum de civitate predicta commendantes, concessimus et licenciam dedimus pro nobis et heredibus nostris quantum in nobis est hominibus de comunitate predicta quod ipsi tenementa et redditus in eadem civitate usque ad valenciam viginti librarum per annum juxta verum valorem eorumdem de hominibus civitatis illius in auxilium sustentacionis cecorum, consternatorum, infirmorum et capellani predictorum adquirere possint sibi et successoribus suis de comunitate misteri predicti ex causis supradictis habendum imperpetuum, statuto de terris et tenementis ad manum mortuam non ponendis, edicto seu aliquo alio statuto vel ordinacione in contrarium factis non obstantibus. Dum tamen per inquisiciones inde in forma debita capiendas et in cancellaria nostra vel heredum nostrorum rite retornandas, compertio sit quod id fieri poterit absque dampno et prejudicio nostri et dictorum heredum nostrorum ac alterius cuiuscumque. In cuius rei testimonium has litteras nostras fieri fecimus patentes. Teste me ipso apud Westmonasterium primo die Maii anno regni nostri Anglie quintodecimo regni vero nostri Francie secundo.

1358 Carta Civitatis Burdegalie in ducatu Acquitanie
Edward par la grace de Dieu roi d'Engleterre et de Fraunce et seignur d'Irlond, a touz ceux qi cestes lettres verrount ou orrount, Salutz. Sachetz qe come a la request des orfeveres de nostre citee de Loundres moustrantz a nous et a nostre conseil en nostre parlement nadgairs tenuz a Westmoustier les deceites et defaltes q'estoient trovez en les overages et la vente d'or et d'argent si bien de plate come de moneie, par assent des prelatz, countes, barouns et la comune

to London on behalf of the said mistery in order to fetch their certain touch of gold and also the punch with the leopard's head to mark their works as it was ordained in ancient times.[36] In witness of which we have had these our letters patent drawn up. Given at Westminster on the thirteenth day of March in the first year of our reign [1327].

Edward by the grace of God King of England and of France and Lord of 1341
Ireland, to all whom these present letters may reach – Greetings. Know that whereas our well-beloved goldsmiths of our City of London have begged us that since there are many men of that mistery blinded by the fire and the smoke of quicksilver, and some worn out by manual work and oppressed and debilitated with various infirmities so that they are unable to help and sustain themselves unless assistance is given them from other sources, and many men of the aforesaid city, having sympathy for the condition of the said blind, wearied and oppressed persons, are disposed to give and concede various tenements and rents in the same city up to the value of twenty pounds per year to the men and the community of the aforesaid mistery | for assistance in sustaining the said blind, p. 20, col. 1
wearied and infirm, and also for a certain chaplain to celebrate mass for these invalids each day for the souls of all the departed according to the ordinance to be made about this, these to be held in perpetuity. And while the same men of the said community should have from us a sufficient licence, we wish graciously to concede to them such a licence. We, commending the pious intention of the said men of the aforesaid city, concede and give licence on behalf of ourselves and our heirs as much as in our power lies to the men of the said community that they may acquire tenements and rents in the same city up to the value of twenty pounds per annum according to a true valuation of them by men of that city, for the assistance in sustaining of the aforesaid blind, wearied, and infirm and a chaplain, to have in perpetuity for themselves and their successors in the aforesaid mistery for the aforesaid reasons, not to be placed in mortmain by the published statute of lands and tenements, notwithstanding the decree or any other statute or ordinance made to the contrary. Meanwhile therefore by inquiries taken in due form and to be returned in proper manner to our chancellery or that of our heirs, it is to be discovered whether this can be done without loss or prejudice to us and our said heirs or to anyone else whomsoever. In testimony of which we have had these our letters patent made. Witnessed by myself at Westminster on the first day of May in the fifteenth year of our reign of England and the second of our reign of France [1341].

Charter of the city of Bordeaux in the dukedom of Aquitaine 1358

Edward by the grace of God King of England and of France and Lord of Ireland, to all those who may see or hear these letters, Greetings. Know that whereas at the request of the goldsmiths of our city of London, revealing to us and to our Council in our Parliament recently held at Westminster the deceits and faults that were to be found in the works and in the sale of gold and silver, both in plate and in coin, we, by the assent of prelates, earls, barons and the

[36] The record has survived of the mandate sent to the mayor and bailiffs of Oxford, dated 14 October 1328, asking them to put this into practice and naming Edward de Worcester as the representative goldsmith of Oxford. See *CPR, Edward III 1327–30*, p. 323.

de n*ost*re roialme a mesme le p*ar*lement assemblez, p*ur* co*mun*e p*ro*fit de no*us* *et* de n*ost*re poeple g*ra*untasmes p*ur* no*us* *et* noz heirs q*e* nul marchant p*ri*vé n'est*ra*nge ne porte en n*ost*re dite roialme nulle man*er*e de monoie forgé mesq*e* plate d'argent fyn, ne q*e* nul or ne argent overé d'orfav*er*ie ne plate d'argent soient venduz a marchauntz p*ur* revendre de porter hors du roialme, mes soient venduz a noz eschaunges ou ov*er*tement en la dite orfav*er*ie p*ur* depescer *et* ne mye p*ur* revendre. Et q*e* nul qi claime estre del dit mestier
col. 2 d'orfev*er*ie | en la dite citee ne teigne shope forsq*e* en Chepe, qe ho*m*me puisse veer q*e* lo*ur* ov*er*ages soient bones *et* covenables; *et* qe eux du dit mestier puissent p*ar* vertue du dit g*ra*unt eslire bones gentz loialx *et* sufficiantz q*e* meltz se conoissent en dit mestier d'enqere des choses susdites et q*e* mesmes ceux issint esluz puissent les defaltes trovez en dit mestier amender p*ar* droit consideraciou*n* de mesme le mestier et s*ur* ceo mettre due punissement as contrariantz les pointz susdites p*ar* eide du meire *et* viscountes qu*a*nt mestier sera, et q*e* touz les citees *et* villes d'Englet*er*re ou orfev*er*es et repair des marchantz sount facent *et* teignent mesmes les ordinances q*e* ceux de Loundres fount, *et* q*e* un ou deux de chescune citee *et* ville avandites veignent a Loundres p*ur* le dit mestier de quere lo*ur* c*er*tein touche d'or *et* ensement le pounchon ové le teste de leopard p*ur* mercher lo*ur* ov*er*ages come ancienement feust ordeigné, sicome en noz l*ett*res patentes s*ur* ceo faites est contenuz plus au plein. Et eioms entendu par relaciou*n* de plusou*rs* q*e* p*ar* cause q*e* nulles ordinances ne sount faites del mestier d'orfav*er*ie en la citee de Burdeux, plusou*rs* defaltes *et* deceites ount esté faites dev*a*nt ces hures *et* sount de jo*ur* en altre en le dit mist*ier* d'orfev*er*ie sibien en la dite cité de Burdeux come aillo*ur*s en n*ost*re Duché de Guyen, *et* fait a douter q*e* greindres s*er*rount faites en temps avenir: Nous, considerantz les damages *et* perdes q*e* p*ar* celles defaltes et deceites purrount avenir sibien a nous come a n*ost*re poeple, voillantz p*ur* tielles damages *et* pertes eschivre p*ur*veoir de remedie covenable a p*ro*fit de no*us* *et* de n*ost*re poeple en celle p*ar*tie, voloms, g*ra*untoms *et* ordeignoms p*ur* no*us* *et* noz heirs q*e* les orfev*er*es de n*ost*re dite cité de Burdeux eiount *et* gardent les poinz south esc*ri*ptez, c'este assavoir: q*e* nul argent de plate ne vessel d'or ne d'argent ne soit vendu en n*ost*re dite cité de Burdeux sinoun p*ar*devant les eschaungou*r*s ou en l'orfev*er*ie dev*a*nt les mestres de celle mestier illoeq*e*s publicment *et* ov*er*tement si qe les gentz du dit mestier puissent estre avisez *et* avoir evidence si le vendo*ur* soit loialment avenuz a tiells vessell*es* ou ne mye, et si le vessel soit de droit alay *et* de bon argent, et q*e* nul qi se cleyme estre du dit mestier ne teigne schope en venelle einz en lieu out*re* ou en rewe publiq*e*, issint q*e* l'em puisse veer q*e* lo*ur* ov*er*ages soient covenables *et* bones; *et* q*e* ceux du dit mestier peussent p*ar*
p. 21, col. 1 vertue de cestes l*ett*res | eslire bones gentz loialx *et* sufficiantz de ceux de lour mestier q*e* se conoissent en ceo q'appent a mesme le mestier, d'enquere des choses susdites *et* de amender les defaltes q*e* s*er*rount p*ar* eux trovez en dit mestier, *et* de ordeigner les poinz necessaires p*ar* droite consideraciou*n* des gentz de mesme le mestier, *et* s*ur* ceo mettre due punissement as cont*ra*riantz les poinz avantditz p*ar* eide des maire *et* jurez de mesme la

commons of our kingdom assembled in that same Parliament, for the common weal of ourselves and our people, granted for ourselves and our heirs that no merchant whether native or alien might bring into our said kingdom any kind of coined money but only plate of fine silver, and that no gold or silver worked as a goldsmith's piece and no plate of silver might be sold to merchants for resale to be taken out of the kingdom, but they are to be sold in our exchanges or openly in the said goldsmiths' quarter to be broken up and not for resale. And that no one who claims to be of the said goldsmiths' mistery | in the said city may keep a shop except in Cheap, so col. 2
that one may see that their works are good and up to standard; and that those who are of the said mistery may by virtue of the said grant elect good, true and competent men who are the most knowledgeable about the said mistery, to inquire into the aforesaid matters, and that those thus elected may correct faults found in the said mistery by a rightful consideration of the same mistery, and according to this may inflict due punishment upon those who go against the aforesaid points, with the assistance of the Mayor and Sheriffs when necessary; and that all the cities and towns of England where goldsmiths are and to which merchants resort shall make and hold to the same ordinances as those of London, and that one or two [men] from each aforesaid city and town shall come to London on behalf of the said mistery in order to obtain their certain touch for gold and also the punch with the leopard's head to mark their works as was ordained in former times, as is set out more fully in our letters patent drawn up on this matter. And we have heard it tell by many people that because there are no ordinances made for the goldsmiths' mistery in the city of Bordeaux, many faults and deceits have been practised before now and are at present practised daily in the said goldsmiths' mistery both in the said city of Bordeaux as well as elsewhere in our Duchy of Guienne, and it is to be feared that greater ones will be practised in the future. We, considering the damage and losses that may come about through these faults and deceits both to us and to our people, wishing in order to eschew such damage and losses to provide a suitable remedy which shall be to the benefit of ourselves and our people in this area, wish, grant and ordain for ourselves and for our heirs that the goldsmiths of our said city of Bordeaux should have and should keep the points written below, that is to say: that no silver in plate nor vessel of gold or silver should be sold in our said city of Bordeaux except before the exchangers or in the goldsmiths' quarter before the masters of that mistery there, publicly and openly so that those of the said mistery may be able to inform themselves and have evidence as to whether the seller has come by such vessels legally or not, and whether the vessel is of true alloy and good silver, and that no one who claims to be of the said mistery should keep a shop in a narrow lane but must rather be in a main place or in a public street, so that one may see that their works are up to standard and well-made; and that those who are of the said mistery may by virtue of these letters | elect good, true and competent men from among those of their p. 21, col. 1
mistery who are knowledgeable about what pertains to the same mistery, to enquire into the aforesaid matters and to amend the faults which shall be found by them in the same mistery, and to ordain necessary ordinances by rightful consideration of the men of the same mistery and then to inflict due punishment on those who go against the aforesaid ordinances with the

citee qu*a*nt mestier s*er*ra. Et auxint voloms q*e* les dites orfev*er*es ov*er*ount bon argent, si bon come ad esté ov*eré* avant ces hures en meme la citee, et q*e* nul ov*er*age d'argent en vessellement n'en altre man*er*e ne soit vendu as est*ra*nges ne en la dite orfav*er*ie s'il ne soit consigné ou altrement soit si bone come cele q'est ov*eré* en la dite citee. Et q*e* en totes les cités *et* villes de n*os*tre dite Duché de Guyene ou orfev*er*es *et* repair des marchantz sount, facent et teignent mesmes les ordinances q*e* ceux de Burdeux fount en celle p*ar*tie, *et* q*e* un ou deux du dit mestier de chescun cité ou ville avantdites veignent a n*os*tre chastel de Burdeux a n*os*tre Conestable illoeq*e*s, p*ur* le dit mestier, de quere lo*ur* c*er*tein touche d'or *et* ensement le punchou*n* ové la teste de leopard p*ur* merch*er* lo*ur* overages. Et n'est mye n*os*tre entenciou*n* ne ne voloms q*e* p*ar* cause de ceste n*os*tre g*ra*unt les ditz orfev*er*es soient exemptz de la jurisdicciou*n* de meire *et* jurez de mesme la citee de Burdeux es altres faitz et contrattz, mesq*e* le meire *et* jurez *et* orfev*er*es avantditez *et* chescun de eux demo*ur*gent en lo*ur* pr*i*vilages en queles eux estoient devant la fesaunce de cestes. En tesmoignance de quele chose no*us* avoms fait faire cestes noz l*et*tres ov*er*tez. Don*é* a Langlé, le vj[me] jour d'av*er*il l'an de n*os*tre regne d'Englet*er*re trentisme secounde *et* de Franc*e* xixme.

1341 Edwardus dei gr*acia* Rex Angl*ie* *et* Franc*ie* *et* d*omin*us Hib*ernie* dil*ect*o sibi Andree Aubreye, maiori civitatis n*os*tre London' *et* Esc*aetori* n*os*tro in eadem civitate, sal*u*tem. Mandam*us* vob*is* q*uo*d p*er* sacr*amentum* p*ro*bor*um* *et* leg*um* ho*m*inu*m* *de* *ci*vitate p*re*d*ic*ta p*er* quos rei v*er*itas melius sciri pot*er*it diligent*er* inquiratis si sit ad dampnu*m* v*e*l p*re*judiciu*m* n*os*trum aut alior*um* si concedam*us* Laurentio de Clyf *et* Joh*ann*i de Bokedene, capellano, executorib*us* test*amen*ti Will*elm*i de Clyf, cl*er*ici, q*uo*d ip*s*i unu*m* mesuagiu*m*
col. 2 cum p*er*tin*enciis* | in eadem civitate dare possint *et* assignare ho*min*ib*us* de co*mun*ita[te] mister*e* aurifabror*um* eiusdem civitatis h*ab*end*um* *et* tenend*um* eisdem ho*min*ib*us* et successorib*us* suis in auxiliu*m* sustentac*io*nis cecor*um,* const*er*nator*um* *et* infirmor*um* de mist*er*a p*re*d*ic*ta necnon cuiusdam capellani missam eisdem infirmis sing*u*lis dieb*us* p*ro* a*n*i*m*ab*us* om*n*i*um* fidelium defunctor*um* jux*ta* ordinac*io*nem inde faciend*um* celebratur*i*, in p*ar*tem satisfact*io*nis ten*ementa* *et* redditu*s* ad valenciam viginta librar*um* que eisdem ho*min*ib*us* mistere p*re*d*ic*t*e* de ho*min*ib*us* civitatis p*re*d*ic*t*e* concessim*us* adquirend*um*, ne*c*ne et si sit ad dampnu*m* v*e*l p*re*judiciu*m* n*os*trum aut alior*um* tunc ad quod dampnu*m* *et* quod p*re*judiciu*m* alior*um* *et* quor*um* *et* qualit*er* *et* quo modo, *et* quantu*m* p*re*d*ic*tu*m* mesuag*ium* valeat p*er* annu*m* in om*n*ib*us* exitib*us* jux*ta* verum valorem eiusdem. Et inquisic*io*nem inde distincte *et* ap*er*te coram nob*is* s*u*b sigillo v*es*tro *et* sigillo eor*um* p*er* quos facta fu*er*it sine dilac*io*ne mittatis *et* hoc l*ett*ere. T*este* meip*s*o apud Westm*onasterium* vii[mo] die septemb*ris* anno r*egni* n*ostri* Angl*ie* quinto decimo, r*egni* v*er*o n*ostri* Franc*ie* sec*un*do.

assistance of the Mayor and the *jurés*[37] of the same city when necessary. And we wish also that the said goldsmiths shall work good silver, of as high a standard as that which has been worked before now in the same city, and that no work of silver as a vessel or other object should be sold to aliens nor in the said goldsmiths' quarter unless it be stamped with a mark or else be [proved to be] of as good a standard as that which is worked in the said city. And that in all the cities and towns of our said Duchy of Guienne where goldsmiths are and to which merchants resort, they should make and hold to the same ordinances as the men of Bordeaux have, and that one or two of the said mistery should come from each aforesaid city or town on behalf of the said mistery to our castle of Bordeaux to our Constable there in order to obtain their certain touch for gold and also the punch with the leopard's head to mark their works. And it is in no way our intention nor do we wish that by reason of this our grant the said goldsmiths should be exempt from the jurisdiction of the Mayor and *jurés* of the same city of Bordeaux in other deeds and contracts, but that the Mayor and *jurés* and goldsmiths aforesaid and each one of them should retain all their privileges which they had before these letters were drawn up. In witness of which we have had drawn up these our letters patent. Given at Langley on the sixth day of April in the thirty second year of our reign of England and the nineteenth [of our reign] of France [1358].

Edward by the grace of God King of England and France and Lord of Ireland, 1341
to his well-beloved Andrew Aubreye, Mayor of our city of London and our Escheator in the same city, Greetings. We command you that on the oath of honest and lawful men of the aforesaid city through whom the truth of a matter may best be known you make inquiries as to whether it may be to our loss or prejudice or that of others if we concede to Laurence de Clif and John de Buckedene, chaplain, executors of the will of William de Clif, cleric, that they should be able to give and assign a messuage with appurtenances |in the same col. 2
city to the men of the community of the mistery of goldsmiths of the same city, to have and to hold by the same men and their successors for assistance in the sustaining of the blind, wearied and infirm of the said mistery and also a certain chaplain who is to celebrate mass for those infirm people every day for the souls of all the faithful departed according to the ordinance to be made about this, in part satisfaction of the tenements and rents to the value of twenty pounds which we conceded might be acquired by the same men of the same mistery from the men of the aforesaid city; and if it were to be to the loss or prejudice or ourselves or of others, then to what loss and what prejudice of others and which others and in what manner or way and how much the aforesaid messuage may be worth per annum from all revenues according to the true value of the same. And you should send the inquisition on that separately and openly to us under your seal and the seal of those who have made the inquiry without delay. Witnessed myself at Westminster on the seventh day of September in the fifteenth year of our reign of England and the second of our reign of France [1341].

[37] The word 'jurés', literally 'sworn men', is used here as in other documents to refer to those who were also known as 'échevins' and had functions similar to those of aldermen. On the wide range of applications of the word in the Middle Ages and beyond see e.g. Littré, vol. 4, pp. 1332–33.

1358–59 Ces sount les nouns des gardeyns del orfev*er*ie de Loundres l'an du regne le
p. 22, col. 1 Roi Edward tierz puis la conquest xxxiie:
Joh*a*n Coraunt
William de Berkyng
Nicholas de Twyford
Edmund de Ippeg*ra*ve

Ces sount les despens*es* faites, c'este a dire de la fest de Seint Dunston l'an susdit tanqe a mesme la fest de Seint Dunston l'an xxxiii^ce^.

Adeprimes, les costages de la fest de Seint Dunston a le diner des dites gardeyns outre le quilett amont a – x li. x s.
Item, paié a les deux povres p*ar* les avantditz Joh*a*n Coraunt, William de Berkyng et Nich*olas* de Twyford mesme l'an – lxxv s.
Item, don*é* a les povres encountre Noel p*ar* les troiz gardeyns avantditz – viii s. viii d.

Item, i g*ra*unt pap*er*e achaté p*ar* les avantditz iii gardeyns p*ur* regist*r*er totes man*er*es remembrances q*e* sount ou s*er*rount faitez p*ar* la compaignie du dit orfev*er*ie, dount les costages du dit pap*er*e amont – xiii s. iiii d.
Item, paié p*ur* la lum*er*e de Seint Dunston a la glise de Seint Joh*a*n Zakarie – xiii s. iiii d.
Item, paié p*ur* soner a Seint Poul *et* pur boire – iiii s. x d.
Item, don*é* a l'encrés de Seint Dunston p*ar* les iii gardeyns avantditz, outre touz les costages *et* despens*es* avant esc*ri*ptz – lx s.

Ces sount les nouns des app*re*ntiz en l'an susdit:

Adeprimes receu de Henr*i* Payn app*re*ntiz Ric*hard* Payn –	ii s.
William atte Chaumbr*e* app*re*ntiz Rauf de Greneford –	ii s.
col. 2 Nichol Marche, Thomas Forest*er* app*re*ntiz Joh*a*n Forst*er* –	iiii s.
Rob*er*t Malerbe app*re*ntiz Thomas de Salesbury –	ii s.
Nichol Ferford app*re*ntiz Thomas de Mundene –	ii s.
Joh*a*n Burgh*e* app*re*ntiz Joh*a*n de Chichestre –	ii s.
Walt*er* Bourchalcote app*re*ntiz Joh*a*n Seybrok –	ii s.
William Picard app*rentiz* Joh*a*n Northwych*e* –	ii s.
William Tann*er*er app*rentiz* William Salesbury –	ii s.
Walt*er* de Westou*n*, Rog*er* Mopas app*rentiz* Berkyn –	iiii s.
Rob*er*t Holm app*rentiz* Ric*hard* Arnold –	ii s.
Henr*i* Malmayn app*rentiz* Thomas de Pantou*n* –	ii s.
Nich*ol* Derneford app*rentiz* Joh*a*n Coraunt –	ii s.

Ces sount les nouns de les issantz de lo*ur* app*re*nticialté: . . .

Joh*a*n Lalh*a*m qe fust a Joh*a*n Littelyngtou*n* –	ii s.
Rob*er*t atte Launde q*e* fust app*rentiz* Joh*a*n Coraunt –	ii s.

These are the names of the Wardens of the Goldsmiths' Mistery of London in the year 32 Edward III [1358]: 1358–59 p. 22, col. 1
John Coraunt
William de Barking
Nicholas de Twyford
Edmund de Ippegrave

These are the expenditures made, i.e. from the feast of St Dunstan in the aforesaid year until the same feast of St Dunstan in the year 33 Edward III [1359]:

Firstly, the costs of the feast of St Dunstan at the dinner of the said wardens over and above the collection amount to – £10 10s.
Item, paid to the two poor men by the aforesaid John Coraunt, William de Barking and Nicholas de Twyford in the same year – 75s.
Item, given to the poor at Christmas time by the three wardens aforesaid – 8s. 8d.

Item, a large paper register bought by the aforesaid three wardens in order to record all manner of matters worthy of memory that have been or shall be done by the company of the said Goldsmiths' Mistery, of which the costs of the said register amount to – 13s. 4d.
Item, paid for the light of St Dunstan in the church of St John Zachary – 13s. 4d.
Item, paid for bell-ringing at St Paul's and for drink – 4s. 10d.
Item, given to the increase of the funds of St Dunstan by the three aforesaid wardens, over and above all the aforewritten costs and expenses – 60 s.

These are the names of apprentices in the aforesaid year:

Firstly, received from Henry Payn, apprentice of Richard Payn –	2s.
William atte Chaumbre, apprentice of Ralph de Greenford –	2s.
Nicholas Marche, Thomas Forester, apprentices of John Forster –	4s. col. 2
Robert Malerbe, apprentice of Thomas de Salisbury –	2s.
Nicholas Fairford, apprentice of Thomas de Mundene –	2s.
John Burghe, apprentice of John de Chichester –	2s.
Walter Bourchalcote, apprentice of John Seybrook –	2s.
William Picard, apprentice of John Northwyche –	2s.
William Tannerer, apprentice of William Salisbury –	2s.
Walter de Weston, Roger Mopas, apprentices of Barking –	4s.
Robert Holm, apprentice of Richard Arnold –	2s.
Henry Malmayn, apprentice of Thomas de Panton –	2s.
Nicholas Dornford, apprentice of John Coraunt –	2s.

These are the names of those coming out of their apprenticeship:

John Lalham who was with John Litlington –	2s.
Robert atte Launde who was John Coraunt's apprentice –	2s.

Ces sount les nouns q*e* sont est*ra*nges entreez:
Nich*ol* Gyne lowys Joh*a*n Seybrok, p*ur* son entré – v s.
Nichol de Bedeford p*ur* son entré – xxvi s. viii d.
William Gerners p*ur* son entré – vi s. viii d.

Am*er*cimentz
Item, rec*eu* de Joh*a*n Buntyng p*ur* ceo q'il mesprist dev*er*s William de Berkyng, gardein p*ur* le temps, p*ar* malveises p*ar*oles – vi s. viii d.

Item, comandé fust p*ar* co*mun*e assent q*e* Joh*a*n Leche q*e* fust app*re*ntiz Henr*i* Brunne q'il ne dusse tenir schope ne forge, mais dusse s*er*vir en le mister auxi come vallet ové ascun bone hom*me* tanqe il fust able, p*ur* ceo q'il ne fust app*re*ntiz qe p*ar* un an *et* de*m*i.

1359–60 p. 23, col. 1 Ces sount les nouns des gardeyns del orfev*er*ie de Loundres l'an du regne le Roi Edward tierz ap*ré*s le conquest xxxiii^{ce}:
Joh*a*n de Hiltofte
Thomas de Hyngston*e*
Walter de Louthe
Joh*a*n de Northewych*e*

Ces sount les despens*es* faites c'este a savoir de la fest de Seint Dunston l'an susdit tanqe a mesme le fest de Seint Dunston l'an xxxiiii^{te}:
Adep*ri*mes, les costages de la dite fest de Seint Dunston a le diner des dites gardeyns, outre le quilet, amonte a xxiii li. xi s.
Item, paié as quatre pov*er*es countre la fest de Noel p*ar* les iiii gardeyns – xiii s. iiii d.
Item, doné a l'encrés de Seint Dunston p*ar* mesme les gardeyns – lii s.
Item, paié a la lumere de Seint Dunston en la eglise de Seint Joh*a*n Zakarie p*ar* mesme les gardeyns – xiii s. xi d.
Item, paié p*ur* soner a Seint Poul *et* pur boire – v s. i d.

Ces sount les nouns des app*re*ntiz en l'an susdit:

Adeprimes, receu de Joh*a*n Gilot app*re*ntiz Thomas de Reynh*a*m –	ii s.
Roger Garston apprentiz William de Burtou*n* –	ii s.
Joh*a*n Daye app*re*ntiz Simon Mazerer –	ii s.
Bartelmeu Merdene app*re*ntiz Joh*a*n Seybrok –	ii s.
Hugh*e*[46] . . . *appre*ntiz Nicholas de Bedeford –	ii s.
William Daye app*re*ntiz Rob*er*t de Guldeford –	ii s.
Joh*a*n Bradele app*re*ntiz Ric*hard* de Bartou*n* –	ii s.
William atte Noke app*re*ntiz Joh*a*n Thorn –	ii s.
Joh*a*n H*e*reford app*re*ntiz Simond Wynter –	ii s.
Joh*a*n Mounfort app*re*ntiz Thomas de Wirlyngworth –	ii s.
col. 2 Robert Hempstede[47] app*re*ntiz Rob*er*t Launde –	ii s.
Waut*er* Halyngge app*re*ntiz Ric*hard* Franceis –	ii s.

[46] A gap has been left for the surname.
[47] This surname is written over a scored 'Henr*i*'.

These are the names of aliens entered:
Nichol Gyne, serving-man of John Seybrook, for his entry – 5s.
Nichol de Bedford for his entry – 26s. 8d.
William Gerners for his entry – 6s. 8d.

Amercements:
Item, received from John Buntyng because he offended against William de Barking, warden at the time, by bad language – 6s. 8d.

Item, it was by common assent commanded that John Leche, who was the apprentice of Henry Bamme, that he should not keep either a shop or a forge, but must serve in the mistery as a servant with some good man until he is competent, because he was an apprentice only for a year and a half.

These are the names of the wardens of the Goldsmiths' Mistery of London in the year 33 Edward III [1359]: 1359–60 p. 23, col. 1
John de Hiltoft
Thomas de Hingston
Walter de Louth
Johan de Northwych

These are the expenses incurred, i.e. from the feast of St Dunstan in the said year until the same feast of St Dunstan in 34 [Edward III] [1360]:
Firstly, the costs of the said feast of St Dunstan at the dinner of the said wardens, over and above the collection, amount to – £23 11s.
Item, paid to the four poor people at Christmas time by the four wardens – 13s. 4d.
Item, given to the increase of the funds of St Dunstan by the same wardens – 52s.
Item, paid for the light of St Dunstan in the church of St John Zachary by the same wardens – 13s. 11d.
Item, paid for bell-ringing at St Paul's and for drink – 5s. 1d.

These are the names of apprentices in the aforesaid year:
Firstly, received from John Gilot, apprentice of Thomas de Raynham – 2s.
Roger Garston, apprentice of William de Burton – 2s.
John Daye, apprentice of Simon Mazerer – 2s.
Bartholomew Merdene, apprentice of John Seybrook – 2s.
Hughe . . . , apprentice of Nicholas de Bedford – 2s.
William Daye, apprentice of Robert de Guildford – 2s.
John Bradele, apprentice of Richard de Barton – 2s.
William atte Noke, apprentice of John Thorn – 2s.
John Hereford, apprentice of Simon Wynter – 2s.
John Mounfort, apprentice of Thomas de Worlingworth – 2s.
Robert Hempstead, apprentice of Robert Launde – 2s. col. 2
Walter Halyngge, apprentice of Richard Fraunceys – 2s.

Richard Suet app*re*ntiz Thomas Bygod – ii s.
Thomas Polle app*re*ntiz William Stour – ii s.
Thomas Notle app*re*ntiz Joh*a*n Fairher – ii s.
Joh*a*n atte Water app*re*ntiz Pieres Hiltofte – ii s.
Thomas Hanlep app*re*ntiz William Liverpol – ii s.
Joh*a*n Pikenh*a*m app*re*ntiz Thomas Hyngston*e* – ii s.
Joh*a*n atte Hawe app*re*ntiz Rob*er*t Godman – ii s.
William atte Forthe app*re*ntiz Wauter de Louthe – ii s.
Joh*a*n Bramle app*re*ntiz William Davyd – ii s.
Waut*er* Freman app*re*ntiz Joh*a*n Croidou*n* – ii s.
Joh*a*n in the Lane, Joh*a*n Gerners app*re*ntiz Ric*hard* atte Welle – iiii s.

Ces sount les nouns de les issantz de lo*ur* app*re*nticialté:
Joh*a*n Pipehurst q*e* fust a Thomas de Lyncoln – ii s.
Ric*hard* Children q*e* fust a dit Thom*as* – ii s.
Joh*a*n de Garwyntou*n* q*e* fust a Rob*er*t de Walcote – ii s.
William Brix q*e* fust a Thomas de Salesbury – ii s.
Henr*i* Abbot q*e* fust a Nichol de Twyford – ii s.
Joh*a*n de Harpele q*e* fust app*re*ntiz Will*iam* de Croidou*n* – ii s.
Joh*a*n Coron*er* q*e* fust app*re*ntiz Ric*hard* Arnold – ii s.

Ces sount les nouns q'ount paié lo*ur* entrez:
Simon Wynter p*ur* son entré – vi s. viii d.

Ces sount les am*er*ciementz:
Adep*ri*mes, reçu de Thomas Willuby pur un trespas q*e* trové fust q'il mist de plumb deinz un bociel rond d'argent – xl s.
Item, de Thomas Leche p*ur* gree faitz a la compaignie – lx s.

1360 Item, fait a remembr*er* de un debat meeu p*ar*entre les bones gentz
p. 24, col. 1 d'orfeve*re*s et un Joh*a*n de Bartou*n* de mesme le mister, p*ur* mals out*ra*ges, les quex ne furent bones, covenables ne loialx, p*ar* qei il fust mys hors de la dite compaignie p*ar* lo*ur* co*mun*e assent *et* de sa vest*ur*e tollu de ly p*ar* cause q'il ne serroit mye conu p*ur* un de eux; p*ar* qei il vynt a la eglise de Seint Piere en Chepe le xiiii jo*ur* ap*rés* la Chaundelur*e* en l'an du regne le Roi Edward tierz ap*rés* le conquest xxxiiii^{te} p*ar* priere de ses amiz. Et la se obligea p*ar* umble cuer et cria m*er*ci a tote la compaignie, *et* les p*ro*fra .x. tonellx de vyn a lo*ur* ordinance; issint q'il purport estre reconcilé p*ur* un de eux. Les bones gentz concilerent ensemble et ly mist en lour g*ra*ce en ceste fourme: q'il paiereit un pipe de vyn et q'il trovereit un pov*er*e hom*m*e de mesme le mister xii d. la simaign*e* continuant un an entier. Et cels .x. tonell*es* de vyn furent mys en surté p*ar* mesmes son obligement *et* p*ar* l'assurance de deux plegges, Joh*a*n Fairher et Thomas de Lincoln*e*, sur tiel condiciou*n* q'il serra bon *et* loial *et* qe nul reprof ne vilenye puet avenir a la dite mister p*ar* cause de ly. Et s'il soit trové de mals outrages ou de

Richard Suet, apprentice of Thomas Bygod – 2s.
Thomas Polle, apprentice of William Stour – 2s.
Thomas Notle, apprentice of John Fairher – 2s.
John atte Water, apprentice of Piers Hiltoft – 2s.
Thomas Hanlep, apprentice of William Liverpool – 2s.
John Pickenham, apprentice of Thomas Hingston – 2s.
John atte Hawe, apprentice of Robert Godman – 2s.
William atte Forthe, apprentice of Walter de Louth – 2s.
John Bramle, apprentice of William Davyd – 2s.
Walter Freman, apprentice of John Croydon – 2s.
John in the Lane, John Gerners, apprentices of Richard atte Welle – 4s.

These are the names of those coming out of their apprenticeship:
John Piphurst, who was with[38] Thomas de Lincoln – 2s.
Richard Children, who was with the said Thomas – 2s.
John de Garwyntoun, who was with Robert de Walcote – 2s.
William Brix, who was with Thomas de Salisbury – 2s.
Henry Abbot, who was with Nicholas de Twyford – 2s.
John de Harpele, who was William de Croydon's apprentice – 2s.
John Coroner, who was Richard Arnold's apprentice – 2s.

These are the names of those who have paid for their entry:
Simon Wynter, for his entry – 6s. 8d.

These are the amercements:
Firstly, received from Thomas Willuby for an offence that it was found[39] that he had put lead in a round silver bowl – 40s.
Item, from Thomas Leche as a sum agreed to the company – 60s.

Item, memorandum about a dispute that arose between the good men of the 1360
Goldsmiths and a John de Barton of the same mistery, on account of evil p. 24, col. 1
outrageous deeds which were not good, suitable nor faithful, for which he was expelled from the said company by their common assent, and his livery clothing was taken from him so that he might never be taken for one of them; and for this reason he came to the church of St Peter in Cheap on the fourteenth day after Candlemas in the year 34 Edward III [16 February 1360 n.s.] by the request of his friends. And there he bowed down with a humble heart and begged mercy of the whole Company, and offered them 10 tuns of wine at their command, thus that he purported to be reconciled as one of them. The good men took counsel together and passed judgment in these terms: that he should pay a pipe of wine and that he should fund support for a poor man of the same mistery at 12d. per week throughout a whole year. And those 10 tuns of wine were placed under guarantee on his own obligation and on the assurance of two mainpernors, John Fairher and Thomas de Lincoln, on the condition that he would be good and faithful and that no reproach nor evil should come to the said mistery because of

[38] The French phrase 'qe fust a' means 'who belonged to', which was indeed the situation during the terms of an apprenticeship.
[39] i.e. that he was found/proved guilty of doing this.

mals p*ar*oles p*ar* qei le dit mist*er* soit mys en esclaundre ou en reprof, q*e* mesmes les dites p*ro*fres de .x. tonell*es* de vyn soient levés de mesme le dit Joh*an* de Bartou*n* p*ar* destresse de ses biens *et* chateux et retenuy entierement tanq*e* les ditz tonell*es* de vyn soient levez.

1361–62 [48]Ceux sount les nou*n*s d'app*re*ntysez *et* lowys de la orfeve*r*ye entrans et issans en temps dez gardeins, c'est assavoir de William de Burtou*n*, Johan Boton, William Salusbury, Richard Fraunceys, l'an du regn*e* n*ost*re s*eignur* le Roi Edward lui tierce puis le conquest xxxv[te]:

Laur*ence* Frekenh*a*m app*re*ntys Johan Godeman –	iis.
William Wodeland app*re*ntys Peres Mazerer –	ii s.
Robert Meryfeld app*re*ntys Adam Merefeld –	ii s.
Will*iam* Spereman app*re*ntys Thomas Lincoln*e* –	ii s.
Joh*an* Som*er*vyle app*re*ntys Joh*an* Fairher –	ii s.
Joh*an* Cressi app*re*ntys Joh*an* Lytlingtou*n* –	ii s.
Joh*an* Seler app*re*nt*ys* Nich*olas* Twyford –	ii s.
Thom*as* atte Grene app*re*nt*ys* Will*iam* Davy –	ii s.
Joh*an* Hayward app*re*nt*ys* Will*iam* Glasen –	ii s.
Thomas Genge app*re*ntys Ric*hard* Frauncey*s* –	ii s.
Baldewyn Slawestou*n* app*re*nt*ys* Symond Mazerer –	ii s.
Rob*er*t Estwyk, Henr*i* de More, app*re*nt*ys* Joh*an* Cappe –	iiii s.
Ric*hard* Savage app*re*nt*ys* Rob*er*t Savage –	ii s.
Thomas Linge app*re*nt*ys* Robert Oxenford –	ii s.
Joh*an* Cowle app*re*nt*ys* Hamond Chose –	ii s.
Joh*an* Fourde app*re*nt*ys* Joh*an* Brugges –	ii s.
col. 2 William Thurstan app*re*nt*ys* Ric*hard* Arnold –	ii s.
Joh*an* Howkyng app*re*nt*ys* Joh*an* Bountyng –	ii s.
Joh*an* Newland app*re*nt*ys* Thom*as* Bygod –	ii s.
Joh*an* Adam app*re*nt*ys* Robert Yppegrave –	ii s.
Thomas Dancastr*e* app*re*nt*ys* Thomas Salisb*ury* –	ii s.
Joh*an* Yppegr*a*ve app*re*nt*ys* Will*iam* Yppegr*a*ve –	ii s.
Will*iam* Glepsfeld app*re*nt*ys* Rob*er*t Goodman –	ii s.
Joh*an* Bryan app*re*nt*ys* Henr*i* Asshele –	ii s.
Rob*er*t Potyn app*re*nt*ys* Michel*et* in la rente –	ii s.
Thom*as* Crups app*re*nt*ys* Henr*i* Crups –	ii s.
Thomas Bartou*n* app*re*nt*ys* Joh*an* Chichestr*e* –	ii s.
Henr*i* atte Chambr*e* app*re*nt*ys* Adam Eynesh*a*m –	ii s.
Joh*an* atte Forde app*re*nt*ys* Peris Hiltoft –	ii s.
Will*iam* atte Egg*er*, Ric*hard* Syward app*re*nt*ys* Joh*an* Cu*r*rant –	iiii s.
Thomas atte Hay, Joh*an* Goldbeter, app*re*nt*ys* Joh*an* Lyhtegr*a*ve –	iiii s.
Joh*an* Blast app*re*nt*ys* Joh*an* Croydou*n* –	ii s.
Richard Benham app*re*nt*ys* Johan Lyndesey –	iis.
Thomas Spyc*er* app*re*nt*ys* Joh*an* Gravele –	ii s.

[48] On the dating problem for this and the next few years see the Introduction, pp. xxiv–xxvii.

him. And if he should be found guilty of evil deeds or evil words through which the said mistery should be disgraced or reproached, then the same proffer of 10 tuns of wine should be levied of the said John de Barton by distraint on his goods and chattels, to be kept in entirety until the 10 tuns of wine should be levied.

These are the names of apprentices and serving-men of the Goldsmiths' Mistery entering and leaving during the term of office of the wardens, i.e. of William de Burton, John Boton, William Salisbury, Richard Frauunceys, in the year 35 Edward III [1361]: 1361–62

Laurence Freckenham, apprentice of John Godman –	2s.
William Woodland, apprentice of Piers Mazerer –	2s.
Robert Mirfield, apprentice of Adam Mirfield –	2s.
William Spereman, apprentice of Thomas Lincoln –	2s.
John Somerville, apprentice of John Fairher –	2s.
John Cressy, apprentice of John Litlington –	2s.
John Seler, apprentice of Nicholas Twyford –	2s.
Thomas atte Grene, apprentice of William Davy –	2s.
John Hayward, apprentice of William Glasen –	2s.
Thomas Genge, apprentice of Richard Fraunceys –	2s.
Baldwin Slawston, apprentice of Simon Mazerer –	2s.
Robert Estwyk, Henry de More, apprentices of John Cappe –	4s.
Richard Savage, apprentice of Robert Savage –	2s.
Thomas Linge, apprentice of Robert Oxenford –	2s.
John Cowle, apprentice of Hamond Chose –	2s.
John Fourde, apprentice of John Bruges –	2s.
William Thurstan, apprentice of Richard Arnold –	2s. col. 2
John Howkyng, apprentice of John Buntyng –	2s.
John Newland, apprentice of Thomas Bygood –	2s.
John Adam, apprentice of Robert Ippegrave –	2s.
Thomas Dancaster, apprentice of Thomas Salisbury –	2s.
John Ippegrave, apprentice of William Ippegrave –	2s.
William Glepsfeld, apprentice of Robert Goodman –	2s.
John Bryan, apprentice of Henry Asshele –	2s.
Robert Potyn, apprentice of Michelet in the rent –	2s.
Thomas Crups, apprentice of Henry Crups –	2s.
Thomas Barton, apprentice of John Chichester –	2s
Henry atte Chambre, apprentice of Adam Eynsham –	2s.
John atte Forde, apprentice of Piers Hiltoft –	2s.
William atte Egger, Richard Syward, apprentices of John Coraunt –	4s.
Thomas atte Hay, John Goldbeater, apprentices of John Litegrave –	4s.
John Blast, apprentice of John Croydon –	2s.
Richard Benham, apprentice of John Lindsey –	2s.
Thomas Spicer, apprentice of John Gravele –	2s.

Ceux sont les nons de lowys yssans:
Joh*an* Clerk de Hanneye – ii s.
Joh*an* Watford – ii s.
Joh*an* Rowland – ii s.
Henr*i* Bradeser – ii s.
Nich*olas* Colkyn – ii s.
Henr*i* Jouste – ii s.
Will*iam* Burdeyn – ii s.
Wat*er* Westou*n* – ii s.
Rob*ert* Shadewell*e* – ii s.
Henr*i* Crups – ii s.
Joh*an* Howkyng – ii s.

Ric*hard* Marchal lowys Thomas Paintou*n* ad fait gré p*ur* son entré – xxvi s. viii d.
George Molasch lowys Wat*er* de Lowthe ad fait gré p*ur* son entré – iii s. iiii d.
Item, Michelet en la rente ad fait gré p*ur* son entré – vi s. viii d.
Ric*hard* Sherold ad fait gré p*ur* son entr*é* – x s.

Don*é* al encrés del almoign*e* de Seint Dunstan – lx s.
Et del devys Janyn Perer – lx s.

Fait a remembr*er* q*e* en le temps dez gardeins suditez furent totz les poys dez orfev*er*es p*ar* tote la cité de Loundres assises *et* faitz d'une acord.

1362–63 p. 25, col. 1 Ces sount les nouns de gardeins del orfev*er*ie de Loundres l'an du regne le Roi Edward tierçz puis le conquest xxxvime:
Johan de Mapelesden*e*
Johan de Croidou*n*
Johan Walsshe
Thomas de Wirlyngworth*e*

Ces sount les despens*es* faites p*ar* les dites gardeins mesme l'an:
Adep*ri*mes p*ur* le fest*e* fait le jo*ur* de Seint Dunston – xiiii li. ii s. iii d.
Item, paié as deux pov*er*es del orfev*er*ie – Cvi s. viii d.
Item, paié p*ur* le sonail de Seint Dunston *et* p*ur* altres costages faites – xiii s. iiii d.
Item, doné al encrés del amoign*e* de Seint Dunstou*n* p*ar* mesme les gardeins – viii li.

These are the names of serving-men coming out [of their term of apprenticeship]:

John Clerk of Hanneye –	2s.
John Watford –	2s.
John Rowland –	2s.
Henry Bradeser –	2s.
Nicholas Colkyn –	2s.
Henry Jouste –	2s.
William Burdeyn –	2s.
Walter Weston –	2s.
Robert Shadwelle –	2s.
Henry Crups –	2s.
John Howkyng –	2s.

Richard Marchal, serving-man of Thomas Paintoun, has settled for his entry – 26s. 8d.
George Molasch, serving-man of Walter de Louth, has settled for his entry – 3s. 4d.
Item, Michelet in the rent has settled for his entry – 6s. 8d.
Richard Sherold has settled for his entry – 10s.

Given to the increase of the alms funds of St Dunstan – 60s.
And from the bequest of Janyn Perer – 60s.

Memorandum that in the time of the aforesaid wardens all the weights of goldsmiths throughout the city of London were sized and made to one uniform standard.

These are the names of the wardens of the Goldsmiths' Mistery of London in the year 36 Edward III [1362]: 1362–63 p. 25, col. 1
John de Maplesdene
John de Croydon
John Walsshe
Thomas de Worlingworth

These are the expenditures made by the said wardens in the same year:
Firstly, for the feast held on St Dunstan's Day – £14 2s. 3d.
Item, paid to the two poor people of the Goldsmiths' Mistery – 106s. 8d.
Item, paid for the ringing of St Dunstan's bell[40] and other costs incurred – 13s. 4d.
Item, given to the increase of the alms funds of St Dunstan by the same wardens – £8

[40] The phrasing used for this regular item of expenditure is here different and presents a small linguistic problem. 'Sonail' is not otherwise yet attested in Anglo-Norman. It is attested in continental French with the meaning of a little bell around an animal's neck (e.g. a cow-bell): see Godefroy, Comp. X, 687b; TL, IX, 834; Wartburg, XII (1966), sub SONARE, pp. 97–101. Later it is used again in these records in this same context looking very much as if it means 'bell', but here it would seem to mean 'the ringing of the bell(s)'. However, the bell itself was probably named 'Dunstan' (see Introduction, p. xxxvi), and the phrasing here is loose and allusive.

Item, en perte de mesme les gardeins p*er*du mesme l'an sur l'ordinance faite de novel[49] p*ar* le mister – xlii s. p*ur* div*er*ses choses p*ri*s sur Cornhull*e*.

Ces sount les nouns des app*re*ntiz:

Joh*a*n de Bannebury app*re*ntiz Joh*a*n de Walden*e* –	ii s.
Joh*a*n de Totenhale app*re*ntiz William de Stameld*e*ne –	ii s.
Stevene de Shareshull*e* app*re*ntiz Thomas de Lincoln*e* –	ii s.
Rob*er*t de Teukesbury *et* Robert Tav*er*ner app*re*ntiz Joh*a*n Fairher –	iiii s.
Thomas Elys app*re*ntiz Rob*er*t de Guldeford –	ii s.
Richard Ive app*re*ntiz Joh*a*n Walsshe –	ii s.
Joh*an* Frekenh*a*m app*re*ntiz Joh*a*n Fraunceis –	ii s.
Edmu*n*d Brandou*n* *et* Hanekyn Vanderhawe app*re*ntiz Henr*i* Chikesond*e* –	iiii s.
Joh*a*n Edmostou*n* app*re*ntiz Thomas Sherholt –	ii s.
Rob*er*t Edlee app*re*ntiz Edmu*n*d Brutou*n* –	ii s.
Joh*a*n Sentou*n* app*re*ntiz Joh*a*n Saybrok –	ii s.
Joh*a*n Smelt app*re*ntiz Adam Elsh*a*m –	ii s.
Joh*a*n atte Fisshewere app*re*ntiz Ric*hard* Arnold –	ii s.
col. 2 Adam Frend*e* app*re*ntiz Thomas Bygod –	ii s.
Rob*er*t Pottere app*re*ntiz Henri Brenle –	ii s.
Thomas Brunstou*n* app*re*ntiz William Fraunc*eis* –	ii s.
Thomas Charletou*n* app*re*ntiz Joh*a*n Hokyng –	ii s.
Joh*a*n Bulstrode app*re*ntiz Thom*as* Wirlyngworth*e* –	ii s.
Richard Bromle app*re*ntiz Sanguynel –	ii s.
Joh*a*n Blakman app*re*ntiz Joh*a*n G*ra*vele –	ii s.
Richard de Apeltou*n* *et* William Boter app*re*ntiz Rauf de Lyme –	iiii s.
William Granth*a*m *et* William Burgylou*n* app*re*ntiz Thomas Munden*e* –	iiii s.
Richard Warderobe app*re*ntiz Joh*a*n Locche –	ii s.
William Maryner app*re*ntiz (Joh*a*n)[50] Fraunceis –	ii s.
William Warde *et* Thomas Payn app*re*ntiz Janyn de Shordich*e* –	iiii s.
William atte Doune *et* Joh*a*n Porter app*re*ntiz Thomas de Salesbury –	iiii s.
Hanekyn Feldasshe app*re*ntiz Willia*m* Aclom –	ii s.
Rich*ard* Brewere app*re*ntiz Wilcons –	ii s.
Adam Bamme app*re*ntiz Will*iam* Berkyngg*e* –	ii s.
Joh*a*n Beche app*re*ntiz Will*iam* de Ippeg*ra*ve –	ii s.
Joh*a*n Mounte *et* Thomas Monte app*re*ntiz Thomas Hyngston*e* –	iiii s.
Joh*a*n Pieres app*re*ntiz William Davy –	ii s.
Thomas Tyderle app*re*ntiz Thomas Wynter –	ii s.
Elys Sp*ri*nger app*re*ntiz Walter atte Hall*e* –	ii s.
Rob*er*t Shadewell*e* app*re*ntiz Adam Shadewell*e* –	ii s.
Joh*a*n Dellom app*re*ntiz Joh*a*n Lalh*a*m –	ii s.
Thomas Forsthull*e* app*re*ntiz Thomas atte Laye –	ii s.

[49] The reference is to Statute 37 Edward III, c. 7. On this see Reddaway and Walker, pp. 31–32, and for a discussion of how this entry affects the dating problem see the Introduction, p. xxvi.

[50] A line has been drawn through this name.

Item, as a loss[41] of the same wardens, lost [i.e. paid out] the same year on the new ordinance made by the mistery – 42s. – for various objects seized on Cornhill.

These are the names of apprentices:

John de Banbury, apprentice of John de Walden –	2s.
John de Totenhale, apprentice of William de Stameldene –	2s.
Stephen de Shareshill, apprentice of Thomas de Lincoln –	2s.
Robert de Tewkesbury and Robert Taverner, apprentices of John Fairher –	4s.
Thomas Elys, apprentice of Robert de Guildford –	2s.
Richard Ive, apprentice of John Walsshe –	2s.
John Freckenham, apprentice of John Fraunceys –	2s.
Edmund Brandon and Hanekyn Vanderhawe, apprentices of Henry Chicksands –	4s.
John Edmostoun, apprentice of Thomas Sherholt –	2s.
Robert Edlee, apprentice of Edmund Bruton –	2s.
John Sentoun, apprentice of John Seybrook –	2s.
John Smelt, apprentice of Adam Elsham –	2s.
John atte Fisshewere, apprentice of Richard Arnold –	2s.
Adam Frende, apprentice of Thomas Bygod –	2s. col. 2
Robert Potter, apprentice of Henry Brenle –	2s.
Thomas Brunston, apprentice of William Fraunceys –	2s.
Thomas Charletoun, apprentice of John Hokyng –	2s.
John Bulstrode, apprentice of Thomas Worlyngworth –	2s.
Richard Bromley, apprentice of Sanguynel –	2s.
John Blakman, apprentice of John Gravele –	2s.
Richard de Appleton and William Boter, apprentices of Ralph de Lyme –	4s.
William Grantham and William Burgyloun, apprentices of Thomas Mundene –	4s.
Richard Warderobe, apprentice of John Leche –	2s.
William Maryner, apprentice of Fraunceys –	2s.
William Warde and Thomas Payn, apprentices of Janyn de Shoreditch –	4s.
William atte Doune and John Porter, apprentices of Thomas de Salisbury –	4s.
Hanekyn Feldasshe, apprentice of William Aclom –	2s.
Richard Brewer, apprentice of Wilcons –	2s.
Adam Bamme, apprentice of William Barking –	2s.
John Beech, apprentice of William de Ippegrave –	2s.
John Mounte and Thomas Monte, apprentices of Thomas Hingston –	4s.
John Pieres, apprentice of William Davy –	2s.
Thomas Tidderle, apprentice of Thomas Wynter –	2s.
Elys Springer, apprentice of Walter atte Halle –	2s.
Robert Shadwell, apprentice of Adam Shadwell –	2s.
John Dellom, apprentice of John Lalham –	2s.
Thomas Forsthulle, apprentice of Thomas atte Laye –	2s.

[41] The word 'perte' ('loss') is used here in something of a technical financial sense. The wardens are reporting the 'loss' to the funds of 42s. which they have had to pay out. The verb 'perdre' and the noun 'perte/perde' are found in other medieval financial accounts used in the same manner, and it is probable, though not entirely certain, that it refers to individual personal paying out, rather than a company expense.

Joh*an* atte Noke app*re*ntiz Joh*an* Thorne –	ii s.
Thomas Dent app*re*ntiz Joh*an* Hiltoft –	ii s.
(Rob*er*t Teukesburi et Rob*er*t Tav*er*ner et Joh*an* . . .	
app*re*ntiz Joh*an* Fairher –	vi s.)[51]
Stevene de Lyme *et* Edmu*n*d Vilers app*re*ntiz Ric*hard* de Burnh*am* –	iiii s.
Joh*an* Rufber app*re*ntiz Sayer van Trike –	ii s.
Joh*an* Bansted app*re*ntiz Mich*el* Andewerp*e* –	ii s.
Rob*er*t Gendren app*re*ntiz Phelipp*e* de Qilere –	ii s.
Rob*er*t Caldecote app*re*ntiz Daventr*e* –	ii s.
Geffrei Emeraude app*re*ntiz Ric*hard* Monden*e* –	ii s.
Steven*e* de Thorp*e* *et* Joh*an* Wyke app*re*ntiz Pieres Hiltoft –	iiii s.
Pieres Chaumpaign*e* app*re*ntiz Briges –	ii s.
Joh*an* Ippeg*ra*ve app*re*ntiz Betaigne –	ii s.
William Hayward app*re*ntiz Will*iam* Glasene –	ii s.
Joh*an* Latimer app*re*ntiz Nicho*las* Cove –	ii s.
Joh*an* Louesh*am* *et* Joh*an* Clopptou*n* app*re*ntiz Nich*olas* Cotou*n* –	iiii s.

Ces sount les nouns dé est*ra*nges q'ount paié lo*ur* entrez:

Edmund de Geynesford*e* –	xiii s. iiii d.
Thomas Russhemere –	xiii s. iiii d.
Thomas atte Leye –	xxxiii s. iiii d.
Mans Irissheman –	vi s. viii d.
Wynant van Waldek de Coloigne –	xiii s. iiii d.
Joh*an* Lincoln*e* –	x s.
Sayer van Trike –	x s.
p. 26, col. 1 Joh*an* Colom[52] . . .	
Arnold Helmstede –	xiii s. iiii d.
Herman van Ruwyel –	vi s. viii d.
Fransekyn de Bonella –	xx s.
Lyoun van Lubek –	xx s.
Phelipp*e* de Guere –	xx s.
Gerard van Swethen –	xx s.
Joh*an* Lyoun –	vi s. viii d.
Henri Garet –	xiii s. iiii d.
Richard Betoigne –	xx s.
Thomas Wynter –	vi s. viii d.
Roulandus van Frankeford –	xiii s. iiii d.
Ricardus Lontri –	vi s. viii d.
Joh*an* van Zarnh*am* –	vi s. viii d.
Johan Yarnemouth*e* –	vi s. viii d.
William Aclom –	x s.
Herman van Mentre –	vi s. viii d.
Dederik van Hokh*am* –	vi s. viii d.
Nicholas Cotou*n* –	vi s. viii d.
Roger de la Fosseye –	x s.
Thomas Marnam –	x s.

[51] The whole of this line has been scored out. The first two apprentices here have been listed above at the top of the list.

[52] No figure is given.

John atte Noke, apprentice of John Thorne –	2s.
Thomas Dent, apprentice of John Hiltoft –	2s.
(Robert Tewkesbury and Robert Taverner and John [. . .] apprentices of John Fairher –	6s)[42]
Stephen de Lyme and Edmund Vilers, apprentices of Richard de Burnham –	4s.
John Rufber, apprentice of Sayer van Trike –	2s.
John Banstead, apprentice of Michel Antwerp –	2s.
Robert Gendren, apprentice of Philippe de Qilere –	2s.
Robert Caldecote, apprentice of Daventry –	2s.
Geoffrey Emeraude, apprentice of Richard Mundene –	2s.
Stephen de Thorpe and John Wyke, apprentices of Piers Hiltoft –	4s.
Piers Champayne, apprentice of Briges –	2s.
John Ippegrave, apprentice of Beteigne –	2s.
William Hayward, apprentice of William Glasene –	2s.
John Latimer, apprentice of Nicholas Cove –	2s.
John Louesham and John Clopton, apprentices of Nicholas Coton –	4s.

These are the names of aliens who have paid for their entry:

Edmund de Geynesforde –	13s. 4d.
Thomas Rushmere –	13s. 4d.
Thomas atte Leye –	33s. 4d.
Mans, Irishman –	6s. 8d.
Wynant van Waldek from Cologne –	13s. 4d.
John Lincoln –	10s.
Sayer van Trike –	10s.
John Colom . . .	
Arnold Helmstede –	13s. 4d.
Hermann van Ruwyel –	6s. 8d.
Fransekyn de Bonella –	20s.
Lyoun van Lübeck –	20s.
Philippe de Guere –	20s.
Gerard van Swethen –	20s.
John Lyoun –	6s. 8d.
Henry Garet –	13s. 4d.
Richard Beteigne –	20s.
Thomas Wynter –	6s. 8d.
Roland van Frankfurt –	13s. 4d.
Richard Lontri –	6s. 8d.
John van Zarnham –	6s. 8d.
John Yarmouth –	6s. 8d.
William Aclom –	10s.
Hermann van Mentre –	6s. 8d.
Dederik van Hokham –	6s. 8d.
Nicholas Cotoun –	6s. 8d.
Roger de la Fosseye –	10s.
Thomas Marnam –	10s.

p. 26, col. 1

[42] See note 51 on opposite page.

[53]Thomas Flete apprentiz Johan Cappe –	ii s.
Joh*a*n Baunsere apprentiz Thomas Lincoln*e* –	ii s.
Geffrei Wych*e* apprentiz Simon Porkele –	ii s.
Joh*a*n Crillyng *et* Albon Stok apprentiz William Stour –	iiii s.
Joh*a*n Bodesh*am* *et* Joh*a*n Gray apprentiz Edmund Ippegrave –	iiii s.
Thomas Lincoln*e* apprentiz Joh*a*n Balauncer –	ii s.
Joh*a*n Lutou*n* apprentiz Joh*a*n Ippeg*ra*ve –	ii s.
William fiz Hugh*e* apprentiz Rob*er*t Prest –	ii s.
Simon Thame apprentiz James de Thame –	ii s.
Thomas Forsthull*e* apprentiz Thomas atte Leye –	ii s.
Simon Olyver apprentiz Ric*hard* Payn –	ii s.

Ces sount les issantz hors de lo*ur* t*er*me q'ount paié:[54]
William de Lettou*n*
Robert Cateneys
Richard Suet
Richard Frend
Joh*a*n Seler
Thomas Briche
Joh*a*n Asshebo*ur*ne
William Jordan
Steph*en* Nortou*n*
Adam de Thorp*e*
Henri atte Lee
Joh*a*n Trentemars
Joh*a*n Brom
William Gaytou*n*
col. 2 Joh*a*n Bonyng*e*
Joh*a*n Ippeg*ra*ve fiz Thomas Ippeg*ra*ve
William Bertilmeu
Joh*a*n Nacheles
Thomas Hanneye
Joh*a*n Cloptou*n*
Joh*a*n Ippegrave fiz Will*iam* Ippeg*ra*ve
Joh*a*n Atheby
Joh*a*n Walsyngh*am*
Joh*a*n Hortou*n*
Joh*a*n van Lyere
William Nassyngtou*n*
Bartilmeu Atoun
Henri Chikesond*e*
Joh*a*n Beworth*e*
Everard van Mynge
Richard Brid
Richard Pecheford*e*

[53] This second separate list of apprentices is unusual and it may well be that these names are out of order and that the scribe has picked up a list he had omitted to copy earlier. See the Introduction, p. xxv and cf. the similar problem on p. 118 of A + a.

[54] No sum of money is listed for any name in the following list; one may presume that each paid the usual 2s.

[43]Thomas Flete, apprentice of John Cappe –	2s.
John Baunsere, apprentice of Thomas Lincoln –	2s.
Geoffrey Wyche, apprentice of Simon Porkele –	2s.
John Crillyng and Albon Stok, apprentices of William Stour –	4s.
John Bottisham and John Gray, apprentices of Edmund Ippegrave –	4s.
Thomas Lincoln, apprentice of John Balauncer –	2s.
John Luton, apprentice of John Ippegrave –	2s.
William Fitzhugh, apprentice of Robert Prest –	2s.
Simon Thame, apprentice of James de Thame –	2s.
Thomas Forsthulle, apprentice of Thomas atte Leye –	2s.
Simon Olyver, apprentice of Richard Payn –	2s.

These are those coming out of their terms [of apprenticeship] who have paid:
William de Lettoun
Robert Catenys
Richard Suet
Richard Frend
John Seler
Thomas Briche
John Ashbourne
William Jordan
Stephen Norton
Adam de Thorpe
Henry atte Lee
John Trentemars
John Brom
William Gayton
John Bonynge col. 2
John Ippegrave, son of Thomas Ippegrave
William Bartholomew
John Nacheles
Thomas Hanneye
John Clopton
John Ippegrave, son of William Ippegrave
John Atheby
John Walsingham
John Horton
John van Lyere
William Nassyngtoun
Bartholomew Atoun
Henry Chicksands
John Beworth
Everard van Mynge
Richard Brid
Richard Pecheford

[43] See note 53 on opposite page.

1363–64 Ces sount les nouns des gardeins de orfev*er*ie de Loundres l'an du regne le
p. 27, col. 1 Roi Edward tierçz puis le conquest trent *et* sept:

Johan Coraunt
Thomas Pipehurst
Thomas Lincoln*e*
Henr*i* Markeby

Ces sont les despens*es* faites par les dites gardeins mesme l'an:
Adep*ri*mes doné a l'encrés del amoigne de Seint Dunstou*n* p*ar* mesme les gardeins – iiii li.
Item, paié p*ur* le sonail de Seint Poul *et* p*ur* altres coustages faites – xiii s. iiii d.
Item, paié as deux pov*er*s del orfev*er*ie p*ur* mesme l'an – Cvi s. viii d.
Item, doné as dites pov*er*s novel vest*ur*e contre la fest de Seint Dunston en mesme l'an – xiii s. iiii d.
Item, en coustages del fest le jour de Seint Dunston – x li.

Ces sont les nouns des app*re*ntiz:

Johan Rigge app*re*ntiz Joh*a*n Pipehurst – ii s.
William Huphull*e* app*re*ntiz William Burdeyn – ii s.
Richard Shene app*re*ntiz Roberd Launde – ii s.
Johan Stoke app*re*ntiz Hugh*e* Bilyngdou*n* – ii s.
Richard Chancy app*re*ntiz Johan Walden*e* – ii s.
Walter Fermer app*re*ntiz Joh*a*n Leche – ii s.
Joh*a*n Vanuche app*re*ntiz Joh*a*n Littlyngtou*n* – ii s.
William Bridford app*re*ntiz Richard Bartou*n* – ii s.
col. 2 Joh*a*n Hunte app*re*ntiz Joh*a*n Broun – ii s.
Joh*a*n West app*re*ntiz Robert Guldeford – ii s.
Walter Rigge app*re*ntiz Joh*a*n Bonyng – ii s.
Joh*a*n Olyve app*re*ntiz Richard atte Wat*er*e – ii s.
Johan Clere app*re*ntiz Thomas Forster – ii s.
Thomas Bounde, Henr*i* Markeby app*re*ntiz Joh*a*n Mapelesdene – iiii s.
William Godefrei app*re*ntiz Joh*a*n Garwyntou*n* – ii s.
Joh*a*n Bernyngh*a*m app*re*ntiz Joh*a*n Pyk – ii s.
Joh*a*n Walyngford app*re*ntiz Robert Oxenford – ii s.
Thomas Dente app*re*ntiz James de Thame – ii s.
Richard Merdene app*re*ntiz Joh*a*n Seybrok*e* – ii s.
Edmund Pri*n*s app*re*ntiz Nichol Gyna – ii s.
Roger Whitewey app*re*ntiz Henr*i* Asshele – ii s.
Phillip*e* Richemond app*re*ntiz Thomas Wynter – ii s.
Joh*a*n Bretou*n* app*re*ntiz Richard Burch*a*m – ii s.
Joh*a*n Gloucestre app*re*ntiz Simon Wynter – ii s.
Joh*a*n Gerv[a]ys app*re*ntiz William Gervays – ii s.
Joh*a*n Em app*re*ntiz Richard Lontri – ii s.

p. 28, col. 1 Ces sont les nouns des issanz:

Richard atte Wade – ii s.
Roger atte Garstou*n* – ii s.
William Som*er*ville – ii s.

These are the names of the wardens of the Goldsmiths' Mistery of London in the year 37 Edward III [1363]: 1363–64 p. 27, col. 1
John Coraunt
Thomas Piphurst
Thomas Lincoln
Henry Markeby

These are the expenditures made by the said wardens in the same year:
Firstly, given to the increase of the alms funds of St Dunstan by the same wardens – £4
Item, paid for the bell-ringing at St Paul's and other costs incurred – 13s. 4d.
Item, paid to the two poor people of the goldsmiths' mistery for the same year – 106s. 8d.
Item, new clothing given to the said poor people at the time of the feast of St Dunstan in the same year – 13s. 4d.
Item, for the costs of the feast on St Dunstan's Day – £10.

These are the names of apprentices:
John Rigge, apprentice of John Piphurst – 2s.
William Huphulle, apprentice of William Burdeyn – 2s.
Richard Sheen, apprentice of Robert Launde – 2s.
John Stoke, apprentice of Hugh Billington – 2s.
Richard Chancy, apprentice of John Waldene – 2s.
Walter Fermer, apprentice of John Leche – 2s.
John Vanuche, apprentice of John Litlington – 2s.
William Bridford, apprentice of Richard Barton – 2s.
John Hunte, apprentice of John Broun – 2s. col. 2
John West, apprentice of Robert Guildford – 2s.
Walter Rigge, apprentice of John Bonyng – 2s.
John Olyve, apprentice of Richard atte Water – 2s.
John Clere, apprentice of Thomas Forster – 2s.
Thomas Bounde, Henry Markeby, apprentices of John Maplesdene – 4s.
William Godfrey, apprentice of John Garwyntoun – 2s.
John Barningham, apprentice of John Pyk – 2s.
John Wallingford, apprentice of Robert Oxenford – 2s.
Thomas Dente, apprentice of James de Thame – 2s.
Richard Merdene, apprentice of John Seybrook – 2s.
Edmund Prins, apprentice of Nichol Gyna – 2s.
Roger Whitewey, apprentice of Henry Asshele – 2s.
Philip Richmond, apprentice of Thomas Wynter – 2s.
John Breton, apprentice of Richard Burcham – 2s.
John Gloucester, apprentice of Simon Wynter – 2s.
John Gervays, apprentice of William Gervays – 2s.
John Em, apprentice of Richard Lontri – 2s.

These are the names of those coming out [of their terms of apprenticeship]: p. 28, col. 1
Richard atte Wade – 2s.
Roger atte Garston – 2s.
William Somerville – 2s.

Joh*an* Adam – ii s.
Thomas Forster – ii s.
Hen*ri* Chaumb*er*lein – ii s.
Thomas Eggesfeld – ii s.
Joh*an* Waldewyne – ii s.
William Shadewell*e* – ii s.

Ces sont les entrés:
Joh*an* Ensfeld
Nichol Lavyntou*n*
Richard Dancastre

Fait a remembrer[55]

1364–65 Ceaux sount les nou*n*s des gardeyns de orfeverie de Loundres l'an du reigne
p. 29, col. 1 le Roi Edward le tie[r]zce puis la conqueste trente *et* oeptisme:
Thomas Hessay
Johan Gravelee
Robert de Launde
Richard de Westou*n*

Ceaux sont les despences faitez p*ar* les ditez gardeins en mesme l'an:
Adep*ri*mes a la feste de Seint Dunstan et altres div*er*ces diners faites p*ar* mesme les d*ic*tes gardeins ap*rés*, q*e* amonte outre la quilet – xlii li.
It*em*, doné a deux pov*er*es ho*m*mes acontr*e* Noel – vi s. viii d.
It*em*, a mesme deux ho*m*mes *et* une fe*m*me *et* un alt*re* ho*m*me del amoigne – en mesme l'an – Cvi s. viii d.
It*em*, a deux pov*er*es del mester doné novel vesture acountre le feste de Seint Dunstan, p*ris* – xiii s. iiii d.
It*em*, p*ur* sonail de Seint Paul *et* p*ur* costages del lumere al glyse Seint Jehan Zakarie, outre la quilet – xv s. vi d.
It*em*, don*é* al encrés del amoigne de Seint Dunstan – iiii li.

Ceaux sount les nou*n*s de ap*re*ntices entrés en mesme l'an:
William Walssh*e* auprentiz Pers Hiltofte – ii s.
Johan[56] Felstede apprentiz Johan Litlingtou*n* – ii s.
Pers Wynnecote app*re*ntiz Johan Walssh*e* – ii s.
Johan Turvey app*re*ntiz Nicolas Twyforde – ii s.
col. 2 Thomas Charltou*n* apprentiz Johan Buntyng – ii s.
Richard *et* Thom*as* Boxcote app*re*ntiz Robert Lucas – iiii s.
Drue Barentyn app*re*ntiz Robert Oxingforde – ii s.
Johan Piphurst app*re*ntiz Richard Westone – ii s.
William Hasregge app*re*ntiz Thomas Salysburi – ii s.
Johan Asshebourne app*re*ntiz Johan Wynd – ii s.

[55] A sentence appears to have been erased here. There is no more written on this page.
[56] MS: Johoan.

John Adam –	2s.
Thomas Forster –	2s.
Henry Chamberlayn –	2s.
Thomas Eggesfield –	2s.
John Waldewyne –	2s.
William Shadwell –	2s.

These are the entries:
John Ensfield
Nichol Lavington
Richard Dancaster

Memorandum:

These are the names of the Wardens of the Goldsmiths' Mistery of London in the year 38 Edward III [1364] 1364–65 p. 29, col. 1
Thomas Hassay
John Gravele
Robert de Launde
Richard de Weston

These are the expenditures made by the said wardens in the same year:
Firstly, at the feast of St Dunstan and various other dinners given afterwards by the same said wardens, which over and above the collection amounts to – £42
Item, given to two poor men at Christmas time – 6s. 8d.
Item, to the same two men and a woman and another man, from the alms,[44] in the same year – 106s. 8d.
Item, to two poor men of the mistery, new clothing given at the time of St Dunstan's feast, cost – 13s. 4d.
Item, for the bell-ringing at St Paul's and for the costs of the light at the church of St John Zachary, over and above the collection – 15s. 6d.
Item, given to the increase of the alms funds of St Dunstan – £4

These are the names of apprentices entered in the same year:

William Walsh, apprentice of Piers Hiltoft –	2s.	
John Felstede, apprentice of John Litlington –	2s.	
Piers Wynnecote, apprentice of John Walsh –	2s.	
John Turvey, apprentice of Nicholas Twyford –	2s.	
Thomas Charltoun, apprentice of John Bunting –	2s.	col. 2
Richard and Thomas Boxcote, apprentices of Robert Lucas –	4s.	
Drew Barantyn, apprentice of Robert Oxenford –	2s.	
John Piphurst, apprentice of Richard Weston –	2s.	
William Hasregge, apprentice of Thomas Salisbury –	2s.	
John Ashbourne, apprentice of John Wynd –	2s.	

[44] Another way of interpreting the French phrasing here would be to read the meaning as '. . . and a woman and another man [who are] on the alms list' (have been granted the right to benefit from payments from the alms fund).

Rob*er*t Taverner app*re*ntiz Johan Fairher – ii s.
William Aras app*re*ntiz Robert de Launde – ii s.
William Russhem*ere* app*re*ntiz Thom*as* Russhemere – ii s.
J[oh]an[57] Hyngde app*re*ntiz Thom*as* Scherhold – ii s.

Ceaux sont les nou*n*s des issantz hors de lour termes:
Thom*as* de Kent – ii s.
Johan Veel – ii s.
Thom*as* Welford – ii s.
Robert Tyngewyk – ii s.
Edmu*n*d Geynisforde – ii s.
William Horsman – ii s.

p. 30, col. 1 Ceaux sont les entrés p*ar* mesme l'an:
Robert Lucas
Bertram van Coloygne
Thomas Forster
William Stoke
Johan Buntyng

9 May 1365 Fait a remembr*er* q*e* le venderdy p*ro*chein ap*ré*s la fest Seint Joh*a*n Portlatyn, l'an n*ost*re S*eignur* le Roi E*dward* tierçz ap*ré*s le conquest xxxixme, les bones gentz del mister d'orfev*er*ie de la Citee de Loundres ensemblement ové les com*un*es, p*ur* co*mun*e p*ro*fit du dit mister furent assemblés en lo*ur* co*mun*e place en la p*ar*oche Seint Joh*a*n Zakar*ie* en la citee avantdite, *et* illoq*e*s estoit ordiné *et* establi p*ar* co*mun*e assent du dit mister q*e* nul qi clamoreit d'estre de la dite compaignie ne usereit nule robe de lo*ur* sute s'il ne soit de la liveree des gardeins du dit mister qe p*ur* le temps y s*er*ront; et q*e* nul qi p*re*igne robe ne face doun ne vente a nul de ses compaignons p*ar* cautele, sur peine de demy marc a paier a l'amoigne de Seint Dunstou*n*; et q*e* la peine avantdite soit levé p*ar* tout auxi bien del vendo*ur* come del acatour. Et a ceste ordinance tenir bien *et* loialment la compaignie avantdite, auxibien les petiz come les g*ra*untz, les jovenes come les veux, le jo*ur* de Seint Dunstou*n* p*ro*chein ensuaunt[58] ap*ré*s la date de cestes sont finalement assentuz.[59]

1364–65[60] Ces sont les nouns des gardeins del orfev*er*ie de la citee de Loundres l'an du
col. 2 regne le Roi Edward tierçz puis le conquest trent *et* oyt:
William de Burtou*n*
Joh*a*n de Northwych*e*
Joh*a*n Seybrok
Thomas de Salesbury

Les dites gardeins despenderent en lo*ur* fest le jo*ur* de Seint Dunstou*n*, outre lo*ur* quillet – xii li. xi s. vi d.

[57] MS: Jhoan.
[58] MS: ensuauat.
[59] See Reddaway and Walker, p. 236.
[60] See the Introduction, pp. xxiv–xxvii, for the problem of whether there might have been two sets of wardens for this year.

Robert Taverner, apprentice of John Fairher[45] – 2s.
William Aras, apprentice of Robert de Launde – 2s.
William Rushmere, apprentice of Thomas Rushmere – 2s.
John Hynde, apprentice of Thomas Sherholt – 2s.

These are the names of those coming out of their terms:
Thomas de Kent – 2s.
John Veel – 2s.
Thomas Welford – 2s.
Robert Tingewick – 2s.
Edmund Geynisford – 2s.
William Horsman – 2s.

These are those who have entered in the same year: p. 30, col. 1
Robert Lucas
Bertram van Cologne
Thomas Forster
William Stoke
John Bunting

Memorandum that on the Friday following the feast of St John ante portam latinam in the year 39 Edward III [9 May 1365], the good men of the Goldsmiths' mistery of the City of London together with the commonalty were assembled for the common benefit of the said mistery in their communal hall in the parish of St John Zachary in the aforesaid city, and there it was ordained and established by common assent of the said mistery that no one who claimed to be one of the said company should use any livery gown unless it be that assigned by the current wardens of the said mistery, and that as a precaution no one who takes a gown may give it or sell it to any of his companions on pain of [a fine of] half a mark to be paid to the alms funds of St Dunstan, and that this aforesaid fine should be levied on both the seller and the buyer. And it was finally agreed by the aforesaid company, by both the high and the low, the young and the old, to keep this ordinance well and loyally from St Dunstan's day next following after the date of these letters. 9 May 1365

These are the names of the Wardens of the Goldsmiths' Mistery of London in the year 38 Edward III [1364] 1364–65 col. 2
William de Burtoun
John de Northwych
John Seybrook
Thomas de Salisbury

The said wardens spent on their feast on St Dunstan's day, over and above their collection – £12 11s. 6d.

[45] This apprentice was listed above, A + a, p. 25, col. 1, in 1362–63. A few other such duplicate entries appear and are most probably due to scribal error in copying up from rough notes. It is of course also possible that this is not the same boy but another with the same name.

It*em*, estre ceo trov*er*ent deux pov*er*es ho*m*mes del mister p*ar* un an – iiii li. xv s. ii d.

Et p*ur* ceo q*e* les bones gentz del mister pristrent dev*er*s eux les p*ro*fitz app*ur*tenantz as dites gardeins, les gardeins ne don*er*ent cest an point d'encrés.[61]

Ordon*a*ncez

Qu*o*d nullus fr*atru*m sit absens in [diem] f*est*i S*anc*ti Dunstani:

Pur ce qe avant ces houres al jo*ur* q*e* le feste de Seinte Dunston soloit estre tenuz, pluso*ur*s de la confrat*er*nité ascunz soi enloigneront hors de ville, ascunz en div*er*s lieus en p*ri*vitez *et* en musceitz, *et* ne voillant ven*ir* *et* honou*r*er le dit feste en le hono*ur* de Dieu *et* de Seint Dunston, a g*ra*nt descrees *et* deshono*ur* de la dite confrat*er*nité:

En le hono*ur* de Dieu *et* de Seint Dunston *et* encrees *et* hono*ur* del dit confrat*er*nité, si est ordeiné *et* assentu p*ar* co*mun*e assent de la dite confrat*er*nité qe le feste de Seinte Dunston desore en avant soit tenuz mesme le jour de S*eint* Dunston *et* q*e* toutz de la dite confrat*er*nité soiont illoqes adonqes *et* qe nully de la dite confrat*er*nité ne soi[t][62] absente sanz resonable *et* v*er*rai encheson, *et* si ascuny le face, il paiera atant come ascuny qe soit al dite feste.

1365–66 Ces sont les nouns des gardeins del orfev*er*ie de la cité de Loundres l'an du
p. 31, col. 1 regne le Roi Edward tierçz puis le conquest trent ixe:

Nicolas Twyfford
Joh*a*n Coraunt
Roberd Oxinford
Joh*a*n Forst*er*

Les dites gardeins despenderent en lo*ur* fest le jo*ur* de Seint Dunstou*n*, outre lo*ur* quillet – xi li. xi s.

Et out*re* ceo trov*er*ent iiii pov*er*es del mist*er* p*ar* un ane chescun semayne xii d. [s'est a dire][63] x li. viii s.

Summa – xxi li. xix s.

Ceux sont les nons dé ap*re*ntis ent*ré*s en mesme l'an:

Joh*a*n Stil app*re*ntiz Ad*am* Marffel –	ii s.
Will*ia*m Harvi app*re*ntiz Th*om*as Bigod –	ii s.
Joh*a*n Payn app*re*ntiz Roberd Launde –	ii s.
Roberd Wrihtte app*re*ntiz Joh*a*n Walche –	ii s.
Joh*a*n Mazerer app*re*ntiz Harri Chehezond –	ii s.
Harri Grene app*re*ntiz Edmond Ippeg*ra*ve –	ii s.
Laurensse Dyland app*re*ntiz Bertram van Coloygne –	ii s.
Roger Grengylford app*re*ntiz Th*om*as ate Nok –	ii s.

[61] See the Introduction, p. xxv.
[62] This emendation is based on the Latin sub-heading; 'ne soi absente' could however be seen as correct, meaning 'should not absent himself'.
[63] MS: s'ast.

Item, besides this, they provided for two poor men of the mistery for a year – £4 15s. 2d.

And since the good men of the mistery took to themselves the profits belonging to the said wardens, the wardens did not in this year give any increase to the funds.

Ordinances

That none of the brothers should be absent on St Dunstan's feast day:
Whereas in recent times on the day that St Dunstan's feast was customarily held many of the fraternity have absented themselves, some going right out of the town, some in various private and hidden places, not wishing to come and honour the said feast in the honour of God and St Dunstan, to the great detriment and dishonour of the said fraternity.
In the honour of God and St Dunstan and to the profit and honour of the said fraternity, it is ordained and agreed by common assent of the said fraternity that the feast of St Dunstan should from henceforth be held on St Dunstan's Day itself, and that everyone of the said fraternity should be present then and that no one of the said fraternity should be absent without reasonable and true excuse, and that if anyone is thus absent he shall pay just as much as one who is at the said feast.

These are the names of the Wardens of the Goldsmiths' Mistery of the city of London in the year 39 Edward III [1365] 1365–66 p. 31, col. 1
Nicholas Twyford
John Coraunt
Robert Oxenford
John Forster

The said wardens spent on their feast on St Dunstan's Day, over and above their collection – £11 11s.
And besides this they provided for 4 poor people of the mistery for a year, at 12d. per week, i.e. £10 8s.
Total: £21 19s.

These are the names of apprentices entered in the same year:

John Style, apprentice of Adam Mirfield –	2s.
William Harvi, apprentice of Thomas Bygod –	2s.
John Payn, apprentice of Robert Launde –	2s.
Robert Wrihtte, apprentice of John Walsh –	2s.
John Mazerer, apprentice of Harry Chicksands –	2s.
Harry Grene, apprentice of Edmund Ippegrave –	2s.
Laurence Dyland, apprentice of Bertram van Cologne –	2s.
Roger Cringleford, apprentice of Thomas atte Noke –	2s.

Gefferey Winch app*re*ntiz Harri Crisp – ii s.
Rechard Hokis app*re*ntiz Rechard Baurnh*am* – ii s.

col. 2 Ceux sount les nou*n*s des issantz hors de lour termes denz le temps de les gardayns avantdit:
Will*ia*m Kelche – ii s.
Joh*a*n Donmawe – ii s.
Nicolas Merffel – ii s.
Joh*a*n Som*er*vile – ii s.
Th*om*as Bounde – ii s.
Stevene Bev*er*ns – ii s.
Roberd Lytlyngto*n* – ii s.
Will*ia*m Wirhale – ii s.
Joh*a*n Chappeler – ii s.
Will*ia*m Dampport – ii s.
Joh*a*n Canoun – ii s.
Th*om*as Dam – ii s.
Joh*a*n Payn – ii s.

Ceux sont les entrés p*ar* mesme l'ane:
Gautroun de la Tour
Roberd Ravin, clerk[64]
Rechard ate Melle
Joh*a*n Esslak

1366 Fayt a remembrer q*e* la co*n*te fayt ent*re* lé bone gens des orffavers *et* lé gardayns avaunt dit, s'est a dire Nicolas Twifford *et* Joh*a*n Coraunt *et* Roberd *et* Johan, le xvj^e jo*ur* de maii l'ane Nost*re* S*eignur* le Roy karaunt: de C*ent et* lxviii li*vres* fust en les maynz [des] dit gardains, de quel C*ent et* lxviii li*vres* fust b*ien* et l[e]alment despendu desur comune place des orffevers p*ur* comune p*r*offit, p*ur* un sale *et* quezine *et* pantri *et* botylrie *et* ii chaumbris ové dowble gette – C xxxvi li. iii d. *et* p*ur* fere sute a la co*n*ssayl p*ur* nost*re* chart*er* p*ar* comune asent fust desspendu xii li. xii s. *et* le remenaunt del argent avaunt dit fust baylé p*ar* les mayns de les gardayns avant dit le jo*ur* de Seint Donstoun a les bones genz *et* comons des orffeveris, q*e* la co*n*te fust leu et lealment fayt denz le mezoun Will*ia*m Tyngewik le xvj^e jo*ur* de maii avant dit – testemoin:
Joh*a*n Chichest*re*
Joh*a*n Heltoft
Will*ia*m Bortoun
Joh*a*n Nortwyck
Joh*a*n Gr*a*vele
Th*om*as Hessay
Th*om*as Rayngh*am*
Joh*a*n Maplisden
Joh*a*n Walsche

64 This may well have been the clerk to the company, being admitted here into the mistery and/or fraternity.

Geoffrey Wynch, apprentice of Harry Crisp – 2s.
Richard Hokis, apprentice of Richard Burnham – 2s.

These are the names of those coming out of their terms during the time of the aforesaid wardens: col. 2
William Kelche – 2s.
John Donmawe – 2s.
Nicholas Mirfield – 2s.
John Somerville – 2s.
Thomas Bounde – 2s.
Stephen Beverns – 2s.
Robert Litlington – 2s.
William Wirral – 2s.
John Chapler – 2s.
William Dampport – 2s.
John Canoun – 2s.
Thomas Dam – 2s.
John Payn – 2s.

These are the entries for the same year:
Gautroun de la Tour
Robert Ravin, clerk
Richard atte Melle
John Esslak

Memorandum that account was made between the good men of the goldsmiths and the aforesaid wardens, i.e. Nicholas Twyford, John Coraunt, Robert [Oxenford] and John [Forster], on 16 May 1366 of £168 which was in the hands of the said wardens, and of these £168, £136 3d. was spent properly and legally on the communal hall of the goldsmiths for their common benefit, for a hall and a kitchen and a pantry and a buttery and two rooms with a double jetty[46] – £136 3d. And for attending court at the [King's] Council for our charter £12 12s was spent by common assent, and the remainder of the aforesaid money was handed over by the aforesaid wardens on St Dunstan's Day to the good men and the commonalty of the goldsmiths. The account was read and legally made in the house of William Tingewick on 16 May aforesaid. Witnesses: 1366
John Chichester
John Hiltoft
William Burton
John Northwych
John Gravele
Thomas Hassay
Thomas Raynham
John Maplesdene
John Walsh

[46] The rooms on the upper floor will have jutted out over the street along two sides of the Hall.

Harri Markeby
Roberd Oxinford
Johan Saybrok
Johan Walden
Nicolas Twifford
Johan Coraunt
Johan Forster
Roberd Launde
Thomas Forster
Johan Fayrher
Bertilme Castre
Thomas Pipherst
Nicolas Cove
Rechard Arnold
William Lythirpol
Rechard Fraunssays
Johan Lincalle
Rechard Bernham
Hamound Joze
Rechard Cheltam
Rechard Alncaster
Simound Mazerer
William Stamelden
William Fraunssays
William Tyngewyk
Johan Wind
Edmound Brauntoun
Johan Hokynge
Johan Broun
Roberd Geldeford

1365 p. 32, col. 1 Fayt a rem[em]brer q*e* le vendirdi p*ro*chayn devant le Pentecost l'an Nost*re* S*eignur* le Roy [Edward][65] terçz aprés le conqu*e*st xxxixme, les bones gens del mist*er* d'orfav*er*ie de la seté de Loundres ensemblement ové les comouns p*ur* comune p*ro*ffit du dit mist*er* furent assemblés en lo*ur* co*mun*e plasce en la p*ar*oche Sent Joh*a*n Zakar*ie* en la seté avauntdit, *et* illoq*e*s estoit ordayné *et* establi p*ar* co*mun*e du dit mist*er* pur ceo q*e* Joh*a*n de Brugis, orfever*e*, fust trové p*ar* li benche mesmes de ii faucimis, s'est a dire le un fauscime fust de un harnés p*ur* un sancture d'argent q*e* fust poyzé devant eus q*e* l'oun achaté, *et* aprés q*e* le dit harnés fust poyzé le dit Joh*a*n p*re*ntt un aultre[66] harnés de le mesme gize q*e* poyze mayns q*e* le harnés avant dit xvi s., a g*ra*nt hounte de li mesmis *et* g*ra*nt rep*ri*ef [du] dit mest*er*. It*em*, l'aut*re* fauscime fust de le poys de un mark de sablount q*e* fust mellé ové lemayle d'argent, *et* vendit p*ur* argent a Th*o*m*a*s de Brandam. P*ur* ses fauscimis p*ar* les bone jenz *et* comunis fust ordayné q*e* le dit Joh*a*n ne dev*er*a mie tyné nul sege devant en Chepe un ane, *et* ausi q*e* le dit Joh*a*n ne dev*er*a mie est*re* vestu de lev*er*é de le dit orfaverie un ane aprés sest

[65] MS: the Tironian 'et'.
[66] MS: alut*re*

Harry Markeby
Robert Oxenford
John Seybrook
John Walden
Nicholas Twyford
John Coraunt
John Forster
Robert Launde
Thomas Forster
John Fairher
Bartholomew Castre
Thomas Piphurst
Nicholas Cove
Richard Arnold
William Liverpool
Richard Fraunceys
John Lincoln
Richard Burnham
Hamond Chose
Richard Cheltam
Richard Alncaster
Simon Mazerer
William Stameldene
William Fraunceys
William Tingewick
John Wynd
Edmund Brandon
John Hokyng
John Broun
Robert Guildford

Memorandum that on the Friday before Whit-Sunday in the year 39 Edward III 1365
[30 May 1365], the good men of the Goldsmiths' mistery of the City of London p. 32, col. 1
together with the commonalty, for the common benefit of the said mistery were assembled in their communal hall in the parish of St John Zachary in the aforesaid city, and there it was ordained and established by the community of the said mistery that, whereas John de Bruges, goldsmith, had been found guilty by the Bench itself of two fraudulencies, i.e. one fraudulency was of the silver harness [metal-work] for a girdle which was weighed before those who purchased it, and after it had been weighed the said John took another harness of the same style which weighed 16s less than the aforesaid harness, to his own great shame and to the great disgrace of the said mistery. Item, the other fraudulency was of one mark's weight of sand which was mixed with silver filings and he sold it for silver to Thomas de Brandam. For his fraudulencies it was ordained by the goodmen and commons that the said John should for a year not hold any front stall in Cheap, and also that for a year after this judgment the said John should not be clothed in the livery of the said Goldsmiths' mistery, unless

jugement, si n'est trové p*ar* iii oue iiii de bones gens q*e* vaust est*re* plegis p*ur* li devant lé iiii gardayns, isi vin le dit Joh*a*n de Brwgis dedenz le dit ane ap*r*iés *et* portount ovesqe[67] li Joh*a*n Fayrher *et* Joh*a*n Broun p*ur* est*re* plege p*ur* le dit Joh*a*n de Brugis *et* lé dit gardayns ount geugé si le dit Joh*a*n est trové ap*r*iés ses euris avesqe ascun fauscime q*e* p*ur*a est*re* trové ové ii co*m*paynuns qe sount de bone co*n*discioun *et* leaus, adounkys qe le dit Joh*a*n Fayrher *et* dit Joh*a*n Broun paya a le co*m*panie le jo*ur* de Sent Dounston p*ro*cheyn suaunt un pipe de vin *et* le dit Joh*a*n de Brugis d'est*re* a dispos[i]sioun[68] dé gardayns *et* lé bone gens [du] dit mest*er*.

1369 Fait a remembr*er* q*e* al feste de S. Dunstan l'an xliii Joh*a*n Fairher *et* Joh*a*n Broun sont deschargez p*ur* plegg*es* de i pipe de vin p*ur* Joh*a*n Brugges.[69]

1365 P*ri*ma ordinacio de non venantib*us*[70]

p. 32, col. 2 Fayt a rem[em]brer q*e* ausi fust ordayné le samadi p*ro*cheyn devant le Pentecost l'an n*ost*re s*eignur* le Roy E.[71] tierçz aprés le conquest xxxixme les bones gens del mist*er* d'orfeve*r*ie de la sitté de Loundres ensembleme*n*t ové les comuns p*ur* co*mun*e proffit *et* p*ur* bone amour du dit mist*er* furent assemblés en lour co*mun*e plasce en la p*ar*oche Sent Joh*a*n Zakar*ie*, q*e* asquin q*e* clayme d'est*re* de dit mist*er* fust maundé p*ar* les brokour*s* p*ur* est*re* devant lé iiii gardaynz *et* ne vin pas, adounkys qe i paya un grot si il ne p*ur*ra covenablement esquzer; *et* ascun de le dit mist*er* est maundé p*ar* asquin de lé dit gardaynz qi sount p*ur* le temps *et* ne vin pas, adounkys q*e* paya xii d. a l'amoyne de Sent Dounstoun; *et* auci q*ua*nt ascun de le co*m*pani est mort de la vesture d'orfave*r*ie q*e* dounkes chescun de la mist*er* s[o]yes a la jo*ur* de l'ent*er*ment si ne p*ur*ra covenablment esquzer, desur le payne avant dit.

1366–67 [72]Ces sunt les nouns dé Gardeyns del orfevré de la Cité de Loundr*es* l'an du regne le Roi Edward tierce puis le conquest quarantisme:
Johan Gravelee
Joh*a*n Walsshe
Richard Arnold
William Lyv*er*epool

It*em*, les dites gardeyns despenderunt le jo*ur* de Seint Dunston en les chaumps en vyn, blaunderell*es*, menestrall*es* *et* autr*es* choses – xxx s.
It*em*, p*ur* le soner del g*ra*untz seyns de Seint Poul *et* p*ur* la lum*er*e en la eglise de Seint Johan Zakarie – xx s.
It*em*, p*ur* la vest*ur*e de ii brokours – xv s.

[67] MS: oue vesqe.
[68] MS: dispossioun. One might also edit to 'disposs[ic]ioun'.
[69] The last entry has been added later in a different hand and different ink.
[70] This heading has been added a little later, in the same hand as wrote the later addition to the case of John of Bruges.
[71] MS: the Tironian 'et'.
[72] A new hand starts here.

3 or 4 good men could be found who would stand surety for him before the 4 wardens; and thus the said John de Bruges came within the said year following and brought with him John Fairher and John Broun to be sureties for the said John de Bruges, and the said wardens made judgement that if the said John should subsequently be found guilty of any fraudulency that could be proved by two honest and loyal members of the company, then the said John Fairher and the said John Broun should pay to the company a pipe of wine on the next St Dunstan's Day, and the said John de Bruges would be at the disposition of the wardens and goodmen of the said mistery.

Memorandum that on St Dunstan's feastday in 1369 John Fairher and John 1369
Broun were discharged of their pledge of a pipe of wine for John Bruges.[47]

First ordinance concerning absentees: 1365
Memorandum that it was also ordained on the Saturday before Whit-Sunday p. 32, col. 2
in the year 39 Edward III [31 May 1365], the goodmen of the Goldsmiths' mistery of the City of London assembled together with the commons for the common benefit and out of good love of the said mistery in their communal hall in the parish of St John Zachary, that anyone who claims to be of the said mistery and is summoned by the brokers to be before the 4 wardens and does not come, that then he should pay one groat if he has no suitable excuse, and that anyone of the said mistery who is summoned by any of the said current wardens and who does not come, that then he should pay 12d. to the alms funds of St Dunstan, and also that if anyone of the company of the livery of the goldsmiths' mistery dies, that then each man of the mistery should be [present] on the day of the burial unless he may have some suitable excuse, upon pain of the aforesaid fine.

These are the names of the Wardens of the Goldsmiths' Mistery of the City 1366–67
of London in the year 40 Edward III [1366]:
John Gravele
John Walsh
Richard Arnold
William Liverpool

Item, the said wardens spent on St Dunstan's Day in the fields on wine, apples, minstrels and other things – 30s.
Item, for the ringing of the great bell[48] at St Paul's, and for the light in the church of St John Zachary – 20s.
Item, for the clothing of 2 brokers – 15s.

47 There is ambiguity in the phrasing as to whether they were discharged of their obligation without payment or after payment.

48 It could be debatable whether the French here means bell or bells, but reference to later entries makes it clear that the singular is intended. On the bells of St Paul's see the Introduction, pp. xxv–xxvi.

Ces sunt les nouns des app*r*entitz entrés en mesme l'an:

Thom*as* Tyngewyk app*r*entiz a Rob*er*t Tyngewyk –	ii s.
Henr*i* atte Well*e* app*r*entiz a Geffrey Walpool –	ii s.
Joh*a*n Rotherh*a*m app*r*entiz a Thom*as* Reynh*a*m –	ii s.
p. 33, col. 1 Roger Ryot app*r*entiz a Nicholas Twyford –	ii s.
Richard Elys app*r*entiz a Richard Burnh*a*m –	ii s.
Andreu Peny app*r*entiz a Simond Mazerer –	ii s.
Thom*as* Stokes app*r*entiz a William Tyngewyk –	ii s.
Joh*a*n Wynt*ur* apprentiz a Adam Alesh*a*m –	ii s.
William Barbo*ur* app*r*entiz a William Wyrhale –	ii s.
Thom*as* Chaler*er*s app*r*entiz a William Liv*er*pool –	ii s.
Thom*as* Mound app*r*entiz a Thom*as* Pantou*n* –	ii s.
Thom*as* Farnh*a*m app*r*entiz a Rob*er*t Burgh*e* –	ii s.
It*e*m, Symon Pykot app*r*entiz Rob*er*t Launde –	ii s.[73]
Andr*eu* Stamenden*e* app*r*entiz William Stamenden*e* –	ii s.

Ces sunt les issauntz hors de lo*ur*s t*er*mes deinz le temps de les gardeyns avantditez:
Rob*er*t Holdrenesse
Joh*a*n Manne
Joh*a*n Walden*e*
Joh*a*n Asshebo*ur*ne
Henr*i* Chaumb*er*leyn
William atte Forde
William Fitzhugh*e*
William Mariner
Rob*er*t Holm
William Horseman
Thom*as* Gildeford
Steph*e*ne de Thorp*e*
Joh*a*n Brackelee
Ric*hard* de Rome
Joh*a*n atte Welle
George Rugges
Waut*er* Deynes.

1367 Fait a remembrer q*e* touz les bones gentz del mestier de orfev*er*ye de
col. 2 Loundr*e*s sunt acordez p*ar* lo*u*r co*mun*e assent le jeody p*ro*sch*ei*n devant la feste de Palmes en l'an n*ost*re s*eignur* le roi quarante p*ri*m*er*e:

C'est assavoir q*e* nully del dit mestier ne venderat nulle vesselement meyn q*e* la li*vr*e p*ar* poys de orfevr*e* ii s. *et* vi d. s*ur* forfaitur*e* del dit vessel.
Item, p*ur* un paire de pootz *et* de ewers la paire nyntmeyns q*e* xxiiii s. s*ur* l'avantdit peyne.

[73] This entry and the next are additions to this list made later in a different ink. S. Pyket must be the same as S. Pygot listed next year also?

These are the names of apprentices entered in the same year:
Thomas Tingewick, apprentice of Robert Tingewick – 2s.
Henry atte Welle, apprentice of Geoffrey Walpole – 2s.
John Rotherham, apprentice of Thomas Raynham – 2s.
Roger Ryot, apprentice of Nicholas Twyford – 2s. p. 33, col. 1
Richard Elys, apprentice of Richard Burnham – 2s.
Andrew Peny. apprentice of Simon Mazerer – 2s.
Thomas Stokes, apprentice of William Tingewick – 2s.
John Wynter, apprentice of Adam Aylsham – 2s.
William Barbour, apprentice of William Wirral – 2s.
Thomas Chalers, apprentice of William Liverpool – 2s.
Thomas Mound, apprentice of Thomas Panton – 2s.
Thomas Farnham, apprentice of Robert Burgh – 2s.
Item, Simon Pykot, apprentice of Robert Launde – 2s.
Andrew Stameldene, apprentice of William Stameldene – 2s.

These are those coming out of their terms during the time of the aforesaid wardens:
Robert Holderness
John Manne
John Waldene
John Ashbourne
Henry Chamberlayn
William atte Forde
William Fitzhugh
William Mariner
Robert Holm
William Horseman
Thomas Guildford
Stephen de Thorpe
John Brackelee
Richard de Rome
John atte Welle
George Rugges
Walter Deynes

Memorandum that all the goodmen of the Goldsmiths' mistery of London agreed by common assent on the Thursday before Palm Sunday in the year 41 Edward III [8 April 1367]: 1367 col. 2
i.e.
That no one of the said mistery should sell any vessel at less than 2s. 6d. per pound goldsmiths' weight[49] on [pain of] forfeiture of the said vessel.
Item, for a pair of pots or ewers, at no less than 24s. the pair, on [pain of] the aforesaid penalty.

[49] These are prices for workmanship, to be paid on top of the price of the silver. 'Goldsmiths' weight' was the Tower pound. This was of 5,400 grains, whereas the pound of Troy weight was of 5,760 grains; the Tower pound was thus less than the Troy pound by 15 pennyweights or ¾oz. See W. Chaffers, *Hall Marks on Gold and Silver Plate . . .*, 6th edn (London, 1883), p. 59.

It*em*, p*ur* un doszeyne de quilher*es*, c'est assav*oir* ové pomelles *et* akeres, meyns q*e* iii s. *sur* la dite peyne.
It*em*, q*e* null*e* de la dit compaignie ne fra nulle peynterye desur nulle seynt*ur*e mes soulement de amaille de colour s'il ne soit q*e* petit chose covenablement, *sur* la peyne avantdit.
It*em*, ordeigné est p*ar* la dit compaignie q*e* q*ui*cu*n*qe p*er*sone q*e* debrise les dites poyntz si avynt q*e* ascun autre p*er*sone se voet pleyndre a les gardeyns ou as bones gentz, q'il av*er*a la tierce p*ar*tie del dite forfait*ur*e p*ur* son t*ra*vail.

1367–68 Ceux sont les nons des gardeinz de orphev*er*ie l'an xlj:
p. 34, col. 1 Thomas Reyngham
Will*elmu*s Tyngewik
Joh*ann*es Broun
Barth*olome*us de Castre

Les despenc*es* des ditz gardeinz:
En p*ri*mes, p*ur* soner la g*ra*unt sonel de Seint Poul *et* p*ur* la lum*er*e al eglise de Seint Joh*a*n Zakarie – xx s. vi d.
It*em*, don*é* al encrés al aumoign*e* de Seint Dunstou*n* – iiii marcz.

Fait a remembr*er* q*e* Thomas Elyz retreta un aqueinte de Geffrey Wynch*e* q*e* voudroit av*er* achaté une seint*ur*e del dit Geffrei *et* mesme cestui Geffrei fist pleinte as ditz gardeinz del t*re*spas suisdit, *et* le dit Thomas fist gree al dit Geffrei – xl d.
Et le dit Thomas paia al aumoign*e* de Seint Dunstou*n* p*ur* le dit t*re*spas – vi s. viii d.

Ceux sont les nouns des app*re*ntiz mesme l'an:
Thomas Hingeston*e* jun*ior* app*re*ntiz de Adam Bamme – ii s.[74]
Walt*er* Iresby app*re*ntiz de Thomas Wilby – ii s.
Ric*hard* atte M*a*rssh*e* app*rent*i*z* de Geffrey Wynch*e* – ii s.
Joh*a*n Bataille app*rent*i*z* Thom*as* Davy – ii s.
Reginald Bacou*n* app*rent*i*z* Ric*hard* Brinchesle – ii s.
Joh*a*n Whitwell*e* app*rent*i*z* Thom*as* Davy – ii s.
Will*iam* atte Stone app*rent*i*z* de Thom*as* Forst*er* – ii s.
Rob*er*t Freman app*rent*i*z* de Joh*a*n Gerwaltou*n* – ii s.
Joh*ann*es Lynde app*rent*i*z* de Joh*a*n Brugges – ii s.
Joh*a*n Almayn*e* app*rent*i*z* de Thom*as* Bygod – ii s.
Joh*a*n Frenssh*e*, Symond Pygot app*rent*i*z* Rob*er*t Laund – iiii s.
Will*iam* Lincoln*e* app*rent*i*z* de Joh*a*n Lincoln*e* – ii s.
Thom*as* Cavendissh*e* app*rent*i*z* Will*iam* Tyngewik – ii s.

[74] This entry has had a line drawn through it.

Item, for a dozen spoons, that is with knops and acorn-knops, at no less than 3s. on [pain of] the said penalty.
Item, that no one of the said company should do any painting on any girdle but should only do colour-enamelling, unless it be a very small thing suitably done, on pain of the above penalty.
Item, it is ordained by the said company that if it should happen that another person should wish to complain to the wardens or the goodmen about whoever it may be who breaks the said ordinances, that he should have for his labour a third part of the forfeit.

These are the names of the Wardens of the Goldsmiths' Mistery in the year 41 [Edward III] [1367]: 1367–68 p. 34, col. 1
Thomas Raynham
William Tingewick
John Broun
Bartholomew de Castre

The expenses of the said wardens:
Firstly, for ringing the great bell[50] of St Paul's and for the light at the church of St John Zachary – 20s. 6d.
Item, given to the increase of the alms funds of St Dunstan – 4 marks

Memorandum that Thomas Elys withdrew an agreement with Geoffrey Wynche that he wished to have bought a girdle from the said Geoffrey and this same Geoffrey complained to the said wardens about the aforesaid offence, and the said Thomas settled with the said Geoffrey – 40d.
And the said Thomas paid to the alms funds of St Dunstan for the said offence – 6s. 8d.

These are the names of apprentices in the same year:

Thomas Hingston, the younger, apprentice of Adam Bamme –	2s.
Walter Iresby, apprentice of Thomas Wilby –	2s.
Richard atte Marsh, apprentice of Geoffrey Wynche –	2s.
John Bataille, apprentice of Thomas Davy –	2s.
Reginald Bacon, apprentice of Richard Brinchisle –	2s.
John Whitwell, apprentice of Thomas Davy –	2s.
William atte Stone, apprentice of Thomas Forster –	2s.
Robert Freman, apprentice of John Gerwaltoun –	2s.
John Lynde, apprentice of John Bruges –	2s.
John Almayne, apprentice of Thomas Bygod –	2s.
John Frenshe, Simon Pikot, apprentices of Robert Launde –	4s.
William Lincoln, apprentice of John Lincoln –	2s.
Thomas Cavendisshe, apprentice of William Tingewick –	2s.

50 'Sonel', later met with as 'sonail' in this same phrasing of later years in these records, could mean 'ringing' or 'pealing' of the bell(s), and the use of 'sonail' in previous years led me to assign this meaning to it there. Here, however, 'sonel' is used in a phrase so similar to that of the previous year: 'p*ur* le soner del gr*a*auntz seyns de Seint Poul', where the 'grauntz seyns' must be the 'great bell', that one is led now to interpret 'sonel' as 'bell' rather than 'peal of bells'. It would seem that the word can carry both meanings in Anglo-Norman.

Joh*a*n Marchall*e* appr*e*nt*iz* de Will*iam* Burtou*n* – ii s.
Petr*e* atte Netherland [appr*e*nt*iz*] de Adam Thorp*e* – ii s.
Ric*hard* Payn appr*e*nt*iz* de Rob*ertus* Oxinford – ii s.
Joh*a*n Chayh*a*m appr*e*ntis Joh*a*n Forst*er* – ii s.

col. 2 Ceux sont les nouns des gentz q*e* issent hors de lo*ur* t*er*me l'an xlj:
Thomas Isle p*ur* issir hors de son t*er*me – ii s.
Wille*lmus* Mariner[75] – ii s.
Joh*a*n Rugg – ii s.
Will*elmu*s Doyer – ii s.
Will*iam* Fitz Hugh – ii s.
Joh*a*n atte Forde – ii s.
Joh*a*n Payn – ii s.
Edmond Brandou*n* – ii s.
Rob*e*rt Wat*e*rmill*e* – ii s.

1368–69 Ceux sont les nouns des gardeinz de orphev*er*ie l'an xlii:
Nich*ola*s Twyford
Joh*anne*s Walssh*e*
Joh*anne*s Walden*e*
Adam Mirfeld

1369 Fayt a remembr*er* q*e* tout chosez acountez le jo*ur* de Seynt Barnabe
p. 35, col. 1 l'apostel*le* l'an xliii[76] entr*e* le companye de les orfeveres[77] Joh*an* Coraunt de tous maneres acsiouns tut guys.[78]

Les nouns de les receyvo*ur*s de lé dynerez:
Will*iam* Borden*e*
Joh*a*n Thorn*e*
La counte fynalment fayt de luy deux entre la companye des orfeveres[79] le jo*ur* de Seynt Barnabe la appostel*le* l'an xliii.[80]

1369 [81]Faite a rememb*r*er q*e* Joh*a*n Coraunt ad acompt*é* le jo*ur* de Seint Dunstan l'an xliii des toutz choses as orphev*er*es solonc le p*ur*port de i bille mys en le co*mune* cesket.[82]

[75] 'Joh*a*n Marin*er*' had been written first and a different hand has corrected this.
[76] MS: lan xliii ans.
[77] MS: orfevefres
[78] There would seem to be some words missing from this entry, and the translation on the opposite page suggests the most likely meaning that should be read here.
[79] MS: orfevefres.
[80] MS: lan xliii ans.
[81] This whole paragraph has been subsequently scored out.
[82] This word is unclearly written and obscure and may be a scribal error in copying. 'cesket' = 'casket' seems perhaps the most probable reading but is not elsewhere attested; it might also perhaps be 'le sket' and the rare ME word 'scat/scatte' meaning 'treasure', with the sense here of 'treasury' i.e. a chest in which precious things were kept.

John Marchalle, apprentice of William Burtoun – 2s.
Peter atte Netherland, apprentice of Adam Thorpe – 2s.
Richard Payn, apprentice of Robert Oxenford – 2s.
John Cheyham, apprentice of John Forster – 2s.

These are the names of those who came out of their terms in the year 1367: col. 2
Thomas Isle, for coming out of his term – 2s.
William Mariner – 2s.
John Rugg – 2s.
William Doyer – 2s.
William Fitzhugh – 2s.
John atte Forde – 2s.
John Payn – 2s.
Edmund Brandon – 2s.
Robert Watermille – 2s.

These are the names of the Wardens of the Goldsmiths' Mistery in the year 1368–69
42 [Edward III] [1368]:
Nicholas Twyford
John Walsh
John Waldene
Adam Mirfield

Memorandum that John Coraunt, having rendered account of all things, 1369
[was discharged] on St Barnabas the Apostle's day in the year 43 Edward III p. 35, col. 1
[11 June 1369] in the presence of the company of the Goldsmiths of all manner of actions in all ways.

The names of the receivers of the money:
William Burdeyn
John Thorne
The account of these two was finally made in the presence of the company of goldsmiths on St Barnabas the Apostle's day in the year 43 [Edward III] [11 June 1369]

Memorandum that John Coraunt rendered account on St Dunstan's Day 43 1369
Edward III [19 May 1369] of all things to the Goldsmiths according to the tenour of a document placed in the common chest.

1368 Burneh*am*:

col. 2 Fait a remembr*er* q*e* Thomas Burneh*am* treia son cotel en l'asemblé del orphev*er*ie q*e* fust le vi jo*ur* d'August l'an xlii *et* auprés il soit mys en la g*ra*ce des gardeinz *et* orphev*er*es *et* il gagea amendes de xx toneux de vin, *et* fuist p*ar*doné le dit vin *et* jugger*ont* a lo*ur* g*ra*ce iiii li., q*ue*ux iiii li. furont baillez as ditz gardeinz *et* p*ar* la co*mun*e assemblé ordeiné fust q*e* les ditz gardeins *et* iiii gentz a eux associ*ez* devont p*re*ndr*e* et jugger ceo q*e* deit estre pris *et* fait des ditz iiii li.

Reynh*am*:

It*em*, auprés as div*er*s assemblez Thomas Reynh*am*, orphev*er*e, vient as ditz gardeinz *et* as bonz gentz de mesme le mestier *et* eaux s*ur*metta q'ils firont tort *et* encontre resou*n* *et* eaux cont*ra*ria p*ar* malveis p*ar*oles *et* cont*ra*rious, *et* dist q'eux ne deivont rien p*re*ndre de dit Thomas Burneh*am* *et* fust desobeisant as ditz gardeinz *et* fist a[83] cont*ra*rie des pointz dont il fust juré adevant *et* mist g*ra*nt delat torcinousment, et auprés il fust somons en l'arches p*ur* ceo q'il fist a cont*ra*rie des pointz dont il fust juré *et* de son s*er*ment; et auprés al co*mun*e assemblé le ix jo*ur* de Nov*embre* l'an xlii, le dit Thomas Reynh*am* humblement p*ur* sa cont*ra*rioustè, torcinous meintenance, *et* p*ur* ceo q'il fist a cont*ra*rie de son s*er*ment, il soi myst humblement en g*ra*ce des gardeinz *et* des bonz gentz del orphev*er*ie p*ar* qi agardé fust p*ar* la dit assemblé q'il paiast le pein q*e* fust ordeiné a devant p*ur* sa cont*ra*rioustè *et* meintenance, quel pein est d*emi* m*arc*.

Burneh*am*:

It*em*, a mesme le jo*ur* q*ua*nt le dit Thomas Reynh*am* soi avoit mys en g*ra*ce, fust agardé p*ar* les bonz gentz de mesme le mest*ier* q*e* iii li. furont rebaillé a lui s*ur* son bon porte, issint si ascun defaut soit trové en lui aup*rés* ses houres qe les ditz iii li. dussont estre levez de lui al oeps del almoign*e* de S. Dunston *et* plus si le q*ua*ntité de t*re*spas le demand, *et* les xx s. en meinz des gardeinz al almoign*e* susdit.

It*em*, fait a remembr*er* q*e* Joh*a*n de Welb*ur*ne vient as ditz gardeinz p*ur* estr*e* enf*ra*nchisé *et* fust g*ra*nté a tiel entent q'il dust ven*ir* *et* av*er* son shop*e* en Chep*e* come custume est des orphev*er*es *et* s'il ne fist mye ou s'il vient en Chep*e* et aup*rés* myst sa dem*ur*e aill*ours*, il paieroit al almoign*e* de S. Dunston xl s. *et* de ceo il affia p*ar* mons*ieur* Joh*a*n Walssh*e* d'y estre al dit ordeinance *et* aup*rés* il vient en Chep*e* *et* fist sa dem*ur*e illoq*es* p*ar* i quart*er* del an *et* aup*rés* . . .[84]

[83] MS: a a.

[84] The text breaks off here.

Burnham: 1368
Memorandum that Thomas Burnham drew his knife in the assembly of the Goldsmiths' Mistery held on 6 August 1368, and afterwards he submitted himself to the judgment of the wardens and goldsmiths, and he pledged amends of 20 tuns of wine, and this was remitted and they decided to sentence him to a fine of £4, which £4 were handed over to the said wardens and it was ordained by the common assembly that the said wardens and 4 men associated with them should take and decide what should be taken and done with the said £4. col. 2

Raynham:
Item, afterwards at various assemblies Thomas Raynham, goldsmith, came to the said wardens and to the goodmen of the same mistery and accused them that they had done wrong and acted unreasonably, and he spoke against them in evil and contrarious words, and said that they should take nothing from the said Thomas Burnham, and he was disobedient to the said wardens and went against the ordinances to which he had previously been sworn, and he wrongfully made a great denouncement, and afterwards he was summoned to the Court of Arches because he had gone against the ordinances to which he had been sworn and against his oath, and afterwards at the common assembly on 9 November 1368 the said Thomas Raynham humbly for his recalcitrance, his wrongful maintenance[51] and because he had gone against his oath, he humbly submitted himself to the judgment of the wardens and goodmen of the Goldsmiths' Mistery, by whom the judgment was awarded at the said assembly that he should pay the penalty which had been ordained previously for his recalcitrance and his maintenance, which penalty is half a mark.

Burnham:
Item, on the same day that the said Thomas Raynham had submitted himself to judgment, it was judged by the goodmen of the same mistery that £3 should be returned to him [Burnham] on [promise of] his good behaviour, on condition that if any fault were to be found in him hereafter then the said £3 should be levied from him for the use of the alms funds of St Dunstan, and even more if the gravity of the offence demanded it, and the 20s. that are in the hands of the wardens should be given to the aforesaid alms funds.

Item, memorandum that John de Welbourne came to the said wardens to be enfranchised and this was granted on the understanding that he should come and have his shop in Cheap as is the custom of goldsmiths, and that if he did not do this, or if he came to Cheap and afterwards moved his home elsewhere, then he would pay 40s. to the alms funds of St Dunstan, and he gave John Walsh as surety promising to keep the said ordinance; and afterwards he came to Cheap and made his home there for a quarter of a year, and afterwards . . .

[51] For the legal sense of 'maintenance' see *OED* sub MAINTENANCE, meaning 6: 'The action of wrongfully aiding and abetting litigation; *spec.* sustentation of a suit or suitor at law by a party who has no interest in the proceedings or who acts from any improper motive.'

1368 Pena p*ro* vendic*ion*e op*er*is aurifabr*ie*:

p. 36, col. 1 Fait a remanbr*er* q*e* Joh*ann*is Chapler, orphev*er*e, il porta c*er*teinz choses d'argent a vendr*e* a Cornhull*e* *et* fust usaité a ceo faire, *et* les gardeinz lui aresoner*ont* de mesme la chose *et* disoient q'il fyst encont*r*e les custumes *et* ordenantz de lo*ur* mest*ier* *et* le dit Joh*a*n disoit q'il voleit feare maugré lo*ur* *et* p*ar*la malveis p*ar*oles *et* maliciouses a eaux *et* fust desobeisant *et* rebel as ditez gardeinz p*ur* q*ue*i il fust mesné a Neugate *et* aup*ré*s viendr*ont* Rob*er*t Launde *et* Joh*a*n Shordich*e*, orphev*er*es, le mekerdy dev*a*[*n*]t Touz Seintz *et* emp*r*istront p*ur* le dit Joh*a*n Chapler de sa bon porte v*er*s les ditz gardeins, p*ar* q*ue*i il fust pris hors de Neugate *et* le dit Joh*a*n Chapler aup*ré*s sa deliv*er*ance est lié a eux p*ar* .i. obligacioun en xl s. p*ur* sa bon porte *et* s'il face ascun t*r*espas ou surfet touchant le dit mest*ier* ou ne soit mye de bon port,[85] les xl s. s*er*ont levez *et* les p*ar*oles del oblig*acioun* ensuont:

1368 Nov*er*int univ*er*si p*er* p*re*sent*es* me Joh*ann*em Chapler aurifabr*um* London' teneri *et* p*er* p*re*sens sc*r*iptum firmit*er* oblig*atum* Nich*ola*o Twyford *et* Joh*ann*i Walden*e*, Joh*ann*i Walssh*e* *et* Ade Mirfeld, civib*us* *et* aur*ifabris* London', in quad*raginta* solid*os* st*er*lingor*um* solvend*os* eisdem Nich*ola*o, Joh*ann*i Walden*e*, Joh*ann*i Walssh*e* *et* Ade ad festu*m* *Sancti* Andr*ee* ap*ost*oli p*roximum* futur*um* post dat*um* p*re*senciu*m* apud London' in Westchepe London', ad q*ua*mquid soluc*ion*em bene *et* fidelit*er* faciend*um* obligo me, her*edes* *et* execut*ores* meos ac om*n*ia bona mea mobilia *et* immobilia p*er* p*re*sent*es*. In cui*us* rei testi*moni*um p*re*sentib*us* sigillu*m* meu*m* apposui. Dat*um* London' die d*omi*nica p*roxima* ante f*estu*m O*mni*um S*anct*or*um* A*nn*o regni Reg*is* Edwardi t*er*cii post conquest*um* xlii.

1368 Hic est ordinac*io* p*ro* apprentic*iis*

col. 2 Al assemblé tenuz al co*m*une assemblé des orphev*er*es le vendredy aup*ré*s le feste de Seint Matheu l'an du regne le Roi E*dward* t*er*ce puis le conquest xlii – Acordé est, ordeiné *et* assentu p*ar* les gardeinz *et* les bonz gentz de la confrat*er*nité des orphev*er*es de Londr*es* q*e* si ascun app*r*entiz des orphev*er*es achate son t*er*me ou p*ar*cel d'ycele de sa p*r*enticiaulté, ou si son mestre lui p*ar*doygn*e* son t*er*me ou relesse a lui, ou si nul chose avigne p*ar* q*ue*i il s*er*roit deschargee de sa app*r*enticiauté deinz son t*er*me, Nep*ur*qant il dem*ur*a lowys atant de temps q'il dust av*er* estee app*r*entiz *et* tanqe tut son t*er*me soit p*ar*empli, et il ne tendra nul shope ne s*er*ra mye enf*ra*nché durant le dit t*er*me, ne il fra nul ov*er*age en chambres n'en aut*r*es privez placez deinz la citee n'en muscet, mes come lowys d'ascuny q*e* soit frank ho*m*me de mesme le mest*ier*, si issint ne soit qe p*ar* assent des gardeinz *et* quatre bonz gentz de mesme le mest*ier* associé as ditz gardeinz *et* lui q'il donne de sa bon gree un c*er*tein so*m*me de monee solom ceo q'ils p*ur*roit acorder al almoigne de Seinte Dunston en eide de sustenance des pov*er*es de mesme le mest*ier* *et* en eide d'allowance des chapleins a chant*er* p*ur* les almes de la confrat*er*nité des orphev*er*es et auxint q'il soit able de p*er*sone et des bienz.

[85] The word 'il' is written but scored out.

Penalty for the sale of goldsmithry work: 1368
Memorandum that John Chapler, goldsmith, took certain silver things to sell p. 36, col. 1
on Cornhill and he was in the habit of doing this, and the wardens spoke to him about this and told him that he was acting against the customs and ordinances of their mistery, and the said John said that he wished to carry on in spite of them, and he spoke evil and malicious words to them and was disobedient and rebellious against the said wardens, for which reason he was taken to Newgate; and afterwards Robert Launde and John Shoreditch, goldsmiths, came on the Wednesday before All Saints'Day [25 October 1368] and mainprized the said John Chapler vouching for his good conduct towards the said wardens, and hence he was taken out of Newgate, and after his release the said John Chapler was bound to them by an obligation in the sum of 40s. for his good conduct,and if he should commit any offence or insolence concerning the said mistery or should not be of good conduct, then the 40s. shall be levied, and the words of the obligation follow:

May all know by these present letters that I, John Chapler, goldsmith of 1368
London, am bound and by this present document am firmly obliged to Nicholas Twyford and John Waldene, John Walsh and Adam Mirfield, citizens and goldsmiths of London, in the sum of 40s. sterling to be paid to the same Nicholas, John Walden, John Walshe and Adam at the Feast of St Andrew the apostle [30 November] next following the date of these present letters in London, in West Cheap, London. To make payment of the same well and faithfully I bind myself, my heirs and my executors, and all my movable and immovable goods by these present letters. In witness of which I have affixed my seal to the present letters. Given in London on the Sunday preceding the Feast of All Saints in the year 42 Edward III [29 October 1368]

This is an ordinance for apprentices: 1368
At the meeting held at the common assembly of the goldsmiths on the Friday col. 2
after the feastday of St Matthew in the year 42 Edward III [22 September 1368] – it was determined, ordained and agreed by the wardens and the goodmen of the Goldsmiths' Fraternity of London that if any goldsmith's apprentice buys out his apprenticeship terms or part of them, or if his master releases him from his terms or remits them to him, or if anything happens which results in his being discharged from his apprenticeship before the expiry of his terms, nevertheless, he shall remain a serving-man for as long a time as he should have been an apprentice and until the whole period of his terms is fulfilled, and he shall not keep a shop nor shall he be enfranchised during the said period, nor shall he work in chambers nor in other private places within the city nor in secret, but shall work as the serving-man of some freeman of the same mistery, unless it shall be by the assent of the wardens and of four goodmen of the same mistery associated with the said wardens, and that he should of his own good will give a certain sum of money, according to what they may determine, to the alms funds of St Dunstan to be used for help in the sustenance of the poor of the same mistery and help in what is paid to chaplains to sing for the souls of the goldsmiths' fraternity; and he must also be able both in person and in goods.

It*e*m, acordé est *et* assentu q*e* si ascun est*ra*nge vigne deinz la citee de Londres q*e* soit de mesme le mest*ier* a dem*ur*er illoqes, q'il dem*ur*a lowys p*ar* sept anz *et* q'il ne tendra mye nul shope ne il s*er*ra mye enf*ra*nchisé durant les sept anz, ne fra nul ov*er*age aut*re*ment mes come avant est dit des app*re*ntiz, si issint ne soit q'il face en mesme le man*ere* come avant est dit des app*re*ntiz.

Ceux sont les nons des orphev*er*es q*ue*ux sont jureez de ten*ir* les bonz pointz *et* ordenantz de mesme le mest*ier*:[86]

Joh*a*n Chichestre
Joh*a*n Norwich*e*
Joh*a*n Corant
Nichol Twyford
Rob*er*t Laund
Joh*a*n Gravele
Thomas Reynh*a*m
William Tyngewyk
Rob*er*t Oxenford
Joh*a*n Walssh*e*
Joh*a*n Fairher
Henr*i* Markeby
Ric*hard* Westou*n*
James de Tame
Rob*er*t Fraunceys
William Stameldene*e*
Barth*olome*us de Castre
Will*elmu*s Fraunceys
Will*elmu*s Ippegr*a*ve
Joh*a*n Walden*e*
Ric*ard*us Arnold
Joh*anne*s Broun
Rob*er*tus Lucas
Galfr*id*us Walpol
Joh*a*n Brugges
Adam Mirfeld
Will*elmu*s Burden*e*
Thomas Bygod
Simon Mazerer
Will*elmu*s Som*er*vill*e*
Adam Bamme
Joh*anne*s Som*er*vill*e*
Joh*anne*s Langrich*e*
Joh*anne*s Veel
Joh*anne*s Forst*er*
Rob*er*tus Gildeford
Thomas Wilby
Joh*anne*s Fraunceys

[86] For discussion of the importance of this entry see Reddaway and Walker, p. 34 and p. 58, n. 61.

Item, it is determined and agreed that if any foreigner who is of the same craft come to the city of London to live there, that he shall remain a serving-man for seven years and that he shall not keep a shop nor be enfranchised during the seven years, nor shall he do any work in any other way than has been said above about apprentices, unless it be that he act in the same way as is said above about apprentices.

These are the names of the goldsmiths who have sworn to keep the good rules and ordinances of the same mistery:
John Chichester
John Norwich
John Coraunt
Nicholas Twyford
Robert Launde
John Gravele
Thomas Raynham
William Tingewick
Robert Oxenford
John Walsh
John Fairher
Henry Markeby
Richard Westoun
James de Thame
Robert Fraunceys
William Stameldene
Bartholomew de Castre
William Fraunceys
William Ippegrave
John Waldene
Richard Arnold
John Broun
Robert Lucas
Geoffrey Walpole
John Bruges
Adam Mirfield
William Burden
Thomas Bygod
Simon Mazerer
William Somerville
Adam Bamme
John Somerville
John Langriche
John Veel
John Forster
Robert Guildford
Thomas Wilby
John Fraunceys

Joh*ann*es Litegr*a*ve
Joh*ann*es Cappe
p. 37, col. 1 Joh*ann*es Thorn*e*
Will*elmu*s Thakstede
Will*elmu*s Gaytou*n*
Joh*ann*es Shordich*e*
Simon atte Wode
Ric*ard*us Burneh*a*m
Joh*ann*es Lincoln*e*
Nich*ola*s Cove
Joh*ann*es Wynd
Steph*an*us de Thorp*e*
Thomas Pantou*n*
Thomas Salesbury
Thomas Extou*n*
Thomas Burneh*a*m
Rob*er*tus Teukesbury
Will*elmu*s Davy
Joh*ann*es Crulling*e*
Edwardus Brountoun
Hamo Chose
Joh*ann*es Salesbury, mazerer
Joh*ann*es Okyng
Ric*ardus* Brenchesle
Joh*ann*es Payn
Henr*icus* Abbot
Will*elmu*s atte Forth*e*
Will*elmu*s Fichet
Will*elmu*s Glasene
Will*elmu*s Selgr*a*vere
Rad*olf*us Lynne
Ric*ard*us Childern*e*
Rob*er*tus Godeman
Petrus Mazerer
Ed*ward*us Forst*er*
Joh*ann*es Botesh*a*m
Ric*ard*us Payn
Andreas Croidou*n*
Will*elmu*s Bartholomeu
Thomas Davy
Galfr*id*us Wynch*e*
Andre*as* Grauntcourt
Ric*ardus* Fraunceys
Will*elmu*s Shordich*e*
Ric*ard*us Bettaign*e*
Joh*ann*es Welb*u*rne
Will*elmu*s Garston*e*
Joh*ann*es Ippegr*a*ve
Thomas Curteys

John Litegrave
John Cappe
John Thorne p. 37, col. 1
William Thaxted
William Gayton
John Shoreditch
Simon atte Wood
Richard Burnham
John Lincoln
Nicholas Cove
John Wynd
Stephen de Thorpe
Thomas Pantoun
Thomas Salisbury
Thomas Exton
Thomas Burnham
Robert Tewkesbury
William Davy
John Crullinge
Edward Brountoun
Hamo Chose
John Salisbury, mazerer
John Okyng
Richard Brinchisle
John Payn
Henry Abbot
William atte Forde
William Fichet
William Glasene
William Sealgraver
Ralph Lynne
Richard Childerne
Robert Godman
Peter Mazerer
Edward Forster
John Bottisham
Richard Payn
Andrew Croydon
William Bartholomew
Thomas Davy
Geoffrey Wynche
Andrew Grauntcourt
Richard Fraunceys
William Shoreditch
Richard Beteigne
John Welbourne
William Garston
John Ippegrave
Thomas Curteys

Johannes Welford
col. 2 Adam de Thorpe
Thomas Hornetoft
Simon Wynter
Johannes Becheswor the
Arnaldus Ercedekene
Thomas Mirfeld
Johannes atte Mount
Robertus Otyngtoun
Ricardus Lincolne
Johannes Halling
Ricardus Punchard
Thomas Chendoun
Johannes Eelman
Willelmus Marny
Walterus Andreu
Johannes Wallingford
Ricardus Jueler
Robertus Godestone
Willelmus Tiryngham
Thomas Tidderle
Thomas Wynter
Johannes Canoun
Rogerus Malpas
Willelmus Wirhale
Johannes Assheburne
Johannes Lutoun
Robertus Burghe
Robertus Holme
Johannes Salesbury
Johannes Trentmarz
Willelmus de Billingesgate
Robertus, prentyz del vyconte[87]
Ricardus atte Water
Johannes Carbonelle
Walterus Deynes
Thomas Polle
Johannes Chapler
Johannes Bartoun
Nicholas Derneford
Ricardus Hungry
Henricus Croidoun
Thomas de Kent
Johannes Broun, mazerer

[87] The two sheriffs in this year were Adam Wymondham and Robert Gurdelere, neither of whom was a goldsmith. The most likely candidate is James de Thame, sheriff 1361–62.

John Welford
Adam de Thorpe col. 2
Thomas Horntoft
Simon Wynter
John Bechesworthe
Arnold Ercedekene[52]
Thomas Mirfield
John atte Mount
Robert Otyngtoun
Richard Lincoln
John Halling
Richard Punchard
Thomas Chendoun
John Eelman
William Marny
Walter Andrew
John Wallingford
Richard Jeweler
Robert Godestone
William Tiryngham
Thomas Tidderle
Thomas Wynter
John Canoun
Roger Malpas
William Wirral
John Ashbourne
John Luton
Robert Burgh
Robert Holme
John Salisbury
John Trentemas
William de Billingsgate
Robert, apprentice of the sheriff
Richard atte Water
John Carbonelle
Walter Deynes
Thomas Polle
John Chapler
John Barton
Nicholas Dornford
Richard Hungry
Henry Croydon
Thomas de Kent
John Broun, mazerer

[52] Or 'Archdeacon'. This is the only reference to this man and one suspects that he is being referred to by his position not his surname, although one cannot be sure. As archdeacon, he might for instance be associated with the fraternity of St Dunstan, rather than himself being a working goldsmith, and an archdeacon might well have responsibilities regarding church plate and ornaments.

Joh*ann*es Sanguynel
Will*elmu*s Ferro*ur*
Joh*ann*es Adam
Joh*ann*es Osbern*e*

1369–70 p. 38, col. 1 Ceux sont les nouns des gardeinz del orphev*er*ie l'an xliii:
William Tyngewyk
Rob*er*tus Oxenford
Rob*er*tus Fraunceys
William Stameldene*e*

Les despence*s* des ditz gardeinz:
En primes, p*ur* soner le *gr*ant sonel de Seint Poul *et* p*ur* la lym*er*e al eglise de S. Joh*a*n Zakarie – xxv s. vi d.

Les ditz gardeinz despenderont le jo*ur* de Seint Dunstou*n* en lo*ur* feste – xxii li. viii s. ix d.
It*em*, le vest*ur*e p*ur* i chaplein – xxii s. iii d.
It*em*, p*ur* le vesture de ii brokours – xiii s. iiii d.

Ceux sont les pov*er*es gentz q*ue*ux sont entreez ceste an:
Petrus Mazerer
Rad*olf*us Makenhenid

Ceux sont les app*re*ntiz entrez ceste an:

Joh*a*n Ely app*re*ntiz de Steph*a*n Thorp*e* –	ii s.
Ed*mund*us[88] Kykely app*rent*iz de Adam Bamme –	ii s.
Martinus Brenlee app*rent*iz de Joh*a*n Fairher –	ii s.
Will*elmu*s Kendale app*rent*iz de Thom*as* Wilby –	ii s.
Robertus	
Thomas Daltou*n* app*rent*iz Joh*a*n Gravele –	ii s.
Joh*ann*es Appelby app*rent*iz Joh*ann*is Walssh*e* –	ii s.
Joh*ann*es Andreu app*rent*iz Henr*ici* Markeby –	ii s.
Will*elmu*s Tiryngham app*rent*iz Joh*ann*is Walden*e* –	ii s.
Nich*ola*s del Grene app*rent*iz Barth*olome*i Castre –	ii s.
Joh*ann*es Bray app*rent*iz Petri Hiltoft –	ii s.
Joh*ann*es Malev*er*er app*rent*iz Thome Burtou*n* –	ii s.
Joh*ann*es Bartou*n* app*rent*iz Joh*ann*is Bodesh*a*m –	ii s.
Ric*ard*us Merden*e* app*rent*iz Johanne Hassdy – [89]	
Joh*ann*es Pant*er* app*rent*iz Joh*ann*is Pieres –	ii s.
Joh*ann*es Clerk app*rent*iz Thome Bygood –	ii s.
Joh*ann*es Orpyk app*rent*iz Thome Tilderle –	ii s.
Joh*ann*es Hamondesham app*rent*iz Will*elm*i Ippeg*r*ave – [90]	

[88] Or 'Ed*ward*us' – he does not appear again in the register.
[89] No sum entered
[90] No sum entered, and no fee may have been paid because of the family relationship mentioned later when this apprentice caused trouble in 1372–73; see below A + a, p. 48 col. 2.

John Sanguynel
William Ferrour
John Adam
John Osborne

These are the names of the Wardens of the Goldsmiths' Mistery in the year 43 [Edward III] [1369]: 1369–70 p. 38, col. 1
William Tingewick
Robert Oxenford
Robert Fraunceys
William Stameldene

The expenses of the said wardens:
Firstly, for ringing the great bell of St Paul's and for the light at the church of St John Zachary – 25s. 6d.

The said wardens spent on their feast on St Dunstan's day – £22 8s. 9d.
Item, the clothing[53] for a chaplain – 22s. 3d.
Item, the clothing for 2 brokers – 13s. 4d.

These are the poor people who have been entered this year [have started to receive regular alms payments]:
Peter Mazerer
Ralph Makenhened

These are the names of apprentices entered this year:

John Ely apprentice of Stephen Thorpe –	2s.
Edmund Kykely, apprentice of Adam Bamme –	2s.
Martin Brenlee, apprentice of John Fairher –	2s.
William Kendal, apprentice of Thomas Wilby –	2s.
Robert	
Thomas Dalton, apprentice of John Gravele –	2s.
John Appleby, apprentice of John Walshe –	2s.
John Andrew, apprentice of Henry Markeby –	2s.
William Tiryngham, apprentice of John Walden –	2s.
Nicholas del Grene, apprentice of Bartholomew Castre –	2s.
John Bray, apprentice of Piers Hiltoft –	2s.
John Maleverer, apprentice of Thomas Burtoun –	2s.
John Barton, apprentice of John Bottisham –	2s.
Richard Merdene, apprentice of John Hassdy	
John Panter, apprentice of John Pieres –	2s.
John Clerk, apprentice of Thomas Bygod –	2s.
John Orpyk, apprentice of Thomas Tilderle –	2s.
John Agmodesham, apprentice of William Ippegrave –	

[53] The clothing listed here for the chaplain and the brokers may very possibly have been issued in the livery colour of the mistery, and to have been worn at the feast.

Remundus Standelf app*r*ent*iz* Thome Tetteswych*e* – ii s.
Ric*ard*us Payn app*r*ent*iz* Rob*er*ti Oxenford – ii s.

p. 38, col. 2 Fait a remembr*er* q*e* les ditz gardeinz paier*ont* as gentz de ley *et* a lo*ur* conseil al Guyhalle *et* as gentz de lo*ur* conseil de ley cristyene, en tut p*ur* le suite encont*r*e Thomas Berch*e*, tutz choses acomptez: – xliii s. iiii d.[91]

Fait a remembr*er* q*e* i. debat fust ent*r*e Joh*a*n Bodesh*a*m *et* Nichol Dorneford le jo*ur* de S. Dunston drein passé *et* le dit Nichol fust trové en defaut *et* dona al almoign*e* de S. Dunston – x s.

Ceux sont les nons q*ue*ux sont entreez en le f*r*anchis*e*:

Adeprimes Joh*a*n Carbonel p*ur* son entr*é* –	v m*a*rz
It*em*, en temps de dreinz gardeinz –	v marz
It*em*, de Thomas Tilderle –	iiii m*a*rz
It*em*, Joh*a*n Canou*n* –	xiii s. iiii d.
It*em*, Thomas atte Noke –	d*em*i m*a*rk
It*em*, Michel Bursiham*e* –	i m*a*rk
It*em*, Joh*a*n Lutou*n* –	i m*a*rk
It*em*, Joh*a*n Beech*e* –	xl d.
It*em*, Rob*er*tus Lucas –	i m*a*rk
It*em*, Flurkyn de Florence –	ii m*a*rz
It*em*, Steph*a*nus de Thorp*e* –	d*em*i m*a*rk
Joh*ann*es de Lincoln*e* –	xx s.

Fait a remembr*er* q*e* les ditz gardeinz doner*ont* le jo*ur* de Seint Dunston al encrees del almoign*e* – x li.
It*em*, des dettou*rs* dont ils ont deliv*er*é gages – xlii [s.] iiii d.
out*r*e les app*r*entiz *et* issanz q*ue*ux paier*ont* devant le confrat*er*nité des orfev*er*es

Ceux sont les nons [des] issantz hors de lo*ur* t*er*me:
Will*elmu*s Grantham
Joh*ann*es Harygtou*n*
Joh*ann*es Covele – ii s.[92]
Thomas Genge
Thomas atte Hay

Fait a remembr*er* q*e* Joh*a*n Rutou*n* fist i. debat ent*r*e le compaignie a Skynneres Well*e* le jour de S. Dunston, p*ur* quel debat les gardeinz lui empleder*ont et* fust mys en prisou*n et* les costages amont*ent* en tut p*ur* le dit plee – xxii s. vi d.

It*em*, le dit Joh*a*n dona al almoign*e* de Seint Dunston ii m*a*rz.

p. 39, col. 1 Fait a remembr*er* q*e* al feste del Nativité de Seint Joh*a*n Baptiste en mesme l'an, en le hon*ur* de Dieu, de Seint Dunstou*n et* en p*r*ofit de roialme *et* del

[91] Thomas Berche or Birch was a jeweller. See *CPR Edward III, 1370–74*, p. 462.
[92] His is the only name with a sum paid beside it.

Raymund Standelf, apprentice of Thomas Tetteswyche – 2s.
Richard Payn, apprentice of Robert Oxenford – 2s.

Memorandum that the said wardens paid to the lawyers and to their counsel at the Guildhall, and to their canon law counsel, in all for the suit against Thomas Berche, all things reckoned – 43s. 4d. p. 38, col. 2

Memorandum that a dispute arose between John Bottisham and Nicholas Dornford last St Dunstan's Day, and the said Nicholas was found at fault and gave to the alms funds of St Dunstan – 10s.

These are the names of those who have been entered into the freedom:
Firstly, John Carbonelle for his entry – 5 marks
Item, during the term of office of the last wardens – 5 marks
Item, from Thomas Tilderle – 4 marks
Item, John Canoun – 13s. 4d.
Item, Thomas atte Noke – ½ mark.
Item, Michael Bursiham – 1 mark.
Item, John Luton – 1 mark.
Item, John Beech – 40d.
Item, Robert Lucas – 1 mark.
Item, Flurkyn de Florence – 2 marks.
Item, Stephen de Thorpe – ½ mark.
John de Lincoln – 20s.

Memorandum that the said wardens gave on St Dunstan's Day to the increase of the alms funds – £10
Item, from debtors whose pledges they have handed over – 42s. 4d.
besides the apprentices and those coming out of their terms which monies they paid out in the presence of the Goldsmiths' fraternity

These are the names of those coming out of their terms:
William Grantham
John Harygtoun
John Covele – 2s.
Thomas Genge
Thomas atte Hay

Memorandum that John Rutoun caused a dispute among the company at Skinners' Well on St Dunstan's Day, for which dispute the wardens impleaded him and he was imprisoned, and the costs of the said plea amount in all to – 22s. 6d.

Item, the said John gave to the alms funds of St Dunstan – 2 marks

Memorandum that on the feast of the Nativity of St John in the same year p. 39, col. 1
[24 June 1369], in the honour of God and of St Dunstan and to the benefit of

amendement de dit mestier, les ditz gardeinz aleront de jour en autre de shope en shope par tut la citee de Londres entre les overours del orpheverie et deliveront le touche de lour mestier d'or et d'argent, et chargeront les gentz de lour mestier sur lour serment q'ils avoient fait a lour mestre et loialté, q'eles ne overont argent pir qe la moné,[93] ne or pir qe la touche de Paris,[94] et q'ils tendront bien et loialment les estatutz, ordenancez et establisementz, et q'ils serront obeisantz et eidantz as toutz chosez ordeinez en profit de dit mestier.

Fait a remembrer qe Thomas Davy fust trové en defaute par les ditz gardeinz et autres bonz gentz de la mestier pur ceo q'il allowast William Tyngewyk hors de son shope encontre les ordenancz faitz d'ancien temps[95] par comune assent de dit mestier, par quei il fust ordeiné par les ditz gardeinz et autres bonz gentz de mesme le mestier q'il paieroit al almoigne de Seint Dunstoun vi s. viii d.[96]

Item, fait a remembrer qe Wauter Deymes, orphevere, fust trové en defaut de ii anels d'argent dorrez queux il avoit resu de un esquier estrange et l'esquier lui avoit bailé un noble en partie de paiement et l'avantdit Wauter lui contredisoit et dit q'il n'avoit bailé qe i groz d'argent et lui contraria par malveis paroles et le revers del responce le dit Wauter fust trové et prové devant les ditz gardeins et orpheveres, par quei comandé fust par les ditz gardeinz a deliverer les ditz anelz deinz certein temps ensemblement ou le noble; quel chose il ne fist point al jour lymyté, mes il taria le dit esquier de jour en autre, par quei fust ajuggé par comune assent des orpheveres q'il paiast al almoigne de S. Dunstoun demi marc.

Item, fait a remembrer qe Johan Trentemas fust trové en defaut devant les gardeinz pur ceo q'il et son apprentiz amesneront i charete de jour en autre continuelment a graunt esclandre et vilanie de dit mestier et auxint il comanda son dit apprentiz d'aler a Smethefeld pur chivacher des chivals preignant pur le chival i d. ou autrement il serroit batu et malment mys; et des cestz choses il fust trové coupable, par quei ajuggé fust par comune assent q'il paieroit al almoigne de S. Dunstoun demi mark et s'il soit trové auprés en ceste defaut ou en ascun autre qe soit en villanie ou damage de dit mestier et de ceo soit convit ou atteint, il paiera al dit almoigne xx s.

Fayt a remembrer qe les ditz gardeinz despenderont en ceste an, fesant et travailant en lour office par tut l'an, es tutz choses acomptez – xl s.

93 The sterling standard was of 11oz. 2dwt. in the pound Troy, and 18dwt. of alloy [92.5%]. See Forbes, *Hallmark*, pp. 15–18, 347.

94 The touch of Paris was at this time gold of the standard of 19.2 carats. See Forbes, *ibid.*

95 See below A + a, pp. 40–41.

96 See the Introduction, pp. xxxii–xxxiii.

the kingdom and to the improving of the said mistery, the said wardens went from day to day and from shop to shop throughout the city of London among all those working as goldsmiths and handed over to them their mistery's touch for gold and silver, and they enjoined those of their mistery upon the oath they had sworn to their master and upon their faith that they shall not work silver of a lower quality than the coinage nor gold of a lower quality than the touch of Paris, and that they shall keep well and faithfully the statutes, ordinances and regulations, and that they shall be obedient and shall help in all matters ordained to the benefit of the said mistery.

Memorandum that Thomas Davy was found at fault by the said wardens and other goodmen of the mistery, in that he evicted William Tingewick from his shop,[54] against the ordinances made in ancient times by common assent of the said mistery, for which cause it was ordained by the said wardens and other goodmen of the same mistery that he would pay to the alms funds of St Dunstan – 6s. 8d.

Item, memorandum that Walter Deynes, goldsmith, was found at fault in the matter of 2 silver-gilt rings that he had received from a foreign squire, and the squire had given him a noble as part payment[55] and the aforesaid Walter denied this and said that he had only given him a silver groat and he spoke insultingly to him, and the reverse of Walter's response was found true and proved before the said wardens and goldsmiths, for which reason it was ordered by the said wardens that he should hand over the said rings within a certain time and also the noble, which thing he did not do by the due day, but rather he kept putting off the said squire from one day to the next, for which reason sentence was passed by common consent of the goldsmiths that he should pay to the alms funds of St Dunstan – ½ mark.

Item, memorandum that John Trentemas was found at fault before the wardens in that he and his apprentice drove a cart around on this day and that and repeatedly, to the great discredit and disgrace of the said mistery, and also that he ordered his said apprentice to go to Smithfield and ride horses, taking 1d. per horse, [threatening that] otherwise [if he did not go] he would be beaten and ill-treated, and he was found guilty of these things, and thus sentence was passed by common assent that he should pay ½ mark to the alms funds of St Dunstan, and if he were afterwards to be found committing the same offence or any other which might bring disgrace or harm to the said mistery and if he were to be found guilty or convicted of it, then he shall pay to the said alms funds 20s.

Memorandum that the said wardens spent this year while carrying out and doing the work of their official functions during the whole year, all things reckoned up – 40s.

[54] See Introduction, pp. xxxii–xxxiii.
[55] i.e. for re-using the silver in the rings to make some other object(s).

col. 2 It*e*m, Gerard van Sweck, p*ur* ceo q'il fust trové en defaut de i. seint*ure* q'il avoit fait al Ducz de Lancastre d'or, *et* puis fust mandé a lui p*ur* remuer *et* enclower *sur* i. novel corps *et* les clowes furont soudez d'esteym, q*ue*ux choses furont en desclandr*e* de dit mest*ier*, p*ar* q*ue*i il obliga de sa volunté al dit compaignie de paier al almoign*e* de S. Dunstan d*em*i m*a*rk.

It*e*m, Bartholmeu de Caastre, orphev*ere*, p*ur* ceo q'il alast a i. feire[97] encont*r*e les ordenantz del mest*ier et* custumes, il fust ajuggé de paier – xiii s. iiii d.

It*e*m, Joh*a*n Betesh*a*m p*ur* ceo q'il ferrist Joh*a*n Beech son compaignou*n* dedeinz son shop*e et* de ceo il fust trové coupable, p*ur* q*ue*i fust ajuggé de paier al almoign*e* de S. Dunston d*em*i m*a*rk *et* de ceo fust p*ar*doné tanqe a xl d.

It*e*m, Will*iam* Horsman p*ur* ceo q'il desp*er*sona Joh*a*n Frаunceis, nadgairs son mestre, en villeinous p*ar*oles, *et* de ceo fust trové coupable p*ar* q*ue*i il soy [mist] en le g*ra*ce le dit Joh*a*n *et* lui gagea amendes de ii m*a*rz, *et* il ne volleit rien p*re*ndre a son oeps demesne mes l'assigna al almoign*e* de Seinte Dunston, p*ar* q*ue*i les gardeinz pristront de lui i. m*a*rk *et* le remenant p*ar*doner*ont*.

It*e*m, Joh*a*n Welb*ur*ne p*ur* ceo q'il alast a i. feire de Salesbury encont*re* les custumes *et* ordenantz del mest*ier,* il fust ajuggé de paier al almoign*e* de Seinte Dunstou*n* – x s.

Fait a remembr*er* q*e* le lundy ap*r*és le feste Seintz Symond *et* Jude,[98] Will*iam* Tyngewyk, Rob*er*t Fraunceys *et* Will*iam* Stameldene paier*ont* a ix mynystrales, c'est assav*oir* Joh*a*n Drake, Joh*a*n Wayte *et* Will*iam* Trumpeur *et* lo*ur* compaignou*ns* p*ur* lo*ur* chaprons ii aunz *et* d*em*i de motlé rouge – v s. ii d. It*e*m, de noir i aun et i q*ua*rt*er* – xl d. It*e*m, chescun de aux[99] avoit xl d. la so*m*me des ditz ix mynyst*ra*les – xxx s. It*e*m, p*ur* lo*ur* chivals vii s. viii d. It*e*m, p*ur* pensell*es* ii aunz de inde sendel de tripe – vi s. It*e*m, al peynto*ur* p*ur* son ov*er*e ii m*a*rz. It*e*m, p*ur* frenges iiii uncz *et* d*em*i – ix s. ix d.

S*um*m*a* total*is* – iiii li. viii s. vii d.

Et de ceo r*eceu* p*ar* les meinz Joh*a*n Broun de la compaignie en Chepe – xxxvii s. iiii d. It*e*m, r*eceu* en Fletstrete *et* a S. Joh*a*n Zakar*ie* – xliiii d. It*e*m, r*eceu* d'encrés des chaprons q*e* amont*e* out*r*e le quillet des petitz *et* des g*ra*ntz, en tut – xvii s. vi d.
S*um*m*a* – lviii s. vi d.

[97] The word 'marché' is scored out and 'feire' written above it.
[98] This dating indicates that the minstrels had been hired to ride with the goldsmiths in the Mayor's procession to Westminster to take his oath of office. See also below, A + b, p. 30 and note.
[99] The last two words written above the scored word 'Trumpour'.

Item, Gerard van Sweck, whereas he was found at fault over a girdle which he col. 2
had made for the Duke of Lancaster of gold, and it was then sent to him for alterations and to be attached with nails to a new corse, and the nails were soldered with tin, which was to the disgrace of the said mistery, and therefore he of his own free will bound himself to the company to pay to the alms funds of St Dunstan ½ mark.

Item, Bartholomew de Castre, goldsmith, whereas he went to a fair against the ordinances and customs of the mistery, he was sentenced to pay – 13s. 4d.

Item, John Bottisham, whereas he struck his companion John Beech inside his shop and was found guilty of this, for this reason he was sentenced to pay half a mark to the alms funds of St Dunstan, and of this all but 40d. was remitted.

Item, William Horsman, whereas he had slandered John Fraunceys, formerly his master, in vile words and was found guilty of this, for this reason he submitted himself to the judgment of the said John and pledged him amends of two marks, and he did not wish to take any of this for his own use but assigned it all to the alms funds of St Dunstan, and for this reason the wardens took from him one mark and remitted the remainder.

Item, John Welbourne, whereas he went to a fair in Salisbury against the customs and ordinances of the mistery, he was sentenced to pay to the alms funds of St Dunstan – 10s.

Memorandum that on the Monday after the Feast of St Simon and St Jude [29 October 1369], William Tingewick, Robert Fraunceys and William Stameldene paid to 9 minstrels, i.e. John Drake, John Wayte and William Trumpeter and their companions, for their hoods: 2½ ells of red motley – 5s. 2d. Item, 1¼ ells of black [cloth] – 40d. Item, each of them received 40d., total for the 9 minstrels – 30s. Item, for their horses 7s. 8d. Item, for pencels, 2 ells of blue mock-sendal[56] – 6s. Item, to the painter for his work – 2 marks. Item, for fringes – 4½ ounces – 9s. 9d.

Sum total: £4 8s. 7d.

And of this, received from the hands of John Broun, member of the company, in Cheap – 37s. 4d. Item, received in Fleet Street and at St John Zachary – 44d. Item, received from the profit on the hoods, which amounts, over and above the collection from both the great men [of the mistery] and those of lesser status, in all – 17s. 6d.
Total: 58s. 6d.

[56] See *OED* sub TRIPE² and SENDAL.

It*em*, les gardeinz doneront al compaignie al Novel Tav*er*ne le jo*ur* de S. Phillip *et* Jacob – xl d. *et* puis outre tant com les aut*re*s.

1370 *Ordinaciones*:[100]

p. 40, col. 1 Amelo*urs* et gravers:[101]

Al hono*ur* de Dieu *et* de Seinte Dunston al co*m*une assemblé d'orfeve*re*s l'an du regne le Roi E*dward* tierçz puis le conquest xliiii, ordeiné est *et* assentu qe toutz ameillo*urs* *et* taillo*ur*s des seals rendront a chescuny son pois d'or *et* d'argent solom lour pouwer, come aut*re*foith fust ordeiné en auncien temps, *et* si ascuny face le contrarie *et* de ceo soit ateint il paiera p*ur* chescun defaut d*em*i m*a*rk al almoign*e* de S. Dunston.

Burnisshers:

It*em*, ordeiné est *et* assentu p*ar* co*mun*e assent des orfeve*re*s p*ur* p*ro*fit de roialme qe nul burniso*ur* ho*m*me ne fe*m*me, ne delive*re* or n'argent hors de lour meinz avant q'il soit veu p*ar* les gardeinz del mest*ier*; *et* si ascuny le face il paiera al almoign*e* de S. Dunston d*em*i m*a*rk; auxint ordeiné est q*e* toutz yceaux qe cleiment d'y estre de dit mest*ier*[102] des burniso*urs* s*er*ront jurez devant les ditz gardeinz de cest*es* choses bien *et* loialment ten*ir* *et* faire.

Des detto*urs* – ad distringend[um]:[103]

It*em*, p*ur* ceo q*e* dive*rs* pleintes *et* clamo*ur*s sont faites des dive*rs* gentz d'orfeve*re*s q'ils deivont c*er*teinz dettes si bien as est*ra*nges come a lo*ur* compaignons de lo*ur* mest*ier*, en g*ra*nt esclandre et deshon*ur* de dit mest*ier*, ordeiné est *et* assentu p*ar* co*m*une assent des ditz orfeve*re*s q*e* si ascun des orfeve*re*s soiont endettez as estranges ou a lo*ur* compaignons, vigne celui a qi la dette est due *et* face sa pleinte as gardeinz des orfeve*re*s, *et* les ditz gardeinz examineront les p*ar*ties, *et* si trové soit q*e* la dette soit duwe, les ditz gardeinz front redresser q*e* la dite dette soit meintenant paié ou aut*re*ment lymit dit i. c*er*tein jo*ur* del paiement, *et* si la dette ne soit mye paié al jo*ur* assis, adonqes eiont les ditz gardeinz pouwer de p*re*ndre destresse des ditz orfeve*re*s q*e* sont dettours *et* de eaux constrendre de feare gree del paiement.

1370 Al co*m*une assemblé d'orphevres faites en temps des gardeinz avant nomez,
col. 2 sy est ordeiné *et* assentu q*e* cestz pointz q'ensuont q*ue*ux sont fait de plus eignié temps q*e* les aut*re*s s*er*roient entrez a durer en p*er*p[et]uel reme*m*b*ra*nce.[104]

[100] Written in the top LH margin as a heading to what follows. The later Book of Ordinances (Goldsmiths' MS 2524) contains many of the same ordinances as are found here, as well as reformulations and later additions. These have been presented by Lorna Walker in modern English translation in Reddaway and Walker, pp. 209–74, along with very informative comments in accompanying footnotes.

[101] This marginal note and those that follow, given here as sub-headings, were written later.

[102] Written then scored out after this word: 'dorfeve*re*s'.

[103] MS: ad distringendend.

[104] Another, later, copy of the ordinances that follow is found in the Register of Deeds, vol. I, f. 374. The scribe of this later copy clearly had some difficulties in reading his exemplar and has

Item, the wardens gave to the company at the New Inn on the feastday of St Philip and St James [1 May 1370] – 40d. and then over and above this the same amount as others.

Ordinances: 1370
Enamellers and engravers: p. 40, col. 1
To the honour of God and of St Dunstan, at the common assembly of goldsmiths in the year 44 Edward III [1370] it was ordained and agreed that all enamellers and engravers of seals shall return to each his weight of gold and silver as far as in their power lies, as it was previously ordained in ancient times, and if anyone should do the contrary and be convicted of this, he shall pay for each offence half a mark [6s. 8d.] to the alms funds of St Dunstan.

Burnishers:
Item, it was ordained and agreed by common assent of the goldsmiths for the benefit of the kingdom that no burnisher, man or woman, should deliver either gold or silver out of their hands until it has been seen by the wardens of the mistery, and if anyone should do this, he shall pay half a mark to the alms funds of St Dunstan, and it is also ordained that all those who claim to be of the said mistery of burnishers shall be sworn before the said wardens to do and to hold to these things well and faithfully.

Debtors – to be distrained:
Item, whereas various complaints and outcries have been made about various men of the goldsmiths' mistery, that they owe certain debts both to aliens and to their companions of their mistery, to the great discredit and dishonour of the said mistery, it is ordained and agreed by common assent of the said goldsmiths that if any goldsmith should be indebted to aliens or to their companions, he to whom the debt is owed should come and make his complaint to the wardens of the goldsmiths, and the said wardens shall examine the parties, and if it is found that the debt is due, the said wardens shall rectify matters so that the said debt should be paid at once or else a certain day for payment set, and if the debt be not paid on the day appointed, then the wardens shall have the power to take distress of the said goldsmiths who are debtors, and to constrain them to settle the payment.

At the common assembly of the goldsmiths held during the term of office of 1370
the aforenamed wardens, it was ordained and agreed that these regulations col. 2
which follow which were made in earlier times than the others should be entered [in the register] so that may endure in perpetual remembrance.

Les p*ro*deshom*m*es jurez p*ur* les estatutz del orfaverie de Londres diont p*ar* lo*ur* s*er*ement q*e* lé statutez soloient estre tieux:

De auro *et* argento ausi bon come la monee n*ost*re seign*ur* le Roy *et*c:
C'est assav*oir* q*e* le mestier soloit estre gardé p*ar* iiii p*ro*deshom*m*es esleus gardeinz de mester *et* jurez a sorver q*e* l'en ov*er*ast argent ausi bon come la monee n*ost*re seigno*ur* le Roi et nul peor mes meillo*ur*, *et* qe l'en ov*er*ast or del assay ou meillo*ur* *et* nul peiour,[105] *et* q*e* l'en asseist dreit piere en or, *et* nul faux. Et si issi fust q*e* or fust[106] trové en meyn d'orfev*er*e ou m*ar*chant q*e* ne vausist le assay, en fermaux ou en aneaux ou en aut*re*s choses, q'ils fussont debrusez[107] et p*er*desist son t*ra*vail del ov*er*aigne *et* amendast son or a son dreit.

De jocalib*us* et lapid*ibus* frangend*is*:
It*em*, si marchant est*ra*nge vensist *et* portast joeaux a vendr*e*, ils soloient estr*e* veus dé iiii p*ro*deshom*m*es gardeinz de mest*er* *et* d'aut*re*s de mest*er* que veissent q*e* la chose fust bon *et* loiale, issint q*e* les hautz[108] hom*m*es de la t*er*re n'aut*re*s ne fussent deceux. It*em*, si joeaux d'or fussont trovez ou faux perre, ils estoient debrusez *et* les pieres moluz en i morter, issi q'ils p*er*dront l'ov*er*aigne *et* les pieres *et* q*e* nul hom*m*e ap*ré*s feust enginé.

Div*erce* ordinac*iones* sequent*ur*:
It*em*, nul ne soloit overer en venels n'en muscettz mes toutz en le haut rue, q*e* l'em peust ver lo*ur* ov*er*aigne q*e* loialment le feissont. It*em*, q*e* nul ne receust hom*m*e en shope s'il ne vousist respondre p*ur* lui auxi bien a p*ri*vez come est*ra*ngez des choses qe hom*m*e lui baillast a overer; et qe latoun ne quivere ne feust overé d'orfev*er*e si ceo ne fust aournement de Seinte Eglise, ne dreit piere ne fust assis en latoun n'en quivere si n'estoit aux[i] aournement de Seinte Eglise. It*em* q*e* nul ne fortreisast ne alopast aut*ri* app*re*ntiz, sergant ne lowys q*e* del mest*er* fust *et* qi q*e* le fist *et* fust atteint q'il donast iiii s. al amoigne q'est

occasionally produced nonsense. His exemplar was not, from the evidence, the version in Book A + a but another copy. Some large passages of A + a are not found in the Register of Deeds copy, and there are some slight differences in word order and the order of ordinances, but the later scribe's difficulties may best account for these. A full collation of readings would therefore not be helpful, but all substantive differences (these amount only to a few differing readings) from the later copy are given as notes here as they may throw some light on the text. The most important point about the later copy is a fairly long extra passage. This occurs just after the point where the scribe of 1370 came to the end of p. 40, col. 2, and this may account for the omission in Book A + a, whether the scribe actually omitted the passage or whether it might have been on a separate sheet of paper now lost. However, the passage would seem rather to be an extra matter dealt with in 1370 partly by consulting old memories, and though it was recorded elsewhere, the earlier scribe of Book A + a may have deliberately chosen to omit it.

105 On all matters concerning the assay and the quality standards for gold and silver one should consult John Forbes, *Hallmark: A History of the London Assay Office* (London, 1999); on the required standard at this date see in particular pp. 15–18 and 347.

106 MS: q*e* or fust qe or fust. Reg. Deeds: q*e* or feut troue oeu*er*e en mayn . . .

107 Reg. Deeds: q*e* ils les feisent debroser.

108 Reg. Deeds: loiaux.

The goodmen sworn for [the purpose of] the statutes of the goldsmiths' mistery of London declare on oath that the statutes used to be as follows:

Gold and silver to be of the standard of the coinage of our Lord the King etc: i.e. that the mistery used to be governed by four goodmen elected as wardens of the mistery and sworn to oversee that silver was worked that was of as good a standard as the coinage of our Lord the King and none of a lesser standard but it might be better, and that gold was worked to the standard of the assay or better and none of a lower standard, and that one should set true gemstones in gold and no false ones. And if it should happen that gold be found[57] in the hands of a goldsmith or merchant that was not up to the assay standard, whether it be in brooches, rings or other objects, they should be broken up,[58] and he should lose his work in the piece, and he had to amend his gold and bring it up to the correct standard.

Jewels and stones to be broken up:
Item, if a foreign merchant should come bringing jewels [precious objects][59] to sell, these used to be looked at by the four goodmen wardens of the mistery and by others of the mistery who had to see that the object was good and true, so that neither the great men[60] of the land nor others might be deceived. Item, if jewels of gold were found with false gemstones, they were broken up and the stones ground in a mortar, so that they lost both the workmanship and the stones and so that no man might thereafter be tricked.

Various ordinances follow:
Item, no one used to work in alleyways nor in secret places, but rather everyone in the high street, so that one might see their work and that they were making it truly. Item, that no one should receive a man in his shop if he did not wish to answer for him both to citizens and to foreigners for that which the man might give him to work; and that latten and copper were not worked by goldsmiths unless it was for a church ornament; nor was a true gemstone set in latten or copper unless also it was a church ornament. Item, that no one should entice away or abduct the apprentice, servant or serving-man of another of the same mistery, and he who

57 Reg. Deeds: that gold be found worked . . .
58 Reg. Deeds: that they should have them broken up.
59 Throughout the medieval period, the word 'jewel' in all three of the languages used in Britain (Middle English, Latin and Anglo-Norman) had the sense of an ornamental piece, made of one of the precious metals and probably set with gemstones.
60 Reg. Deeds: the loyal/faithful men.

p*ur*veu a susten*ir* les pov*er*es *et* les malades de mest*er* *et* ceux q*e* sont cheus en age *et* ne se pount aider. It*em*, qe nul ne lowast aut*r*e hors de son shope *et* qi qe le fist *et* fust atteint q'il donast le tierz den*ier* de la so*m*me q*e* le lowage de la shope amont*er*eit en i an al amoigne avandit; et qe nul ne treisist marchant d'aut*r*i shope et q*i* q*e* le fist *et* feust atteint q'il donast xii d. al amoigne avandite. It*em*, q*e* nul ne resceust app*ren*tiz s'il ne feust fiz de frank ho*m*me ne a meindre t*er*me q*e* x anz s'il ne feust son parent ou q'il ust estee avant en le mest*er* *et* qi q*e* le fist *et* fust atteint q'il donast al amoigne avandit ii besanz *et* p*er*desist le vadlet. Et q*e* chescun app*ren*tiz qe entrast en le mest*er* donast al amoigne i. besant al entré *et* i. aut*r*e al issue.

It*em* q*e* nul forein n'est*ra*nge ne feust resceu en shope sanz congé de mester *et* s'il ne portast garant de son païs de bon conv*er*sacio*un* p*ur* g*ra*nt damages q*e* sont avenuz a mest*er* par teux, *et* qi le fist *et* fust atteint q'il donast d*em*i m*a*rk al amoigne avandit *et* feust l'estrange remué.
Et est assav*oir* que totes cest*es* choses soloiont ils user auxi bien en feires come en la citee de Londres pur foi *et* loiaulté meinten*ir* *et* fauxime destruire.

Reg. Deeds . . . *et* unt dyt les av*a*nt[ditz] jurrez q*e* cestes choses furent p*ur*veux *et* ordeignez:
f. 374r p*ur* ceo q*e* p*ar* feblesse, maladie, age, veillesse, *et* p*ar* chaunce de feu *et* de robbery *et* de p*er*te surve[n]aunt, ascuns del mistier q*e* p*ro*dho*m*mes avoient estee en pov*er*té cheierount dount ils ne poent resurdre saunz eyde, ascuns p*ro*dho*m*mes del mistier diviseront c*er*tein rente a la recov*er*aunce mettre de ceux q*a*nt mistier feust de nul tiel eyder. Et q*e* ceux iiii Gardeyns en la Citee avoyent de ceo la garde, le quel devys pryent a n*ost*re s*eignur* le roy q'il lour voil g*ra*untier *et* ceo qi devise a ceo est et desormés serrad si luy plest, kar cest oev*er*e de charité ferreient volunt*ier*s les bons gentz a Loundres si il veisen[t][109] q*e* le roy les vousist q*e* le chose fuist establié. Et en eyde de cell*e* susten*a*nce g*ra*untier si luy plest les peynes av*a*ntditz come de argent asseus p*ur* tielx t*re*spacis.

1370 Al co*m*une assemblé d'orphevres de Loundres de la confrat*er*nité de Seinte
A + a [Dunston] faite l'an du regne le Roi Edward t*er*ce puis le conquest
p. 41, col. 1 d'Engl[e]t*err*e quarant quart, fust ordeiné *et* assentu q*e* les pointz *et* ordeinantz faitez en auncien temps p*ar* co*mun*e assent des orphev*er*es faitz adonq*es* s*er*roient entreez en ceste paper a durer en remembrance p*er*petuelment, quels pointz *et* ordeinantz ensuont en ceste forme:

[109] MS: veisens.

did this and was convicted of it, he should give 4s. to the alms funds set up for the sustenance of the poor and sick of the mistery and those who are old and cannot provide for themselves. Item, that no one should evict another from his shop, and he who did this and was convicted, that he should give every third penny of the sum that the rent of the shop would bring in in a year to the aforesaid alms funds; and that no one should extract a merchant from the shop of another, and he who did this and was convicted of it that he should give 12d. to the aforesaid alms funds. Item, that no one should take on an apprentice unless he were the son of a freeman, nor should he take him on for a shorter term than 10 years unless he be his kinsman or that he had previously been in the mistery, and he who did this and was convicted of it, that he should give 2 bezants [4s.] to the aforesaid alms funds and he should lose the boy. And that every apprentice who entered the mistery should give one bezant [2s.] to the alms funds on entry and another on issue from his terms.

Item, that no outsider nor alien should be admitted to a shop [as a workman] without the mistery's leave and not unless he bring a guarantee from his homeland of his good character and his skill, and this because of the great harm that has come to the mistery from such men, and he who did this and was convicted of it, he had to pay half a mark to the aforesaid alms funds and the alien was to be removed.
And it is to be known that these regulations used to be kept to at fairs as well as in the City of London, in order to maintain faith and trustworthiness and to eliminate deception.

. . . and the aforesaid sworn men said that these things had been provided for Reg. Deeds f. 374r
and ordained: since, as a result of weakness, illness, increasing years, old age, and by the accidents of fire, robbery and loss arising, some of the mistery who had been worthy men have fallen into poverty from which they cannot rise without assistance, some worthy men of the mistery bequeathed a certain rent to be used for their succour and recoverance when need arose to help any such men. And that those four wardens in the City were in charge of this, the which bequest they pray our lord the King that he may allow them to be granted this and any other such bequests that may come in the future, if it please him, for the goodmen of London would willingly make such charitable donations if they saw that it was the king's wish for this to be established. And as help towards this sustenance may he grant if it please him that the aforesaid penalties may go to these funds, i.e. the monetary fines laid down for such offences.

At the common assembly of the goldsmiths of London of the fraternity of 1370
St Dunstan held in the year 44 Edward III [1370] it was ordained and agreed A + a
that the regulations and ordinances made in ancient times by the common p. 41, col. 1
assent of the goldsmiths should be entered into this register in order to endure in memory for ever, the which regulations and ordinances follow in this form:

Ad diverc*as* ordinac*iones* sequent*es* ordinat*as* p*ro* tot*a* co*m*munit*ate*

1271 – copied in 1370 [E]n[110] l[e][111] hono*ur* de deux et n*ost*re dame Seinte Marie et toutz les seintz et toutz seintes et de Seinte Dunston et a p*ro*fit de roialme *et* amendement de mester, purveu est p*ar* les p*ro*des ho*m*mes d'orpheve*re*s del orpheve*ri*e de Londres qe toutz soient entreroulee del confrarie de Seint Doneston. Et si nul de la confrarie meurt, toutz viendront a l'enterement s'ils n'eiont resonable encheson sur peine de ii deniers a don*er* p*ur* l'alme. Et si nul de la confrarie moert hors de la ville q*e* l'em fra p*ur* lui si com il fust mort en la ville. Et ceux q*e* m*ur*ront q*e* sont de la confrarie regardent a la confrarie a lo*ur* voluntez p*ur* lour almes. Et q*e* nul overe pir oor de l'asay ne pir argent de la moneie. Et qe nul n'eit forsq*ue* une man*er*e de pois, et ceo soit encelez. Et qe nul ne scee faux piere en or ne dreit piere en quivere n'en latun, c'est assav*oir* en anel ne en firmail ne en ceinture, ne deorrer nul de ceo trois. Ne nul ne face hanap*e* de quivere ne de latun dorrez. N[e] nul ho*m*me ne dorre nul ov*er*aigne de quivere ne de latun ne n'y mette dreit piere si ceo ne soit aournement de Seinte Eglise. Et q*e* nul n'y mette foile d'estein s*ur* piere dreiturele. Et qe nul retigne or ne argent q*e* l'om lui baille a overer de compaignou*n* ne d'est*ra*nge s*ur* peine de perdre la confrarie. Et si nul recet ou lui baille a overer en shope ou en meson ap*ré*s ceo q'il soit garni, et soit atteint, q'il doigne demy m*a*rk a la confrarie Seinte Dunston. Et q*e* nul fortreie autri aprentiz ne autri lowiz, s'il soit atteint q'il donne demy m*a*rk a la confrarie. Et q*e* nul ne p*re*igne app*re*ntiz q*e* il ne soit aroulee en la Guyhalle et doygn*e* une besant a la confrarie a soun entré. Et qe nul ne lowe autri hors de sa shope s'il ne p*re*igne a aunz ou l'achate, *et* s'il faite *et* soit atteint q'il doigne demy m*a*rk a la confrarie. Et qe nul ne baille rienz q*e* appent a orpheve*ri*e ne a porteresse ne a portour s'il ne vend sanz rien ret*ur*ner, et s'il soit atteint paie un m*a*rk a la confrarie. Qe nul ne overe a nul ho*m*me estraunge qe sasche q'il voille vendre avaunt si ne p*re*igne treis ataunt plus q'il ne freit d'un compaignou*n* del orfeverie p*ar* le s*er*ement q'il ad fet, et s'il soit atteint q'il paie demy m*a*rk a la confrarie. Qe nul ne face anel s'il ne soit a double caston[112] ne nul mette blaunche sire en croyse plaunche et s'il fait *et* soit
col. 2 atteint ils | s*er*ront depescee et il paiera i besaunt al confrarie. Qi vodra overer de neit overe de la Seinte Michel dekes le Nowel et nient pluis, et s'il fet *et* soit atteint p*ur* chescun neit paie xii deniers a la confrarie. Et qe les Wardeyns facent serche chescun quarter ii fethe.[113] Et qe nul ne resceive

[110] Space is left for a large initial E; this will probably have been due to this entry having been copied from a document which had the initial.

[111] MS: lo.

[112] The text is clearly corrupt here, for only a minority of rings were made with a double bezel. Without another text with which to compare this, one can only guess at what the correct version might have been: perhaps 'Qe nul ne face anel a double caston s'il ne soit . . .'?

[113] A marginal note here: 'de scrutinat' [g]ardianorum [MS: dardianorum] per quarter'.

Re the various following ordinances ordained for the whole community:

In the honour of God and of Our Lady St Mary and of all the saints and of St Dunstan and for the benefit of the kingdom and for the improvement of the mistery, it is provided by the goodmen of the goldsmiths of the goldsmiths' mistery of London that all should be enrolled in the fraternity of St Dunstan. And if any of the fraternity should die, all shall come to the burial unless they have reasonable excuse, on pain of 2d. to be given for the soul. And if any of the fraternity should die outside the city, one shall act for him in the same way as if he had died in the city. And those who belong to the fraternity should at their death consider for their soul's sake the fraternity in their wills. And no one should work gold of a lower standard than the assay nor silver of a lower standard than the coinage.[61] And that no one should have more than one kind of weights, and they should be [officially] sealed. And no one shall set a false gemstone in gold nor a true gemstone in copper or latten, i.e. in a ring or a clasp or a girdle, nor should any of these three be gilded. Nor should anyone make a goblet of gilded copper nor of gilded latten. Nor should any man gild any work of copper or latten nor set any true gemstone in it unless it be a church ornament. And no one should put tinfoil over a true gemstone. And that no one should keep back any of the gold and silver that he has been given to work either by a companion or by an alien, on pain of being expelled from the fraternity. And if anyone hides himself away or sets himself to work in his workshop or house after he has been summoned,[62] and if he be convicted of this, he should give half a mark to the fraternity of St Dunstan. And that no one should entice away the apprentice or serving-man of another, and if he be convicted, he should give half a mark to the fraternity. And no one should take on an apprentice unless he has been enrolled at the Guildhall, and he should give a bezant [2s.] to the fraternity at his entry. And no one should evict another from his shop unless taking it on by the year or buying it, and if he does this and is convicted of it, he should give half a mark to the fraternity. And no one should hand over any object that pertains to the goldsmiths' craft to a hawker whether it be a man or a woman unless he be selling it outright, and if he be convicted of this that he should pay a mark to the fraternity. That no one should do work for any alien knowing that he intends to sell it on to another, unless he take from him three times the price he would from a companion of the Goldsmiths' mistery according to the oath he has sworn, and if he be convicted of this, that he should pay half a mark to the fraternity. That no one should make a ring with a double bezel unless it be . . .,[63] nor should he put any white wax into a hollow flat piece, and if he does this and is convicted of it, they should be broken up and he shall pay one bezant to the fraternity. He who wishes to work at night time may work thus between Michaelmas and Christmas but at no other time, and if he does this and is convicted of it, he should pay for each night 12d. to the fraternity. And that the wardens should make an inspection twice each quarter. And that no one should receive any

1271 – copied in 1370

[61] One may note the differing phrasing in these 1271 ordinances and that neither the 'touch of Paris' nor the 'sterling' standard is referred to.

[62] i.e. by the wardens or another to come before them or to an assembly.

[63] See note 112 on opposite page.

estraunge orphev*er*e en sa shope saunz moustrer as Wardeyns sur peine de demy m*ar*k. Et les Wardeyns des toutz cestz choses avanditz loialment fournieront *et* loial acompte rendront p*ar* le s*er*ement q'ils ount fait. Et chescun purverrunt les pov*er*es. A cestes choses tenier *et* garder avom no*us* toutz juree co*m*munalment. Et a cestes choses tesmoigner q*e* altre foithe ne soit dedit, si ount mys les p*ro*deshom*m*es de la ruwe lur seals. Cestes choses furont g*ra*ntez *et* jureez la veille de la Trinité l'an du g*ra*ce Nostr*e* Seign*ur* Mil CC lxxi.

De assaie argenti *et* auri ut patet:
[O]rdeiné est q*e* nul orfievere d'Englet*er*re ne d'aillo*ur*s de la seign*ur*ie le Roi ne overe ne face de cy enavant nul man*er*e de vessel ne jeuaux ne aut*r*es choses d'or ne d'argent qe ne soit et de verrei alay, c'est assav*oir* oor de c*er*tein touche *et* argent del alay del est*er*ling*e* ou de meillo*ur* alay solomc la volunté de celui a qi les overes sount; qe nul ne overe pir argent qe monaye. Et qe nul man*er*e de vessel d'argent ne soit porté hors des mains as ov[*ere*]res[114] taunt qe ele soit assaié p*ar* les gardeins del mester et q*e* ele [soit] signee de une teste de leopart. Qe nul ne ovre pir or q*e* touche de Paris.[115] Et q*e* les gardeins del mester aillont de shope en shope entre les overers assaiauntz qe le or soit tiel comme la touche avandit. Et s'il troevent nul pir qe la touche qe le ovre soyt forfaite a Roi. Qe nul ne face anels croises ne firmaux croises; qe nul ne mette piere en or si ele ne soit naturele; qe taillours de seals *et* de amaux q'ils rendont a chescuny son pois d'argent *et* d'or auxi avant come ils pount sauver[116] sur lo*ur* loiaulté. Et les jeuaux d'or q'ils ont entremayns del veil oure, q'ils s'en deliveront a plus tost q'ils poent, et s'ils achatent de sel overe mesmes desoreenavant q'ils l'achatent pur reover[117] et ne mye pur revendre.[118]Et en toutz les bones villes d'Englet*er*re ou ayt orfev*er*es, q'ils facent mesmes les estatutz qe ceux de Londr*es* fount, et qe un vigne de chescun ville p*ur* touz a Loundres, de quere lo*ur* c*er*tein touche [et][119] lour punçon. Et si nul orfev*er*e soit atteint
p. 42, col. 1 q*e* aut*re*ment face | qe desus n'est ordeiné, soit puny p*ar* prisoun *et* raunson a la volunté le Roi.

Purveu est d'aut*r*e part qe nul orfev*er*e ovre de neyt et qe nul ne tigne shope fors en haute ruwe. Qe nul ne p*re*nte creese d'or saudé,[120] ne seient feruz p*ur* chapeux

114 Reg. Deeds: ne parte hors des meyns as oeu*er*ers. In A + a, 'parte' had been written, was changed to 'porte' and an omission mark preceding the word was added and above the line 'soit'.
115 A marginal note in a different hand and ink to others at this point: ore de parys.
116 Reg. Deeds: savoir.
117 This word has been inserted at the end of a line; the next line has had the word 'depesceer' expuncted and later scored out. The Reg. Deeds version has 'despescher'.
118 A later marginal note at this point: de scrutinit' in tot' bon' vill' ut patet.
119 MS: a. Reg. Deeds: et.
120 Reg. Deeds: croesse de Orfande.

alien goldsmith into his shop without presenting him to the wardens, on pain of half a mark. And the wardens shall faithfully see to all these aforesaid things and shall render faithful account on the oath they have sworn. And all shall support the poor. To hold and keep to these things we have all sworn communally. And as witness to these things, in order that no denial of them may be made at another time, the goodmen of the street[64] have affixed their seals. These things were granted and sworn to on the eve of Trinity Sunday [30 May] in the year of grace 1271 A.D.

Of the assay of silver and gold, as it appears:
It is ordained that no goldsmith of England or elsewhere from one of the lordships of the King shall from henceforth work or make any kind of vessel or any ornamental object or any other things of gold or silver which be not of true alloy, that is to say gold of the certain touch and silver of the alloy of sterling or better according to the wish of he whose works they are; that no one should work silver of a lower standard than the coinage. And that no manner of silver vessel shall be taken from[65] the hands of the workers until it has been assayed by the wardens of the mistery and been stamped with a leopard's head. That no one should work gold of a lesser standard than the touch of Paris. And that the wardens of the mistery shall go from shop to shop among the workers assaying that the gold be up to the aforesaid touch standard. And if they should find any of a lesser standard than the touch then that piece is to be forfeit to the King. That no one shall make either hollow rings or hollow clasps, and that no gemstone shall be set in gold unless it be genuine (natural); that engravers of seals and of enamels shall render to each his weight of gold and silver as much as they can save[66] of it and this upon their faith. And gold ornaments of olden times which they have in their hands, they should dispose of as soon as they can, and if from henceforth they buy such pieces, they should buy it in order to rework[67] it and not for resale. And in every good town in England where there are goldsmiths, they should draw up the same statutes as those of London, and one man should come from each town on behalf of all to London, to obtain their certain touch and their punch. And if any goldsmith be convicted of acting otherwise | than is ordained above, he should be punished by p. 42, col. 1
imprisonment and his release to be procured by payment of a sum at the King's pleasure.

It is besides decreed that no goldsmith shall work by night, and that no one shall keep a shop elsewhere than in the high street. That no one shall take any extra profit from soldered gold,[68] nor should such be used beaten out for

[64] Goldsmiths' Row in Cheap.
[65] Reg. Deeds: shall leave.
[66] Reg. Deeds: know.
[67] Reg. Deeds: break into pieces.
[68] The Reg. Deeds version would not appear to make any sense.

ne pur tressours. Qe un face aneaux a bares[121] cymoises a gerneitures rivez *et* nient soudez. Qe ho*m*me face en la guise qe ho*m*me voudra mes qe la plaunche ne seit mye croese, et la ou y ad double chaston qe le chaston desouth*e* soit parté a treis parties qe un puisse veere p*ar*my, *et* le chaston p*ar*amont [seit] a baas filet, et les nouches en mesme le man*ere*; *et* aneaux a bases caroles s'ils le voilont faire a double chaston en la fourme avandit. Qe firmaux d'argent enplantés et a braunches soient percez p*ar*desouth*e* le piere ensi qe ho*m*me puisse veer p*ar*my; qe les poys soient faitz de une acordance; et q*e* nul ne poise mes q*e* des poys m*er*chez. Qe nul ne tigne pise. Q*e* nul ne garnice ceintures furrez de fil. Qe nul ne vend*e* oor ars s'il ne soit dreit fyn.

1370 En le hono*ur* de Dieu *et* de Seint Dunston est ordeiné *et* assentu p*ar* tut la confrat*er*nité de Seint Dunston en l'an du regne le Roi E*dward* tierz puis le conquest xliiii, q*e* nul des orfeve*re*s ne meintigne nully des orfeve*re*s encont*re* les gardeinz, ne compaignou*n* encont*re* compaignou*n* de mesme le mest*ier*, *et* si ascuny de mesme le mest*ier* le face nient resonablement *et* de ceo soit atteint, il paiera al almoign*e* de Seint Dunston d*em*y m*ar*k.

It*em*, p*ur* ceo q*e* dive*r*s meschefs, p*er*des *et* damages sont escheuz *et* avenuz al mest*ier* des orfeveres p*ar* cause q*e* dive*r*s gentz de mesme le mest*ier* ont resceuz *et* faitz app*re*ntiz p*ri*vément *et* en muscetz al dit mest*ier* sanz saschantz les gardeinz *et* aut*re*s bonz gentz de mesme le mest*ier*, *et* ascun foith*e* ont fait app*re*ntiz meindre t*er*me q*e* l'estatut de la Citee *et* d'orfeve*re*s, *et* ascunz q*ue*ux ne sont mye ables de p*er*sone ne de linage *et* en dive*r*s man*er*es encont*re* resou*n*, p*ar* q*ue*i dive*r*s meschefs, grevancz *et* esclandres sont avenuz a mesme le mest*ier*.

Ordinanc*io* p*ro* apprent*iciis* ad p*re*sent*andum* gardian*is* ut pat*et*:
En le hon*ur* de Dieu *et* de Seint Dunston *et* en honou*r* *et* amendement del dit

[121] Reg. Deeds: bases.

chaplets or tressures.[69] If one makes rings with 'cyma' bars [holding an ornament or stone within two bands][70], the ornament or stone should be rivetted on and not soldered. One may make [rings] of any type that one likes, but the flat piece of it must not be hollow, and where there is a double bezil, the lower bezil must be divided into three parts so that one may be able to see through it, and the upper bezil should be with a low fillet; and the same similarly should apply to ouches [clasps or brooches]; and if they wish to make rings with a low circle of stones set round with a double bezil, then it should be done in the aforesaid manner. That clasps of silver set into a solid ground and with a decorative design of branches and foliage shall be pierced below the gemstone, so that one may be able to look through. That all weights shall be made to one common standard, and that no one shall weigh except with [officially]-stamped weights. That no one should keep a 'pise'.[71] That no one shall ornament girdles that are lined with thread. That no one shall sell gold that has been refined unless it is of the correct fine standard.

In the honour of God and of St Dunstan it was ordained and agreed by the 1370
whole fraternity of St Dunstan in the year 44 Edward III [1370] that no goldsmith should maintain the cause of any goldsmith against the wardens, nor should any companion maintain anyone against another companion of the same mistery, and if any of the same mistery should unreasonably do this and be convicted of it, he shall pay to the alms funds of St Dunstan half a mark [6s. 8d.].

Item, whereas various misfortunes, losses and harm have befallen and happened to the goldsmiths' mistery because various people of the same mistery have taken on apprentices privately and in secret from the said mistery without the knowledge of the wardens and other goodmen of the same mistery, and sometimes they have taken on apprentices for a shorter term than is laid down by statute of the City and that of the goldsmiths, and some of these are unfit in their persons or by birth, and in various ways unreasonable, and because of this various misfortunes, grievous things and scandals have befallen the same mistery.

Ordinance for the presentation of apprentices to the wardens, as follows:
To the honour of God and St Dunstan, and to the honour and improvement of

[69] 'chapeux' and 'tressours' may refer to a wide variety of head wear and ornaments for the hair. See the article on 'Hair Accessories', pp. 291–96 in Geoff Egan and Frances Pritchard *et al.*, *Dress Accessories c. 1150–c .1450.*

[70] 'Cymaise' = 'cyma' is an architectural term: 'A moulding of the cornice, the outline of which consists of a concave and a convex line; an ogee' (*OED*). It is not recorded as applied to jewellery, but could well apply to rings with holding bars, the lower concave and the upper convex. An alternative but similar meaning could be seen as relating to the word 'cimois' (see the *Dictionnaire de la langue française du seizième siècle*, ed. E. Huguet, vol. 2 (Paris, 1932), p. 292) which has a given meaning of 'lisière, bande servant à attacher l'enfant dans le berceau'. (I am most grateful to Michèle Bimbenet-Privat for this latter information.) No instances are recorded of this word being used in relation to jewellery, but rings exist which could be seen as describable in this way. The Reg. Deeds version with 'bases' not 'bars' seems unlikely.

[71] Some sort of measuring and weighing instrument. John Cherry makes the excellent suggestion that this may have been a set weighing balance rather than a set of scales which have weights that can be checked.

mest*ier*, p*ar* tut la confrat*er*nité de Seint Dunston en l'an du regne le R*oy*
col. 2 E*dward* t*erce* puis le conq*uest* xliiii, ordeiné est *et* assentu p*ar* co*m*une assent | q*e* nully de mesme le mest*ier* resceive nul app*re*ntiz sanz assent des gardeinz *et* bonz gentz de mesme le mest*ier*, *et* si ascuny le face desore enavant *et* de ceo soit atteint, il paiera al almoign*e* de S. Dunstou*n* d*em*i m*a*rk.

De apprent*iciis*:
It*em*, p*ur* ceo q*e* ascunz de mesme le mest*ier* sont custumables d'aler al Guyhalle *et* d'enfrancher app*re*ntiz *et* aut*re*s gentz del dit mest*ier* sanz assent des gardeinz *et* a g*ra*nt damage del dit mest*ier*, p*ar* q*ue*i ordeiné est *et* assentu q*e* nully ne s*er*ra enf*ra*nché sanz [assent] [d]es[122] gardeinz de dit mest*ier*, *et* si ascuny del dit mest*ier* voise al Guyhall*e* p*ur* enfranch*er* ascuny sanz assent des gardeinz, chescuny q*e* voise paiera al almoign*e* de S. Dunston i besant, *et* cestuy q'est enf*ra*nché il paiera d*em*i m*a*rk al almoign*e* susdit.

It*em*, ordeiné est *et* assentu q*e* si les gardeinz de dit mest*ier* busoign*ont* de conseil ou d'eide des gentz de lo*ur* mest*ier* es ascunz choses touchant l'office des gardeinz, q*e* chescuny de dit mest*ier* q*ue*ux sont requis p*ar* les ditz gardeinz soient tenuz de eaux conseiler, eider *et* ovesque eaux aler de feare *et* meinteign*er* les bonz choses touchant lo*ur* office en eide *et* lou meinteignance de lo*ur* mest*ier*, s'ils n'eiont resonable encheson d'y estr*e* escusee, *et* si ascuny le refuse ou sei retret es pointz susditz aup*ré*s q'il soit requis p*ar* les ditz gardeinz, sanz resonable escusaciou*n* ou encheson, il paiera al almoign*e* de S. Dunston i besant.[123]

Fait a remembr*er* q*e* les ditz gardeinz acompt*ont* le mardy aup*ré*s le feste de Seint Dunstan en l'an susdit, tutz choses acomptez la compaignie del confrat*er*nité tignent les ditz gardeinz quitz *et* deschargez des resceites *et* des toutz choses touchant lo*ur* office.

1370–71 A*nn*o xliiii^{to}[124]
p. 43, col. 1 Ceux sount lez nounz des Gardeynz d'Orfev*er*ye l'an xliiii^{te}:
Thom*a*s de Renh*a*m
Will*ia*m Fraunceys
Joh*a*n Fraunceys
Thomas Bygood

Les despences des ditz gardeyns:
Primes, p*ur* soner le g*ra*unt sonel de Seint Poul et p*ur* la lumere a l'esglise de Seint Joh*a*n Zakarye – xix s. viii d.

[122] MS: sanz les gardeinz.
[123] This amount is inserted, at the same time, after the scored words 'd*em*i m*a*rk'.
[124] This annotation-cum-heading at the top of the page, partly cropped off, leads one to think that each year was perhaps given such a heading, the binding of the book leading to the subsequent cropping off.

the said mistery, it was ordained and agreed by the whole fraternity of St Dunstan in the year 44 Edward III [1370] by common assent |that no one col. 2 of the same mistery shall take on any apprentice without the assent of the wardens and goodmen of the same mistery, and if anyone henceforth should do this and be convicted of it, he shall pay half a mark to the alms funds of St Dunstan.

Of apprentices:
Item, whereas some men of the same mistery have been in the habit of going to the Guildhall and giving their freedom to apprentices and others of the said mistery without the assent of the wardens and to the great harm of the said mistery, for this reason it is ordained and agreed that no one shall be enfranchised without [the consent of] the wardens of the said mistery, and if anyone of the said mistery should go the Guildhall to enfranchise anyone without the consent of the wardens, each who should thus go shall pay to the alms funds of St Dunstan one bezant [2s.], and he who has been enfranchised shall pay half a mark [6s. 8d.] to the aforesaid alms funds.

Item, it is ordained and agreed that if the wardens of the said mistery shall be in need of advice or help from people of their mistery in anything concerning their function as wardens, that each and everyone of the said mistery who is asked by the said wardens shall be obliged to advise and help them and go with them to do and maintain all good matters concerning their duties in aid and upkeep of their mistery, unless they may have some reasonable cause to be excused, and if anyone should refuse or withhold himself from the aforesaid rules after he be asked by the said wardens, if he be without reasonable excuse or cause, then he shall pay to the alms funds of St Dunstan one bezant [2s.]

Memorandum that the said wardens presented their accounts on the Tuesday after the feast of St Dunstan in the aforesaid year [21 May 1370]; with all things accounted for the company of the fraternity held the said wardens to be quit and discharged of all receipts and of all matters concerning their term of office.

These are the names of the wardens of the Goldsmiths' Mistery in the year 1370–71
44 [Edward III] [1370]: p. 43, col. 1
Thomas de Raynham
William Fraunceys
John Fraunceys
Thomas Bygod

The expenses of the said wardens:
Firstly, for ringing the great bell of St Paul's and for the light at the church of St John Zachary – 19s. 8d.

It*em*, p*ur* drap*e* achaté al vesture del chapelein: C'est ass*avoir* iiii v*er*ges d*em*i p*ur* i. robe, p*ri*s le v*er*ge xliiii d. – S*umm*a – xvi s. iiii d.
It*em*, p*ur* le forou*r* a ycelle robe – ii s. vi d.
It*em*, lez ditz Gardeynz despenderent le jo*ur* de Seint Dunston en lo*ur* feste – xxv li. iiii s. v d.
It*em*, p*ur* la vesture de ii brokours – x s.

Ceux sount lez pov*er*es gentz paiez ceste aan del almoigne de x li. *et* viii s., c'est ass*avoir*:
Petre Durstalle
Petre Hungry
Joh*ann*i Compes
Johan*n*e Lyncolne

Ceux sount lez nounz dez app*re*ntiz entreez ceste aun xliiii^{te} s*us*dit:

Joh*a*n Salman app*re*ntis Thom*as* Polle –	ii s.
Edward Huwelyn app*re*ntis Ad*am* Bam –	ii s.
Rich*ard* Brook app*re*ntis Rob*er*t Guldeford –	ii s.
Rich*ard* Haper app*re*ntis Joh*a*n Lutou*n* –	ii s.
Joh*a*n Wyot app*re*ntis Will*ia*m G*ra*ntham –	ii s.
Joh*a*n Crowhurst app*re*nt*is* Joh*a*n Pieres –	ii s.
Joh*a*n Gassenby app*re*ntis Thom*as* Herntoft –	ii s.
Will*ia*m Esselyng app*re*ntis Rob*er*t F*ra*unceis –	ii s.
Waut*er* Godestokne app*re*ntis Michelet de Alemaygne –	ii s.
Will*ia*m Spark*e* app*re*ntis Will*ia*m Fichet –	ii s.
Joh*a*n Lynk*e* app*re*ntis Thom*a*s Burneh*a*m –	ii s.
col. 2 Nich*olas* Cappe app*re*ntis Thom*as* Burneh*am* –	ii s.
Joh*a*n Lucas app*re*ntis Simond G*ra*vele –	ii s.
Elias Matefeu app*re*ntis Steph*e*ne Thorp*e* –	ii s.
Rob*er*t Pyk app*re*ntis Thomas atte Noke –	ii s.
Reignald[125] Derby app*re*ntis Joh*a*n de Bartou*n* –	ii s.
Joh*a*n Norman app*re*ntis Thom*as* Gynge –	ii s.
Simond Rotherh*a*m app*re*ntis Thom*as* Renh*am* –	ii s.
Rob*er*t Ulkotes app*re*ntis Joh*a*n F*ra*unceys –	ii s.
Joh*a*n de Herdyngtou*n* app*re*ntis Will*iam*[126] F*ra*unces –	ii s.
Joh*a*n Broun app*re*ntis Henr*i* Chyksond –	ii s.

Lowys:
Ceux sount lez nounz des lowys ysantz hors de lo*ur* t*er*mes le temps dez gardeynz avantditz:

Will*ia*m Grantha*m* –	ii s.
Thom*as* Essex –	ii s.
Dru Barentyn –	ii s.
Joh*a*n Lytherpool –	ii s.
Will*ia*m Lucas –	ii s.
Will*ia*m Burland –	ii s.

[125] *Sic.*
[126] This name written above the scored word 'Rob*er*t'.

Item, for cloth bought for the clothing of the chaplain, i.e. 4½ yards for a gown, at 44d. the yard – total 16s. 4d.[72]
Item, for the lining of the same gown – 2s. 6d.
Item, the said wardens spent on their feast on St Dunstan's Day – £25 4s. 5d.
Item, for the clothing of 2 brokers – 10s.

These are the poor people paid £10 8s. this year from the alms funds, i.e.
Peter Dunstalle
Peter Hungry
John Compes
Joanna Lincoln

These are the names of apprentices entered in this 44th year aforesaid:

John Salman apprentice of Thomas Polle –	2s.
Edward Huwelyn apprentice of Adam Bamme –	2s.
Richard Brook apprentice of Robert Guildford –	2s.
Richard Haper apprentice of John Luton –	2s.
John Wyot apprentice of William Grantham –	2s.
John Crowhurst apprentice of John Piers –	2s.
John Gassenby apprentice of Thomas Horntoft –	2s.
William Esselyng apprentice of Robert Fraunceys –	2s.
Walter Godestokne apprentice of Michelet from Germany –	2s.
William Sparke apprentice of William Fichet –	2s.
John Lynk apprentice of Thomas Burnham –	2s.
Nicholas Cappe apprentice of Thomas Burnham –	2s. col. 2
John Lucas apprentice of Simon Gravele –	2s.
Elias Matefeu apprentice of Stephen Thorpe –	2s.
Robert Pyk apprentice of Thomas atte Noke –	2s.
Reginald Derby apprentice of John de Barton –	2s.
John Norman apprentice of Thomas Genge –	2s.
Simon Rotherham apprentice of Thomas Raynham –	2s.
Robert Ulkotes apprentice of John Fraunceys –	2s.
John de Herdyngtoun apprentice of William Fraunceys –	2s.
John Broun apprentice of Henry Chicksands –	2s.

Serving-men:
These are the names of serving-men coming out of their terms during the term of office of the aforesaid wardens:

William Grantham –	2s.
Thomas Essex –	2s.
Drew Barantyn –	2s.
John Liverpool –	2s.
William Lucas –	2s.
William Burland –	2s.

[72] *Recte* 16s. 6d.?

Rog*er* Kryngelford – ii s.
Joh*a*n West – ii s.
Thom*as* Genge – ii s.

Ceux sount lez nounz entrez en lez f*ra*unchises l'an suisdit:
Joh*a*n Walsh*a*m p*ur* son entree – xiii s. iiii d.
Joh*a*n Regge – x s.
Will*ia*m Horsman – x s.

Lez Exequies dez testamentz deliv*er*ez:
It*em*, lez ditz gardeinz ount paiez *et* deliv*er*ez a la compeignie del devys du testament Will*ia*m de Burtou*n* al almoigne de Seint Dunston xiii s. iiii d. Et xxvi s. viii d. queux il remaneit en dette de la co*m*peignie, dont lez dit gardeinz ount fait une acquitance as executo*ur*s le dit Will*ia*m.

It*e*m, fait a remembrer q*e* Will*ia*m Iryssch*e* avoit pris une app*re*ntis q*e* n'estoit mye able per qoi estoit ordeigné p*ar* lez ditz gardeynz s*ur* la reconissance le piere le dit app*re*ntis q*e* conust q'il estoit fitz a un chapeleyn, q'il durroit al almoigne – vi s. viii d. et s*ur* ceo estoit deliv*er*é de [. . .][127] du dit Will*ia*m.

p. 44, col. 1[128] Item, p*ur* ceo q*e* le vadlet Buntyng retreist une m*ar*chaunt de autrui shope countre la ordinance – xii d.

It*em*, p*ur* ceo q*e* le vadlet Rob*er*t F*ra*unceys retreist une m*ar*cha*n*t de la shope Henr*i* M*a*rkeby countre l'ordinance – xii d.

It*em*, p*ur* ceo q*e* est defenduz p*ar* la ordinance q*e* nul ne baillereit rienz a vendre a nulle porteresse, trové fust q*e* Th*omas* Horntoft bailla a sa fe*m*me div*er*ses aneux, fermailles *et* alt*re*s choses del mestier, de quelle chose le dit Thom*as* estoit atteynt *et* se confessa – de paier al almoigne de Seint Dunston – x s. *et* les paia.

It*em*, Esmond de Brumptou*n* p*ur* ceo q'il estoit rebel *et* revylla lez gardeyns p*ur* une seynt*ur*e q'il avoit fait q*e* feust trové en defaute, si q'il estoit ajuggé p*ar* tout la compaignie de paier al almoigne Seint Dunston x s. *et* lez paia.

Fait a remembrer q*e* p*ur* ceo [qe] une discord estoit p*ar*entre Thom*as* de Renh*a*m, Will*ia*m F*ra*unceys, Joh*a*n F*ra*unceis *et* Thomas Bygood, orfev*er*es *et* gardeyns del mestier del orfev*er*ie de Loundres *et* toutes lez aultr*e*s bones gentz du dite mestier dez orfev*er*es de la dite citee d'une p*ar*t, et Rob*er*t F*ra*unceys, orfev*er*e, d'aultre p*ar*t: si feust une asse*m*blé *et* une acord fait p*ar*entre lez p*ar*ties avantditz meskerdy le xj^{e} jo*ur* de Decembre l'an du r*egne du* r*oi* E*dward* tierce puis le conq*uest* xliiii^{te}, Joh*a*n de Bernes adonqes meire de Loundr*e*s,

[127] A short phrase must have been omitted here by the scribe in copying.
[128] The second column of this page has been left blank.

Roger Cringleford – 2s.
John West – 2s.
Thomas Genge – 2s.

These are the names [of those] who have entered into the freedom in the aforesaid year:
John Walsham, for his entry – 13s. 4d.
John Regge – 10s.
William Horsman – 10s.

Executorship of wills carried out:
Item, the said wardens have paid and delivered to the company from the bequest in the will of William de Burton to the alms funds of St Dunstan – 13s. 4d. And also 26s. 8d. for which he remained in debt to the company, for which the wardens have given a receipt to the said William's executors.

Item, memorandum that William Fitzhugh (*alias* Iryssche) had taken on an apprentice who was unsuitable, for which reason it was ordained by the said wardens on the recognizance of the father of the said apprentice who admitted that he was the son of a chaplain, that he would give to the alms funds – 6s. 8d. and upon this he was released from [his apprenticeship] with the said William.

Item, whereas Buntyng's boy took a merchant away from the shop of another p. 44, col. 1
against the ordinances – 12d.

Item, whereas Robert Fraunceys' boy took a merchant away from Henry Markeby's shop against the ordinances – 12d.

Item, whereas it is forbidden by ordinance that anyone should give anything to any hawker to sell, it was found that Thomas Horntoft had given to his wife various rings, clasps and other things of goldsmithry, and of this the said Thomas was found guilty and admitted this – to be paid to the alms funds of St Dunstan – 10s. – and this he has paid.

Item, Esmond de Brumptoun, whereas he was rebellious and insulted the wardens on account of a girdle he had made and which was found defective, thus he was sentenced by all the company to pay to the alms funds of St Dunstan 10s., and he has paid this.

Memorandum that whereas a dispute arose between Thomas de Raynham, William Fraunceys, John Fraunceys and Thomas Bygod, goldsmiths and wardens of the mistery of goldsmiths of London, and all the other goodmen of the said goldsmiths' mistery of the said city on the one hand, and Robert Fraunceys, goldsmith, on the other hand, an assembly was held and an agreement was made between the aforesaid parties on Wednesday 11 December 44 Edward III [1370], John de Barnes then being Mayor of London, William

Will*ia*m Walworth *et* Rob*er*t de Caytou*n* adonqes viscount*es* du dite citee, c'est assav*oir* en la fo*ur*me q*e* s'ensuist: Le dit Rob*er*t se conust avoir t*re*spacé a lez ditz gardeyns *et* bones gentz *et* se myst a lo*ur* gr*a*ce *et* ordinance al award de sis bones gentz du dite mestiers, queux bones gentz agarderent q*e* le dit Rob*er*t Fraunceis paiereit une pipe de vyn a la compeignie s'il poet estre trovee en temps avenir q*e* le dit Rob*er*t Fr*a*unceis t*re*space, saunz nul alt*re* agard.[129]

1371–72 Ceux sount lez nounz des gardeyns d'orfeve*r*ye de Loundres comensant lo*ur*
p. 45, office le jo*ur* de Seynt Dunston l'an xlv[te]:
col. 1[130] Nicholl*e* de Twyford
Joh*a*n Broun
Will*ia*m Burdeyn
Thom*a*s Pantou*n*

Les despences des dites gardeyns:
Primes, p*ur* soner le gr*a*unt sonel de Seint Dunston al esglise de Seint Poul *et* p*ur* la lumiere a l'esglise de Seint Joh*a*n Zakarye – xx s.

It*em*, p*ur* vesture achaté al chapeleyn, c'est assavoir iiii v*er*ges, p*ri*s le v*er*ge v s. – *summa* – xx s.
It*em*, p*ur* une furro*ur* al dit chapeleyn – ii s. vi d.
It*em*, p*ur* la vesture de iii pov*er*es gentz broko*ur*s – xxi s.

It*em*, paié a Joh*a*n Salesburi p*ur* son drap*e* del liv*er*é de Seint Dunston – x s.

Ceux sount lez pov*er*es gentz paiez ceste an del almoigne de x li. *et* viii s., c'est ass*avoir*:
Pieres Durstalle
Pieres Hungry
Joh*a*n Caumpes
Johane Lyncoln*e*

It*em*, lez dites gardeyns acomptent avoir paié p*ur* i. novel pap*ier* achaté q*e* currera dez gardeyns en gardeyns *et* q*e* ceste gr*a*unt papier s*er*ra mys p*ur* i. lygg*ere*,[131] a gyser en une cofr*e* ovesq*e* aultr*es* choses: p*ri*s del novelle papier – ii s. x d.

[129] A marginal note near the end of this entry: 'Robertus Fraunceis solvit unum pripade vino [*sic*] pro inobediencie suo gardianis fact*e* ut patet.'
[130] The entries on this page are found also on the first page of Book A + b, which, as the entries in both books tell us, was purchased and came into use at this time. From this point forward in this edition, the entries from the two books have been interwoven in chronological sequence. For the first few years only there is an overlap, almost identical entries appearing in both books. Where the two books have these identical entries, Book A + a has been followed, and minor spelling variants of Book A + b have not been noted. All substantive variant readings have been noted and are included, either by printing the alternative text below the first text or by use of a footnote. See further, Introduction, pp. xxiii–xxiv.
[131] The abbreviated 'p*ur*' has had a line scored through here.

Walworth and Robert de Caytoun then being sheriffs of the said City, i.e. in the following form: The said Robert admitted to having offended against the said wardens and goodmen and submitted himself to their judgment to be sentenced by six goodmen of the said mistery, which goodmen sentenced the said Robert Fraunceys to pay a pipe of wine to the company if he should at any time in the future be found guilty of any offence, and no other penalty was set.[73]

These are the names of the wardens of the Goldsmiths' Mistery of London, taking up their office on St Dunstan's Day in the year 45 [Edward III] [19 May 1371]: 1371–72 p. 45, col. 1

Nicholas Twyford
John Broun
William Burdeyn
Thomas Panton

The expenses of the said wardens:
Firstly, for ringing the great bell of St Dunstan[74] at the church of St Paul's, and for the light at the church of St John Zachary – 20s.

Item, for clothing bought for the chaplain, i.e. 4 yards, at 5s. the yard – total 20s.
Item, for a lining for the said chaplain – 2s. 6d.
Item, for the clothing of 3 poor brokers – 21s.

Item, paid to John Salisbury for his cloth of the livery of St Dunstan – 10s.

These are the poor people paid £10 8s. from the alms funds this year, i.e.
Piers Dunstalle
Piers Hungry
John Compes
Joanna Lincoln

Item, the said wardens account for having paid for a new paper register that shall be handed from one set of wardens to the next, and this large register shall be placed as a ledger to be kept in a chest with other things: cost of the new paper register – 2s. 10d.

[73] Marginal note: Robert Fraunceys paid a pipe of wine for his disobedience to the wardens as stated.
[74] See Introduction, p. xxxvi.

A + b p. 1 It*em*, les dites Gardeyns acomptent avoir acheté ceste novelle papier q*e* currera des Gardeyns en gardeyns, et q*e* l'alt*re* g*ra*unt papier s*er*ra gysa*n*t en une cofre ovesq*e* ault*re*s choses p*ur* un remembrauncer; p*ri*s de ceste novelle papier – ii s. x d.

A + a p. 45, col. 1[132] Ceux sount les nounz des app*re*ntices entrez en le mestier puis le jo*ur* de Seint Dunston l'an suisdit:

	Primes, Thom*as* Conyn app*re*ntis Simond Maszerer –	ii s.
	It*em*, Joh*a*n Watekyn app*re*ntis Joh*a*n Veel –	ii s.
	Joh*an*nes Goodenche app*re*ntis Thomas Extou*n* –	ii s.
	It*em*, Joh*a*n Mayheu app*re*ntis Joh*a*n Lyncoln*e* –	ii s.
col. 2	Rob*er*t Wylle app*re*ntis Thomas Pantou*n* –	ii s.
	Joh*a*n Bery app*re*ntis Joh*a*n Carbonel –	ii s.
	Joh*a*n Balshale app*re*ntis Joh*a*n Botesh*a*m –	ii s.
	Joh*a*n Barbet app*re*ntis Joh*a*n F*ra*unceys –	ii s.
	Joh*a*n Kele app*re*ntis Joh*a*n Walssche –	ii s.
	Joh*a*n Bumpsted app*re*ntis Will*ia*m Wyndout –	ii s.
	Eustace atte Pyrie app*re*ntis Joh*a*n Forster –	ii s.
	Rauf My*m*mynglond*e* app*re*ntis Thom*as* Burnh*a*m –	ii s.
	Richard Parsoun app*re*ntis Nich*olas* Twyford –	ii s.
	Joh*a*n Gloucestre app*re*ntis Joh*a*n Hynde –	ii s.
	Richard Sybely app*re*ntis Joh*a*n Gravelee –	ii s.
	Rog*er* Rademoore app*re*ntis Henr*i* Markeby –	ii s.
	Richard Gurdlere apprentis Will*ia*m Bodyer –	ii s.
	Stephene Kyng app*re*ntis Joh*a*n Payn –	ii s.
	Will*ia*m Taylllo*ur* app*re*ntis Joh*a*n Welford –	ii s.
	Rob*er*t Haddelee app*re*ntis Esmond Brumptou*n* –	ii s.[133]
	Joh*a*n atte Stone app*re*ntis Joh*a*n Fayrher –	ii s.

Ceux sount lez nounz des lowys q*e* viegnont hors de lo*ur* t*er*me puis le jo*ur* de Seint Dunston l'a[n] xlv[te] suisdit:[134]

Primes, Joh*a*n Bulstrod*e* –	ii s.
Stephene Mapelesden*e* –	v s. iiii d.
Richard atte Noke –	viii s. viii d.
Richard M*er*edeune –	ii s.
Joh*a*n Hynde –	ii s.
Henr*i*[135] atte Grene –	v s. iiii d.
Will*ia*m Cupp*er*e –	viii s. viii d.
Joh*a*n Blakeman –	v s.
Joh*a*n Greneville –	vi s. viii d.
Rog*er* Kryngelford –	vi s. viii d.
Joh*a*n Mapelesden*e* –	ii s.

[132] The following list is also on p. 2 of A + b.

[133] See the Name Index. It would seem not impossible that this entry has been misplaced and should be in the list of serving-men.

[134] The following list is on pp. 2–3 of A + b.

[135] In A + b, p. 2 this name is given as 'Johan', but it seems likely that Henry is correct. See Name Index.

Item, the said Wardens account for having bought this new paper register which shall be handed from one set of wardens to the next, and the other large register shall be kept in a chest with other things as a memorandum book, cost of this new paper register – 2s. 10d. A + b p. 1

These are the names of apprentices who have entered the mistery since St Dunstan's Day in the aforesaid year [19 May 1371]: A + a p. 45, col. 1

Firstly, Thomas Conyn apprentice of Simon Mazerer –	2s.	
Item, John Watekyn apprentice of John Veel –	2s.	
John Goodenche apprentice of Thomas Exton –	2s.	
Item, John Mayhew apprentice of John Lincoln –	2s.	
Robert Wylly apprentice of Thomas Panton –	2s.	col. 2
John Bery apprentice of John Carbonelle –	2s.	
John Balshale apprentice of John Bottisham –	2s.	
John Barbet apprentice of John Fraunceys –	2s.	
John Kele apprentice of John Walshe –	2s.	
John Bumpstead apprentice of William Wyndout –	2s.	
Eustace atte Pyrie apprentice of John Forster –	2s.	
Ralph Mymmynglond apprentice of Thomas Burnham –	2s.	
Richard Parson apprentice of Nicholas Twyford –	2s.	
John Gloucester apprentice of John Hynde –	2s.	
Richard Sibele apprentice of John Gravele –	2s.	
Roger Radmore apprentice of Henry Markeby –	2s.	
Richard Gurdlere apprentice of William Bodyer –	2s.	
Stephen Kyng apprentice of John Payn –	2s.	
William Tayllour apprentice of John Welford –	2s.	
Robert Haddelee apprentice of Edmund Brumptoun –	2s.	
John atte Stone apprentice of John Fairher –	2s.	

These are the names of serving-men who have come out of their terms since St Dunstan's Day in the aforesaid 45th year [19 May 1371]:

Firstly, John Bulstrode –	2s.
Stephen Maplesdene –	5s. 4d.
Richard atte Noke –	8s. 8d.
Richard Merdene –	2s.
John Hynde –	2s.
Henry atte Grene –	5s. 4d.
William Cuppere –	8s. 8d.
John Blakeman –	5s.
John Greneville –	6s. 8d.
Roger Cringleford –	6s. 8d.
John Maplesdene –	2s.

Conred Schillyng de Coloyne est admis en la Compeignie del Frat*er*nité d'orfev*er*ie *et* ad paié p*ur* sa admission – xx s.[136]
Herman van Gloie est admis a la co*m*peignie paiant vi s. viii d.
Pieres atte Neerlond – iii s. iiii d.
Pieres de Prestou*n* admys a la co*m*peignie – xl s.

p. 46, col. 1[137] It*em*, fait a remembrer q*e* a meisme le temps q*e* meisme ceux gardeyns estoient choisés, ordeigné estoit *et* assentuz p*ar* co*mun*e asse*n*t de touz lez orfev*er*es assemblés, q*e* quecu*n*q*ue* p*er*sone able du dit mestier s*er*roit choisé p*ur* gardeyn p*ur* le temps p*ar* co*mun*e assent et il av*er*eit ew desport *et* ese de iiii ans del dit office de gardeyn; et cellui ou ceux q*e* reffusent de faire la dite office, quelle hure q'ils soient issint choysez, paient al almoigne de Seint Dunston – xl s.

It*em*, p*ur* ceo q*e* Joh*a*n Bruges estoit trovee p*ar* lez gardeyns q'il poisa vessel d'argent, c'est assavoir une doszeine d'esquelles d'argent *et* demy doszeine des sauciers, queux il poisa a la vente p*ar* monoye des grotes choysés sibien des deniers, ii deniers *et* grotes nient resonables, queux esquelles *et* sauciers estoient poisés a div*er*ses foitz p*ar* le pois de xvii s. du dite monoie, issint q*e* defaulte estoit trovee en le pois du dit vessel p*ar* le pois des droiturelles grotes de droit pois de xl s., en desclaundre del mestier, queux xl s. le dit Joh*a*n g*ra*unta de paier al almoigne de Seynt Dunston p*ar* l'agard des dites gardeyns *et* bones gentz du dite mestier. S*ur* quelle defaulte trovee, ordeigné *et* assentuz est p*ar* co*mun*e assent des dites bones gentz q*e* quecu*n*q*ue* p*er*sone en temps avenir soit trovee en mesme la defaulte, q*e* tout l'avantage q*e* dev*er*oit avenir al dit vendo*ur* en tielle man*er*e receux, chece al almoigne de Seint Dunston. Et oult*r*e ceo facent gree a lez gardeyns du dit mestier q*e* p*ur* le temps s*er*ront solonc la quantité du trespas.

It*em*, p*ur* ceo q*e* Joh*a*n Lyripool estoit trovee rebel countre les gardeyns du dit mestier countre son s*er*ement, agardé est q*e* le dit Joh*a*n paie al almoigne de Seint Dunston vi s. viii d. Et oult*r*e ceo ordeigné *et* assentuz est p*ar* co*mun*e assent q*e* si desoremays trovee soit q*e* le dit Joh*a*n trespace en tielle man*er*e ou en nul ault*r*e, dont il p*ur*ra estre atteynt, q'il paie al almoigne de Seint Dunston une pipe de vyn a meisme le pris *et* coustage q'il p*ur*ra estre achaté solonc l'agard des gardeyns du dit mestier q*e* p*ur* le temps s*er*ront *et* des bones gentz du dite mestier.

1372 col. 2[138] It*em*, fait a remembrer q*e* Nicholle de Twyford, Joh*a*n Broun, Will*ia*m Burdeyn *et* Thomas Pantou*n*, adonqes gardeyns du dit mestier p*ur* le temps p*ur* l'an passé, deliv*er*ere*n*t a tout la compeignie d'orfev*er*ye le jo*ur* de Seint Dunston l'an xlvj^{e} une obligac*io*u*n* ovesq*e* une endent*ur*e de Henr*i* Palm*er*e, orfev*er*e, Waut*er* de Roka, clerk, *et* Thomas de Saine, tayllo*ur*, faite a Thom*as* de Renh*a*m, Will*ia*m F*ra*unceys, Thomas Bygood et Joh*a*n Fraunceys, gardeynz du dit mestier l'an devant, en xl li. d'est*er*l*inges*, s*ur*

[136] These entries are also on p. 3 of A + b.
[137] The first two entries here are also on p. 3 and the third on p. 4 of A + b.
[138] The next two entries are also on p. 4 of A + b.

Conrad Schillyng of Cologne has been admitted into the company of the Goldsmiths' Fraternity and has paid for his admission – 20s.
Hermann van Gluye has been admitted to the company on payment of 6s. 8d.
Piers atte Netherland – 3s. 4d.
Piers de Preston, admitted to the company – 40s.

Item, memorandum that at the same time as those same wardens were elected, it was ordained and agreed by common assent of all the assembled goldsmiths, that if any able person of the said mistery should be elected warden for that time by common assent, and provided that he had not been warden during the preceding four years, and if he or they were to refuse to carry out the said office, then at the time that they were thus elected, they should pay to the alms funds of St Dunstan – 40s. p. 46, col. 1

Item, whereas John Bruges was found guilty by the wardens in the weighing of some silver vessels, that is a dozen silver bowls and half a dozen saucers, which he weighed when they were being sold against money in groats, having selected pennies, twopences and groats that were not true, and those bowls and saucers were weighed several times at 17s. of the said money, which was found to fall short by 40s. for the weight of the said vessels weighed by true groats of correct weight, this to the discredit of the mistery. The said John agreed to pay those 40s. to the alms funds of St Dunstan, according to the judgment of the said wardens and goodmen of the said mistery. On being found guilty of such an offence, it was ordained and agreed by common assent of the said goodmen that whoever in the future should be found guilty of the same offence, the whole profit that would have gone to the vendor in such a manner should go to the alms funds of St Dunstan. And besides this, settlement should be made with the current wardens of the said mistery according to the severity of the offence.

Item, whereas John Liverpool was found guilty of rebelling against the wardens of the said mistery in contravention of his oath, it was judged that the said John should pay to the alms funds of St Dunstan 6s. 8d. And it was besides ordained and agreed by common assent that if from henceforth the said John should be found guilty of offending in such a manner or any other, and might be convicted of this, that he should pay to the alms funds of St Dunstan a pipe of wine to be bought at the price and expenses to be determined by the current wardens of the said mistery and by the goodmen of the said mistery.

Item, memorandum that Nicholas Twyford, John Broun, William Burdeyn and 1372
Thomas Panton, then wardens of the said mistery for last year, handed over to col. 2
the whole company of the Goldsmiths' Mistery on St Dunstan's Day in the year 46 [Edward III] [19 May 1372] an obligation with an indenture from Henry Palmere, goldsmith, Walter de Roka, clerk, and Thomas de Saine, tailor, made out to Thomas de Raynham, William Fraunceys, Thomas Bygod and John Fraunceys, wardens of the said mistery for the previous year, in the sum of £10

tielle condic*iou*n q*e* si le dit Henr*i* Palm*ere*, orfev*ere*, en nulle temps avenir soit trovee t*re*spasant ou rebel env*ers* les gardeyns *et* bones gentz du dit mestier, q'adonqes la dite obligac*iou*n de xl li. estoise en sa force *et* v*er*tue.

It*em*, fait a remembrer q*e* lez avantditz[139] gardeyns acomptent en despences *et* div*er*ses coustages v*ers* la lei, de p*ur*sure p*ur* iii fauces lyens des hanaps des mazer, queux lienz estoient de laton *et* endorrez, p*ur* queux hanaps lez dites gentz avoient lo*ur* juggement del pillory, q'amounte en tout – vii s. i d. It*em*, fait a rememb*rer* q*e* i. de les ditz iii hanaps[140] est en le co*mun*e chest.[141]

It*em*, fait a rememb*rer* q*e* Adam Bamme *et* Thom*as* Burnh*a*m, renters p*ur* l'an passé,[142] render*ont* lo*ur* acompte le lundy p*ro*schein aup*rés* le feste de la Trinité l'an xlvi *et* paier*ont* en tut – xxiii li. v s. ix d.

It*em*, fait a rememb*rer* q*e* les ditz gardeinz del dit an doner*ont* p*ur* l'encrees del an passé al almoign*e* de S. Dunston – xx m*a*rz.[143]

It*em*, fait a rememb*rer* q*e* Joh*a*n in the Lane doit s*ur* i. mazer quel est en le chest – d*em*i mark et i. besant.

A + b p. 5 It*em*, Joh*a*n atte Lane ad i mazer en gage en le co*mun*e cheste – p*ur* d*em*i m*a*rk et i besant.

A + a p. 46, col. 2 It*em*, en le dit chest est iiii bendes de Joh*a*n Wadyngtou*n* p*ur* gage de – ii m*a*rz.

A + b p. 5 It*em*, fait a rememb*rer* qe Joh*a*n Wadyngton[144] ad iii lienz d'argent p*ur* mazers (*et* i auncien mazer lié d'argent quel est en le co*mun*e chest p*ur* ii m*a*rz *et* i besant),[145] quel est en le cheste. – p*aié* ii mars[146]

A + a p. 46, col. 2 It*em*, Thom*as* Burche de Cornhull*e* ad xi quilers q*ue*ux sont faux en le forc*er*.

It*em*, le dit Thom*as* Burche ad viii botons de latou*n* endorré en le dit forc*er*.

139 MS: avantdititz.
140 A + b: qe i hanap de les iii.
141 This last sentence is added later in a different hand and ink. This hand then continues forward and is clearly the new clerk taking over at this point.
142 This is the first mention of the renters, for whom see Reddaway and Walker, *passim* (use Index).
143 This entry is also on p. 5 of A + b, as are the following ones with the differences noted.
144 This name is written above a scored 'atte Lane'.
145 The section bracketed has all been scored out.
146 These three words are written beside the name 'Wadyngton', presumably added at the time he redeemed the pledge.

sterling, with the condition that if the said Henry Palmere, goldsmith, should at any time in the future be found guilty of any offence or rebellion against the wardens and goodmen of the said mistery, that then the said obligation of £10 should be brought into force.

Item, memorandum that the aforesaid wardens account for the expenses and various legal costs arising from a prosecution for 3 false bands on mazer goblets, the which bands were made of latten that had been gilded, and for those goblets the said persons received sentence to the pillory, the costs amounted in all to 7s. 1d.
Item, memorandum that one of the said 3 goblets is in the common chest.

Item, memorandum that Adam Bamme and Thomas Burnham, renters for the last year, presented their account on the Monday following Trinity Sunday in the year 46 [Edward III] [24 May 1372], and paid over in all £23 5s. 9d.

Item, memorandum that the said wardens for the said year gave to the increase of funds for the last year to the alms funds of St Dunstan – 20 marks.

Item, memorandum that John in the Lane owes on a mazer which is in the chest – half a mark and 1 bezant.

Item, John atte Lane has a mazer as a pledge in the common chest for half a mark and 1 bezant. A + b p. 5

Item, in the said chest are 3 bands of John Waddington's as a pledge for 2 marks. A + a p. 46, col. 2

Item, memorandum that John Waddington has three silver bands for mazers (and an old mazer with a silver band which is in the common chest [as a pledge] for 2 marks and 1 bezant) which is in the chest. – paid 2 marks. A + b p. 5

Item, Thomas Burche of Cornhill has 11 spoons which are false (sub-standard) in the coffer. A + a p. 46, col. 2

Item, the said Thomas Burche has 8 buttons of gilded latten in the said coffer.

A + b p. 5 Item, Thomas Burche ad viii botons de latoun endorré gisont en le dit forcer.

A + a p. 46, col. 2 Item, Robert Lynne ad ii esquilers blanchez queux sont faux en le dit forcer.

Item, i barre ou iiii foilles qe Michelet fist a Johan Dancastre, copersmyth, al oelle ma dame la princesse, queux sont faux[147] *et* les remnantz sont debrusez.

1372–73 p. 47, col. 1[148] Ceux sont les nouns des Gardeinz d'Orfeverie de Londres comensant lour office le jour de Seint Dunston l'an xlvj:
Johan Walsshe
Johan Fraunceys
Adam Bamme
Johan Thorne

Les despences des ditz gardeinz:
Primes, pur soner le graunt sonel de Seint Dunston al eglise de Seint Poul *et* pur la lu[m]ere[149] al eglise de Seint Johan Zakarie – xx s.
Item, pur vesture achaté al chaplein, c'est assavoir ii verges de drap *et* demi, pris le verge v s. iiii d. qe amonte – xiii s. ii d.[150]
Item, pur le furrour al dit chaplein – ii s. vi d.

Item, pur le vesture des treis poveres gentz brokours – xx s. vi d.

Ceux sont les poveres gentz paiez cest an del almoygne de Seint Dunston:
Pieres Dunstalle
Johane Lincolne } paiez par les meinz Johan Fraunceys – v li. iiii s.

Johan Caumpes
Pieres Hungry } paiez par les meinz Johan Walsshe – v li. iiii s.

Pieres Mazerer, paié par les meinz Adam Bamme
Rauf Makenhened, paié par les meinz Johan Thorne[151]

Ceux sont les nouns des apprentiz entrez en le mestier d'orfeverie puis le jour de Seint Dunston l'an susdit:[152]

Primes, Johan Bedeford apprentiz Geffrey Walpol –	ii s.
Johan Eylesham apprentiz Johan Mount –	ii s.
Robert Langetoun apprentiz Thomas Forster –	ii s.

147 A + b, p. 5: qe fust faux.
148 The following entries for this year are also on p. 7 of A + b.
149 MS: lunere.
150 A + b, p. 7: xiii s. iiii d.
151 No figure of money is given for either of the last two.
152 This list is also on p. 8 of A + b.

Item, Thomas Burche has 8 buttons of gilded latten lying in the said coffer. A + b p. 5

Item, Robert Lynne has 2 white silver spoons which are false (sub-standard) in the said coffer. A + a p. 46, col. 2

Item, a metal bar with quatrefoils, which Michelet made for John Dancastre, coppersmith, to a pattern of[75] Milady the Princess, which was sub-standard, and the remnants have been broken up.

These are the names of the wardens of the Goldsmiths' Mistery of London, taking up their office on St Dunstan's Day in the year 46 [Edward III] [19 May 1372]: 1372–73 p. 47, col. 1

John Walshe
John Fraunceys
Adam Bamme
John Thorne

The expenses of the said wardens:
Firstly, for ringing the great bell of St Dunstan[76] at St Paul's church, and for the light at the church of St John Zachary – 20s.
Item, for clothing bought for the chaplain, i.e. 2½ yards of cloth at 5s. 4d. the yard, which amounts to – 13s. 2d.[77]
Item, for the said chaplain's lining – 2s. 6d.

Item, for the clothing of 3 poor men, brokers – 20s. 6d.

These are the poor people paid this year from the alms funds of St Dunstan:
Piers Dunstalle, Joanna Lincoln } paid by[78] John Fraunceys – £5 4s.

John Compes, Piers Hungry } paid by John Walshe – £5 4s.

Piers Mazerer, paid by Adam Bamme
Ralph Makenhened, paid by John Thorne

These are the names of apprentices who have entered the goldsmiths' mistery since St Dunstan's Day in the aforesaid year:

Firstly, John Bedford, apprentice of Geoffrey Walpole –	2s.
John Aylsham apprentice of John Mount –	2s.
Robert Langton apprentice of Thomas Forster –	2s.

[75] Alternatively, this might mean 'to the order of', 'at the wishes of'.
[76] See note 74 above.
[77] A + b, p. 7: 13s. 4d.; this sum seems correct.
[78] Literally, the text says: by the hands of.

Richard [Huntyngdon][153] apprentiz William Burdene –	ii s.
Richard Persoun apprentiz Nichol Twyford –	ii s.
Johan Hadlowe apprentiz Johan Davy –	ii s.
William Baldewyne apprentiz William Willay –	ii s.
Johan Bedles apprentiz de Thomas Hay –	ii s.
William Clement apprentiz Johan Crullyng –	ii s.
Johan Henny apprentiz Johan Rugge –	ii s.
Henry Clay apprentiz Johan Carbonel –	ii s.
Johan Walkere apprentiz Johan Lanham –	ii s.
Johan Trokkyng apprentiz William Aylesham –	ii s.
Firmyn Morel apprentiz de William Glasen –	ii s.[154]
col. 2 Roger Hedersete apprentiz Richard Betaygne –	ii s.
William Lecham apprentiz Johan Yernemuthe –	ii s.
Johan Gilmyn apprentiz Johan Lutoun –	ii s.
William Holt apprentiz Johan Welburne –	ii s.
Johan Bramptoun apprentiz Johan Hokyng –	ii s.
Johan Devy apprentiz[155] Melburne –	ii s.
Richard Shrovesbury apprentiz Robert Teukisbury –	ii s.
Roger Horntoft apprentiz Thomas Horntoft –	ii s.
Johan Poyntel apprentiz Johan Walsshe –	ii s.
Johan Seybrok apprentiz Johan Thorne –	ii s.
Hugo Wetherby apprentiz Richard Dancastre –	ii s.[156]

Ceux sont les nouns des lowys qe issont hors de lour terme puis le jour de Seint Dunston l'an xlvj:[157]

Primes, William Bretford –	ii s.
Richard Elyz –	ii s.

Fait a remembrer qe Godekyn[158] , orfevere, myst en i anel d'or i piere de veer, en grant damage *et* esclandre del mestier d'orfeverie, sur qei il fust aresoné par les gardeinz *et* les bonz gentz del mestier; quel trespas *et* mesprision il conust, et profri al almoigne de Seint Dunston pur le dit trespas – xx tonels de vin en grace des ditz gardeinz *et* bonz gentz, sur qei lui fust pardoné pur xiii s. iiii d. de paier al almoygne susdit.

Item, Symond Gravele pur exitement de mesme la cause al almoigne susdit profri – xl s. sur qei lui fust pardoné pur – xl d.

Item, Johan Payn pur mesme la cause de i autre anel il profri al almoygne de Seint Dunston xx tonels de vin, sur qei lui fust pardoné pur – xx s.

153 The name 'Huntyngdon' is given only in Book A + b, p. 8. In Book A + a, a space follows the name 'Richard'.

154 This entry (not in A + b) was added later in different ink by another scribe, and was preceded by another line then scored through, no doubt when the scribe saw it was a faulty version of the entry at the top of the next column: 'Roger Etercestre apprentiz de Richard Beteyn – ii s.'

155 A space follows.

156 This line (not in A + b) is an addition in a later hand, not the same as that which added two lines to the foot of col. 1.

157 This entry and those concerning Godekyn, Gravele and Payn are also on p. 9 of A + b.

158 A space follows; as also in Book A + b; clearly his surname was unknown.

Richard [Huntingdon] apprentice of William Burdeyn – 2s.
Richard Persoun apprentice of Nicholas Twyford – 2s.
John Hadlowe apprentice of John Davy – 2s.
William Baldewyne apprentice of William Willay – 2s.
John Bedles apprentice of Thomas Hay – 2s.
William Clement apprentice of John Crullyng – 2s.
John Henny apprentice of John Rugge – 2s.
Henry Clay apprentice of John Carbonelle – 2s.
John Walker apprentice of John Lanham – 2s.
John Trokkyng apprentice of William Aylsham – 2s.
Firmyn Morel apprentice of William Glasen – 2s.
Roger Hedersete apprentice of Richard Beteigne – 2s. col. 2
William Lecham apprentice of John Yarmouth – 2s.
John Gilmyn apprentice of John Luton – 2s.
William Holt apprentice of John Welbourne – 2s.
John Bramptoun apprentice of John Hokyng – 2s.
John Devy apprentice of Melburne – 2s.
Richard Shrewsbury apprentice of Robert Tewkesbury – 2s.
Roger Horntoft apprentice of Thomas Horntoft – 2s.
John Poyntel apprentice of John Walshe – 2s.
John Seybrook apprentice of John Thorne – 2s.
Hugo Wetherby apprentice of Richard Dancastre – 2s.

These are the names of serving-men who have come out of their terms since St Dunstan's Day in the year 46 [Edward III] [19 May 1372]:
Firstly, William Bretford – 2s.
Richard Elys – 2s.

Memorandum that Godekyn, goldsmith, set a glass gemstone in a gold ring, to the great harm and discredit of the goldsmiths' mistery, about which he was questioned by the wardens and goodmen of the mistery, the which offence and wrong-doing he confessed to, and he offered for the said offence to the alms funds of St Dunstan – 10 tuns of wine, and submitted to the judgment of the said wardens and goodmen, at which sentence was remitted and he had to pay only 13s. 4d. to the aforesaid alms funds.

Item, Simon Gravele for incitement to the same offered to the aforesaid alms funds – 40s., and sentence was remitted to 40d.

Item, John Payn for the same cause with another ring offered to the alms funds of St Dunstan 20 tuns of wine, and sentence was remitted to 20s.

p. 48, col. 1[159] Fait a remembr*er* qe William Fitz Hugh*e et* Joh*a*n Ippegr*a*ve, orfeve*r*es, p*ar* cause q'ils furont rebeles v*er*s les gardeinz *et* les bones gentz del orfev*er*ie *et* ne volloient estre justefiez p*ar* eaux, ils furont enprisonez en Neugate, *et* aupr*é*s ils les mystront en la gr*a*ce des ditz gardeinz *et* bonz gentz del orfev*er*ie, *et* aupr*é*s le dit William gr*a*unta al almoygn*e* de Seint Dunston p*ur* le dit t*re*spas – x s.
Et auxint il *et* William Buddere[160] sont obligez as bonz gentz del orfeverie en – xx li. p*ur* son bon port en temps aven*ir*.

It*em*, Joh*a*n Ippegr*a*ve, p*ar* cause q'il fust pov*er*es, lui fust p*ar*don*é et* il *et* Rob*er*t Ippegr*a*ve son frere sont obligez en mesme la man*er*e en – x li.

It*em*, Henry atte Grene p*ur* mesme la cause q'il fust rebel il p*ro*fri al almoygn*e* de S. Dunston – vi s. viii d.

Et out*re* ceo il *et* William Fitz Hugh*e*[161] sont obligez en mesme la man*er*e p*ur* son bon port en – x li.[162]

It*em*, Joh*a*n Beech*e* p*ur* mesme la cause q'il fust rebel il don*e* al almoygn*e* suisdit – vi s. viii d.
It*em*, Steph[e]ne Maplesden*e* p*ur* mesme la cause il don*e* al almoygn*e* suisdit – xl d.
It*em*, Richard atte Nook p*ur* mesme la cause il don*e* [al] almoygn*e* suisdit – xl d.

Fait a remembr*er* q*e* al co*mun*e assemblé des orfev*er*es fait en temps des ditz gardeinz fust ordeiné *et* assentu q*e* chescun an deivont aler as div*er*s feires les gardeinz qe s*er*ront p*ur* l'an p*ur* assay feare des choses touchant le mest*ier* d'orfev*er*ie, *et* ferront lo*ur* assay des toutz choses touchant lo*ur* mest*ier* trovez en les meinz des m*er*ceres, haburdassheres come des orfev*er*es, *et* si bien en feires p*ar*dehors villes come en villes.

Et auxint fust ordeiné en le dit assemblé qe les orfev*er*es de Londres qe ne sont mye gardeinz *et* voisont as feires p*ur* vendre choses touchant lour mest*ier* paieront p*ur* les costages des ditz gardeinz a cel temps, s*ur* q*e*i les ditz gardeinz aleront al feire de Wynchestre *et* trov*er*ont illoqes c*er*teinz gentz d'orfev*er*es de Londres p*ur* vendre choses touchant lo*ur* mest*ier*, q*ue*ux nouns ensuont aupr*é*s, *et* sont mys en c*er*tein q*e* chescun de eaux paiera:
Bartholmeu Castre p*ur* costages des ditz gardeinz al feire suisdit – x s.
William Granth*a*m p*ur* mesme la cause – vi s. viii d.
William Louth*e* p*ur* mesme la cause – vi s. viii d.
Joh*a*n Welb*ur*ne p*ur* mesme la cause – viii s. iiii d.

[159] The following entries concerning FitzHugh, Ippegrave and Grene are also on p. 9 of A + b.
[160] This man is not mentioned in A + b, whose entry is otherwise the same.
[161] This man is not mentioned in A + b, whose entry is otherwise parallel.
[162] This entry and the following ones down to that concerning Welbourne are also on p. 10 of A + b.

Memorandum that William Fitzhugh and John Ippegrave, goldsmiths, whereas they rebelled against the wardens and goodmen of the Goldsmiths' Mistery and did not wish to be judged by them, they were imprisoned in Newgate, and afterwards they submitted to the judgment of the said wardens and goodmen of the Goldsmiths' Mistery, and afterwards the said William granted to the alms funds of St Dunstan for the said offence – 10s. p. 48, col. 1
And also he and William Buddere are under an obligation in the sum of £20 to the goodmen of the Goldsmiths' Mistery, for his good behaviour in the future.

Item, John Ippegrave, because he was poor had his sentence remitted and he and Robert Ippegrave, his brother, are under an obligation in the same manner in the sum of £10.

Item, Henry atte Grene for the same reason that he was rebellious offered to the alms funds of St Dunstan 6s. 8d.

And besides, he and William Fitzhugh are under an obligation in the same manner for his good behaviour in the sum of £10.

Item, John Beeche for the same reason that he was rebellious gave to the aforesaid alms funds – 6s. 8d.
Item, Stephen Maplesdene for the same reason gave to the aforesaid alms funds – 40d.
Item, Richard atte Nook for the same reason gave to the aforesaid alms funds – 40d.

Memorandum that at the common assembly of the goldsmiths held during the term of office of the said wardens, it was ordained and agreed that each year the current wardens for that year must go the various fairs in order to make assay of objects that pertain to the goldsmiths' craft, and they shall make their assay of all objects that pertain to their mistery that may be found in the hands of mercers and haberdashers as well as goldsmiths, and they should do this at fairs held both outside and inside towns.

And it was also ordained at the said assembly that those goldsmiths of London who are not wardens and who go to fairs to sell objects pertaining to their mistery shall pay the costs of the said wardens at that time. And then the said wardens went to Winchester Fair, and there they found certain goldsmiths of London there to sell things pertaining to their mistery, whose names follow here, and they were informed of how much each of them shall pay:
Bartholomew Castre, for the expenses of the said wardens at the aforesaid fair – 10s.
William Grantham for the same cause – 6s. 8d.
William Louth for the same cause – 6s. 8d.
John Welbourne for the same cause – 8s. 4d.

col. 2[163] Fait a remembr*er* qe Joh*a*n Agmodesh*a*m qe fust app*r*entiz a Margrete, nadgairs la fe*m*me William Ippegr*a*ve *et* meere al dit Joh*a*n, il fust de mal port *et* rebel v*er*s le dit Margrete. Et auxint covygne avient p*a*rent*r*e le dit Joh*a*n *et* Joh*a*n de Lutou*n*, Henr*y* atte Grene *et* aut*r*es qe si ascunz des ditz Joh*a*n Lutou*n* ou les aut*r*es esposa la dite Margrete, qe celui qe l'esposa ferroit une acquitance meintenant aup*r*és les esposailes al dit Joh*a*n Agmodesh*a*m de son app*r*enticialté. Et aup*r*és avient qe le dit Joh*a*n Lutou*n* esposa la dite Margrete, s*ur* qei aup*r*és les esposailes le dit Joh*a*n Agmodesh*a*m vient al dit Joh*a*n Lutou*n* *et* lui d*ema*nda de feare acquitance *et* il nel voleit feare; p*ar* qei gr*a*nt debat fust ent*r*e eaux, *et* s*ur* ceo les p*ar*ties soi mystront en agard des gardeinz *et* d'aut*r*es bons gentz del mest*ier*, *et* moustreront lo*ur* causes a eux; s*ur* qei fust agardé qe la ou iiii anz et iii quart*er*s furont avenuz del app*r*enticialté le dit Joh*a*n Agmodesh*a*m, q*e* le dit Joh*a*n Lutou*n* ferroit une acquitance de i an *et* de iii quart*er*s al dit Joh*a*n Agmodesh*a*m *et* qe les iii anz il dem*ur*eit app*r*entiz ovesqe Thomas Reynh*a*m *et* le dit Thomas durreit viii m*a*rz p*ur* av*er* le dit Joh*a*n Agmodesh*a*m app*r*entiz les ditz iii anz, des queux viii m*a*rz iiii m*a*rz furont donez al almoign*e* de Seint Dunston *et* les aut*r*es iiii m*a*rz a Joh*a*n Lutou*n* *et* Margrete sa fe*m*me.

It*e*m, la ou gr*a*nt debat fust p*a*rent*r*e Thomas Wynt*er*, orfev*er*e, *et* son app*r*entiz, *et* les ditz p*ar*ties furont as gr*a*ntz costages en p*ur*suite p*ar* la ley de t*er*re, aup*r*és les ditz p*ar*ties soy mystr*ont* en agard des gardeinz *et* aut*r*es bonz gentz del mest*ier*, les q*ue*ux agarderont qe le dit app*r*entiz devoit don*er* a son mestre une c*er*tein so*m*me d'argent, de quel so*m*me viii s. furont donez al almoign*e* de Seint Dunston *et* le remenant al dit Thomas, son mestre.

It*e*m, la ou Joh*a*n de Tourstrete avoit mys en une pee d'argent de une hanap qe l'en appele une Note c*er*tein plum en deceite, quel defaut fust ap*er*ceu p*ar* les gardeinz, p*ar* qei agardé fust p*ar* les ditz gardeinz qe le dit Joh*a*n devoit don*er* al almoign*e* de S. Dunston vi s. viii d., *et* le pee fust debrusé.

p. 49, col. 1[164] Fait a remembr*er* qe la ou Richard Arnold avoit mys son fitz a William de Gaytou*n* p*ur* estre son app*r*entiz *et* le dit Richard avoit paié al dit William v m*a*rz, aup*r*és avient debat p*a*rent*r*e le dit Richard *et* William p*ar* cause qe les faitz d'ap*r*enticialté ne furont faites, s*ur* qei les p*ar*ties soy mistront en agard des gardeinz *et* aut*r*es bons gentz del mest*ier*, q*ue*ux agarderont qe le dit William Gaytoun rebailereit al dit Richard ii m*a*rz *et* le dit William av*er*eit xl s. *et* les ditz p*ar*ties doneront al almoign*e* de S. Dunston i besant.

A + b p. 13 Fait a remembr*er* qe al co*mun*e assemblé tenuz en le feste de Seint Dunston l'an xlvii p*ar* les orfev*er*es de Londres p*ar* co*m*une assent est ordeigné q*e* eaux tindront lo*ur* feste chescun an mesme le jo*ur* de Seint Dunston, s*ur*

[163] The entries concerning Agmodesham, Wynter and Tourstrete are also on p. 11 of A + b.
[164] The following entry is also on p. 12 of A + b.

Memorandum that John Agmodesham, who was the apprentice of Margaret, formerly the wife of William Ippegrave and mother of the said John, behaved badly and rebelled against the said Margaret. And also there was an agreement between the said John and John de Luton, Henry atte Grene and others, that if either John Luton or one of the others should marry the said Margaret, that he who married her should immediately after the wedding discharge the said John Agmodesham from his apprenticeship. And afterwards it happened that the said John Luton married the said Margaret, and after the wedding the said John Agmodesham came to the said John Luton and asked him for his discharge, but he did not wish to give it to him; there was thus a great quarrel between them, and therefore the parties brought the case to be judged by the wardens and other goodmen of the mistery, and they stated their cases to them; and it was then judged that as there were 4 years left of his apprenticeship, the said John Luton would give the said John Agmodesham a discharge of 1 years, and that he would for the 3 years remain an apprentice with Thomas Raynham, and the said Thomas would give 8 marks to have the said John Agmodesham as an apprentice for the said 3 years, and of those 8 marks, 4 marks were given to the alms funds of St Dunstan and the other 4 marks to John Luton and his wife Margaret. col. 2

Item, whereas a great quarrel arose between Thomas Wynter, goldsmith, and his apprentice, and the said parties went to great expense in prosecuting the matter by the law of the land, afterwards the said parties brought the case to be judged by the wardens and other goodmen of the mistery, and they gave judgment that the said apprentice should give his master a certain sum of money, of which sum 8s. were given to the alms funds of St Dunstan and the remainder to the said Thomas, his master.

Item, whereas John of Tower Street[79] had deceitfully put some lead within the silver base of a goblet of the type called a coconut-cup, the which misdeed was noticed by the wardens, and for this reason it was judged by the said wardens that the said John should give 6s. 8d. to the alms funds of St Dunstan, and the base was broken up.

Memorandum that whereas Richard Arnold had placed his son with William de Gaytoun to be his apprentice, and the said Richard had paid 5 marks to the said William, and afterwards a quarrel arose between the said Richard and William because the apprenticeship deeds had not been drawn up, and therefore the parties brought the case to be judged by the wardens and other goodmen of the mistery, and they judged that the said William Gaytoun should return 2 marks to the said Richard, and the said William should keep 40s. and the said parties gave one bezant to the alms funds of St Dunstan. p. 49, col. 1

Memorandum that at the common assembly held by the goldsmiths of London on St Dunstan's feastday in the year 47 [Edward III] [19 May 1373] it was ordained by common assent that they should hold their feast each year on A + b p. 13

[79] Tower Street is both a street and a ward within the City of London. Although 'de Tourstrete' might be seen as a surname, it seems perhaps more likely that it is a designation.

peine q*e* les gardeinz novels eslieux doneront de lo*ur* burse p*ro*pre al aunciens gardeinz iiii li. mesme le jo*ur* de S*eint* Dunston p*ur* despendre ent*re* les bons gentz del mest*ier*.[165]

1373–74 A + a p. 49, col. 1[166] [167]Ceux sont les nons de les gardeyns de le mester del Orfeve*r*ie de Londres, comenceant lo*ur* office le jo*ur* de Seint Dunstou*n* l'an du regne le roi E*dward* tierce puis le conquest d'Englet*er*re xlviime. Les nons de les:
Will*ia*m Tyngewyk
Joh*a*n Waldene
Will*ia*m Geytou*n* et
Joh*a*n Carbonell*e*

Dispenses de les ditz gardeyns mesmes l'an susdit:
Primes, p*ur* soner none en le belfray[168] de Seint Poul de dive*r*ses costagies – vii s. iii d.
It*em*, le lumere al esglise de Seint Joh*a*n Zakarie – xvii s.
It*em*, doné al encrés del almoigne de Seint Dunstou*n* – vii li.
It*em*, p*ur* vesture achaté a trois povres ho*m*mes – xxi s.
It*em*, p*ur* vesture a S*ire* Philipp*e*, le prestre, iiii aunes le aune a v s., et xl d. p*ri*s le pane – la su*m*me xxiii s. iiii d.
It*em*, ceux sont les nons des povres gentz paier ceste an del almoigne de Seint Dunstou*n*:
Joh*a*n Compes, Thom*a*s Salesbury } paié p*ar* la meyn de Will*ia*m Tyngewyk – v li. xvi s.[169]
Joh*a*ne Lyncoln*e* paié p*ar* la meyn de Joh*a*n Walden*e* – lii s.
Pieres Dunstall*e* paié p*ar* la meyn de Will*ia*m Gaytou*n* – lii s.
Pieres Hungry paié p*ar* la mayn Joh*a*n Carbonell*e* – lii s.

col. 2 It*em*, S*ire* Philipp*e*, prestre, Pieres Mazerer, Rauf Makenehe[ne]d[170] } paié p*ar* les meyns de les renters l'an susdit, c'est assav*oir* Thom*a*s Extou*n* *et* Thom*a*s Polle.

Ceux sont les nons des apprentices entrés en le mester d'orfeve*r*ie l'an susdit:[171]
Will*el*m*us* Ligthtegr*a*ve apprentys ové Nichol*e* Twyford – ii s.[172]
Rogerus Lawtou*n* apprent*icius* cu*m* Roberto Tewkesbery – ii s.

[165] See below, p. 25 of Book A + b, for this ruling being put into practice differently in 1381, the old wardens who have not held a feast giving £4 to the new wardens.
[166] The following entries for this year are also on p. 14 of A + b.
[167] A new hand starts here.
[168] One may note the specific mention here of the bell-tower. For further information on this see Christopher Wilson's forthcoming book: *The Honour and Glory of London: The Architecture of St Paul's Cathedral 1087–1547*.
[169] This figure, and those below in this list, have been written in later in a different hand.
[170] The name is spelt 'Makenet' in Book A + b.
[171] The following two lists are also on p. 15 of A + b.
[172] The rest of this column has been entered by another hand, and then the rest of the page below in the former hand; this scribe must have left a blank space to be filled in later.

St Dunstan's Day itself, on pain that [if no feast were held] the newly-elected wardens should give to the former wardens on that same St Dunstan's Day £4 from their own pockets to be spent out among the goodmen of the mistery.

These are the names of the wardens of the Goldsmiths' Mistery of London, taking up their office on St Dunstan's Day in the year 47 Edward III [19 May 1373]. Their names: 1373–74 A + a p. 49, col. 1

William Tingewick
John Walden
William Gaytoun
John Carbonelle

Expenses of the said wardens in the same aforesaid year:
Firstly, for ringing out noon in the belfry of St Paul's, various expenses – 7s. 3d.
Item, the light in the church of St John Zachary – 17s.
Item, given to the increase of the alms funds of St Dunstan – £7
Item, for clothing bought for three poor men – 21s.
Item, for clothing for Sir Philip, the priest, 4 ells at 5s. the ell, and 40d. the cost of the 'pane'[80] [lining] – total 23s. 4d.
Item, these are the names of the poor people paid this year from the alms funds of St Dunstan:
John Compes, Thomas Salisbury } paid by[81] William Tingewick – £5 16s.
Joanna Lincoln, paid by John Walden – 52s.
Piers Dunstalle, paid by William Gaytoun – 52s.
Piers Hungry, paid by John Carbonelle – 52s.

Item, Sir Philip, priest, Piers Mazerer, Ralph Makenhened } paid by the renters of the aforesaid year i.e. Thomas Exton and Thomas Polle col. 2

These are the names of apprentices who have entered the goldsmiths' mistery in the aforesaid year:

William Ligthtegrave, apprentice with Nicholas Twyford –	2s.
Roger Lawtoun apprentice with Robert Tewkesbury –	2s.

[80] A soft kind of cloth with a long nap used to make linings.
[81] Literally, the text says 'by the hand of'.

Joh*anne*s Berkham apprent*icius* cu*m* Joh*anne* Welborne –	ii s.
Walterus Michel apprent*icius* cu*m* Joh*anne* Bulstrod*e* –	ii s.
Henricus Heyward apprent*icius* cu*m* Henr*ico* Bamme –	ii s.
Joh*anne*s Shithby apprent*icius* cu*m* Thom*e* Wylby –	ii s.
Thom*as* Pountfrett apprent*icius* cu*m* Will*elmo* de Louth*e* –	ii s.
Thom*as* Cresselowe apprent*icius* cu*m* Thom*e* Davy –	iis.
Joh*anne*s Boston apprent*icius* cu*m* Robert*o* Godma*n* –	ii s.
Joh*anne*s Walgrave apprent*icius* cu*m* Joh*anne* Lutone –	ii s.
Joh*anne*s Laget apprent*icius* cu*m* Nichol*ao* Merfeld*e* –	ii s.
Will*elmus* Brerelee apprent*icius* cu*m* Joh*anne* Ascheburn*e* –	ii s.
Joh*anne*s Howgtou*n* apprentic*ius* cu*m* Will*elmo* Horsman –	ii s.
Joh*anne*s Sadelere apprentic*ius* cu*m* Joh*anne* Ipegrave –	ii s.
Joh*anne*s Bette, Nichol*as* Nygent apprentic*ii* cu*m* Will*el*m*o* Pevere –	iiii s.
Will*elmus* Baldeswell*e* apprent*icius* cu*m* Ricard*o* Brunh*am* –	ii s.
Thom*as* Secroft apprentic*ius* cu*m* Henr*ico* Abot –	ii s.
Joh*anne*s Stanes apprentis cu*m* Joh*anne* Adam –	ii s.

Ceux sont les nons des lowés q*e* sont hors de lo*ur* te*r*mes:

Rog*er* Riot –	ii s.
Thom*as* Foxcote –	ii s.
Remund Standel[f] –	ii s.
Ricardus Savage –	ii s.
Robertus Langelee –	ii s.
Symon Pykot –	ii s.

Ordinacio de vessellers[173]

Fait a remembrer q*e* une ordinance fust ordiné entre les vesselers q*e* null*e* de eux vende null*e* vessel a null*e* estrang*er* meins le lb de ii s., south peine de xl s. appaier al almoigne de Seint Dunstou*n*, *et* un Will*ia*m Yrissh*e* q*e* l'en appelle Will*iam* fitz Hughe fust trové q*e* il vendy a Cornhull*e* une dozeine d'esquelys le lb meyns de xviii d.[174] La il paia la peine al almoigne de Seint Dunstou*n*, viendront Joh*a*n de Chichestre *et* Nichole Twyford *et* prieront remedie a les gardeins de p*ar*tie del dit argent, *et* les gardeyns lui ont rebaillez xx s. et les autres xx s. il paia. Et acordé fust si il fusse aut*re*foitz trové en tiele defaute il repaiera les xx s. et xl s. plus al almoigne.

p. 50, col. 1 Giffrey Walpoul ad vendu son apprentys sans congé de les gardeyns le te*r*me de v ans, *et* ledit apprentys avoit a nou*n* Estephene Clerc, *et* p*ur* ceo il dona al almoigne de Seint Dunston – iiii li. des queux iiii li. il paia xx s. le mesme an a les gardeyns *et* trois ans aprés le jo*ur* de Seint Dunston il paiera chescun an xx s. si son dit apprentis vive *et* demure en la ville. Et de ceo ledit Giffrey est obligé a les ditz gardeyns en viii li. p*ar* une l*ett*re obligatorie.

[173] Cf. above, p. 33, col. 2. This ordinance, and the following entry concerning Walpole, are also on p. 15 of A + b.

[174] MS: xviii s.

John Barkham apprentice with John Welbourne –	2s.
Walter Michel apprentice with John Bulstrode –	2s.
Henry Heyward apprentice with Henry Bamme –	2s.
John Shithby apprentice with Thomas Wilby –	2s.
Thomas Pountfrett apprentice with William de Louth –	2s.
Thomas Cresselowe apprentice with Thomas Davy –	2s.
John Boston apprentice with Robert Godman –	2s.
John Walgrave apprentice with John Luton –	2s.
John Laget apprentice with Nicholas Mirfield –	2s.
William Brerelee apprentice with John Ashbourne –	2s.
John Houghtoun apprentice with William Horsman –	2s.
John Saddler apprentice with John Ippegrave –	2s.
John Bette, Nicholas Nygent, apprentices with William Pevere –	4s.
William Baldeswelle apprentice with Richard Burnham –	2s.
Thomas Seacroft apprentice with Henry Abbot –	2s.
John Staines apprentice with John Adam –	2s.

These are the names of serving-men who have come out of their terms:

Roger Ryot –	2s.
Thomas Foxcote –	2s.
Raymund Standelf –	2s.
Richard Savage –	2s.
Robert Langley –	2s.
Simon Pykot –	2s.

Ordinance of vessellers:
Memorandum that an ordinance was ordained among the vessellers that none of them should sell any vessel to any alien at less than 2s. the lb.,[82] on pain of paying 40s. to the alms funds of St Dunstan, and a William Yrisshe, called William FitzHugh, was found guilty of selling on Cornhill a dozen bowls at less than 18d. the pound. When he paid the penalty to the alms funds of St Dunstan, John de Chichester and Nicholas Twyford came and begged the wardens that a part of the said money should be remitted, and the wardens returned 20s. to him and he paid the other 20s. And it was agreed that if he were to be found guilty again of such a misdeed, then he shall repay the 20s. and another 40s. to the alms funds.

Geoffrey Walpole sold his apprentice without permission of the wardens five p. 50, col. 1
years of his apprenticeship, and the said apprentice's name was Stephen Clerk, and for this reason he gave to the alms funds of St Dunstan – £4, of the which £4 he paid 20s. the same year to the wardens and for each of the next 3 years he shall pay 20s. on St Dunstan's Day if his said apprentice shall live and shall remain in the city. And for this the said Geoffrey is bound by letters obligatory in the sum of £8 to the said wardens.

[82] This must be the price of the workmanship, over and above the price of the metal etc.

Fait a remembrer q*e* Estephene Clerc est obligé a lesditz gardeyns en x m*a*rcz d'est*er*lingz p*ar* une l*ett*re obligatorie, nep*ur*qant lesditz gardeins volunt *et* g*ra*untont si ledit Estephene des*er*ve a gentz de le dit mester de sa art b*ie*n *et* loialment *et* a null*e* autre ho*m*me q*e* voet revendre sa chose arere durant le t*er*me de .v. ans q*e* il ne paie rien. Et si il face, la obligacion tieigne sa force.[175]

[176]Pensez q*e* Richard Burnh*a*m ad vendu son apprentys p*ur* C. s. sans congé ou gree faire a les gardeins.

Pensés q*e* Joh*a*n Laneh*a*m ad vendu son apprentys[177] a lui mesmes p*ur* v m*a*rcz *et* d*em*i sanz congé ou gree faire a les gardeyns.

1374–75 [178]Ceux [sont] lé nouns des gardeins de mestr*ier* d'orffev*er*ie comenceant a
col. 2 Loundres lo*ur* office le jo*ur* de Seint Dunston l'an du regn*e* le Roy Edward puis le conquest quarant oetisme:

Nicholas Twyfford
Petrus Prestou*n*
Thomas Reinh*a*m
Robertus Lucas
} no*m*i*n*a custodu*m*

Despenses des ditz gardeyns l'an susdit, c'est assav*oir*:
Primes, p*ur* sonere non*e* le veile de Seint Dunstan en la Belfray de Seint Poule p*ur* div*er*s costages – vi s. viii d.
It*em*, p*ur* le lum*er*e al esglise Seint Joh*a*n Zakarie c'est ass*avoir* p*ur* xii ceir*es* *et* ii torch*es* poissant xviii libr*as* q*e* amont – x s. vi d.

It*em*, p*ur* vest*ur*e achaté a S*ire* Gaweyn de Southorp*e*. Et p*ur* S*ire* Randolp*he*, chapeleyn. Et p*ur* lé panez – xxiii s. iii d.

It*em*, p*ur* vest*ur*e achaté a iiii[179] pov*er*e ho*m*mes – xvi s. ix d.

Ceux sont les nou*n*s des pov*er*es gentz paié del almoigne de Seint Dunstan ceste an:

Pers Hungri
Pers Durstall*e*
Will*ia*m Stoure
Joh*a*n[e][180] Lincolln*e*
} paié p*ar* lez gardeins – x li. viii s.

It*em* S*ire* Gaweyn Southorp*e* paié p*ar* Nich*olas* Twyford p*ar* chescun semayn – ii s. – xviii s.

[175] This entry and the following two are also on p. 16 of A + b.
[176] This entry and the next have been added later but in the same hand as those above.
[177] This is presumably, although not certainly, John Walker, listed above, who does not appear again in the records, and who may well have gone to practise his trade outside London.
[178] A new hand starts here.
[179] This number has been written over the scored word 'trois'.
[180] This person is everywhere else spelt with a feminine '-e' ending to the name; see Name Index.

Memorandum that Stephen Clerk is bound by letters obligatory to the said wardens in the sum of 10 marks sterling, nevertheless the said wardens wish and grant that if the said Stephen shall serve people of the said mistery well and faithfully in his craft, and shall not do work for any other man who might wish to sell his pieces retail, this during the period of 5 years, then he shall pay nothing. And if he does this, then the obligation shall be brought into force.

Memo that Richard Burnham sold his apprentice for 100s. without permission from and without making a settlement with the wardens.

Memo that John Lanham sold his apprentice his own terms for 5½ marks without the permission of and without making a settlement with the wardens.

These are the names of the wardens of the goldsmiths' mistery, taking up their office in London on St Dunstan's Day in the year 48 Edward III [19 May 1374]: 1374–75 col. 2

Nicholas Twyford
Piers Preston
Thomas Raynham
Robert Lucas } the names of the wardens

Expenses of the said wardens in the aforesaid year, i.e.
Firstly, for ringing out noon on the eve of St Dunstan's Day in the belfry of St Paul's, for various expenses – 6s. 8d.
Item, for the light at the church of St John Zachary, i.e. for 12 wax candles and 2 torches [large candles] weighing 28 lbs. which amount to – 10s. 6d.

Item, for clothing bought for Sir Gawain de Southorpe. And for Sir Randolph, chaplain. And for the linings – 23s. 3d.

Item, for clothing bought for 4 poor men – 16s. 9d.

These are the names of poor people paid this year from the alms funds of St Dunstan:

Piers Hungry
Piers Dunstalle
William Stour
Joanna Lincoln } paid by the wardens £10 8s.

Item, Sir Gawain Southorpe paid by Nicholas Twyford, each week – 2s. – 18s.

Item, Pers Mazarer
Rauphe Makenhe[ne]d } paié [par les] renteres pur chescun semayn – iii s.

Item, Thomas Aras paié par Pers de Prestoun pur chescun symayn – xii d.
– totalis[181]

Item, Sire Randolphe, prest, paié par les renteres pernaunt par l'an – vi li.
– par le semayn[182]
Item, a William Hathfeld, paié par Nicholas Twyford et Thomas Reynham del almoynge – xl s.

p. 51, col. 1 Faite a remembrer qe les avantdittz gardeins ont paiés as homes de la ley pur certeins bosoins touchant la mestier, c'est assavoir a Johan Midiltoun, [183]Rikille, a sergans demurranz ovek la meyre et autres, en diversez costages.

Fait a remembrer qe les gardeins avantditz ont doné al encrés de almoigne Seint Du[n]stoun ceste an – x li.

Pensez qe Geffray Walpole vint devant les bones gentz de dit mestier et illoqes paiat – xx s. le jour Seint Du[n]stoun, en queux vintz soulsz il est obligé pur soun apprentis[184] vendu sanz coungé des gardeyns, a paier chescun an de trois anz aprés la acorde. Et ici reste a paier[185]

Fait a rem[em]brer qe Richard Durham vint devant les gardeins et se mist en lour grace pur la vendicioun de soun apprentiz et ilz ont agreez o luy pur paier al almoigne de Seint Dunston avandit demi marc, quel demi marc est paié.

Johan Laneham vint devant lez gardeins avantditz et il [se] meste en lour grace par cause q'il ad vendu soun apprentiz sanz congé dé ditz gardeins. De quel Johan lez gardens susditz avont consideracioun de soun poverté[186] et luy ont pardoné le trespas en huvre de charité.

Ceux sount les nouns des apprentiz entrés en le mestier d'orpheverie l'an susditz:

Johannes Henney apprenticius cum Johanne Canoun –	ii s.
Johannes Duse apprenticius cum Johanne Lutoun –	ii s.
William Britoun aprenticius cum Henrico Malmeyn –	ii s.
Thomas atte Wode aprenticius cum Stephano Maplesdene –	ii s.
Richard Hotoft aprenticius cum Hugone Wetherby –	ii s.
Walter atte Water aprenticius cum Johanne Thorne –	ii s.

181 No sum has been filled in.
182 No sum has been filled in.
183 A space has been left, clearly the first name was not known.
184 See above, A + a, p. 50, col. 1.
185 No sum has been filled in.
186 MS: povererte.

Item, Piers Mazerer } paid by the renters, each week – 3s.
Ralph Makenhened

Item, Thomas Aras paid by Piers de Preston, each week – 12d. – total

Item, Sir Randolph, priest, paid by the renters, taking for the year – £6
– per week
Item, to William Hatfield, paid by Nicholas Twyford and Thomas Raynham from the alms funds – 40s.

Memorandum that the aforesaid wardens paid to the lawyers for certain necessary matters pertaining to the mistery, i.e. to John Middleton, Rikille, to the Mayor's serjeants and others, for various expenses – p. 51, col. 1

Memorandum that the aforesaid wardens gave to the increase of the alms funds of St Dunstan this year – £10.

Memo that Geoffrey Walpole came before the goodmen of the said mistery and there paid – 20s. on St Dunstan's Day, the which twenty shillings he was bound to pay for having sold his apprentice without the permission of the wardens, this to be paid each year for three years after the agreement. And there now remains to be paid –

Memorandum that Richard Durham came before the wardens and submitted himself to their judgment for the sale of his apprentice, and they settled with him to pay half a mark to the aforesaid alms funds of St Dunstan, the which half mark is paid.

John Lanham came before the aforesaid wardens and submitted himself to their judgment for having sold his apprentice without permission of the said wardens. The aforesaid wardens, having consideration for his poverty, gave the said John a pardon for his offence as an act of charity.

These are the names of apprentices admitted into the goldsmiths' mistery in the aforesaid year:

John Henney apprentice with John Canon –	2s.
John Dusse apprentice with John Luton –	2s.
William Britoun apprentice with Henry Malmayn –	2s.
Thomas atte Wood apprentice with Stephen Maplesdene –	2s.
Richard Hotoft apprentice with Hugh Wetherby –	2s.
Walter atte Water apprentice with John Thorne –	2s.

Joh*ann*es Beste ap*r*ent*icius* cum Georg*io* Reg – ii s.
Sander*s* Withe ap*r*ent*icius* cum Joh*ann*e Ippeg*ra*ve – ii s.
Laur*ence* Dunhide ap*r*ent*icius* cum Thoma Tidirle – ii s.
Ric*hard* Kegge ap*r*ent*icius* cum Joh*ann*e F*ra*nceis – ii s.
Will*ia*m Markesdene ap*r*ent*icius* cum Nich*olao* Fairford – ii s.
Neel Saunford app*r*ent*icius* cum Joh*ann*e S[h]ordich*e* – ii s.
Janekyn Coraunt app*r*ent*icius* cum Joh*ann*e Coraunt – ii s.[187]

col. 2 Ceux sont les nouns de strangers q'ount paié p*ur* lo*ur* entré al almeingne de Seint Donstou*n*:

Joh*ann*es Doubler –	xx s.
Joh*ann*es Fox –	xx s.
Joh*ann*es Coloyn Heghlow –	xiii s. iiii d.
Wynaunt Vangeyn –	xvi s. viii d.
Mich*ael* Lokherst –	xiii s. iiii d.
Hans Selslider –	xx s.
Joh*ann*es Holscombe Westfelyng –	x s.
Joh*ann*es Brissels –	xxvi s. viii d.
Widikyn Wathle –	xiii s. iiii d.
Herman de Souste –	xx s.
Joh*ann*es le Freynshe –	xiii s. iiii d.
Michelet n*ihil* valet[188] –	xiii s. iiii d.
Hans Vinbe –	xx s.
Godkyn milliz g*ra*nis –	xiii s. iiii d.
Joh*ann*es Durdraiche –	x s.
Rouland de Coloyn –	xiii s. iiii d.
Hardwyn de Scriwesbure –	xiii s. iiii d.

It*e*m, paié p*ur* un esc*ri*veyn p*ar* l'an p*ur* totez man*er*es chose q'amount en tout[189]

1375 It*e*m, pensez q*e* Nich*olas* Twyford, Pers de P*re*stou*n*, Thom*as* Reynh*a*m *et* Rob*er*t Lucas ont paié a Joh*ann*e Salusburi l'an xlixe –
xx li. dont ills ont de le dit Joh*a*n un aquitaunce de dit so*m*me receuz.[190]

1375 Fait a remembrer q*e* Will*ia*m F*ra*unceys, Joh*a*n Bodish*a*m, Joh*a*n Welforde
p. 52 *et* Rob*er*t Launde, gardeinz de mester des orfev*er*s, ont resceu de la cu*m*paignye de dit mestier le veigle de Seint Thom*as* le T*ra*nslac*io*n en l'an xlixe p*ur* rebailer al dit cu*m*paignie al feste de Seint Dunstan p*ro*schein a venir apr*és* la date d'icestez, en cler – xv li.
c'est asavoir, chescun dez ditez gardeinz p*ur* sou*n* p*ar*tie lxxiiii s. xi d.

187 This last line appears to be a slightly later addition by the same scribe.
188 This appears to be a nickname, and one wonders whether it has not been translated into Latin by the scribe? Alternatively, it might be a note to mark the entry as invalid.
189 No figure has been filled in.
190 This paragraph has been added later in a different hand.

John Beste apprentice with George Reg –	2s.
Sanders Withe apprentice with John Ippegrave –	2s.
Laurence Dunhide apprentice with Thomas Tidderle –	2s.
Richard Kegge apprentice with John Fraunceys –	2s.
William Markesdene apprentice with Nicholas Fairford –	2s.
Neil Sanford apprentice with John Shoreditch –	2s.
Janekyn Coraunt apprentice with John Coraunt –	2s.

These are the names of aliens who have paid to the alms funds of St Dunstan for their entry: col. 2

Johan Dobler –	20s.
John Fox –	20s.
Johan Cologne Heghlow –	13s. 4d.
Wynant Vangeyn –	16s. 8d.
Michael Lokherst –	13s. 4d.
Hans Selslider –	20s.
John Holscombe of Westphalia –	10s.
John Brissels –	26s. 8d.
Widikyn Wathle –	13s. 4d.
Hermann de Souste –	20s.
John le Frenshe –	13s. 4d.
Michelet 'worthless' –	13s. 4d.
Hans Vinbe –	20s.
Godkyn 'milliz granis'[83] –	13s. 4d.
Johan Durdrecht –	10s.
Roland de Cologne –	13s. 4d.
Hardwyn de Shrewsbury –	13s. 4d.

Item, paid for a scribe (scrivener) for a year, for all manner of things, amounting in total

Item, memo that Nicholas Twyford, Piers de Preston, Thomas Raynham and Robert Lucas have paid to John Salisbury in 1375 – £20, for which they have a receipt in full from the said John.

Memorandum that William Fraunceys, John Bottisham, John Welford and Robert Launde, wardens of the Goldsmiths' Mistery, received from the company of the said mistery on the eve of the Translation of St Thomas in the year 49 [Edward III] [6 July[84] 1375], these monies to be restored to the company at the feast of St Dunstan next following the date of this – £15 net. i.e. each of the said wardens as his portion – 74s. 11d.[85] p. 52

[83] This might be a surname but is more probably another nickname, 'a thousand grains'.

[84] This if one assumes that St Thomas a Becket is meant. If the translation of St Thomas the Apostle, then the eve of this is 2 July.

[85] 4d. would appear to be unaccounted for.

1375–76 No*min*a de novo jur*atorum* indigen*orum*:
p. 53, col. 1[191] In primis, de Will*elm*o Stuwardy appr*enticius* cum Rob*er*to Boteller – ii s.
It*em*, de Joh*ann*e Clyff appr*enticius* cum Will*elm*o Cheyne – ii s.
It*em*, de Will*elm*o Swetyng app*renticius* cum Joh*ann*e Waryn – ii s.
It*em*, de Thoma Hall*e* filio Joh*ann*is Hall*e* nup*er* aurifabri – ii s.
Rog*er*us Ernstou*n* app*renticius* cum Jacobo Tregustok – ii s.
It*em*, de Will*elm*o Melsomby app*renticius* cum Joh*ann*e Sturdys – ii s.
It*em*, de Roge Jertou*n* app*renticius* cum Joh*ann*e Jertou*n* p*at*re suo – ii s.
It*em*, de Joh*ann*e Jertou*n* app*renticius* cum Joh*ann*e Jertou*n* p*at*re suo – ii s.
It*em*, de Joh*ann*e Burnh*a*m app*renticius* cum Ric*ard*o Bradcok – ii s.
Will*elmu*s Knyght app*renticius* cum Walt*er*o atte Stokkes – ii s.
Will*elmu*s Percy app*renticius* cum Henr*ico* Pole – ii s.

col. 2 No*min*a de novo jur*atorum* de lez ducheman:
In primis, de Gyes Glokvim – ii s.
It*em*, de Helme Spayn cum Walter Rocandelle – ii s.
It*em*[192]
It*em*, de Cristyan Jouhnson – ii s.
It*em*, de Arnold Denchrode – ii s.
It*em*, de Jone Feselard cum eodem – ii s.
It*em*, de Nich*ol*o Myleagard cum eodem – ii s.
It*em*, de Georgio Shees et de Joh*a*n Joh*a*nson cum Arnaldo Aumoner – iiii s.
It*em*, Geriardus Ibyng de Westfale , Lubard of Midewold de Freseland, cum Mangnus Goldsmyth – Item idem Mangnus – vi s.
It*em*, Garlodre Madewell*e* cum Will*elm*o Garrard in Suth*e*werk – ii s.
It*em*, Denyse Tristram cum Matheo Phelipp*e* – ii s.
It*em*, Hans Bremer cum Joh*ann*e Seynne – ii s.
It*em*, Andreas Cape cum Henr*ico* Luton – ii s.
It*em*, Gyes Spenser cum Semetr*i*ps – ii s.
It*em*, Clays Henrykson cum Arnold Denchrode – ii s.
It*em*, Deryk of Orysewyk *et* Syvran Ovserdesse cum Walt*er*o Roucandell*e* – iiii s.
It*em*, Germyn Lynch*e* of Ierland cum Bisshop – ii s.
It*em*, Wyghtte Johnson – ii s.[193]
It*em*, Cristian Rodloff dwellyng with Garrard Hanerboke – ii s.

p. 54 It*em*, resceyved of Arnold Annore, ducheman, for a fyne to have leve to occupye John Johnson as his app*re*ntyse for þe tyme of app*re*ntysode – xiii s. iiii d.

It*em*, resceyved of Barthelodee Lamspyng for þe kepyng of Lenard Milleward for þe same cause – xiii s. iiii d.[194]

[191] A new hand starts here.
[192] The rest of the line is blank.
[193] The name has been written over the scored phrase 'a ducheman dwellyng beside Benet of Dorkyng'.
[194] It would seem probable that the two apprentices listed in the above entries were men who were in fact already well-trained but who were forced by the Goldsmiths' ordinances into spending time as apprentices in order later to gain acceptance and entry into the mistery. See above, A + a, pp. 40–41.

The names of denizens recently sworn: 1375–76
Firstly, from William Stuwardy apprentice with Robert Boteler – 2s. p. 53, col. 1
Item, from John Clyff apprentice with William Cheyne – 2s.
Item, from William Swetyng apprentice with John Waryn – 2s.
Item, from Thomas Halle, son of John Halle, late a goldsmith – 2s.
Roger Ernstoun apprentice with James Tregewstek – 2s.
Item, from William Melsomby apprentice with John Sturdys – 2s.
Item, from Roger Jertoun apprentice with John Jertoun, his father – 2s.
Item, from John Jertoun apprentice with John Jertoun, his father – 2s.
Item, from John Burnham apprentice with Richard Bradcok – 2s.
William Knyght apprentice with Walter atte Stokkes – 2s.
William Percy apprentice with Henry Pole – 2s.

The names of 'Dutchmen' recently sworn: col. 2
Firstly, from Gyse Glokvim – 2s.
Item, from Helme Spayn, with[86] Walter Rocandelle – 2s.
Item,
Item, from Christian Jouhnson – 2s.
Item, from Arnold Denchrode – 2s.
Item, from John Feselard, with the same man[87] – 2s.
Item, from Nicholas Myleagard, with the same man – 2s.
Item, from George Shees and from John Johanson, with Arnold Aumoner – 4s.
Item, Gerard Ibyng of Westphalia, Lubard of Midewold in Friesland, with Magnus Goldsmith – Item, the same Magnus – 6s.
Item, Garlodre Madewelle, with William Garrard in Southwark – 2s.
Item, Denis Tristram, with Matthew Philipp – 2s.
Item, Hans Bremer, with John Seynne – 2s.
Item, Andrew Cape, with Henry Luton – 2s.
Item, Gyse Spenser, with Semetrips – 2s.
Item, Clays Henrykson, with Arnold Denchrode – 2s.
Item, Derek of Orysewyk and Syvran Ovserdesse, with Walter Rocandelle – 4s.
Item, Germyn Lynche of Ireland, with Bisshop – 2s.
Item, Wight Johnson – 2s.
Item, Christian Rodloff, living with Garrard Hanerboke – 2s.

Item, received from Arnold Annore, 'Dutchman', as a fee to obtain permission to employ John Johnson as his apprentice during the time of his apprenticeship – 13s. 4d. p. 54

Item, received from Bartholodee Lamspyng for keeping Leonard Milleward for the same reason – 13s. 4d.

[86] i.e. who is his serving-man.
[87] Presumably this means that John Feselard is the serving-man of Arnold Denchrode, as is the next named Nicholas Myleagard?

1376–77 A + b p. 17[195] Ceux su*n*t les nouns queux ou*n*t baylé en p*re*sticioun en onour, dedew e ayde del mest*er* de orf[ev]erie e p*ur* aver alouaunce de lo*ur* rente, checun de xviii co*m*paynou*n*s – xx s.[196]

Ce est a savoyr p*ri*mere*r*ment:

Will*iam* Tingewyk –	xx s.
Adam Ba*m*me –	xx s.
Will*iam* Borden –	xx s.
Thom*as* Davy –	xx s.
Harri Ba*m*me –	xx s.
Joh*an* Botisham –	xx s.
Joh*an* Walshe –	xx s.
Joh*an* Fraunceys –	xx s.
Thom*as* Pantone –	xx s.
Thom*as* Polle –	xx s.
Will*iam* Lucas –	xx s.
Joh*an* Luton –	xx s.
Joh*an* Maplisdene –	xx s.
Joh*an* Lincolle –	xx s.
Will*iam* Lowþe –	xx s.
Joh*an* Thorn –	xx s.
Estep*hanus* Thorp –	xx s.
Joh*an* Welbourne –	xiii s. iiii d.[197]

p. 18 Ceux su*n*t les nou*n*s q*ue*ux furu*n*t rebel e co*ntra*[r]ious enco*ntr*e les bons ordinaunces ordeynés p*ar* comune assent de les bons gens de le mest*er* orf[ev]erie, p*ur* quey il su*n*t mys hors de la liv*er*é de lo*ur* co*m*paynie p*ar* les dit gardeyns e aut*re*s bons gens de la co[*m*]panie en l'an su dit:

Peris de P*re*ston
Goffrey Walpol
Peris Hiltoft
Thom*as* Findene
Robe*r*t Godema*n*
Joh*an* Blacman
Gorge Rigge
Joh*an* Canon
Will*iam* Fichet
Rolond Van de Bush
Will*iam* Fis Hwe
Will*iam* Everad
Robe*r*t P*re*ntis

195 The following entries from Book A + b have no date within them but must by their position in the book date from between 1374 and 1377, and they can be dated 1376–77 for the loans, the date of which is given later when they are repaid (see below, A + b, p. 23). On this p. 17 a new hand, a somewhat poor and ill-formed one, takes over the writing and continues to p. 20; this hand does not appear in Book A + a.

196 When repayments start to be listed, in addition to the following names, those of John Broun and Thomas Usk are given (see Name Index).

197 No explanation is given but perhaps he promised 20s. but was in the event unable to raise the whole sum?

These are the names of those who have made a loan for the honour, pleasure and assistance of the Goldsmiths' mistery and to be set off against rent-money due,[88] each of 18 companions – 20s. 1376–77 A + b p. 17
i.e. firstly:

William Tingewick –	20s.
Adam Bamme –	20s.
William Burdeyn –	20s.
Thomas Davy –	20s
Harry Bamme –	20s.
John Bottisham –	20s.
John Walshe –	20s.
John Fraunceys –	20s.
Thomas Panton –	20s.
Thomas Polle –	20s.
William Lucas –	20s.
John Luton –	20s.
John Maplesdene –	20s.
John Lincoln –	20s.
William Louth –	20s.
John Thorn –	20s.
Stephen Thorp –	20s.
John Welbourne –	13s. 4d.

These are the names of those who have been rebellious and have gone against the good ordinances ordained by common assent of the goodmen of the Goldsmiths' Mistery, for which reason they have been taken out of [forbidden to wear] the livery of their company by the said wardens and other goodmen of the company in the aforesaid year: p. 18

Piers de Preston
Geoffrey Walpole
Piers Hiltoft
Thomas Findon
Robert Godman
John Blakman
George Rigge
John Canon
William Fichet
Roland van de Busshe
William FitzHugh
William Everad
Robert Prentys

[88] Presumably, these men rent either workshops or rooms to live in in property owned by the company, and in return for their loan at this time they will not have to pay a part or the whole of their rent due. The monies loaned here are repaid at various times, for which one may check the Name Index.

Joh*an* Lincolle, seler
Schilling

It*e*m, ceux su*n*t les nou*n*s ke furu*n*t co*ntra*[r]ious en maner*e* su dit, q*ue*us n'aveyu*n*t auqkes de la liv*eré*
Water Fis Joh*an*
Thom*as* ate Noke
Joh*an* Jerveine Wye
Joh*annes* Clopton
Will*ia*m of Bilingate
Joh*an* Colman
Will*ia*m Horsma*n*
Will*ia*m Bader
Simo*n* Wintir
Reynol of the Brige
Joh*an* Ipeg*ra*ve
Rog*er* K[r]yngylford[198]
Joh*an* Watford

p. 19 Ceux su*n*t les nou*n*s quex su*n*t entrés en la liv*er*é en l'an avandite e ressus p*ar* les quat*re* gardeyns e lé bon gens de la co*m*paynie:
Premerem*en*t:
Harri Malmayn
Roger Riot
Emond Forster
Johan Cheyham
Robert Ernold
} quex ne payu*n*t rien p*ur* lo*ur* entr*é*
William Hapir – vi s. viii d.

It*e*m, Goffrey Wapol ad fayt treys bendis de argent a un est*ra*unge poysant p*ar* poys x s. e ad doré les bendis ové la value de cink s. de or, ke fut or a la dit est*ra*unge, e ne p*ri*st p*ur* la ov*er*aigne de le pece de la dit bendis fors ke viii d.,[199] p*ur* quex il fut ajugé de payer de Seint Donston p*ur* la amoyne – vi s. viii d.

Fayt a rem*em*brer ke Ricard ate Yoke fut trové en deffaute ke il avoyt lowé su*n* apre*n*tys a Joh*a*n Freysel de Colchest*re* enco*n*t*re* [les bons ordinancis] del mester e fut ajugé p*ar* les gardeyns al amoyne de Seyn Donston de payer – xl d.

Fayt a r*e*me*m*brer ke Will*ia*m ate Stockys fit un chalis a l[es][200] gardeyns de la glise de Wolcherche e miht en la pomel un d*em*i ounce de plu*m* e ensi fut rebel enco*n*tre les gardeyns e les bons ordinancis de la mest*er* e ne voloyt fayr*e* gré a dite co*m*paynie mes p*ur* tews deffautis e plusours autris fui a Westmohter.[201]

198 The 'r' of this name was written and then overwritten with the first 'y'.
199 See the ordinance for vesselers of 1373, A + a, p. 49 above.
200 MS: la.
201 *Sic*, as also the 'h' in the word 'miht' above and below. One may wonder whether the scribe in copying has not misinterpreted an 's' of another writer?

John Lincoln, sealer[89]
[Conrad] Schilling

Item, these are the names of those who rebelled in the aforesaid manner, who had never received livery:
Walter FitzJohn
Thomas atte Noke
John Jerveine Wye
John Clopton
William of Billingsgate
John Colman
William Horsman
William Bader
Simon Wynter
Reynol of the Bridge
John Ippegrave
Roger Cringleford
John Watford

These are the names of those who entered the livery in the aforesaid year and were admitted by the four wardens and the goodmen of the company: p. 19
Firstly:
Harry Malmayn
Roger Ryot
Edmund Forster
John Cheyham
Robert Ernold
} who did not pay anything for their entry
William Haper – 6s. 8d.

Item, Geoffrey Walpole made three silver bands weighing 10s. for an alien, and he gilded the bands with 5s. worth of gold, which was gold belonging to the said alien, and he only took 8d. for his workmanship for each of the said bands, for which he was sentenced to pay to the alms funds of St Dunstan – 6s. 8d. p. 19

Memorandum that Richard atte Yoke was found at fault for having hired his apprentice to John Freysel of Colchester against [the good ordinances] of the mistery, and he was sentenced by the wardens to pay to the alms funds of St Dunstan – 40d.

Memorandum that William atte Stockys made a chalice for the wardens of the church of Woolchurch, and he put half an ounce of lead in the knop, and was rebellious against the wardens and the good ordinances of the mistery and he did not wish to make a settlement to the said company, but for such faults and several others he fled to Westminster.

[89] Here the word probably means one who makes and engraves seals, although the *OED* and *MED* list other meanings.

p. 20 Fayt a rem*em*brer ke Joh*a*n Flete avoyt un valet demoront en sa cosine *et* se m[i]ht en s'op[er]e e le mostroyt lé secrés del mest*er* tank il avoyt fayt deux viergis de arg*e*nt e se fut trové e p*ro*vé devant les dits gardeyns e autris gens de la co*m*payne, p*ur* quex il fut ajugé de payer al amoyne de Seynt Donston sulu*n* la ordinance, e ne voet est*re* justicé p*ar* les dit gardeyns, eyns est rebel enco*n*tre su*n* sereme*n*t.

1377–78 Ceux sont les nou*n*s dez gardeins del orfeverie de Londres l'an du regne le
p. 21[202] roi Richard s*eco*nde puis le conquest primer, finantz lour office en le jour de Seint Dunstan l'an susdit:

col. 1 Adam Bamme
Joh*a*n Carbonel
Joh*a*n Lincoln*e*
Will*ia*m atte Forde

Lez desp*e*nc*e*z des ditz Gardeins:
P*ri*mes, pur sonner le *gra*nt sonel de Seint Dunston en l'eglise de Seint Poul *et* pur le lumer de Seint Joh*a*n Zakery – xxii s.
Item, p*ur* vesture achaté p*ur* le chapellein, c'est assav*er* iii v*er*ges de draps p*ri*s la v*er*ge iiii s. x d. – xiiii s. vi d.
It*em*, pur le furrure al chapellein – ii s.
It*em*, p*ur* la vesture de deux povres genz – xi s. vi d.

Ceux sont lez nou*n*s dez app*re*ntiz entrez en le mister del Orfeverie:

Joh*a*n Wadevile app*re*ntiz de Reymond Standelve –	ii s.
Joh*a*n Cokes app*re*ntiz de Rob*er*t Teukesbury –	ii s.
Thom*a*s Lauton*e* app*re*ntiz Rog*er* Riot –	ii s.
Joh*a*n Lemyng app*rentiz* Joh*a*n Covele –	ii s.
Joh*a*n Barre app*rentiz* Rich*ard* M*er*ssh*e* –	ii s.
Mark Munden app*rentiz* de Will*ia*m G*ra*ntha*m* –	ii s.
Thom*as* Wilton*e* app*rentiz* Piers[203] –	ii s.

Ceux sont les nou*n*s dez lowiz venuz[204] hors de lo*ur* t*er*me:

Thom*a*s Stoke –	ii s.
Joh*a*n Halle –	ii s.
Joh*a*n Lynk –	ii s.
Richard Broke –	ii s.
Joh*a*n Notton*e* –	ii s.

Ceux sont lez genz du dit mister enf*ra*nchisez en la Gildhall*e*:

Joh*a*n Luton*e* –	xx s.
Joh*a*n Clopton*e* –	x s.

202 A new hand starts here, a fully-trained, very neat and careful hand, not one that appears in Book A + a.
203 This is perhaps John Piers: see Name Index.
204 MS: venduz.

Memorandum that John Flete had a boy living in his kitchen, and he engaged him in his work and showed him the secrets of the mistery sufficiently until he had made two bars[90] of silver, and he was proved guilty of this before the said wardens and others of the company, for the which he was sentenced to pay to the alms funds of St Dunstan the amount laid down by ordinance, but he did not wish to accept judgment from the said wardens, but instead rebelled against his oath. p. 20

These are the names of the wardens of the Goldsmiths' Mistery of London in the year 1 Richard II, their term of office ending on St Dunstan's Day in the aforesaid year [19 May 1378]: 1377–78 p. 21

Adam Bamme col. 1
John Carbonelle
John Lincoln
William atte Forde

The expenses of the said wardens:
Firstly, for ringing the great bell of St Dunstan in St Paul's church, and for the light at St John Zachary – 22s.
Item, for clothing bought for the chaplain, i.e. 3 yards of cloth at 4s. 10d. per yard – 14s. 6d.
Item, for the lining for the chaplain – 2s.
Item, for the clothing of two poor people – 11s. 6d.

These are the names of apprentices admitted into the Goldsmiths' Mistery:

John Wadevile apprentice of Raymund Standelf –	2s.
John Cokes apprentice of Robert Tewkesbury –	2s.
Thomas Lautoun apprentice of Roger Ryot –	2s.
John Lemyng apprentice of John Covele –	2s.
John Barre apprentice of Richard Marsshe –	2s.
Mark Munden apprentice of William Grantham –	2s.
Thomas Wilton apprentice of Piers –	2s.

These are the names of serving-men who have come out of their term [of apprenticeship]:

Thomas Stoke –	2s.
John Halle –	2s.
John Lynk –	2s.
Richard Brook –	2s.
John Notton –	2s.

These are the men of the said mistery who have been enfranchised at the Guildhall:

John Luton –	20s.
John Clopton –	10s.

[90] Bars, rods of silver seems more probable in context than 'virgins' which is linguistically possible. The boy will have been taught how to melt and refine silver and make it into bars.

Joh*a*n Flete –	xl s.
Joh*a*n Brackele –	iii s. iiii d.
Joh*a*n Hynde –	xiii s. iiiid.
Joh*a*n Grenefeld –	xxvi s. viii d.
Joh*a*n Soviry –	xx s.

Ceux sont lez est*ra*nges q'ont paiez lo*ur* entrez:

Joh*a*n Deneh*a*m –	xii s.
Joh*a*n Pope –	vi s. viii d.

1377 Ceux sont lez costages *et* despen*c*ez queux lez gardeins ont faitz:[205]
col. 2 Pr*i*mes, paiez as ministralx le jo*ur* de la coronacion du roi – xl s.
It*em*, p*ur* chap*er*ons *et* p*ur* boir*e* as ditz ministralx – xii s. ii d.
It*em*, pur pensels – xlii s.
It*em*, p*ur* clowes, ropes *et* tarre pur le chastell*e* – ii s. ii d. ob.
It*em*, p*ur* portage – xxii d.
It*em*, p*ur* foyl *et* orsandy – xxi s.
It*em*, pur hanaps[206] – xvi d.
It*em*, pur vin – iii s.
It*em*, pur carpent*er*s – iii s. iiii d.
It*em*, pur drap pur lez damiseles[207] – xxiii s. vi d.
It*em*, p*ur* ministralx al chivachure du Mair*e* – x s.
It*em*, p*ur* le lomer, *et* le soner, pain et c*er*voise de Seint Dunston – xxii d.
It*em*, p*ur* vesture del chapellein – xiiii s. vi d.
It*em*, p*ur* un furrure – ii s.
It*em*, p*ur* vesture p*ur* lez povres genz – xi s. vi d.
It*em*, p*ur* p*ur*suit fait p*ur* la compaignie p*ar* Joh*a*n Carbonel – viii s. vi d.
Item, p*ar* Adam Bamme – xiii s. ii d.
Item, p*ar* Johan Lincoln – xiiii s. ii d.
It*em*, pur vesture de Sire Thom*a*s Org*ra*ve – xv s.
It*em*, pur vesture de Richard Forster[208] – x s. vi d.
It*em*, paié al escrivein pur div*er*ses choses – ii s.
S*um*m*a*: xiii li. xiii s. viii d. ob.

1377–78 Fait a remembr*er* de lez receites:
Primes, receu de lez renteres – iiii li. iii s.

[205] On this pageant and the later one of 1382 (see below, A + a, p. 57) see the article by R.H. Osberg, 'The Goldsmiths' "Chastell" of 1377', *Theatre Survey* 27 (1986), 1–15.

[206] The use of these 'hanaps' is described in Walsingham: 'Cum autem ante castellum venisset, ciphos aureos acceperunt, et implentes eos vino ad fistulas dicti castelli, Regi atque Dominis obtulerunt.' Thomas Walsingham, *Historia Anglicana*, ed. H.T. Riley, 2 vols, Rolls Series 28.1 (London, 1863–64), p. 332.

[207] Walsingham tells us there were four of these and that they wore white: 'In turribus autem ejus quatuor virgines speciosissimae collocatae fuerant, staturae et aetatis regiae, vestibus albis indutae, in qualibet turri una; quae adventati Regi procul aurea folia in ejus faciem efflaverunt, et propius accedenti, florenos aureos, sed sophisticos, super eum et ejus dextrarium projecerunt.' (*Ibid.*, pp. 331–32).

[208] In several subsequent years also an amount is listed for his clothing. These entries may well indicate that he was the beadle.

John Flete – 40s.
John Brackele – 3s. 4d.
John Hynde – 13s. 4d.
John Greenfield – 26s. 8d.
John Soviry – 20s.

These are the aliens who have paid for their entry:
John Deneham – 12s.
John Pope – 6s. 8d.

These are the costs and expenses of the wardens: 1377
Firstly, paid to the minstrels on the day of the King's coronation – 40s. col. 2
Item, for hoods and for drink for the said minstrels – 12s. 2d.
Item, for pencels[91] – 42s.
Item, for nails, ropes and tar for the castle – 2s. 2½d.
Item, for carriage – 22d.
Item, for foil[92] and arsedine[93] – 21s.
Item, for drinking-cups – 16d.
Item, for wine – 3s.
Item, for carpenters – 3s. 4d.
Item, for cloth for the maidens – 23s. 6d.
Item, for minstrels in the Mayor's procession – 10s.
Item, for the light, and the bell-ringing, the bread and ale for St Dunstan's Day – 22d.
Item, for clothing for the chaplain – 14s. 6d.
Item, for a lining – 2s.
Item, for clothing for the poor – 11s. 6d.
Item, for a lawsuit brought on behalf of the company by John Carbonelle – 8s. 6d.
Item, by Adam Bamme – 13s. 2d.
Item, by John Lincoln – 14s. 2d.
Item, for the clothing of Sir Thomas Orgrave – 15s.
Item, for the clothing of Richard Forster – 10s. 6d.
Item, paid to the scribe for various things – 2s.
Total: £13 13s. 8½d.

Memorandum of receipts:
Firstly, received from the renters – £4 3s.

[91] Small pennons or streamers (*OED*).
[92] Probably here gold foil; Walsingham's account of this pageant refers to 'aurea folia' – 'golden leaves', but one should perhaps not forget that this was written considerably after the event from unknown sources. The word 'foyl' could refer to any metal foil. See Thomas Walsingham, *Historia Anglicana*, ed. H.T. Riley, vol. I, pp. 331–32.
[93] A gold-coloured alloy of copper and zinc rolled into very thin leaf, and used to ornament objects. Osberg, *op. cit.*, p. 13 states that this was used to manufacture the counterfeit florins ('florenos aureos sed sophisticos') noted by Walsingham, and he may well be right about this.

It*em*, receeu de lez enf*ra*nchisez – vi li. xiii s. iiii d.
It*em*, receeu de lez lowiz – xxvi s. viii d.
It*em*, receeu del entré dez app*re*ntices – xiiii s.
It*em*, receeu de William Mariner p*ur* allower Henri Bamme hors de sa maisone – vi s. viii d.

Summa: xiii li. iii s. viii d.

1378–79 p. 23 Ceux sont les nou*n*s dez gardeins del Orfeve*r*ie de Loundres l'an du regne le roi Richard s*econ*de puis le conquest s*econ*de, finantz lour office en le jour de Seint Dunston l'an susdit:

col. 1 Joh*a*n Fr*a*unceis
Thomas Panton
Thom*a*s Polle
Joh*a*n Luyton*e*

Lez despe*n*ce*z* dez ditz gardeins:
P*ri*mes, p*ur* sonner le g*ra*nt sonal de Seint Dunston en l'eglise de Seint Poul *et* pur le lumer a Seint Joh*a*n Zakarie – xxii s.
It*em*, p*ur* vesture achaté p*ur* le chapellein, c'est assav*er* iii v*er*ges de drap – xv s. vi d.
It*em*, p*ur* le furrure al chapellein – ii s. vi d.
It*em*, p*ur* la vesture de ii povres ho*m*mes – xi s. iiii d.

Ceux sont les nou*n*s dez app*re*ntiz entrez en le mister del Orfeve*r*ie:

Joh*a*n Waldeg*ra*ve apprentis de Nichol Twyford –	ii s.
Simon Chestrefeld app*re*nt*is* de Rob*er*t Launde –	ii s.
James Southe app*re*nt*is* Henr*i* Abbot –	ii s.
Joh*a*n Conyngton app*re*nt*is* de Joh*an* Lyv*er*pole –	ii s.
Thom*as* Bokyl app*re*nt*is* de Thom*as* Exton –	ii s.
Joh*a*n Borkelow app*re*nt*is* Joh*a*n Rudh*a*m –	ii s.
Rob*ert* Croft app*re*nt*is* de Will*iam* fiz Hugh*e* –	ii s.
Joh*a*n Pecche app*re*nt*is* de Will*iam* fiz Hugh*e* –	ii s.
Will*iam* Skele app*re*nt*is* de Rob*er*t Lynne –	ii s.
Thom*as* Throckyng app*re*nt*is* de Will*iam* Burdeyn –	ii s.
Joh*a*n Scoudone *et* Henr*i* Richemond app*re*ntis de Joh*a*n Fairehere –	iiii s.
Joh*a*n Spicer app*re*nt*is* de Will*ia*m Geyton*e* –	ii s.
Giles Goce app*re*nt*is* de Thom*as* Essex –	ii s.
Joh*a*n Patcheford app*re*nt*is* de Will*ia*m Forde –	ii s.
Joh*a*n Kele app*re*nt*is* de Stephen Mapesden*e* –	ii s.
Ric*hard* Haketon*e* app*re*nt*is* de Henr*i* Grene –	ii s.

Ceux sont lez nou*n*s dez lowiz q*i* sont venuz hors de lour t*er*me:

Rog*er* Gay –	ii s.
Will*ia*m Lincoln*e* –	ii s.
Joh*a*n Mazerer –	ii s.

Ceux sont les nou*n*s du dit mister qi sont enf*ra*nchisez en la Gilde Halle:
Adam de Thorp*e* – iii s. iiii d.

Item, received from those who have been enfranchised – £6 13s. 4d.
Item, received from serving-men – 26s. 8d.
Item, received from the entry of apprentices – 14s.
Item, received from William Mariner for having evicted Henry Bamme from his house – 6s. 8d.
Total: £13 3s. 8d.

These are the names of the wardens of the Goldsmiths' Mistery of London in the year 2 Richard II, their term of office ending on St Dunstan's Day in the aforesaid year [19 May 1379]: 1378–79 p. 23
John Fraunceys col. 1
Thomas Panton
Thomas Polle
John Luton

The expenses of the said wardens:
Firstly, for ringing the great bell of St Dunstan in St Paul's church, and for the light at St John Zachary – 22s.
Item, for clothing bought for the chaplain, i.e. 3 yards of cloth – 15s. 6d.
Item, for the lining for the chaplain – 2s. 6d.
Item, for the clothing of 2 poor men – 11s. 4d.

These are the names of apprentices admitted into the Goldsmiths' mistery:

John Waldegrave apprentice of Nicholas Twyford –	2s.
Simon Chesterfield apprentice of Robert Launde –	2s.
James South apprentice of Henry Abbot –	2s.
John Conyngton apprentice of John Liverpool –	2s.
Thomas Bokyl apprentice of Thomas Exton –	2s.
John Borkelow apprentice of John Rudham –	2s.
Robert Croft apprentice of William FitzHugh –	2s.
John Pecche apprentice of William FitzHugh –	2s.
William Skele apprentice of Robert Lynne –	2s.
Thomas Throckyng apprentice of William Burdeyn –	2s.
John Scoudone and Henry Richmond apprentices of John Fairher –	4s.
John Spicer apprentice of William Gaytoun –	2s.
Giles Goos apprentice of Thomas Essex –	2s.
John Patcheford apprentice of William Forde –	2s.
John Kele apprentice of Stephen Maplesdene –	2s.
Richard Haketone apprentice of Henry Grene –	2s.

These are the names of serving-men who have come out of their terms:

Roger Gay –	2s.
William Lincoln –	2s.
John Mazerer –	2s.

These are the names of those of the said mistery who have been enfranchised at the Guildhall:
Adam de Thorpe – 3s. 4d.

col. 2 Fait a remembr*er* dez paiementz faitz as gentz qi app*re*sterent del arge*n*t au temps q*e* Joh*a*n Forster, Rob*ert* F*ra*unceis, Thom*as* Hay *et* Thom*as* Exton fure*n*t gardeins:[209]

A Stephen de Thorp*e* – xx s.	quit
Joh*a*n Lincoln*e*	quit
Thom*as* Davy	quit
Henr*i* Ba*m*me	quit
Joh*a*n Brou*n*	quit
Will*ia*m Burdeyn	quit
Joh*a*n F*ra*nceis	quit
Thom*as* Panton	quit
Joh*a*n Luton	quit
Thom*as* Polle	quit

et examinez de la remenant

1379–80 Ceux so*u*nt les no*u*ns dez gardaynz del orfeve*r*ye de Loundres l'an du regne
A + a le Roy Richard *secon*de puis le conquest tierce, finauntz lo*ur* office en le jo*ur*
p. 55[210] de Seynt Dunstoun l'an susdit:

col. 1 Rob*ert* Lucas
Joh*a*n Coraunt
Harr*i* Ba*m*me
Harr*i* Malmayne

Lez despensez de ditz gardayns:
Primes, pur soner le g*ra*unt sonel de Seint Dunstou*n* en l'esglise de Seint Poul *et* pur le lumer a Seynt Joh*a*n Zakarie – xvii s.

Ite*m*, p*ur* vesture pur iii prestres *et* pur S*ire* Thom*as* Org*ra*ve *et* pur Richard Forster *et* pur lez deux brokours – iii li. ii s.

Ceux so*u*nt lez no*u*ns dez app*re*ntiz entrez en le mest*ier* d'orfeve*r*ye l'an susdit:

Joh*a*n Ede app*re*ntiz Ric*hard* Ede –	ii s.
Thom*as* Dawe app*re*ntiz Joh*a*n Peris –	ii s.
Harr*i* Hochedes app*re*ntiz Joh*a*n Canou*n* –	ii s.
Nich*ol*as Birche app*re*ntiz Ric*hard* Jeweler –	ii s.
Joh*a*n Smyth*e*, Phelipp*e* Northene app*re*nt*iz* Rob*er*t Godman –	iiii s.
Joh*a*n Deneristo*u*n app*re*ntiz Joh*a*n Bernys –	ii s.
Will*ia*m Eddyngh*a*m app*re*ntiz Drw Barantyn –	ii s.
Thom*as* Cove app*re*ntiz Harr*i* Bamme –	ii s.
Hug*o* atte Spitil app*re*ntiz Will*ia*m Pever –	ii s.
Rob*er*t Payn app*re*nt*iz* Joh*a*n Walsch*e* –	ii s.
Joh*a*n Baker*e* *et* Ric*hard* Suttou*n* app*re*ntiz Joh*a*n Maplesden*e* –	iiii s.
Will*ia*m Snoksille app*re*ntiz Joh*a*n Bulstrode –	ii s.
Thom*as* Stanlowe app*re*ntiz Ric*hard* Merden*e* –	ii s.

209 See above, A + b, p. 17.
210 A new hand starts here.

Memorandum of payments made to the men who lent money at the time when John Forster, Robert Fraunceys, Thomas Hay and Thomas Exton were wardens [1376–77]: col. 2

To Stephen de Thorpe – 20s. – quit
John Lincoln quit
Thomas Davy quit
Henry Bamme quit
John Broun quit
William Burdeyn quit
John Fraunceys quit
Thomas Panton quit
John Luton quit
Thomas Polle quit
and consideration has been given to the remainder.

These are the names of the wardens of the Goldsmiths' Mistery of London in the year 3 Richard II, their term of office ending on St Dunstan's Day in the year aforesaid [19 May 1380]: 1379–80 A + a p. 55

Robert Lucas col. 1
John Coraunt
Harry Bamme
Harry Malmayn

The expenses of the said wardens:
Firstly, for ringing the great bell of St Dunstan in the church of St Paul's and for the light at St John Zachary – 17s.

Item, for clothing for 3 priests and for Sir Thomas Orgrave and for Richard Forster and for the two brokers – £3 2s.

These are the names of apprentices admitted into the Goldsmiths' Mistery in the aforesaid year:

John Ede apprentice of Richard Ede –	2s.
Thomas Dawe apprentice of John Pieres –	2s.
Harry Hoccedys apprentice of John Canon –	2s.
Nicholas Birch apprentice of Richard Jeweler –	2s.
John Smythe, Phillip Northene, apprentices of Robert Godman –	4s.
John Deneristoun apprentice of John Barnes –	2s.
William Eddyngham apprentice of Drew Barantyn –	2s.
Thomas Cove apprentice of Harry Bamme –	2s.
Hugo atte Spitil apprentice of William Pevere –	2s.
Robert Payn apprentice of John Walsh –	2s.
John Baker and Richard Sutton, apprentices of John Maplesdene –	4s.
William Snoksille apprentice of John Bulstrode –	2s.
Thomas Stanlowe apprentice of Richard Merdene –	2s.

Harr*i* Glede app*re*nt*iz* Thom*a*s Fyndene – ii s.
Joh*a*n Chaumbyrlayn app*re*nt*iz* Joh*a*n Squiry – ii s.
Will*ia*m Smetou*n* app*re*nt*iz* Thom*a*s Bygod – ii s.
Joh*a*n van Bonygghe app*re*nt*iz* Herman van Gluye – ii s.
Will*ia*m Cozin *et* Joh*a*n Phelpot app*re*nt*iz* Joh*a*n Thorn*e* – iiii s.
Joh*a*n Roo de Schoreham app*re*nt*iz* Hankyn Reinbake – ii s.

col. 2 Ceux so*u*nt lez no*u*ns dez lowys q*e* so*u*nt venuz hors de lo*ur* te*r*me l'an susdit:

Joh*a*n Westou*n* – ii s.
Joh*a*n He*n*neye – ii s.
Joh*a*n Broun – ii s.
Will*ia*m Bart – ii s.
Joh*a*n Stainys – ii s.
Joh*a*n Appilby – ii s.
Joh*a*n Busch*e* – ii s.

Fait a rememb*rer* en le temps de lez gardayns avantditz, c'est a dire Rob*er*t Lucas, Joh*a*n Cora*u*nt, Harr*i* Ba*m*me, Harr*i* Malmayns, al comencement de lour office p*ar* assent de bons gentz de le compaignie *et* co*mun*es, ils fo*u*nt une feste, a quele feste furo*u*nt s*eign*o*r*s *et* dames, adep*ri*mes ma t*re*shonu*r*able Madame Izabell*e,* file Roy d'Englet*er*e, *et* sa file Countasse de Oxinfford *et* le s*eignur* de Latemer *et* le p*ri*ncipal mestre de Seynt Joh*a*n de Clerkenwell*e* *et* le Maire de Loundr*e*s, ovesq*es* a[ul]tr*e*s[211] bons gentz de la Cité. P*ar* quoy lez ditz gardayns furo*u*nt a g*ra*untz costagez, p*ar* quoy lez ditz gardayns prieunt q*e* ils pu*r*rount estre alowé de sez g*ra*untz costagez, ové a[ul]trement[212] q*e* chescun dez gardayns q*e* vient ap*ré*s, q*e* ils fount une feste desus une payne fait ent*re* lez bons gentz *et* co*mun*es de dit mester.

1368–69 Compo*s*ic*i*o Joh*an*nis de Hyltoft[213]
p. 56 Unive*r*sis s*anct*e matris eccl*es*ie filiis p*re*sentes l*itte*ras inspetturis Joh*anne*s, decanus, *et* capit*u*l*u*m eccl*es*ie S*anct*i Pauli London' sal*ute*m in d*omi*no. Nov*er*it unive*r*sitas v*est*ra q*uo*d cum d*omin*us Will*el*m*us* de Swynflet, archidiaconus Norwicen*sis*, Joh*anne*s de Bures, civis *et* pannar*ius* London', Joh*anne*s Coraunt *et* Henricus Markeby, cives *et* aurifabri London', *et* d*omin*us Will*el*m*us*

211 MS: alutr*e*s.
212 MS: alutrement.
213 John Hiltoft died in 1368, see Reddaway and Walker, p. 297. There appears to be no other copy of this present document extant, and there is no date contained within it, but it must be presumed to date from 1368–69, although placed here in the record book between the entries for 1378–79 and 1380–81, and therefore copied in here at this time. The reference within it to 'ven*er*abilem prev*endarium* d*omin*um Simone*m* dei gra*cia* London' Ep*iscopu*m' (see next note) indicates that the document was drawn up before 1375. We also know that a contract was drawn up on 7 April 1369 between the Dean and Chapter of St Paul's and two carpenters who were undertaking to carry out work in the area specified: see L.F. Salzman, *Building in England down to 1540*, rev. edn (Oxford, 1967), pp. 441–43. (I am most grateful to Dr Christopher Wilson for bringing this text to my notice.) Other references to Hiltoft's bequest and his obit may be found in W. Dugdale, *The History of St Paul's Cathedral* (London, 1658), p. 25; *ibid.* (London, 1818 edn with additions), Appendix p. 382; W. Sparrow Simpson, ed., *Documents Illustrating the History of St Paul's Cathedral* (London: Camden Society, 1880), pp. 66, 83–84. His obit on 17 May is marked on the Goldsmiths' calendar.

Harry Glede apprentice of Thomas Findon –	2s.
John Chamberlayn apprentice of John Squiry –	2s.
William Smetoun apprentice of Thomas Bygod –	2s.
John van Bonygghe apprentice of Hermann van Gluye –	2s.
William Cozin and John Philpot apprentices of John Thorne –	4s.
John Roo of Shoreham, apprentice of Hanekyn Reinbake –	2s.

These are the names of serving-men who have come out of their terms in the aforesaid year: col. 2

John Weston –	2s.
John Henney –	2s.
John Broun –	2s.
William Bart –	2s.
John Staines –	2s.
John Appleby –	2s.
John Busshe –	2s.

Memorandum that during the term of office of the aforesaid wardens, i.e. Robert Lucas, John Coraunt, Harry Bamme, Harry Malmayn, at the beginning of their term of office, by the consent of the goodmen of the company and the commonalty, they held a feast at which lords and ladies were present, firstly the most honourable Lady Isabelle, daughter of the King of England,[94] and her daughter the Countess of Oxford, and Lord Latimer, and the High Master of St John of Clerkenwell, and the Mayor of London, with other goodmen of the City. For this the wardens had great expenses, and they beg to have their great expenses authorized, and otherwise that each of the wardens who shall follow, that they should hold a feast subject to a penalty settled upon between the goodmen and the commonalty of the said mistery.

The composition[95] of John de Hiltoft:[96] 1368–69

To all sons of Holy Mother Church who shall inspect these present letters, John, p. 56
the dean, and the chapter of the church of St Paul in London, greetings in the Lord. May it be known to you all that whereas Sir William de Swinefleet, archdeacon of Norwich, John de Bures, citizen and draper of London, John Coraunt and Henry Markeby, citizens and goldsmiths of London, and

[94] Edward III's daughter.

[95] i.e. the statement of the final financial settlement made.

[96] See Reddaway and Walker, p. 297 for a brief biography and further references to sources on John de Hiltoft. See also *ibid.*, p. 186 for the later history of Hiltoft's bequest.

Calseby, capellanus, executores testamenti bone memorie *et* devoti viri deo *et* eccl*es*ie n*ost*re Joh*ann*is de Hyltoft, nup*er* civis *et* aurifabri London', defuncti, de ip*s*ius defuncti bonis quingentas *et* viginti libras st*er*lingor*um* p*ro* sal*u*te anime ip*s*ius *et* Alicie quond*a*m ux*or*is sue *et* a*ni*mar*um* om*n*ium p*ar*entum *et* b*e*nefattor*um* suor*um* *et* om*ni*u*m* fidel*iu*m defunctor*um*, ad construendu*m* de novo totam aream n*ost*ram a porta pistrini d*ict*e eccl*es*ie n*ost*re usq*ue* ad corneriu*m* eiusd*e*m pistrini v*er*sus austrum *et* ab eod*e*m cornerio usq*ue* ad quend*a*m locu*m* vocat*um* Gibbeshawe v*er*sus occidentem, in quo quidem loco domus ruinose *et* inutiles dudum existebant, p*ro* om*ni*b*us* nobis incumbent*ibus* melius *et* lenius supportand*is* dederint *et* integralit*er* lib*er*av*er*unt num*er*at*as*. De qua quidem pecunie su*m*ma nos totam aream n*ost*ram p*re*d*ict*am in longitudi*n*e a d*ict*o cornerio versus occidentem quinquaginta *et* nove*m* virgas ferr*eas* *et* ab eod*e*m cornerio v*er*sus aquilonem viginti *et* sex virgas ferr*eas* continent*em* de novo edificari faciemus. De quor*um* quidem edificior*um* redditib*us* possunt cunctis futuris temporib*us* o*mn*i*a* subscripta congrue supportari. Nos, ampliorem min*or*u*m* ministror*um* in eccl*es*ia n*ost*ra p*re*dicta habitus gesta*cion*em diviniq*ue* cultus augmentu*m* phirmu*m* affectantes necnon considerantes co*m*modu*m* q*uo*d sp*er*am*us* ult*ra* o*mn*i*a* octon*ari*e p*re*missor*um* nobis incumbencia reportare diligenti in hac p*ar*te t*ra*ctatu *et* solempni requisic*ion*e int*er* ven*er*abilem prev*endarium* d*omi*n*um* Simone*m*[214] dei gra*cia* London' Ep*iscop*u*m* *et* nos p*re*habito de ip*s*ius patris conce*n*ssu *et* n*ost*ri unanimi concensu, assensu *et* voluntate concedim*us* p*ro* nobis *et* successorib*us* n*ost*ris futuris quibuscumq*ue*, *et* eciam ordinamus q*uo*d in d*ict*a eccl*es*ia n*ost*ra sit unus sac*er*dos p*er*petuus qui p*ro* a*ni*mabus d*ictorum* Joh*ann*is *et* Alicie defunctor*um* quor*um* corpora in cimiterio n*ost*ro canonicor*um* iacent humata, p*ar*entum *et* b*e*nefactor*um* suor*um* ac a*ni*mab*us* om*ni*u*m* fideliu*m* defunctor*um* in capella S*anct*i Dunstani in p*ar*te australi nove fabrice d*ict*e eccl*es*ie n*ost*re iux*ta* capellam gl*ori*ose virg*in*is Marie cotidie nisi justo *et* legiti*m*o impedimento fu*er*it impeditus, divina imp*er*petuu*m* celebrabit, *et* debeat celebrare, cui quidam capellano nos *et* successores n*ost*ri pane*m*, vinu*m*, *et* lumen p*ro* celebrac*ion*e huius*m*odi di*vin*or*um* inve*n*iemus q*uo*dq*ue* id*e*m capellanus p*er*cipiet annuati*m* de tenementis p*re*d*ict*is p*er* manus cam*er*ar*ii* n*ost*ri *et* successor*um* suor*um* qui p*ro* temp*or*e fu*er*int decem marcas st*er*lingor*um* eid*e*m in quatuor compot*is* d*ict*e cam*e*re camerarie annuati*m* equalit*er* reddend*as* videl*ice*t die sabb*at*i p*roxima* post festu*m* Assensionis d*omi*ni, die sabb*at*i p*roxima* ante festu*m* S*anct*i Petri q*uo*d dicit*ur* ad Vinc*u*la, die sabb*at*i p*roxima* ante festu*m* S*anct*i Martini, *et* die sabb*at*i

[214] Simon Sudbury, Bishop of London from 1361 until translated to Canterbury in 1375.

Sir William Calseby, chaplain, the executors of the will of John de Hiltoft, deceased, of good memory and devoted to God and our church, lately a citizen and goldsmith of London, have given and entirely handed over counted in full £520 sterling from the possessions of the said deceased, for the good of his own soul and that of Alice, once his wife, and of the souls of all his relatives and benefactors and of all the faithful departed, to be used to rebuild the whole of the part of our precinct from the door of the bakehouse of our said church as far as the corner of the same bakehouse on the south side, and from the same corner as far as a certain place called Gibbeshawe on the western side, in which place until now useless buildings in a state of ruin have been standing, and this to be for the better and more comfortable support of all our incumbents. With which sum of money we shall build anew the whole of our aforesaid grounds which contain in length from the said corner on the western side 59 yards[97] and from the same corner towards the north 26 yards. From the rents of which buildings all those written below may be properly supported for all future time. We, devoted to the fuller support of the way of life of the lesser clergy of our church and to the solid increase in divine services, and also considering the good which we hope may be brought to us in incumbencies, after all taxes of an eighth on the above, having diligently dealt in this matter and having obtained a solemn requisition between the venerable prebendary Sir Simon, by the grace of God Bishop of London, and ourselves, with the consent of his own father and our unanimous consent, assent and will, we concede for ourselves and our future successors whoever they may be, and we ordain also that in our said church there shall be in perpetuity one priest who shall and shall be obliged to celebrate daily a divine service, unless he shall be impeded by just and legal impediment, for the souls of the said departed John and Alice, whose bodies lie buried in our canons' cemetery, and of their relatives and benefactors, and for the souls of all the faithful departed, in the chapel of St Dunstan in the southern part of the New Work[98] of our said church next to the chapel of the glorious virgin Mary, to the which chaplain we and our successors shall provide the bread, wine and lighting for such celebrations of divine service, and also the same chaplain shall receive annually from the income from the aforesaid tenements 10 marks sterling to be paid by hand of our chamberlain and his successors whoever they shall be at the time, the money to be paid to him annually in perpetuity in equal portions by the chamberlain on the four accounting days of the said treasury that is on the Saturday following Ascension Day, on the Saturday preceding the Feast of St Peter ad Vincula, on the Saturday preceding the Feast of St Martin, and on the Saturday

[97] 'virgas ferreas' – yards measured by an iron measuring rod. Dr Christopher Wilson has pointed out that St Paul's had its own foot (referred to in contexts other than the cathedral also) which appears to have been the same as the standard English statute foot, but which may have necessitated by tradition the use of an iron measuring rod when measuring anything in the precinct.

[98] The 'New Work' on St Paul's was started in 1259 and the building was finished by 1294–1300 although fitting it out went on until 1327. I am most grateful for this information to Dr Christopher Wilson whose forthcoming book, *The Honour and Glory of London: The Architecture of St Paul's Cathedral 1087–1547* will provide full details. The altar of St Dunstan was consecrated in 1313. See Dugdale, *The History of St Paul's Cathedral* and A. Dimock, *The Cathedral Church of St Paul* (London, 1900), p. 45; G.H. Cook, *Old St. Paul's Cathedral* (London, 1955).

proxima ante diem Cinerum, per equales porciones annuatim imperpetuum persolvendas. Et si contingat nos in aliquo termorum predictorum deficere nisi infra mensem continuum pro termino illum dicto capellano satisfacerimus, nos *et* successores nostri solvemus pro quolibet die quo postea retardata fuerit solucio dimidiam marcam argenti quousque dicto capellano plenariter fuerit satisfactum quatuor magistris de artificio aurifabrorum cuius medietas applicetur fabrice veteris operis Sancti Pauli *et* alia medietas distribuatur inter pauperes per manus dictorum magistrorum vel deputatorum eorum. Et eciam singulis annis imperpetuum die obitus dicti defuncti quinque marcas sterlingorum de eisdem tenementis modo inferius describendo per manus dicti camerarii distribuendas videlicet maioribus canonicis stagiariis presentibus triginta solidos, minoribus canonicis necnon capellanis cantarias in eadem ecclesia habentibus *et* vicariis eiusdem ecclesie similiter presentibus duas marcas, choristis *et* aliis servientibus ecclesie virgas in eadem spectantibus quadraginta denarios, necnon magistris predictis qui pro tempore fuerint quos presentes esse volumus in missa die obitus dicti defuncti imperpetuum ad superindendum quod obitus predictus competenter fiat singulis annis prout decet pro labore suo dimidiam marcam, dividi *et* fideliter distribui faciemus sub pena prescripta. Predicti vero magistri artificii predicti qui pro tempore fuerint quociens ipsam cantariam per mortem, cessionem, resignacionem vel aliam causam vacare contigerit, alium capellanum ydoneum nobis *et* successoribus nostris infra quindecim dies a tempore note vacacionis eiusdem in ecclesia nostra antedicta presentabunt. Nosque *et* successores nostri huiusmodi capellanum sic presentatum dum tamen aliquod canonicum non obstiterit ad dictam cantariam admittemus *et* instituemus *et* ipsi nostri successores instituent debite in eadem. Et si contingat dictos magistros in presentacione huiusmodi capellani in forma predicta ultra quindecim dies huiusmodi deficere, tunc nos, decanus *et* capitulum *et* successores nostri dictam cantariam alicui capellano ydoneo nullum aliud beneficum seu officium ecclesiaticum habenti in communi conferremus infra alios quindecim dies tunc proximos sequentes alioquin pro quolibet die quo ipsa cantaria post eosdem quindecim dies perseveraverit vel steterit vacans eciam donec per nos aut successores nostros aut episcopum London' perpetuam necgligenciam eorum vel nostram huiusmodi de capellano ydoneo prefate cantarie fuerit iuxta huiusmodi ordinacionem bene *et* laudabiliter provisum, nos *et* successores nostri predicti solvemus unam marcam argenti magistris predictis dividendam in duas partes quarum una elemosine domini episcopi London' *et* alia arbitrio dictorum magistrorum in pios usus pro animabus predictis distribuentur illa vice; set si dictam cantariam inter predictum diem sabbati proximum ante festum Sancti Petri quod dicitur Ad Vincula *et* vigiliam Sancti Michaelis proximam sequentem vacare contingat, inter que festa nos *et* dicte ecclesie nostre canonici stagiariis pro fructibus autumpnalibus colligendis absentari consuemus ab eadem,[215] quod tempus nobis non currat medio tempore ad dictam cantariam conferendos, set quod tempus quindecim dierum tunc incipiat contra nos currere post lapsum vigilie beati Michaelis

[215] Dr Christopher Wilson has suggested that this may be a 'fossil' from the time when, in the more benign climate before c. 1300, they had vineyards on their estates.

preceding Ash Wednesday. And if it should happen that we default on this at any of the aforesaid terms, unless the matter be settled to the satisfaction of the said chaplain within a month after that term, we and our successors shall pay for each day that the payment shall be late half a mark of silver until the said chaplain shall have full satisfaction, this to be paid to the four wardens of the Goldsmiths' Mistery, and half of it shall be applied to the fabric of the the Old Work[99] in St Paul's and the other half shall be distributed among the poor by hand of the said wardens or their deputies. And also each year in perpetuity on the day of the obit of the said deceased, 5 marks sterling from the income of the said tenements shall be distributed by hand of the said chamberlain in the manner described below, i.e. to the major stagiary canons present 30s., to the minor canons and chaplains having chantries in the same church and to vicars of the same church similarly present 2 marks, to the choristers and other servants of the church in respect of their offices in the same 40d., and to the aforesaid wardens whoever they may be at each time, and whom we wish to be present at mass on the day of the obit of the said deceased in perpetuity in order to supervise that the said obit shall be properly carried out each year as is fitting, for their pains shall receive half a mark, all the above amounts we shall give out and faithfully distribute on pain of the penalty prescribed. And the aforesaid wardens of the aforesaid mistery, whoever they may be at the time, as often as that chantry become vacant through death, retirement, resignation or any other cause, shall present to us and our successors in our aforesaid church another suitable chaplain within fifteen days from the date of notification of the said vacancy. And we and our successors shall admit such a chaplain thus presented, provided however that no canonical reason prevents this, to the said chantry and shall institute him, and our same successors shall carry out all that is due in this matter. And if it should happen that the said wardens shall fail to present such a chaplain in the aforesaid manner within fifteen days, then we, the dean and chapter and our successors shall in common confer the said chantry on some suitable chaplain who holds no other benefice or ecclesiastical office within the next following fifteen days, and otherwise for each day after those same fifteen days that the chantry shall stand vacant until through us or our successors or the bishop of London, our or their continuing negligence in the matter of a suitable chaplain for the aforesaid chantry shall be well and worthily remedied according to the above ordinance, we and our aforesaid successors shall pay one mark of silver to the aforesaid wardens, this to be divided into two portions, of which one shall go to the almsbox of the Lord Bishop of London and the other according to the decision of the said wardens shall be distributed at that time on pious uses for the sake of the aforesaid souls. But if the said chantry shall chance to be vacant between the aforesaid Saturday preceding the Feast of St Peter ad Vincula and the eve of St Michael next following, during which time between these feasts we and the stagiary canons of our said church are accustomed to be absent from the same for the gathering the fruits of autumn, then at this time we shall not be held due to confer the said chantry in the meanwhile, but the fifteen-day period shall start to run against us after the end of the eve of the blessed Michael, if within the fifteen days

[99] i.e. the Romanesque nave, transepts and crossing tower of the cathedral, which it was the duty of the bishops to maintain. I am grateful to Dr Christopher Wilson for this information.

si in*fra* illos qui*n*decim dies d*ict*am vigil*iam* immediato sequentes de d*ict*a cantar*ia* pe*r* nos ut p*re*mittit*ur* v*e*l successores n*ost*ros non sit p*ro*visum. It*em*, ordinamus q*uo*d id*em* capellanus qui p*ro* temp*or*e fu*er*it chorum d*ict*e eccl*es*ie n*ost*re de die more humano sequi teneat*ur* *et* p*re*senciam suam exhibeat, habitu*m* portando tam in d*ict*a eccl*es*ia n*ost*ra q*ua*m pe*r* civitatem quociens chorus p*ro*cessionem fec*er*it *et* dicet fidelit*er* officiu*m* mortuor*um* cum co*m*mendac*io*ne sing*u*lis dieb*us*. It*em*, ordinamus q*uo*d id*em* capellanus jurabit q*uo*d nullu*m* aliud h*ab*eat aut teneat nec acceptet beneficiu*m* sive officiu*m* eccl*es*iasticu*m* cum cura v*e*l sine cura cum cantar*ia* p*re*d*ic*ta *et* statim cu*m* aliud hui*us*modi b*e*n*e*ficiu*m* v*e*l officiu*m* h*ab*uit v*e*l irregular*iter* v*e*l alit*er*, inhabil*is* ad officiu*m* suu*m* hui*us*modi p*re*t*er*q*ua*m ex corporis infirmitate fu*er*it effectus, sit ip*s*a cantar*ia* ip*s*o iur*e* p*ri*vatus *et* p*ro* sic privato *et* d*ict*a cantar*ia* p*ro* vacant*e* habeat*ur*. Om*n*ino jurabit insup*er* d*ict*us capellanus qui p*ro* temp*or*e fu*er*it in admissione sua.

1380–81 A + b p. 25[216] Ceux sou*n*t les nou*n*s dez Gardeynis del Orfeve*r*ye de Londrez l'an du regne le Roy Richard s*ec*o*n*de puis le qonquest quarte, finantz lo*ur* office en le jo*ur* de Saynt Donston l'an susditz:

Thom*a*s Renh*a*m, Aldirman del le garde del Aldristgate en le vant ditz aune
Thom*a*s Hexton
Joh*a*n Welbo*ur*ne
Drw Barantyne

Lez despensez dé ditz Gardeynis:

Primez, pur soner le grantz sonel de Saint Donsto*n* en l'esglise de Saynt Poul – s*umma*: iii s. iiii d.

It*em*, p*ur* lumer en le eglise de Saint Joh*a*n Zakarye, p*ur* xv sergis *et* ii tortys – s*umma*: viii s. x d.

It*em*, p*ur* payn *et* s*er*voyse *et* formage p*ur* le ditz soner – s*umma*: iii s. vi d.

Pur ceo q*e* le ditz Thom*a*s *et* Thom*a*s, Joh*a*n *et* Drew ne fesoit null*e* fest en le vant dit aune, illez doneront a lez gardeinez, c'est asavoire Joh*a*n Fost*er*, Barthelemew Castre, Will*ia*m Glasene *et* Joh*a*n Mapisden – s*umma*: iiii li.[217]

It*em*, p*ur* vesture p*ur* une priest *et* p*ur* S*ire* Thom*a*s Olg*ra*ve *et* p*ur* Richard Fost*er* *et* p*ur* les iii brokorez – s*umma*: l s. vi d. ob.

It*em*, p*ur* div*er*sez costagis de div*er*sez hommez de le lay, c'es[t a]ssavoire[218] acontre le lowez de Saxson en le temps devant le mair*e* Joh*a*n Addele[219] – s*umma*: vi s. vii d.

Auxi acont*re* Will*ia*m Orsman en le temps Will*ia*m Walworth.[220]

216 A new hand starts here.
217 See, above, the ruling of 1372–73, p. 13 of Book A + b, where however it is said that the fine should be given to the old wardens, not, as here, to the newly elected ones.
218 MS: cessavoire.
219 John Hadley was Mayor from October 1379–October 1380.
220 William Walworth was Mayor from October 1380–October 1381.

immediately following the said eve the said chantry shall not have been provided for by us as aforesaid or by our successors. Item, we ordain that that same chaplain whoever he may be at the time shall be obliged every day in person to follow the choir of our said church and to show himself present there, wearing his habit both within our said church and while in the city, this as often as the choir shall make a procession, and he shall faithfully say the Office of the Dead with a commendation every day. Item, we ordain that the same chaplain shall swear that he neither has nor holds nor will he accept any other benefice or ecclesiastical office with or without cure of souls at the same time as the aforesaid chantry, and immediately that he may have another such benefice or office whether irregularly or otherwise, he shall be disqualified from his office, unless it shall be out of bodily infirmity, and he shall be deprived *ipso jure* of that same chantry and once thus deprived the said chantry shall be held to be vacant. And besides the said chaplain, each whoever it may be at any time, shall swear to all the above at the time of his admission.

These are the names of the wardens of the Goldsmiths' Mistery of London 1380–81
in the year 4 Richard II, their term of office ending on St Dunstan's Day in A + b p. 25
the aforesaid year [19 May 1381]:
Thomas Raynham, alderman of Aldersgate Ward in the aforesaid year
Thomas Exton
John Welbourne
Drew Barantyn

The expenses of the said wardens:
Firstly, for ringing the great bell of St Dunstan in St Paul's church – total 3s. 4d.
Item, for the light in the church of St John Zachary, for 15 candles and 2 torches – total 8s. 10d.
Item, for bread and ale and cheese at the said bell-ringing – total 3s. 6d.

Whereas the said Thomas and Thomas, John and Drew did not hold a feast in the aforesaid year, they gave to the wardens, i.e. John Forster, Bartholomew Castre, William Glasen and John Maplesdene – total £4.

Item, for clothing for a priest and for Sir Thomas Orgrave and for Richard Forster and for the 3 brokers – total 50s. 6½d.

Item, for various expenses for various lawyers, i.e. against Saxon's servingman at the time before the Mayor John Hadley – total 6s. 7d.
Also against William Horsman during the time of William Walworth.

Fait a rem*em*br*er* que nous avoumez paié p*ur* une faucon faucement fait a Joh*a*n Geddyng, squier, que le vant ditz lowez de Saxon feyt a le dit Joh*a*n – s*umma*: xiii s. iiii d.

p. 26[221] Feat a remembr*er* q*e* Joh*a*n Mapplestone est payez del argent quel yl app*re*sta en temps q*ua*nt Joh*a*n Forst*er*, Rob*er*t Fr*a*nceys, Thom*as* Hexton*e* *et* Thom*as* Hay furent gardeyns – quyt.

Feat a remembr*er* q*e* sur Lodewyk de Saxoyn*e* p*ar* les gardeyns del miest*er* des orfev*er*s de Londr*e*s fuit trovez q'il eyt feat un faux faukon de cup*er* dargentés deceyvable, a tort *et* a g*ra*nt vilenye *et* esclandr*e* del miest*er* des orfev*er*s, p*ur* quey p*ar* assent *et* pleynt des ditz gardeyns Joh*a*n Hadle, mair de Londr*e*s, fist arrest*er* le dit Lodowyk *et* ly fist enprison*er* p*ar* un q*ua*rt*er* del an, ap*ré*s quel q*ua*rt*er* yl fuit deliv*er*ez, s*ur* condicion d'avoyr esté p*re*st a quel ho*ur*e q*e* le co*m*panye del dit miest*er* le vorroyt avoyr dev*a*nt eux a r*e*spondr*e* del dit t*re*spas, *et* s*ur* ceo le dit Lodowyk fuy *et* est eschapé sauns aut*re* redressement *etc*.

It*em*, feat a remembr*er* q*e* en temps de Will*ia*m Waleworth, mayr de Londr*e*s, l'an q*ua*rte du r*e*gne le Roy Ric*hard* s*e*co*n*de, un accord fuit feat ent*re* les gardeyns del miest*er* *et* Will*ia*m Horsman, *et* accordé fuit q*e* a chescun t*re*spas quel le dit Will*ia*m face encont*re* les gardeyns ou le co*m*panye del dit miest*er*, q'adonq*e*s yl payera xx s. dount la moyté s*er*ra al chambr*e* del Gyhall*e* *et* l'aut*re* moyté al almoygn*e* del dit miest*er*, come pleynement appiert p*ar* la record ent enrollés en la Gyhall*e* en le temps du dit mair l'an suisdit.

Les nouns des app*re*ntices:

Joh*a*n Tylbury app*re*nt*is* Will*ia*m Lyncoln*e* –	ii s.
Will*elmu*s Arsham app*re*nt*is* de Stephen Mapplesden*e* –	ii s.
Esmond Davy app*rentis* de Barth*olome*u Castr*e* –	ii s.
Thom*as* Halle app*rentis* Joh*a*n Halle –	ii s.
Joh*an* Kyng app*rentis* Joh*a*n Welbo*ur*ne –	ii s.
Joh*a*n Nedersol app*rentis* Joh*a*n Godard –	ii s.
Joh*a*n Hanow app*rentis* Joh*a*n Covele –	ii s.
Ric*hard* Snell*e* app*rentis* Joh*a*n Andreu –	ii s.
Joh*a*n Corby app*rentis* Will*ia*m Burgylon*e* –	ii s.
Joh*a*n Brygge app*rentis* Henry Markby –	ii s.
Joh*a*n del Hay app*re*nt*is* Henry Grene –	ii s.
Will*elmu*s Harpell*e* app*re*nt*is* Joh*an* Rodh*a*m –	ii s.
Joh*a*n Wymbulton*e* app*rentis* Reymond Standelf –	ii s.
Thom*as* Brygh*a*m app*re*nt*is* Henry Chiksond –	ii s.

Les nou*n*s des lowys q*ue*ux sou*n*t hors de lo*ur* t*er*me:

Joh*a*n Wylby – ii s.

[221] A new hand starts here.

Memorandum that we have paid for a falcon deceitfully made for John Gedding, squire, which the aforesaid serving-man of Saxon made for the said John – total – 13s. 4d.

Memorandum that John Maplesdene has been paid the money he lent at the p. 26
time when John Forster, Robert Fraunceys, Thomas Exton and Thomas Hay were wardens – quit.

Memorandum that Ludwig of Saxony was found guilty by the wardens of the Goldsmiths' Mistery of London of having made a false falcon of copper silvered in deceitful manner, wrongly and to the great shame and discredit of the Goldsmiths' Mistery, for which reason, with the assent and following a complaint of the said wardens, John Hadley, Mayor of London, had the said Ludwig arrested and he imprisoned him for a quarter of a year, after which he was released on condition that he be ready at whatever time the company of the said mistery should wish him to come before them to answer for the said offence, and at this the said Ludwig fled and escaped, without any other action being taken etc.

Item, memorandum that during the term of office of William Walworth, Mayor of London, in the year 4 Richard II [1380–81], an agreement was made between the wardens of the mistery and William Horsman, and it was agreed that for each offence which the said William might commit against the wardens or the company of the said mistery, he should then pay 20s., of which half shall go to the Guildhall Chamber and the other half to the alms funds of the said mistery, as appears fully in the record of this enrolled at the Guildhall during the time of the said Mayor in the aforesaid year.

The names of apprentices:

John Tilbury apprentice of William Lincoln –	2s.
William Arsham apprentice of Stephen Maplesdene –	2s.
Esmund Davy apprentice of Bartholomew Castre –	2s.
Thomas Halle apprentice of John Halle –	2s.
John Kyng apprentice of John Welbourne –	2s.
John Nedersol apprentice of John Godard –	2s.
John Hanow apprentice of John Covele –	2s.
Richard Snelle apprentice of John Andrew –	2s.
John Corby apprentice of William Burgyloun –	2s.
John Brygge apprentice of Henry Markeby –	2s.
John del Hay apprentice of Henry Grene –	2s.
William Harpele apprentice of John Rodham –	2s.
John Wimbledon apprentice of Raymund Standelf –	2s.
Thomas Brygham apprentice of Henry Chicksands –	2s.

The names of serving-men who are out of their term [of apprenticeship]:

John Wilby –	2s.

Joh*an* Bedyk – ii s.
Will*iam* Kendale – ii s.
Walt*er* Thorn – ii s.
Joh*an* Howton*e* – ii s.

Ces sount les nouns q*ue*ux sou*n*t a la Gylhal[222] enfr*a*nch[isez]:[223]
Ric*hard* Broun – vi s. viii d.

1381–82 Ces sount les nouns des gardeyns del miest*er* des orfeve*r*s p*ur* l'an quinte du
A + a p. 57, regne le Roy Richard *seconde* finant le jo*ur* de Seint Dunsto*u*n l'an av*an*tdit:
col. 1[224] Joh*anne*s Forster
Barth*olomeu*s Castr*e*
Will*elmu*s Glasen
Joh*anne*s Mapplesden*e*

Les despens featz p*ar* les ditz gardeyns:
Pur soner le *gra*unt sonel de Seint Poul en le veille de Seint Dunsto*u*n *et* p*ur* lumer en la chapell*e* de Seint Dunsto*u*n a Seint Poul – xiii s. i d.

It*em*, p*ur* la vestur*e* de S*ire* Thom*as* Orgrave, p*ur* iii v*er*ges – xiii s.

It*em*, p*ur* l'amendement des trompes pois*ant* p*ar* poys d'orf*everie* – de*m*i m*ar*.

Ces sount les nouns des app*re*ntys:
Will*elmu*s Owbrugg*e* app*re*nt*icius* Joh*anni*s Grenefeld – ii s.
Joh*anne*s Barto*u*n app*re*nt*icius* Joh*ann*is Flete – ii s.
Joh*anne*s Dykele app*re*nt*icius* Joh*ann*is Norman – ii s.
Rog*er*us Donne app*re*nt*icius* Joh*ann*is Cheyh*am* – ii s.
Joh*anne*s Games app*re*nt*icius* Ade Bamme – ii s.
Ric*ar*dus Spritford app*re*nt*icius* Thom*e* Davy – ii .s
Ric*ar*dus Sydon app*re*nt*icius* Hervici Rokehaw – ii s.
Will*elmu*s Dene app*re*nt*icius* Joh*ann*is Blakme – ii s.
Will*elmu*s Sutton app*re*nt*icius* Rob*erti* Brynle – ii s.
Ric*ar*dus Aas app*re*nt*icius* Joh*ann*is Canoun – ii s.
Thom*as* Took app*re*nt*icius* Will*elm*i Barbo*ur* – ii s.
Will*elmu*s Garto*u*n app*re*nt*icius* Thom*e* Poll*e* – ii s.
Joh*annes* fitz Hugh app*re*nt*icius* Will*elm*i fitz Heugh – ii s.
Gyves Mando*u*n app*re*nt*icius* Radl*er*i van Dussh*e*, p*ur* sou*n* entré et p*ur* sou*n* issue – iiii s.[225]

Ces sount les nouns des lowys:
Joh*anne*s Bury – ii s.
Henr*icus* Heyward – ii s.

[222] 'a la Gylhal' has been added above the line in a different but contemporary hand.
[223] The word has been truncated as it is inserted into the modern paper page.
[224] A new hand starts here.
[225] Below this the start of a further line has been scored out: 'Joh*anne*s Bu'.

John Bedyk –	2s.
William Kendal –	2s.
Walter Thorn –	2s.
John Houghtoun –	2s.

These are the names of those who have been enfranchised at the Guildhall:
Richard Broun – 6s. 8d.

These are the names of the wardens of the Goldsmiths' Mistery for the year 5 Richard II, [their term] ending on St Dunstan's Day in the aforesaid year [19 May 1382]: 1381–82 A + a p. 57, col. 1

John Forster
Bartholomew Castre
William Glasen
John Maplesdene

The expenditures made by the same wardens:
For ringing the great bell of St Paul's on the eve of St Dunstan's Day, and for the light in the chapel of St Dunstan at St Paul's – 13s. 1d.

Item, for the clothing of Sir Thomas Orgrave, for 3 yards – 13s.

Item, for repair of the trumpets, weighing by goldsmiths' weight[100] – ½ mark.

These are the names of apprentices:

William Owbrugge apprentice of John Greenfield –	2s.
John Barton apprentice of John Flete –	2s.
John Dykele apprentice of John Norman –	2s.
Roger Donne apprentice of John Cheyham –	2s.
John Games apprentice of Adam Bamme –	2s.
Richard Sprotford apprentice of Thomas Davy –	2s.
Richard Sydon apprentice of Harvey Rookhawe –	2s.
William Dene apprentice of John Blakme –	2s.
William Sutton apprentice of Robert Brinle –	2s.
Richard Aas apprentice of John Canon –	2s.
Thomas Took apprentice of William Barbour –	2s.
William Gartoun apprentice of Thomas Polle –	2s.
John FitzHugh apprentice of William FitzHugh –	2s.
Gyves Mandoun apprentice of Radler van Dusshe, for his entry and his release from terms –	4s.

These are the names of serving-men:

John Bury –	2s.
Henry Heyward –	2s.

[100] i.e. the Tower pound – see p. 103, note 49 above.

Ces sount les nou*ns* q*e* sou*n*t f*ra*nchisés en la Gyhall*e*:
Joh*anne*s Pope – xiii s. iiii d.

It*em*, les ditz gardeyns resceyvront de:
Joh*a*n Welbourn et Joh*a*n Mapplesden*e*, de lo*ur* accomptes aderere[226]
– ii m*ars*

q*ue*ux treys[227] m*ars* furent payez a Thom*as* Exto*u*n en p*ar*tie de payement de la so*m*me a ly due p*ur* le rente.[228]

1382 col. 2 Feat a reme*m*br*er* q*e* le vendirdy apr*é*s le feste del Epiph*an*ie cest an les meir*e et* aldermans *et* comu*n*es furent arrayés p*ur* chevacher encontr*e* la Reyne, soer al Emp*erour,*[229] *et par* cause q*e* touz les miest*er*s de la cité avoyent en charge q'ils ne duissent avoyr autr*e* vestur*e* q*e* rouge *et* blank, les orfev*er*s furent arrayez de mesme les colo*ur*s, et p*ur* ceo q*e* touz aut*re*s miest*er*s avoy[e]nt div*er*s conisances, les ditz orfev*er*s furent en le rouge p*ar*tie barrés de selverwir *et* poudrés de treys foylles d'argent [de] perles, et chescun ho*m*me de mesme le miest*er* al nombr*e* de vii^{xx} avoy[e]nt s*ur* le senestr*e* p*ar*tie g*ra*untz nouches d'or *et* de p*er*reye *et* s*ur* lo*ur* testes chapell*es* cov*er*és de rouge *et* poudr*é*s des ditz treys foylles, q*ue*ux chevacheront ovec la royne p*ar*my la cité *et* les ditz gardeyns payeront dev*er*s custages p*ur* mesme le chevaché c'est assav*oir*:

En p*ri*mes, a les vi mynstrall*es* – lx s.
It*em*, p*ur* vestur*e* de mesme les mynstrall*es* – xxiiii s. v d.
It*em*, p*ur* foyll*es* a diaprer a geter s*ur* le royne – v s.
It*em*, p*ur* selverskynnes – iii s. iiii d.
It*em*, al porter de Seint Barth*olome*u *et* so*u*n s*er*v*a*nt – xiiii d.
It*em*, a un peynto*ur* p*ur* les garneme*n*tz des mynst*ra*ll*es* – ii s. ii d.
S*um*m*a*: iiii li. xvi s. i d.

Et feat a remembr*er* q*e* desuis Chepe feut un som*er*castell*e* b*ie*n arrayés, pendant en quel furent treys virgyns p*ur* geter foyll*es*, quel castel costa:
En primes, p*ur* vi v*er*ges de rouge p*ri*s le v*er*ge xviii d.
i v*er*ge *et* i q*u*art*er* rouge, p*ri*s le v*er*ge – xxx d.
iii v*er*ges blank, p*ri*s le v*er*ge xxviii d.
Joh*a*n Garoun[230] p*ur* carpentrie – xliii d.

[226] John Welbourne was warden in the previous year, 1380–81, and John Maplesdene is warden this year, 1381–82, and thus this reference to their accounts being in arrears must refer to an earlier year when they were renters, to which there is no other reference.
[227] i.e. the sum paid by John Pope and that paid by John Welbourne and John Maplesdene.
[228] See below, A + a, p. 58.
[229] Anne of Bohemia.
[230] Osberg, p. 4, reads the name as Baroun but (at length in a footnote) can find no record of a carpenter of this name; the initial is identical with other instances of capital G in this scribe's hand.

These are the names of those who have been enfranchised in the Guildhall:
John Pope – 13s. 4d.

Item, the said wardens have received from:
John Welbourne and John Maplesdene, from their accounts in arrear – 2 marks.

– the which three marks were paid to Thomas Exton as part payment of the sum due to him for the tenement.

Memorandum that on the Friday after the Feast of the Epiphany this year 1382
[11 January 1382 n.s.] the Mayor, aldermen and the commons were arrayed to col. 2
ride in procession with the Queen, the Emperor's sister, and whereas all the city misteries were instructed that their clothing must be of red and white,[101] the goldsmiths were dressed in these same colours, and since all the other misteries had various cognizances, the goldsmiths had the red part of their clothing barred with silver wire and powdered with silver pearl trefoils, and each of the seven score men of the said mistery wore on their left side a large gold clasp with gemstones, and on their heads they wore chaplets covered in red material powdered with the said trefoils, and they rode with the queen throughout the city, and the said wardens paid various expenses for the said riding as follows:

Firstly, to the 6 minstrels – 60s.
Item, for the clothing of the same minstrels – 24s. 5d.
Item, for leaves to be diapered to throw over the queen[102] – 5s.
Item, for 'silverskins'[103] – 3s. 4d.
Item, to the porter of St Bartholomew's and his servant – 14d.
Item, to a painter for the minstrels' ornaments – 2s. 2d.
Total: £4 16s. 1d.

Memorandum also that a summer-castle[104] was set up in Cheap and well decorated, and three virgins leaned out of it to throw leaves, and this castle cost:
Firstly, for 6 yards of red cloth at 18d. the yard –
1¼ yards of red cloth at 30d. the yard –
3 yards of white cloth at 28d. the yard –
John Garoun, for carpentry work – 43d.

[101] These are the colours of the City of London. For another occasion when these colours were worn by all citizens greeting the King in the City on 10 November 1387, see Hector and Harvey, *The Westminster Chronicle*, p. 206.

[102] i.e. as a sort of confetti.

[103] These are probably silvered over animal skins or hides, used here perhaps for horse ornaments (?) and below in the coverings of the summer castle. I find Osberg's suggestion (*op. cit.*, note 13) that 'seluer' here is a form of 'celure' unconvincing and unnecessary.

[104] A movable tower used in sieges (the etymology is from 'somer' = packhorse), but here clearly in peace-time and for pageantry and ceremonial procession use: a decorative model castle-tower made of wood used as a decorative object in pageants and processions. Osberg's article concentrates on this 'castle' and gives many illustrations of other similar ones and is most illuminating on this whole matter.

It*em*, p*ur* i corde – vi s. viii d.
It*em*, p*ur* selverskynnes – viii s. x d. ob.
S*um*m*a*: xxxv s. ix d. ob.

dount ressu p*ur* le drap *et* le cord*e* – x s.

Feat a remembr*er* q*e* les ditz gardeyns ount resseu de la co*m*panye p*ur* les ditz costages encontr*e* la venue de la dite royne – vii li.

Feat a remembr*er* q*e* p*ar* co*m*une assent de tut le co*m*panye Thom*as* Vok feut resseu d'estr*e* clerk de mesme le co*m*panye *et* jur*é* feut a mesme le co*m*panye *et* ordiné feut q'il duist avoyr p*ar* an sou*n* vestur*e* *et* i m*ar*c p*ur* loyalment s*er*vyr mesme le co*m*panye en lo*ur*s affair*es* *etc*.

1381 It*em*, feat a remembr*er* q*e* Thom*as* Hexto*u*n, orfev*er*e, ad resceux le jo*ur* des
p. 58 Innocentz l'an av*a*ntdit xx li. des ditz gardeyns *et* de la co*m*panye des orfev*er*s de Londr*es* en p*ar*tie de payement de C m*ar*s p*ur* la rev*er*sion del ten*ement* apellé "le Ship on the Hop" apr*é*s la decesse de *Christ*ine, la fe*m*me de Will*iam* Chipelden*e*, issint q*e* le dit Thom*as* ore est payez de iiii^{xx} m*ar*s en p*ar*tie de payement des ditz C m*ar*s ové une aut*re* so*m*me de .l. m*ar*s payez dev*a*nt, de queux xx li. les ditz gardeyns avoy[e]nt des rent*er*s del co*m*panye xxiiii m*ars* *et* de Matill*e* Chardou*n* xxv s. *et* de Joh*a*n Pope xiii s. iiii d. *et* de Joh*a*n Welbo*ur*ne *et* Joh*a*n Mappelesden*e* ii m*ars*.

1381–82 Et issint touz choses q*ue*ux lez ditz gardeyns ount resceux amontent en tut
– xxviii li. ix s.
Et les ditz gardeyns ount payés come piert p*ar* p*ar*cell*es* av*a*ntditz
– xxviii li. vii s. iii d. ob.
Et les novell*es* gardeyns ount ressu les xxi d. residues de la so*m*me av*a*ntdit.
Et les ditz vielx gardeyns ount de lo*ur* bon*ne* gree donez al almoigne de Seint Dunsto*u*n xx s.

1382–83 Ces sount les nou*n*s des gardeyns de la feste de Seint Dunsto*u*n l'an v tanq*e*
p. 59 a mesme le feste l'an vj^{me}:
Will*elmu*s Tyngewyk
Joh*anne*s Carbonel
Thom*as* Davy *et*
Joh*anne*s Bulstrode

Ces sont les despences feat p*ar* les ditz gardeyns:
En p*ri*mes, p*ur* le sono*ur* del g*ra*unt sonel de Seint Poul *et* p*ur* autr*es* custages del berfray – viii s. ii d. It*em*, p*ur* lum*er*e de Seint Dunsto*u*n, p*ur* ix Judas, le feso*ur* vii s. It*em*, p*ur* peyntu*r*e de mesme les Judas iii s. It*em*, p*ur* ix

Item, for a rope – 6s. 8d.
Item, for 'silverskins' – 8s. 10½d.
Total: 35s. 9½d.

of which has been received for the cloth and the rope – 10s.

Memorandum that the said wardens have received from the company for the said expenses at the arrival of the said queen – £7

Memorandum that by common assent of the whole company Thomas Vok was admitted as clerk of the same company and was sworn to the said company, and it was ordained that he should receive each year clothing and 1 mark for his loyal service to the same company in their affairs etc.

Item, memorandum that Thomas Exton, goldsmith, has received on Holy 1381
Innocents Day of the aforesaid year [28 December 1381] £20 from the said p. 58
wardens and the company of the Goldsmiths of London, as part payment of 100 marks for the reversion of the tenement called 'The Ship on the Hoop' after the death of Christine, the wife of William Chipeldene, and thus the said Thomas has now been paid 80 marks in part payment of the said 100 marks, with another sum of 50 marks paid previously, of the which £20 the said wardens received 24 marks from the company's renters, and 25s from Matilda Chardoun, and 13s. 4d. from John Pope and from John Welbourne and John Maplesdene 2 marks.

And thus the wardens receipts amount in all to – £28 9s. 1381–82
And the said wardens have paid out as appears in the aforesaid items – £28 7s. 3½d.
And the new wardens have received the 21d. remainder of the aforesaid sum.
And the said previous wardens have of their goodwill given to the increase of the alms funds of St Dunstan – 20s.

These are the names of the wardens from the Feast of St Dunstan in the 1382–83
year 5 [Richard II] until the same Feast in the year 6 [Richard II] p. 59
[19 May 1382 – 19 May 1383]:
William Tingewick
John Carbonelle
Thomas Davy and
John Bulstrode

These are the expenditures made by the said wardens:
Firstly, for the ringing the great bell of St Paul's and for other costs in the bell-tower – 8s. 2d. Item, for the light of St Dunstan, for the making of 9 judas[105] 7s. Item, for the painting of the same judas – 3s. Item, for 9 dishes

[105] A 'judas' was a rounded length of wood imitating a candle and often painted decoratively, at the top of which a candle was attached. Those used at Easter time were especially elaborate. See *OED*: 'The paschal candlestick in churches, which was usually of brass, had seven branches, from the seventh or middle one of which a tall thick piece of wood, painted like a candle, and called the Judas of the Paschal, rose nearly to the roof, and on the top of this was placed at Eastertide the paschal candle of wax.'

disshes p*ur* les tapr*e*s – iii s. ix d. It*em,* in cir*e* – xviii s. viii d. It*em,* p*ur* le wast de ii torches xxii d. It*em,* p*ur* un barr*e* de ferr*e* *et* p*ur* mettr*e* illoeq*e*s – vii s. x d. It*em,* p*ur* i l*ett*re d'or en la gr*a*unt Ch*art*re del rente – xx d. It*em,* p*ur* enroller i feat p*ar* quel Thom*as* Exto*un* ad vendus al companye la r*e*versio*un* del rente del Shippe q*e* feut a Waut*er* atte Grene en le Bocherie – xxx d. It*em,* a Thom*as* Exto*un* p*ur* la r*e*versio*un* del dite rente appellé la Shippe – xx li.

S*um*ma: xxii li. xiiii s. v d.

p. 59, col. 1 Ces so*u*nt les no*u*ns des appr*e*ntys en le dit an – ii s.[231]

Joh*anne*s Moreby app*rentys* ové Joh*an* Grenefeld –	ii s.
Fraunceys app*rentys* ové Dru[232] Barantyn –	ii s.
Henr*icus* Maserer app*rentys* ové Joh*an* Bulstrode –	ii s.
Joh*anne*s Halyday app*rentys* ové Will*ia*m Lucas –	ii s.
Will*elmu*s atte Mille app*rentys* ové Joh*an* Pope –	ii s.
Will*elmus* Elys, Thom*as* Warmesto*un* app*rentys* Joh*an* Busshe –	iiii s.
Laur*encius* Mortymer app*rentys* ové Joh*an* Luyto*un* –	ii s.
Ranulphus Langrave app*rentys* ové Henr*i* Heyward –	ii s.
Joh*anne*s Chatr*e* app*rentys* ové Will*iam* Harre –	ii s.
Joh*anne*s Cheke, Will*elmu*s Halteby app*rentys* ové Thom*as* Chalers –	iiii s.
Rob*er*tus London app*rentys* ové Rob*er*t Betoigne –	ii s.
Rog*er*us Polhill*e* app*rentys* Will*elm*i Horsman –	ii s.
Joh*anne*s Bray app*rentys* ové Will*ia*m Heyward –	ii s.
Walt*er*us Hammes app*rentys* Andr*ew* Stameldén*e* –	ii s.
Rog*er*us Ramides app*rentys* Rob*er*ti Huggevile –	ii s.
Joh*anne*s Fyfhide *et* Joh*anne*s Watford app*rentys* Adam Ba*m*me –	iiii s.
Thom*as* Ufford app*rentys* ové mo*nsire* Nichol Twyford –	ii s.

Ces so*u*nt les no*u*ns des lowys:

Ric*ardus* Cranesle[233]	
Jacobus Buntyng –	ii s.
Joh*anne*s Thorkyng –	ii s.
Joh*anne*s Waldegrave –	ii s.
Joh*anne*s Waddesley –	ii s.
Ric*ard*us Cranesle[234] –	ii s.

p. 59, col. 2 Feat a remembr*er* q*e* les ditz gardeyns ount resseux de Will*ia*m Lucas *et* Joh*an* Cheyh*a*m del surplusage del rent – xviii li. vi s. ob.[235]

It*em,* ressu des vielx gardeyns p*ur* dette quel Joh*an* Lyncoll*e* devoyt p*ur* sa rente – xiii s. iiii d.

[231] Clearly, the scribe has gone down this list adding 'ii s.' at the end of each line including, mistakenly, this first line; he also put it at the end of the sixth line following, then changing this to the correct 'iiii s.'

[232] MS: Dru Dru.

[233] In the LH margin beside this name has been written 'vac'', i.e. this name to be cancelled (see below).

[234] The surname has been substituted for the name 'Knare', scored out.

[235] This entry must imply that William Lucas and John Cheyham were renters in either this year or the previous one.

for tapers – 3s. 9d. Item, for wax – 18s. 8d. Item, for the consumption of a certain amount[106] from 2 torches – 22d. Item, for an iron bar and for setting it up there – 7s. 10d. Item, for a gold initial letter on the great charter of the tenement – 20d. Item, for enrolling a deed by which Thomas Exton has sold to the company the reversion of the tenement of the Ship which belonged to Walter atte Grene in the Shambles[107] – 30d. Item, to Thomas Exton for the reversion of the said tenement called the Ship – £20.

Total: £22 14s. 5d.

These are the names of apprentices in the said year: p. 59, col. 1

John Moreby, apprentice with John Greenfield –	2s.
Fraunceys,[108] apprentice with Drew Barantyn –	2s.
Henry Mazerer, apprentice with John Bulstrode –	2s.
John Halyday, apprentice with William Lucas –	2s.
William atte Mille, apprentice with John Pope –	2s.
William Elys, Thomas Warmestoun, apprentices of John Busshe –	4s.
Laurence Mortimer, apprentice with John Luton –	2s.
Ranulph Langrave, apprentice with Henry Heyward –	2s.
John Chatre, apprentice with William Harre –	2s.
John Cheke, William Halteby, apprentices with Thomas Chalers –	4s.
Robert London, apprentice with Robert Beteigne –	2s.
Roger Polhille, apprentice with William Horsman –	2s.
John Bray, apprentice with William Heyward –	2s.
Walter Hamme, apprentice of Andrew Stameldene –	2s.
Roger Ramides, apprentice of Robert Huggevile –	2s.
John Fifehead and John Watford, apprentices of Adam Bamme –	4s.
Thomas Ufford, apprentice with Sir Nicholas Twyford –	2s.

These are the names of serving-men:

Richard Cranesle	
James Buntyng –	2s.
John Thornkyn –	2s.
John Waldegrave –	2s.
John Waddesley –	2s.
Richard Cranesle –	2s.

Memorandum that the said wardens have received from William Lucas and John Cheyham for the surplusage[109] of the tenement – £18 6s. ½d. p. 59, col. 2
Item, received from the previous wardens for the debt which John Lincoln owed for his rent – 13s. 4d.

[106] See Jefferson, 'The Language and Vocabulary . . .', p. 211.
[107] This was in Newgate Street.
[108] It is perhaps more likely that this is a surname rather than a first name.
[109] In charge and discharge accounting, which is being used here, the surplusage or superplusagium is the amount that e.g. a reeve on an estate when presenting his accounts for the year has if he has spent more than he has received, i.e. money will be owed to him from somewhere to reimburse him for this extra expenditure; such a superplusagium could be dealt with in a number of ways. Here it would appear that W.L. and J.C. are reimbursing the wardens for their, the wardens, extra expenditure on the new tenement of the Ship on the Hoop.

It*em*, de mesmes les gardeyns p*ur* lo*ur* encresse – xxi s. ix d.
It*em*, ressu de Thom*as* Renh*am* p*ur* C s. de quitrente p*ur* t*er*me de sa vye – lii li.
It*em*, des exec*utours* de Alice Chichestr*e* en moneye – x li., *et* i sale ové iiii costers, iiii banqers *et* xxiiii quiss*yns* de plum*e*.
It*em*, de Dru Barrantyn del argent q*e* r*e*maynt en sa mayn q*ua*nt yl fu gardeyn – xxiiii s. iiii d.
It*em*, ressu de Joh*a*n Park*e* p*ur* so*u*n entré en la companye – v m*ars*; dont abbatus xii s. viii d. p*ur* sa robe.
It*em*, deliv*er*é a Thomas Panto*u*n, Joh*an* Thom*as*, Esteph*ene* Thorp *et* Joh*an* Cheyh*a*m, ii masers q*ue*ux Walt*er* Brent dona a la companye
P*ur* ceo q*e* Richard Bro*u*n fuist trovez en defaute p*ur* esquelers q'il vendust en mesme an, ordeigné fuist q*e* si le dite Rich*ard* fuist trovez en defaute un autr*e* temps, q'il paiera al almoign*e* de Seint Donston vi s. viii d. Outr*e* ceo, si ascun autr*e* fuist trovez en mesme defaute paiera mesme peyne.[236]

p. 59 It*em*, p*ur* ceo q*e* Joh*a*n Pope trové feut p*a*r les gardeyns ovec c*er*tein vessell*e* q*e* feut defectyf, le quel vessel le dit Joh*an* enprist a les ditz gardeyns de amesner arer*e* a feare ent ceo q*e* dreyt le voet, *et* p*a*r cause q*e* le dit Joh*an* fist defaute *et* ne voleyt soy justicer a les gardeins de amesner ar*ere* les ditz vessell*es,* le dit Joh*an* soy myst en le g*ra*ce de ses gardeyns en d*em*i m*a*r a payer al almoign*e* de Seint Dunsto*u*n.

p. 60 Ces sount les custages ento*ur* le novel p*a*rlo*ur*:
En p*ri*mes baillé a Thom*as* Reynh*a*m en erres del so*m*me quel yl paya – xii d. It*em*, payé a Mathu, carpent*er*, del p*a*rlo*ur* – xxv li. It*em*, a un maso*u*n p*ar* xxxii jo*u*rs p*er*nant p*ar* le jo*ur* viii d. p*ur* la fesance des fundementz del meso*u*n *et* del privé – xxii s. iiii d. It*em*, p*ur* chalk *et* cariage – xxvii s. It*em*, p*ur* i laborer p*ar* xxxii jo*u*rs p*ar* le jo*ur* v d. – S*umma*. xiii s. iiii d. It*em*, p*ur* C charrettés de lomb *et* sond – xxvi s. viii d. It*em*, p*ur* iiii^{C} et .v. sacz de lym – xxvii s. iiii d. It*em*, payé al daub*e*re p*ar* xlii jo*u*rs d*em*j, p*er*nant le jo*ur* vii d. – xxiiii s. iii d.[237] It*em*, payé a un s*er*vant p*ar* xlii jo*u*rs *et* d*em*j, v d. le jo*ur* – xvii s. ix d. It*em*, p*ur* un autr*e* s*er*v*a*nt p*ar* vii jo*u*rs d*em*j, v d. le jo*ur* – iii s. ii d. It*em*, al tyler*e* – xii s. It*em*, p*ur* iiii^{Ml} tieles, p*ri*s xxvi s. viii d. It*em*, p*ur* rooftiel – ii s. vii d. It*em*, p*ur* tylpyns vii d. ob. It*em*, p*ur* lathes al celo*ur* – x s. x d. It*em*, p*ur* lathenayll*e* a tut l'ov*er*aygne – xx s. v d. ob. It*em*, M^{l} M^{l} M^{l} M^{l} CCC *et* d*em*i des clowes blank *et* autr*es* – xx s. It*em*, p*ur* henges *et* hokes *et* renges p*ur* vii hoes *et* iii fenestr*es* – vii s. viii d. It*em*, p*ur* bord appellé plaunchebord p*ur* les mures del p*a*rlo*ur et* a les goters *et* p*ur* le novel oes a la seler *et* ii stulpes p*ur* l'oes del seler *et* p*ur* l'ov*er*aigne –

[236] This paragraph has been added in a different hand and ink in a space previously blank between the columns.
[237] He was apparently slightly underpaid.

Item, from the same wardens for the increase given by them [to the alms funds] – 21s. 9d.
Item, received from Thomas Raynham for 100s. quitrent [p.a.] until the end of his life – £52
Item, from the executors of Alice Chichester in money – £10 and 1 set of furnishings for a hall with 4 costers [wall-hangings], 4 bankers [tapestry coverings for benches or chairs] and 24 feather cushions.
Item, from Drew Barantyn for the money remaining in his hands from the time when he was a warden[110] – 24s. 4d.
Item, received from John Parke for his entry into the company – 5 marks, of which 12s. 8d. is rebated for his gown.
Item, delivered to Thomas Panton, John Thomas, Stephen Thorp and John Cheyham, 2 mazers which Walter Brent gave to the company.
Whereas Richard Broun was found guilty of an offence over spoons which he sold in the same year, it was ordained that if the said Richard should once again be found guilty of an offence, then he shall pay to the alms funds of St Dunstan 6s. 8d. And besides, if anyone else shall be found guilty of the same offence, he shall pay the same penalty.

Item, whereas John Pope was found by the wardens to have certain vesselware p. 59
which was defective, and the said John gave an undertaking to the said wardens to take back the said vesselware and to do with it as required by rights, and whereas the said John failed in this, and did not wish to have judgment from the wardens of taking back the said vessels, the said John submitted himself to the judgment of his wardens to pay half a mark to the alms funds of St Dunstan.

These are the expenses incurred over the new parlour:[111] p. 60
Firstly, handed to Thomas Raynham as a deposit on the sum which he has paid out – 12d. Item, paid to Matthew, the carpenter, for the parlour – £25. Item, to a mason for 32 days at 8d. per day for the making of the foundations of the room and the privy – 22s. 4d. Item, for chalk, and carriage – 27s. Item, for a labourer for 32 days at 5d. per day – total 13s. 4d. Item, for 100 cartloads of clay and sand – 26s. 8d. Item, for 405 bags of lime – 27s. 4d. Item, paid to the dauber [plasterer] for 42½ days at 7d. per day – 24s. 3d. Item, paid to a servant for 42½ days at 5d. per day – 17s. 9d. Item, to another servant for 7½ days at 5d. per day – 3s. 2d. Item, to the tiler – 12s. Item, for 4,000 tiles, cost 26s. 8d. Item, for roof tiles – 2s. 7d. Item, for tile-pins 7½d. Item, for laths for the storeroom – 10s. 10d. Item, for lath-nails for the whole of the works – 20s. 5½d. Item, 4,350 white nails and others – 20s. Item, for hinges and hooks and rings for 7 doors and 3 window-frames – 7s. 8d. Item, for boards called 'plaunchebord' [planks] for the walls of the parlour and for the gutters and for the new door to the storeroom, and 2 posts

[110] This was two years previously.
[111] The 'parlour' would have been the main living-room where the wardens and others would meet on an everyday basis, where meals might be served, where all sorts of business might have been transacted, and where the records might have been kept. The 'hall' would have been a larger room and used for more formal occasions such as the annual feast and general assemblies of the whole company.

xxvi s. i d. Item, pur plumbe a les goters *et* pur chymenees *et* pur les stulpes, vii weyes ix clowes – iiii li. pris le wey xiii s., *et* pur le fesance de viii clowes de nostre propre plumb viii d. summa – iiii li. xviii s. Item, pur plumb a les privees – xvi d. Item, pur piche *et* talgh a mesme les privees – iiii d. Item, al rakiere pur portage del plumbe – iii d. Item, pur netter le privé – ii d. Item, pur fesance de deux chemenés – iiii mars. Item, pur fesance d'un mur desus le novel privé – xii s. Item, a un tylere aprés ceo qe les chemenés furent levés – xxii d. Item, pur oker *et* oyle – vi s. ix d. Item, pur cole – iiii d. Item, pur i laborer par v jours pur netter le novel mesoun – xxv d. Item, pur i styrope de ferre al chemeney – xviii d. Item, a i tylere pur amender les defautes en la sale *et* del rente a cause del novel mesoun – vi s. vi d.

Summa – xlviii li. xiiii s. x d.

Item, pur ii stulpes al graunt port – xiii s. iiii d. Item, pur ferre a mesme les stulpes – xii s. x d. Item, pur clowes des stulpes appellés lednaylle – iii d. Item, pur le celer ii lokkes, i barre de ferre, ii boltes, pris – ii s. Item, pur ii carpenters par v jours pur feare choses en la celer *et* le oes devers le sale – vi s. viii d. Item, i servant pur netter le seler par ii jours – x d. Item, i plankbord al oes del celer – viii d. Item, pur i tristelle pur le seler – xviii d. Item, pur grees al seler xxv sak de lym – xl d. Item, pur vi charrettés de sond pris – xviii d. Item, a Johan Cot de Maydeston pur le oes *et* xii grees – xxiii s. viii d. Item, pur cariage – xvi d. Item, pur i corbel pur le seler – x d. Item, iiii hokes pur le seler – xvi d. *et* pur iiii henges – xviii d. Item, pur le masoun pur soun travaille – vi s. viii d. Item, pur i servant par ii jours – x d. Item, pur amender les autres defautes en autres mesouns queux furent feat a cause del novel mesoun avantdit: payé a iii carpenters par iii jours pur i mesoun desus le seler – v s. iii d. Item, pur i autre carpenter par i jour a mesme le mesoun – viii d. Item, pur i daubere *et* soun vadlet – iiii s. viii d. Item, pur CC lathes – viii d. Item, pur M[l] M[l] lattenaylle – ii s. Item, a Julian Bristow pur voyder mesme la mesoun – i marc. Item, delyveré as novelles gardeyns pur i pipe de vyn quel Thomas Renham dona – xl s.

Summa – vi li. xii s. viii d.

Feat a remembrer qe tut le resceyte amounte – iiii[xx] viii li. xviii s. i d. ob.
Et touz les custages amontent – lxxviii li. xxiii d.
Et issint rest due al companye – x li. xvi s. ii d. ob., la quele somme est deliveré a Thomas Pantoun, Johan Thomas, Stephen Thorpe *et* Johan Cheham, novelles gardeyns.[238]
Item, yls ount deliverés a les ditz novelles gardeyns xx s. d'encrés.

[238] See below, A + b, p. 30.

for the door of the storeroom and for the workmanship – 26s. 1d. Item, for lead for the gutters and for the fireplaces and for the posts, 7 wayes 9 cloves – £4, at 13s. the waye, and for the making up of 8 cloves of our own lead – 8d., total £4 18s. Item, for lead for the privies – 16d. Item, for pitch and tallow for the same privies – 4d. Item, to the rakier [street-cleaner] for porterage of the lead – 3d. Item, for cleaning of the privy – 2d. Item, for the making of 2 fireplaces – 4 marks. Item, for the making of a wall over the new privy – 12s. Item, to a tiler after the installation of the fireplaces – 22d. Item, for ochre and oil – 6s. 9d. Item, for size [glue] – 4d. Item, for a labourer for 5 days to clean the new building – 25d. Item, for an iron stirrup for the fireplace – 18d. Item, to a tiler for repairing the defects in the hall and in the tenement which arose because of the new building – 6s. 6d.

Total: £48 14s. 10d.

Item, for 2 posts for the big doorway – 13s. 4d. Item, for iron for these same posts – 12s. 10d. Item, for nails for the posts called 'lead-nails' – 3d. Item, for the storeroom, 2 locks, 1 iron bar, 2 bolts, cost – 2s. Item, for 2 carpenters for 5 days to do work in the storeroom and on the door leading to the hall – 6s. 8d. Item, a servant to clean the storeroom for 2 days – 10d. Item, 1 plank for the storeroom-door – 8d. Item, for a trestle for the storeroom – 18d. Item, for steps to the storeroom – 25 bags of lime – 40d. Item, for 6 cartloads of sand, cost – 18d. Item, to John Cot of Maidstone for the door and 12 steps – 23s. 8d. Item, for carriage – 16d. Item, for a corbel[112] for the storeroom – 10d. Item, 4 hooks for the storeroom – 16d. and for 4 hinges – 18d. Item, for a mason for his work – 6s. 8d. Item, for a servant for 2 days – 10d. Item, for repairing the other defects in other rooms which have arisen on account of the aforesaid new building: paid to 3 carpenters for 3 days for a room above[113] the storeroom – 5s. 3d. Item, for another carpenter for one day working on the same room – 8d. Item, for a plasterer and his boy – 4s. 8d. Item, for 200 laths – 8d. Item, for 2,000 lath-nails – 2s. Item, to Julian Bristow for vacating[114] the same room – 1 mark. Item, delivered to the new wardens for a pipe of wine given by Thomas Raynham – 40s.

Total: £6 12s. 8d.

Memorandum that the receipts in all amount to – £88 18s. 1½d.
And all the expenses amount to – £78 23d.
And thus the remainder due to the company – £10 16s. 2½d., the which sum has been handed over to Thomas Panton, John Thomas, Stephen Thorpe and John Cheyham, the new wardens.
Item, they have handed over to the new wardens 20s. increase.[115]

[112] It is possible that the 10d. was spent on a basket (also 'corbel' in Anglo-Norman), an object which would indeed be necessary in a storeroom, but the reference afterwards to the mason leads me to prefer 'corbel'.

[113] 'desus' can mean both 'above' and 'below' in Anglo-Norman, dependent on context. Here it would seem impossible to be sure which.

[114] 'voyder' could also mean 'to clear, to empty' but 'to vacate' seems more probable and that he had been a tenant.

[115] No mention is made here of the alms funds, as is usual. This may just be an omission, or it may be that the monies received as interest this year are going straight into the general funds held by the wardens.

1383–84 *Anno* vj° regni Reg*is* Ric*ard*i sec*und*i

A + b p. 29[239] Ces su*n*t les nou*n*s dé Gardeyns[240] de la feste de Seint Donston l'an vj^e tank a mesme feste l'an viie:

Thom*as* Panton
Joh*ann*es Thorn
Steph*anus* Thorp
Joh*ann*es Cheyh*am*

En p*ri*mes, p*ur* soner le g*ra*unt sonail de Seint Poul *et* en autr*es* costages en le belfray – vii s. vii d.
It*em*, en costag*es* de cir*e* p*ur* les vii serges du pois iii^xx li. *et* xv, *et* p*ur* le wast de les torches *et* le faç*oun* – xxxviii s. i d. ob.

S*um*ma: xlv s. iiii d. ob.[241]

Ceux sount les nouns de app*re*ntys resceux mesme aan:

Joh*a*n Sheffelde app*re*ntys de George Lynforde –	ii s.
Joh*a*n Huddesone app*re*ntys de Remond Standel –	ii s.
Will*ia*m Parker app*re*ntys de Henri Chiksond –	ii s.
Joh*a*n Rasene app*re*ntys de Joh*a*n Bulstrode –	ii s.
Joh*a*n Sotherne app*re*ntys de Thom*as* Fyndon*e* –	ii s.
Ric*hard* Sulg*ra*ve app*re*ntys de Thom*as* Davy –	ii s.
Thom*as* Meseng*er* app*re*ntis de Thom*as* Broune –	ii s.
Joh*a*n Maldon*e* app*re*ntis de Joh*a*n Walsh*e* –	ii s.
Ric*hard* Marchal app*re*ntys de Joh*a*n Somerfile –	ii s.
Ric*hard* Crafforde app*re*ntys de Thom*as* Polle –	ii s.
Jeames Moriel app*re*ntys de Joh*a*n Hynde –	ii s.
Joh*a*n Colyn app*re*ntis de Will*ia*m Haper –	ii s.
Will*ia*m Whetle app*re*ntys de Thom*as* Panton*e* –	ii s.
Joh*a*n Franns app*re*ntys de Joh*a*n Frenshe –	ii s.
Nich*ol*as Breton*e*, Joh*a*n Martyn app*re*ntis de Joh*a*n Bodesh*am* –	iiii s.
Barth*olom*eu Bylyngh*am* app*re*ntis de Thom*as* Essex –	ii s.

Ceux sount les nouns de lowys mesme aan:

Thom*as* Cresselowe –	ii s.
Thom*as* Lamport –	ii s.
Will*ia*m Baldeswell*e* –	ii s.
Will*ia*m Hugate –	ii s.
Ric*hard* Sage –	ii s.

Fait a reme*m*br*er* q*e* les gardeins ount resceu l'an du roy avantdit de les vieux gardeinz, c'est assavoir Will*ia*m Tyngewyk, Joh*a*n Carbonel *et* lo*ur* compaignons *et* de les renteres xxvi li. xv s. x d. ob.
It*em*, ount resceu ii cuppes de mazer*e*, des q*ue*ux le un est venduz p*ur* –

[239] A new hand has written the introduction ('Ces su*n*t . . .') and another new hand then continues with the list of names and the rest of this page and the next. The year at the top of the page has been written in yet another and probably slightly later hand.
[240] The words 'de le mester de Seynt' have been written but scored out here.
[241] This sum does not tally with the amounts given above.

The year 6 Richard II 1383–84
These are the names of the wardens from the feastday of St Dunstan in the year 6 [Richard II] until the same feastday in the year 7 [Richard II] [19 May 1383 – 19 May 1384] A + b p. 29
Thomas Panton
John Thorn
Stephen Thorp
John Cheyham

Firstly, for ringing the great bell of St Paul's and for other expenses in the bell-tower – 7s. 7d.
Item, for the costs of wax for the 7 candles weighing 60lb. and 15[116] and for the consumption of torches and the making-up [of candles] – 38s. 1½d.
Total: 45s. 4½d.[117]

These are the names of apprentices admitted the same year:

John Sheffield apprentice of George Lynford –	2s.
John Huddesone apprentice of Raymund Standelf –	2s.
William Parker apprentice of Henry Chicksands –	2s.
John Rasen apprentice of John Bulstrode –	2s.
John Southern apprentice of Thomas Findon –	2s.
Richard Sulgrave apprentice of Thomas Davy –	2s.
Thomas Messenger apprentice of Thomas Broun –	2s.
John Maldon apprentice of John Walsh –	2s.
Richard Marchal apprentice of John Somerville –	2s.
Richard Crafford apprentice of Thomas Polle –	2s.
James Moriel apprentice of John Hynde –	2s.
John Colyn apprentice of William Haper –	2s.
William Whetle apprentice of Thomas Panton –	2s.
John Franns apprentice of John Frenshe –	2s.
Nicholas Breton, John Martyn, apprentices of John Bottisham –	4s.
Bartholomew Billingham apprentice of Thomas Essex –	2s.

These are the names of serving-men in the same year:

Thomas Cresselowe –	2s.
Thomas Lamport –	2s.
William Baldeswelle –	2s.
William Hugate –	2s.
Richard Sage –	2s.

Memorandum that in the aforesaid year the wardens received from the previous wardens, i.e. William Tingewick, John Carbonelle and their fellow wardens, and from the renters – £26 15s. 10½d.
Item, they received 2 mazer cups, of the which one has been sold for 23s. 4d.

[116] It is not impossible that the weight meant was 75lb (three score and fifteen), but the position of the 'li.' leads one to think that the 'xv' was an amount of a lower denomination.
[117] *Recte*: 45s. 8½d.?

xxiii s. iiii d. Et le autr*e* est deliv*er*ez a Joh*a*n Coraunt *et* Henri Ba*m*me *et* lo*ur* compaignons.
It*em*, resceu de Thom*a*s Broune p*ur* entrer eins le liv*eré* – iii s. iiii d.
It*em*, de Robert Lynne p*ur* entr*er* – iii s. iiii d.
It*em*, resceu de draps d'or *et* de soy ap*ur*tinaunt a le frat*er*nité – v peces.
It*em*, resceu ii trompes d'argent.
It*em*, viii peces de draps de nap*eré* ap*ur*tinant a le sale.
[242](It*em*, resceu un toret dorr*é* de Joh*a*n Bodesh*a*m p*ur* iiii s. en plegg*e* p*ur* ii app*re*ntys.)
It*em*, resceu de[243]   Ponchon p*ur* sou*n* entr*é* – v m*a*rcs.

P*ur* ceo q*e* discord fuist p*ar*entr*e* Rob*er*t de Lynne *et* Joh*a*n Osborne, les ditz Joh*a*n *et* Rob*er*t ount paiez – xl d.
It*em*, p*ur* ceo q*e* Michel Hongry fuist trové en defaute en le faç*oun* de un seint*ur*e a un taylo*ur* paia – xx d.
It*em*, p*ur* ceo q*e* Joh*a*n Andrew fuist trové en defaute en le faç*oun* de un batelment paia – ii s.
It*em*, p*ur* ceo q*e* Joh*a*n Pope fuist trové en defaute en faç*oun* de meyne a un tabler paia – ii s.
It*em*, p*ur* ceo q*e* Jeames de Coloign*e* fuist trové en defaute en faç*oun* de barres paia – ii s.
It*em*, p*ur* ceo q*e* Ric*hard* Broke fuist defenduz p*ar* les gardeins q'il ne devoit vendr*e* certeinz perles q'il avoit achatez, les q*ue*ux furront chalangez, le q*ue*le Rich*ard* encount*re* le defens de les gardeinz vendust, p*ur* ceo paia – xx d.

p. 30 Ceux sount les despenses fait p*ar* mesme gardeins, c'est assavoir*e* de les x li. xvi s. ii d. ob. q*ue*ux Joh*a*n Cheyh*a*m ad resceu:[244]
En p*ri*mes, paié a Adam Ba*m*me en le eglise de Seint Matheu – ii s.
It*em*, a Thom*a*s Usk mesme jo*ur* – xx s.
It*em*, a Joh*a*n Walsh*e* – xx s.
It*em*, a Will*ia*m Lowthe – xx s.
It*em*, a Barth*olom*eu Castr*e* – ii s.
It*em*, a Joh*a*n Carbonel – vi s. viii d.
It*em*, a Thom*a*s Reynh*a*m – iii s. iiii d.
It*em*, a les mynst*ra*les p*ur* chivacher ové le vicecompt*e*[245] – vi s.
S*um*m*a* de despens*es* – iiii li. xviii s.

[242] This whole entry has been scored out, presumably at the time when the pledge was redeemed.
[243] A blank space has been left for the man's first name.
[244] See above, A + a, p. 60.
[245] Adam Bamme was Sheriff 1382–83. At this period, the sheriffs were elected on 21 September (St Matthew) at the Guildhall and the Mayor was elected on 13 October (the feast of the Translation of St Edward the King). Two weeks later, on 28 October (the feast of the Apostles St Simon and St Jude), the Mayor took his oath, and the next day rode in procession from the Guildhall along Cheapside and to Westminster, accompanied by the sheriffs and men from the city misteries along with minstrels. See below, A + a, p. 146. See also Valerie Hope, *My Lord Mayor: Eight Hundred Years of London's Mayoralty* (London, 1989); R.R. Sharpe, *Calendar of Letter-Books Preserved among the Archives of the Corporation of the City of London, A-H* (London, 1899–1907), *passim* for this period in Letter Book G.

And the other has been handed over to John Coraunt and Henry Bamme and their fellow wardens.
Item, received from Thomas Broun for his entry into the livery – 3s. 4d.
Item, from Robert Lynne for his entry – 3s. 4d.
Item, received: of cloths of gold and of silk belonging to the fraternity – 5 pieces.
Item, received: 2 silver trumpets.
Item, 8 pieces of table linen belonging to the hall .
(Item, received: a gilded torret[118] from John Bottisham, for a pledge for 4s. for 2 apprentices.)
Item, received from Ponchon for his entry – 5 marks.

Whereas there was a quarrel between Robert de Lynne and John Osborne, the said John and Robert paid – 40d.
Item, whereas Michael Hungry was found at fault in the making of a girdle for a tailor, he paid – 20d.
Item, whereas John Andrew was found at fault in the making of a battlement[119], he paid 2s.
Item, whereas John Pope was found at fault in the making of the pieces for a backgammon board, he paid 2s.
Item, whereas James de Cologne was found at fault in the making of bands, he paid 2s.
Item, whereas Richard Brook was forbidden by the wardens from selling certain pearls which he had bought, and which were in dispute, the which Richard sold in contravention of the wardens' prohibition, and for this he paid – 20d.

These are the expenditures made by the same wardens, i.e. out of the £10 16s. 2½d. which John Cheyham received: p. 30
Firstly, paid to Adam Bamme in St Matthew's church – 2s.
Item, to Thomas Usk on the same day – 20s.
Item, to John Walsh – 20s.
Item, to William Louth – 20s.
Item, to Bartholomew Castre – 2s.
Item, to John Carbonelle – 6s. 8d.
Item, to Thomas Raynham – 3s. 4d.
Item, to the minstrels for their riding with the sheriff – 6s.
Total expenses – £4 18s.

[118] 'A ring or the like, often moving on a swivel, whereby an object can be attached to a chain' (*OED*).
[119] An indented or crenelated rim or brim to a vessel e.g. a cup.

1384–85 Ceux sount les nouns dé Gardeyns de la feste de Seint Donston l'an vii[e]
A + a tank*e* a mesme feste l'an viiie:
p. 61[246] Henri Ba*m*me
Joh*a*n Coraunt
Joh*a*n Som*er*file
Thom*as* Fyndo*u*n

Fait a remembr*er* q*e* les gardeins avantditz ount deliverez au Joh*a*n Honte *et* Hervi Rookhawe, rent*ers* p*ar* mesme an, xlvii li. p*ur* le faç*oun* de les tenementz en Bredstrete.

En p*ri*mes, en costages fait p*ar* Henri Ba*m*me en vyn en mesme jo*ur* avantdit – xxii d.[247]
It*em*, paié a le clerk – vi s. viii d.
It*em*, paié en almoign*e* a Alic*e* Fraunceys – xx s.
It*em*, a Johan Payn – vii d.
Fait a remembr*er* q*e* est gr*a*unté a Rich*ard* Fraunceis le almoign*e*, c'est assavoir ii s. p*ar* le symaign*e*.

Les despenses fait p*ar* mesme gardeins l'an avant dite:
En p*ri*mes, p*ur* soner le gr*a*unt sonaile de Seint Poul – iii s. iiii d.
It*em*, en payn, formage, *et* servoise mesme temps – iii s. iiii d.
It*em*, en cir*e* novelement fait encountr*e* le jo*ur* de Seint Donston – xiii s. xi d.
It*em*, en disches p*ur* lé serges fait mesme an – iiii s. i d.
It*em*, p*ur* deliverance de Joh*a*n Salisbury hors de p*ri*so*u*n – xxvi s viii d. *et* ii d. p*ur* i acquitance.[248]
It*em*, paié p*ur* un dyner a Rob*er*t Boxforde p*ur* div*er*ses monument – v s. ii d.
It*em*, paié *et* despenduz a le recordo*ur* p*ur* appeller un monument – xvi d. ob.
It*em*, paié a les clerkes de Seint Vedast – v s.

Ceux sount les nouns de app*re*ntys resceux mesme aan:

Cristofre Tyddeslee app*re*nt*ys* de Joh*a*n Grenefeld –	ii s.
Nicholas Bemond app*re*nt*ys* Joh*a*n Flete –	ii s.
Nicholas Josep app*re*nt*ys* Joh*an* Covele –	ii s.
Thom*as* Glade app*re*nt*ys* Will*iam* Maryn*er* –	ii s.
Joh*a*n Corierthe *et* Joh*a*n Ferberde app*re*nt*ys* Joh*a*n Forst*er* –	iiii s.
Joh*a*n Mapelesden*e* app*re*nt*ys* de Steven*e* Mapelesden*e* –	ii s.
Joh*a*n Exetr*e* app*re*nt*ys* Henr*i* Markeby –	ii s.
Joh*a*n Sonnynge app*re*nt*ys* Joh*a*n Bro*u*n –	ii s.
Ric*hard* Ov*er*done app*re*nt*ys* Will*elm*i Forthe –	ii s.
Will*iam* Byntre et Henr*i* Mites app*re*nt*ys* Will*elm*i Pev*er*e –	iiii s.
Rob*ertus* Howe app*re*nt*ys* Rog*er* Ryot –	ii s.
Nicholas Bokel[249] app*re*nt*ys* Nich*ol*ai Merfeld –	ii s.

246 A new hand starts here.
247 This figure has been substituted for a scored 'xvi d.'
248 The last phrase is a very slightly later addition.
249 See the Name Index. This may be the same man who later appears as the apprentice of John Edmund.

These are the names of the wardens from the feast of St Dunstan in the year 7 [Richard II] until the same feast in the year 8 [Richard II] [19 May 1384 – 19 May 1385]: 1384–85 A + a p. 61
Henry Bamme
John Coraunt
John Somerville
Thomas Findon

Memorandum that the aforesaid wardens have handed over to John Honte and Harvey Rookhawe, the renters for the same year, £47 for the building of the tenements in Bread Street.

Firstly, for the expenses incurred by Henry Bamme on wine on the same aforesaid day – 22d.
Item, paid to the clerk – 6s. 8d.
Item, paid as alms to Alice Fraunceys – 20s.
Item, to John Payn – 7d.
Memorandum that Richard Fraunceys has been granted alms, i.e. at 2s. per week.

The expenditures made by the same wardens in the aforesaid year:
Firstly, for ringing the great bell of St Paul's – 3s. 4d.
Item, for bread, cheese and ale at that time – 3s. 4d.
Item, for wax newly made up for St Dunstan's Day – 13s. 11d.
Item, for dishes for the candles made the same year – 4s. 1d.
Item, for the release of John Salisbury from prison – 26s. 8d., and 2d. for an acquittance.
Item, paid for a dinner for Robert Boxforde, for various documents – 5s. 2d.
Item, paid and spent out to the Recorder for reading out a document[120] – 16½d.
Item, paid to the clerks of St Vedast – 5s.

These are the names of apprentices admitted the same year:

Christopher Tyldesley apprentice of John Greenfield –	2s.
Nicholas Bemond apprentice of John Flete –	2s.
Nicholas Josep apprentice of John Covele –	2s.
Thomas Glade apprentice of William Mariner –	2s.
John Corierthe and John Ferberde, apprentices of John Forster –	4s.
John Maplesdene apprentice of Stephen Maplesdene –	2s.
John Exeter apprentice of Henry Markeby –	2s.
John Sonnyng apprentice of John Broun –	2s.
Richard Overdone apprentice of William Forth –	2s.
William Byntre and Henry Mites, apprentices of William Pevere –	4s.
Robert Howe apprentice of Roger Ryot –	2s.
Nicholas Bokyl apprentice of Nicholas Mirfield –	2s.

[120] The sense of this is probably either that of calling for the granting of legal status, validity, to the document, or that of demanding that the provisions of the document be enacted. On the various meanings of 'appeler' see Godefroy I, 329; Hatzfeld and Darmesteter, *Dictionnaire général de la langue française*, vol. I (Paris, 1890), 116–17; and F. Lecoy's remarks in *Romania* 76 (1955), 537.

Joh*ann*es Sowtham app*r*ent*y*s Henr*i* Bamme –	ii s.
Joh*ann*es Bryg app*r*ent*y*s Will*elm*i Boder –	ii s.
Steph*anu*s Goodman app*r*ent*y*s Henri Ware –	ii s.
Joh*ann*es Bradle app*r*ent*y*s Joh*a*n Squyry –	ii s.
Rob*ertus* de la Pantrie app*r*ent*y*s Rob*er*t Wylly –	ii s.

Ceux sount les nouns de lowys mesme aan:

Joh*ann*es Laget –	ii s.
Laurenc*e* Flekenh*a*m –	ii s.
Joh*ann*es Standulf –	ii s.
Steph*anus* Goodma*n* –	ii s.
Ric*ardus* Gegge –	ii s.
Will*elmu*s Downe –	ii s.
Rich*ard* Bartone –	ii s.
Will*elmu*s Falle –	ii s.

p. 62 Item, mesme gardeins ount resceu de Will*ia*m Fyhewe en aidaunce a n*ost*re rente[250] – xx s.
It*em*, de Joh*a*n Blakeman en eaidaunce de mesme rente – vi s. viii d.
It*em*, de Joh*a*n Pieres p*ur* defaute fait a les gardeins *et* le mestier – vi s. viii d.
It*em*, de Joh*a*n Walsh*a*m p*ur* le executrie de la fe*m*me de Thom*a*s Skreveyn*er*[251] – vi s. viii d.
It*em*, p*ur* le entré de Rich*ard* Brok – iii s. iiii d.
It*em*, de Hanes Dobler en amendement de la rente – xi s.
It*em*, de un Reynkyn, duchma*n*, p*ur* un defaute – xx d.
It*em*, de Jacob van Coloigne p*ur* i defaute – ii s.
It*em*, de Henr*i,* duchman, p*ur* defaute – xvi d.
It*em*, de Joh*a*n Pieres p*ur* defaute – ii s.
It*em*, de Stevene Carler p*ur* defaute – ii s.
It*em*, de Wilkyn, duchman, p*ur* un defaute – ii s.

Fait a remembr*er* q*e* Joh*a*n Coraunt, Henri Bamme, Thomas Fyndo*un* *et* Joh*a*n Som*er*file ount deliverez a Dru Barentyn, Joh*a*n Bodesh*a*m, Steven*e* Mapelesden*e*, Hervy Rookhawe, gardeins p*ur* l'an suivant:
En p*ri*mes, vi draps[252] d'or *et* de soy ap*ur*tinant a le auter
It*em*, viii peces de drap de naprie
It*em*, ii trompes du pois[253]
Item, deliv*er*é a mesmes gardeins avantditz – lii s. vi d.
It*em*, deliv*er*é a mesmes – i maser g*ra*unt
It*em*, de Gilb*er*t Pr*in*ce – xl s.

[250] Presumably the tenement in Bread Street referred to above, p. 61.
[251] Is it possible that this was Thomas Vok, appointed clerk in 1382? A new hand has taken over above however, but the meaning of this entry is unclear and it might be he who has died (see opposite page).
[252] There were only five pieces listed for the previous year, and only five are listed for the following year.
[253] A figure should have been filled in here, but has not been.

John Southam apprentice of Henry Bamme –	2s.
John Brig apprentice of William Bodyer –	2s.
Stephen Goodman apprentice of Henry Ware –	2s.
John Bradle apprentice of John Squiry –	2s.
Robert de la Pantrie apprentice of Robert Wylly –	2s.

These are the names of serving-men in the same year:

John Laget –	2s.
Laurence Freckenham[121]–	2s.
John Standelf –	2s.
Stephen Goodman –	2s.
Richard Gegge –	2s.
William Downe –	2s.
Richard Barton –	2s.
William Falle –	2s.

Item, the same wardens have received from William Fitzhugh as a subsidy p. 62
for our tenement – 20s.
Item, from John Blakeman as a subsidy for the same tenement – 6s. 8d.
Item, from John Pieres for an offence committed against the wardens and mistery – 6s. 8d.
Item, from John Walsham for the obsequies[122] of Thomas Scrivener's wife – 6s. 8d.
Item, for the entry of Richard Brook – 3s. 4d.
Item, from Hans Dobler, for repairs to the tenement – 11s.
Item, from one Reynkyn, a 'Dutchman', for an offence – 20d.
Item, from Jacob van Cologne for an offence – 2s.
Item, from Henry, a 'Dutchman', for an offence – 16d.
Item, from John Piers for an offence – 2s.
Item, from Stephen Carler for an offence – 2s.
Item, from Wilkyn, a 'Dutchman', for an offence – 2s.

Memorandum that John Coraunt, Henry Bamme, Thomas Findon and John Somerville have handed over to Drew Barantyn, John Bottisham, Stephen Maplesdene, Harvey Rookhawe, the wardens for the following year:
Firstly, 6 cloths of gold and silk which belong to the altar
Item, 8 pieces of table linen
Item, 2 trumpets weighing
Item, handed over to the same aforesaid wardens – 52s. 6d.
Item, handed over to the same – 1 large mazer
Item, from Gilbert Prince – 40s.

[121] See Name Index. Unless there are two different men here, his apprenticeship must have lasted over twenty years.

[122] This translation is uncertain, but seems the most probable. The Latin word 'executoria' can mean 'obsequies', although the Anglo-Norman 'executrie' is also found elsewhere with the meaning of 'executorship [of a will]'. The phrase 'de la femme' can mean either 'of the wife' or 'from the wife', and it is thus possible that it was money given for the funeral rites (or executorship of the will) by the wife.

1386 Fait a remembr*er* q*e* Joh*a*n Sokes, app*re*ntys de Joh*a*n Hynde, luy ad surmys a les gardeyns avantditz le xv jo*ur* de Janvi*er* l'an du roy Rich*ard* ixe, q*e* si puist estr*e* p*ro*vé q*e* le dite Joh*a*n ad estez chivachant de jo*ur* en jo*ur* achatant le poys de li*vre* d'argent xxvii s. p*ar* faux[254] poys *et* nou*n*[255] loial, q*e* p*er*de tout q*e* il ad p*ar* execuciou*n* de xx li.

1385–86 Ceux sount les nouns dé Gardeyns de la feste de Seint Donston l'an viii^{e}
p. 63 tank*e* a mesme feste l'an ixe:
Joh*a*n Bodesh*a*m
Dru Barentyn
Steph*ene* Maplesden*e*
Hervie Rookhawe

Les despenses fait p*ar* mesmez gardeyns mesme l'an avant dit:
En p*ri*mes, p*ur* soner le g*ra*unt sonail*e* de Seint Poul – iii s. iiii d.
It*em*, en payn, furmage *et* servoise – iii s. viii d.
It*em*, en cir*e* novelment fait – xxiii s. ix d.
It*em*, en p*ur*sute v*er*s les duches *et* foreynes orfev*er*es, en gentz de loy, serjauntz *et* autr*e*s costag*es* – xl s.
(It*em*, pur un Chiseldene,[256] pur un plé mové encount*re* no*us,* paié a gentz de loy *et* conseil – xiii s. iiii d.
It*em*, a menstrales – xvi s. viii d.)[257]
It*em*, a lé seoures a Seint Jeame – xx s.

Ceux sount les nouns de app*re*ntys:

Thom*as* Presto*u*n app*re*nt*ys* de Joh*a*n Luto*u*n –	ii s.
Thom*as* Whitchirch*e* app*rentys* de Joh*a*n Andrew –	ii s.
Joh*anne*s Hale, Joh*anne*s Bischop, app*renticii* Will*elm*i Hap*er* –	iiii s.
Ric*ard*us atte Welle app*renticius* cu*m* Joh*anne* Peris –	ii s.
Joh*anne*s Foxcote app*renticius* cu*m* Will*elm*o Horsma*n* –	ii s.
Thom*as* Wedone app*renticius* cu*m* Will*elm*o Falle –	ii s.
Thom*as* Oxenforde app*renticius* cu*m* Simo*ne* Wynt*er* –	ii s.
Nich*o*las Angetyn app*renticius* cu*m* [258]Beteyne Senior*e* –	ii s.
Thom*as* Pipe app*renticius* cu*m* Joh*anne* Maserer –	ii s.
Will*elmu*s Keer app*renticius* Hugonis Wetherby –	ii s.
Ric*ardus* Blithe app*renticius* Will*elm*i Lucas –	ii s.
Joh*anne*s Halle app*renticius* Joh*annis* Frau*n*ceis – [259]	
Joh*anne*s Perechild app*renticius* cu*m* Joh*anne* Appelby –	ii s.
Edmu*n*de Langeyn app*renticius* cu*m* Joh*anne* Norema*n* –	ii s.

254 This word written above a scored 'bone'.
255 This word added suprascript.
256 This might perhaps be William de Chesulden, John of Gaunt's receiver. See the index to *John of Gaunt's Register, 1379–1383*, ed. E.C. Lodge and R. Somerville, Camden Society 3rd ser. 56, 57, 2 vols (London, 1937). There were however several men with the surname Chiseldene/Chesulden active in the City of London at this time: see the indexes to *CPR*, *CCR* etc.
257 The section placed here within brackets has been scored out, perhaps because the expenses had not been allowed by the auditors?
258 A gap precedes this name. See Name Index.
259 The sum has here been partially erased, partially scored out.

Memorandum that John Sokes, the apprentice of John Hynde, submitted himself[123] to the aforesaid wardens on 15 January 9 Richard II [1386], that if it could be proved that the said John had been riding around from day to day buying up silver by weight at 27s. the pound using false and illegal weights, then he should lose all that he has by order to pay up to the sum of £20. 1386

These are the names of the Wardens from the Feast of St Dunstan in the year 8 [Richard II] until the same feast in the year 9 [Richard II] [19 May 1385 – 19 May 1386]: 1385–86 p. 63

John Bottisham
Drew Barantyn
Stephen Maplesdene
Harvey Rookhawe

The expenditures made by the same wardens in the same aforesaid year:
Firstly, for ringing the great bell of St Paul's – 3s. 4d.
Item, for bread, cheese and ale – 3s. 8d.
Item, for wax newly made up – 23s. 9d.
Item, for the prosecution against 'Dutchmen' and foreign goldsmiths, to lawyers, serjeants-at-law and other expenses – 40s.
(Item, for Chiseldene, for a plea brought against us, paid to lawyers and counsel – 13s. 4d.
Item, to minstrels – 16s. 8d.)
Item, to the nuns of St James – 20s.

These are the names of apprentices:

Thomas Preston apprentice of John Luton –	2s.
Thomas Whitchurch apprentice of John Andrew –	2s.
John Hale, John Bishop, apprentices of William Haper –	4s.
Richard atte Welle apprentice with John Piers –	2s.
John Foxcote apprentice with William Horsman –	2s.
Thomas Weedon apprentice with William Falle –	2s.
Thomas Oxenford apprentice with Simon Wynter –	2s.
Nicholas Angetyn apprentice with Beteigne, the elder –	2s.
Thomas Pipe apprentice with John Mazerer –	2s.
William Keer apprentice of Hugh Wetherby –	2s.
Richard Blithe apprentice of William Lucas –	2s.
John Halle apprentice of John Fraunceys –	2s.
John Perechild apprentice with John Appleby –	2s.
Edmund Langeyn apprentice with John Norman –	2s.

[123] There is an ambiguity in the language here and in that both men are called John. It is possible that John Sokes is accusing John Hynde of doing this: 'surmettre' can mean 'to accuse' and is also used to mean 'to submit to'; the pronoun 'luy' is frequently in Anglo-Norman used reflexively where in continental French one finds 'se'.

Jacobus Chaumb*er*leyn app*renticius* cu*m* Steph*ano* Clerk – ii s.
Joh*annes* Bery apprentic*ius* cu*m* Remu*n*do Standev*e* – ii s.
Thom*as* Senycle app*rent*ic*ius* d*omi*ni Nichol*a*i Twyforde – ii s.
Thom*as* Clevemayde app*rent*ic*ius* Hervici Rookhawe – ii s.[260]
Summa: xxxvi s.

Ceux sount les nouns de lowys:
Thom*as* Wedon*e* – ii s.[261]
En p*ri*mes, Nel Salforde – ii s.
Thom*as* Langtou*n* – ii s.
Nich*ol*a*s* Baylolf – ii s.
Joh*annes* Dusse – ii s.
Will*elmu*s Frraunceis, junior – ii s.
Thom*as* Barker*e* – ii s.
Joh*anne*s Howesone – ii s.
Henric*us* Dertynghole – ii s.
Thom*as* Philpot[262]
Thom*as* Fraunceis – ii s.
S*um*m*a*: xviii s.[263]

Ceux sount les entr*é*s:
En p*ri*mes de Rouland, orfev*er*e – xl s.
It*em*, de Schillyng, orfev*er*e – xxvi s. viii d.
It*em*, de Joh*an*[264] White – xxvi s. vi d.
It*em*, de Joh*a*n Maserer – xx s.
It*em*, de Joh*a*n, goldbet*ere* – xiii s. iiii d.
It*em*, de Ric*hard* Beteynne *et* sou*n* fitz – xiii s. iiii d.
It*em*, de Joh*a*n Leycetr*e* – xx s.
It*em*, de Thom*as* Boner*e* – xl s.
It*em*, de Joh*a*n Rudh*a*m – vi s. viii d.

1386 Fait a remembr*er* q*e* Joh*a*n Bodesh*a*m, Dru Barentyn, Stephen*e* Mapelesden*e*
p. 64 *et* Hervy Rookhawe ount deliverés le xxiiiie jo*ur* de Maii l'an du Roy Rich*ard* ixe a Thom*as* Exton*e*, Thom*as* Davy, Joh*a*n Frenshe *et* Joh*a*n Honte, gardeins de orfev*er*ie p*ur* l'an ensuaunt, xx m*a*rs iii s. iiii d.

It*e*m, Dru Barentyn ad plegg*es* de Hanes Dowbler de C s. de paier a la feste Nat*ivité* Seint Joh*a*n Baptiste
It*em*, de reward de Rog*er* Elys – iiii s.
It*em*, ount resceu v draps d'or *et* de soy
It*em*, vii peces de naprie[265]

260 This name has been added later in a different ink.
261 Although in the same hand and ink, this line must have been added later, since the next starts 'En p*ri*mes'.
262 No sum is listed against this name.
263 This total sum must have been made before the addition of the top name in the list, and one may note that it takes account that no sum is entered against the name of one man.
264 Scored out here is the word 'ysmong*er*'.
265 8 pieces have been listed for the previous two years.

James Chamberlayn apprentice with Stephen Clerk –	2s.
John Bery apprentice with Raymund Standelf –	2s.
Thomas Senycle apprentice of Sir Nicholas Twyford –	2s.
Thomas Clevemayde apprentice of Harvey Rookhawe –	2s.
Total: 36s.	

These are the names of serving-men:

Thomas Weedon –	2s.
Firstly, Nel Salford –	2s.
Thomas Langton –	2s.
Nicholas Baylolf –	2s.
John Dusse –	2s.
William Fraunceys, the younger –	2s.
Thomas Barker –	2s.
John Howesone –	2s.
Henry Dertynghole –	2s.
Thomas Philpot –	
Thomas Fraunceys –	2s.
Total: 18s.[124]	

These are the entries:

Firstly, from Rouland, goldsmith –	40s.
Item, from Schillyng, goldsmith –	26s. 8d.
Item, from John White –	26s. 6d.[125]
Item, from John Mazerer –	20s.
Item, from John, goldbeater –	13s. 4d.
Item, from Richard Beteigne and his son –	13s. 4d.
Item, from John Leicester –	20s.
Item, from Thomas Bonere –	40s.
Item, from John Rudham –	6s. 8d.

Memorandum that John Bottisham, Drew Barantyn, Stephen Maplesdene 1386
and Harvey Rookhawe have on 24 May 1386 handed over to Thomas p. 64
Exton, Thomas Davy, John Frenshe and John Honte, wardens of the Goldsmiths' Mistery for the following year – 20 marks 3s. 4d.

Item, Drew Barantyn has sureties from Hans Dobler in the sum of 100s. to be paid on the feast of the Nativity of St John the Baptist [24 June].
Item, as a payment from Roger Elys – 4s.
Item, they have received 5 cloths of gold and of silk
Item, 7 pieces of table-linen

124 *Recte* 20s.?

125 On the scored out word 'ysmonger' (see n. 264 opposite), had he previously been an ironmonger? Or should one ignore this as an error since it is scored out?

It*em*, ii trompes
It*em*, i maser gr*a*unt

Ut mult*i* app*r*entic*ii* vender*entur* p*er* m*agist*ru*m* suu*m* sine consenc*ia* gardianor*um* sub pena C s.[266]
P*ur* ceo q*e* div*er*se gentz del mestier d'orfev*er*ie p*r*eignont app*r*entys *et* tost q'ils poy aprys en mesme mestier *et* sachent les privités d'icell*e* ils achatount lo*ur* t*er*mes de lo*ur* mestres *et* ils s'en alount a autres citees, burgh*es* *et* villes *et* la ils eov*er*ount nient covenableme*n*t ne loialment come dev*a*nt ces heures sovent ad estee p*r*ovez a gr*a*unt disclaundr*e* de les gentz du dite mestier. Sur quel ordeign*é* est p*ar* co*mun*e assent de to*us* hon*ur*ables gentz *et* co*mun*alté de mesme mestier q*e* nully disoremés vende le t*er*me de sou*n* app*r*entys a luy mesmez ne a autri d'autr*e* mestier, mes solement a un du mesme mestier q*e* soit frank ho*m*me de mesme cité; *et* s'il face, paiera al almoign*e* de Seint Donston la moyté del monoye q'il ad resceu del vende [de] sou*n* dite app*r*entys, saunz ascun countredir*e*, et ne fra null*e* acquitanc*e* a sou*n* dite app*r*entys tank*e* mesme app*r*entys ad estee dev*a*nt sez gardeins p*ur* illoq*e*s jurrer de tenir to*us* les ordeignanc*es* du dite mestier, sur peyne de paier au dite almoign*e* de Seint Donston – C s.

1386–87 Ceux sount les nouns dé gardeyns l'an du Roi Rich*ard* neofisme tank*e* l'an
p. 65[267] du mesme Roy x[e]:
Thom*as* Exton*e*
Thom*as* Davy
Joh*ann*es Frenshe
Joh*ann*es Honte

Lequel an avantdite ordeigné est p*ar* les ditz gardeins *et* toutz hon*ur*ables gentz du dite mestier q*e* nule du dit mestier ne eov*er*e en sa vestur*e* de le lyveré sur peyne de p*er*dre al almoign*e* de Seint Donston – iiii d.

It*em*, ils s*er*rount prest qaunt ils soient garniz p*ar* deputez ou p*ar* broco*ur* ové lo*ur* gardeins sur mesme peyne si ils ne eaiount resonable excusacio*un*.

It*em*, q*e* nule du dite mestier ne resceyve nule app*r*entys ne nule foreyne lowys saunz vieu *et* assent de les gardeins q*e* serrount p*ur* le an, sur peyne de p*er*dre au dite almoigne – xl s.

[266] This is a LH marginal note.
[267] A new hand starts here.

Item, 2 trumpets
Item, 1 large mazer

Whereas many apprentices have been being sold by their master without the consent of the wardens, under penalty of 100s.
Whereas various people of the goldsmiths' mistery take on apprentices and as soon as they have learnt a little of the same craft and know its privities [trade secrets],[126] they buy out their terms from their masters and go off to other cities, boroughs and towns, and there they do work that is not proper and not up to the legal standard, as has often before now been proved, to the great discredit of the people of the said mistery. Therefore it is ordained by common assent of all the honourable people and the commonalty of the same mistery that no one henceforth shall sell the terms of his apprentice either to the apprentice himself or to anyone else of another mistery, but only to one of the same mistery who is a freeman of the said city; and if anyone should do this, he shall pay to the alms funds of St Dunstan half of the money which he has received from the sale of his said apprentice, without any appeal against this, and he shall give no acquittance to his said apprentice until the same apprentice has been before the wardens to swear to keep to all the ordinances of the said mistery, on pain of paying to the said alms funds of St Dunstan – 100s.

These are the names of the Wardens in the year 9 Richard II until 10 Richard II [1386–87]: 1386–87 p. 65
Thomas Exton
Thomas Davy
John Frenshe
John Honte

In the which year it was ordained by the said wardens and all honourable people of the said mistery that no one of the said mistery shall work in his livery clothing, on pain of having to pay to the alms funds of St Dunstan – 4d.

Item, they shall, when summoned by deputies or by a broker, promptly be with their wardens, on pain of the same penalty, unless they have a reasonable excuse.

Item, that no one of the said mistery shall take in any apprentice or foreign[127] serving-man without the inspection and the assent of the wardens for that year, on pain of having to pay to the said alms funds – 40s.

[126] As for other crafts and trades, the 'privities' were special techniques learned which the mistery tried to keep as closely guarded secrets to avoid unauthorised work and workers. A long ordinance of 12 April 1484, recorded in the *Book of Ordinances*, ff. 67r–71r, lists these 'privities' of the Goldsmiths as including the valuing of precious stones and pearls by carat weight and 'moldyng, chalke daubyng, rechyng of golde, quykenyng, chargyng, gyldyng, colorysshyng, wexyng, withes ustum and letyng up . . . enamelyng, blak enelyng, enelyng, boylyng and burnysshyng with meltyng of lymell bothe of golde and sylvyr and how hyt shall be broute togedyr. And to make all maner sowdors of golde and sylver . . .'. See also Reddaway and Walker, p. 270, note 1.

[127] i.e. from outside the City of London.

It*em*, ordeigné fuist *et* est enrollez en le Gildehalle le temps q*e* Joh*a*n Warde fuist Meir*e* de Loundres *et* Will*ia*m Halden*e* recordo*ur*, sur Joh*a*n Boinon *et* Ric*hard* Bore, Michel Hakeney *et* autres q'ils ne deargentont tielx choses q*e* sount desceyvables, sur peyne de paier al chaumbr*e* le prim*er* foitz xl s. *et* al secounde temps C s. *et* al tierce x m*a*rs *et* al quarte temps forjur*er* la dite cité, le quel Joh*a*n Boinon fuist trové en defaute p*ur* quel paia al chaumbr*e* – xl s.

Despenses fait p*ar* mesmes gardeins:
En p*ri*mes, p*ur* soner le g*ra*unt sonaill*e* – iii s. iiii d.
It*em*, en payn, formage *et* s*er*voise – iii s. ii d.
It*em*, en cir*e* novelment fait – xxii s. ob.
It*em*, en div*er*ses costages p*ur* closer les alienes, a gentz de loy *et* serjau*n*tz – xi s. i d.

Fait a remembr*er* q*e* Giles Goos fuist trové en defaute de un harnois fait a Kat*er*ine Goldbet*er*e q*e* fuist de quiover*e* enargentez *et* certeinz p*ar*cell*es* d'argent, p*ur* quel fuist atteint faux *et* adjugé si fuist trové en mesme defaute autr*e* temps paiera al almoigne solonc jugement de les gardeins.

p. 66 Ceux sount app*re*ntys:

Ric*ard*us Wylde app*renticius* Henric*i* Grene –	ii s.
Joh*ann*es Fermerie app*renticius* Thome Exton*e* –	ii s.
Nich*ol*as Bokyl[268] app*renticius* Joh*ann*is Edmu*n*d –	ii s.
Joh*ann*es Hewet app*renticius* Will*elm*i Baldewyne –	ii s.
Ric*ard*us Kyllehog app*renticius* Thome Pantou*n* –	ii s.
Thom*as* Snoth app*renticius* Joh*ann*is Canou*n* –	ii s.
Thom*as* Danefor*e* app*renticius* Thome Lamport –	ii s.
Joh*ann*es Pat app*renticius* Will*elm*i Heyward –	ii s.
Thom*as* Wylkes app*renticius* Joh*ann*is Lagehatch*e* –	ii s.
Joh*ann*es Reel app*renticius* Ric*ard*i Sibile –	ii s.
Joh*ann*es Poykyn app*renticius* Joh*ann*is Schillyng –	ii s.
Will*elmu*s Sotby app*renticius* Rob*er*ti Hugfelde –	ii s.
Will*elmu*s Schirborne app*renticius* Remundi Standelf –	ii s.
Joh*ann*es Gilberd app*renticius* Rob*er*ti Brynle –	ii s.
Henric*us* Lamport app*renticius* cu*m* Joh*ann*e Welborn*e* –	ii s.
Will*elmu*s Kyng app*renticius* Joh*ann*is Rudh*a*m –	ii s.
Joh*ann*es Drynge app*renticius* Thome Cresselowe –	ii s.

Les nouns dé lowys:

Thom*as* Frаunceis –	ii s.
Thom*as* Bokyl –	ii s.

268 See the list of apprentices for the previous year and the Name Index.

Item, it was ordained and has been enrolled in the Guildhall at the time when John Warde was Mayor of London and William Haldene Recorder, against John Boinon and Richard Bore, Michael Hackney and others, that they shall not silver such objects as may be deceptive, on pain of paying to the Chamber[128] on the first occasion 40s., on the second 100s., on the third 10 marks, and on the fourth occasion they shall forswear the said City, and the said John Boinon was found at fault, for which he paid to the Chamber 40s.

Expenditures made by the same wardens:
Firstly, for ringing the great bell – 3s. 4d.
Item, for bread, cheese and ale – 3s. 2d.
Item, for wax newly made up – 22s. ½d.
Item, for various expenses in closing down the aliens[129], to lawyers and serjeants – 11s. 1d.

Memorandum that Giles Goos was found at fault regarding a set of mountings made for Katherine Goldbeater, which were of silvered copper[130] and some partly of silver, and for this he was convicted of deceit and it was judged that if he were once again to be found guilty of the same offence then he shall pay to the alms funds as sentenced by the wardens.[131]

These are the apprentices: p. 66

Richard Wylde apprentice of Henry Grene –	2s.
John Fermerie apprentice of Thomas Exton –	2s.
Nicholas Bokyl apprentice of John Edmund –	2s.
John Hewet apprentice of William Baldewyne –	2s.
Richard Kyllehog apprentice of Thomas Panton –	2s.
Thomas Snoth apprentice of John Canon –	2s.
Thomas Danefore apprentice of Thomas Lamport –	2s.
John Pat apprentice of William Heyward –	2s.
Thomas Wylkes apprentice of John Lagehache –	2s.
John Reel apprentice of Richard Sibile –	2s.
John Poykyn apprentice of John Schillyng –	2s.
William Sotby apprentice of Robert Hugfelde –	2s.
William Sherborne apprentice of Raymund Standelf –	2s.
John Gilbert apprentice of Robert Brynle –	2s.
Henry Lamport apprentice with John Welbourne –	2s.
William Kyng apprentice of John Rudham –	2s.
John Drynge apprentice of Thomas Cresselowe –	2s.

The names of serving-men:

Thomas Frauncey s –	2s.
Thomas Bokyl –	2s.

[128] *sc*. of the Guildhall.
[129] i.e. in getting their businesses closed down.
[130] On the techniques of silvering on copper alloy see the article by Susan La Niece, 'Silver Plating on Copper, Bronze and Brass', *The Antiquaries Journal* LXX (1990), 102–14; and D. Hook, S. La Niece and J. Cherry, 'A Fifteenth-Century Mercury Silvered Buckle from Hillington, Norfolk', *ibid.* LXVIII (1988), 301–05. (I am most grateful to John Cherry for these references.)
[131] See below, A + a, p. 68.

Thom*as* Waryn – ii s.
Joh*ann*es Huesone – ii s.[269]
Joh*ann*es Dontone – ii s.
Joh*ann*es Edmu*n*d – ii s.
Joh*ann*es Northryng – ii s.
Joh*ann*es Pachforde – ii s.
Will*elmu*s Kempe – ii s.
Joh*ann*es Fyfhede – ii s.
Rob*er*tus Godesfeld – ii s.
Joh*ann*es Scherston – ii s.

1387–88 p. 67 Ceux sount les nouns dé Gardeyns l'an du regne le Roy Ric*hard* x^e tank al feste de Seint Donston xj^e:
Joh*ann*es Forster
Will*ia*m Forthe
Rob*ertus* Wadefile
Will*elmu*s Burgelon

Despenses fait p*ar* mesme gardeyns:
En p*ri*mes, p*ur* soner lé g*ra*untz sonayles de Seint Poul – iii s. iiii d.
It*em*, en payn, formage *et* s*er*voise – v s. v d.
It*em*, en cire novell*e* fait – xxii s. v d.
It*em*, paié a menstrales p*ur* chivacher v*er*s le roy *et* v*er*s le meir*e* – iii li. xiii s. iiii d.
It*em*, p*ur* baneres a lo*ur* trompes – xxvi s. viii d. dou*n*t resceu de ceo q*e* fuist quilez de gros – xxvi s. vi d.
It*em*, p*ur* drap achaté a viii[270] menstrel*es* – xxviii s. iiii d.

It*em*, p*ur* ceo qe Aleyn[271] Palmer*e*, Simond atte Wode, Hanes Bugelyn[272], *et* Thom*as* Richardso*u*n,[273] pedder*e*, *et* i frer*e* carme furrount arestez p*ur* xxii esquilers lesq*ue*ux fure*n*t trovez en le mayn le avant dit Simo*n*d, *et* i cuppe q*e* fuist trové en le mayn Joh*a*n van Berwe, Duchman, q*e* furront de alkenamye *et* faux argent, *et* i staylet pece trové en le mayn du dit Simond *et* autres yngotys peces trovez ové le dite Aleyn Palmer*e,* p*ur* queux ils furrount emprisonez en temps Nichol*as* Exto*u*n, meir*e*, *et* les chosez avant nomez lessez en le chaumbr*e* del Gildehall*e,* as costages des ditz gardeyns – xxvi s. viii d.

It*em*, despenduz p*ur* ensercher les ordinanc*es* de coteleres a Henri Perot – xii d.
It*em*, en jonkes encountr*e* le feste de Seint Donston – v d. ob.
It*em*, paié a un cordewan*er* en n*ost*re rente a Newegate p*ur* un pece de faux argent achaté de dit frer*e* carme – iii s. iiii d.

269 This line has been scored out. To the right of it, and referring either to this name or the one above, is the word 'Juré'.
270 A same hand has later in different ink inserted 'viii', after scoring out 'viii ' and 'ix', with an omission mark mistakenly before the word 'a'. Other later such amendments are noted below.
271 Here and below, this name is written above a scored 'Joh*a*n'.
272 This name has been added later.
273 This surname has been added later.

Thomas Waryn – 2s.
John Huesone – 2s.
John Dontone – 2s.
John Edmund – 2s.
John Northryng – 2s.
John Patcheforde – 2s.
William Kempe – 2s.
John Fifehead – 2s.
Robert Godesfeld – 2s.
John Sherston – 2s.

These are the names of the Wardens from the year 10 Richard [II] until the feast of St Dunstan in 11 [Richard II] [1387 – 19 May 1388]: 1387–88 p. 67
John Forster
William Forth
Robert Wadevyle
William Burgyloun

Expenditures made by the same wardens:
Firstly, for ringing the great bells of St Paul's – 3s. 4d.
Item, for bread, cheese and ale – 5s. 5d.
Item, for wax newly made up – 22s. 5d.
Item, paid to minstrels for riding in procession with the king and the Mayor – £3 13s. 4d.
Item, for banners on their trumpets – 26s. 8d. of which received from the lump sum of the collection made – 26s. 6d..
Item, for cloth bought for 8 minstrels – 28s. 4d.

Item, whereas Alan Palmer, Simon atte Wood, Hans Bugelyn and Thomas Richardson, pedlar, and a Carmelite friar were arrested for 22 spoons which were found in the possession of the aforesaid Simon, and a cup which was found in the possession of John van Berwe, 'Dutchman', which were made of alchemy[132] and fake[133] silver, and a small piece of a bar found in the possession of the said Simon and other pieces of ingots found in the possession of Alan Palmer, for which they were imprisoned in the time of Nicholas Exton, Mayor, and the aforenamed objects were left in the Guildhall Chamber, to the costs of the said wardens – 26s. 8d.

Item, spent on an examination of the Cutlers' ordinances, to Henry Perot – 12d.
Item, for rushes at the time of St Dunstan's Feast – 5½d.
Item, paid to a cordwainer in our tenement in Newgate for a piece of fake silver bought from the said Carmelite Friar – 3s. 4d.

[132] The *OED* gives this as 'a metallic composition imitating gold', and John Cherry has suggested that it might have been used to designate a metal imitating either precious metal, and that the whole of this entry might concern objects of false, fake silver.

[133] Rather than 'fake', this might refer to sub-standard silver, but in conjunction with the 'alchemy' one wonders if this was e.g. highly polished pewter?

Item, paié a mynstrales encountre le feste de Seint Donston – xxvii s. iiii d.[274]
Item, paié a Johan Somervyle pur i box qe fuist doné al femme del maire – vi s. viii d.
Item, paié a un serjaunt pur closer les heous de aliens – xx d.
Item, paié a Whitelok pur pursuer pur l'esquier – viii d.

1388 Fait a remembrer qe le jour de Seint Donston l'an du regne le Roy Richard secounde xj^e graunté est a Richard Fraunceys par touz les bonez gent de orfeverie xviii d. par symaigne.[275]

1387–88 Les nouns de apprentys:
p. 68 Richard Spicer apprentys de Robert Lyme – ii s.
Thomas Aleyn apprentys Simond Chesterfelde – ii s.
Johan Gryffyn apprentys Thomas Langtoun – ii s. per vadum i pendant[276]
Johannes Lenyng apprentys Adam Merfeld – ii s.
Johan Broun apprentys de Johan Bulstrode – ii s.
Johan Payn apprentys William Downe – ii s.
Johan de Ther apprentys Richard Bartoun – ii s.
Walterus Cope apprentys Robert Wylly – ii s.
Johannes Herteshorn apprentys Johan Bury – ii s.
Willelmus Reygate apprentys William Lyncolne – ii s.
William Mortemer apprentys Johan Lutoun – ii s.
Johan Broun apprentys Johan Standelf – ii s.
William Cowpere apprentys William Fallee – ii s.
Gy Naylond apprentys Robert Beteigne – ii s.
Richard Howard apprentys Thomas Mounde – ii s.
William Stantoun apprentys Jeames Bontyng – ii s.
Johan Ellerworthe apprentys Johan White – ii s.
Richard Halmestede apprentys George Cressy – ii s.
William Emede apprentys Adam Bamme – ii s.

Les nouns de lowys:
Johannes Huberd – ii s.
Johannes Stamdoun – ii s.

Pur ceo qe Johan Piers fuist trové en defaute en façoun de esquilers paia – ii s.
Item, pur ceo [qe] Johan Fairher le puisné fuist trové en defaute en façoun d'un bokyl paia – ii s.
Item, pur ceo qe Giles Goos qe fuist ové Thomas Essex fuist trové en defaute en façoun d'un bokel, i pendaunt et xx barres paia – ii s.

[274] The three items below have all been added later.
[275] In 1384–85 he was granted 2s. per week alms payments. Is this a reduction, or, more probably, an increase to 3s. 6d. per week?
[276] See the further paragraph below about this.

Item, paid to minstrels at the time of St Dunstan's Feast – 27s. 4d.
Item, paid to John Somerville for a box which was given to the Mayor's wife – 6s. 8d.
Item, paid to a serjeant for closing down the aliens' workshops – 20d.
Item, paid to Whitelock for pursuing an action for the squire[134] – 8d.

Memorandum that on St Dunstan's day in the year 11 Richard II 1388
[19 May 1388] Richard Fraunceys was by all the goodmen of the Goldsmiths' granted 18d. per week.

The names of apprentices: 1387–88
Richard Spicer apprentice of Robert Lyme – 2s. p. 68
Thomas Aleyn apprentice of Simon Chesterfield – 2s.
John Gryffyn apprentice of Thomas Langton – 2s. – as a pledge – 1 pendant[135]
John Lemyng apprentice of Adam Mirfield – 2s.
John Broun apprentice of John Bulstrode – 2s.
John Payn apprentice of William Downe – 2s.
John de Ther apprentice of Richard Barton – 2s.
Walter Cope apprentice of Robert Wylly – 2s.
John Herteshorn apprentice of John Bury – 2s.
William Reigate apprentice of William Lincoln – 2s.
William Mortimer apprentice of John Luton – 2s.
John Broun apprentice of John Standelf – 2s.
William Cowper apprentice of William Falle – 2s.
Gy Nayland apprentice of Robert Beteigne – 2s.
Richard Howard apprentice of Thomas Mounde – 2s.
William Stanton apprentice of James Buntyng – 2s.
John Ellerworthe apprentice of John White – 2s.
Richard Holmstead apprentice of George Cressy – 2s.
William Emede apprentice of Adam Bamme – 2s.

The names of serving-men:
John Huberd – 2s.
John Stamdoun – 2s.

Whereas John Piers was found at fault in the making of spoons, he paid – 2s.
Item, whereas John Fairher the younger was found at fault in the making of a buckle, he paid – 2s.
Item, whereas Giles Goos, who was with Thomas Essex,[136] was found at fault in the making of a buckle, a pendant and 20 bars, he paid – 2s.

[134] It is unclear to what this entry refers. The 'squire' was probably a City officer of some kind. It is possible that the payment was not for a legal prosecution, but just for 'pursuer' in the literal sense of searching or seeking out, but a legal action seems more likely.
[135] i.e. the pendant of a girdle.
[136] The phrasing might imply that G. G. was still working with Th. Essex at the time of this offence (he was listed as his apprentice in 1378–79), but he was fined last year also for sub-standard work, and seems clearly to have set up work on his own, although there is no record of his issue from apprenticeship terms.

(It*em*, p*ur* defaute q*e* Thom*as* Langto*un* p*ri*st app*re*ntys *et* ne voil*e* paier p*ur* mesme, i pendant est p*ri*s p*ur* ii s.)[277]
It*em*, resceu p*ur* fraunchiser Rob*er*t Wadesle – x s.
It*em*, de Joh*a*n Pant*er* p*ur* un defaute en fesaunce d'esquilers – ii s.
It*em*, resceu de Hanes Dobler – C s.
It*em*, resceu de Simond Chesterfeld p*ur* luy fraunchiser – vi s. viii d.

1388 Fait a remembr*er* q*e* Joh*a*n Forster, Will*ia*m Forthe, Rob*er*t Wadefile, Will*ia*m Burgylo*un*, les gardeins de l'an avant dite, ount deliverez a Thom*as* Panto*un*, Thom*as* Polle, Remu*n*d Standelf *et* Andrew Stameldene*e* le xiie jo*ur* d'August – iiii li. xviii s.
It*em*, ils ount resceu de mesme Joh*a*n Forster, Will*ia*m Forthe, Rob*er*t Wadefile, Will*ia*m Burgylo*un* i cuppe d'argent *et* xvi esquilers *et* vii s. iiii d.
It*em*, de assaiez d'argent, pois i m*a*rc ix d. de pois de Troye – It*em*, en or debrosé – ii d. ob. de pois.
Puys, de encrees ount deliv*er*ez – iiii li. – les q*ue*ux furrount paiez a Thom*as* Panto*un* *et* Thom*as* Polle p*ur* le feste, *et* rewarde a Joh*a*n Forst*er* *et* ses compaigno*un*s xxvi s. viii d.
Dount repaiez a Th-[278]
Ency remeynt as gardeins en cler – xxiii s. vii d. en le forser.

1388–89 Ceux sount les nouns dé gardeins l'an du regne le Roi Rich*ard* xj^{e} tank al
p. 69 feste Seint Donston xiie:
Thom*as* Panto*un*
Thom*as* Polle
Remu*ndus* Standelf
Andreas Stameldene*e*

Despenses p*ar* mesme gardeins:
En p*ri*mes, p*ur* soner lez g*ra*untz sonail*es* de Seint Poul*es* – iii s. iiii d.
It*em*, en payn, furmage *et* s*er*voise – iiii s. x d.
It*em*, en cire novell*e* fait – vi s. ix d.
It*em*, paié a menstrales p*ur* chivacher ové le Meir*e* – iiii m*a*rc
It*em*, paié as gentz de loy – xl s.
It*em*, en costag*es* fait a un dyn*er* p*ur* mesme gentz de loy *et* as bones gentz del companye – xxvi s. x d.

Ceux sount les nouns de app*re*ntys:

Philipp*us* Bowyer*e* app*renticius* Joh*ann*is Style –	ii s.
Ric*ard*us Kendale app*renticius* Thome Exto*un* –	ii s.
Walt*er*us Langerherst app*renticius* Ric*ardi* Arnold –	ii s.
Ric*ard*us Knappyng app*renticius* Ric*ard*i Brook*e* –	ii s.

[277] This line has been scored out, perhaps at the time when the pledge was redeemed?
[278] This entry is unfinished and an attempt has been made to erase it.

Item, for the offence that Thomas Langton took an apprentice and does not wish to pay for him, a pendant has been taken for 2s.
Item, received for enfranchising Robert Waddesley – 10s.
Item, from John Panter for a fault in the making of spoons – 2s.
Item, received from Hans Dobler – 100s.
Item, received from Simon Chesterfield for his enfranchisement – 6s. 8d.

Memorandum that John Forster, William Forthe, Robert Wadevyle, William 1388
Burgyloun, the wardens of the aforesaid year, have handed over to Thomas Panton, Thomas Polle, Raymund Standelf and Andrew Stameldene on 12 August – £4 18s.
Item, they received from the same John Forster, William Forthe, Robert Wadevyle, William Burgyloun 1 silver cup and 16 spoons and 7s. 4d.
Item, from assays[137] of silver, weight 1 mark 9d. Troy weight – Item, for broken gold, 2½d. in weight.
Then, as increase they have handed over £4 – which was paid to Thomas Panton and Thomas Polle for the feast, and a payment to John Forster and his fellow-wardens of 26s. 8d.
Of which repaid to Th . . .
Thus there remains net to the wardens – 23s. 7d. in the chest.[138]

These are the names of the wardens in the year 11 Richard [II] until the feast 1388–89
of St Dunstan in the year 12 [Richard II] [1388 – 19 May 1389]: p. 69
Thomas Panton
Thomas Polle
Raymund Standelf
Andrew Stameldene

Expenditures of the same wardens:
Firstly, for ringing the great bells of St Paul's – 3s. 4d.
Item, for bread, cheese and ale – 4s. 10d.
Item, for new wax made up – 6s. 9d.
Item, paid to minstrels for riding with the Mayor – 4 marks.
Item, paid to the lawyers – 40s.
Item, for the costs of a dinner for the same lawyers and the goodmen of the company – 26s. 10d.

These are the names of apprentices:

Phillip Bowyer apprentice of John Style –	2s.
Richard Kendal apprentice of Thomas Exton –	2s.
Walter Langerherst apprentice of Richard Arnold –	2s.
Richard Knappyng apprentice of Richard Brook –	2s.

137 i.e. samples of silver scraped from articles in order to test its standard. These were at one time the perquisite of the wardens but were then by ordinance made the benefit of the company as a whole. See Book A (MS 1520), p. 137; the Book of Ordinances ff. 57r–58v; S. Hare, 'The History of the Goldsmiths' Company from their Records', *Proceedings of the Society of Silver Collectors* II (Spring 1982), 174–79; Reddaway and Walker, pp. 260–61; and Forbes, *Hallmark*, pp. 26, 34, 39.

138 The amounts listed above do not seem to arrive at this final figure.

Joh*anne*s Bernes, Henric*us* Snokeshulle, Joh*anne*s Brigge,
app*renticii* Thome Panto*u*n – vi s.
Joh*anne*s Warwell*e* app*renticius* Will*elm*i Lucas – ii s.
Thom*as* Dadcastr*e* app*renticius* Joh*ann*is Wadeslee – ii s.
Joh*anne*s Waldeg*r*ave app*renticius* Ric*ard*i Sibile – ii s.
Ric*ard*us Smyth app*renticius* Joh*ann*is Honte – ii s.
Will*elmu*s atte Wode app*renticius* Marg*er*ie Fithewe – ii s.
Andreas Leef *et* Dere app*renticius* Will*elm*i Fichet – ii s.
Joh*anne*s Moto*u*n app*renticius* Thome Chalers – ii s.
Rob*er*tus Pycot app*renticius* Pet*er* Hiltoft – ii s.
Will*elmu*s Chepstede app*renticius* Will*elm*i Burgylo*u*n – ii s.
Walt*er*us Brewes app*renticius* Thome Langto*u*n – ii s.
Rog*er*us Belho*m*me app*renticius* Joh*ann*is Tewkesbury – ii s.

Les nouns de lowys:
Henric*us* Richemond – ii s.
Edmu*ndus* Davy – ii s.
Joh*anne*s Blakeden*e* – ii s.
Walt*er*us Bochet – ii s.
Will*elmu*s Skele – ii s.
Thom*as* Lynk – ii s.

Fait a remembr*er* q*e* Rog*er* Swynarto*u*n dona al almoign*e* p*ur* so*u*n entré – xl s.
It*em*, de Will*ia*m Fithewe – xx s.

1389–90 Ceux sount les no*u*ns dé gardeyns l'an du regne le Roi Rich*ard* xiie tank al
p. 70 an xiiie:
Joh*anne*s Bodesh*a*m
Joh*anne*s Bulstrode
Joh*anne*s Corant le puisné
Will*ia*m Lucas

Rent*er*s p*ar* mesme an:
Ric*hard* Barto*u*n
Stephen*e* Clerk

Les nouns de app*r*entys:[279]
Joh*anne*s Coch*e* app*renticius* Rob*er*t Bromle
Rob*ertus* Halle app*renticius* Joh*annis* Standelf
Thom*as* South app*renticius* Thome Exto*u*n
Aubre*us* Bleseforde app*renticius* Joh*annis* Turpyn
Will*elmus* Hergh*a*m app*renticius* Ric*ard*i Brok
Joh*anne*s Cokeram app*renticius* Steph*an*i Mapelesden*e*
Rob*ertus* Valence app*renticius* Will*elm*i Maryn*er*
Thom*as* Lyncoln*e* app*renticius* Huch*e* Wetherby

[279] No sums of money are written against any names on this page, but one should probably assume this to be a scribal omission only.

John Barnes, Henry Snokeshulle, John Brigge, apprentices of Thomas Panton –	6s.
John Whirwelle apprentice of William Lucas –	2s.
Thomas Dadcastre apprentice of John Waddesley –	2s.
John Waldegrave apprentice of Richard Sibile –	2s.
Richard Smyth apprentice of John Honte –	2s.
William atte Wood apprentice of Margery FitzHugh –	2s.
Andrew Leef & Dere[139] apprentice of William Fichet –	2s.
John Motoun apprentice of Thomas Chalers –	2s.
Robert Pycot apprentice of Peter Hiltoft –	2s.
William Chipstede apprentice of William Burgyloun –	2s.
Walter Brewes apprentice of Thomas Langton –	2s.
Roger Belhomme apprentice of John Tewkesbury –	2s.

The names of serving-men:

Henry Richmond –	2s.
Edmund Davy –	2s.
John Blakedene –	2s.
Walter Bochet –	2s.
William Skele –	2s.
Thomas Lynk –	2s.

Memorandum that Roger Swynnerton gave for his entry to the alms funds – 40s.
Item, from William Fitzhugh – 20s.

These are the names of the wardens in the year 12 Richard [II] until the year 13 [Richard II] [1389–90]: 1389–90 p. 70
John Bottisham
John Bulstrode
John Coraunt the younger
William Lucas

Renters for the same year:
Richard Barton
Stephen Clerk

The names of apprentices:
John Coche apprentice of Robert Bromley
Robert Halle apprentice of John Standelf
Thomas South apprentice of Thomas Exton
Aubrey Bleasford apprentice of John Turpyn
William Hergham apprentice of Richard Brook
John Cokeram apprentice of Stephen Maplesdene
Robert Valence apprentice of William Mariner
Thomas Lincoln apprentice of Hugh Wetherby

139 This seems a very odd name, but it is how it appears. It has been suggested that one might interpret it as 'Andrew Leef, *alias* Dere'.

Will*elmus* Faunt app*renticius* Thome Gyenge
Rob*ertus* Northawe app*renticius* Thome Broune
Thom*as* Hout*ou*n app*renticius* Joh*ann*is Noreman
Joh*annes* Grene app*renticius* Will*elmi* Pever*e*
Will*elmus* Bro*u*n app*renticius* Rob*er*d Savage
Joh*annes* Gofair*e* app*renticius* Joh*annis* Chayh*a*m
Joh*annes* Reygat*e* app*renticius* Rob*er*ti de Lynne
Joh*annes* Frer*e* app*renticius* Joh*ann*is Welbo*u*rne
Joh*annes* Chestr*e*, Rob*er*t Thom*as* app*renticii* Rob*er*ti Bech*e*
Joh*annes* P*a*rker app*renticius* Joh*annis* Mounte
Walt*er* Westby app*renticius* Thom*e* Davy
Rob*er*t Neylond app*renticius* Rob*er*ti Beteygne
Joh*annes* Lanhari app*renticius* Will*elmi* Fithewe
Joh*annes* Fyge app*renticius* Salema*n* Oxeneye
Will*elmus* Parker app*renticius* Joh*a*n Hynde
Joh*annes* Crawlond app*renticius* Rob*er*ti Becheswort*he*
Will*elmus* Burt*ou*n app*renticius* Joh*ann*is Lut*ou*n
Henr*icus* Camayle, Joh*annes* Hertewell*e* app*renticii* Joh*ann*is Bodesh*a*m

Les nouns de lowys:
Ric*ardus* Sprotford*e*
Philipp*us* Oxenford
Joh*annes* Grene
Rob*ertus* Godesfeld
Ric*ardus* Marchall*e*

1390 [281]Fait a remembr*er* q*e* le p*ri*m*er* jo*ur* de Jull*et* l'an du r*egne* [le] Roy Ric*hard*
p. 71[280] secounde xiiii^e^, en p*r*esenc*e* Joh*an* Lincoln*e*, Stephen*e* de Thorp, Ric*hard* Brook, Will*ia*m Grantha*m*, gardeins d'orfeve*r*ie, Joh*a*n Forster, Thom*as* Ext*ou*n, Dru Barentyn, Thom*as* Davy, Will*ia*m Lowthe , Will*ia*m Baldeswell*e* porta un obligaci*ou*n d'un Thom*as* Throkkyng a la sale d'orpheve*r*ie *et* illoq*e*s la dite obligaci*ou*n sa p*ro*pres mayns debrosa.[282]

Rob*er*tus Hamelton app*rentys* Joh*an* Tewkysbury, jun*ior*[283]
Ric*hard* George pet*us*(?)[284]

J*o*h*ann*es Kyng lowys de Joh*ann*e Walsch*e* – ii s.
Henr*icus* van Andynak lowis cu*m* Al van Andynak – ii s.

[280] This sheet has been damaged and then repaired, part of the lower section has been torn away, and the whole has clearly been thought of as rough paper to make quick notes on.

[281] A LH marginal note gives the date here: a° 14 Rich. 2.

[282] The rest of this page has been used for scribbling rough notes, and this presumably indicates that the register was for some time left open with this page on the top; the names and other information are scribbled in various places, different inks show different times of writing and various hands, all very rough and untidy. The writing seems at times indecipherable. Some of the information contained can be dated from later entries in the books to 1414–15, some to 1418–19, some to 1428–29, some information here however cannot be checked against other information elsewhere. Notes indicate the different dates.

[283] This entry is found 1428–29.

[284] Richard George is listed in entries dating from 1391–2 until 1422–23.

William Faunt apprentice of Thomas Genge
Robert Northawe apprentice of Thomas Broun
Thomas Houtoun apprentice of John Norman
John Grene apprentice of William Pevere
William Broun apprentice of Robert Savage
John Gofair apprentice of John Cheyham
John Reigate apprentice of Robert de Lynne
John Frere apprentice of John Welbourne
John Chester, Robert Thomas apprentices of Robert Beech
John Parker apprentice of John Mount
Walter Westby apprentice of Thomas Davy
Robert Neyland apprentice of Robert Beteigne
John Lanhari apprentice of William Fitzhugh
John Fyge apprentice of Solomon Oxney
William Parker apprentice of John Hynde
John Crawlond apprentice of Robert Bechesworth
William Burton apprentice of John Luton
Henry Camayle, John Hertewelle apprentices of John Bottisham

The names of serving-men:
Richard Sprotford
Phillip Oxenford
John Grene
Robert Godesfeld
Richard Marchal

Memorandum that on 1 July 14 Richard II [1390], in the presence of John Lincoln, Stephen de Thorp, Richard Brook, William Grantham, wardens of the goldsmiths' mistery, and of John Forster, Thomas Exton, Drew Barantyn, Thomas Davy and William Louth, William Baldeswelle brought a bond obligatory from a certain Thomas Throkkyng to the Goldsmiths' Hall and there with his own hands he tore up the said obligation. 1390 p. 71

Robert Hamelton, apprentice of John Tewkesbury the younger
Richard George [?]

John Kyng, serving-man of John Walsh – 2s.
Henry van Andirnak, serving-man with Albrecht Van Andirnak – 2s.

Tom*as* Whitmor*e* lowys cu*m* Joh*ann*e Cresben – ii s.
– mynstr*al*
Joh*an* Beynton*e* lowys cu*m* Will*elm*o Belverge – ii s.[285]

Alex Ferrentyne
Din*er*eus de Villan*e*
Franciscus Sophet[286] } florentynis in CC li.

Nalldelwynus Tregaree app*rentys* Th*omas* Blithe,[287] h*an*c diem eff'
med(?) Andru in Anderages v

Hans van Andirnak*e* – vi s. viii d.
Hans Holthous – xl s.
Hans Ekhorn*e* – xx s.
Herma*n* Spryg – vi s. viii d.
Ph*ilipp*us Langveld – vi s. viii d.[288]

p. 72[289] quarto die Augusti deliv*eratur* Will*elm*o Granth*am*[290] xxix li. xv s. ii d.

1412 Fait a remembr*er* qe le xi jo*ur* de Julet l'an du Henr*i* q'or est xiii° Will*ia*m Randolf *et* cez compaigons doient al Cumpany toutz chosez abatez mesme le jo*ur* – vii li. ii s. v d.
Henr*i* Gutz – vi s. viii d.
T*homas* Exto*u*n
Ric*hard* Barto*u*n
Joh*an* Norman
Ric*hard* George
Jh*es*u Jh*es*u
Jh*es*u n*ost*ro redemp*tor*e
Math
Mathus van Holand
Amen dico vobis sup*er* a*n*ima bona sua
Henric*us* de Lym*erene*(?) oblig*atur* in v. li. sol*vendas* ad festu*m* Pasche.

1390–91 Ceux sount les nouns dé gardeins l'an du regn*e* le Roi Rich*ard* xiiie tank al
p. 73 an xiiii:
Steven de Thorp*e*
Joh*an* Lincoln*e*
Will*ia*m Granth*am*
Ric*hard* Brook } les q*ue*ux ount resceu xxxiii s. iiii d. close en le ferser.

[285] These four entries seem to date from 1418–19, where however William Belverge's serving-man appears as 'Bevyngton' not 'Beyntone'.
[286] These three men are not found listed anywhere else. They can probably however be dated to 1427–28, since they are in the same hand as the entry below.
[287] N. Tregaree is listed as T. Blithe's apprentice in 1427–28.
[288] These five Dutchmen would appear to be listed as paying licence fees. Three of these are listed in 1414–15 and also in other years, the other two are listed in other years. See the Name Index for all of these.
[289] This page has also been used for rough notes and the same problems of decipherment apply. Dating seems more straightforward for most of the entries. The reasons for the religious interjections remain obscure.
[290] William Grantham was the first-listed warden in 1403–04 and in 1409–10, and this entry might therefore refer to one of these years?

Thomas Whitmore, serving-man with John Cresbien – 2s.
– minstrel
John Beyntone, serving-man with William Belverge – 2s.

Alex Ferrentyne
Dinereus de Villane } Florentines, £200
Franciscus Sophet

Nalldelwynus Tregaree, apprentice of Thomas Blithe, this day ?
? Andrew in Anderages ?

Hans Van Andirnak – 6s. 8d.
Hans Holthous – 40s.
Hans Ekhorn – 20s.
Hermann Spryg – 6s. 8d.
Phillip Langveld – 6s. 8d.

On 4 August there was handed over to William Grantham – £29 15s. 2d. p. 72

Memorandum that on 11 July 13 Henry IV [1412], William Randolf and his companions owe to the Company, all subtractions having been made on the same day – £7 2s. 5d. 1412
Henry Gutz – 6s. 8d.
Thomas Exton
Richard Barton
John Norman
Richard George
Jesus Jesus
Jesus our Redeemer
Math
Mathus van Holland
Amen I say to you upon his good soul
Henry de Lymerene is bound in the sum of £5 to be paid at Easter.

These are the names of the wardens in the year 13 Richard [II] until the year 14 [Richard II] [1390–91]: 1390–91 p. 73
Stephen de Thorpe
John Lincoln
William Grantham } who have received 33s. 4d. locked in the chest.
Richard Brook

Fait a remembr*er* q*e* Estiephen de Thorp, Joh*an* Lincoln*e*, Will*iam* Grantham *et* Ric*hard* Brook o*u*nt resc*eu* de Thom*as* Panto*un*, Thom*as* Polle, Remu*nd* Standelf *et* Andreu Stameldene de encrés – xl s. v d.
It*em*, resceu deux trompes poisaunt – x m*a*rcs *et* d*em*i ounce.

Despenses dé mesme gardeyns p*ar* mesme an:
En p*ri*mes, p*ur* soner le g*ra*unt sonaill*e* – iii s. iiii d.
It*em*, en payn, formage *et* cervoise – v s. iii d.
It*em*, en cire:
En p*ri*mes, en novel cire xv li. *et* i q*uar*t – vii s. vii d. ob.
It*em*, p*ur* le fesure de viii li. *et* i q*ua*rt*er*e de veel cere – iiii d. ob.
It*em*, p*ur* ii tortys poisaunt xi li. *et* d*em*i – v s. ix d.

col. 1 Appr*en*tys:
Will*iam* Bette app*rentys* Remu*nd* Standelf – ii s.
Ric*hard* Rous app*rentys* J*ohan* Lincoln*e*[291] – ii s.
Will*elmus* Tetirlee app*rentys* Joh*an* Thornkyn – ii s.
Joh*ann*es Walyngforde app*renticius* cu*m* Rog*er*o Ryot – ii s.
Thom*as* Selby app*renticius* cu*m* Ric*ard*o Barto*un* – ii s.
Ric*hard* De la Mar*e* app*renticius* cu*m* Joh*ann*e Blakedo*un* – ii s.
Rog*er*us Pichaunt app*renticius* cu*m* Joh*ann*e Bulstrode – ii s.
Joh*an* Bywatre app*renticius* cu*m* Will*elm*o Burgylo*un* – ii s.
Joh*an* Glos app*renticius* cu*m* Will*elm*o Baldeswell*e* – ii s.
Will*elmu*s Godolf app*renticius* cu*m* Will*elm*o Fraunceys – ii s.
Joh*an* Gentilman app*renticius* cu*m* Joh*ann*e Luto*un* – ii s.
Andreas Dynby app*renticius* cu*m* Joh*ann*e Rudh*am* – ii s.
Joh*an* Brynkele app*renticius* cu*m* Joh*ann*e Hynde – ii s.
Rob*er*tus Brennalsto*un* app*renticius* cu*m* Rob*er*to Wylly – ii s.
Galfridus Hore, Thom*as* Seyntcler app*renticii* Joh*ann*is Som*er*vile – iiii s.
Will*elmu*s Northwode app*renticius* Will*elm*i Harpele – ii s.
Joh*an* Langwelle app*renticius* cu*m* Rolando van Bussh*e* – ii s.
Henr*i* Bo*ur*ne app*renticius* cu*m* Ric*ard*o Ponchard – ii s.
Thom*as* Wynto*un* app*renticius* Thome Davy – ii s.
Joh*annes* Stodbarn app*renticius* Joh*annis* Davy – ii s.
Joh*annes* Appelby app*renticius* Will*elm*i de Lowth*e* – ii s.
Simon app*renticius* Stephe*n*i Clerk – ii s.
col. 2 Henric*us* Mallynge app*renticius* Andree Stameldene – ii s.
Ric*ardus* Ingelby app*renticius* Thome Polle – ii s.
Thom*as* Thomer app*renticius* eiusde*m* Thome Polle – ii s.
Joh*annes* Neyland app*renticius* Rob*er*ti Beteigne – ii s.
Joh*annes* Surbyto*un* app*renticius* Ric*ard*i Kirkeby – ii s.
Joh*annes* Warde app*renticius* Will*elm*i Lincoln*e* – ii s.

Lowys:
Thom*as* Throkkyng jur*at et* sol*vit* – ii s.
Rich*ard* Marchal – ii s.
Reginald*us* Lang*ra*ve – ii s.

[291] This name has been written in after a complete erasure of another name.

Memorandum that Stephen de Thorp, John Lincoln, William Grantham and Richard Brook have received from Thomas Panton, Thomas Polle, Raymund Standelf and Andrew Stameldene, as increase – 40s. 5d.
Item, received 2 trumpets weighing 10 marks and ½ ounce.

Expenses of the same wardens in the same year:
Firstly, for ringing the great bell – 3s. 4d.
Item, for bread, cheese and ale – 5s. 3d.
Item, for wax:
Firstly for new wax 15¼ lbs. – 7s. 7½d.
Item, for the making up of 8¼ lbs. of old wax – 4½d.
Item, for 2 torches weighing 11½ lbs. – 5s. 9d.

Apprentices:		col. 1
William Bette apprentice of Raymund Standelf –	2s.	
Richard Rous apprentice of John Lincoln –	2s.	
William Tetirlee apprentice of John Thornkyn –	2s.	
John Wallingford apprentice with Roger Ryot –	2s.	
Thomas Selby apprentice with Richard Barton –	2s.	
Richard de la Mare apprentice with John Blakedene –	2s.	
Roger Pichaunt apprentice with John Bulstrode –	2s.	
John by the Water apprentice with William Burgyloun –	2s.	
John Glos apprentice with William Baldeswelle –	2s.	
William Godolf apprentice with William Fraunceys –	2s.	
John Gentilman apprentice with John Luton –	2s.	
Andrew Dynby apprentice with John Rudham –	2s.	
John Brinkley apprentice with John Hynde –	2s.	
Robert Brennalstoun apprentice with Robert Wylly –	2s.	
Geoffrey Hore, Thomas Seyntcler, apprentices of John Somerville –	4s.	
William Northwood apprentice of William Harpele –	2s.	
John Langwelle apprentice with Roland van Busshe –	2s.	
Henry Bourne apprentice with Richard Punchard –	2s.	
Thomas Wyntoun apprentice of Thomas Davy –	2s.	
John Stodbarn apprentice of John Davy –	2s.	
John Appleby apprentice of William de Louth –	2s.	
Simon apprentice of Stephen Clerk –	2s.	
Henry Mallyng apprentice of Andrew Stameldene –	2s.	col. 2
Richard Ingleby apprentice of Thomas Polle –	2s.	
Thomas Thomer apprentice of the same Thomas Polle –	2s.	
John Nayland apprentice of Robert Beteigne –	2s.	
John Surbiton apprentice of Richard Kirkby –	2s.	
John Warde apprentice of William Lincoln –	2s.	

Serving-men:	
Thomas Throkkyng swore and paid –	2s.
Richard Marchal –	2s.
Reginald Langrave –	2s.

Ric*ard*us[292]
Will*elmu*s Egh*a*m – ii s.
Henric*us* Hoccedys[293] – ii s.
Walt*er*us Sprynget – ii s.
Barth*olome*us Byllyngto*un* – ii s.
Joh*anne*s Norynge – ii s.
Will*elmu*s Holteby – ii s.
Joh*anne*s Burto*un* – ii s.
Thom*as* Popelto*un* – ii s.

1391–92 Ceux sount les nouns des Gardeyns eslutz le jo*ur* de Seint Donston l'an du
p. 74 regne le Roi Rich*ard* secounde xiiii^e^ tank al xv^e^:
Thom*as* Davy
Joh*a*n Honte
Thom*as* Lamport
Will*elmu*s Haper

Fait a remembr*er* q*e* Estevene de Thorp, Joh*a*n Lyncoln*e*, Rich*ard* Brook *et* Will*ia*m Granth*a*m ount deliv*er*ez de novel fait tru*m*pes, clarions *et* pipes, c'est assavoir a Thom*as* Davy, Joh*a*n Honte, Thom*as* Lamport *et* Will*ia*m Hap*er*, gardeyns, les tru*m*pes poisant x m*a*rcs viii[294] ounc*es et* d*em*i de pois de Troye.
It*em*, les clarions poisaunt vii m*a*rcz x d. du pois de Troye.
It*em*, schalmuse petit pois*aunt* xi ounc*es et* viii d. du pois de Troye.
It*em*, un bombard poisant iiii m*a*rcs d*em*i[295] i ounc*e et* v d. de mesme pois, ové le porto*ur*.
It*em*, un g*ra*unt schalmuse poisaunt ii li. ix s. ii d. de pois de Troye ové le porto*ur*.
It*em*, un cornmuse – i m*a*rc *et* xi d. de mesme pois.
It*em*, p*ur* les iiii pipes, paié al menstrall*e* – xxv s. iiii d.
Summa del pois – xxviii m*a*rcs i ounce *et* xiiii d.

It*em*, deliv*er*é mesme jo*ur* le composiciou*n* de Joh*a*n Hiltoft a Thom*as* Davy, Joh*an* Honte, Will*ia*m Hap*er et* Thom*as* Lamport p*ar* mesmes Joh*a*n Lincoln*e*, Steven*e* Thorp, Will*ia*m Granth*a*m *et* Ric*hard* Brook.[296]

Et g*ra*unté fuist a Joh*a*n Lalh*a*m xviii d. p*ar* symaign*e* tank a temps q*e* sou*n* dette soit paiez *et* sou*n* rente en sa mayn.

Les nouns d'ap*r*entys:[297]
Joh*anne*s Watevile app*renticius* Joh*a*n Cheyh*a*m
Joh*annes* Suttou*n* app*renticius* Thome Davy
Thom*as* Aylesbury app*renticius* Rog*er*i Ryot

292 This name has been left but would appear to be in error.
293 This man's name has been put in the list again four lines below and has then been scored out.
294 This figure for the ounces has been written above a scored figure of 'ii'.
295 This word added superscript at this point.
296 See A + a, p. 56 above.
297 None of the following names on this page have any figure paid marked against them, but this is probably a scribal oversight.

Richard

William Egham –	2s.
Henry Hoccedys –	2s.
Walter Sprynget –	2s.
Bartholomew Billington –	2s.
John Norynge –	2s.
William Holteby –	2s.
John Burton –	2s.
Thomas Poppleton –	2s.

These are the names of the Wardens elected on St Dunstan's Day in the year 1391–92
14 Richard II until the year 15 [Richard II] [19 May 1391 – 1392]: p. 74
Thomas Davy
John Honte
Thomas Lamport
William Haper

Memorandum that Stephen de Thorp, John Lincoln, Richard Brook and William Grantham have handed over newly made trumpets, clarions and pipes [wind instruments], i.e. to Thomas Davy, John Honte, Thomas Lamport and William Haper, wardens, the trumpets weighing 10 marks 8½ ozs. Troy weight.
Item, the clarions weighing 7 marks 10d. Troy weight.
Item, a small shawm weighing 11 oz. 8d. Troy weight.
Item, a bombard weighing 4½ marks 1 oz. 5d. of the same weight, with a carrier[140].
Item, a large shawm weighing £2 9s. 2d. Troy weight, with a carrier.
Item, a horn-pipe – 1 mark 11d. of the same weight.
Item, for the 4 pipes, paid to the minstrel – 25s. 4d.
Total weight – 28 marks 1 oz. 14d.

Item, on the same day the composition[141] of John Hiltoft was handed over to Thomas Davy, John Honte, William Haper and Thomas Lamport by the same John Lincoln, Stephen Thorp, William Grantham and Richard Brook.

And 18d. per week was granted to John Lalham until the time that the debt owing to him may be repaid and he may have his rent-money in his hands.

The names of apprentices:
John Watevile apprentice of John Cheyham
John Sutton apprentice of Thomas Davy
Thomas Aylesbury apprentice of Roger Ryot

140 This might be either a strap or a carrying case, the former perhaps being more probable.

141 It is unclear whether they are handing over the document itself or the monies due according to its provisions (see above, A + a, p. 56), but the former is perhaps more probable since no sum is given.

Thom*as* Rougeye app*renticius* Th*omas* Extou*n*
Will*elmus* Sawyer app*renticius* Th*omas* Thomkyn
Joh*annes* Dusse, Adam Westou*n* app*renticii* Joh*ann*is Lutou*n*
Will*elmus* Hertewelle app*renticius* Will*elmi* Downe
Ric*ardus* Meryot app*renticius* Joh*ann*is Lagehach*e*
Rog*erus* Veel app*renticius* Thome Lamport
Thom*as* Pope app*renticius* Rob*er*ti Beteygne
Will*elmus* Bysmer*e* app*renticius* Joh*ann*is Perys
Rob*ertus* Spenser app*renticius* Joh*ann*is Honte
Thom*as* Lye app*renticius* Salamonis Oxeneye
Joh*ann*es Rog*er* app*renticius* Thome Polle.

Lowys:
Joh*ann*es Flete quond*am* app*renticius* Will*elm*i atte Forth*e*
Joh*ann*es Honte quond*am* app*renticius* Joh*ann*is Coraunt
Ric*ardus* George quond*am* app*renticius* Joh*annis* Som*er*vile

1393–94 Ceux sount les nouns des gardeins eslutz *et* jurrez le jo*ur* de Seint Donston
p. 75 l'an du regne le Roy Rich*ard* secounde xvj^{e} tanq*ue* a mesme feste l'an xviie:
Thom*as* Pantou*n*
Thom*as* Extou*n*
Rog*erus* Ryot
Will*elmu*s Maryner

Fait a remembr*er* q*e* pur ceo q*e* Will*ia*m Lucas, orfev*er*e, revyla dispitousement un de sez gardeins av*a*ntditz *et* luy mentust, sur quel enapr*é*s dev*a*nt to*us* les hon*ur*ables gentz du dite mestier d'orfev*er*ie cria m*er*cy *et* se mist en g*ra*ce des ditz gardeins et se offry d'estr*e* a lo*ur* ordinance p*ur* mesme trespace, les q*ue*ux gardeins ové autres hon*ur*ables gentz du dite mestier ount ordeignez q*e* mesme Will*ia*m lessereit sou*n* vestur*e* de Seint Dunston *et* paieret al almoign xx li. sur g*ra*ce, *et* les q*ue*ux gardeins enapr*é*s ount pris le dite Will*ia*m a lo*ur* g*ra*ce *et* luy ount g*ra*unté le vestur*e* *et* q'il paiereit al almoign*e* de Seint Donston chescun symaign*e* a un de les pov*er*ez de mesme almoign*e* xviii d. durant un an entier, c'est assavoir del feste del Nativité de N*ost*re Dame l'an du regne le roy Rich*ard* secounde puys le conqueste xviie tank a mesme feste adonq*es* p*ro*schein ensuant. Et auxi si le dite Will*ia*m d'iceo en av*a*nt soit trovez rebell*e* ou disp*er*sone ascun des gardeins av*a*ntditz ou ascun autr*e* gardein q*e* serra p*ur* le temps, q*e* paiera au dite almoign*e* de Seint Donston xx li. *et* a iceo ad trové plegg*es*, c'est assavoir Joh*a*n Bodesh*a*m *et* Joh*a*n Welbourne.

Auxi p*ur* ceo q*e* Will*ia*m Pev*er*e revyla ses gardeins av*a*ntditz *et* eux fauxa *et* auxi disclaundra les gentz del mestier d'orfev*er*ie, se mist en g*ra*ce de sez gardeins *et* to*us* les hon*ur*ables gentz du dite mestier *et* eux cria m*er*cy *et* se offry d'estr*e* a lo*ur* ordinance p*ur* mesme trespace, les queux gardeins ové autres hon*ur*ables gentz du dite mestier ount ordeignez q*e* mesme Will*ia*m lessereit sa vestur*e* de Seint Dunston *et* paiereit al almoign*e* xx li. sur g*ra*ce,

Thomas Rougeye apprentice of Thomas Exton
William Sawyer apprentice of Thomas Thomkyn
John Dusse, Adam Weston, apprentices of John Luton
William Hertwelle apprentice of William Downe
Richard Mariot apprentice of John Lagehache
Roger Veel apprentice of Thomas Lamport
Thomas Pope apprentice of Robert Beteigne
William Bismere apprentice of John Piers
Robert Spenser apprentice of John Honte
Thomas Lye apprentice Solomon Oxney
John Roger apprentice of Thomas Polle

Serving-men:
John Flete formerly apprentice of William atte Forthe
John Honte formerly apprentice of John Coraunt
Richard George formerly apprentice of John Somerville

These are the names of the wardens elected and sworn on St Dunstan's Day in the year 16 Richard II until the same feast in the year 17 [Richard II] [19 May 1393 – 19 May 1394]: 1393–94 p. 75
Thomas Panton
Thomas Exton
Roger Ryot
William Mariner

Memorandum that whereas William Lucas, goldsmith, contemptuously insulted one of his aforesaid wardens and lied to him, for this afterwards before all the honourable people of the said goldsmiths' mistery he begged pardon and submitted himself to the judgment of the said wardens and offered to do whatever they might command for this same offence, the which wardens with other honourable men of the said mistery ordered that the same William should be deprived of his livery clothing of St Dunstan and should pay to the alms funds £20, and afterwards these wardens decided to make the judgment that they granted him the livery clothing and that he should pay to the alms funds of St Dunstan 18d. each week for a whole year for one of the poor men of the same alms, i.e. from the Feast of the Nativity of Our Lady in the year 17 Richard II until the same subsequent feastday. [8 September 1393–8 September 1394]. And also that if the said William should from henceforth be found guilty of rebelling against or slandering any of the aforesaid wardens or any other current warden, that he shall pay to the said alms funds of St Dunstan £20, and for this he found sureties i.e. John Bottisham and John Welbourne.

Also, whereas William Pevere insulted his aforesaid wardens and was false to them and he also slandered the people of the goldsmiths' mistery, he submitted himself to the judgment of his wardens and of all the honourable men of the said mistery and begged pardon of them and offered to do whatever they might command for the same offence, the which wardens with other honourable men of the said mistery ordained that the same William should be deprived of his

les queux gardeins de lo*ur* gr*a*ce ount gr*a*untez au dite Will*ia*m sa vestur*e* *et* q'il paiereit al almoign*e* de Seint Dunston chescun symaign*e* a un de les pov*er*es de mesme almoign*e* xviii d. durant un an entier c'est assavoir del feste de Seint Donston l'an du regne le Roy Rich*ard* secounde puys le conqueste xviie tank a mesme feste adonq*es* p*ro*schein ensuant. Et auxi si le dite Will*ia*m d'iceo enav*a*nt soit trovez rebell*e* ou disp*er*sone ascun des gardeins av*a*ntditz ou ascun autr*e* gardein q*e* serra p*ur* le temps, q*e* paiera al dite almoign*e* de Seint Donston xx li. *et* a iceo ad trové plegg*es*, c'est assavoir Joh*a*n Bulstrode *et* Rob*er*t Wadevyle.

1394 Fait a remembr*er* q*e* Will*ia*m Hastorp*e*, orfev*er*e, est resceux *et* jurrez devant les gardeins av*a*ntditz le xv jo*ur* de Maii l'an du Roy av*a*ntdite.

1393–94 Ceux sount les despens*es* fait p*ar* mesmes gardeyns av*a*ntditz:
p. 76[298] En p*ri*mes, p*ur* soner le gr*a*unt sonayles de Seint Poul*es* – iii s. iiii d.
It*em*, en payn *et* formage – xii d.
It*em*, en cervoise – iii s. ix d.
It*em*, en cir*e* fait encountr*e* le jo*ur* de Seint Donston – vii s. vi d. ob.
It*em*, paié p*ur* cir*e* q*e* Joh*a*n Bodesh*a*m *et* Joh*a*n Bulstrode *et* lo*urs* compaignou*ns* ount ordeignez – xi s. vi d.

col. 1 Ceux sount les nouns de app*re*ntys:
Joh*an*nes Halle[299] app*renticius* Joh*ann*[is][300] Welforde sol*vit* – ii s.
Thom*as* Fenler*e* app*renticius* Thome Pantou*n* sol*vit* – ii s.
Will*elmu*s Belverge app*renticius* Joh*ann*is Bulstrode sol*vit* – ii s.
Will*elmu*s Brakenh*a*m app*renticius* Jacobi Bontyng sol*vit* – ii s.
Thom*as* Westle app*renticius* Joh*ann*is Coraunt sol*vit* – ii s.
Thom*as* Maheu app*renticius* Ade Merfeld sol*vit* – ii s.
Joh*ann*es Seynclowe app*renticius* Joh*ann*is Knyvesworth*e* sol*vit* – ii s.
Ric*ardus* Bagenor*e* app*renticius* Rob*er*ti Hugfeld sol*vit* – ii s.
Will*elmu*s Parys app*renticius* Ric*ard*i George sol*vit* – ii s.
Ric*ard*us Oxenford app*renticius* Will*elm*i Baldewyne sol*vit* – ii s.
Rog*erus* Cabourne app*renticius* Rob*er*ti Brynle sol*vit* – ii s.
Joh*ann*es Cole app*renticius* Thome Wiltou*n* sol*vit* – ii s.
Will*elmu*s Heed app*renticius* Will*elm*i Kirkeby sol*vit* – ii s.
Joh*ann*es Hattele app*renticius* Joh*ann*is Tewkesbury sol*vit* – ii s.
Rob*er*t Lyncoln*e* app*renticius* Ric*ard*i Brook sol*vit* – ii s.
Joh*ann*es Cook app*renticius* Joh*ann*is Panter sol*vit* – ii s.
Joh*ann*es Alkam app*renticius* Salamonis Oxeneye sol*vit* – ii s.

Ceux sount les nouns de lowys:[301]
Joh*ann*es Gale quond*am* app*renticius* Joh*ann*is Osterlee sol*vit* – ii s.
Thom*as* Oxenford quond*am* app*renticius* Simo*n*is Wynt*er* sol*vit* – ii s.

[298] A new hand starts here.
[299] This name is followed by 'app' p*ro*', the former word only scored out.
[300] MS: Johanne.
[301] The first five of the following names have the LH marginal note against them: 'jur' = 'juré' or 'juratus'.

livery clothing of St Dunstan and should pay to the alms funds £20, the which wardens then decided to grant to the said William his livery clothing and that he should pay to the alms funds of St Dunstan 18d. each week for a whole year to one of the poor men of the same alms, i.e. from the feastday of St Dunstan in the year 17 Richard II until the same subsequent feastday [19 May 1394 – 19 May 1395]. And also that if the said William should from henceforth be found guilty of rebelling against or slandering any of the aforesaid wardens or any other current warden, that he shall pay to the said alms funds of St Dunstan £20, and for this he found sureties, i.e. John Bulstrode and Robert Wadevyle.

Memorandum that William Hastorpe, goldsmith, has been admitted and sworn before the aforesaid wardens on 15 May of the aforesaid year. 1394

These are the expenditures made by the same aforesaid wardens: 1393–94
Firstly, for ringing the great bell of St Paul's – 3s. 4d. p. 76
Item, for bread and cheese – 12d.
Item, for ale – 3s. 9d.
Item, for wax made up for St Dunstan's Day – 7s. 6½d.
Item, paid for wax ordered by John Bottisham and John Bulstrode and their fellow-wardens – 11s. 6d.

These are the names of apprentices: col. 1

John Halle apprentice of John Welford, paid –	2s.
Thomas Fenlere apprentice of Thomas Panton paid –	2s.
William Belverge apprentice of John Bulstrode paid –	2s.
William Brackenham apprentice of James Buntyng paid –	2s.
Thomas Westley apprentice of John Coraunt paid –	2s.
Thomas Maheu apprentice of Adam Mirfield paid –	2s.
John Seynclowe apprentice of John Knyvesworthe paid –	2s.
Richard Bagnore apprentice of Robert Hugfeld paid –	2s.
William Paris apprentice of Richard George paid –	2s.
Richard Oxenford apprentice of William Baldewyne paid –	2s.
Roger Cabourne apprentice of Robert Brinle paid –	2s.
John Cole apprentice of Thomas Wilton paid –	2s.
William Heed apprentice of William Kirkby paid –	2s.
John Hattele apprentice of John Tewkesbury paid –	2s.
Robert Lincoln apprentice of Richard Brook paid –	2s.
John Cook apprentice of John Panter paid –	2s.
John Alkam apprentice of Solomon Oxney paid –	2s.

These are the names of serving-men:

John Gale formerly apprentice of John Osterlee paid –	2s.
Thomas Oxenford formerly apprentice of Simon Wynter paid –	2s.

Will*elmus* Gartou*n* quond*am* app*renticius* Thome Polle sol*vit* – ii s.
Ric*ardus* Flecchere quond*am* app*renticius* Thome Hay sol*vit* – ii s.
Joh*annes* Halyday quond*am* app*renticius* Will*elm*i Lucas sol*vit* – ii s.
Joh*annes* Hilles quond*am* app*renticius* Rob*er*ti Brynle sol*vit* – ii s.

col. 2 Fait a remembr*er* q*e* Joh*a*n P*ur*chas dona p*ur* estre enfraunchisez – xx s.
It*em*, Barth*olom*eu Seman p*ur* le lyv*er*é entrer d'orfev*er*ie paia – xiii s. iiii d.
It*em*, de Wynant van Wermes p*ur* entrer en le lyv*er*é paia – vi s. viii d.
It*em*, Thom*a*s Langetou*n* p*ur* ceo q'il vendust un lowys *et* un app*re*ntys paia – xl s.
It*em*, de Petre Torold p*ur* entrer en le liv*er*é d'orfev*er*ie – iii s. iiii d.
It*em*, de Perot Tounvyle p*ur* entrer en le liver*é* d'orfev*er*ie – v. s.
It*em*, resceu de Joh*a*n Tewkesbury p*ur* sou*n* trespas de aler al feir*e* – vi s. viii d.
It*em*, pur Joh*a*n Huberd p*ur* sou*n* entr*é* en le lyver*é* – iii s. iiii d.[302]

1394–95 p. 77[303] Ceux sount les nouns des Gardeyns eslutz *et* jurrez le jo*ur* de Seint Donston l'an du regne le Roy Rich*ard* secounde puys le conqueste xviie tank a mesme feste [l'an] xviiie:
Joh*a*n Forster
Joh*ann*es Bulstrode
Joh*a*n Standelf
Will*ia*m Downe

Fait a remembr*er* q*e* mesme an fuist ordeigné q*e* nuly du dite mestier n'achate de null*e* est*ra*ung*er* le li*vre* d'argent blank debrosez pluys cher*e* q*e* le li*vre* a xxvii s., *et* si ascun achate a pluys haute p*ri*s, paiera al almoign*e* de Seint Donston p*ur* chescu*n* li*vre* – ii s.
It*em*, null*e* argent debrosez endorrez a pluys haute p*ri*s q*e* a xxviii s. vi d., sur peyne [de] paier au dite almoign*e* p*ur* chescu*n* li*vre* – iii s. iiii d.

Item, q*e* nully p*re*igne app*re*ntys mes a t*er*me de vii ans ové C s.[304] *et* si ascun p*re*igne app*re*ntys ové meyns q*e* C s. paiera al almoign*e* de Seint Donston – C s.

It*em*, q*e* nule foreigne ne alien soit p*ri*s de eov*er*er ové nully du dite mestier tank il soit moustr*é* as Gardeyns *et* apporte ové luy l*ett*res de sa conv*er*saciou*n* *et* de sa bone porte, *et* trove suffisantz plegg*es* de estre

[302] I would not change the 'pur' after 'Item' since although it might be an error for 'de' it might indicate that someone else had paid for this man.
[303] The hand is again here that of the scribe who wrote p. 75 etc.; p. 76 only has been in a different hand.
[304] There has been some scoring out and additions to these figures: the figure of 7 years has been scored, but then 'vii' has again been written above; the sum of 100s. has been scored out and 'vii li.' written above, but this has then been scored; a further addition has been made above the line: 'oue x m*a*rcs *et* x ans oue C s.'

William Garton formerly apprentice of Thomas Polle paid – 2s.
Richard Flecchere formerly apprentice of Thomas Hay paid – 2s.
John Halyday formerly apprentice of William Lucas paid – 2s.
John Hilles formerly apprentice of Robert Brinle paid – 2s.

Memorandum that John Purchas gave for his admission to the freedom – 20s. col. 2
Item, Bartholomew Seman for his entry to the livery of the Goldsmiths' mistery paid – 13s. 4d.
Item, from Wynant van Worms for his entry to the livery paid – 6s. 8d.
Item, Thomas Langton, whereas he sold a serving-man and an apprentice, paid – 40s.
Item, from Piers Thorold for entry into the livery of the Goldsmiths' mistery – 3s. 4d.
Item, from Peter Tounvyle for entry into the livery of the Goldsmiths' mistery – 5s.
Item, received from John Tewkesbury for his offence in going to the fair – 6s. 8d.
Item, for John Huberd for his entry into the livery – 3s. 4d.

These are the names of the wardens elected and sworn on St Dunstan's Day in the year 17 Richard II until the same feast in the year 18 [Richard II] [19 May 1394 – 19 May 1395]: 1394–95 p. 77
John Forster
John Bulstrode
John Standelf
William Downe

Memorandum that the same year it was ordained that no one of the said mistery shall buy from any foreigner broken-up white [ungilded][142] silver at more than 27s. the lb., and if anyone should buy it at a higher price then he shall pay to the alms funds of St Dunstan for each pound – 2s.
Item, no broken-up gilded silver at a higher price than 28s. 6d., on pain of paying to the said alms funds for each pound – 3s. 4d.

Item, that no one shall take on an apprentice except for a term of 7 years, with 100s.[143], and if anyone takes on an apprentice for less than 100s. he shall pay to the alms funds of St Dunstan – 100s.

Item, that no one from outside the City of London nor from abroad should be taken on to work with anyone of the said mistery before he has been presented to the wardens, and he must bring with him letters regarding his skill and his good behaviour, and he must find sufficient sureties that he will be good and

142 David Beasley has pointed out that 'white silver' is the term used to designate silver in its usual polished state. One very frequently finds the term used in apposition to 'gilded silver', 'gilt plate', and it can thus take on the meaning of 'ungilded silver', although its primary meaning is 'white (polished) silver'.
143 The note: 'with 10 marks, and 10 years with 100s.'

bone *et* loiall*e* au dite mestier *et* p*ur* garder to*us* les bones ordinanc*es* du dite mestier. Et si ascun p*re*igne ascun tiel, paiera al almoign*e* de Seint Donston tant come il paiera au dite lowys.[305]

It*em*, q*e* nully du dite mestier d'orfeve*r*ie ne eove*r*e en schope ne en mesou*n* de null*e* autre d'autr*e* mestier, sur peyne de p*er*dre au dite almoign*e* – C s.[306]

It*em*, p*ur* ceo q*e* Will*elmu*s Nichol*e* ferist un Elys Coher*e* de Kyngestou*n* nient droiturelem*en*t al schope de Joh*a*n Som*er*vyle *et* ne voill*e* estr*e* justefiez p*ar* ses gardeins, mes rebelem*en*t eux respondist, ordeigné est q*e* si soit trové en defaute d'issor*e*enav*a*nt de reviler ascun est*ra*ung*er* come il fist mesme Elys ap*ré*s le acord fait p*ar* ses gardeyns paiera al almoign*e* de Seint Donston – xx s.

It*em*, p*ur* ceo q*e* Will*ia*m Holteby fuist rebell*e* a ses gardeyns, ordeign*é* est q*e* si desoreenav*a*nt soit trové rebell*e* a ses gardeyns, paiera al almoign*e* xx s. *et* av*er*a sa penaunce solonc l'ordinance des rebell*es* ordeign*é* en la Guyhall*e* – xx s.

It*em*, si les gardeins ne levount les peynes a lo*ur* poair paieront al almoigne de Seint Donston – C s.

Fait a remembr*er* q*e* Joh*a*n Vangav*er*e fuist enfraunchisez l'an av*a*ntdite *et* resceu al lyv*e*r*é* d'orfeve*r*ie *et* paia p*ur* sou*n* entr*é* – C s.
It*em*, Philipp*e* Castill*e* paia mesme an p*ur* estr*e* fraunchisez – v m*a*rcs
It*em*, resceu de Joh*a*n Carbonell*e* – xl s.
It*em*, p*ur* assayez resceu de mesme Joh*a*n Carbonell*e* – ix s.

p. 78 Ceux sount les nouns d'app*re*ntys resceu en mesme an av*a*ntdite:

En p*ri*mes, Will*ia*m Fyfhede app*re*ntys de Perot Tounvile –	ii s.
Item, Philippe Skele app*rentys* William Skele –	ii s.
William Nortoun app*rentys* Johan Standelf –	ii s.
Robert	
Johannes Adam app*re*ntys de William Downe –	ii s.
Thomas Brakenham app*re*ntys de Johan Exetre –	ii s.
Thomas Noreys app*rentys* Willelmi Maryner –	ii s.
Rauf Fyfhede app*rentys* de Thomas Langtoun –	ii s.
William Willy app*rentys* de Hugh Wetherby –	ii s.
Johan Barde app*rentys* de William Barde –	ii s.
Richard[307] Totenham app*rentys* de Robert Frauncеys –	ii s.
Johan Fest app*rentys* Thome Mounde –	ii s.

[305] A further phrase here has been scored right through, as has the sum of money at the side which went with this: 'ou si il p*re*ign*e* ascun mes al meyns p*ar* un an sur peyne de p*er*dre al almoign*e* – C s.'
[306] The same hand has written an addition to this later (in different ink): 'ne lesse null*e* autr*e* veer les p*ri*vités du dite mestier sur mesme peyne'.
[307] An omission mark follows this name and interlinearly has been written: 'Taylo*ur* do*n*us/dou*n*s'.

loyal to the said mistery and will keep all the good ordinances of the said mistery. And if anyone should take on any such, he shall pay to the alms funds of St Dunstan the amount he shall pay to the said serving-man.[144]

Item, that no one of the said Goldsmiths' mistery shall work in the shop or the house of anyone else of another mistery, on pain of having to pay to the said alms funds – 100s.[145]

Item, whereas William Nichole unlawfully struck one Ellis Cohere of Kingston in the shop of John Somerville, and did not wish to be judged by his wardens, but replied to them rebelliously, it was ordered that if he should be found guilty from this day forward of insulting any foreigner in the way he did to the same Elys, according to the decision made by his wardens he shall pay to the alms funds of St Dunstan – 20s.

Item, whereas William Holteby rebelled against his wardens, it was ordained that if from henceforth he should be found guilty of rebellion against his wardens, he shall pay to the alms funds – 20s., and he shall have his penance as decreed in the ordinance against rebels at the Guildhall – 20s.

Item, if the wardens do not do their utmost to levy penalties, they shall pay to the alms funds of St Dunstan – 100s.

Memorandum that John van Gavere was enfranchised in the aforesaid year and admitted into the livery of the Goldsmiths' mistery, and he paid for his entry – 100s.
Item, Philip Castille paid in the same year for being enfranchised – 5 marks.
Item, received from John Carbonelle – 40s.
Item, for assays[146] received from the same John Carbonelle – 9s.

These are the names of apprentices admitted in the same aforesaid year: p. 78

Firstly, William Fifehead apprentice of Piers Tounvile –	2s.
Item, Phillip Skele apprentice of William Skele –	2s.
William Nortoun apprentice of John Standelf –	2s.
Robert	
John Adam apprentice of William Downe –	2s.
Thomas Brackenham apprentice of John Exeter –	2s.
Thomas Noreys apprentice of William Mariner –	2s.
Ralph Fifehead apprentice of Thomas Langton –	2s.
William Wylly apprentice of Hugh Wetherby –	2s.
John Barde apprentice of William Barde –	2s.
Richard Tottenham apprentice of Robert Fraunceys –	2s.
John Fest apprentice of Thomas Mounde –	2s.

144 The note: 'or if he takes on anyone but at least for a year, on pain of having to pay to the alms funds – 100s.'
145 The note: 'nor let anyone else see the privities of the said mistery, on the same pain'. See above, p. 219, note 126.
146 See above, p. 227, n. 137

Johan Batelkyng app*rentys* Johan Halle – ii s.
Thomas Stolkene app*rentys* Johan Bulstrode[308] – ii s.
Roger Nykke app*rentys* William Nicolas – ii s.
Richard West app*rentys* Saleman Oxeneye – ii s.
Johan Hawe app*rentys* Johan Waldene – ii s.
Thomas Gybbe app*rentys* Robert Brinlle, pynnere[309] – ii s.
William Godeston app*rentys* Johan Forster – ii s.

col. 2 Les nouns de lowys:[310]
Joh*an* Corby jadys app*r*entys Will*iam* Burgelou*n*
Geffrey Serjeant ové Th*omas* Bygood
Cristofr*e* Tydesle jadys app*rentys* Joh*an* Grenefeld
Nich*olas* Fairher app*rentys* Steph*en* Clerc
Joh*an* Mapelesdene[311] app*rentys* Steph*en* Mapelesden*e*
Th*omas* Ufford app*rentys* Nich*ola*i Twyford
Will*iam* Coupere app*rentys* Will*iam* Falle
Joh*an* Martyn app*rentys* quond*am* Joh*an* Bodesh*am*
Walt*er* Ha*m*me app*rentys* Andr*eu* Stameldene

– mesme jo*ur* fuist g*ra*unté xii d. a Thom*a*s Rokyngh*a*m.

Les despens*es* fait p*ar* mesme gardeins:
En p*ri*mes, a Rog*er* Elys p*ur* cir*e* encountr*e* le feste de Seint Donston – viii s. ii d. ob.
It*em*, paié a George Cressy *et* Remu*n*d Standelf p*ur* p*ur*suite al treso*ur*er p*ur* le chaunge – xxvi s. viii d.

1395–96 Ceux sount les nouns des Gardeyns eslutz *et* jurrez le jo*ur* de Seint Donston
p. 79 l'an du regne le Roi Rich*ard* secounde puis le conqueste xviii tank a mesme feste de Seint Donston [l'an] xix^e^:
Thom*as* Polle
Rob*ertus* Fraunceys
Ricard Bartou*n*
Joh*annes* Edmu*n*d

Ceux sount les p*ar*cell*es* despenduz p*ar* mesmez gardeyns:
En p*ri*mes, p*ur* soner le g*ra*unt sonaill*e* en le belfrey a Poules – iii s. iiii d.
It*em*, en novell*e* cir*e*, i li. *et* d*em*i, p*ri*s – x d. ob.
It*em*, p*ur* le faç*oun* de xxii li. *et* d*em*i – xi d. ob.
It*em,* p*ur* ii tortices pois*aunt* x li., p*ri*s le li. a vii d. – v s. x d.
Summa – xi s.

[308] This line has been scored out and the note 'mortu*us*' written in the LH margin. Below this in the margin is written 'pleg-' – one cannot be sure against which name.
[309] This last word seems to have been added very slightly later.
[310] No sums of money are listed for the following, but the writing here goes so close to the RH side that it is not impossible (although not probable) that they are either hidden in the gutter or were cropped off at the time of binding.
[311] This name has the word 'pleg-' written in the margin to the left of it.

John Batelkyng apprentice of John Halle –	2s.
Thomas Stolkene apprentice of John Bulstrode –	2s.
Roger Nykke apprentice of William Nicolas –	2s.
Richard West apprentice of Solomon Oxney –	2s.
John Hawe apprentice of John Walden –	2s.
Thomas Gybbe apprentice of Robert Brinle, pinner –	2s.
William Godeston apprentice of John Forster –	2s.

The names of serving-men: col. 2
John Corby, formerly apprentice of William Burgyloun
Geoffrey Serjeant with Thomas Bygod
Christopher Tyldesley, formerly apprentice of John Greenfield
Nicholas Fairher, apprentice of Stephen Clerk
John Maplesdene apprentice of Stephen Maplesdene
Thomas Ufford aprentice of Nicholas Twyford
William Coupere apprentice of William Falle
John Martyn formerly apprentice of John Bottisham
Walter Hamme apprentice of Andrew Stameldene

– on the same day 12d. was granted to Thomas Rockingham.

The expenditures made by the same wardens:
Firstly, to Roger Elys for wax for St Dunstan's feastday – 8s. 2½d.
Item, paid to George Cressy and Raymund Standelf for making suit to the Treasurer for the exchange[147] – 26s. 8d.

These are the names of the wardens elected and sworn on St Dunstan's Day 1395–96
in the year 18 Richard II until the same feast of St Dunstan in the year 19 p. 79
[Richard II] [19 May 1395 – 19 May 1396]:
Thomas Polle
Robert Fraunceys
Richard Barton
John Edmund

These are the items of expenditure made by the same wardens:
Firstly, for ringing the great bell in the bell-tower at St Paul's – 3s. 4d.
Item, for new wax, 1½ lbs., price – 10½d.
Item, for the making up of 22½ lbs. [of wax into candles] – 11½d.
Item, for 2 torches weighing 10 lbs., at 7d. per lb. – 5s. 10d.
Total: 11s.

[147] i.e. to try to obtain the office of King's Exchanger, in which they were unsuccessful. See Reddaway and Walker, pp. 76–77.

col. 1 Ceux sount les nouns de app*re*ntisez p*ri*sez mesme l'an:
Nich*ola*s Wodhull*e* app*re*ntys de Will*ia*m Lowthe – ii s.
Henric*us* Valent app*re*ntys de Hereman van Glew – ii s.
Will*elmu*s Alkeh*a*m app*re*ntys de Saleman Oxeneye – ii s.
Joh*anne*s Bauer app*re*ntys de Wynant van Wermes – ii s.
Ric*ardus* atte Watr*e* app*re*ntys de Thom*a*s Langetou*n* – ii s.
Thom*a*s Covele, Joh*a*n Pycot app*re*ntis*es* de Joh*a*n Lutou*n* – iiii s.
Radulph*us* Alem app*re*ntys de Rich*ard* Bartou*n* – ii s.
Will*elmu*s Horewode app*rentys* Thome Lamport – ii s.

Ceux sount les nouns q*e* ount entrez en le lyver*é*
Nanfre Molken, chaungeo*ur* – xl s.
Thom*a*s Middeltou*n* – xxvi s. viii d.

col. 2 Lowys p*ar* mesme temps:[312]
Joh*anne*s[313] Whirwell*e* jadys app*re*ntis Will*iam* Lucas
Joh*anne*s Mapelesden*e* jadys app*rentys* Steph*e*n Mapelesden*e*
Joh*anne*s Lemyng jadys app*rentys* Adam Merfeld

It*em*, deliv*er*é mesme temps, i [p]eir*e*[314] bedes de latou*n* endorr*é,* i anell*e* d'or stuffé ové plumb*e*, *et* un glas, p*ri*s en le schope de Bussh*e*.
It*em*, un ouche de cop*er* ové un cerf.[315]
It*em*, petit*es* bedes de cop*er* en un pice de drap linge.
It*em*, ii bokclapses[316] de cop*er* endorrez.
It*em*, belles de tyn q*e* furent mys en un seynt*ur*e d'argent p*ar* Joh*a*n Gyles.
It*em*, un autr*e* seynt*ur*e de metall*e* p*ri*s en la schope de mesme Joh*a*n Giles.
It*em*, i paxbrede d'argent deliv*er*é a Honte *et* sez compaignons.

Fait a remembr*er* q*e* Joh*a*n Lutou*n*, Joh*a*n Honte, Joh*a*n Godard *et* George Cressy ount resceu de les rent*er*s Will*iam* Lincoln*e et* Joh*a*n Lagehach*e* – ix s. viii d.

1396–97 Ceux sount les nouns dé Gardeyns eslutz *et* jurez le jo*ur* de Seint Donston
p. 80 l'an du regne le Roi Rich*ard* secounde xixe tank a mesme feste l'an xxe:
Joh*anne*s Honte
Joh*anne*s Lutou*n*
Joh*anne*s Godard
George Cressy

Ceux sount les p*a*rcell*es* despenduz p*ar* mesme gardeyns:
En primes, p*ur* soner le g*ra*unt sonaill*e* de Seint Poull*es* – iii s. iiii d.
It*em*, en payn a mesme lieu – v d.

[312] No sums of money are listed against the following names. The writing goes very near to the RH side (as on p. 78), this time being at the outer edge.
[313] This name has been written over a scored 'Thom*a*s'.
[314] MS: beire.
[315] This line has been scored out.
[316] *Sic.*

These are the names of apprentices taken on in the same year: col. 1

Nicholas Woodhille apprentice of William Louth –	2s.
Henry Valent apprentice of Hermann van Gluye –	2s.
William Alkam apprentice of Solomon Oxney –	2s.
Johan Bauer aprentice of Wynant van Worms –	2s.
Richard atte Water apprentice of Thomas Langton –	2s.
Thomas Covele, John Pycot, apprentices of John Luton –	4s.
Ralph Alom apprentice of Richard Barton –	2s.
William Horwood apprentice of Thomas Lamport –	2s.

These are the names of those who have entered the livery:
Nanfre Molakyn, [the King's] exchanger[148] – 40s.
Thomas Middleton – 26s. 8d.

Serving-men during the same time: col. 2
John Whirwelle formerly apprentice of William Lucas
John Maplesdene formerly apprentice of Stephen Maplesdene
John Lemyng formerly apprentice of Adam Mirfield

Item, handed over at the same time: 1 rosary of gilded copper, 1 gold ring plugged[149] with lead, and a glass [fake gemstone], seized in Busshe's workshop.[150]
Item, a copper clasp with a stag.
Item, small copper beads in a piece of linen cloth.
Item, 2 book-clasps of gilded copper.
Item, tin bells which were fixed to a silver girdle by John Gyles.
Item, another metal girdle seized in the workshop of the same John Gyles.
Item, a silver pax handed over to Honte and his fellow-wardens.

Memorandum that John Luton, John Honte, John Godard and George Cressy have received from the renters William Lincoln and John Lagehache – 9s. 8d.

These are the names of the wardens elected and sworn on St Dunstan's Day 1396–97
in the year 19 Richard II until the same feast in the year 20 [Richard II] p. 80
[19 May 1396–19 May 1397]:
John Honte
John Luton
John Godard
George Cressy

These are the items of expenditure made by the same wardens:
Firstly, for ringing the great bell of St Paul's – 3s. 4d.
Item, for bread at the same place – 5d.

148 He was a Florentine, and was also Master of the Mint. See Reddaway and Walker, p. 77.
149 i.e. deceitfully stuffed into an empty space.
150 This might have been either Roland van Busshe or John Busshe: see Name Index.

It*em*, en formage – vi d.
It*em*, en servoise – iiii s.
It*em*, en novell*e* cir*e*, un li. *et* de*m*i, p*r*is – x d. ob.
It*em*, p*ur* le faç*oun* de xxii li. cir*e* *et* de*m*i – xi d. ob.
It*em* en ii tortices pois*aunt* xiii li. – vi s. vi d.

p. 81, col. 1 Lowys:

Joh*anne*s Mene – qu*i*t –	vi s. viii d.[317]
Will*elmu*s Falle –	ii s.
Thom*as* Glade –	ii s.
Rog*er*us Aleyn –	ii s.
Joh*anne*s Payn –	ii s.
Will*elmu*s Adys –	ii s.
Rob*ertus* Halle –	ii s.
Joh*anne*s Saleman –	ii s.
Ric*ard*us Bussh*e* –	ii s.
Rog*erus* Downe –	ii s.
Henric*us*[318] Camell*e* –	ii s.
Joh*anne*s Frer*e* –	ii s.
Joh*anne*s Pake –	ii s.
Thom*as* Aleyn –	ii s.
Thom*as* Derlyng –	ii s.
Joh*anne*s Bisshop senior, goldbet*ere* –	ii s.
Joh*anne*s Bisshop junior, goldbet*ere* –	ii s.
Joh*anne*s Hale, goldbet*ere* –	ii s.
Joh*anne*s Fiherberd –	ii s.
Rob*ertus* Howes –	ii s.
Henric*us* Snokeshull*e* –	ii s.
Joh*anne*s Terne –	ii s.
Joh*anne*s Orped –	ii s.
Joh*anne*s Bontyng –	ii s.
Rob*ertus* Brou*n* –	ii s.

No*min*a app*r*enticior*um*:

Henric*us* Plumstede app*renticius* Thome Pantou*n* –	ii s.
Thom*as* Frambold app*renticius* Joh*ann*is Standelf –	ii s.
Rog*er*us Warburgh*e* app*renticius* Remu*n*d Standelf –	ii s.
Clemens Wilmott app*renticius* Will*ia*m Fithewe –	ii s.
Ric*ard*us Loudyer app*renticius* Joh*a*n Frer*e* –	ii s.

col. 2 Ceux sount les nouns de novell*es* entrés en le lyv*eré*:
Joh*a*n Wynne, jeweler – xxvi s. viii d.

p. 82 Corby:[319]

P*ur* ceo q*e* Joh*a*n Corby se mist en agard de sez gardeins *et* aprés countredist le agard *et* disclaundra mesmez gardeyns *et* fist mayntenance encountr*e* eux p*ar* esquiers en le Guyhall encountr*e* sou*n* serement *et* a g*ra*unt repreof *et*

[317] This sum of money has been written in slightly later.
[318] This name has a note against it in the LH margin: 'Jur'.
[319] This has been written in the LH margin.

Item, for cheese – 6d.
Item, for ale – 4s.
Item, for new wax, 1½ lbs., price – 10½d.
Item, for the making up of 22½ lbs. of wax – 11½ d.
Item, for 2 torches weighing 13 lbs. – 6s. 6d.

Serving-men: p. 81, col. 1

John Mene – quit –	6s. 8d.
William Falle –	2s.
Thomas Glade –	2s.
Roger Aleyn –	2s.
John Payn –	2s.
William Adys –	2s.
Robert Halle –	2s.
John Saleman –	2s.
Richard Busshe –	2s.
Roger Downe –	2s.
Henry Camelle –	2s.
John Frere –	2s.
John Pake –	2s.
Thomas Aleyn –	2s.
Thomas Derlyng –	2s.
John Bisshop the elder, goldbeater –	2s.
John Bisshop the younger, goldbeater –	2s.
John Hale, goldbeater –	2s.
John FitzHerbert –	2s.
Robert Howes –	2s.
Henry Snokeshulle –	2s.
John Terne –	2s.
John Orped –	2s.
John Buntyng –	2s.
Robert Broun –	2s.

The names of apprentices:

Henry Plumstead apprentice of Thomas Panton –	2s.
Thomas Frambold apprentice of John Standelf –	2s.
Roger Warburgh apprentice of Raymund Standelf –	2s.
Clemens Wilmott apprentice of William FitzHugh –	2s.
Richard Loudyer apprentice of John Frere –	2s.

These are the names of those who have newly entered the livery: col. 2
John Wynne, jeweller – 26s. 8d.

Corby: p. 82
Whereas John Corby submitted himself to the jurisdiction of his wardens, and afterwards he disputed their sentence and slandered the same wardens, and he committed maintenance[151] against them, bringing litigation in the name of some

[151] For the legal sense of this word, see *OED*: 'The action of wrongfully aiding and abetting litigation; *spec.* sustentation of a suit or suitor at law by a party who has no interest in the proceedings or who acts from any improper motive.'

disclaundr*e* de sez gardeyns *et* de tout la mestier, jugé fuist p*ar* Joh*a*n Lutou*n*, Joh*a*n Honte, Joh*a*n Godard *et* George Cressy, p*ar* assent des autres gentz de mesme mestier a eux eslutz,[320] c'est assavoir Joh*a*n Forster, Will*ia*m Lowthe, Thom*a*s Pantou*n*, Joh*a*n Frensshe, Ric*hard* Bartou*n*, Will*ia*m Maryner, Will*ia*m Burgylou*n*, Stephen*e* Mapelesden*e*, q*e* mesme Joh*a*n Corby paiera al almoigne de Seint Donston vi s. viii d. Et si d'iceo enav*a*nt soit trové en defaute ou rebell*e* v*er*s sez gardeins, paiera al almoign*e* C s. Et ap*ré*s al prier*e* de Will*ia*m Burgelou*n* furent remys les av*a*ntditz vi s. viii d.

Fait a remembr*er* q*e* Will*ia*m de Lowth*e*, Joh*a*n Frensh*e*, Saleman Oxeneye, Joh*a*n Blakedou*n* ount resceu de Joh*a*n Honte *et* ses compaignons av*a*ntditz – iii li. xviii s. iiii d.

1400–01 Corby:[321]

P*ur* ceo q*e* Joh*a*n Corby disclaundra Joh*a*n Knyvesworth*e* en temps q*e* fuist gardeyn, fuist adjuggé p*ar* Joh*a*n Standelf, Ric*hard* Bartou*n*, Joh*a*n Noreman, ses compaignou*n*s gardeyns, *et* vi autres a eux eslutz, de paier al almoign*e* de Seint Donston vi s. viii d., q*ue*ux il paia. Et enoutr*e* si mesme Joh*a*n Corby disclaundr*e* desoreenav*a*nt le dite Joh*a*n Knyvesworth*e* ou ascun autr*e* gardeyn ou ascun del lyv*er*é paiera xxxiii s. iiii d. sauns redempciou*n*.

1409 [322]Pur ceo q*e* Joh*a*n Corby disclaundra Will*ia*m Granth*a*m, Will*ia*m Randolf, Joh*a*n Wat*er* *et* Joh*a*n Pake, ses gardeins, le xme jo*ur* de juyll*et* l'an du regne le Roi Henr*i* quart puis le conquest xme, la est ordeigné *et* juggé p*ar* assent q*e* il paiera la so*m*me av*a*ntdit p*ur* la rebelté q*e* en luy fuist trovez a cell*e* temps.

1397–98 Ceux sount les nouns dé Gardeyns eslutz *et* jurrez l'an du Roy xxe le jo*ur* de
p. 83 Seint Donston tank a mesme feste l'an xxj^e^:

Will*ia*m de Lowthe
Joh*a*n Frenssh*e*
Saleman Oxeneye
Joh*a*n Blakedou*n*

Ceux sount les p*a*rcell*es* despenduz p*ar* mesmes gardeins l'an av*a*ntdite:
En p*ri*mes, p*ur* son*er* les g*ra*untz sonaill*es* de Seint Poul*es* – iii s. iiii d.
It*em,* en payn et formage – xviii d.
It*em*, en servoise – iii s. iiii d.
It*em*, en un cheste p*ur* le mynstralcie – iiii s.

[320] This is interesting as an early mention of men elected or appointed to give assistance to the wardens. This led ultimately to the establishment of the Court of Assistants, still in existence today. See the other such entries, e.g. A + a, pp. 108, 114, 128.

[321] Written as above in the LH margin.

[322] This paragraph has been written later in a different hand, the same as has written e.g. pp. 103–112.

esquires in the Guildhall, in contravention of his sworn oath and to the great disgrace and shame of his wardens and of the whole mistery, judgment was made by John Luton, John Honte, John Godard and George Cressy, with the assent of others of the same mistery elected [to sit] with them [on this case], i.e. John Forster, William Louth, Thomas Panton, John Frenshe, Richard Barton, William Mariner, William Burgyloun, Stephen Maplesdene, that the said John Corby shall pay to the alms funds of St Dunstan 6s. 8d. And if from this day forward he shall be found at fault or shall rebel against his wardens, he shall pay to the alms funds 100s. And afterwards, at the entreaty of William Burgyloun, the aforesaid 6s. 8d. was remitted.

Memorandum that William de Louth, John Frenshe, Solomon Oxney, John Blakedene have received from John Honte and his aforesaid fellow-wardens – £3 18s. 4d.

Corby: 1400–01
Whereas John Corby slandered John Knyvesworthe during his term of office as warden,[152] it was judged by John Standelf, Richard Barton, John Norman, his fellow wardens, and 6 others elected [to sit] with them [on this case], that he should pay to the alms funds of St Dunstan 6s. 8d., which he paid. And further, that if the same John Corby shall from henceforth slander the said John Knyvesworthe or any other warden or anyone who is of the livery, he shall pay 33s. 4d. without any remission.

Whereas John Corby slandered William Grantham, William Randolf, John 1409
Water and John Pake, his wardens, on 10 July of the year 10 Henry IV [1409], it was then ordained and judged by assent that he shall pay the aforesaid sum for the rebelliousness of which he was found guilty at that time.

These are the names of the wardens elected and sworn in the year 20 1397–98
[Richard II] on St Dunstan's Day until the same feastday in the year 21 p. 83
[Richard II] [19 May 1397 – 19 May 1398]:
William de Louth
John Frenshe
Solomon Oxney
John Blakedene

These are the items of expenditure made by the same wardens in the aforesaid year:
Firstly, for ringing the great bells of St Paul's – 3s. 4d.
Item, for bread and cheese – 18d.
Item, for ale – 3s. 4d.
Item, for a chest for the musical instruments – 4s.

[152] 1400–01.

Ceux sount les nouns d'app*re*ntis resceux mesme an:
Denis Tillesle app*re*ntis Cristofre Tillesle – ii s.
Rob*er*t Child app*re*ntis Thom*as* Langtou*n* – ii s.
Walt*er* Coggere app*re*nt*is* Rob*er*t Brynle – ii s.
Ric*hard* Spenser app*re*nt*is* Joh*a*n Frer*e* – ii s.
Will*iam* Barle app*re*nt*is* Thome Glade – ii s.
Will*elmu*s Merfeld app*re*nt*is* Joh*a*n White – ii s.
Joh*a*n Colneye app*re*nt*is* Joh*a*n Blakedou*n* – ii s.
Will*iam* Tideswell*e* app*re*nt*is* Rog*er* Aleyn – ii s.
Reginald*us* Verneye app*re*nt*is* Joh*a*n Wynne – ii s.
Ric*hard* Hogge app*re*nt*is* Thome Bokyll*e* – ii s.
Will*iam* Tynwich app*rentis* Egidii Oxeneye – ii s.
Steph*an*us Knight, Will*iam* Matheu app*re*nt*is* Georgii Cressy – iiii s.
Nich*ola*us Harlestoke app*re*nt*is* Ph*ilipp*i Castill*e* – ii s.
Will*elmu*s Pomfreit app*rentis* Ric*ard*i Bartou*n* – ii s.

Lowys mesme l'an:
Joh*a*n Bernes jadys app*re*ntys Thom*as* Pantou*n* – ii s.
Rog*er* Brenastou*n* jadys app*re*ntys Rob*er*t Willy – ii s.
Joh*a*n Herteshorn jadys app*re*ntys Will*iam* Lincoln*e* – ii s.
Will*iam* Cokkele jadys app*re*nt*y*s Rob*er*t Hugfeld – ii s.
Joh*ann*es South*a*m jadys app*rentys* Henri Ba*m*me – ii s.[323]

Mesme an Giles Oxeneye paia p*ur* so*u*n entr*é* xiii s. iiii d.

1398 Fait a remembr*er* q*e* Will*iam* Lowth*e*, Joh*a*n Frensh*e*, [Saleman][324] Oxeneye *et* Joh*a*n Blakedou*n* ount deliv*eré* a Thom*as* Extou*n*, Andreu Stameldene*e*, Will*iam* Fithewe *et* Joh*a*n Halle le xiii jo*ur* de June l'an xxie lxx s. ix d. Et Will*iam* Burdeyne, rent*er*, ad deliv*er*é mesme temps – lxvii s. iii d.

1398–99 p. 84 P*ur* ceo q*e* Joh*a*n Bontyng le puisné disclaundra Thom*as* Extou*n*, Andreu Stameld*e*n*e*, Will*iam* Fithewe *et* Joh*a*n Halle, ses gardeyns p*ur* le temps, ordeigné est q*e* mesme Joh*a*n criera mercy, le quel fist eov*er*tement en la sale *et* puys ordeigné est q*e* si d'iceo enav*a*nt soit trové rebell*e* v*er*s ses gardeyns ou defame ascun de eux, unq*u*es ne serra resceu en la vestur*e* des orphev*er*s ne null*e* benefice touchant la mestier av*er*a durant sa vie.

1398–99 Ceux sount les nouns des Gardeins eslutz le jo*ur* de Seint Donston l'an xxj^e tank a mesme feste l'an xxiie:
Thom*as* Exto*u*n
Andreas Stameldene*e*
Will*elmu*s Fithewe
Joh*ann*es Halle

Ceux sount despens*es* fait p*ar* mesme gardeins:
En p*ri*mes, p*ur* le g*ra*unt sonaill*e* a Seint Poull – iii s. iiii d.

323 This line has been added slightly later, by the same scribe, in different ink.
324 MS: Giles.

These are the names of apprentices admitted in the same year:
Denis Tyldesley apprentice of Christopher Tyldesley – 2s.
Robert Child apprentice of Thomas Langton – 2s.
Walter Coggere apprentice of Robert Brinle – 2s.
Richard Spenser apprentice of John Frere – 2s.
William Barle apprentice of Thomas Glade – 2s.
William Mirfield apprentice of John White – 2s.
John Colney apprentice of John Blakedene – 2s.
William Tideswelle apprentice of Roger Aleyn – 2s.
Reginald Verney apprentice of John Wynne – 2s.
Richard Hogge apprentice of Thomas Bokyl – 2s.
William Tynwich apprentice of Giles Oxney – 2s.
Stephen Knight, William Matthew, apprentices of George Cressy – 4s.
Nicholas Harlestoke apprentice of Phillip Castille – 2s.
William Pomfreit apprentice of Richard Barton – 2s.

Serving-men the same year:
John Barnes formerly apprentice of Thomas Panton – 2s.
Roger Brenaston formerly apprentice of Robert Wylly – 2s.
John Herteshorn formerly apprentice of William Lincoln – 2s.
William Cokkele formerly apprentice of Robert Hugfeld – 2s.
John Southam formerly apprentice of Henry Bamme – 2s.

In the same year Giles Oxney paid for his entry – 13s. 4d.

Memorandum that William Louth, John Frenshe, Solomon Oxney and John Blakedene handed over to Thomas Exton, Andrew Stameldene, William Fitzhugh and John Halle on 13 June 21 [Richard II] [1398] – 70s. 9d. 1398
And William Burdeyn, renter, handed over at the same time – 67s. 3d.

Whereas John Buntyng the younger slandered Thomas Exton, Andrew Stameldene, William Fitzhugh and John Halle, his current wardens, it was ordered that the same John shall beg forgiveness, the which he did publicly in the Hall, and it was then ordered that if from this day forward he should be found guilty of rebelling against his wardens or slandering any of them, he shall never be admitted into the livery of the Goldsmiths, nor shall he obtain any benefit connected with the mistery during his whole lifetime. 1398–99 p. 84

These are the names of the wardens elected on St Dunstan's Day in the year 21 [Richard II] until the same feastday in the year 22 [Richard II] [19 May 1398–19 May 1399]: 1398–99
Thomas Exton
Andrew Stameldene
William Fitzhugh
John Halle

These are the expenditures made by the same wardens:
Firstly, for the great bell at St Paul's – 3s. 4d.

Item, en cire al chaundelere – viii s. xi d.
Item, en payn et servoise al belfrey – xxii d.
Item, paié as mynstrales – xiii s. iiii d.

col. 1 Ceux sount les nouns d'aprentys resceux mesme an:
Johan Sompter apprentys Petri Tounvile – ii s.
Walter Bentele apprentys Johan Scherston – ii s.
Johan Samforde apprentys Thomas Bokylle – ii s.
Johan Honte apprentys Johan Hille – ii s.
Johan Cotelle apprentys Richard Bartoun – ii s.
Johan Goodchild apprentys Johan Herteshorn – ii s.
Roger Kirkam apprentys Willelmi Pevere – ii s.
Thomas atte Watre apprentys Salamon Oxeney – ii s.
Johan Molkyn apprentys Gilis Oxeneye – ii s.
Robert Constable apprentys Edmund Nethersole – ii s.
Johan Piryman apprentys Johannis Halle junior – ii s.
Thomas Lyes apprentys Johan Thorne – ii s.
Thomas Wayte apprentys Johannis Lutoun – ii s.
William Dodyngherst apprentys Johan Noreman – ii s.
Thomas Horwode, Johannes Cowbrigge, Nicholaus Twyforde apprenticii Drugonis Barentyn, tunc Maioris London' – vi s.
Johannes de Trite apprenticius Johannis Frenshe – ii s.

col. 2 Ceux sount les nouns de lowys mesme an:
William Byntre jadis apprentys William Pevere – juré – ii s.
Richard Smyth apprentys jadys Johan Honte – juré – ii s.
Johan Malory jadys apprentys Johannis Rudham – juré – ii s.
Rogerus Veel apprentys jadys Thomas Lamport – ii s.
Johannes Brigge apprentys jadys Thomas Pantoun – ii s.
William Chipstede jadys apprentys Willelmi Lowthe – ii s.
Thomas Dancastre jadys apprentys George Cressy – ii s.
Richard Holmestede jadys apprentys de mesme George – ii s.
William Scharbroun apprentys jadys Remund Standelf – ii s.
Johannes Wiltschire jadys apprentys William Sparke – ii s.
Johannes Chestre apprentys jadys Robert Beche – ii s.
Item, de Ricardo Stanshalt jadys apprentys Mathie Goldbetere – ii s.

1399 Fait a remembrer qe Johan Farltoun fuist entré come lowys le xiiii jour de Maii l'an xxiie et paia pur soun entré xx s.
Item, Robert Serle fuist entré a mesme temps et paia pur soun entré – lx s. et trova plegge William . . .

p. 84[325] Fait a remembrer qe Johan Lincolne, Estephen de Thorp, William Lyncolne et Jeames Bontyng ount resceu de Thomas Extoun, Andreu Stameldene, William Fithewe et Johan Halle en monoye et plegges – xix li. iii s.
Item, de Thomas Dodesole et Johan Knyvesworth[326]

[325] This is now written right across the page below the two columns.
[326] No sum is entered but this can be calculated at £12 7s. 3d. from the total given below (although previous partial accounts where figures do not tally should make one beware).

Item, for wax, [paid] to the chandler – 8s. 11d.
Item, for bread and ale in the bell-tower – 22d.
Item, paid to the minstrels – 13s. 4d.

These are the names of apprentices admitted in the same year: col. 1

John Sompter apprentice of Piers Tounvile –	2s.
Walter Bentele apprentice of John Sherston –	2s.
John Samforde apprentice of Thomas Bokyl –	2s.
John Honte apprentice of John Hilles –	2s.
John Cotelle apprentice of Richard Barton –	2s.
John Goodchild apprentice of John Herteshorn –	2s.
Roger Kirkham apprentice of William Pevere –	2s.
Thomas atte Water apprentice of Solomon Oxney –	2s.
John Molkyn apprentice of Giles Oxney –	2s.
Robert Constable apprentice of Edmund Nethersole –	2s.
John Piryman apprentice of John Halle the younger –	2s.
Thomas Lyes apprentice of John Thorne –	2s.
Thomas Wayte apprentice of John Luton –	2s.
William Doddinghurst apprentice of John Norman –	2s.
Thomas Horwood, John Cowbrigge, Nicholas Twyford, apprentices of Drew Barantyn, then Mayor of London –	6s.
John de Trite apprentice of John Frenshe –	2s.

These are the names of serving-men the same year: col. 2

William Byntre formerly apprentice of William Pevere –	sworn	– 2s.
Richard Smyth formerly apprentice of John Honte –	sworn	– 2s.
John Malory formerly apprentice of John Rudham –	sworn	– 2s.
Roger Veel formerly apprentice of Thomas Lamport –		2s.
John Brigge formerly apprentice of Thomas Panton –		2s.
William Chipstede formerly apprentice of Wiliam Louth –		2s.
Thomas Dancastre formerly apprentice of George Cressy –		2s.
Richard Holmstead formerly apprentice of the same George –		2s.
William Sherborne formerly apprentice of Raymund Standelf –		2s.
John Wiltshire formerly apprentice of William Sparke –		2s.
John Chester formerly apprentice of Robert Beech –		2s.
Item, from Richard Stanshalt formerly apprentice of Matthew Goldbeater		– 2s.

Memorandum that John Farleton was admitted as a serving-man[153] on 14 May 1399 and paid for his entry 20s. 1399
Item, Robert Serle was admitted at the same time and paid for his entry – 60s. – and he found as a surety[154] William . . .

Memorandum that John Lincoln, Stephen de Thorp, William Lincoln and James Buntyng have received from Thomas Exton, Andrew Stameldene, William FitzHugh and John Halle in money and pledges – £19 3s. p. 84
Item, from Thomas Dodesole and John Knyvesworthe – [£12 7s. 3d.]

[153] i.e. he was allowed entry to the freedom (and possibly the livery?) but had not been an apprentice but a serving-man to someone and therefore had to pay for his entry, as did e.g. 'Dutchmen'.
[154] Either for the money if not paid immediately (but it is said to have been paid), or, perhaps more likely, as a guarantor of his skill and his good behaviour.

It*em* un obligaciou*n* de Will*ia*m Burdeyne – C s.
S*umma* – xxxvi li. x s. iii d.

1399–1400 Ceux sount les nouns des gardeyns d'orfev*er*ie eslutz le jo*ur* de Seint
p. 85 Donston l'an du regne le Roy Rich*ard* secounde xxii^{e} tank a mesme feste l'an du regne le Roy Henri quarte puys le conqueste primer*e*:
Joh*a*n Lincoln*e*
Steph*e*n de Thorp*e*
Will*ia*m Lincoln*e*
Jeames Bontyng

Despens*es* fait p*ar* mesme gardeyns:
En p*ri*mes, p*ur* son*er* les sonaill*es* – iii s. iiii d.
It*em*, en payn *et* formage – xi d.
It*em*, en servoise – iii s. ix d.
It*em*, as mynstral*les* – xiii s. iiii d.

col. 1 Ceux sount les nouns d'ap*re*ntys resceux mesme an:[327]
Joh*a*n Eustas app*rentys* Will*ia*m Lowthe
Rob*er*t Downe ap*prentys* Rog*er* Downe
Thom*a*s Gabrull*e* app*rentys* Will*ia*m Randolf
Steph*e*n Walssh app*rentys* Joh*a*n Bernes
Joh*a*n Badbursh*a*m app*rentys* Will*ia*m Drayto*u*n
Steph*e*n[328] app*rentys* Will*ia*m Adys
Joh*a*n Bray app*rentys* Joh*a*n Forster
Will*ia*m Cook app*rentys* Joh*a*n Som*er*vile
Joh*a*n Lemyng app*rentys* Rob*er*t Lemyng
Hugh*e* de Stainyngstrete app*rentys* Joh*a*n Watyr
Godefrey Byntre app*rentys* Thom*a*s Popelto*u*n
Rog*er* Kirkam app*rentys* Will*ia*m Pevere
Fraunceys Frer*e* app*rentys* Joh*a*n Honte
Joh*a*n Newento*u*n app*rentys* Will*ia*m Garto*u*n
Thom*a*s Parker app*rentys* Rich*ard* Holstede
Thom*a*s Lynforde app*rentys* George Cressy
Joh*a*n Halle app*rentys* Joh*a*n Huberd
Simu*n*d Hulle app*rentys* Joh*a*n Stile[329]
Joh*a*n Bette app*rentys* Joh*a*n Granth*a*m
Ric*hard* Bonre app*rentys* Joh*a*n Whirwell*e*
Henr*i* Hillon app*rentys* Joh*a*n Houghto*u*n
Joh*a*n Onger app*rentys* Will*ia*m Fithewe
Rob*er*t Grene app*rentys* Nichol*as* Payn
Rob*er*t Bocher app*rentys* Rob*er*t Hugfeld
Joh*a*n Horold app*rentys* Joh*a*n Lenham
Joh*a*n Norto*u*n app*rentys* Joh*a*n Bulstrode
Nich*ola*us Covele app*rentys* Joh*a*n Fynk

[327] No sums of money are listed against the following names, but this is no doubt a scribal omission again.
[328] A gap follows.
[329] This surname has been written after a scored 'Lenh*a*m'.

Item, an obligation from William Burdeyn – 100s.
Total £36 10s. 3d.

These are the names of the wardens of the Goldsmiths' Mistery elected on St Dunstan's Day in the year 22 Richard II until the same feastday in the year 1 Henry IV [19 May 1399 – 19 May 1400]: 1399–1400 p. 85
John Lincoln
Stephen de Thorpe
William Lincoln
James Buntyng

Expenditures made by the same wardens:
Firstly, for ringing the bells – 3s. 4d.
Item, for bread and cheese – 11d.
Item, for ale – 3s. 9d.
Item, to the minstrels – 13s. 4d.

These are the names of apprentices admitted the same year: col. 1
John Eustace apprentice of William Louth
Robert Downe apprentice of Roger Downe
Thomas Gabrielle apprentice of William Randolf
Stephen Walsh apprentice of John Barnes
John Badbursham apprentice of William Draytoun
Stephen apprentice of William Adys
John Bray apprentice of John Forster
William Cook apprentice of John Somerville
John Lemyng apprentice of Robert Lemyng
Hugh de Stanystreet apprentice of John atte Water
Godfrey Byntre apprentice of Thomas Poppleton
Roger Kirkham apprentice of William Pevere
Francis Frere apprentice of John Honte
John Newton apprentice of William Garton
Thomas Parker apprentice of Richard Holmstead
Thomas Lynford apprentice of George Cressy
John Halle apprentice of John Huberd
Simon Hulle apprentice of John Style
John Bette apprentice of John Grantham
Richard Bonre apprentice of John Whirwelle
Henry Hillon apprentice of John Houghton
John Nongyl apprentice of William FitzHugh
Robert Grene apprentice of Nicholas Payn
Robert Bocher apprentice of Robert Hugfeld
John Horold apprentice of John Lenham
John Norton apprentice of John Bulstrode
Nicholas Covele apprentice of John Fynk

[330]apprentys Henri Hochedes
Thomas[331] apprentys Fithherberd

col. 2 Lowys:[332]
Edmund Page jadys apprentys Dru Barentyn
William Thelby jadys apprentys Piers Torold
Nicholas Bokyl jadys apprentys Johan Edmund
Richard Botlee jadys apprentys Thomas Lamport

Forfetures encountre l'ordeignance de apprentys:[333]

Johan Lutoun –	l s.
Roger Ryot –	l s.
Willelmus Adys –	xl s.
Johan Honte –	xx s.
Johan Panter –	vi s. viii d.
Johan Grantham –	vi s. viii d.
Johan Style –	xvi d.
Johan Scherston –	xiii s. iiii d.
Johan Somervile –	vi s. viii d.
William Gilbert –	vi s. viii d.
William Heyward –	iii s. iiii d.

Johan Lagehache pur un covenant fait de maseres – xx s.
Laurence Cornhulle pur faux eoveraigne – iii s. iiii d.
Item, pur vende d'un apprentys, c'est assavoir Johan Wulyngforde, venduz a Johan Therme – vi s. viii d.

p. 86 Ceux sount entrés en le lyveré:

Henri Goldbetere –	xxvi s. viii d.
Johannes Bisshop junior –	xx s.
Simon Chesterfelde –	iii s. iiii d.
William Gilbert –	iii s. iiii d.
De Johan Hille –	iii s. iiii d.
Johan atte Watre –	iii s. iiii d.
Walter Sprynget –	xvi d.
Johan Fithherberd –	iii s. iiii d.
Johan Herteshorn –	iii s. iiii d.

Summa de les revenuz: xlj[334] li. xix d.

1400 Summa totallis – lix li. iiii s. x d. – deliveré a les gardeyns aprés escriptz, c'est assavoir Johan Standelf, Richard Bartoun, Johan Noreman et Johan Knyvesworthe par Estephen de Thorpe, Johan Lincolne, William Lincolne et Jeames Bontyng.

[330] The apprentice's name was clearly unknown.
[331] A gap follows.
[332] No sums of money are listed here either, but one must assume the usual 2s. was paid.
[333] See above, A + a, p. 64.
[334] This figure is unclear and it might be only £40.

apprentice of Henry Hochedes
Thomas apprentice of FitzHerbert

Serving-men: col. 2
Edmund Page formerly apprentice of Drew Barantyn
William Thelby formerly apprentice of Piers Thorold
Nicholas Bokyl formerly apprentice of John Edmund
Richard Botlee formerly apprentice of Thomas Lamport

Fines for offences against the ordinance for apprentices:

John Luton –	50s.
Roger Ryot –	50s.
William Adys –	40s.
John Honte –	20s.
John Panter –	6s. 8d.
John Grantham –	6s. 8d.
John Style –	16d.
John Sherston –	13s. 4d.
John Somerville –	6s. 8d.
William Gilbert –	6s. 8d.
William Heyward –	3s. 4d.

John Lagehache for an agreement made about mazers – 20s.
Laurence Cornhill for false workmanship – 3s. 4d.
Item, for the sale of an apprentice, i.e. John Wallingford, sold to John Thorne – 6s. 8d.

These are those who have entered the livery: p. 86

Henry Goldbeater –	26s. 8d.
John Bisshop the younger –	20s.
Simon Chesterfield –	3s. 4d.
William Gilbert –	3s. 4d.
From John Hilles –	3s. 4d.
John atte Water –	3s. 4d.
Walter Sprynget –	16d.
John FitzHerbert –	3s. 4d.
John Herteshorn –	3s. 4d.

Total receipts: £41 19d.

Sum total: £59 4s. 10d. handed over to the wardens named below i.e. John Standelf, Richard Barton, John Norman and John Knyvesworthe, by Stephen de Thorpe, John Lincoln, William Lincoln and James Buntyng. 1400

It*em*, deliv*er*é en anelx d'or faux *et* stoppés de cop*er*:
En p*ri*mes, un anell*e* fait al maner*e* d'un signet stoppé de cop*er*
It*em*, iii rynge*s* d*em*i round cover*é* d'or *et* stoppé de lato*u*n
It*em*, i anell*e* d'or bon pois*aunt* v s. ové un verr*e*
It*em*, un autr*e* anell*e* cov*er*é d'or, stoppé de plumb, ové un verr*e*
It*em*, un papenyay d'argent pois*aunt* – xii d. ob.[335]
It*em*, un signet de lato*u*n endorr*é*.

1400 Anno p*ri*mo H*enrici* quarti q*uid*libet apprent*icius* solver*e* tenet*ur* xx s.[336]
Fait a remembr*er* q*e* le jo*ur* de Seint Donston l'an du regne n*ost*re s*eignur* le Roy Henri quarte puis le conqueste primer*e,* al general assemblé en lo*ur* sale en Fastres Lane, ordeigné fuist p*ar*entre toutz les hon*ur*ables gentz *et* co*mun*es du dite mestier p*ar* lo*ur* co*mun*e assent q*e* si ascun du dite mestier d'iceo enav*a*nt p*re*igne ascun app*re*ntys, q*e* mesme app*re*ntys serra moustr*é* a les gardeyns de mesme mestier come av*a*nt ces heours ad esté usez, sur peyne de paier le peyne av*a*nt ordeignez, *et* q*e* tantost q'il ad resceu sou*n* app*re*ntis paiera xx s. a sez ditz gardeyns.

1400–01 Ceux sount les nouns des gardeyns eslutz le jo*ur* de Seint Donston l'an du
p. 87 regne le Roy Henri quarte puys le conqueste primer*e* tank a mesme feste l'an de mesme Roy secounde:
Joh*a*n Standelf
Rich*ard* Barto*u*n
Joh*a*n Noreman
Joh*a*n Knyvesworth*e*

col. 1 Ceux sount les nouns d'ap*re*ntys en mesme an:

Joh*a*n Peny app*re*ntys Will*ia*m Fithewe –	xx s.
It*em*, Joh*a*n Caumbrigg*e* app*rentys* Joh*a*n Palyng –	xx s.
Ed*mundu*s Seyntclowe app*rentys* Thome Dodesole –	xx s.
Will*elmu*s atte Welle app*rentys* Joh*a*n Standelf –	xx s.
Ric*ard*us Chircheman app*rentys* Joh*a*n Therne –	xx s.
Ric*ard*us Borne app*r*ent*ys* George Cressy –	xx s.
Joh*anne*s Biker app*r*ent*ys* Joh*ann*is Herteshorn –	xx s.
Ro*bertus*[337] Bekyngh*a*m *et* Rob*ert*us Ferybe app*rentys* Petri Torold –	xl s.
Will*ia*m Castilcary app*rentys* Joh*ann*is Oxenford –	xx s.
Joh*anne*s Buker*e* app*rentys* Steph*en* Mapelesden*e* –	xx s.
Thom*a*s Merfeld app*rentys* Rob*er*ti Lemyng –	xx s.

[335] John Cherry has pointed out the great interest of this item in the list, and that popinjays were popular for a variety of reasons, one of which is that they were part of the insignia of Flemish and English archery fraternities. A fascinating article that studies popinjays in literature, art, sport and ritual is that of Malcolm H. Jones, 'Popinjay, jolly May! Parrot-badges and the Iconography of May in Britain, France and the Netherlands', *Gevonden Voorwerpen. Lost and Found. Opstellen over middeleeuwse archeologie/Essays on Medieval Archaeology for H.J.E. Van Beuningen*, ed. D. Kicken, A.M. Koldeweij, J.R. ter Molen (Rotterdam, 2000), [Rotterdam Papers, vol. 11], pp. 214–29.

[336] This heading is written in the LH margin.

[337] This name has been written above a scored 'Joh*anne*s'.

Item, the following gold rings handed over which were false and plugged with copper:
Firstly, a ring made in the manner of a signet-ring and plugged with copper
Item, 3 semi-circular rings[155] gilded and plugged with latten
Item, 1 ring of good quality gold weighing 5s. with a glass gemstone
Item, another ring gilded, plugged with lead, with a glass gemstone
Item, a silver popinjay weighing 12½d.
Item, a signet ring of gilded latten.

In the year 1 Henry IV [1400], every apprentice to have to pay 20s. 1400
Memorandum that on St Dunstan's Day in the year 1 Henry IV [19 May 1400] at the general assembly in their Hall in Foster Lane, it was ordained by all the honourable people and the commonalty of the said mistery by their common assent that if anyone of the said mistery from henceforth takes on any apprentice, then the same apprentice shall be presented to the wardens of the same mistery, as has been the custom in former times, on pain of paying the penalty previously ordained, and that as soon as he has taken on his apprentice he shall pay 20s. to his said wardens.

These are the names of the wardens elected on St Dunstan's Day in the year 1 Henry IV until the same feastday in the year 2 Henry IV [19 May 1400–19 May 1401]: 1400–01 p. 87
John Standelf
Richard Barton
John Norman
John Knyvesworthe

These are the names of apprentices in the same year: col. 1

John Peny apprentice of William FitzHugh –	20s.
Item, John Cambridge apprentice of John Palyng –	20s.
Edmund Seyntclowe apprentice of Thomas Dodesole –	20s.
William atte Welle apprentice of John Standelf –	20s.
Richard Chircheman apprentice of John Therne –	20s.
Richard Boorne apprentice of George Cressy –	20s.
John Biker apprentice of John Herteshorn –	20s.
Robert Bekyngham and Robert Ferybe, apprentices of Piers Thorold –	40s.
William Castlecary apprentice of John Oxenford –	20s.
John Bukere apprentice of Stephen Maplesdene –	20s.
Thomas Mirfield apprentice of Robert Lemyng –	20s.

[155] These would very probably have been rings to affix to e.g. a girdle, or perhaps some other sort of dress fitting.

Will*elm*us Northewich app*rentys* Joh*ann*is atte Watr*e* – xx s.
Ric*hard* Derby app*rentys* Joh*ann*is Noreman – xx s.
Will*iam* Holcroft app*rentys* Remu*n*d Standelf – xx s.
Walt*er* Will*ia*m app*rentys* Thome Exto*u*n – xx s.
Joh*ann*es Bukto*u*n app*rentys* Joh*ann*is Fraunceys – xx s.
Reginald*us* Camayll*e* app*rentys* Rob*er*ti Halle – xx s.
Joh*ann*es Strete app*rentys* Will*ia*m Downe – xx s.
Walt*er* Prata app*rentys* Joh*ann*is Lincoln*e* – xx s.
Ric*hard* atte Grene app*rentys* Will*elm*i Chalphonte – xx s.
Will*ia*m de Assh*e* app*rentys* Will*elmi* Burgylo*u*n – xx s.
Nich*olas* Bette app*rentys* Henr*ici* Grene – xx s.
col. 2 Joh*ann*es Halle app*rentys* Petri Tounvile – xx s.
Walt*er* Chadesle app*rentys* Joh*an* Halle – xx s.
Will*iam* Titlyngto*u*n app*rentys* Henri Ba*m*me – xx s.
Joh*ann*es More app*rentys* Ed*mund*i Nethersole – xx s.
Joh*ann*es Cressebien app*rentys* Joh*a*n Bernes – xx s.
Thom*as* Caumse app*rentys* Joh*a*n Sonnyng – xx s.
Joh*ann*es Marwe app*rentys* Joh*a*n Knyveswort*he* – xx s.
Thom*as* Flete app*rentys* Rob*er*t Fraunceys – xx s.
Thom*as* Driffeld app*rentys* Joh*ann*is Lincoln*e* – xx s.
Item, de eodem Thom*a*[338] *pro* app*renticio* Will*elm*i Fithewe – xx s.
Joh*ann*es Mabyan app*rentys* Will*ia*m Burgylo*u*n – xx s.
Will*iam* Robyn app*rentys* Thome Popelto*u*n – xx s.
Rob*ertus* Scot app*rentys* Rob*er*t Lemyng – xx s.
Nich*ol*aus Birch*e* app*rentys* Ric*hard* Withihale – xx s.
Joh*ann*es Gadesle app*rentys* Joh*a*n Chestr*e* – xx s.
Joh*ann*es Tiwyn app*rentys* Joh*a*n Lagehach*e* – xx s.
Will*elmus* Wolforde app*rentys* Joh*a*n Halle – xx s.
Ric*hard* Hydyngh*a*m app*rentys* Henr*i* Hochedes *per* vadiu*m*
Joh*ann*es Luk app*rentys* Joh*a*n Martyn *per* vad*ium*

Lowys:
Will*ia*m Bismer*e* quond*am* app*renticius* Joh*annis* Peres[339] – ii s.
Joh*ann*es Foxcote quond*am* [app*renticius*] Joh*annis* Lenam – ii s.
Rob*er*t Heved quond*am* app*renticius* Will*iam* Chalphont*e* – ii s.
Joh*ann*es Parker quond*am* app*renticius* Thome Fyndo*u*n – ii s.
Will*ia*m Willy quond*am* app*renticius* Hug*onis* Wetherby – ii s.

p. 88 P*ur* ceo q*e* Joh*a*n Martyn fuist rebell*e* a ses gardeyns, fuist condempnés a priso*u*n, sur quel le dite Joh*a*n soy mist a g*r*ace *et* p*ar* prier*e* de Thom*as* Exto*u*n, Will*ia*m Lowthe, Joh*a*n Lincoln*e*, Estephe*n* de Thorp, Joh*a*n Bulstrode, Joh*a*n Honte, Will*ia*m Granth*a*m *et* autres hon*ur*ables gentz de mesme mestier fuist remys a mesme Joh*a*n sur condicio*u*n q*e* si le dite Joh*a*n

[338] This Th. Driffield, though an apprentice, must have come from an affluent background, and one may wonder whether he and FitzHugh's apprentice were not perhaps related? Presumably this was not the apprentice named above for FitzHugh but another?

[339] The last four words have been added later though in the same hand; the last two letters of 'Peres' have apparently been deleted.

William Northwich apprentice of John atte Water –	20s.	
Richard Derby apprentice of John Norman –	20s.	
William Holcroft apprentice of Raymund Standelf –	20s.	
Walter William apprentice of Thomas Exton –	20s.	
John Buktoun apprentice of John Fraunceys –	20s.	
Reginald Camaylle apprentice of Robert Halle –	20s.	
John Strete apprentice of William Downe –	20s.	
Walter Prata apprentice of John Lincoln –	20s.	
Richard atte Grene apprentice of William Chalfont –	20s.	
William de Asshe apprentice of William Burgyloun –	20s.	
Nicholas Bette apprentice of Henry Grene –	20s.	
John Halle apprentice of Peter Tounvyle –	20s.	col. 2
Walter Chaddesley apprentice of John Halle –	20s.	
William Titlyngtoun apprentice of Henry Bamme –	20s.	
John More apprentice of Edmund Nethersole –	20s.	
John Cresbien apprentice of John Barnes –	20s.	
Thomas Caumse apprentice of John Sonnyng –	20s.	
John Marwe apprentice of John Knyvesworthe –	20s.	
Thomas Flete apprentice of Robert Fraunceys –	20s.	
Thomas Driffield apprentice of John Lincoln –	20s.	
Item, from the same Thomas for the apprentice of William FitzHugh –	20s.	
John Mablean apprentice of William Burgyloun –	20s.	
William Robyn apprentice of Thomas Poppleton –	20s.	
Robert Scot apprentice of Robert Lemyng –	20s.	
Nicholas Birche apprentice of Richard Withihale –	20s.	
John Gadesle apprentice of John Chester –	20s.	
John Tiwyn apprentice of John Lagehache –	20s.	
William Wolforde apprentice of John Halle –	20s.	
Richard Hydyngham apprentice of Henry Hochedes –	by a pledge	
John Luke apprentice of John Martyn –	by a pledge	

Serving-men:

William Bismere, formerly apprentice of John Piers –	2s.
John Foxcote, formerly [apprentice] of John Lenam –	2s.
Robert Heved, formerly apprentice of William Chalfont –	2s.
John Parker, formerly apprentice of Thomas Findon –	2s.
William Wylly, formerly apprentice of Hugh Wetherby –	2s.

Whereas John Martyn rebelled against his wardens, he was condemned to p. 88
prison, at which the said John submitted himself to judgment and by the entreaty of Thomas Exton, William Louth, John Lincoln, Stephen de Thorp, John Bulstrode, John Honte, William Grantham and other honourable people of the same mistery, this was remitted him on condition that if the said John

d'iceo enav*a*nt soit trové rebell*e* encountr*e* ses gardeyns, paiera al almoign*e* de Seint Donston – C s.

1401 En le jo*ur* de Seint Donston l'an du regne n*ostr*e s*eignur* le Roy [Henri] quarte secounde, ordeigné est q*e* si ascun del mestier d'orfeve*r*ie porte ou maunde ascun chose d'orfeve*r*ie a ascun fe*m*me espousez a ascun ho*m*me d'autr*e* mestier, paiera a chescun foitz q*e* soit trové en defaute vi s. viii d., de quel celuy q*e* prove mesme fait ave*r*a p*ur* so*u*n t*ra*vaill*e* xx d.

1401 Fait a remembr*er* q*e* fuist delive*r*é a Joh*a*n Carbonell*e*, Joh*a*n Coraunt, Will*ia*m Pev*er*e *et* Thom*a*s Dodesole p*ar* Joh*a*n Standelf, Ric*hard* Bart*ou*n, Joh*a*n Knyvesworth*e* – iiii^{xx}xviii li. iii s. xi d.
It*em* de Perys Torold *et* Joh*a*n Halle, renters – ix li. iii s. iii d.

1401–02 A + b p. 33[340] Ceux sount les nouns des Gardeyns eslutz le jo*ur* de Seint Donston l'an du regne le Roy Henri quarte secounde tank a mesme feste l'an du Roy av*a*ntdite tierce:
Joh*a*n Carbonell*e*
Joh*a*n Coraunt
Will*ia*m Pev*er*e
Thom*a*s Dodesole[341]

Costag*es* fait mesme an:
En p*ri*mes, p*ur* soner le g*ra*unt sonayll*e* de Seint Poull*e* – iii s. iiii d.
It*em*, en payn *et* formage a mesme temps – xii d.
It*em*, en s*er*voise a mesme temps – iii s. x d.
It*em*, en cir*e* novell*e* xiiii li. – vii s.
It*em*, p*ur* faç*on* de viell*e* cir*e* – xxxvii li. – xviii d.
It*em*, p*ur* ii tortices pois*ant* x li. – v s.
It*em*, as viii menstrales paié – xvi s.

Ceux sount les nouns d'ap*re*ntys:
Thom*a*s Curteys app*re*ntys de Joh*a*n Frer*e* – xx s.
Thom*a*s Fairhurst app*re*ntys de Jeames Bontyng – xx s.
Mathe*us* Rodeleye app*re*ntys Joh*a*n Bythewatir – xx s.
Edm*undu*s Parker app*re*ntys Will*el*m*us* Fraunceys – xx s.
Joh*a*n Oxendon app*re*ntys Joh*a*n Corbyn – xx s.
Joh*a*n atte Soler app*re*ntys Will*ia*m Kirkeby – xx s.
Thom*a*s Warde app*re*ntys de Rog*er* Brenaston*e* – xx s.
Rob*er*t Chambr*e* app*re*ntys Cristofr*e* Tillesle – xx s.
Joh*a*n Cotiller app*re*ntys Joh*a*n Therme – xx s.
Thom*a*s Lincoln app*re*ntys Henri Ba*m*me – xx s.
Joh*a*n Pateslee app*re*ntys Joh*a*n Osborn*e* – xx s.
Joh*a*n Phelip app*re*ntys Tidrik Van Watir – xx s.
Steven*e* Colle app*re*ntis Joh*a*n Ficherberd – xx s.

340 A new hand starts here.
341 A sixteenth-century hand has written in the LH margin beside these four names: 'John Fr*a*unc*is* beyng Mayr*e* this yer*e*.'

should from this day forward be found guilty of rebellion against his wardens, he shall pay to the alms funds of St Dunstan – 100s.

On St Dunstan's Day in the year 2 Henry IV [19 May 1401] it was ordained that if anyone of the goldsmiths' mistery should take or send any piece of goldsmiths' ware to any woman married to a man of another mistery, he shall pay for each time he is found guilty of the offence 6s. 8d., of which he who may prove this same fact shall have for his labour – 20d. 1401

Memorandum that there was handed over to John Carbonelle, John Coraunt, William Pevere and Thomas Dodesole by John Standelf, Richard Barton, John Knyvesworthe – £98 3s. 11d. 1401
Item, from Piers Thorold and John Halle, renters – £9 3s. 3d.

These are the names of the wardens elected on St Dunstan's Day in the year 2 Henry IV until the same feastday in the year 3 Henry IV [19 May 1401 – 19 May 1402]: 1401–02 A + b p. 33
John Carbonelle
John Coraunt
William Pevere
Thomas Dodesole

Expenditures made the same year:
Firstly, for ringing the great bell of St Paul's – 3s. 4d.
Item, for bread and cheese at the same time – 12d.
Item, for ale at the same time – 3s. 10d.
Item, for 14lb. of new wax – 7s.
Item, for the making-up of 37lb. of old wax – 18d.
Item, for 2 torches weighing 10lb. – 5s.
Item, paid to the 8 minstrels – 16s.

These are the names of apprentices:

Thomas Curteys apprentice of John Frere –	20s.
Thomas Fairhurst apprentice of James Buntyng –	20s.
Matthew Rodeleye apprentice of John atte Water –	20s.
Edmund Parker apprentice of William Fraunceys –	20s.
John Oxendon apprentice of John Corbyn –	20s.
John atte Soler apprentice of William Kirkby –	20s.
Thomas Warde apprentice of Roger Brenaston –	20s.
Robert Chambre apprentice of Christopher Tyldesley –	20s.
John Cotiller apprentice of John Therne –	20s.
Thomas Lincoln apprentice of Henry Bamme –	20s.
John Pattesley apprentice of John Osborne –	20s.
John Philippe apprentice of Tidrik Van Wetter –	20s.
Stephen Colney apprentice of John FitzHerbert –	20s.

Will*iam* Brayles app*re*ntys Rob*er*t Brynle – xx s.
Edward Gaver*e* app*re*ntys Joh*a*n Lagehach*e* – xx s.
Rob*er*t Pecche app*re*ntys de Rich*ard* George – xx s.
Rob*er*t Stanford app*re*ntys Rog*er* Cryngelford – xx s.
Joh*a*n Dekne app*re*ntys de Rob*er*t Brou*n* – xx s.
Thom*as* Essex app*re*ntys Barth*olom*eu Billyngdon – xx s.
p. 34 Joh*a*n Ednoye app*re*ntys de Will*ia*m Downe – xx s.
Will*ia*m Ryver*e* app*re*ntys de Joh*a*n Bussh*e* – xx s.
Henri Seber*e* app*re*ntys de Joh*a*n Lenh*a*m – xx s.
Joh*a*n Cook app*re*ntys Joh*a*n Sonnyng – xx s.
Joh*a*n Braunston*e*, Guy Doser app*re*ntys Will*ia*m Forde – xx s.[342]
Joh*a*n Kebil app*re*ntys de Rich*ard* Burton – xx s.
Joh*a*n Turnell*e* app*re*ntys Thom*as* Dodesole – xx s.
Joh*a*n Edward app*re*ntys Will*ia*m Edward – xx s.

Lowys p*ar* mesme an:[343]
Ric*hard* Hayles jadys app*re*ntys Will*ia*m Burdeyne – jur*é*
Joh*a*n Northov*er*e jadys app*re*ntys Will*ia*m Randolf – jur*é*
Joh*a*n Warde jadys app*re*ntys Will*ia*m Lincoln*e* – jur*é*
Thom*as* Noreys jadys app*re*ntys Steven*e* Mapelesden*e* – jur*é*
Remu*n*d Chambr*e* jadys app*re*ntys Joh*a*n Fraunceys – jur*é*
Rog*er* Peraund jadys app*re*ntys Joh*a*n Bulstrode – jur*é*
Ric*hard* Trewyn jadys app*re*ntys George Cressy – jur*é*
Ric*hard* Litle jadys app*re*ntys Joh*a*n Welbo*ur*ne – jur*é*
Will*iam* Edward jadys app*re*ntys Joh*a*n Beston*e* – jur*é*
Ric*hard* Meriot jadys app*re*ntys Joh*a*n Lagehache – jur*é*
Ric*hard* Delamar*e* jadys app*re*ntys Joh*a*n Blakeden*e* – jur*é*
Will*iam* Bette jadys app*re*ntys Remu*n*d Standelf – jur*é*
Joh*a*n Gofair jadys app*re*ntys Joh*a*n Cheyh*a*m – jur*é*
Will*iam* White jadys app*re*ntis Joh*a*n White – jur*é*
Joh*a*n Picard jadys app*re*nt*y*s Joh*a*n Forster – jur*é*
Ric*hard* West jadys app*re*nt*ys* Saleman Oxeney – jur*é*
Henri Goldsmyth jadys app*rentys* Joh*a*n Lincoln*e* – jur*é*
Will*ia*m Faunt [jadys] app*re*ntys de mesme Joh*a*n – jur*é*
Joh*a*n Watervile [jadys] app*re*ntys Joh*a*n Cheyh*a*m – jur*é*

1402–03 Ceux sount les nouns dé Gardeyns eslutz le jo*ur* de Seint Donston l'an du
A + a p. 89 regne le Roy Henri quarte puys le conqueste tierce tank a mesme feste l'an de mesme Roy quarte:
Will*ia*m Lowthe
Joh*a*n Blakeden*e*
Cristofr*e* Tildesle
Will*ia*m Fraunceys

Despens*es* fait p*ar* mesmes gardeyns:
En p*ri*mes, p*ur* soner les sonaill*es* de Seint Poull*es* – iii s. iiii d.[344]

342 One presumes this figure must be incorrect and a scribal error.

343 No sums of money are indicated but one must presume that each serving-man listed paid the usual 2s. for his exit from apprenticeship terms.

344 This is the last mention of expenses paid out for bell-ringing at St Paul's. It may well be that the

William Brayles apprentice of Robert Brinle –	20s.	
Edward Gavere apprentice of John Lagehache –	20s.	
Robert Pecche apprentice of Richard George –	20s.	
Robert Stanford apprentice of Roger Cringleford –	20s.	
John Dekne apprentice of Robert Broun –	20s.	
Thomas Essex apprentice of Bartholomew Billington –	20s.	
John Ednoye apprentice of William Downe –	20s.	p. 34
William Ryvere apprentice of John Busshe –	20s.	
Henry Seburghe apprentice of John Lenham –	20s.	
John Cook apprentice of John Sonnyng –	20s.	
John Braunstone, Guy Doser, apprentices of William Forde –	20s.	
John Kebbell apprentice of Richard Burton –	20s.	
John Turnelle apprentice of Thomas Dodesole –	20s.	
John Edward apprentice of William Edward –	20s.	

Serving-men in the same year:

Richard Hayles, formerly apprentice of William Burdeyn –	sworn
John Northover, formerly apprentice of William Randolph –	sworn
John Warde, formerly apprentice of William Lincoln –	sworn
Thomas Noreys, formerly apprentice of Stephen Maplesdene –	sworn
Raymund Chambre, formerly apprentice of John Fraunceys –	sworn
Roger Peraund, formerly apprentice of John Bulstrode –	sworn
Richard Trewyn, formerly apprentice of George Cressy –	sworn
Richard Litle, formerly apprentice of John Welbourne –	sworn
William Edward, formerly apprentice of John Bestone –	sworn
Richard Mariot, formerly apprentice of John Lagehache –	sworn
Richard de la Mare, formerly apprentice of John Blakedene –	sworn
William Bette, formerly apprentice of Raymund Standelf –	sworn
John Gofair, formerly apprentice of John Cheyham –	sworn
William White, formerly apprentice of John White –	sworn
John Picard, formerly apprentice of John Forster –	sworn
Richard West, formerly apprentice of Solomon Oxney –	sworn
Henry Goldsmith, formerly apprentice of John Lincoln –	sworn
William Faunt, [formerly] apprentice of the same John –	sworn
John Watevile, [formerly] apprentice of John Cheyham –	sworn

These are the names of the wardens elected on St Dunstan's Day in the year 3 Henry IV until the same feastday in the year 4 Henry IV [19 May 1402 – 19 May 1403]: 1402–03 A + a p. 89

William Louth
John Blakedene
Christopher Tyldesley
William Frauncеys

Expenditures made by the same wardens:
Firstly, for ringing the bells of St Paul's – 3s. 4d.

It*em*, en payn *et* formage – xii d.
It*em*, en s*er*voise a mesme temps – iii s. vi d. *et* portage i d.
It*em*, p*ur* fesur*e* de xli li. – xx ob.
It*em*, p*ur* ii torches pois*aunt* xii li. – vi s. iiii d.
It*em*, paié as menstral*les* – x s.

Ceux sount les nouns d'ap*re*ntys:

Joh*a*n Launden*e* app*rentys* Joh*a*n Lincoln*e* –	xx s.
Will*iam* Longe app*rentys* Will*iam* Adys –	xx s.
Joh*a*n Per*ou*n app*rentys* Rob*er*t Howys –	xx s.
Will*iam* Bodenh*am* app*rentys* Thome Langt*ou*n –	xx s.
Joh*a*n Gredele app*rentys* Joh*a*n Mapelesden*e* –	xx s.
Ric*hard* Chaumbr*e* app*rentys* Remu*n*d Chaumbr*e* –	xx s.
Joh*a*n Horwell*e* app*rentys* Joh*a*n Br*ou*n –	xx s.
Joh*a*n Crowe app*rentys* Thom*a*s Rokell*e* –	xx s.
Dru Bet*ou*n app*rentys* Joh*a*n Somervile –	xx s.
Ric*hard* Ryecroft app*rentys* Joh*a*n Noreman –	xx s.
Ric*hard* Bot*ou*n app*rentys* Rob*er*t Serle –	xx s.
Joh*a*n Prentys app*rentys* Thom*a*s Lamport –	xx s.
Thom*a*s Stemen*e* app*rentys* Thom*a*s Mounde –	xx s.
Joh*a*n Pecok app*rentys* Will*iam* Horsman –	xx s.
Thom*a*s Wedoun[345] app*rentys* Joh*a*n Stoke –	xx s.
Joh*a*n Bury app*rentys* Andrew Stameldene –	xx s.
Nich*ol*aus Claver app*rentys* Joh*a*n Lut*ou*n –	xx s.
Will*iam* Bot*ou*n app*rentys* Henri Ba*m*me –	xx s.
Reginald*us* Launde app*rentys* Joh*a*n Blakeden*e* –	xx s.
Thom*a*s Wakforde app*rentys* Thom*a*s Ext*ou*n –	xx s.

Lowys:[346]
Joh*a*n Fynegod jadys app*rentys* Thom*a*s Pant*ou*n
Joh*a*n Ert*ou*n jadys app*rentys* Thome Bygood

p. 90 Fait a remembr*er* q*e* p*ur* ceo q*e* un Will*iam* Wilby fuist trové en defaute dev*a*nt ces gardeyns, ordeigné est q*e* si desoremés soit trové en tiell*e* defaute paiera al almoign*e* de Seint Donston C s.,
– *et* p*ur* quel*le* Joh*a*n Knyvesworth*e* est devenuz plegg*e*.

1402 It*em*, p*ur* ceo q*e* le xiie jo*ur* de Jun*e* l'an du regne le Roy Henri quarte puisse le conqueste tierce, Joh*a*n Pecche fuist trové en defaulte en eov*er*aign*e* d'argent *et* d'iceo fuist atteynt, adjugé est *et* ordeyné q*e* si mesme Joh*a*n disoremés soit

bells continued to be rung on St Dunstan's day or its eve at the costs of the Goldsmiths' Mistery, and that changes in record-keeping mean that we have no further records. However, Dr Christopher Wilson has pointed out that shortly after this date, in 1405–06, the bells were all recast, four huge new bells being made for the campanile, and the old bells becoming just 'old metal'. It could be that a break in continuity resultant for the Goldsmiths led to a discontinuance of the custom. See Introduction pp. xxxv–xxxvi.

345 There is an interlinear addition here: ?'l*er*et'?

346 No sums of money are listed against the following names.

Item, for bread and cheese – 12d.
Item, for ale at the same time – 3s. 6d. and porterage 1d.
Item, for the making-up of 41 lbs. [of wax into candles] – 20½d.
Item, for 2 torches weighing 12 lbs. – 6s. 4d.
Item, paid to the minstrels – 10s.

These are the names of apprentices:

John Laundene apprentice of John Lincoln –	20s.
William Longe apprentice of William Adys –	20s.
John Peroun apprentice of Robert Howes –	20s.
William Bodenham apprentice of Thomas Langton –	20s.
John Gredele apprentice of John Maplesdene –	20s.
Richard Chaumbre apprentice of Raymund Chaumbre –	20s.
John Orwell apprentice of John Broun –	20s.
John Crowe apprentice of Thomas Rokelle –	20s.
Drew Bethun apprentice of John Somerville –	20s.
Richard Ryecroft apprentice of John Norman –	20s.
Richard Botoun apprentice of Robert Serle –	20s.
John Prentys apprentice of Thomas Lamport –	20s.
Thomas Stemene apprentice of Thomas Mound –	20s.
John Peacock apprentice of William Horsman –	20s.
Thomas Weedon apprentice of John Stoke –	20s.
John Bury apprentice of Andrew Stameldene –	20s.
Nicholas Claver apprentice of John Luton –	20s.
William Botoun apprentice of Henry Bamme –	20s.
Reginald Launde apprentice of John Blakedene –	20s.
Thomas Wakforde apprentice of Thomas Exton –	20s.

Serving-men:
John Fynegod, formerly apprentice of Thomas Panton
John Ireton, formerly apprentice of Thomas Bygod

Memorandum that whereas a certain William Wilby was found guilty before his p. 90
wardens of an offence, it was ordered that if he should henceforth be found guilty of such an offence he shall pay to the alms funds of St Dunstan – 100s.
– and for this John Knyvesworthe has stood surety.

Item, whereas on 12 June 3 Henry IV [1402] John Pecche was found guilty of 1402
faulty workmanship of silver and was convicted of this, it was judged and ordered that if the same John should from henceforth be found at fault and if

trové en defaute *et* ne eov*er*e argent bon *et* loiall*e* come l'esterlyng *et* l'or tochant le allay de .v., q*e* paiera al almoign*e* de Seint Donston C s.
– *et* p*ur* quel*le* Will*ia*m Horsman est plegg*e*.

1400–03 It*em*, p*ur* ceo q*e* Joh*a*n Scherston revyla Esteph*e*n de Thorp en temps q*e* fuist gardeyn, adjugé est q*e* si le dite Joh*a*n disoreenav[*a*]nt revyle ou desclaundr*e* le dite Esteph*e*n ou ascun autr*e* gardeyn q*e* serra en temps avenir, paiera al almoign*e* de Seint Donston un pipe de vyn.

1402–03 It*em* p*ur* ceo q*e* Joh*a*n Bussh*e* revyla *et* disclaundra Joh*a*n Flete, orfev*er*e de Loundres, ordeigné est q*e* si mesme Joh*a*n Bussh*e* desoreenav*a*nt revile ou desclaundre le av*a*ntdite Joh*a*n Flete q*e* puist estre provez p*ar* loialx gentz, il paier*a* al almoign*e* de Seint Donston C s.

Et en l'autr*e* p*ar*tie p*ur* ceo q*e* Joh*a*n Flete av*a*ntdite revyla *et* disclaundra le av*a*ntdite Joh*a*n Bussh*e*, ordeigné est q*e* si le av*a*ntdite Joh*a*n Flete disor*e*enav*a*nt r*e*vile ou disclaundr*e* le dite Joh*a*n Bussh*e* q*e* puist estr*e* p*ro*vez p*ar* loialx gentz, il paiera al almoigne de Seint Donston C s.

It*em*, p*ur* ceo q*e* Henri Wortesburgh*e*, Duchman, est trové en defaute de pois*es* fauxes, ascuns trop legiers *et* ascun[s] trop pois*auntes*, en desceit del people du roialme, ordeigné est q*e* si desor*e*enav*a*nt soit trové en mesme defaute paiera al almoign*e* de Seint Donston xx li., et si soit trové en defaute en eov*er*er d'or *et* d'argent paiera mesme so*m*me, p*ur* quel*le* est obligez p*ar* un obligaci*ou*n.

It*em*, p*ur* ceo q*e* Thom*a*s Cove trespasssa v*er*s Joh*a*n Flete, orfev*er*e, le eisné, fuist juggé p*ar* Will*ia*m Lowth*e*, Joh*a*n Blakeden*e*, Will*ia*m Fraunceys *et* Cristophr*e* Tilleslee q*e* paiera a mesme Joh*a*n xl li.
– p*ur* queux Andreu Stamelden*e*, Joh*a*n Halle le puisné *et* Will*ia*m Adys sount plegg*es* *et* p*ur* quel*le* so*m*me le dite Thom*a*s est obligez as ditz Andreu, Joh*a*n Halle *et* Will*ia*m p*ur* eux garder hors damage, le quel*le* agard fuist fait le xxv jo*ur* d'aprill*e*.

It*em*, p*ur* ceo q*e* Edmond Page fuist trové en defaute en ix barres[347] . . .

1403 Fait a remembr*er* q*e* le xxiie jo*ur* de March*e* l'an du regne le Roy Henr*i* quarte
p. 91 puys le conqueste quarte, accordé fuist p*ar* toutz les hon*ur*ables gentz ap*rés* escriptz, c'est assavoir Drew Barentyn, Joh*a*n Fraunceys, Joh*a*n Forster, Henri Ba*m*me,[348] Thom*a*s Exto*u*n, Thom*a*s Hay, Joh*a*n Honte, Ric*hard* Barto*u*n, Joh*a*n Noreman, Remu*n*d Standelf, Will*ia*m Fithewe, Joh*a*n Standelf, Will*ia*m Granth*a*m, Joh*a*n Lyncoln*e*, Steph*e*n de Thorp, Will*ia*m Downe, Joh*a*n Frenssh*e*, Joh*a*n Luto*u*n, Andrew Stamelden*e*, Joh*a*n Bulstrode, Will*ia*m Lowthe, Joh*a*n Blakeden*e*, Cristofr*e* Tildesle *et* Will*ia*m Fraunceys, q*e* Thom*a*s

[347] The text breaks off here (plenty of blank space remains on the page).
[348] This man's name has been added, in the same hand and at the same time for the surname, the first name having been added slightly later.

he does not work silver to the good legal standard of sterling and gold of the assay of the fifth,[156] that he shall pay to the alms of St Dunstan – 100s.
– and for this William Horsman has stood surety.

Item, whereas John Sherston insulted Stephen de Thorp during the time when 1400–03
he was warden, it was judged that if the said John should henceforth insult or slander the said Stephen or any other future warden, he shall pay to the alms funds of St Dunstan a pipe of wine.

Item, whereas John Busshe insulted and slandered John Flete, goldsmith of 1402–03
London, it was ordered that if the same John Busshe should from henceforth insult or slander the aforesaid John Flete and that this can be proved by trustworthy people, he shall pay to the alms funds of St Dunstan – 100 s.

And on the other hand, whereas the aforesaid John Flete insulted and slandered the aforesaid John Busshe, it was ordered that if the aforesaid John Flete should from henceforth insult or slander the said John Busshe, and that this can be proved by trustworthy people, he shall pay to the alms funds of St Dunstan – 100s.

Item, whereas Henry Wortesburgh, 'Dutchman', was found guilty of the offence of having false weights, some too light and some too heavy, to the deceit of the people of the kingdom, it was ordered that if he should from henceforward be found guilty of the same offence, he shall pay to the alms funds of St Dunstan £20, and if he should be found guilty of any offence in the working of gold and silver, he shall pay the same sum, for the which he is bound by an obligatory deed.

Item, whereas Thomas Cove offended against John Flete the elder, goldsmith, it was judged by William Louth, John Blakedene, William Fraunceys and Christopher Tyldesley that he should pay to the same John £40
– for the which Andrew Stameldene, John Halle the younger and William Adys are sureties, and for the which sum the said Thomas is bound to the said Andrew, John Halle and William, in order to prevent their suffering any loss, the which judgment was made on 25 April.

Item, whereas Edmund Page was found guilty of an offence over 9 bars . . .

Memorandum that on 22 March of the year 4 Henry IV [1403] it was agreed 1403
by all the honourable people whose names follow, i.e. Drew Barantyn, John p. 91
Fraunceys, John Forster, Henry Bamme, Thomas Exton, Thomas Hay, John Honte, Richard Barton, John Norman, Raymund Standelf, William FitzHugh, John Standelf, William Grantham, John Lincoln, Stephen de Thorp, William Downe, John Frenshe, John Luton, Andrew Stameldene, John Bulstrode, William Louth, John Blakedene, Christopher Tyldesley and William Fraunceys, that Thomas Polle shall be paid £10 annually on the

[156] i.e. 19.2 carats (the Touch of Paris); this standard was revised in 1478. See Reddaway and Walker, p. 233, note 1.

Polle serra paié annuelement al feste de Seint Donston x li. tank a temps q*e* soit paiez de iiii^{xx} li. a luy duez p*ur* rep*ar*aciou*n* del rente d'Orfev*er*ie.

1403–04 Fait a remembr*er* q*e* Edmu*n*d Nethersole fuist jurré deva*n*t Will*ia*m Granth*a*m, Saleman Oxeneye, Rob*er*t Halle *et* Thom*a*s Senycle, l'an du r*egne le* R*oi* Henri quarte quinte.

Fait a remembr*er* q*e* la acompt*e* fait p*ar*entr*e* Thom*a*s Polle d'un p*ar*tie *et* Henri
1407 Ba*m*me, Joh*a*n Blakeden*e*, Joh*a*n Bernes *et* Thom*a*s Popeltoun d'autre p*ar*tie le xiiii^{e} jo*ur* de Novembr*e* l'an du r*egne le* R*oi* Henri quarte puys le conqueste ix^{e} issint q*e* a mesme jo*ur* fuist duez au dite Thom*a*s Polle lvi li. vi s. viii d, de sa endent*ur*e a luy fait del tenement Thom*a*s Langeport.[349]

1403–04 Ceux sount les nouns des gardeins eslutz le jo*ur* de Seint Dunston l'an du regne le
p. 92 Roy Henr*i* quarte puys le conqueste quarte tank a mesme feste l'an ensuant:
Will*ia*m Granth*a*m
Saleman Oxeneye
Rob*er*t Halle
Thom*a*s Senycle

App[*re*]ntys resceu mesme an:[350]

A + b Fait a remembr*er* q*e* p*ar* assent *et* bone examinaciou*n* de les gardeyns av*a*ntditz
p. 37[351] Joh*a*n Standelf, Joh*a*n Halle le eisné, Will*ia*m Fraunceys, le xxiii jo*ur* de Maii l'an du r*egne le* r*oi* Henri quarte puys le conqueste quarte, Joh*a*n Cokfelde[352] fitz a Geffrey Cokfelde, jadys groc*er et* citezein de Loundres, fuist resceu p*ur* estr*e* app*re*ntys a Joh*a*n Hilles p*ur* luy servir en man*er*e d'ap*re*ntys p*ar* t*er*me de x ans, paié – xx s.

Fait a remembr*er* q*e* le xvi jo*ur* de Jull*et* p*ar* bone examinaciou*n* de les gardeyns av*a*ntditz Joh*a*n Gybon del counté de Caumbrigg*e* fuist resceu p*ur* estr*e* app*re*ntys ové Thom*a*s Welles p*ur* luy servir en maner*e* d'ap*re*ntys p*ar* t*er*me x ans, paia – xx s.

It*em*, Will*ia*m Sawyer le vi jo*ur* d'Augst l'an du regne le Roy Henri quarte fuist resceu d'estr*e* app*re*ntys a Joh*a*n Tewkesbury p*ur* luy servir del feste de Seint Piet*er* ad vincul*a* tank al fyn xiii ans – paia xx s.

It*em*, Adam Fraunceys fitz a Will*ia*m Fraunceys, orfev*er*e, l'an du Roy av*a*ntdite fuist resceu d'estr*e* app*re*ntys a Joh*a*n Bulstrode p*ur* luy servir a t*er*me de x ans – paia xx s.

349 This paragraph has clearly been added later, but has been written by the same scribe.

350 Book A + a has at this point a normally laid-out list of apprentices, but we have here substituted for this the entries on pp. 37–38 of Book A + b, which contain significant further information. The first entry for John Cokefield, for example, in Book A + a has no more than: 'Joh*a*n Cokefelde app*re*ntys Joh*a*n Hilles – xx s.' Spelling variants and further information from Book A + a have been given in footnotes below.

351 Several different hands have been at work on this page, each writing one paragraph except that the same hand has written the paragraphs concerning William Sawyer, Adam Fraunceys, John Fraunceys and William Lolham.

352 A + a: Cokefelde.

feastday of St Dunstan until the time when he shall have been repaid the £80 due to him for the repairs to the tenement of the Goldsmiths' Mistery.

Memorandum that Edmund Nethersole was sworn before William Grantham, Solomon Oxney, Robert Halle and Thomas Senycle in the year 5 Henry IV [1403–04]. 1403–04

Memorandum that account was made between Thomas Polle on the one hand and Henry Bamme, John Blakedene, John Barnes and Thomas Poppleton on the other, on 14 November 1407, thus that on the same day £56 6s. 8d. was due to Thomas Polle from his indenture made with him regarding the tenement of Thomas Langport.[157] 1407

These are the names of the wardens elected on St Dunstan's Day in the year 4 Henry IV [19 May 1403] until the same feastday the next year: 1403–04 p. 92

William Grantham
Solomon Oxney
Robert Halle
Thomas Senycle

Apprentices admitted the same year:

Memorandum that by the assent and [after] careful examination of the aforesaid wardens and of John Standelf, John Halle the elder, William Fraunceys, on 23 May 1403 John Cockfield, son of Geoffrey Cockfield, formerly a grocer and citizen of London, was admitted to be an apprentice of John Hilles, to serve him as an apprentice for a term of 10 years – paid – 20s. A + b p. 37

Memorandum that on 16 July after careful examination by the aforesaid wardens, John Gybon of the County of Cambridge was admitted to be an apprentice with Thomas Welles, to serve him as an apprentice for a term of 10 years – he paid – 20s.

Item, on 6 August 1403 William Sawyer was admitted to be an apprentice of John Tewkesbury to serve him from the feastday of St Peter ad vincula until the end [of his term of] 13 years – he paid 20s.

Item, Adam Fraunceys, son of William Fraunceys, goldsmith, was admitted in the aforesaid year to be an apprentice of John Bulstrode to serve him for a term of 10 years – he paid 20s.

[157] This is probably Thomas Lamport. See Name Index.

It*em*, Joh*a*n Fraunceys fitz a mesme Will*ia*m Fraunceys fuist resceu p*ur* estr*e* app*re*ntys a Will*ia*m Lyncoln*e* p*ur* s*er*vir a t*er*me – x ans – paia xx s.

It*em*, Will*ia*m Lolh*a*m[353] fuist resceu p*ur* estr*e* app*re*ntys a Joh*a*n Therm*e*[354] p*ur* luy servir del feste de Toutz Seintz l'an quinte tank au fyn x ans.

Fait a remembr*er* q*e* Joh*a*n Horforde[355] est devenuz app*re*ntys a Joh*a*n Wenne p*ur* luy s*er*vir come app*re*ntys – paia xx s.

p. 38[356] It*em*, Joh*a*n Lyver est devenuz app*re*ntys de Joh*a*n Corby de luy servir come app*re*ntys del feste de Pask l'an du Roy Henri [quarte] quinte tank a fyn xii ans – xx s.

It*em*, Nicholas Ryecroft fuist vendus p*ar* Thom*as* Noreys a Rich*ard* Withihale – paia xx s.[357]
It*em*, Joh*a*n Catesby est devenuz app*re*ntys a Saleman Oxeneye[358]
It*em*, Will*ia*m atte Nye[359] est devenuz app*re*ntys a Joh*a*n Lagehach *et* paia xx s.
It*em*, Joh*a*n Dene est devenuz app*re*ntys a Rob*er*t Beteigne p*ur* luy s*er*vir a t*er*me de ix ans *et* ad paié – xx s.
It*em*, Will*elmu*s Aleyn est devenuz app*re*ntys a Edmu*n*d Nethersole p*ur* luy servir a t*er*me de xii ans.[360]

A + a p. 92 Lowys en mesme an:

Will*elmu*s Bolverge jadys app*rentys* Joh*an* Bulstrode –	ii s. – jur*é*[361]
Joh*a*n Naylond jadys app*rentys* Robert Beteyne –	ii s. – jur*é*
Thom*as* South*e* jadys app*rentys* Thom*as* Extou*n* –	ii s. – jur*é*
Will*elmu*s Parys jadys app*rentys* Rich*ard* George –	ii s. – jur*é*

p. 93 Defautes:[362]
Thom*as* Langetou*n* p*ur* ceo q'il mist [en eoveraigne] un vadlet Duchman q*e* fuist sou*n* cook, il fuist amercié en xx s. *et* se mist en g*ra*ce *et* paia – vi s. viii d.[363]

353 A + a: Lelom.
354 A + a: Therne.
355 A + a: Hertforde.
356 A new hand starts here.
357 A + a: LH marginal note: jadys app*rentys* Joh*a*n Noreman.
358 No sum is given as paid by this man.
359 A + a: Will*elmus* atte Neye quond*am* app*renticius* Joh*a*n (Lagehach), / iam app*renticius* Joh*annis* Lagehach – xx s.' The name 'Lagehach', bracketed here, has been scored out, as has the figure of 20s. beside it, and there has clearly been some confusion; one might assume that W. atte N. was formerly the apprentice of another John (but no record exists of this).
360 No sum is given as paid by this man.
361 The 'jur*é*' against this name and the next appears to have been written in somewhat later.
362 Book A + b has a long list of offences for this year, some of which entries are parallel to those in A + a, some are different. The entries from A + b are presented here below those from A + a and footnotes indicate those entries that have a parallel.
363 See also below.

Item, John Fraunceys, son of the same William Fraunceys, was admitted to be an apprentice of William Lincoln to serve a term of 10 years – he paid 20s.

Item, William Lelom was admitted to be an apprentice of John Therne to serve him from the feast of All Saints Day in the year 5 [Henry IV] [1 November 1403] until the end [of a term of] 10 years.

Memorandum that John Hertford has become an apprentice of John Wenne to serve him as an apprentice – he paid 20s.

Item, John Lyver has become the apprentice of John Corby to serve him as p. 38
an apprentice from the feast of Easter in the year 5 Henry IV [30 March 1404] until the end [of a term of] 12 years – 20s.

Item, Nicholas Ryecroft was sold by Thomas Noreys to Richard Withihale – he paid 20s.[158]
Item, John Catesby has become an apprentice of Solomon Oxney.
Item, William atte Neye has become an apprentice of John Lagehache and paid 20s.
Item, John Dene has become an apprentice of Robert Beteigne to serve him for a term of 9 years and he has paid 20s.
Item, William Aleyn has become an apprentice of Edmund Nethersole to serve him for a term of 12 years.

Serving-men the same year: A + a p. 92
William Belverge, formerly apprentice of John Bulstrode – 2s. – sworn
John Nayland, formerly apprentice of Robert Beteigne – 2s. – sworn
Thomas South, formerly apprentice of Thomas Exton – 2s. – sworn
William Paris, formerly apprentice of Richard George – 2s. – sworn

Offences: p. 93
Thomas Langton, whereas he set to work [i.e. to goldsmiths' work] a 'Dutch' lad who was his cook, he was amerced in the sum of 20s. and he submitted himself to judgment and paid 6s. 8d.

[158] The marginal note in Book A + a says that he was formerly the apprentice of John Norman.

It*em*, Joh*a*n Frer*e* p*ur* ceo q*e* fuist trové en defaute de sez pois*es*, c'est assavoir*e* de ii piles l'un fuist trop poisaunt l'autre trop leggier encountr*e* l'ordeignance ent fait, paia p*ar* gr*a*ce – vi s. viii d.[364]

It*em*, Joh*a*n Scherston p*ur* ceo q'il ad ov*er*tement disclaundrés un Will*ia*m Hert de latrocinie, *et* puis ad desclaundré les gardoyns q'ils furent mayntenou*rs* *et* susteignou*rs* de mesme felou*n*, il paia p*ar* prier*e* des bones gentz – vi s. viii d. Et si desoreenav*a*nt soit trové en tiel defaute paiera – C s.[365]

It*em*, p*ur* ceo q*e* Philip Castill*e* vendust a un Thom*as*, servant de Henri Grene, orfev*er*e, un anell*e* d'or p*ur* iiii s. *et* i d. *et* vendust mesme anell*e* a un des customers du dite Henri,[366] au quel custom*er* le dite Phelip eov*er*tement dist q*e* le anell*e* ne costa pluys q*e* iiii s. et i d. en disclaundr*e* du dite Thom*as* *et* p*er*de de sou*n* custom*er*, p*ur* quel paia – vi s. viii d.[367]

It*em*, p*ur* ceo q*e* Will*ia*m Bismer*e* vendust certeins choses d'orfev*er*ie encountr*e* l'estatut ent ordeignez, il paia xiii s. iiii d., des q*ue*ux furent paiez a celuy q*e* aspia – vi s. viii d.[368]

It*e*m, Joh*a*n Corby vendust sou*n* app*re*ntys saunz licence des sez gardeins, paia – vi s. viii d.[369]

It*em*, p*ur* ceo q*e* Joh*a*n Tewkesbury vendust sou*n* app*re*ntys saunz licence de sez gardeyns al p*re*ntys mesmes, paia[370]

It*em*, p*ur* ceo q*e* Thom*as* Dodesole vendust sou*n* app*re*ntys a luy mesmes paia[371]

It*em*, p*ur* ceo q*e* Joh*a*n Honte vendust certeins choses d'orfev*er*ie encountr*e* l'estatut *et* ordeignance a deux foitz[372]

[364] See also below.
[365] See also below.
[366] See also below, and note that the account in Book A + b is both fuller and gives a slightly different price paid.
[367] See also below.
[368] See also below. The ordinance referred to here and in various other offences below is probably that of 1401: see A + a, p. 88 above; the ordinances entered on p. 41 of A + a also contain rules about to whom objects may be sold etc., and this is referred to later on p. 51 of Bk A + b below. However, the amount of the fines paid does not correspond with any recorded ruling and this is worth noting.
[369] See also below. This entry has been picked out by a LH marginal note: 'Corby'.
[370] See also below. No sum is given. Note that the other sums given on this page appear to have been written in slightly after the record of the reason for the fines.
[371] No sum given.
[372] See also below. No sum given.

Item, John Frere, whereas he was found at fault with his weights, i.e. of two piles[159] one was too heavy and the other too light, in contravention of the ordinance made about this, he paid after judgment given – 6s. 8d.

Item, John Sherston, whereas he had openly slandered one William Hert, accusing him of theft, and then he slandered the wardens, accusing them of being maintainers[160] and supporters of the same felon, he paid following the advice of the goodmen – 6s. 8d.
And if he should henceforth be found guilty of such an offence, he shall pay – 100s.

Item, whereas Philip Castille sold to one Thomas, the servant of Henry Grene, goldsmith, a gold ring for 4s. 1d. and he sold the same ring to one of the customers of the said Henry, to the which customer the said Philip openly said that the ring did not cost more than 4s. 1d., to the discredit of the said Thomas and the loss of his customer, for the which reason he paid – 6s. 8d.

Item, whereas William Bismere sold certain objects of goldsmithry against the statute ordained about this, he paid 13s. 4d., of which was paid to the man who caught him out – 6s. 8d.

Item, John Corby sold his apprentice without the permission of his wardens, he paid 6s. 8d.

Item, whereas John Tewkesbury sold his apprentice without the permission of his wardens to the apprentice himself,[161] he paid

Item, whereas Thomas Dodesole sold his apprentice to [the apprentice] himself, he paid

Item, whereas John Honte twice sold certain objects of goldsmithry against the statute and ordinance

[159] i.e. a pile = 'a series of weights fitting one within or upon another, so as to form a solid cone or other figure' (*OED*).
[160] This word often had a pejorative sense at this time, and may well here carry the legal meaning of 'one who unlawfully supports a suit in which he is not concerned' (*OED*).
[161] i.e. the apprentice bought out the remaining portion of his term of apprenticeship.

It*em*, p*ur* ceo q*e* Joh*a*n Lagehach*e* enforma un enfaunt male *et* un enfaunt femele en le mestier d'orfev*er*ie *et* ne furent app*r*entys, il fuist jugez de paier C s., de quel paia – xx s. – *et* app*r*esta al mestier viii li.[373]
Et s'il desor*e* soit trové en defaute paiera – x li.

It*em*, Albright de Aldernak enforma un page Duch*e* encountr*e* sou*n* serement, il fuist jugé de paier C s. p[374]

It*em*, p*ur* ceo q*e* Rich*ard* Bartou*n* fuist trové en mesme defaute en vende[375]

It*em*, p*ur* ceo q*e* Will*ia*m Donne fuist trové en defaute q'il vendust encountr*e* l'ordeignance[376]

1403 Defautes

A + b p. 39 En p*ri*mes, p*ur* ceo q*e* Joh*a*n Panter, orfev*er*e, le xxv jo*ur* de Maii l'an du regne le Roy Henr*i* quarte puys le conqueste quarte, [fuist trové en defaute][377] en esquilers fait p*ar* mesme Joh*a*n, les q*ue*ux sount defectif, p*ur* quel il se mist en g*ra*ce de ses gardeyns *et* fuist condempnés de paier ii s., les q*ue*ux furont remys sur condiciou*n* q*e* si desoremés soit trové en defaute paiera – vi s. viii d. sauns remissiou*n*.

It*em*, p*ur* ceo q*e* Joh*a*n Newelyn le xxvii jo*ur* de Maii l'an du roi av*a*ntdite quarte, fuist trové en defaute de barres fait a un seynt*ur*e, de soudur*e* al fifthe, p*ur* quel il se mist en g*ra*ce de sez gardeyns *et* fuist condempné en ii s., q*ue*ux furent remys sur condiciou*n* q*e* si desormés soit trové en defaute paiera vi s. viii d. *et* les ii s. av*a*ntditz, *et* est jurrez.

It*em*, p*ur* ceo [q*e*] Ric*hard* Holmstede fuist trové en defaute, le sisme jo*ur* Juni l'an av*a*ntdite, de iii barres q*e* ne furent fait soloncq*es* le allay, fuist condempnés en ii s., les q*ue*ux furent remys sur condiciou*n* q*e* si le dite Ric*hard* fuist desormés trové en defaute paier*a* vi s. viii d.

It*em*, p*ur* ceo q*e* Joh*a*n Welforde fuist trové en defaute le xxj[e] jo*ur* de Juni, de ii lokett*es* *et* un harnois d'un corn d'argent q*e* le li*vre* fuist peio*ur* de vii d., fuist condempnez en ii s., p*ur* le quel se mist en g*ra*ce *et* fuist remys – sur condiciou*n* q*e* soit desormés trové en defaute paier*a* vi s. viii d.

It*em*, p*ur* ceo q*e* Joh*a*n Frer*e* fuist trové en defaute de ii piles du pois pois*ant* viii m*ar*cz, dount l'un fuist trop legier *et* l'autr*e* trop poisans p*ar* ii unc*es*, fuist amercié en vi s. viii d., *et* s'il soit trové en defaute desor*e*enav*a*nt paier*a* – xl s.[378]

[373] See also below. This last phrase has been added at the side slightly later by the same scribe.
[374] See also below. This 'p' is probably the first letter of 'paia' and for some reason the scribe has broken off and not entered the sum paid.
[375] See also below. The text breaks off.
[376] See also below. The text breaks off.
[377] This phrase, supplied here from other entries below, is needed for the sense and must have been omitted as an oversight.
[378] See also above.

Item, whereas John Lagehache instructed one male child and one female child in the craft of goldsmithing, and they were not apprenticed, he was sentenced to pay 100s., of the which he paid 20s. – and he has lent the mistery £8.
And if he should henceforth be found guilty of an offence he shall pay – £10.

Item, Albright de Aldernak instructed a 'Dutch' pageboy in contravention of his oath, he was sentenced to pay – 100s.

Item, whereas Richard Barton was found guilty of the same offence of selling

Item, whereas William Donne was found at fault in that he had sold against the ordinance

Offences A + b p. 39

Firstly, whereas John Panter, goldsmith, on 25 May 1403 [was found at fault over] spoons made by the same John which are defective, for the which he submitted himself to the judgment of his wardens, and he was sentenced to pay 2s., and this was remitted him on condition that if from henceforth he should be found at fault he shall pay – 6s. 8d. without remission.

Item, whereas John Newlyn on 27 May 1403 was found at fault over bars made for a girdle, of soldering to the fifth,[162] for which he submitted himself to the judgment of his wardens and was sentenced [to a fine of] 2s., which was remitted on condition that if henceforth he should be found at fault he shall pay 6s. 8d. and the aforesaid 2s., and he was sworn.

Item, whereas Richard Holmstead was found at fault on 6 June 1403 over 3 bars which were not made of the correct assay standard, he was sentenced [to a fine of] 2s., which was remitted on condition that if the said Richard should henceforth be found at fault he shall pay 6s. 8d.

Item, whereas John Welford was found at fault on 21 June over 2 lockets[163] and a mount for a horn made of silver of which the pound was below standard by 7d., he was sentenced [to a fine of] 2s., for the which he submitted himself to judgment and it was remitted on condition that if henceforth he should be found at fault he shall pay 6s. 8d.

Item, whereas John Frere was found at fault over 2 piles of weights weighing 8 marks, of the which one was too light and the other too heavy by 2 ounces, he was fined 6s. 8d. and if he should henceforth be found at fault he shall pay – 40s.

[162] On the techniques of soldering see Aimé Thouvenin, 'La soudure dans la construction des oeuvres d'orfèvrerie antique et ancienne', *Revue archéologique de l'Est et du Centre-Est* XXIV (1973), 11–68. Theophilus devotes a lot of attention to this technique: see e.g. the translation *On Divers Arts*, trans. John G. Hawthorne and Cyril Stanley Smith (Chicago, 1963), pp. 107–08, 121–25, etc. (see index).

[163] David Beasley has pointed out that 'on items of mounted wares there appears usually a fixing which joins the metal mount to a harness which secures the object within the harness', and that the 'lokettes' referred to here will most probably have been these fixings on the horn (in all likelihood here a drinking-horn).

p. 40 It*em*, p*ur* ceo q*e* Thom*as* Langeton mist un duch*e* vadlet q*e* fuist sou*n* cook en eov*er*aign*e* d'orfev*erie*, *et* ascun temps en schope, ascun temps en cusyne, *et* p*ur* port*er* eawe, p*ur* quel fuist amercié en vi s. viii d. et puys ordeigné est q*e* si mesme ou ascun autr*e* soit trové en sa schope p*ur* eov*er*er, si ne soit app*re*ntys ou lowys duement p*ris*, paiera xx s.[379]

It*em*, p*ur* ceo q*e* George Cressy mist en eoveraign*e* un enfaunt p*ar* long temps *et* le quel enfaunt ne fuist app*re*ntys, fuist amercié en[380] vi s. viii d. *et* si disoremés soit[381] trové en defaute paiera xx s.

It*em*, p*ur* ceo q*e* Nichol Bokyll fuist trové en defaute de xv[382] barres, un bokel *et* pendant d'un seynt*ure*, il fuist amerciez en ii s. d'iceo q*e* le li*vre* ne fuist auxi bon p*ar* xviii d. q*e* ne duist estr*e*, *et* si desoremés soit trové en defaute paiera – vi s. viii d.

It*em*, p*ur* ceo q*e* Rob*er*t Howes fuist trové en defaute p*ur* ceo q*e* moust*ra* a (un)[383] est*ra*ungers les privités del mestier – en melter d'argent[384] – il se mist en g*ra*ce de sez gardeyns, remys, *et* si [desoremés] soit trové en defaute paier*a* xx s.

It*em*, p*ur* ceo q*e* Joh*a*n Thorne ad pris deux enfauntz *et* eux enfo*ur*més en la mestier *et* ne fait eux ap*re*ntys, fuist condempnés en xiii s. iiii d. p*ur* paier en le feste de Seint Gile p*ro*schein avenir.

It*em*, p*ur* ceo q*e* Joh*a*n Scherston ad eov*er*tement disclaundrez Will*ia*m Hert de latrocinie *et* ad disclaundr*é* les gardeyns q'ils sount susteign*ours* de mesme Will*ia*m Hert, il est adjugé q'il paiera al almoigne de Seint Donston vi s. viii d., *et* puys si ascun de les p*ar*ties av*a*ntditz disclaundr*e* l'autre q*e* puist estre p*ro*vez paiera al almoign*e* de Seint Dunston – C s.[385]

1403–04 p. 41[386] These be the poynt*es* which that Walter Prata, app*re*ntys of John Lyncoln, goldsmyth, hath don to his mayster. Wherfor*e* the same Walter was by his owne knowlech convict & forswor the Cite & ȝif he wer*e* ev*er*e founde in the Cite to be justefied after the lawe of the Cite:

[379] See also above.
[380] A word or numerals have been efficiently erased after this word.
[381] MS: si soit disoremes soit.
[382] This figure has been added as an afterthought above the line.
[383] 'un' has been scored out and an indecipherable number written over, and an 's' added to the next word.
[384] These three words have been added as an afterthought above the line.
[385] See also above.
[386] The whole section on Walter Prata would appear to be in a different hand, but it is just possible that it is the same scribe using a formal, careful hand. One may also note that this scribe uses yogh but not thorn for which he writes 'th'.

Item, whereas Thomas Langton set a 'Dutch' servant who was his cook to work at goldsmith's work, and sometimes [he worked] in his shop, sometimes in the kitchen, and at fetching and carrying water, for the which he was fined 6s. 8d., and it was then ordained that if the same boy or any other should be found working in his shop and be not either an apprentice or a serving-man duly hired, he shall pay – 20s. p. 40

Item, whereas George Cressy set a child to work over a long period and the said child was not an apprentice, he was fined 6s. 8d., and if from henceforth he should be found at fault he shall pay – 20s.

Item, whereas Nicholas Bokyl was found at fault over 15 bars, a buckle and a pendant of a girdle, he was fined 2s. because the pound [of silver] was below the standard it should be by 18d., and if he should henceforth be found at fault he shall pay 6s. 8d.

Item, whereas Robert Howes was found at fault in that he had demonstrated to some aliens the privities of the craft – in the melting of silver – he submitted to the judgment of his wardens, his fine was remitted, and if he should [henceforth] be found at fault he shall pay 20s.

Item, whereas John Thorne has taken on two children and has instructed them in the craft and has not made them apprentices, he was sentenced [to a fine of] 13s. 4d. to be paid at the next feast of St Giles [1 September].

Item, whereas John Sherston openly slandered William Hert accusing him of larceny, and slandered the wardens saying they were sustaining the same William Hert, it was judged that he shall pay to the alms funds of St Dunstan 6s. 8d., and further that if either of the aforesaid parties should slander the other and this can be proved, he shall pay to the alms funds of St Dunstan – 100s.

These are the offences which Walter Prata, apprentice of John Lincoln, goldsmith, has committed against his master, for the which the same Walter was by his own admission convicted, and he foreswore the City, and if ever he be found in the City then he shall be tried according to City laws. p. 41

Furst, he knowleched that noman schuld take hym an unce of selver to weye that he ne wolde take iii or iiii peny wighte therof.

Also, ther as the same John Lyncoln tok hym thyng wrouȝt of gold to the t*ur*nours, whan he com hom, therwith*e* ther failed of the wighte – iiii d.

Also, ther as the same John Lyncoln sent hym w*ith* a noble to chaunge, whan he com hom, ther failede – vii d.

Also, the same John sente the same Walt*er* to Tyse with gylt selver, whan he com hom, ther failede the wighte of – x d.

Also, ther as the same John tok Will*ia*m Faunt his servant a peir*e* basynes gylt for to lote hem up in colorynge, & he had the foreseid Walter make a feer & for unlust & evel wyl he wolde no feer make but tok awey the basynes whil the same Will*ia*m was at his dyner & the same Walt*er* let hem up hym self til the gold went awey.

Also, the same Walter tok a swage of gold weyeng iii unces out of the tye of the foreseid Will*ia*m Faunt & kepte it thre dayes that noman wiste wher it was til atte laste that s*er*vaunt*es* in the schoppe hadden suspecion upon the same Walt*er*, & thanne the same Walt*er* com to Henri Goldsmyth, servant of the same John & seide "Henri, lo I have hyd this swage sethon Saterday & I priye ȝow Henri, sey ȝe that ȝe founde it for to excuse me that ȝe mowe make the foreseid Will*ia*m paie a peny worth ale for the fyndynge." & in this wyse he made moche dissese among the meyne, & thanne theruppon the same Henri com & tolde it to his mayster & to the foreseid Will*ia*m al this mater.

Also, the same Walter wente to Hert, jeweler upon the brigge, & borwede a cuppe of selver on his maystres name w*ith*oute wytyng of his mayster & what he dede therwith his maist*er* can nat seye.

p. 42 Also, he tok awey his maystres sal armonyak & salt pet*er* for to make a watir of, & p*ro*frede to a man x s. for to lerne to make it.

Also, he countr*e*feted the keye of his maystres counto*ur* chaumbr*e* & of his cheste, of which he confessed hym that his entent was to have take cuppes of gold & of selver gylt & gon awey in to Flaundres w*ith* John Sasse, Flemyng, & ther openly he confessed hym to his mayst*er*, to Ric*hard* Fraunceys & to al the meyne.

Also, he countr*e*feted the keye of Will*ia*m Faunt*es* chaumbre & wente in & dede al that hym luste, the which keye aft*er* was founde in the bed straw of the same Walt*er*.

Also, whan the mayne of the same John Lyncoln be at her*e* mete, the same Walt*er* wente in to the schoppe & wossh*e* the asshes of the herth*e* & pyked out the greynes both of gold & selver.

First, he admitted that if ever any man took an ounce of silver to him to weigh he would take three or four dwt. (pennyweight)[164] of it.
Also, when the same John Lincoln sent a wrought gold object to the turners,[165] when he came home with it 4 dwt. weight was missing.
Also, when the same John Lincoln sent him to change a noble, when he came home 7d. was missing.
Also, the same John sent the same Walter to Tyce[166] with some gilt silver, and when he came home 10dwt. was missing.
Also, when the same John brought to his servant William Faunt a pair of gilt basins for him to give them a fine polish, and he asked the aforesaid Walter to make a fire,[167] and out of ill-will and wickedness he refused to make a fire, and instead he took away the basins while the same William was at dinner, and the same Walter himself polished them until all the gold was removed from them.
Also, the same Walter took a gold swage weighing three ounces out of the aforesaid William Faunt's casket, and he kept it for three days so that no one knew where it was, until at last the servants in the workshop began to suspect the said Walter, and then the said Walter came to Henry Goldsmith, John Lincoln's serving-man, and said: 'Look, Henry, I have had this swage hidden since Saturday, and I beg you, Henry, to get me out of trouble will you say that you have found it, and you can get the aforesaid William to pay for a pennyworth of ale as a reward for the finding of it.' And in this way he caused a great deal of trouble in the household, and then the same Henry came and told his master and the aforesaid William the whole story.
Also, the same Walter went to Hert,[168] a jeweller on the bridge,[169] and borrowed a silver cup in his master's name, this without any knowledge of his master, and what he has done with it is completely unknown to his master.
Also, he took his master's sal ammoniac and saltpetre in order to make p. 42
aquafortis,[170] and he offered a man 10s. to teach him how to make this.
Also, he made duplicates of the keys to his master's counter-room and of his chest, and he confessed that his intention in this had been to take gold and silver-gilt cups and to go to Flanders with John Sasse, a Fleming, and then he openly made confession of this to his master, to Richard Fraunceys and to the whole household.
Also, he made a duplicate of the key to William Faunt's room, and he went in there and did whatever he wanted to, and afterwards this key was found in the said Walter's bedstraw.
Also, when the household of the same John Lincoln were all eating their meal, the same Walter went into the workshop and washed through the ashes of the hearth, and picked out the grains of both gold and silver.

164 A pennyweight (dwt.) was either 22½ grains if weighed by the Tower pound (goldsmiths' weight) or 24 grains Troy weight (one twentieth of an ounce Troy).

165 A turner was an ancillary worker in the goldsmiths' craft, who 'turned' and cleansed gold and silver objects.

166 John Tyce or Tyse was a goldbeater: see Name Index.

167 It is possible that this type of polishing was done by application of a special solution which needed to be heated, but John Cherry has queried this and suggests that the order to light the fire may have had nothing to do with the polishing.

168 This is perhaps William Hert: see Name Index.

169 i.e. London Bridge.

170 A powerful solvent, dilute HNO^3 (nitric acid).

Also, many other thing*es* ther ben that the meyne of the ho*us* knowe that he hath don & they be examyned therof they coune telle, wherfor*e* that he is nat worthi to be no goldsmyth.

It*em*, p*ur* ceo q*e* Rob*er*t Howes fuist trové[387]

It*em*, p*ur* ceo q*e* Edmu*n*d Page fuist trové en defaute de ix barres, il se mist en g*ra*ce de sez gardeyns[388] *et* fuist remys le besaunt, *et* g*ra*unt*er* q*e* si disor*e*enav*a*nt soit trové en defaute, de paier ii s. *et* le besaunt dev*a*nt remys.

It*em*, p*ur* ceo q*e* Anneis Sauvage fuist trové en defaute de xi barres, p*ur* quel ele se mist en g*ra*ce *et* fuist jugés de paier un besaunt, le quel fuist remys, *et* si desor*e*enav*a*nt soit trové en defaute paier*a* mesme besaunt *et* un autr*e* besaunt p*ur* mesme trespas.

1403–04 p. 43 Fait a remembr*er* q*e* Rog*er* Veell*e* ad g*ra*unté paier au Joh*a*n Fitherberd en le feste de Seint Piet*re* ad vincula – viii s. iiii d.

It*em*, p*ur* ceo q*e* Thom*a*s Wylwes fist un bond blank a un est*ra*ung*er* *et* mesme est*ra*ung*er* fist endorrer mesme bond *et* reporta au dite Thom*a*s p*ur* mettre sur le hanap, *et* mesme Thom*a*s mist mesme bond sur le hanap, p*ur* quel il se mist en g*ra*ce de sez gardeyns *et* ils ount juggez q*e* si desoreenav*a*nt le dite Thom*a*s soit trové en mesme defaute, paiera al almoign*e* de Seint Donston – xl s.

It*em*, p*ur* ceo q*e* Piers Torold disclaundra sez gardeyns *et* disobeisant a eux p*ar*la, il se myst en arbitrement de Joh*a*n Fraunceys, Will*ia*m Lowthe, Thom*a*s Polle, Thom*a*s Exton *et* moultz autres hon*ur*ables gentz, les q*ue*ux ount ordeignés q*e* mesme Piers Torold duist crier ses gardeyns m*er*cy, le quel fist, *et* enoutr*e* fuist juggez de paier p*ur* sou*n* trespace v tonelx de vyn, al ordeignance de les hon*ur*ables gentz du dit mestier *et* les av*a*ntditz hon*ur*ables gentz.

Item, p*ur* ceo q*e* Johan Thorne fuist trové en defaute de xiii boses p*ur* un seynt*our* a un corn, est juggé de paier un besaunt, c'est assavoir – ii s – remys[389]

It*em*, Rog*er* Cryngelforde p*ur* ceo q*e* il fuist trové en defaute de ii bokell*es* *et* ii pendauntz q*e* furent faux, est juggé de paier – ii s. – remys

It*em*, p*ur* ceo q*e* Phelip Castill*e* ad venduz a Thom*a*s, servant de Henri Grene, orfev*er*e, un anell*e* d'or p*ur* iiii s. i d. meyns, *et* mesme Thom*a*s vendust mesme anell*e* p*ur* v s., *et* sur quel le dite Phelip certefia a mesme q*e* achata le anell*e* du dite Thom*a*s q*e* ne costa pluys qe iiii s., en disclaundr*e*

[387] This phrase has been partially deleted, the scribe (the same as he who wrote p. 40) having realised he had already written up this entry on the preceding page. It is his hand writing the next two entries on this page and that continues on the next.

[388] It would seem that a phrase must have been left out here, saying that he was fined a besant.

[389] The word 'remys' against the sum of this fine and the next has been written in by the same scribe but perhaps a little later.

Also, there are many other things that those of the household know he has done, and which they could tell about if they were questioned, and for all these reasons he is not worthy to be a goldsmith.

Item, whereas Robert Howes was found guilty

Item, whereas Edmund Page was found at fault over 9 bars [and was fined one bezant], he submitted himself to his wardens' judgment, and the bezant was remitted, and it was granted that if he should henceforth be found at fault, he shall pay 2s. plus the aforesaid remitted bezant.

Item, whereas Agnes Sauvage was found at fault over 9 bars, for the which she submitted herself to judgment and was sentenced to pay a bezant, the which was remitted, and if from henceforth she should be found at fault, she shall pay the same bezant and one other bezant for the same offence.

Memorandum that Roger Veel has agreed to pay John FitzHerbert at the feast p. 43
of St Peter ad Vincula – 8s. 4d.

Item, whereas Thomas Wylwes made a white silver band for an alien, and the same alien had the same band gilded and brought it back to the said Thomas to set it on the goblet, and the same Thomas fixed the same band on the goblet, and for this he submitted himself to the judgment of his wardens and they judged that if from henceforth the said Thomas should be found guilty of the same offence, he shall pay to the alms funds of St Dunstan – 40s.

Item, whereas Piers Thorold slandered his wardens and spoke disobediently to them, he submitted himself to the arbitration of John Fraunceys, William Louth, Thomas Polle, Thomas Exton and many other honourable men, who ordered that the same Piers Thorold should beg mercy of his wardens, which he did, and he was further sentenced to pay 5 tuns of wine for his offence, this to be as ordered by the honourable men of the said mistery and the aforesaid honourable men.

Item, whereas John Thorne was found at fault over 13 bosses for a girdle for a horn, he was sentenced to pay one bezant, i.e. 2s. – remitted

Item, whereas Roger Cringleford was found at fault over 2 buckles and 2 pendants which were of sub-standard silver,[171] he was sentenced to pay 2s. – remitted

Item, whereas Phillip Castille sold a gold ring to Thomas, the servant of Henry Grene, goldsmith, for 1d. less than 4s., and the same Thomas sold the same ring for 5s., and at this the said Phillip declared to the man who bought the ring from the said Thomas that it had not cost more than 4s., to the discredit of the

[171] Literally: which were false.

du dite Thom*as* *et* a p*er*de del custom*er* du dite Thom*as*, p*ur* quel il se mist en g*ra*ce *et* fuist condempnés en vi s. viii d. q*ue*ux il paia.[390]

p.44 It*em*, p*ur* ceo q*e* Thom*as* Noreys revyla Joh*a*n Walsshe *et* treya cutell*e* p*ar* cause q*e* il demaunda son rente, il est juggé de crier luy m*er*cy *et* de paier vi s. viii d.

It*em*, p*ur* ceo q*e* mesme Thom*as* revyla *et* fauxa Andreu Stameldene*e* en p*re*sence de ses gardeyns, il fuist jugez de luy crier m*er*cy *et* de paier al almoign*e* de Seint Donston – sur g*ra*ce[391] – vi s. viii d.

Et si le dite Thom*as* desoreenav*a*nt trespace v*er*s ascun du dite mestier en ascun poynt av*a*ntdite, paiera au dite almoign*e* – xx s.

It*em*, p*ur* ceo q*e* Remu*n*d Chaumbre ad revylés Joh*a*n atte Watre, orfev*ere*, et luy fauxa, est juggés – vi s. viii d. – remys

It*em*, p*ur* ceo q*e* Rog*er* Cryngelforde fuist trové en defaute del ordeignance en le vende d'orfev*er*ie *et* il alegg*a* q*e* mesme ordeignance ne fuist confermez a mesme temps, nep*ur*qant il ad paié a les gardeyns – xl s. sur lo*ur* grace.

[392]It*em*, p*ur* ceo q*e* Joh*a*n Honte fuist trové en defaute de mesme ordeignance, il paia xl s. sur g*ra*ce dé mesmez gardeyns.[393]

It*em*, p*ur* ceo q*e* Rich*ard* Barton fuist trové en defaute de mesme ordeignance, il paia xl s. sur g*ra*ce dé mesme gardeyns.[394]

It*em*, p*ur* ceo q*e* Will*ia*m Bysmer*e* est trové en defaute de mesme ordeignance, paia xl s. sur g*ra*ce dé mesmez gardeyns, les q*ue*ux gardeyns ount considerez q*e* est le p*ri*m*er* temps q*e* fuist trové en defaute *et* ount g*ra*unté q'il paiera xiii s. iiii d., de quel ils ount paié a celuy q'ad aspié – vi s. viii d.[395]

p.45 Sacr*amentum* liber*orum* London' in Guyhalda[396]
Vous jurrez q*e* vo*us* serrez foiall*e* *et* loyall*e* a n*os*tre s*eignur* le Roy Henr*i* Roy d'Englet*er*re *et* ses heirs *et* serrez obeisant au Meir*e* *et* ministres q*e* gardent la Citee, *et* les fraunchises *et* customes de la Cité meyntendrez a v*os*tre poair, *et*

[390] See also above.

[391] 'sur g*ra*ce' has been added as an afterthought in the space between the end of the reason and the stated sum of money.

[392] The word 'remys' is written in the space of the empty line above the first two words of this item; it probably applies to this entry, but might apply to the previous one.

[393] See also above.

[394] See also above.

[395] See also above.

[396] The oath at the top of this page is written in the same hand as that which wrote the whole section on Walter Prata (pp. 41–42). What follows is in the same hand as p. 44.

said Thomas and the loss of the said Thomas's customer, for the which he submitted himself to judgment and he was sentenced to pay 6s. 8d, which he paid.

Item, whereas Thomas Noreys insulted John Walsh and drew a knife on him because he was asking for his rent, he was sentenced to beg mercy of him and to pay 6s. 8d. p. 44

Item, whereas the same Thomas insulted Andrew Stameldene and accused him of lying in the presence of his wardens, he was sentenced to beg mercy of him and to pay to the alms funds of St Dunstan – subject to judgment – 6s. 8d.

And if the said Thomas shall from henceforth offend against anyone of the said mistery in any such way as on the above occasions, he shall pay to the said alms funds – 20s.

Item, whereas Raymund Chaumbre insulted John atte Water, goldsmith, and accused him of lying, he was sentenced to pay – 6s. 8d. – remitted

Item, whereas Roger Cringleford was found guilty of offending against the ordinance concerning the sale of goldsmiths' wares, and he claimed that the said ordinance had not at the time been confirmed, nevertheless he paid the wardens – 40s. subject to their judgment

Item, whereas John Honte was found guilty of offending against the same ordinance, he paid 40s. subject to the same wardens' judgment

Item, whereas Richard Barton was found guilty of offending against the same ordinance, he paid 40s. subject to the same wardens' judgment

Item, whereas William Bismere was found guilty of offending against the same ordinance, he paid 40s , subject to the same wardens' judgment, the which wardens took into consideration that this was the first time that he had been found guilty of offence and they granted that he should pay 13s. 4d., of the which they paid 6s. 8d. to the man who caught him out.

The oath of freemen of London at the Guildhall[172] p. 45
You shall swear that you will be faithful and loyal to our lord King Henry, King of England, and his heirs, and that you will be obedient to the Mayor and the ministers who govern the City, and that you will maintain as far as

[172] On citizenship and the freedom of the City of London, and the obligations and privileges of this and the forms and content of oaths sworn see the introduction to the *Calendar of Plea and Memoranda Rolls, 1364–81*, ed. A.H. Thomas (Cambridge, 1929), pp. xviii-lxiv.

mesme la Cité qaunt en v*ous* est saunz damage garderez, *et* p*ar*cener serrez de toutz chargez touchant la Cité come en somoncez, contribucions, veilles, taillages *et* autres charges come autr*e* frank de la Cité, vo*us* ne avowerez mye les biens de foreyns come v*ost*res, dount le Roy purra p*er*dre sa custume; vo*us* ne prendrez null*e* app*re*ntys meyns de sept auns *et* les freez enroller si eins deins le primer an de v*ost*re covenant *et* au fyn de sou*n* terme, si vo*us* eit bien *et* loialment servy, sou*n* issue freez enroller. Et si vo*us* savez null*e* foreigne merchaunder en la Citee, vo*us* garnerez le chaumb*er*leyn ou les serjauntz del chaumbr*e*; vo*us* n'enplederez null*e* homme q'est del fraunchise de la dite Cité hors de mesme la Cité si vous purrez avoir droit dev*a*nt les ministres de la Cité. Et si saverez ascun congregaciou*n*, assemblé ou affinité faitz encountr*e* la pees, vo*us* garnerez le Meir*e* q'est p*ur* le temps. Et vo*us* ne prendrez null*e* app*re*ntys si ne soit frank ho*m*me *et* nemye nef.

It*em*, p*ur* ceo q*e* Rog*er* Brenaston fuist trové en defaute d'un seynt*ur*e ové vi barres les q*ue*ux furent debrosez *et* il fuist amerciez en ii s. remys[397]

It*em*, p*ur* ceo q*e* Thom*as* Oxenforde ad disclaundr*é* Huchon Wetherby en disaunt q*e* ne savoit eover*er* ne fair*e* un cuppe, p*ar* quel p*er*dust sou*n* custom*er*, p*ur* quel il fuist juggez de paier vi s. viii d. – remys

It*em*, p*ur* ceo q*e* Henri Burneye revyla *et* desclaundra sez gardeyns, il se myst en g*ra*ce dé mesmes gardeyns.

It*em*, mesme Henri p*ur* ceo q*e* il encountr*e* les comaundement de sez gardeins fist arrestier Joh*a*n Gale, un del lyver*é* d'orfeve*r*ie, il fuist condempnés selon l'estatut *et* ordeignance ordeignez – vi s. viii d. – remys

p. 46 Fait a remembr*er* q*e* Henri Burneye est obligez a Will*ia*m Granth*a*m, orfev*er*e de Loundres, en C li., la quel*e* obligaciou*n* est en garde de Drew Barentyn. Et la condiciou*n* de mesme obligaciou*n* est tiell*e* q*e* si le dite Henri dep[erso]ne[398] le dite Will*ia*m Granth*a*m v*er*s ascun p*er*sene ou ascun autr*e* du dite mestier p*ar* quel*e* ascun damage puist asso*ur*der a mesme Will*ia*m, q'adonq*es* la dite obligaciou*n* estoise en sa force *et* v*er*tue ou autrement p*er*de sa force *et* p*ur* rien soit tenuz.

It*em*, p*ur* ceo q*e* Rich*ard* Litlee fuist trové en defaute de vi boses appellé anelett*es* p*ur* un jakke, q*ue*ux pois*ent* i li*vre*, le quel li*vre* ne vaut forsq*ue* xx s.,[399] p*ur* quel*e* fauxté il se mist en g*ra*ce de ses gardeyns.

[397] As before, the 'remys' here and below look like slightly later additions.

[398] MS: 'depne', with perhaps a smudged abbreviation mark over.

[399] At this date the base-line mint price for a pound weight of silver was 25s. This mint price referred to a Tower pound of silver, but a Troy pound of silver would at this date have been worth just under 25s. 7¼d. Thus Richard Litlee's silver was worth either 80% of what it should have been if the Tower pound is being used, or 78% if the Troy pound. (I am most grateful to Dr B.J. Cook for this and other information and explanation.)

you are able all the freedoms and customs of the City, and that you will as far as in you lies keep the same City free from any harm, and that you will participate along with other freemen of the City in all charges concerning the City such as summonses, contributions, watches, tallages and other charges, that you will never declare as yours the goods of foreigners, by which act the King's customs could be lost, that you will not take on any apprentice for a term of less than seven years and that you will have them enrolled during the first year of the contract and at the end of his term, if he has well and faithfully served you, you will enroll his issue from apprenticeship terms. And if you should know of any foreigner trading in the City, you shall inform the chamberlain or the Mayor's serjeants; you shall not implead outside the City any man who is of the freedom of the said City if you may obtain justice before the City officials. And if you know of any congregation, assembly or association made against the peace, you shall inform the current Mayor. And you shall take on no apprentice unless he be a free man and no bondman.

Item, whereas Roger Brenaston was found at fault over a girdle with 6 bars, the which were broken up and he was fined 2s. – remitted

Item, whereas Thomas Oxenford slandered Hugh Wetherby saying that he did not know how to work or make a cup, as a result of which he lost his customer, for this he was sentenced to pay 6s. 8d. – remitted

Item, whereas Henry Burneye insulted and slandered his wardens, he submitted to the judgment of the same wardens.

Item, whereas the same Henry against the orders of his wardens had John Gale, one of the liverymen of the Goldsmiths' Company, arrested, he was sentenced in accordance with the statute and ordinance ordained concerning this – 6s. 8d. – remitted

Memorandum that Henry Burneye is bound in the sum of £100 to William Grantham, goldsmith of London, and the bond obligatory is in the keeping of Drew Barantyn. And the condition of the same bond is such that if the said Henry should slander the said William Grantham towards anybody or [should he slander] anyone else of the said mistery as a result of which any harm might arise for the same William, that then the said bond obligatory should come into full force and strength, and otherwise it should lose its force and be held as null and void. p. 46

Item, whereas Richard Litle was found at fault over 6 bosses called annulets for a jack,[173] which weigh 1lb., the which lb. is only worth 20s., for which deceit he submitted himself to the judgment of his wardens.

[173] 'A coat of fence, a kind of sleeveless tunic or jacket, formerly worn by foot-soldiers and others, usually of leather quilted, and in later times often plated with iron; sometimes applied to a coat of mail' (*OED*).

It*em*, mesme Rich*ard* fist un seynt*ure* ové x barres de mesme metall*e* *et* furent ryvés ové ryvett*es* de soudur*e*, p*ur* quel il se mist en *gra*ce, sur quel ordeigné est q*e* si desoreenav*a*nt soit trové en mesme defaute *et* fauxté, il p*ar*jura la Cité p*ar* to*us* jo*urs*.

It*em*, p*ur* ceo q*e* Joh*a*n Pake fuist trové faux en eov*er*aign*e* de x barres a un seynt*ure*, il se mist en *gra*ce de sez gardeyns *et* il paia un besant solonc l'ordeignance p*ar* cause q*e* est le prim*er* defaute.

It*em*, p*ur* ceo q*e* Joh*a*n Welforde fuist trové faux en eov*er*aign*e* de ix barres fait a Edmu*n*d Chambr*e*, *et* p*ur* ceo q*e* fuist trové en defaute dev*a*nt, il paier*a* al almoign*e* de Seint Donston vi s. viii d. solonc l'ordeignance.

It*em*, p*ur* ceo q*e* Rob*er*t Howys lessa un est*ra*unger veer les privités del mestier encountr*e* l'estatut du dite mestier, paiera C s. sur *gra*ce de les gardeyns.

p. 47 De foreyns

Corby:

It*em*, p*ur* ceo q*e* Joh*a*n Corby vendust app*re*ntys a un autr*e* de sa p*ro*p*re* mister encountr*e* volonté *et* assent de sez gardeyns, il fuist juggé de paier
xx s. dount fuist remys p*ar* priere dé bones gentz xiii s. iiii d. *et* paia
– vi s. viii d.[400]

It*em*, p*ur* ceo q*e* Joh*a*n Whitwell*e* fuist trové en defaute d'un helm a un escuchou*n* d'un mynstrall*e*, fuist jugé de paier un besaunt.

It*em*, p*ur* ceo q*e* Jacob Bukke fuist trové en defaute d'un bokyll*e* *et* pendant paia en nou*n* d'un besaunt – ii s.

Item, Joh*a*n Welforde fuist trové en defaute en iii bokell*es* *et* iii pendantz q*e* furent faux, *et* fuist trové deux temps dev*a*nt faux come apiert en mesme paper*e*, paier*a* – xx s.

It*em*, p*ur* ceo q*e* Thom*a*s Noreys disclaundra sez gardeyns fuist juggé de crier m*er*cy dev*a*nt tout la companye *et* se mist en *gra*ce de les gardeyns.

It*em*, p*ur* ceo q*e* Albright Aldernak ad enfo*ur*més certeins p*er*sones en la mestier q*ue*ux ne furent app*re*ntys, ount jugés de paier C s. p*ur* quel*e* il ad mys plegg*es*.[401]

[400] See also above.
[401] See also above.

Item, the same Richard made a girdle with 10 bars of the same metal and they were rivetted on with rivets of solder, for the which he submitted himself to judgment, and it was ordered that if from henceforth he should be found guilty of the same offence and deceit, he shall forswear the City for ever.

Item, whereas John Pake was found guilty of deceit in the working of 10 bars to a girdle, he submitted himself to the judgment of his wardens and he paid one bezant in accordance with the ordinance because this was his first offence.

Item, whereas John Welford was found guilty of deceit in the working of 9 bars made for Edmund Chambre, and whereas he had previously been found guilty of this offence, he shall pay to the alms funds of St Dunstan 6s. 8d. in accordance with the ordinance.

Item, whereas Robert Howes allowed an alien to see the privities of the mistery in contravention of the statute of the said mistery, he shall pay 100s. subject to the judgment of the wardens.

Of foreigners p. 47

Corby:
Item, whereas John Corby sold an apprentice to another man of his own mistery against the wishes and without the consent of his wardens, he was sentenced to pay 20s., of which 13s. 4d. was remitted at the request of the goodmen, and he paid – 6s. 8d.

Item, whereas John Whitwelle was found at fault over a helm for a minstrel's shield,[174] he was sentenced to pay one bezant.

Item, whereas Jacob Bukke was found at fault over a buckle and pendant, he paid, as the equivalent of a bezant – 2s.

Item, John Welford was found at fault over 3 buckles and 3 pendants which were faulty, and he had been found guilty of deceit twice before as appears in this same register, he shall pay – 20s.

Item, whereas Thomas Noreys slandered his wardens, he was sentenced to beg their mercy before the whole company, and he submitted himself to the judgment of the wardens.

Item, whereas Albright Aldernak trained certain persons in the craft who were not apprentices, they sentenced him to pay 100s. for the which sum he has provided pledges.

[174] This was presumably a decorative shield to be worn perhaps while riding in a procession. The word 'helm' here probably refers not to a helmet but either to a crest above the shield or perhaps to a handle (see *OED* sub HELM).

It*em*, Johan Lagehach p*ur* ceo q*e* il ad enfo*ur*mé un enfaunt – et un fe*m*me[402] – q*e* ne fuist mye sou*n* app*re*ntys, il est jugé de paier C s., les q*ue*ux sount paié en mayn sur g*ra*ce; les q*ue*ux furent remys a xx s., q*ue*ux paia[403]

It*em*, p*ur* ceo q*e* Joh*a*n Tewkesbury vendust sou*n* app*re*ntys a luy mesmes[404]

It*em*, Thom*as* Dodesole vendust sou*n* app*re*ntys a luy mesmes

p. 48[405] It*em*, p*ur* ceo q*e* Thom*as*, app*re*ntys de Will*ia*m Randolf, voil*e* se treyer hors s*er*vise de sou*n* mestre, fuist amesné al sale *et* la avoit de sou*n* mestr*e* vi. coupes ové un whippe *et* de chescu*n* de les gardeins trois coupes.

Will*ia*m Merifeld, app*re*ntys Joh*a*n White, p*ur* rebelté encountr*e* sou*n* mestre, *et* p*ur* ceo q*e* vendust certeins choses de sou*n* mestr*e* encountr*e* sa volonté, avoit vi. coupes de sou*n* mestre *et* chescun gardein iii. coupes, *et* enoutr*e* fuist juggé si desoreenav*a*nt fuist trové en defaute, av*er*eyt le double, *et* al tierce forjura le mestier.

It*em*, p*ur* ceo q*e* Albright Aldernak enforma Henri van Aldernak, sou*n* cosyn, en la mestier d'orfev*er*ie saunz assent de les gardeyns *et* encountr*e* l'estatut ent ordeignez, fuist dev*a*nt les gardeins le veill*e* de Seint Dunston l'an av*a*ntdite[406] – q*e* mesme Henri servera a mesme Albright p*ar* t*er*me de sept ans ap*ré*s le veill*e* av*a*nt escrit, *et* p*ur* quel il paia lx s. p*ur* estre suffri en la fo*ur*me av*a*ntdite.[407]

It*em*, p*ur* ceo q*e* Will*ia*m Donne fuist trové en defaute del vende d'orfev*er*ie encountr*e* l'ordeignance de mesme orfev*er*s, est jugé de paier le payne ent ordeignez.[408]

It*em*, p*ur* ceo q*e* Giles Oxeney vendust sou*n* app*re*ntys a luy mesmes, il paia xiii s. iiii d.
Et sou*n* dite app*re*ntys est obligez au dite Giles p*ur* luy paier d'un certein so*m*me d'argent.

p. 49

De foreyns faux

P*ur* ceo q*e* Joh*a*n T*ur*nour, fitz a Simond T*ur*no*ur*, fuist trové faux en bondes de cuppes q*e* furent faux *et* desceyvables les bondes de cuppes,[409] p*ur* quel*e* fuist ordeigné d'avoir jugement al pilory, *et* les gardeyns ount fait g*ra*ce a mesme, *et* fuist obligé p*ar* obligaciou*n* en xl li. a Will*ia*m Granth*a*m *et* sez compaignons,

[402] These three words have been added as an afterthought not here but at the end of the line following the word 'fuist', where there is room in the margin. The most logical place for these words is here.
[403] See also above.
[404] See also above. The sentence stops abruptly here for this entry and the next. Selling an apprentice's term to the apprentice himself was strictly forbidden in the ordinances. See above, A + a, p. 64.
[405] This page has clearly been written at different times and there may possibly be different hands at work, although I think the same but with a much smaller nib for the central paragraph.
[406] Something appears to be missing here, but the sense is clear.
[407] See also above.
[408] See also above.
[409] The previous four words seem redundant.

Item, whereas John Lagehache trained a child – and a woman – who was not his apprentice, he was sentenced to pay 100s., which was paid into their hands, subject to judgment; and the fine was remitted down to 20s., which he paid.

Item, whereas John Tewkesbury sold his apprentice to [the apprentice] himself

Item, Thomas Dodesole sold his apprentice to [the apprentice] himself

Item, whereas Thomas, the apprentice of William Randolf, wished to withdraw p. 48
himself from his master's service, he was brought to the hall and there he received from his master 6 stripes of the whip, and 3 stripes from each of the wardens.

William Mirfield, apprentice of John White, for rebelling against his master, and because he sold certain of his master's objects against his wishes, received 6 stripes from his master and 3 stripes from each warden, and it was besides decided that if he should from henceforth be found at fault, he should receive double this, and at a third offence he shall forswear the mistery.

Item, whereas Albright Aldernak trained Henry van Aldernak, his cousin, in the craft of goldsmithry without the consent of the wardens and in contravention of the statute ordained about this, he was brought before the wardens on the eve of St Dunstan's Day in the aforesaid year – that the same Henry shall serve the same Albright for a term of 7 years dating from the aforesaid eve, and for this he paid 60s. to have licence to do this in this way.

Item, whereas William Donne was found at fault over the selling of goldsmiths' wares in contravention of the goldsmiths' own ordinance, he was sentenced to pay the penalty ordained for this offence.

Item, whereas Giles Oxney sold his apprentice to [the apprentice] himself, he paid 13s. 4d.
And his said apprentice is bound to the said Giles to pay him a certain sum of money.

Of foreigners who have committed offences p. 49

Whereas John Turnour, son of Simon Turnour, was found guilty of offence over bands for cups which were faulty and deceitfully made, for the which he was ordered to be sentenced to the pillory, and the wardens showed him mercy and instead he was bound by letters obligatory in the sum of £40 to William

sur condicioun qe si soit desoreenavant trové en defaute paiera les avantditz xl li. *et* avera jugement pur soun defaute.

[410]Item, pur ceo qe Henri Clerk, Duchman de Durdreight, fuist prové en defaute de moustrer les pryvytés del mestier en dorrure d'un bonde, il vient devant les gardeyns le x jour d'Octobre l'an du regne le Roi Henri quarte puis le conqueste quinte, il se mist en grace de sez gardeyns, c'est assavoir William Grantham, Saleman Oxeney, Robert Halle *et* Thomas Senycle *et* cria mercy humblement *et* graunta qe si desoreenavant il moustre ascun privité du dite mestier a ascun estraunger, de paier al almoigne du dite mestier xx li., *et* a ceo est jurrez sur un lyvere de paier la somme avantdite saunz countredire.

p. 50 [blank]

1403–04 p. 51 Fait a remembrer qe Johan van Bonne, Duchman, goldbetere, est obligez par sa obligacion a William Grantham, Saleman Oxeney *et* sez compaignons, gardeyns, *et* a Johan Bisshop *et* Johan Bisshop, goldbeters, en x li., la condicion qe si le dite Johan Bonne bien *et* loialment garde les estatutz de lour mestier fait *et* devant escrit, qe la obligacioun perde[411] sa force *et* pur rien soit tenuz.

Item, pur ceo qe Henri atte Felde, goldbetere, fuist trové en defaute d'iceo qe ses moldes ne furent fait de mesure ne assise qe ils duissent estre, il fuist amerciez en xl s. a grace de les gardeins, *et* il mist en plegges un seynture *et* daggere harneisez, sur quel les gardeins ount de lour grace [juggé][412] qe mesme Henri paiera xiii s. iiii d. des queux lé diz mestres d'orbatours averont la moyté. Et si le dite Henri soit trové disoreenavant en ascun defaute, ne avera nulle grace mes come en l'estatut est ordeigné.

Item, pur ceo qe Nicholas Croft, goldbetere, fuist trové en defaute d'iceo qe il [ad fait][413] encountre l'ordeignance du dite mestier la ou il est ordeigné qe nulle du dite mestier duist aler a nulle hostelrie ne nulle autre place hors lour schopes pur vendre or ne argent, il paiera x s., et sur ceo il se mist en award et paia x s. al grace des ditz gardeyns.

Item, William Hardy en mesme cause fuist trové en partie, *et* fuist al supplicacioun de orbatours remys, et si ascun de eux fuist trové d'iceo enavant en defaute paiera x s.

[410] A sixteenth-century hand has written '5. H. 4' in the margin here.

[411] This has been written to replace the scored word 'estoise'.

[412] This word has been added by analogy with other similar phrases, since the sentence otherwise is incomplete.

[413] These two words are added by analogy with the phrasing in the next entry but one in order to complete the sense.

Grantham and his fellow wardens, on the condition that if he should from henceforth be found guilty of offence, he shall pay the aforesaid £40 and shall be sentenced for the offence.

Item, whereas Henry Clerk, 'Dutchman' of Durdrecht, was found guilty of demonstrating the privities of the mistery as concerns the gilding of a band, he came before the wardens on 10 October 1403 and submitted himself to the judgment of his wardens, i.e. William Grantham, Solomon Oxney, Robert Halle and Thomas Senycle, and he humbly begged pardon and he accepted that if from henceforth he should demonstrate any of the privities of the mistery to any alien, then he shall pay £20 to the alms funds of the mistery, and to this he was sworn on the book, to pay the aforesaid sum without any dispute.

[blank] p. 50

Memorandum that John van Bonne, 'Dutchman' and goldbeater, is bound by p. 51 letters obligatory to William Grantham, Solomon Oxney and their fellow wardens, and also to John Bisshop and John Bisshop, goldbeaters, in the sum of £10, the condition being that if the said John Bonne keep and observe well and faithfully the statutes of their mistery as drawn up and as written previously, that then the bond shall lose its force and be held as null.

Item, whereas Henry atte Field, goldbeater, was found guilty of offence in that his moulds[175] were not of the correct standard size and measure as they should have been, he was fined 40s. subject to the judgment of the wardens, and he placed as sureties a girdle and a dagger with silver mountings, and the wardens then made judgment that the said Henry shall pay 13s. 4d. of which the said masters of the goldbeaters shall receive half. And if the said Henry should from henceforth be found guilty of any offence, he shall be granted no favours but shall be fined in full according to the relevant ordained statute.

Item, whereas Nicholas Croft, goldbeater, was found guilty of offence in that he had acted in contravention of the ordinance of the said mistery which states that no one of the said mistery may go to any hostel or any other place outside their shops in order to sell gold or silver, he shall pay 10s., and he then submitted himself to judgment and paid 10s. subject to the judgment of the said wardens.

Item, William Hardy was found partly guilty of the same offence, and on the supplication of the goldbeaters his fine was remitted, and if from henceforth any of them should be found guilty of this offence, he shall pay 10s.

[175] See *OED* sub MOULD^3, meaning 7: 'A package of leaves of gold-beaters' skin between which gold-leaf is placed for beating. – 1727–52 Chambers *Cycl.*, *Mould*, among gold-beaters, a certain number of leaves of velom . . . between which they put the leaves of gold and silver which they beat on the marble with the hammer. – 1879 *Encycl. Brit.* X. 753/1 A "mould", composed of about 950 of the finest gold-beaters' skins.' One may note how very late these two examples are, although the methods used were the same in the medieval period.

It*em*, p*ur* ceo q*e* Joh*a*n Bonne, goldbet*ere*, ad fait encountr*e* l'ordeignance du dite mestier paia – vi s. viii d.

It*em*, p*ur* ceo q*e* Nich*olas*, goldbet*ere*, fuist trové en defaute paia iiii s. vi d.

1404 A + a p. 94 Fait a remembr*er* q*e* a un p*ar*lement gen*er*all*e* ordeigné a Westm*oustier* [l'endemeyne][414] de Seint Hiller*e* p*ar* n*ost*re tresredouté s*eignur* le Roy Henri q*ua*rte l'an de sou*n* regne quinte, le viell*e* chartre de Edward tierce g*ra*untés as orfev*er*es p*ar* mesme Roy Henri *et* tout la p*ar*lement fuist confermés *et* ratefiez *et* en outre un autr*e* novell*e* chartre de mesme Roy Henri fuist as ditz orfev*er*s g*ra*untez. Au quel an *et* temps Will*ia*m Grant*ha*m, Saleman Oxeneye, Rob*er*t Halle *et* Thom*as* Senycle furent gardeyns de mesme mestier d'orfev*er*ie.

Reg. Deeds, f. 377 1404 Petition to Parliament [415] A n*ost*re t*re*sredouté *et* t*re*ssov*er*aigne s*eignur* le Roy *et* a lez t*re*ssages s*eignur*s de cest p*re*sent p*ar*leme*n*t:

Supplient voz hu*m*ble lieges William Grantham, Salamon Oxeney, Thom*as* Senycle *et* Robert Halle, citezeins *et* orfeours de v*ost*re citee de Loundres *et* gardeyns del mistier d'orfeours de v*ost*re dite citee *et* tout la co*mun*ialté de mesme le mistier, q*e* come les ditz gardeins *et* touz autres qi ount esté gardeyns de la dite mistier en la dite citee de temps dount memorie ne court, ount ewez *et* usez d'avoir la serche, survieu, assaie *et* governaunce de tout manere oor *et* argent ov*er*ez, si b*ie*n deinz mesme la citee co*m*e aillours deinz v*ost*re roialme d'Englet*er*re; et come le t*re*snoble Roy Edward v*ost*re ayel (q*e* Dieu assoyle) sur certeins defautes moustrés a luy *et* a son counceyl en son p*ar*lement tenuz a Westm*oustier* l'an de son regne prim*er*e, touchaunt l'ov*er*aigne d'argent p*ar* les cotillers fait du dite citee sur cotels, grauntea patentz a les orfeours de mesme la citee q'ils puissent eslire bons gentz *et* suffisauntz de lo*ur* mistier d'orfeours d'enquere *et* serchier, les ditz defautes trovez en la dit mistier amender *et* redresser, *et* due punissement mettre as contrariauntz p*ar* eyde des Mair *et* viscountz du dite citee q*ua*unt mistier s*er*ra; et ore les ditz cotillers use*n*t d'ov*er*er or *et* argent en autre man*ere* q*e* ne userent au temps du g*ra*unte suisdit; sur quoy p*ar* les defautes *et* subtiltees en l'ov*er*aigne des ditz cotillers g*ra*unde esclaundre *et* arrerisem*en*t y purra avenir au dit mistier de orfeours si remedie ne soyt mys. Qe please a v*ost*re roial maiesté g*ra*untier as ditz suppliauntz q*e* les ditz cotillers n'autris artificers q*e*conq*e*s ne usent enapr*é*s autre man*ere* de ov*er*aigne d'or ou argent q'ils ne userent au temps du g*ra*unt de v*ost*re

[414] MS: al quinsisme. This parliament was held from the day after the feast of St Hilary, in the Latin phrasing 'in crastino Sancti Hillarii', and the scribe has somehow become confused here. See *Rotuli Parliamentorum* III, 522.

[415] Below is the main petition sent by the Goldsmiths to Parliament which resulted in the following charter. This petition was followed by a flurry of petitions and counter-petitions to Parliament from both the Goldsmiths and the Cutlers; Parliament ordered the Mayor to look into the matter and advise, and then report back to the King's Council in Parliament. The charter is the result of that advice. (See Register of Deeds, ff. 377–78 for copies of all the various petitions and other documents. See also *Rotuli Parliamentorum* III, 536–37; and see Reddaway and Walker, pp. 93–95.)

Item, whereas John Bonne, goldbeater, acted in contravention of the ordinance of the said mistery, he paid 6s. 8d.

Item, whereas Nicholas, goldbeater, was found guilty of offence, he paid 4s. 6d.

Memorandum that at a parliament called to Westminster by our most redoutable lord King Henry IV the day after St Hilary in the fifth year of his reign [Monday 14 January 1404 n.s.] the old charter of Edward III granted to the goldsmiths was confirmed and ratified by the same King Henry and the whole parliament, and besides another new charter was granted to the said goldsmiths by the same King Henry. In the which year and at this time William Grantham, Solomon Oxney, Robert Halle and Thomas Senycle were the wardens of the same goldsmiths' mistery. 1404 A + a p. 94

To our most redoubtable and most sovereign lord the King and to the most wise lords of this present parliament: Your humble lieges William Grantham, Solomon Oxney, Thomas Senycle and Robert Halle, citizens and goldsmiths of your City of London and Wardens of the Goldsmiths' Mistery of your City and the whole commonalty of the same mistery beg you that since the said wardens and all others who have been wardens of the said mistery in the said City from time immemorial have had and been accustomed to have the search, supervision, assay and governance of all manner of worked gold and silver both within this same City as also elsewhere in your kingdom of England; and since the most noble King Edward your ancestor (may God absolve him) because of certain faults demonstrated to him and to his Council in his Parliament held at Westminster in the first year of his reign, which concerned the working of silver done by the cutlers of the said city on knives, he granted letters patent to the goldsmiths of the same City that they might elect good and competent men of their Goldsmiths' mistery who should make enquiry and search, who should amend and correct the said faults found in the said mistery, and inflict due punishment on those who infringe the ordinances, with the aid of the Mayor and sheriffs of the said City when necessary. And now the said cutlers have taken to working gold and silver in other ways than they did at the time of the aforesaid grant. And regarding this, because of the faults and deceptions in the work of the said cutlers great detriment and discredit could come to the said mistery of goldsmiths if matters are not remedied. May it please your royal majesty to grant to the said suppliants that neither the said cutlers nor any other craftsmen whatsoever may from henceforth use any other methods of working gold and silver than they used at the time of the grant of Reg. Deeds, f. 377

tresnoble ayel suisdit. Et outre ceo de vostre pluis haboundaunte grace grauntier as ditz gardeins q'ils *et* lour successours gardeyns du dite mistier d'orfeverye ayent as touz jours le serche, survieu, assaye *et* governaunce de toute manere d'overaigne overez *et* a overer d'or *et* d'argent *et* d'enorrez *et* suisorrez par ascune persone de qeconqes mistier, sibien deinz la dite citee come aillours deinz vostre dit roialme, *et* sur ceo de mettre due punissement *et* redresse en lez overaignes defectives *et* deceivables, sibien par ayde des Mair *et* viscountz du dite citee quaunt bosoigne serra, come par ayde des Mair, viscountz, baillifs ou autres officers qeconqes aillours parmy le roialme pur le temps esteauntz quaunt busoigne serra, en manere come mesmes les orfeours ount usez devant ses heures, touz jours reservant a les seignurs de fraunchises les profites qe a eux puissent parteigner a cause de tielz faux overaignes issint trovez *et* provez deinz lour fraunchises par les gardeins de la mistier suisdite, pur dieu *et* en oevere de charitee.

f. 10[416] New Charter . . . Nos autem concessiones predictas ratas habentes *et* gratas eas pro nobis *et* heredibus nostris quantum in nobis est dilectis nobis nunc aurifabris dicte civitatis London' *et* eorum heredibus *et* successoribus aurifabris eiusdem civitatis de assensu dominorum tam spiritualium quam temporalium in presenti parliamento nostro nobis assistencium concedimus et confirmamus sicut carta predicta rationabiliter testatur. Preterea volentes eisdem aurifabris graciam uberiorem facere in hac parte, de assensu predicto concessimus pro nobis *et* heredibus nostris eisdem aurifabris *et* hac carta nostra confirmavimus quod licet ipsi vel antecessores sui libertatibus in dicta carta contentis aut earum aliqua aliquo casu emergente hactenus plene usi non fuerint, ipsi tamen *et* eorum heredes *et* successores aurifabri civitatis predicte libertatibus predictis et earum qualiter decetero plene gaudeant *et* utantur sine occasionatione vel impedimento nostri vel heredum nostrorum, justiciarum, escaetorum, vicecomitum aut aliorum ballivorum seu ministrorum nostrorum quorumcumque. Concessimus insuper de assensu dominorum predictorum eisdem aurifabris quod ipsi *et* eorum successores imperpetuum habeant scrutinium, supervisum, assaiam *et* gubernacionem omnimodorum auri *et* argenti operatorum *et* operandorum infra civitatem London' *et* suburbia eiusdem ac in comunibus feriis per totum regnum nostrum *et* ad defectus in eisdem operacionibus inventos puniendos *et* corrigendos per auxilium Maioris *et* vicecomitum civitatis predicte ac aliorum officiariorum quorumcumque in feriis predictis quociens *et* quando necesse fuerit, proviso semper quod iidem aurifabri scrutinium, supervisum, assaiam, correccionem vel gubernacionem alicuius operis deaurati vel argentati per sellarios, calcarios sive zonarios de cupro vel auricalco confecti ad artificia eorundem sellariorum, calcariorum vel zonariorum pertinentes seu de eo quod ad currus pro dominabus de cupro vel auricalco confectis seu conficiendis pertinet non habeant seu se inde in

416 The full text appears copied out in the *Register of Deeds*, f. 10, but since the first part, the *inspeximus* of Henry IV, simply repeats the previous charter as recorded above, A + a, pp. 19–20, we have omitted this and include here only the new charter. See Reddaway and Walker, p. 114 for further discussion and references to other copies of these and other relevant documents.

your aforesaid most noble ancestor. And besides may it please you in your most abundant grace to grant to the said wardens that they and their successors as wardens of the said mistery of goldsmiths may for ever have the rights of search, supervision, assay and governance of all manner of work done and to be done with gold and silver and of all forms of gilding done by anyone of whatever mistery both within the said City as also elsewhere within your said kingdom, and to be able to inflict due punishment and correction as to faulty and deceitful works, with the aid both of the Mayor and sheriffs of the said City when necessary as also of the Mayor, sheriffs, baillifs or any other officer whatsoever in office at the time elsewhere throughout the kingdom whenever the necessity shall arise, this to be in the manner which has been accustomed previously to the same Goldsmiths, saving always to those who hold liberties and franchises any profits that may pertain to them as a result of such faulty works being thus found and proved to be offences within their franchises by the wardens of the aforesaid mistery, for God and and as a work of charity.[176]

. . . We however, having approved the aforesaid concessions grant them on our own behalf and that of our heirs as far as in us lies to our well-beloved goldsmiths of the said City of London and their heirs and successors as goldsmiths of the same City with the assent of the lords both spiritual and temporal present with us in this our present parliament and we confirm them as witnessed in due form in the aforesaid charter. And besides, wishing to show more abundant grace to these same goldsmiths over these matters, with the assent aforesaid we grant to the same goldsmiths on our own behalf and that of our heirs and by this our charter we confirm that whereas they and their predecessors have until now not made full use of the privileges contained in the said charter nor of any causes that might in any way derive from them, yet they themselves and their heirs and successors as goldsmiths of the aforesaid City may from henceforth fully enjoy and make use of the aforesaid privileges and all that pertains to them without any interference or hindrance from us or our heirs or from any of our judges, escheators, sheriffs or any other bailiff or minister of ours whatsoever. We grant besides to the same goldsmiths with the assent of the aforesaid lords that they and their successors may in perpetuity have the rights of scrutiny, supervision, assay and governance of all those who work or may work with gold and silver within the City of London and its suburbs and also in common fairs throughout the whole of our kingdom, and the right to punish and correct as often and whenever it may be necessary those found guilty of offence in the working of the same, with the assistance of the Mayor and sheriffs of the aforesaid City and of other officials whoever they may be in the aforesaid fairs, provided always that the same goldsmiths shall not have rights of scrutiny, supervision, assay, correction nor governance of any work of gilding or silvering done by saddlers, spurriers or girdlers on copper or orichalc[177] on anything which belongs to the misteries of the same saddlers, spurriers or girdlers, nor in anything that pertains to copper or orichalc articles made or to be made for ladies' carriages, nor shall they in any

Reg. Deeds, f. 10

[176] The last phrase is a standard formula ending petitions.

[177] The use of the Latin 'auricalcus' is noteworthy. See *OED* for its derivation and meaning: 'Some yellow ore or alloy of copper, highly prized by the ancients; perhaps brass. Applied by Strabo to brass, though some Greek writers treated it as a fabulous metal; in the Middle Ages, *aurichalcum*

aliquo intromittant. Hiis testib*us* ven*er*abilib*us* p*resbiter*ib*us* Th*oma* Cantuar', tocius Angl*ie* primate, R. Ebor', Angl*ie* primate archiep*iscop*is, H. Lincoln', cancellar' n*ost*ro, H. Norwicen', epis*copo*, carissimo f*rat*re n*ost*ro Johanne Soms', cam*er*ario n*ost*ro, Rad*ulph*o Westm*er*land, marescallo Angl*ie*, comitib*us* Will*elm*o de Roos de Hamelak, thes' n*ost*ro, Ric*ard*o de Grey de Codenore, Thoma Erpyngham, senescallo hospicii n*ost*ri, Thoma de Longeley, custode privati sigilli n*ost*ri *et* aliis. Dat*um* p*er* manu*m* n*ost*ram apud Westm*onasterium* decimo nono die Marcii anno regni n*ost*ri quinto.[417]

1403–04 Ceux apr*é*s escriptz furrount del vestur*e* d'orfev*er*ie mesme an:
A + a p. 94 Drugo Barentyn
col. 1 Joh*ann*es Fraunceys
Thom*as* Polle
Henri Ba*m*me
Will*elmu*s Lowthe
Joh*ann*es Forster
Thom*as* Extou*n*
Thom*as* Hay
Joh*ann*es Carbonell*e*
Cristofre Tildesle
Joh*ann*es Hygyn
Joh*ann*es Blakeden*e*
Will*ia*m Fitzhewe
Joh*ann*es Lutou*n*
Joh*ann*es Lyncoln*e*
Joh*ann*es Frenssh*e*
Joh*ann*es Bulstrode
Joh*ann*es Standelf
Walt*er*us Marwe
Thom*as* Lamport
Joh*ann*es Lenh*a*m
Remu*n*d*us* Standelf
Georgi*us* Cressy
Will*elmu*s Burgylou*n*
Jacobus Bontyng
Joh*ann*es Lagehach*e*
Will*elmu*s Donne
Joh*ann*es Noreman

[417] One of most important points of the above is that no exclusion is made of rights over the Cutlers, and indeed the Goldsmiths' rights over gold and silver work done by the former are fully upheld by the King, and the Goldsmiths exercised these rights publicly very soon after this (see below, p. 55 of Book A + b).

way interfere in these matters. Witnessed by the venerable priests the archbishops Thomas of Canterbury, Primate of all England,[178] and R. of York, Primate of England,[179] H. of Lincoln, our Chancellor,[180] H. bishop of Norwich,[181] our dearest brother John Somerset, our Chamberlain,[182] Ralph of Westmorland, Marshal of England, the earls William de Roos de Hamlake, our Treasurer, Richard Lord Grey of Codnor, Thomas Erpyngham, seneschal of our household, Thomas de Longley, guardian of our privy seal, and others. Given by our own hand at Westminster on 19 March in the fifth year of our reign (1404).

Those listed below were of the livery of the goldsmiths in the same year: 1403–04 A + a p. 94 col. 1

Drew Barantyn
John Frounceys
Thomas Polle
Henry Bamme
William Louth
John Forster
Thomas Exton
Thomas Hay
John Carbonelle
Christopher Tyldesley
John Hygyn
John Blakedene
William FitzHugh
John Luton
John Lincoln
John Frenshe
John Bulstrode
John Standelf
Walter Marwe
Thomas Lamport
John Lenham
Raymund Standelf
George Cressy
William Burgyloun
James Buntyng
John Lagehache
William Donne
John Norman

is often mentioned as a very precious metal known only by report.' Here however it would seem probable that it refers to brass or latten.

178 Thomas Arundel, Archbishop of Canterbury.

179 Richard le Scrope, Archbishop of York.

180 Henry Beaufort, Bishop of Lincoln.

181 Henry Dispenser, Bishop of Norwich.

182 John Beaufort, Earl of Somerset.

Ric*ardus* Bartou*n*
Andreas Stamelden*e*
Joh*ann*es Canou*n*
Joh*ann*es Halle junior
Hanes Dobler
Joh*ann*es Dobler
Joh*ann*es Palynge
Will*elmu*s Lucas
col. 2 Will*elmu*s Lyncoln*e*
Joh*ann*es Tewkesbury
Joh*ann*es Wynne
Joh*ann*es White
Pet*ru*s Torold
Thom*a*s Popeltou*n*
Joh*ann*es Frer*e*
Will*elmu*s Adys
Joh*ann*es Bernys
Joh*ann*es Bussh*e*
Henr*icus* Grene
Ric*ardus* George
Pet*ru*s Tounvyle
Joh*ann*es Granth*a*m
Will*elmu*s Barde
Joh*ann*es Whitwell*e*
Walt*er*us Sprynget
Philipp*us* Castill*e*
Mathias Goldbet*er*e
Barth*olome*us Goldbet*er*e
Joh*ann*es Bisshop junior
Will*elmu*s Gylberd
Will*elmu*s Randolf
Ed*mundu*s Page
Will*elmu*s Horsman
Ed*mundu*s Nethersole
Will*elmu*s Gartou*n*
Simon Chesterfelde
Joh*ann*es Hilles
Joh*ann*es Gale
Joh*ann*es van Gaver*e*
Wynant van Wermes
Ric*ard*us Forster
Joh*ann*es Huberd
Thom*a*s Glade
Henr*icus* atte Felde
col. 3 Will*elmu*s Pevere
Joh*ann*es Coraunt
Thom*a*s Dodesole

Richard Barton
Andrew Stameldene
John Canon
John Halle, the younger
Hans Dobler
John Dobler
John Palyng
William Lucas
William Lincoln col. 2
John Tewkesbury
John Wynne
John White
Piers Thorold
Thomas Poppleton
John Frere
William Adys
John Barnes
John Busshe
Henry Grene
Richard George
Peter Tounvyle
John Grantham
William Barde
John Whitwelle
Walter Sprynget
Phillip Castille
Matthew Goldbeater
Bartholomew Goldbeater[183]
John Bisshop, the younger
William Gilbert
William Randolf
Edmund Page
William Horsman
Edmund Nethersole
William Garton
Simon Chesterfield
John Hilles
John Gale
John van Gavere
Wynant van Worms
Richard Forster
John Huberd
Thomas Glade
Henry atte Field
William Pevere col. 3
John Coraunt
Thomas Dodesole

[183] i.e. Bartholomew Seman.

Rob*ertus* Beteigne
Joh*anne*s Watyr
Nich*ola*us Croft
Thom*a*s Bokyll*e*
Joh*anne*s Edmu*n*d
Joh*anne*s Walssh*e*
Joh*anne*s Martyn
Joh*anne*s Brigge
Joh*anne*s Pake
Will*elmu*s Bismer*e*
Rob*ertus* Childerle
Ric*ardus* Cranesle
Egide*us* Oxeneye
Joh*anne*s Osborne
Hervic*us* Rokhawe
Joh*anne*s Halle senior
Joh*anne*s Thornkyn
Joh*anne*s Flete
Hugo Wetherby
Rob*ertus* Hugfelde
Joh*anne*s Som*er*vyle
Joh*anne*s Walsh*a*m
Ric*ard*us Fraunceys
Joh*anne*s Cappe
Joh*anne*s Knyvesworth*e*
Joh*anne*s Brou*n*
Rob*ertus* Brou*n*

col. 4 Jeovenes gentz de mesme mestier:
Rob*ertus* Lemyng
Joh*anne*s Parker
Rob*er*t Serle
Thom*a*s Wottou*n*
Barth*olome*us Bylingtou*n*
Nich*ola*us Angetyn
Thom*a*s Lynk
Will*elmu*s Bette
Ric*ardus* Ede

Robert Beteigne
John Water
Nicholas Croft
Thomas Bokyl
John Edmund
John Walsh
John Martyn
John Brigge
John Pake
William Bismere
Robert Childerle
Richard Cranesle
Giles Oxney
John Osborne
Harvey Rookhawe
John Halle the elder
John Thornkyn
John Flete
Hugh Wetherby
Robert Hugfeld
John Somerville
John Walsham
Richard Fraunceys
John Cappe
John Knyvesworthe
John Broun
Robert Broun

Yeomen[184] of the same mistery: col. 4
Robert Lemyng
John Parker
Robert Serle
Thomas Wootton
Bartholmew Billington
Nicholas Angetyn
Thomas Lynk
William Bette
Richard Ede

[184] Literally: young men. They belonged at this date to the freedom but not the livery. In later years the terms 'bachelor' and 'yeoman' (which etymologically means 'young man') came to be applied to junior members of a trade or craft who had not yet been admitted to full membership of the mistery (see e.g. Pearl, 'A Revolt in 1529 by Yeomen . . .'), but at this date no standard term was in use. The term 'bachelor' is found in the Grocers' Accounts, the earliest usage being in 1397 but where it does not however have the later full technical meaning. See P. Nightingale, *A Medieval Mercantile Community*, p. 341. An early instance of the term 'yeoman' is found in the Skinners' records for the year 1402 (the 'yemen companye' – see E. Veale, *The English Fur Trade in the Later Middle Ages*, pp. 112–13) and one finds it also in the Merchant Taylors' Accounts for the year 4 Henry VI [1425–26]: 'Item ressu des gardeins del yemon taillours pur soun felawschip – xl s.' By this time these yeomen of the Skinners and Tailors were organised into their own company. See Veale, *English Fur Trade*; C.M. Clode, *The Early History*, I, 60–68.

Rob*ertus* Northenere
Joh*anne*s Scherston
Will*elmu*s Tholby
Remu*ndus* Chaumbr*e*
Ric*ard*us Aas
Joh*anne*s Bedeforde
Thom*a*s Wellys
Rob*ertus* Langeley
Henri Goldsmyth*e*
Ric*ardus* Hayle
Hereman Vynk
Ric*ardus* de la Mar*e*
Will*elmu*s Chipstede
Rog*er* Poiaunt
Will*elmu*s Belverge
Thom*a*s Mounde
Will*elmu*s Coup*er*e
Ric*ardus* West
Will*elmu*s Guppeye
Thom*a*s Wedou*n*
Henr*i* Champleyn
Simon Foryng*er*
Joh*a*n Rokhawe
Joh*a*n Farle
Rich*ard* Withihale
Will*elmu*s Edward
Joh*anne*s Chestr*e*
p. 95, col. 1 Rob*ertus* Suttou*n*
Joh*annes* Fynegod
Thom*a*s Wareyn
Joh*anne*s Corbyn
Joh*anne*s Mene
Joh*anne*s Warde
Joh*anne*s Brian
Joh*anne*s Alyngtou*n*
Joh*anne*s White
Joh*anne*s Foxcote
Will*elmu*s Hert
Joh*anne*s Houghtou*n*
Rob*ertus* Howys
Ric*ardus* Helmstede
Joh*anne*s Sonnyng
Joh*anne*s Wadevile
Ric*ardus* Sage
Joh*anne*s Therne
Joh*anne*s Hertewell*e*
Rog*erus* Veell*e*
Ric*ardus* Brou*n*
Ed*mundu*s Davy

Robert Northenere
John Sherston
William Thelby
Raymund Chaumbre
Richard Aas
John Bedford
Thomas Welles
Robert Langley
Henry Goldsmith
Richard Hayle
Hermann Vynk
Richard de la Mare
William Chipstead
Roger Poiaunt
William Belverge
Thomas Mound
William Couper
Richard West
William Guppeye
Thomas Weedon
Henry Champleyn
Simon Forynger
John Rookhawe
John Farle
Richard Withihale
William Edward
John Chester
Robert Sutton p. 95, col. 1
John Fynegod
Thomas Wareyn
John Corby
John Mene
John Warde
John Brian
John Allington
John White
John Foxcote
William Hert
John Houghtoun
Robert Howes
Richard Holmstead
John Sonnyng
John Wadevile
Richard Sage
John Therne
John Hertwell
Roger Veel
Richard Broun
Edmund Davy

Thom*as* Westley
Will*elmu*s Faunt
Rob*ertus* Londou*n*
Will*elmu*s Sawyer*e*
Will*elmu*s Baldeswell*e*
Rob*ertus* Pycot
Thom*as* Aleyn
Will*elmu*s Falle
Ric*ardus* Ponchard
Joh*anne*s Stile
Ric*ardus* Wynter
Will*elmu*s atte Wode
Joh*anne*s Chervell*e*
Will*elmu*s Schirbo*ur*ne
Joh*anne*s Mounte
Ric*ardus* Wylde
Thom*as* Cresselowe
Thom*as* Oxenforde
Austyn Porter
Joh*anne*s Welforde
Thom*as* Willkes
Will*elmu*s Harpele

col. 2[418] Fait a remembr*er* q*e* est gr*a*unté p*ar* Will*ia*m Granth*a*m, Saleman Oxneye, Thom*as* Senycle *et* Rob*er*t Halle, gardeins d'orfeve*r*ie, *et* p*ar* autres bones gentz de mesme mestier a eux eslutz, q*e* Jacob Bulke serra suffriz de eove*r*er en la mestier d'orfeve*r*ie sur condiciou*n* q'il ne vende null*e* chose d'orfeve*r*ie ove*r*és tank'yl ad les moust[r]és as orfeve*r*s engleys, s'ils voilent achatier ou nou*n*,[419] *et* est jurrez de tenir les ordeignanc*es* en la pap*er*[420] ordeynés de Duchmen *et* ad paié – iiii m*arces*

It*em*, Nich*olas* Leygey est suffry sur condiciou*n* q'il ne face null*e* eove*r*aigne mes solement as orfeve*r*s *et* ad paié xx s. *et* est jurrez de tenir les ordeignanc*es* av*a*ntditz.

It*em*, Wynant van Coloign*e* est suffry en mesme condiciou*n* q*e* Jacob Bulke est suffriz et paia xl s.

1404–05 p. 96[421] Ceux sount les nouns des gardeyns eslutz le jo*ur* de Seint Dunston l'an du regne le Roy Henri quarte puys le conqueste quinte tank*e* a mesme feste l'an ensuant:
Joh*a*n Standelf
Will*ia*m Fithewe
Will*ia*m Randolf
Joh*a*n Halle le puisné

418 A new hand writes the rest of this page.
419 'ou nou*n*' is a slightly later superlinear addition.
420 See A + b, pp. 64 and 66.
421 A new hand starts here. The list of wardens is also given on p. 53 of A + b.

Thomas Westley
William Faunt
Robert London
William Sawyer
William Baldeswelle
Robert Pycot
Thomas Aleyn
William Falle
Richard Punchard
John Style
Richard Wynter
William atte Wood
John Chervelle
William Sherborne
John Mount
Richard Wylde
Thomas Cresslowe
Thomas Oxenford
Austin Porter
John Welford
Thomas Wilkes
William Harpele

Memorandum that it has been granted by William Grantham, Solomon Oxney, col. 2
Thomas Senycle and Robert Halle, wardens of the goldsmiths' mistery, and by other goodmen of the same mistery elected as their associates, that Jacob Bulke shall be permitted to work in the goldsmiths' craft on condition that he should sell no object of worked goldsmithry before showing it to the English goldsmiths to see if they wish to buy it or not, and he has been sworn to keep the ordinances that are in the register and ordained for 'Dutchmen', and he has paid – 4 marks.

Item, Nicholas Leygey has been given permission on condition that he makes works only for the goldsmiths, and he has paid 20s. and has been sworn to keep the aforesaid ordinances.

Item, Wynant van Cologne has been given permission on the same condition as that on which Jacob Bulke was given permission, and he paid 40s.

These are the names of the wardens elected on St Dunstan's Day in the year 1404–05
5 Henry IV [19 May 1404] until the same feastday the following year: p. 96
John Standelf
William FitzHugh
William Randolf
John Halle the younger

col. 1 Apprentys resceux mesme an:[422]
Johan Hoke apprentys de William Grantham
Thomas Stapeles apprentys de Robert Broun
George Codesmore apprentys de Johan Standelf
Tileman Gaye apprentys de Johan Bernes
William Ryvere apprentys de Johan Busshe
Huhe Tildeslee apprentys de Richard Bartoun
Johan Bray apprentys de Johan Forster
Johan Bedeforde apprentys William Gartoun
William Werketoun apprentys de Thomas Extoun
Radulfus Wardele apprentys Johan Brigge
Thomas Grene apprentys William Gylbert
Simond Sotherne apprentys Johan Martyn
Thomas Willy apprentys Robert Suttoun
(Johan Pynwyncle apprentys Johan Fraunceys)[423]
Robert Bowyer apprentys Johan Foxcote
(Johan Thomas apprentys Johan Gale)[424]
Roger Erdestone apprentys William Fithewe
Johannes Mage apprentys Ulrik van Beyre
Johannes Trevilyas apprentys Henri Wortesburghe

col. 2 Lowys en mesme an:

Henri Grantham jadys apprentys *William* Grantham –	ii s.
Henri Plomstede jadys apprentys Thomas Pantoun –	ii s.
Thomas Covele jadys apprentys Johan Lutoun –	ii s.
Petrus Stokes jadys apprentys Richard George –	ii s.
Johan Joce jadys apprentys *William* Baldeswelle –	ii s.
Simond[425] jadys apprentys *William* Lucas –	ii s.
Rauf Alom jadys app*rentys* Richard Bartoun –	ii s.
Thomas Longe jadys app*rentys* Johan Huberd –	ii s.
Nich*olas* Wodhulle jadys app*rentys* Will*iam* Lowthe –	ii s.
Johan Adam jadys app*rentys* Will*iam* Downe –	ii s.
William atte Wode jadys app*rentys* Will*iam* Fithewe –	ii s.
Joh*an* Motoun app*rentys*[426]	
Thomas Brynkele jadys apprentys Th*omas* Lamport –	ii s.
Nich*olas* Bette jadys app*rentys* Henri Grene –	ii s.
Will*iam* Ketille jadys app*rentys* Hervy Rokhawe –	ii s.
Robert Botulf jadys app*rentys* Robert Beteigne –	ii s.
Johan Lane jadys app*rentys* Andrew Stameldene –	ii s.
Ric*hard* Bagard jadys app*rentys* Robert Hugfeld –	ii s.

A + b Les defautes en mesme an:
p. 53[427] Primerement, le xe jour de Jullet l'an avantdite William Covele, apprentys de

[422] No sums of money are listed against the names in the following column.
[423] This line has been scored through.
[424] This line has been scored out and a LH margin note explains: 'adnullat*ur* quia m*odo* est appren*ticius* Cissorio*rum* ac p' p^{t}tea in papiro'. See further A + a, p. 108.
[425] A space follows this name.
[426] The rest of this line is blank. Th. Chalers is listed in 1388–89 as his master.
[427] A new hand starts with the list of wardens at the top of this page.

Apprentices admitted the same year: col. 1
John Hoke apprentice of William Grantham
Thomas Staplehurst apprentice of Robert Broun
George Codesmore apprentice of John Standelf
Tileman Gaye apprentice of John Barnes
William Ryvere apprentice of John Busshe
Hugh Tyldesley apprentice of Richard Barton
John Bray apprentice of John Forster
John Bedford apprentice of William Gartoun
William Werketoun apprentice of Thomas Exton
Ralph Wardele apprentice of John Brigge
Thomas Grene apprentice of William Gilbert
Simon Southern apprentice of John Martyn
Thomas Willy apprentice of Robert Sutton
(John Pynwyncle apprentice of John Fraunceys)
Robert Bowyer apprentice of John Foxcote
(John Thomas apprentice of John Gale)[185]
Roger Erdestone apprentice of William FitzHugh
John Mage apprentice of Ulrik van Beyre
John Trevilyas apprentice of Henry Wortesburgh

Serving-men in the same year: col. 2

Henry Grantham formerly apprentice of William Grantham –	2s.
Henry Plumstead formerly apprentice of Thomas Panton –	2s.
Thomas Covele formerly apprentice of John Luton –	2s.
Peter Stokes formerly apprentice of Richard George –	2s.
John Joce formerly apprentice of William Baldeswelle –	2s.
Simon formerly apprentice of William Lucas –	2s.
Ralph Alom formerly apprentice of Richard Barton –	2s.
Thomas Longe formerly apprentice of John Huberd –	2s.
Nicholas Woodhille formerly apprentice of William Louth –	2s.
John Adam formerly apprentice of William Downe –	2s.
William atte Wood formerly apprentice of William FitzHugh –	2s.
John Motoun apprentice	
Thomas Brinkley formerly apprentice of Thomas Lamport –	2s.
Nicholas Bette formerly apprentice of Henry Grene –	2s.
William Ketille formerly apprentice of Harvey Rookhawe –	2s.
Robert Botulf formerly apprentice of Robert Beteigne –	2s.
John Lane formerly apprentice of Andrew Stameldene –	2s.
Richard Bagard formerly apprentice of Robert Hugfeld –	2s.

Offences in the same year: A + b p. 53
Firstly, on 10 July of the aforesaid year [1404], whereas William Covele,

185 LH marginal note: 'annulled because he is now an apprentice of the Tailors and therefore [score his name out?] in the register'.

Will*ia*m Granth*a*m, p*ur* ceo q*e* fuist rebell*e* a sou*n* mestr*e* *et* maistresse *et* p*ur* un defaute fait v*er*s eux, avoit certeins coupes ové un whippe de sou*n* mestr*e* *et* de chescun de les gardeyns.

It*em*, p*ur* ceo q*e* Tidrik van Watir fuist trové en defaute de eov*er*aign*e* de viii barres, les q*ue*ux ne furent covenables, paia un besaunt *et* les barres furrount debrosez – ii s.

It*em*, p*ur* ceo q*e* Simond Canyngtou*n* est trové en defaute d'iceo q'il fist vii seynt*ur*es ové bokell, pendant *et* barres a Joh*a*n Wottone, haberdassher*e*, les q*ue*ux furount faux, fuist juggez – ii s.

1405 It*em*, p*ur* ceo q*e* Will*ia*m Granth*a*m fuist rebell*e* *et* cont*ra*ri*ous* a sez gardeyns al assemblé fait en la sale le iiie jo*ur* de Fev*er*er l'an av*a*ntdite, vient *et* humblement sur ces genux cria m*er*cy *et* se myst en g*ra*ce de ses ditz gardeins en p*re*sence de Dru Barentyn, Joh*a*n Frauncey*s*, Thom*a*s Polle, Will*ia*m Lowthe, aldermans, *et* moultz autres hon*ur*ables gentz de mesme mestier.

1404–05 It*em*, p*ur* ceo q*e* Albright *et* Hanes, Duchmen, ount ov*er*ez en la mesou*n* d'un
p. 54 brewer ount paiez – ii s.

[428]Come etc. Henr*i* de Coleyn, orfev*er*e, soit tenuz *et* obligez a Will*ia*m Granth*a*m *et* sez compaygnons, orfev*er*ez de Loundr*es* *et* gardeins de mesme la mistier, en x li. d'est*er*ling*es* a paier come en mesme l'oblig*acion* ent fait pluis pleinem*en*t app*er*t la cause *et* declarac*i*on, *et* cause q*e* la dit l'oblig*acion* fuist fait est tiell*e* q*e* si le dit Henr*i* en temps a ven*ir* b*ie*n, honestem*en*t *et* loialm*en*t se porte en toutz pointz, en ditz *et* faitz, si b*ie*n env*er*s toutz les ho*m*mes de mesme la mister*e* come env*er*s toutz aut*re*s qiconq*e*s saunz ascun empecheme*nt*, defaut ou t*re*spas, q'adonq*e*s la dit oblig*acion* soit p*ur* null*e*. Et si le dit Henr*i* soit trové en ascuns dez pointz suisditz issint q'il poet estr*e* trové p*ar* bon*e* *et* loiall*e* declarac*i*on, q'adonq*e*s la dit oblig*acion* estoise en sa forse *et* v*er*tue saunz ascun allegeance en temps a ven*ir*.

1404 Fait a remembr*er* q*e* le iiie jo*ur* de Decembr*e* l'an du regne le Roy Henri quarte
p. 55[429] puis le conqueste sisme, serche *et* assay fuist fait p*ar* Will*ia*m Fithewe, Joh*a*n Standelf, Will*ia*m Randolf *et* Joh*a*n Halle sur toutz les cotillers, *et* Pichard fuist assignés p*ar* Joh*a*n Hende, meir*e* de Loundres, p*ur* aler ové eux p*ur* enforcier eux p*ar* comaundement du Roy av*a*ntdite.[430]

1404 It*em*, apr*é*s le feste de Seint Thom*a*s apostle l'an av*a*ntdite, les gardeyns av*a*ntditz ount fait lo*ur* serche *et* assay sur mesmez cotillers saunz ascun officer.

p. 56–57 [blank]

[428] This paragraph is written in a different hand.
[429] The same hand as that writing p. 53.
[430] See above, Reg. Deeds, f. 10 for the charter that confirmed these powers to the goldsmiths.

apprentice of William Grantham, rebelled against his master and mistress and for an offence committed against them, he received a number of stripes of the whip from his master and from each of the wardens.

Item, whereas Tidrik van Wetter was found guilty of offence in the working of 8 bars which were not up to standard, he paid one bezant and the bars were broken up – 2s.

Item, whereas Simon Canyngtoun was found guilty of offence in that he made 7 girdles with buckles, pendants and bars for John Wootton, haberdasher, which were faulty, he was sentenced [to pay] – 2s.

Item, whereas William Grantham rebelled and opposed his wardens at the 1405
assembly held in the Hall on 3 February of the aforesaid year [1405], he came and humbly on his knees begged pardon and submitted himself to the judgment of his said wardens in the presence of Drew Barantyn, John Fraunceys, Thomas Polle, William Louth, aldermen, and many other honourable men of the same mistery.

Item, whereas Albright and Hans, 'Dutchmen', had worked in the house of a p. 54
brewer, they paid – 2s.

As etc. Henry de Cologne, goldsmith, is bound to William Grantham and his fellow wardens, goldsmiths of London and wardens of the same mistery, in the sum of £10 sterling to be paid according to the cause and declaration as are more fully stated in the same bond of obligation, and the cause of making the same bond is such that if the said Henry in future behaves in all ways in an honest and faithful manner, in words and deeds, both towards all men of the same mistery and also towards all others whatsoever, and is free of all hindrances, faults and offences, that then the said bond should be null and void. And if the said Henry should be found guilty in any aforesaid way such that this may be proved by a true and faithful declaration, that then the said bond should come into full force and strength with no leniency in the future.

Memorandum that on 3 December 1404 search and assay were carried out p. 55
on all cutlers by William FitzHugh, John Standelf, William Randolf and John Halle, and Pichard was appointed by John Hende, Mayor of London, to accompany them to reinforce them by command of the aforesaid King.

Item, after the feastday of St Thomas the Apostle in the aforesaid year [21 December 1404] the aforesaid wardens carried out their search and assay on the same cutlers without any officer.

[blank] pp. 56–57

p. 59[431] Fait a remembr*er* q*e* Rich*ard* Heyward est resceu p*ar* les gardeyns av*a*nt ditz p*ur* estr*e* suffry sur condicion q'il paiera iiii m*a*rcz come apiert p*ur* ii obligacions, les q*ue*ux il ad paié al eops del dite mestier *et* p*ur* ceo les obligacions voidé.

Fait a remembr*er* q*e* Wynant van Cologne fuist g*ra*unté d'estr*e* suffry de dem*ur*rer *et* eover*er* en chambre en temps de Will*ia*m Grantham, Saleman Oxeneye, Rob*er*t Halle *et* Thom*a*s Senycle,[432] p*ur* paier al mestier xl s. Et ap*r*és le dite Wynant paia a mesmes Will*ia*m Granth*a*m *et* ses compaignons xx s., et puys ap*r*és le dite Wynant accorda ové les gardeins ap*r*és escriptz[433] de eux paier xl s. nient encountr*e* esteant les xx s. dev*a*nt paiez, *et* issint ad paiez lx s., *et* p*ar* cause q'il fuist app*r*entys en mesme mestier ové un f*ra*nc ho*m*me de mesme cité, suffri est d'avoir un enfaunt al man*er*e de app*r*entice p*ar* certeins ans p*ar*entr*e* eux accordés.

p. 60 [blank]

1404 En p*ar*lement[435]

p. 61[434] It*em*, ordeigné est *et* establez q*e* nully desoreenav*a*nt use de multeplier or ou argent, ne use le art de multeplicacion, *et* si nully le face *et* d'iceo soit atteynt, q'il enco*ur*ge le peyne de felonye en ceo caas.

1404 It*em*, p*ur* ceo q*e* pluso*ur*s disloialx artificers ymaginantz a desceyv*er* le co*mun*e people fait de jo*ur* en autr*e* firmeux, anelx, bedes, chaundelures, gipserryng*es*, chalices, hiltes et pomelx d'espeyes, pouderboxes, liens *et* burcelx p*ur* hanapes, de cupr*e* *et* de latou*n*, *et* les susorrount *et* susargentount semblables a or *et* argent *et* les vendent *et* mettent a gage as pluso*ur*s ho*m*mes nient eaiantz plein conisance de ceo p*ur* or entier *et* argent entier, a g*ra*unt desceit, p*er*de *et* arrerisement du co*mun*e people *et* anientisement *et* destruction d'or *et* d'argent: Ordeignez est *et* establiez q*e* null*e* arteficer n'autr*e* ho*m*me queconq*uez* desorenav*a*nt suisor*e* ne suisargente null*e* tielx firmaux, anelx, bedes, chaundelures, gipserryng*es*, chalices, hiltes ne pomelx p*ur* espeies, pouderboxes, liens ne bursels p*ur* hanapes faitz de cupre ou de latou*n*, sur

[431] Accurate dating of the entries in this section of this register is very difficult, since most individual entries are not given a year date, and since it is clear that at times blank pages were left which were sometimes used subsequently to record a matter which took place later than another already recorded on a following page. Thus here it seems possible that the first entry on p. 58 was written out a few years later than pp. 59ff. and it has therefore been incorporated, with due reservation, at a later point below. The further entry on p. 58 is clearly dated to 1420–21 and is so placed below. An additional problem is that all these pages have been mounted within modern paper and the pagination is subsequent to this. The problems might therefore have arisen at the time this mounting and binding was done, but close examination of the leaves in fact makes this seem unlikely.

[432] i.e. 1403–04.

[433] Unfortunately these wardens' names have not been written in and the date of this entry is uncertain. See also the entry below, A + b, p. 67 and above, A + a, p. 95.

[434] A different hand starts here.

[435] See *Rotuli Parliamentorum* III, 540. The first day of the parliament was 14 January 1404 n.s.

Memorandum that Richard Heyward has been accepted to have a licence by the aforesaid wardens on condition that he shall pay 4 marks as according to 2 bonds obligatory, the which he has paid to the funds[186] of the said mistery and therefore the bonds have been nullified. p. 59

Memorandum that Wynant van Cologne was granted licence to live and work in chambers during the period of office of William Grantham, Solomon Oxney, Robert Halle and Thomas Senycle, in return for paying 40s. to the mistery. And afterwards the said Wynant paid 20s. to the same William Grantham and his fellow wardens, and then later the said Wynant made an agreement with the wardens whose names are written below to pay them 40s. notwithstanding the 20s. paid before, and thus he paid 60s., and because he had been an apprentice in the same mistery with a freeman of the same city, he has been permitted to take on a child as an apprentice for a certain number of years agreed between them.

[blank] p. 60

In Parliament: 1404
Item, it was ordained and established that no one from henceforth may practise the multiplying of gold or silver, nor may anyone use the art of multiplication,[187] and if anyone should do so and be found guilty of this, he shall incur the penalty of felony in this case. p. 61

Item, whereas many unfaithful craftsmen scheming to deceive the common people have from day to day made clasps, rings, beads,[188] candlesticks, gipser-rings,[189] chalices, hilts and pommels of swords, powder-boxes,[190] bands and bossells[191] for hanaps, out of copper and latten and they gild or silver them to resemble gold or silver and sell them or place them as pledges as if they were wholly of gold or silver to many men who do not have full knowledge of such matters, to the great deceit, loss and detriment of the common people and to the waste and destruction of gold and silver. It is ordained and established that no craftsman nor any other man whatsoever from henceforth may gild or silver any such clasps, rings, beads, candlesticks, gipser-rings, chalices, hilts or pommels for swords, powder-boxes, bands or bossels for hanaps made of copper or latten,

[186] Literally: to the works of.
[187] The words 'multiply' and 'multiplication' were applied to what later became known also as 'alchemy', the claims to be able to increase an amount of gold or silver by the addition of base metal. The results of such experiments could deceitfully be presented and used for supposedly fine gold or silver ware. See for instance the case recorded on pp. 222–23 above. See also Sir Thomas Phillipps, '*Mappae Clavicula*: A Treatise . . .; the text edited here by Phillipps presents a wide range of recipes for making and 'duplicating' or 'doubling' gold and silver. The text has been translated by Cyril Stanley Smith and John G. Hawthorne, *Mappae Clavicula: A Little Key to* . . . As Smith and Hawthorne point out in their introduction: 'There is no hint of making gold, only of imitating it and making a limited amount of it go further' (p. 18). The introductions to both the Phillipps edition and the translation list a large number of medieval manuscripts containing this text.
[188] Especially rosary beads.
[189] Rings by which a purse or bag might be suspended from a girdle.
[190] Probably at this date to contain either spices or salt and be used at table.
[191] The 'print' or ornamental medallion fixed in the bottom of a mazer or drinking bowl (see *OED*).

peyne de forfair*e* au Roy C s. a chescun foitz q'il serra trové coupable, *et* de fair*e* gré au p*ar*tie p*ur* sez damag*es*. Mes q*e*, chalys toutdys except*és*, les ditz artificers p*ur*rount fair*e* *et* eov*er*er ornementz a Seint Esglise de cupr*e* *et* latou*n* *et* les suisorrer *et* suisargentier p*ar* ainsy toutz foitz q*e* la pee ou autr*e* p*ar*tie de chescun ornement ensi affair*e* soit le cupr*e* ou latou*n* pleyn au fyn q*e* ho*m*me purra veer dount la chose est fait p*ur* eschivr*e* le desceit av*a*ntdite. Et le av*a*ntdit statute fuitz faitz a Westm*oustier* l'endemeyne de Seynt Hillar*e* l'an du regne le Roy Henry quart ap*rés* le conquest quinte.[436]

pp. 62–66[437]

1404? p. 67[438] (Hanes Cokeban est jurr*é* [*et*] voil paier ii nobles p*ur* estre suffry tank al feste de Pask *et* s'il dem*ur*re en outr*e*, *gr*aunte de fair*e* fyn ové les gardeyns.)

(Ingel Boteler est jurrez *et* *gr*aunte de paier p*ur* estr*e* suffrez xxvi s. viii d., c'est assavoir al feste de Noell xiii s. iiii d., *et* al feste de Pask xiii s. iiii d., *et* il ne eov*er*a as merceres ne a jewelers.)

(Henri Bussh in Schab*our*ne Lane est jurr*é* *et* ad *gr*aunté de paier lx s. p*ur* estr*e* suffry, c'est assavoir al festes del Noell, Purificacion de N*ost*re Dame et Pask, a chescun feste xx s.)

Wynant van Coloigne est jurrez *et* ad *gr*aunté de paier p*ur* estre suffriz xl s., c'est assavoir al feste de Noell *et* le Purificacion de N*ost*re Dame et ov*er*a p*ar* t*er*me de les ans q*e* est obligez.[439]

(Andrew Gast est jurrez *et* *gr*aunte de paier p*ur* estre suffriz xxvi s. viii d. c'est assavoir al feste de Toutz Seint *et* la feste del Purificacion.)

Nich*olas* Leygay est jurr*é* *et* *gr*aunte de paier xx s. p*ur* estr*e* suffriz al feste de Noell – ne s*er*vera a null merc*er* ne jeweler.

(It*em*, Joh*a*n Van Heous jurr*é*)
(It*em*, Gerard Van Braban)

1404 Jacob*us*[440] Bulke dem*ur*rant en Cricherche Aley – iiii m*ar*c*s* de paier le dymenge p*ro*schein dev*a*nt le feste de Pentecost l'an v^{te}, p*ur* estre suffrez d'ov*er*er en la dite mestier, *et* ceo q'il eov*er*a il les moust*ra* as orfev*er*s

[436] This last sentence has been added in a different hand and ink, probably the same hand that wrote the scribbled note upside down on p. 58.
[437] See below for the entries to these pages which were written at later dates.
[438] The hand of this page and the next is probably the same as that of p. 59. A number of entries on this page have been struck through by means of a line scored through the beginning and sometimes also the end of the entry, apparently by the scribe himself. No reasons are given. The entries affected are indicated here by round brackets around them.
[439] See also above, A + b, p. 59.
[440] This name is written above the scored 'Nich*o*l*a*us'.

on pain of forfeiture to the King of 100s. for each occasion on which he is found guilty, and of having to compensate the other party for his losses. However, with the exception always of chalices, the said craftsmen may make and decorate church ornaments of copper and latten and may gild and silver them, provided always that the base or some other part of each such ornament to be made shall be of plain copper or latten, so that one may see of what the object is made in order to avoid such aforesaid deceit. And the aforesaid statute was made at Westminster on the day after the feast of St Hilary in the year 5 Henry IV [14 January 1404 n.s.].

(Hans Cokeban has been sworn and will pay 2 nobles in order to obtain permission to work until Easter, and if he shall stay longer then he consents to agree with the wardens to a [further] fee.) p. 67

(Ingel Boteler has been sworn and consents to pay 26s 8d. for permission to work, i.e. 13s. 4d. at Christmas and 13s. 4d. at Easter, and he shall do no work for either mercers or jewelers.)

(Henry Busshe in Sharebourne Lane has been sworn and has consented to pay 60s. for permission to work, i.e. 20s. at each of the feastdays of Christmas, Candlemas and Easter.)

Wynant van Cologne has been sworn and has consented to pay 40s. for permission to work, i.e. at the feasts of Christmas and of Candlemas, and he shall work for the term of years to which he is bound.

(Andrew Gast has been sworn and consents to pay 26s. 8d. for permission to work, i.e. at the feasts of All Saints and Candlemas.)

Nicholas Leygey has been sworn and consents to pay 20s. at Christmas time for permission to work – he shall do no work for any mercer or jeweler.

(Item, Johan van Heous has been sworn)
(Item, Gerard van Brabant)

Jacob Bulke who lives in Christchurch Alley – 4 marks to be paid on the Sunday before Whit Sunday in the year 5 Henry IV [11 May 1404], for permission to work in the said mistery, and he is to show all that he makes

engleis p*ur* achater, *et* s'ils[441] ne voilent achater adonq*es* q'il[442] vende a autr*es*.

1404 p. 68 Fait a remembr*er* q*e* Henri Wortesburgh est examinez, jurrez *et* resceux en la mestier d'orfev*er*ie le lundy p*ro*schein apr*és* le feste de Seint Piet*er* ad vincul*a* l'an du r*egne le* r*oi* Henri quarte puys le conqueste quinte *et* ad paié p*ur* sou*n* entr*é* – xx m*ar*c*s*.

1405 It*em*, Gys Akerman est examinez, jurrez *et* resceux en la mestier d'orfev*er*ie le eoptisme jo*ur* de Fever*er* l'an du r*egne le* r*oi* [Henri] quarte sisme, *et* paia p*ur* sou*n* entr*é*[443]

1406–07 A + a p. 97 Ceux sount les nouns des Gardeyns eslutz *et* jurrez le jo*ur* de Seint Donston l'an du r*egne le* R*oi* Henri quarte puys le conqueste viie tanq*ue* a mesme feste l'an ensuant:

Thom*as* Extou*n*
Ric*hard* Bartou*n*
Joh*a*n Noreman
Ric*hard* George

App*r*entys resceux mesme an:

Ric*hard* Broune app*r*ent*y*s de Will*ia*m Barde –	xx s.
Thom*as* Mar*e* app*r*ent*y*s Ric*hard* Wythihale –	xx s.
Joh*a*n Laxman app*rentys* Joh*a*n Canou*n* –	xx s.
Rauf Botulf app*rentys* Rob*er*t Botulf –	xx s.
Will*ia*m Payn app*rentys* Joh*a*n Wyn –	xx s.
Harri Rageley app*rentys* George Cressy –	xx s.
Joh*a*n Flo*ur* app*rentys* Joh*an* Honte le puisné –	xx s.
app*rentys* Richa*rd*[444]	
Thom*as* Yernemowth*e* app*rentys* Joh*a*n Alyngtou*n* –	xx s.

Lowys en mesme an:

col. 1 Joh*a*n Botreux jadys app*r*entys Thom*as* Lamport –	ii s.
Joh*a*n Honte jadys app*r*entys Joh*a*n Hill*es* –	ii s.
Ric*hard* Prentys jadys app*r*entys Joh*a*n Frer*e* –	ii s.
George Geffrey jadys app*r*entys Will*ia*m Lyncoln*e* –	ii s.
Joh*a*n Bon jadys app*rentys* Will*ia*m Fithewe –	ii s.
Thom*as* Harwode jadys app*rentys* Dru Barentyn –	ii s.
Peres Goldesburgh*e* jadys app*rentys* Dru Barentyn –	ii s.
Joh*a*n Cottou*n* jadys app*rentys* Rich*ard* Bartou*n* –	ii s.
Joh*a*n Bray jadys app*rentys* Joh*a*n Forst*er* –	ii s.
Joh*a*n Ferro*ur* jadys app*rentys* Thom*as* Cresselowe –	ii s.
Joh*a*n Paulyn jadys app*rentys* Joh*a*n Canou*n* –	ii s.

441 MS: s'il ils.
442 MS: qils.
443 No sum is given.
444 These two words are on their own in the middle of a line.

to English goldsmiths for them to have the chance to buy it, and if they do not wish to buy anything then he may sell it to others.

Memorandum that Henry Wortesburgh has been examined, sworn and admitted into the goldsmiths' mistery on the Monday after the feastday of St Peter ad Vincula in the year 5 Henry IV [4 August 1404], and he has paid for his entry – 20 marks. 1404 p. 68

Item, Guy Akerman has been examined, sworn and admitted into the goldsmiths' mistery on 8 February 1405 n.s., and he paid for his entry 1405

These are the names of the wardens elected and sworn on St Dunstan's Day in the year 7 Henry IV [19 May 1406] until the same feastday in the following year: 1406–07 A + a p. 97

Thomas Exton
Richard Barton
John Norman
Richard George

Apprentices admitted the same year:

Richard Broun apprentice of William Barde –	20s.
Thomas Mare apprentice of Richard Withihale –	20s.
John Laxman apprentice of John Canon –	20s.
Ralph Botulf apprentice of Robert Botulf –	20s.
William Payn apprentice of John Wynne –	20s.
Harry Ragley apprentice of George Cressy –	20s.
John Flour apprentice of John Honte the younger –	20s.
apprentice of Richard	
Thomas Yarmouth apprentice of John Allington –	20s.

Serving-men in the same year:

John Botreux formerly apprentice of Thomas Lamport –	2s.	col. 1
John Honte formerly apprentice of John Hilles –	2s.	
Richard Prentys formerly apprentice of John Frere –	2s.	
George Geffrey formerly apprentice of William Lincoln –	2s.	
John Bon formerly apprentice of William FitzHugh –	2s.	
Thomas Harwood formerly apprentice of Drew Barantyn –	2s.	
Piers Goldsborough formerly apprentice of Drew Barantyn –	2s.	
John Cotton formerly apprentice of Richard Barton –	2s.	
John Bray formerly apprentice of John Forster –	2s.	
John Ferrour formerly apprentice of Thomas Cresselowe –	2s.	
John Paulyn formerly apprentice of John Canon –	2s.	

Thom*as* Thomer*e* jadys app*rentys* Rob*er*t Bech*e* –	ii s. – juré[445]
Rob*er*t Stanford jadys app*rentys* Rog*er* Cryngelforde –	ii s. – juré
Denys Tildesle [jadys] app*rentys* de Cristofr*e* Tildesle –	ii s.
Thom*as* Wylde jadys app*rentys* Henri Grene –	ii s.
Joh*an* Fitz Rob*er*t jadys app*rentys* Will*iam* Fithewe –	ii s.
col. 2 Joh*an* Suttone jadys app*rentys* Joh*an* Blakeden*e* –	ii s.
Thom*as* Brakenh*am* jadys app*rentys* Thom*as* Extou*n* –	ii s.
Henr*i* Mallynge jadys app*rentys* Andr*ew* Stamelden*e* –	ii s.
Rob*er*t Standelf jadys app*rentys* Joh*an* Standelf –	ii s.
Will*iam* Alkam jadys app*rentys* Salamon Oxeneye –	ii s.
Joh*an* Pope jadys app*rentys* Joh*an* Tewkesbury –	ii s.

Fait a remembr*er* q*e* un barr*e* al maner*e* d'un squirell*e* fuist pris en la schope de Piet*er* van Hous en Suthewerk come apiert p[*ar*][446] un bille sur mesme penduz.

It*e*m, un autr*e* barr*e* al maner*e* d'un chapelet fuist pris de Will*ia*m Markeby come apiert p*ar* bille sur mesme penduz.

1407 Fait a remembr*er* q*e* Will*ia*m Chipstede, jadys orfeve*re* de Loundr*es*,
p. 98 fauxement *et* disloialment disclaundra les gardeyns del mestier d'orfeve*r*ie de mesme la cité *et* toutz les hon*ur*ables gentz *et* la co*mun*ealté d'icell*e*, eux accusant dev*a*nt Rich*ard* de Whityngtou*n,* adonq*ues* Meir*e* de Loundres, vicecompt*es et* Aldermans de Loundres, *et* autres hon*ur*ables commu*n*s du dite cité, q*e* ové toutz les p*ro*fitz *et* rentes p*ro*venantz de les tenementz *et* rentes app*ur*tenantz au dite mestier, q*e* contient al so*m*me come il disoit dev*a*nt le dite Meir*e et* autres av*a*ntditz viii^{xx} ou ix^{xx} li., le quel est faux come ov*er*tement dev*a*nt lé ditez Meir*e et* Aldermans fuist provez, q*e* p*ar* mesmes gardeyns la dite monoye fuist despenduz en mayntenance de contecou*r*s, co*mun*es meffesou*r*s, fauxe quereles, en arrerisement *et* diffesaunce de les jeofnes gentz de mesme mestier q*e* voilent labou*r*er p*ur* lo*ur* susteignance gaign*er et* p*ur* emplet*er* gentz d'autres mestiers. Et puys[447] mesme Will*ia*m Chipstede ové autres de sa covygne a luy confiderez, c'est assavoir*e* Rog*er* Osborne, Will*ia*m Markeby, Will*ia*m Litherpoull*e*, Thom*as* Wylde *et* Henri Burneye ount ordeignez p*ur* avoir tuez[448] lo*ur* gardeyns del dite mestier d'orfeve*r*ie en lo*ur* co*mun*e sale en Fastres Lane de Loundres, p*ar* cause q*e* les ditz gardeyns ount entretés p*ar*entr*e* hon*ur*ables gentz del mestier dé Pelters de dite cité *et* les av*a*ntditz Rog*er et* sez compaignons av*a*nt nomez, p*ur* quel certeins p*er*sones de mesmes rebellés ensemble ové le dite Will*ia*m Chipstede furent arrestuz p*ur* lo*ur* rebelté. Et le dite Rog*er* Osbo*ur*ne, encountr*e* la fraunchise du dite cité *et* encountr*e* sou*n* serement fait al dite mestier, p*ur*sua al chaunceler d'Engl[e]ter*e* p*ur* avoir le dite Will*ia*m Chipstede dev*a*nt le dite Chaunceler p*ar* brief appellé 'corpus cu*m*

[445] It is unclear why only this and the next name have 'juré' written against them. All apprentices on coming out of their terms, paying 2s. and becoming regular workers in the mistery, were supposed to be sworn to keep the statutes and ordinances.

[446] MS: p*ur*.

[447] Above this word, in what appears to be the same hand but written scrappily, is the word 'aftward'. It and the other two instances below were written after the main text, i.e. as a gloss.

[448] Above this word is written: slayn.

Thomas Thomere formerly apprentice of Robert Beech – 2s. – sworn
Robert Stanford formerly apprentice of Roger Cringleford – 2s. – sworn
Denis Tyldesley [formerly] apprentice of Christopher Tyldesley – 2s.
Thomas Wylde formerly apprentice of Henry Grene – 2s.
John FitzRobert formerly apprentice of William FitzHugh – 2s.
John Sutton formerly apprentice of John Blakedene – 2s. col. 2
Thomas Brackenham formerly apprentice of Thomas Exton – 2s.
Henry Mallyng formerly apprentice of Andrew Stameldene – 2s.
Robert Standelf formerly apprentice of John Standelf – 2s.
William Alkam formerly apprentice of Solomon Oxney – 2s.
John Pope formerly apprentice of John Tewkesbury – 2s.

Memorandum that a girdle-bar in the form of a squirrel was seized in the shop of Pieter van Hous in Southwark, as is stated in a document attached to the same.

Item, another girdle-bar in the form of a chaplet was seized from William Markeby, as is stated in a document attached to the same.

Memorandum that William Chipstead, formerly a goldsmith of London, 1407
falsely and disloyally slandered the wardens of the goldsmiths' mistery of the p. 98
same city and all the honourable people and the commonalty of the same, accusing them before Richard de Whittington, then Mayor of London, the sheriffs and aldermen of London, and other honourable commoners of the said city, that they had spent all the money from the profits and rents coming from the tenements and rents belonging to the said mistery (which, as he said before the said Mayor and the other aforesaid people, comes to £160 or £180, which is untrue as was openly proved before the said Mayor and aldermen), on the maintenance of conteckers,[192] common miscreants, and false quarrels, to the detriment and the prejudice of the young men of the same mistery who wish to work to earn their living and to implead men of other misteries.[193] And afterwards the same William Chipstead with others who had joined in collusion with him, i.e. Roger Osborne, William Markeby, William Liverpool, Thomas Wylde and Henry Burney, drew up plans to kill their wardens of the said goldsmiths' mistery in their communal hall in Foster Lane in London, for the reason that the said wardens had negotiated between honourable men of the Skinners' mistery of the said city and the aforesaid Roger and his aforenamed companions, as a result of which certain persons who had also rebelled alongside the said William Chipstead were arrested for their rebellion. And the said Roger Osborne, in contravention of the liberties of the said city and of his oath sworn to the said mistery, brought a suit to the Chancellor of England to bring the said William Chipstead before the said Chancellor by writ of 'corpus cum causa'. And the said Chancellor, seeing the

[192] An obsolete word for 'one who contends at law, or is at strife or discord; a quarrelsome contentious person, etc.' *OED*.

[193] Rivalry between the different misteries was rife in London perhaps, but one still raises an eyebrow at this. It may well be that these are reported words of a somewhat allusive and wildly phrased accusation, the full intended sense being that the wardens should not be making trouble for men of their own mistery but those of others.

causa'. Et le dite Chaunceler, voyant la cause, luy remist a les vicecompt*es* de Loundres p*ur* estr*e* justefié solonc l'ordeignance du dite cité. Et ap*rés*, le dite Will*ia*m Chipstede disclaundra ses ditz gardeyns en les co*ur*tes du Roy *et* de Roign*e* del matier*e* av*a*ntdite, p*ur* quel la Roigne maunda sez hon*ur*ables l*ett*res al Meir*e* *et* les gardeyns av*a*ntditz p*ur* deliv*er*ance du dite Will*ia*m, come p*ar* la copie du dite l*ett*re desouz escrit pleynement piert. Sur quel, le dite Rich*ard* de Whityngtou*n* adonq*es* deliv*er*a mesme Will*ia*m Chipstede saunz assent de les gardeyns du dite mestier d'orfev*er*ie. Et enoutr*e*[449] le dite Will*ia*m Chipstede ad renunciez la mestier d'orfev*er*ie *et* dist eov*er*tement q'il ne voill*e* estr*e* al gov*er*nayle de sez gardeyns ne unq*es* claymer d'estr*e* orfev*er*e p*ur* M^1 li.[450]

La copie del brief p*ur*chasez p*ar* Rog*er* Osbo*ur*ne
Henric*us* dei gra*cia* Rex Anglie *et* Franc*ie* *et* D*omin*us Hib*erni*e vic*ariis* London' sal*ute*m. Precipim*us* vobis q*uo*d Will*ia*m Chipstede p*er* vos capt*us* *et* in prisona n*ost*re civitat*is* p*re*dict*e* ut dicit*ur* detent*us* h*abentes* coram nobis in cancellar*ia* n*ost*ra die sab*ba*ti p*roximo* futur*o* ubicu*nque* tunc fu*eri*t, una cu*m* causa capc*io*nis *et* detenc*io*nis eiusd*e*m. Et hoc nullaten*us* omitt*ere*. Et h*ab*eat*ur* ibi hoc l*itt*ere T*este* meip*s*o apud Westm*onasterium* xxi die April*is* anno r*egni* n*ost*ri octavo.

La copie del l*ett*re la Roign*e*.
Tresch*er* *et* bien amez: p*ur* ceo q*e* no*us* autrefoitz eousoms escrit a n*ost*re tresch*er* *et* tresentierement bien amé le Meir*e* de Loundres p*ur* la deliv*er*ance d'un Will*ia*m Chipstede q*e* estoit enprisoné en la cité s*us*d*ic*te p*ur* un certeyn mot q'il avoit dit, de verité a ceo q*e* no*us* adonq*es* estoioms enfo*ur*mez; Nesp*ur*qaunt, p*ur* ceo q*e* no*us* sumes enformez a p*re*sent coment le dite Will*ia*m luy ad apporté nyent g*ra*ciousement dev*er*s vo*us* ne les mestres de sou*n* art des orfev*er*s, dount il no*us* displest a cause de sou*n* orgelouseté *et* necligence cell*e* p*ar*tie; Nientmayns no*us*, desirauntz le bien de le dite Will*ia*m q*e* vo*us* prioms *et* p*ur* la chierté q*e* no*us* portons a sa p*er*sone, vo*us* prioms treschierement q*e*, p*ur* cause q*e* est del lynage de mou*n* tresch*er* *et* tresamé chapelayn S*ire* Joh*a*n Cleseby, q*e* vo*us* luy vuylez fair*e* desport *et* ease q*e* vo*us* purretz, ainsi toutfoitz q'a cause d'iceste n*ost*re prier*e* *et* p*ur* am*our* de no*us* q'il puisse estr*e* deliv*er*é hors de prisou*n* saunz fyn ou ra[u]nsou*n*[451] p*ur* sou*n* orgelouseté *et* necligence s*us*ditz ent fair*e* deinz la cité susd*ic*te. Et outre no*us* vo*us* saioms tresbone gree *et* autrefoitz de fair*e* chose a v*ost*re pleaser d'estr*e* pluys enclyné ceste. N*ostre* S*eignur* vo*us* eit toutz

[449] Above this word is written: More ouere.
[450] One may note a further document referring to this matter dated Westminster, 9 June 1407, a writ to the sheriffs of London in favour of Thomas Exton, Richard Barton, John Norman and Richard George at the suit of William Chepstede. See *Calendar of the Close Rolls preserved in the Public Record Office: Henry IV*, vol. III: *1405–1409* (London, 1931), p. 294. Chipstead makes a further appearance in the records in 1440–41, see below, A + b, p. 98.
[451] MS: 'rainsoun', almost certainly an orthographic error with one minim missing.

case, sent him back to the sheriffs of London to be judged according to the said city's ordinance. And afterwards, the said William Chipstead slandered his said wardens in the King's and the Queen's courts over the aforesaid matter, as a result of which the Queen sent her respectful letters to the Mayor and to the aforesaid wardens, asking for the said William to be released, as appears in full in the copy of the said letter written out below. As a result, the said Richard de Whittington then freed the same William Chipstead without the consent of the wardens of the said goldsmiths' mistery. And besides the said William Chipstead has renounced the mistery of goldsmiths and said in public that he did not wish to be under the rule of his wardens, nor did he ever wish to claim to be a goldsmith, not for a thousand pounds.

The copy of the writ obtained by Roger Osborne:
Henry by the grace of God King of England and of France and Lord of Ireland, to the sheriffs of London: Greeting. We command you that William Chipstead, who was arrested by you and whom, so it is said, you have in detention in a prison of our aforesaid city, shall from wherever he may then be be brought to our presence in our Chancellery next Saturday together with the cause of his arrrest and detention. And this you shall in no way omit to do. And this letter is to be brought there. Witnessed in person at Westminster on 21 April in the eighth year of our reign [1407].

The copy of the Queen's letter:
Dearest and well-beloved: whereas we has previously written to our most dear and entirely well-beloved the Mayor of London to ask for one William Chipstead to be set free, who had been imprisoned in the aforesaid city for certain words he had spoken, these being truthful ones as we had been informed at that time. Nevertheless, whereas we are at present informed as to how the said William has behaved towards you in a discourteous manner, as also towards the wardens of his craft of goldsmiths, which displeases us because of his overweening pride and careless disregard in this matter, nevertheless we, desiring the good of the said William which we beg you for, and for the fondness which we bear towards him, beseech you most dearly that since he is a relative of my most dear and most beloved chaplain Sir John Cleseby you will feel inclined to treat him with all the favour and leniency possible, so that in any case as a result of this our request and out of your love for us he may be released from prison without paying either fine or ransom within the aforesaid city for his overweening pride and careless disregard. And besides we are most grateful to you and shall on another occasion be more inclined to be favourable to carry out your wish. May our Lord hold you always in His most holy

j*o*urs en sa tressantisme garde *et* vo*us* doign*e* tresbone vie *et* long. Escript al Manoir*e* de Benyngtou*n*[452] le xxviii jo*ur* d'Aprill*e*.

1407–08 p. 99[453] Ceux sount les nouns des gardeyns eslutz al feste de Seint Donston l'an du *regne le* R*oi* Henri quarte puys le conqueste viii^{e} tank a mesme feste l'an ensuant:

Henri Ba*m*me
Joh*a*n Blakeden*e*
Joh*a*n Bernes
Thom*as* Popeltou*n*

1491–1562 Renters:[454]

a*nno* 7 H 7 ad 14 enrl?[455] –	A
a*nno* 15 H 7 ad 22 enrl? –	B
a*nno* 23 H 7 ad 8^{vi} H 8 –	C
a*nno* 9 H 8 ad 23 H 8 –	D
a*nno* 24 H 8 ad 4 Elis. –	E

1407–08 Joh*ann*es Luk apprent*icius*[456] Ric*ard*i George –	ii s. – jur*atus*
Joh*ann*es Bette app*r*ent*icius* Joh*ann*is Granth*a*m –	ii s. – jur*atus*
Thom*as* Wayt app*renticius* Joh*ann*is Lutou*n* –	ii s. – jur*atus*
Will*elmu*s Hope app*renticius* Joh*ann*is F*ra*unceys –	ii s. – jur*atus*
Joh*ann*es Colneye app*renticius* Joh*ann*is Blakeden*e* –	ii s. – jur*atus*
Fraunceys Frere jadys app*rentys* Joh*a*n Hounte –	ii s. – jur*atus*
Joh*ann*es Cresbyn jadys app*rentys* Joh*ann*[i]s[457] Biernys –	ii s. – jur*atus*
Rog*er* Wayland(?) jadys app*rentys* Remu*n*d Standelf –	ii s. – jur*atus*

[452] It would seem probable that this is a scribal copying error and that the Queen was at Kennington. The manor of Bennington = Long Bennington, Lincs., is mentioned in documents of the period (see e.g. J.L. Kirby, ed., *Calendar of Inquisitions post mortem*, vol. XVIII (London, 1987), via index), but there is no evidence of the Queen's having spent time there. Bevington, Warwicks., seems even less possible. Kennington however, was a king's manor on the Surrey bank of the river Thames about two miles south of London Bridge and was a frequent royal residence. See H.M. Colvin, *The History of the King's Works,* vols I and II (London, 1963), esp. pp. 967–69. I have been unable to trace any other copy of this letter from the Queen.

[453] Unfortunately, there is considerable damage to this page, rendering much of it illegible. It appears that the page may have been much faded and that someone has used a chemical to bring out the writing, but that this has now done further damage. The page has also clearly been used as scrap on which to scribble figures and sums of money, and it has also been torn (this mended in modern times). The five lines concerning the renters' books have been scrawled in a sixteenth-century hand in what was a blank space on this page; the space would appear to have been left for names of apprentices to be filled in later. The 'heading': 'Renters' is written twice in the LH margin; sideways on to these lines, in the LH margin, is written: 'Antoine Bate etc / mother Coverley etc'. A number of sums, figures, are written near these lines (most in Arabic notation e.g. '5.2.6', 43.14.4.'), some are also found at the bottom of the page, at the far RH side, and across the text in places; they appear to be scribbled calculations, and seem to indicate that this page was being considered as worthless scrap in the sixteenth century.

[454] This scribbling is interesting as it must refer to the Renters' Accounts books, now lost. They are listed as still surviving in an inventory of 1628–29: Goldsmiths' Company Archives MS E III, 4 (1), *olim* Guildhall MS 8749.

[455] It is uncertain but this may refer to these records being enrolled.

[456] This list is clearly one of serving-men sworn that year, the word 'jadys' being omitted from the first five entries.

[457] MS: Joh*ann*es.

protection and may he grant you a most good and long life. Written at the Manor of [Kennington][194] on 28 April [1407]

These are the names of the wardens elected on the feastday of St Dunstan in the year 8 Henry IV [19 May 1407] until the same feastday in the following year: 1407–08 p. 99

Henry Bamme
John Blakedene
John Barnes
Thomas Poppleton

Renters: 1491–1562

7 Henry VII to 14 [1491–2 – 1498–99] –	A
15 Henry VII to 22 [1499–1500 – 1506–07] –	B
23 Henry VII to 8 Henry VIII [1507–08 – 1516–17] –	C
9 Henry VIII to 23 Henry VIII [1517–18 – 1531–32] –	D
24 Henry VIII to 4 Elizabeth [1532–33 – 1561–62] –	E

John Luke apprentice of Richard George –	2s. – sworn	1407–08
John Bette apprentice of John Grantham –	2s. – sworn	
Thomas Wayt apprentice of John Luton –	2s. – sworn	
William Hope apprentice of John Fraunceys –	2s. – sworn	
John Colney apprentice of John Blakedene –	2s. – sworn	
Francis Frere formerly apprentice of John Honte –	2s. – sworn	
John Cresbien formerly apprentice of John Barnes –	2s. – sworn	
Roger Wayland formerly apprentice of Raymund Standelf –	2s. – sworn	

[194] See note on opposite page.

Juré – William Waltoun jadys apprentys Roger Aleyn – ii s. – juratus
Juré – Johannes Colnye jadys apprentys Robert Halle – ii s. – juratus
Johannes Halle jadys apprentys Petri Tounvile – ii s. – juratus
Robertus Waltoun jadys apprentys Johan Whirwelle – ii s. – juratus

1407 A + b p. 68 *cont.* Nichol Deveroun fuist jurrez le xxiie jour de Jullet l'an du regne le roi Henri eoptisme.

1407 A + a p. 99 Fait a remembrer qe le veille de Seint Pieter et Poulle l'an du regne le Roy Henri quarte puys le conqueste viiie, William Stevenessone de Lameslee del counté de Durham d.. . . . . a Piers Torold pur luy servir del feste del Nativité de [Seint Johan?] . . . . . . bien et loialment come servant tank al feste del Nativité [de Seint Johan?] . . . ans ensuantz. Pur quel Johan Willy . . . . . . et le dite William Stevenessone . . . . . . et issint servir a terme de ?vii? ans . . .

1407–08 Item, Gobelle, Ducheman, fuist . . .
Item, Hanes . . . fuist . . . defaute en anelx . . .
Item, Hanes . . . .., Duchman, fuist trové en defaute en firmaulx . . .
Item, pur ceo qe Johan Herwick fuist trové en defaute d'un lien d'un note et r . . . . . . de mesme . . . paié . . . companye – . . .

Memorandum quod generalis comitiva aurifabrorum London' debebant Christophiro . . . . . . tempore . . . viginta marcas quas quia . . . . . . Ricardo Bartonie.., aur.., ... Ricardo Bartonie recepit in partem . . . . . . eodem tempore existentibus – xl s. et residuum inde recipiet . . . reddit . . . .

p. 100 15?? Thomas Lodge { William Alleyn[458]
Richard Chamberlayne }

1407–08 [459]Nouns d'aprentys:
Johan Wylkensane de Geynesburghe apprentys Peris Torold – xx s.
Thomas Rammy de Comitatu Cantabrigh' apprenticius Petri Mayre – xx s.
Thomas Ledbarne de Comitatu Hertford' apprenticius Johannis Halle nuper apprenticius Petri Tounvile – xx s.
Thomas Turvyle de Comitatu Essex' apprenticius Johannis Parker – xx s.
Johannes Witleseye de Comitatu Cantabrigg' apprenticius Johannis Halle senioris – xx s. – nul, quia mortuus fuerat antequam indenture sue fuerunt sigillate.

[460]Fait a remembrer qe Johan Colneye pur i apprentys del counté de Barkshire appellé Walter Colneye[461] – xx s.

[458] These three names have been written at the top RH corner of the page in a sixteenth-century hand. Right at the top and partly cut off is written: Amphitract..??.
[459] A new hand starts here.
[460] A new hand starts here.
[461] The last three words have been added above the line slightly later.

Sworn – William Walton formerly apprentice of Roger Aleyn – 2s. – sworn
Sworn – John Colney formerly apprentice of Robert Halle – 2s. – sworn
John Halle formerly apprentice of Peter Tounvyle – 2s. – sworn
Robert Walton formerly apprentice of John Whirwelle – 2s. – sworn

Nichol Deveroun was sworn on 22 July 1407. 1407 A + b p. 68 *cont.*

Memorandum that on the eve of the feast of St Peter and St Paul in the year 8 Henry IV [28 June 1407] William Stevenson of Lamesley in the County of Durham [. . .] to Piers Thorold to serve him from the feast of the Nativity of St John[195] [. . .] well and faithfully as his servant until the feast of the Nativity of St John [?] years later. For whom John Willy [. . .] and the said William Stevenson [. . .] and thus to serve for a term of [7?] years [. . .] 1407 A + a p. 99

Item, Gobelle, 'Dutchman', was . . . 1407–08
Item, Hans [. . .] was [found] at fault over rings . . .
Item, Hans [. . .], 'Dutchman', was found at fault over clasps . . .
Item, whereas John Herwick was found at fault over the band for a coconut-cup and . . . of the same [. . .] paid [. . .] company

Memorandum that the general company of goldsmiths of London owed to Christopher [. . .] at the time [. . .] twenty marks, which because [. . .] to Richard Barton, goldsmith, [. . .] to Richard Barton, received in part [. . .] living at the same time – 40s. and receive the remainder from [. . .] hand over [. . .]

Thomas Lodge { William Alleyn / Richard Chamberlayne } p. 100

Names of apprentices: 1407–08
John Wylkensane of Gainsborough apprentice of Piers Thorold – 20s.
Thomas Remy from the County of Cambridge apprentice of Peter Mayre – 20s.
Thomas Ledbarne from Hertfordshire apprentice of John Halle, recently the apprentice of Peter Tounvile – 20s.
Thomas Turvyle from Essex apprentice of John Parker – 20s.
John Whittlesey from the County of Cambridge apprentice of John Halle the elder – 20s. annulled, because he died before his indentures were sealed

Memorandum that John Colney for an apprentice from Berkshire called Walter Colney – 20s.

195 It can be made out that the feast is of a Nativity and that of St John the Baptist (24 June) is the most probable.

Nich*ola*us Breto*u*n app*renticius* de Com*itatu* Suff' app*renticius* Will*ia*m Hertwell*e* – xx s.
Joh*annes* Hoker*e* app*renticius* Will*elm*i Downe de Com*itatu* Notyngh*a*m – xx s.
– unde d*ic*tus Will*elmus* r*ecepit* d*ic*tos xx s. in manu sua p*ro*p*ri*a ut patet in rotula debitor*um*.
Rog*er*us Kendale de London' app*renticius* Ric*ard*i Barto*u*n – xx s.
Will*elmus* Schrovysbury de Com*itatu* Buk*ingham* app*renticius* Joh*ann*is Granth*a*m – xx s.
– unde d*ic*tus Joh*ann*es r*ecepit* d*ic*tos xx s. in manu sua p*ro*p*ri*a ut p*atet* in rotula debitor*um*
Will*elmus* Hampston*e* de Com*itatu* Lyncoln' app*renticius* Petri Thorold – xx s.
Joh*ann*es Arnwaye de Com*itatu* Essex' app*renticius* Thome Lynke – xx s.
Thom*a*s Bart de Com*itatu* Sussex' app*renticius* Will*elm*i Bart – xx s.
Symon Collissone de Com*itatu* Northamppton' app*renticius* Will*elm*i Fyhug' – xx s.

?1407–08? A + b p. 58[462]

Johannes Forster
Johan Standelf
Joh*a*n Coraunt
Richard Barton
Johan Honte
Johan Blakedone
Johan Noreman
William Wawne
Richard George
Petrus Torald
Petrus Tounvyle
Johan Flete
Johan Huberd

} *pur* Perot Tounvyle *et* sou*n* app*re*ntys

1407–08 A + a p. 100 *cont.* [463]M*emorandum* q*uo*d eodem anno Joh*ann*es Wissyngsete recept*us* est in lib*er*ata eiusdem mistere ad eff*ec*tu*m* de essend*o* de co*mun*i consilio mistere p*re*dicte *et* ad hoc fecit fidem *et* sup*er* hoc concessu*m* est ei p*er* assensum tam custodu*m* mistere p*re*dic*t*e q*ua*m tocius co*mun*itatis eiusdem q*uo*d ip*s*e lib*er*atam p*re*dic*t*am annuatim h*ab*ebit de dono absq*ue* aliquo p*ro* eadem lib*er*at*a* solvend*o*.

Fait a remembr*er* q*e* del assent dez gardeyns *et* autr*e*s hon*ur*ables gentz del mistier d'orfeverie, Jacob Grace fytz Thomas Grace, cop*er*smyth*e*, *et* prentice

[462] This entry is incorporated here with all due reservations as to date. It is not at all obvious what this list is of, nor why the names are all bracketed to the remark at the RH side. However, it seems possible that the date is 1407–08 and that these men have approved the transfer of Tounvile's apprentice Thomas Ledbarne to a new master, John Halle. See A + a, p. 100 above.
[463] A new hand starts here.
[464] This page has been quite extensively scribbled over by the same sixteenth-century hand that was scribbling figures etc. also on p. 99. The page has also been repaired in modern times.

Nicholas Breton from the County of Suffolk apprentice of William Hertwelle – 20s.
John Hokere from the County of Nottingham apprentice of William Downe – 20s.
– from whom the said William received into his own hands the said 20s. as it appears in the roll of debtors
Roger Kendal of London apprentice of Richard Barton – 20s.
William Shrewsbury of the County of Buckingham apprentice of John Grantham – 20s.
– from whom the said John received into his own hands the said 20s. as it appears in the roll of debtors
William Hampston from the County of Lincoln apprentice of Piers Thorold – 20s.
John Arnwaye from Essex apprentice of Thomas Lynk – 20s.
Thomas Bart from Sussex apprentice of William Bart – 20s.
Simon Collissone from the County of Northampton aprentice of William FitzHugh – 20s.

John Forster A + b p. 58
John Standelf
John Coraunt
Richard Barton
John Honte
John Blakedene
John Norman
William Wawne
Richard George
Piers Thorold
Peter Tounvyle
John Flete
John Huberd
} for Piers Tounvyle and his apprentice

Memorandum that in the same year John Wissyngsete[196] was admitted to the livery of the same mistery to the effect that he should be of common counsel to the aforesaid mistery, and he swore to be faithful in this, and it was then granted to him by the assent both of the wardens of the aforesaid mistery as also of the whole company of the same that he should have as a gift each year the aforesaid livery without having to pay anything for the same livery. A + a p. 100

Memorandum that by the assent of the wardens and other honourable men of the goldsmiths' mistery, it was ordained that Jacob Grace, son of Thomas

[196] He is clearly a lawyer.

Ric*hard* Mariot, ordeigné est p*ar* lez hon*ur*ables av*a*ntditz desoreenav*a*nt ne s*er*ra p*ri*s p*ar* le dit Ric*hard* ne p*ur* null*e* autr*e* du dit mistier, sur pey[n]e de payer s*umm*a x li. Et le dit Jacob est juggé q*e* jammés ne vendra en le mistier av*a*ntdit.

p. 101[464] JC[465]

Pur ceo q*e* Joh*a*n Cottou*n* fuist trové en defaut del ov*er*aigne dez colers appellez 'S',[466] des queux S quatre[467] sount en garde come appiert p*ar* un bill*e* le xxme jo*ur* d'apprill*e*; il ad payé a cell*e* temps – iii s. iiii d.

Joh*ann*es Chervell*e*:

Pur ceo q*e* Joh*a*n Chervell*e* fuist trové en defaut del ov*er*aigne del garnyscho*ur* d'un note le xme jo*ur* d'aprill*e* et issint t*r*ové p*ar* dieux foitz, dount ad payé al almoigne de Seint Dunstou*n* – iii s. iiii d.

Nicho*la*us Bokyll*e*:

Pur ceo q*e* Nicholas Bokyll*e* le xiime jo*ur* d'aprill*e* fuist trové en defaut del ov*er*aigne dez bokyls [et] pendantz dount soun ov*er*aigne fuist trové ez mayns de div*erses* gentz p*ar* div*erses* foitz dount ad payé – ii s.

Thomas Willow*us*:

Pur ceo q*e* Thom*a*s Wilw*us*, orfev*er*e,[468] *et* Will*ia*m Schoryn, herberg*er*, furent trovez en defaut dez c*er*teins debat*es* p*ar*entr*e* eux pendauntz de sclaundr*e* *et* mals p*ar*ols, les gardeins p*ur* le an esteantz ount ordeinez q*e* chescun d'eux s*er*ra obligé a autr*e* en un obligac*io*u*n* de xl s. s*ur* le condiciou*n* qu'ensuit:

La condic*io*u*n* de cest obligac*io*u*n* est tiell*e* q*e* si l'av*a*ntdit Thom*a*s Willew*us* desclaundra ou defama p*ar* luy ou p*ar* ascun autr*e* en sou*n* nou*n* issint q*e* poet estr*e* p*r*ové p*ar* dieux foialx ho*m*mes de cez vicines l'av*a*ntdit Wi[lliam],[469] q'adonq*es* il payera sou*n* obligac*io*u*n* de xl s. Et en mesme la man*er*e q*e* si l'av*a*ntdit Will*ia*m Schoryn defama ou disclaundra l'av*a*ntdit Thom*a*s Wilew*us* p*ar* luy ou p*ar* ascun autr*e* en sou*n* nou*n*, issint q*e* poet estr*e* p*r*ové p*ar* dieux ho*m*mes foyalx, q'adonq*es* il payera sou*n* obligac*io*u*n* de xl s.

Joh*ann*es Chervell*e*:

Pur ceo q*e* Joh*a*n Chervell*e* le xj^me^ jo*ur* de Maii fuist t*r*ové en default dev*a*nt lez

465 These initials (for Johan Cottoun) have been written as a sort of sub-heading in the LH margin, and below the full name of each offender is similarly written.

466 These collars of SS were very expensive items. A contemporaneous (1407) document (PRO, E403/589) records a payment to Christopher Tyldesley of £385 6s. 8d. by the king 'pro uno colari auri operato cum hoc verbo "soveignez" et litteris de S et X, aymellato et garnizato cum ix grossis perlis, duodecim grossis dyamandis, viii^to^ Baleys, viii^to^ sapharis, una cum uno grandi Rubi in eo infixo et garnisato cum iiii^or^ grossis perlis, quodquidem colare cum toto apparatu supradicto eidem domino Regi apud Wynton' liberat*um* extitit . . .'.

467 This word has been scored out and 'iii' is written above it.

468 MS: dorfeu*er*e.

469 The text runs off the outer edge of the page, which has been cropped.

Grace, coppersmith, and apprentice of Richard Mariot, shall from henceforward not be taken on by the said Richard nor by anyone else of the said mistery, on penalty of paying the sum of £10. And judgment was given that the said Jacob shall never enter the aforesaid mistery.

J.C. p. 101
Whereas John Cotton was found at fault in the workmanship of collars called 'collars of SS',[197] four of the which are being kept in custody, as is stated in a certificate of 20 April, he paid at this time – 3s. 4d.

John Chervelle:
Whereas John Chervelle was found at fault on 10 April in the workmanship of the garnishings of a coconut-cup, and was thus found guilty twice, for which he has paid to the alms funds of St Dunstan – 3s. 4d.

Nicholas Bokylle:
Whereas Nicholas Bokylle was on 12 April found at fault in the workmanship of buckles and pendants, of which his work has been found in the hands of various people at different times, and for which he has paid – 2s.

Thomas Wylwes:
Whereas Thomas Wylwes, goldsmith, and William Schoryn, inn-keeper, were found at fault over certain quarrels between them concerning slander and evil words, the current wardens have ordered that each of them shall be bound to the other by letters obligatory in the sum of 40s. with the following condition:

The condition of this obligatory letter is such that if the aforesaid Thomas Wylwes shall slander or defame the aforesaid William, if either he himself do this or has it done by someone else in his name, and thus that this can be proved by two loyal men from among his neighbours,[198] that then he shall pay his bond of 40s. And in the same manner, if the aforesaid William Schoryn shall defame or slander the aforesaid Thomas Wylwes , either doing this himself or having it done by another in his name, thus that it can be proved by two loyal men, that then he shall pay his bond of 40s.

John Chervelle:
Whereas John Chervelle was on 11 May found at fault before the wardens over

[197] Livery collars formed of chains of linked letters S – the livery of the house of Lancaster, granted by Henrys IV, V, and VI. See A.P. Purey-Cust, *The Collar of SS*; Joan Evans, *A History of Jewellery 1100–1870*, pp. 66–68. The King paid Christopher Tyldesley 'for a collar of gold worked with the word 'Remember' and the letters S and X, enamelled and garnished with nine large pearls, twelve large diamonds, eight balas rubies, eight sapphires, together with a large ruby set into it and garnished with 4 large pearls'.

[198] There are later references also to 'neighbours' in the same type of phrase. There would appear to have been no specific technical legal definition of such, but in a London context they would probably have been required to have been from the same parish, and for one of the larger parishes, perhaps from the same area. (I am grateful to Dr Paul Brand for this information.)

gardeins del ov*er*aigne[470] d'un cup*e*bonde ennorez, ils ount ordeignez q'il s*er*ra obligé as eux en un obligac*i*oun de .x. li. *sur* cest co*n*dic*i*oun q*e* si le dit Joh*a*n Chervell*e* soit t*ro*vé desoreenav*a*nt faulx en sou*n* ov*er*aigne, q'adonq*e*s il paiera la so*m*me av*a*ntdit al almoign*e* de Seint Dunston.

Hans Van Tyoll*e*:
Pur ceo q*e* Hans Van Tyol de Geldirland vient en la sale le xj^{me} jo*ur* de Maii *et* la ad jur*é* *sur* le liv*er*e p*ar* cause q*e* fuist t*ro*vé p*ar* sou*n* p*ro*p*re* record en defaut, q*e* fuist ov*er*aunt ovesq*e*s Jak*e*s Davy, cotillere, q'il ja*m*més ne ov*er*a ové null*e* autr*e* ho*m*me de null*e* man*er*e mistier mes soulm*en*t ové un orfev*er*e *et* *sur* ceo est jur*é* *sur* le liv*er*e dev*a*nt eux. Et outr*e* est obligé en un obligac*i*ou*n* de .x. li.[471] as gardeins p*ur* l'an esteantz q*e*, si soit t*ro*vé desoreenav*a*nt ov*er*aunt ové ascun autr*e* ho*m*me qe orfe*vere*, q'adonq*e*s il payera al almoigne de Seint Dunstou*n* la so*m*me av*a*ntdit.

1408–09 Ceux sount lez nouns des gardeins eslutz al fest de Seint Dunstou*n* l'an du regne
A + a le Roi Henr*i* quart puis le conquest ixme tanq*e* al mesme feste l'an ensuant:
p. 102[472] Salamannus Oxneye
Rob*er*tus Hall*e*
Joh*ann*es Palyng
Will*el*m*us* Adys

1409 Gaunt[473] . . . Gerard Alfkyn:
Fait a remembr*er* q*e* le p*ri*m*er* jour de March*e* l'an du regne le Roi Henr*i* quart puis le conquest xme Joh*a*n de Gaunt, Gobell*e* de Coleyn*e*, Gerloff Vlythik,[474] Ducheman, Gerard Alfkyn[475] de Utrawt veignent dev*a*nt lez gardeyns p*ur* l'an esteantz *et* Dru Barantyn adonq*e*s esteantz Mair*e* de Loundr*es*, Will*ia*m Louth*e*, Joh*a*n Bulstrode, Ric*hard* George, Will*ia*m Granth*a*m, Joh*a*n Frensch*e*, Joh*a*n Downe, Joh*a*n Walsch*e* *et* Thom*a*s Well*es*, *et* la ount juré *sur* le liv*er*e dev*a*nt toutz eux de bien *et* loialment tener *et* mainteyn*er* lez poyntz *et* articles au dit mestier app*ur*tenantz, *et* *sur* ceo s*er*rount suffrez d'ov*er*er ez lieux covenablez al ordinanc*e* dez gardeins p*ur* l'an esteantz . . .

Stykeneye:
Fait a remembr*er* q*e* la xvme jour d'Aprill*e* l'an du regne le Roi Henr*i* quart puis le conquest xme, Will*ia*m Stykeneye de Coventr*e* vient dev*a*nt lez Gardeins p*ur* l'an esteantz *et* la ad juré de bien *et* loyalment s*er*ver Joh*a*n Palyng sou*n* meist*re* p*ar* iii ans et aprés de bien et loyalment garder *et* teingn*er* lez articlez *et* pointz

[470] MS: ov*er*aignde.
[471] This amount has been added above the line after an omission mark, but in the same hand and ink.
[472] This page has also been scribbled over and has smudges of ink.
[473] These sub-headings are once again in the LH margin. The paper is damaged near this first one; the information also appears here that Ghent paid the sum of 'vi li.' and below this paragraph is written in later that Gobelle paid £6 also. The other scribbled figures here appear to be later and not to concern this entry.
[474] This surname has been added above the line.
[475] This surname has also been added above the line.

the workmanship of a gilded ornamental band for a cup, they ordered that he shall be bound to them by letters obligatory in the sum of £10 on this condition, that if the said John Chervelle should henceforward be found defective in his workmanship, that then he shall pay the aforesaid sum to the alms funds of St Dunstan.

Hans van Tyol:
Whereas Hans van Tyol of Gelderland came to the Hall on 11 May and there, because he had been found guilty by his own record of working with Jakes Davy, cutler, he swore on the book that never shall he work with any other man of any mistery whatsoever except only with a goldsmith, and to this he was sworn before them on the book. And besides he was bound by letters obligatory to the current wardens in the sum of £10, that if he should from henceforward be found working with any man other than a goldsmith, that then he shall pay to the alms funds of St Dunstan the aforesaid sum.

These are the names of the wardens elected at the feast of St Dunstan in the year 9 Henry IV [19 May 1408] until the same feastday in the following year: 1408–09 p. 102
Solomon Oxney
Robert Halle
John Palyng
William Adys

Ghent . . . Gerard Alfkyn:
Memorandum that on 1 March 1409 John de Ghent, Gobelle de Cologne, Gerloff Vlythik, 'Dutchman', Gerard Alfkyn of Utrecht came before the current year's wardens and Drew Barantyn, then Mayor of London, William Louth, John Bulstrode, Richard George, William Grantham, John Frenshe, John Downe, John Walsh and Thomas Welles, and there they swore before them all on the book to keep and maintain well and faithfully all the ordinances and regulations pertaining to the said mistery, and upon this they shall be permitted to work in suitable places as ordained by the current wardens.

Stickney:
Memorandum that on 15 April 1409 William Stickney of Coventry came before the current year's wardens and there he swore to serve well and faithfully John Palyng, his master, for 3 years and afterwards to hold and keep well and faithfully the regulations and ordinances pertaining to the mistery in his work

ou mistier app*ur*tenantz en soun ov*er*e de mesme, *et* a ceo ad payé as ditz Gardeins al oeps du dit mistier – v m*ar*cz. Et a quell*e* temps q*e* le dit Will*ia*m poet garn*er* ascuns amys de luy ayder d'estr*e* frenk*e* a la Guyldehall*e*, q'adonq*es* lez Gardeins p*ur* l'an esteantz alerount *et* eayderount ovesq*e* le dit Will*ia*m en taunt q'ils p*ur*rount.

Constantyne:
Fait a remembr*er* q*e* le xxme jour de Maii Constantyn*e* de Heyde de Westvale, l'an du regne le Roi Henr*i* quart puis le conquest xme, vient dev*a*nt lez gardeins av*a*ntdit del mistier d'orfev*er*ie *et* la ad jur*é* *sur* le liv*er*e dev*a*nt eux de bien *et* loialment ten*er* et mainteign*er* toutz lez pointz *et* articles au dit mistier app*ur*tenantz et de bien *et* loialment ov*er*er or *et* argent, *et* *sur* ceo s*er*ra suffr*i* d'ov*er*er del mistier av*a*ndit ez lieux covenablez.

Fait a remembr*er* q*e* le jour de Seint Dunstou*n* l'an du regne le Roi Henr*i* quart puis le conquest xme p*ar* co*mun*e assent *et* avys dez on*ur*ables gentz, Mair*e* *et* Aldermans, Gardeins *et* autr*es* del mistier d'orfev*er*ie, ount gr*a*untez a Thomas Cove, comune s*er*vant al dit mistier,[476] xviii d. p*ar* le semayn*e*. Issint q*e* le dit Thom*as* Cove s*er*ra a toutz temps pr*e*st al comaundem*en*t dez Gardeins p*ur* l'an esteantz p*ur* faire ceo q'ils luy comaunderont p*ur* l'on*ur*e *et* av*a*nttag*e* del mistier av*a*ndit. Et sy le dit Thom*as* Cove soit ou p*ur*roit est*re* trové defective p*ar*ount lez on*ur*ables gentz ou la Companye d'orfev*er*ie p*ur*rount estr*e* disclaundrez ou defamez, q'adonq*es* soit voidé *et* oustee p*ar* assent dez on*ur*ablez gentz av*a*ntditz.

1408–09 Lowys:

p. 103	Nichol*a*us Twyford [quond*a*m] app*re*ntic*ius* Drugonis Barantyn*e* –	ii s. – jur*atus*
	Joh*ann*es Clerk quond*a*m app*re*ntic*ius* Will*elm*i Burguloun –	ii s. – jur*atus*
	Joh*ann*es Alkam quond*a*m app*re*ntic*ius* Salamonis Oxney –	ii s. – jur*atus*
	Joh*ann*es Marwe quond*a*m app*re*ntic*ius* Will*elm*i Lyncoln*e* –	ii s.[477]
	Walt*er*us Foundour quond*a*m app*re*ntic*ius* Thome Extou*n* –	ii s.
	Will*elmu*s atte Welle quond*a*m app*re*ntic*ius* Joh*ann*is Standelf –	ii s. jur*atus*
	Cows Harry quond*a*m app*re*ntic*ius* Joh*ann*is Davy –	ii s. – jur*atus*
	Joh*ann*es Nongyl quond*a*m app*re*ntic*ius* Will*elm*i Fytzhugh*e* –	ii s. – jur*atus*
	Thom*as* Nowentone quond*a*m app*re*ntic*ius* Joh*ann*is Gale –	ii s. – jur*atus*

Apprentic*es*:

Rog*er*us Roskyn*e* app*re*ntic*ius* Joh*ann*is Whyte –	xx s.
Joh*ann*es Parantyn*e* app*re*ntic*ius* Salamonis Oxney –	xx s.
Adam Fytz Hugh*e* app*re*ntic*ius* Will*elm*i Wodma*n* –	xx s.
Thomas Crowe app*re*ntic*ius* Ric*ard*i George –	xx s.
Rog*er*us Extou*n* app*re*ntic*ius* Thome Extou*n* –	xx s.
Thom*as* Gyllyng app*re*ntic*ius* Rob*er*ti Lemyng –	xx s.
Will*elmu*s Genyows app*re*ntic*ius* Joh*ann*is Hall*e* –	xx s.

476 The word 'p*re*ndra' has been added above the line by the same scribe, in the same ink; it does not fit into the syntax of the sentence, although its sense ('will take') is clear.

477 There appears to be an erasure here of the word 'jur''.

of the same, and he then paid to the said wardens for the use of the said mistery – 5 marks. And at whatever time the said William may be able to provide some friends to help him to be made free at the Guildhall, that then the current year's wardens shall go and assist the said William in as far as they shall be able.

Constantyne:
Memorandum that on 20 May 1409 Constantyne de Heyde from Westphalia came before the aforesaid wardens of the goldsmiths' mistery and there he swore on the book before them to keep and maintain well and faithfully all the regulations and ordinances pertaining to the said mistery and to work gold and silver well and faithfully, and upon that he shall be permitted to work within the aforesaid mistery in suitable places.

Memorandum that on St Dunstan's Day in the year 10 Henry IV [19 May 1409], by common assent and advice of the honourable men the Mayor and Aldermen, the Wardens and others of the goldsmiths' mistery, they granted to Thomas Cove, beadle of the said mistery, 18d. per week. Thus that the said Thomas Cove shall be at all times ready at the command of the current wardens to do what they shall command him for the honour and the advantage of the aforesaid mistery. And if the said Thomas Cove should be or could be found at fault in any way whereby the honourable men or the goldsmiths' company could be slandered or defamed, that then he shall be dismissed and removed from his office by the assent of the aforesaid honourable men.

Serving-men: 1408–09
Nicholas Twyford formerly apprentice of Drew p. 103
Barantyn – 2s. – sworn
John Clerk[199] formerly apprentice of William Burgyloun – 2s. – sworn
John Alkam formerly apprentice of Solomon Oxney – 2s. – sworn
John Marwe formerly apprentice of William Lincoln – 2s.
Walter Foundour formerly apprentice of Thomas Exton – 2s.
William atte Welle formerly apprentice of John Standelf – 2s. – sworn
Cows Harry formerly apprentice of John Davy – 2s. – sworn
John Nongyl formerly apprentice of William FitzHugh – 2s. – sworn
Thomas Nowentone formerly apprentice of John Gale – 2s. – sworn

Apprentices:
Roger Roskyne apprentice of John White – 20s.
John Parantyne apprentice of Solomon Oxney – 20s.
Adam FitzHugh apprentice of William Woodman – 20s.
Thomas Crowe apprentice of Richard George – 20s.
Roger Exton apprentice of Thomas Exton – 20s.
Thomas Gilling apprentice of Robert Lemyng – 20s.
William Junyos apprentice of John Halle – 20s.

[199] *alias* Mablean: see Name Index.

Thom*as* ȝung*er* app*re*ntic*ius* Joh*ann*is Standelf – xx s.
Petrus Gosse app*re*ntic*ius* Joh*ann*is Cottou*n* – xx s.
Will*elmu*s Helston*e* app*re*ntic*ius* Ric*ard*i Wethyale – xx s.
Will*elmu*s Furneys app*re*ntic*ius* Joh*ann*is Farletou*n* – xx s.
Thom*as* Lagage app*re*ntic*ius* Joh*ann*is Lagage – xx s.
Thomas Spegernell*e* app*re*ntic*ius* Will*elm*i Adys – xx s.

1409–10 Ceux sount lez nouns des gardeins eslutz al feste de Seint Dunston*e* l'an du
p. 104 regne le Roi Henr*i* quart puis le conquest xme tanq*e* al dit feste de Seint Dunston*e* l'an ensuant:
Will*elmu*s Grantha*m*
Will*elmu*s Randolf
Joh*ann*es Wat*er*
Joh*ann*es Pake

1410 Galeas: Fait a remembr*er* q*e* [le] iiime jo*ur* de Janev*er* l'an du regne le Roi Henr*i* quart puis le conquest xj^{me} Galeas Tav*er*ne de Amelon vient dev*a*nt lez Gardeins dev*a*nt esc*ri*ptz *et* la ad jur*é* *sur* le liv*er*e de bien *et* loialment teign*er*, mainteign*er* *et* s*er*v*er* toutz les pointz *et* articles au dit mistier app*ur*tenantz *et* *sur* ceo s*er*ra suffr*y* d'ov*er*er d'or *et* d'argent *et* p*er*r*ie*[478] ez lieux covenablez – x m*ar*cz.

Notu*m* sit om*n*ib*us* q*uo*d nos Will*elmu*s Grantha*m*, W.R.,[479] J. Wat*er*, J. Pake, Custodes artis aurifabror*um*, dedim*us* licencia*m* Galeas Taverne de Amelon*e* ad op*er*andu*m* opus artis p*re*dic*t*e in domo vel in cam*er*a secrete set no*n* tam*en* ap*er*te p*er* strata*m*, p*ro* sum*m*a dece*m* marcar*um* nob*is* p*re*manib*us* p*er*solut*a*. Unde id*e*m Galeas nob*is* juravit sup*er* libru*m* ben*e* *et* fidelit*er* op*er*ar*e* *et* secreta artis custodir*e* ac p*ro*mte ad sum*moniciones* art*is* venir*e*. In cui*us* rei testi*monium* custodes sigilla sua apposuer*unt*[480] Dat*um* xxviii° die Martii A*nn*o r*egni* r*egis* undecimo.

Henr*i* Busch*e*:
M*emorandum* q*uo*d xvi die Maii Henr*icus* Bussch*e* de Braban venit cora*m* Will*elm*o Grantha*m*, Will*elm*o Randolf, Joh*ann*e atte Wat*er* *et* Joh*ann*e Pake, a*nno* r*egni* r*egis* Henr*ici* quarti xj°, *et* ib*id*em juravit sup*er* libru*m* ben*e* *et* fidelit*er* op*er*ar*e* auru*m* *et* argentu*m* *et* ben*e* custodir*e* om*n*es articulos art[i][481] p*re*dict*e* p*er*tinent*es*, p*ro* quada*m* su*m*ma pecunie – iii li.. Et sup*er* p*re*dic*tam* custodes ded*er*unt p*re*dic*t*o Henrico licencia*m* op*er*ar*e* secrete locis honestis – iii li.

Henri Entz:
M*emorandum* q*uo*d xvj° die Maii a*nno* r*egni* r*egis* Henr*ici* quarti xj°, Henr*icus* Entz de Colonya venit cora*m* Will*elm*o Grantha*m*, Will*elm*o Randolf, Joh*ann*e atte Wat*er* *et* Joh*ann*e Pake, custodes artis aurifabror*um*, *et* ib*id*em juravit sup*er* libru*m* ben*e* *et* fidelit*er* op*er*ar*e* auru*m* *et* argentu*m* *et* ben*e* custodir*e* om*n*es

[478] '*et* p*er*r*ie*' has been added above the line, with an omission mark, at a slightly later time.
[479] *Sic.*
[480] The previous four words here have been added interlinearly but at the same time as the rest.
[481] MS: arte.

Thomas Younger apprentice of John Standelf –	20s.
Peter Gosse apprentice of John Cotton –	20s.
William Helston apprentice of Richard Withihale –	20s.
William Furneys apprentice of John Farleton –	20s.
Thomas Lagage apprentice of John Lagage –	20s.
Thomas Spegernelle apprentice of William Adys –	20s.

These are the names of the wardens elected on the feastday of St Dunstan in 1409–10
the year 10 Henry IV [19 May 1409] until the said feastday of St Dunstan in p. 104
the following year:
William Grantham
William Randolf
John Water
John Pake

Galeas:
Memorandum that on 3 January 1410 [n.s.] Galeas Taverne of Amelon came before the aforenamed wardens and there he swore on the book to keep, maintain and to serve well and faithfully all the regulations and ordinances pertaining to the said mistery, and upon this he shall be permitted to work gold and silver and precious stones in suitable places – 10 marks.

Be it known to all that we, William Grantham, William Randolf, John Water, John Pake, wardens of the goldsmiths' mistery, have given permission to Galeas Taverne of Amelon to be a practitioner in work of the aforesaid mistery in his house or in private chambers, but not openly on the street, for the sum of ten marks paid to us into our hands. For which reason the same Galeas swore to us on the book to work well and faithfully and to guard the secrets of the mistery and promptly to come to the summons of the mistery. In witness of which the wardens have affixed their seals. Given on 28 March 1410.

Henry Busshe:
Memorandum that on 16 May 1410 Henry Busshe of Brabant came before William Grantham, William Randolf, John atte Water and John Pake, and there swore on the book well and faithfully to work gold and silver and to keep well all the regulations pertaining to the aforesaid mistery, for a certain sum of money – £3. And upon this the wardens gave permission to the aforesaid Henry to work in private in honest places – £3.

Henry Entz:
Memorandum that on 16 May 1410 Henry Entz of Cologne came before William Grantham, William Randolf, John atte Water and John Pake, wardens of the goldsmiths' mistery, and there he swore on the book to work gold and silver well and faithfully and to keep well all the ordinances of the

articulos artis p*redic*te *pro* quada*m* su*m*ma pecunie – v m*arcas*. Et sup*er* hoc p*redicti* custodes dederu*n*t p*redic*to Henr*ico* licencia*m* ben*e* op*erare* locis honest*is* – v m*ar*cz.

1409 A + b p. 68 *cont.* Nich*ola*us Holonder fuist jurez le xme de Juyll*et* l'an du regne le Roi Henr*i* quart xme de bien *et* loialment ten*ir et servir* lez pointz av*a*ntescr*i*ptz – ii s. iiii d.[482]

1409 A + a p. 105 Fait a remembr*er* q*e* le pr*imer* jo*ur* d'aust Henr*i* Mallyng fuist jurré dev*a*nt Will*iam* Granth*am et* Will*iam* Randolff, Joh*a*n Wat*er et* Joh*a*n Pake de bien *et* loialment ten*ir et servir* lez pointz au ditz mistier*e* app*ur*tenantz.

1409–10 Appr*entys*:[483]

col. 1 In p*rimis* Ric*ard*us Cowlyng appr*enticius* Will*elm*i Granth*am*
It*em*, Elys Harewod*e* appr*enticius* Will*elm*i Randolf
It*em*, Thom*as* Swynysco appr*enticius* Johannis atte Wat*er*
It*em*, Petrus Lawdy appr*enticius* Joh*ann*is Paake
It*em*, Thom*as* Ba*m*me appr*enticius* Rob*er*ti Hall*e*
It*em*, Joh*ann*es Byrlyng appr*enticius* Joh*ann*is Wynne
It*em*, Nich*ola*us Lovet appr*enticius* Henr*ici* Wortysburgh*e*
It*em*, Ric*ard*us Wynne appr*enticius* Joh*ann*is Palyng
It*em*, Ric*ard*us Mallyng appr*enticius* Will*elm*i atte Wode
It*em*,Ric*ard*us Gybb*e* appr*enticius* Thome Foxcote
It*em*, Joh*ann*es Paraunt appr*enticius* Will*elm*i Hertwell*e*
It*em*, Reynold Clyppyng appr*enticius* Joh*ann*is Colney
It*em*, Joh*ann*es Reep appr*enticius* Joh*ann*is Botereux
It*em*, Joh*ann*es Kyng appr*enticius* Joh*ann*is Walsch*e*
It*em*, Will*elmu*s Smyth*e* appr*enticius* Nich*ola*i Wodhill*e*
It*em*, Will*elmu*s Goolde appr*enticius* Will*elm*i Bysmer*e*
It*em*, Joh*ann*es Wykes appr*enticius* Joh*ann*is Brou*n*
It*em*, Joh*ann*es Bastard appr*enticius* Joh*ann*is Alyngton*e*
It*em*, Thom*as* Baarfoot appr*enticius* Will*elm*i Baldyswell*e*
It*em*, Cristoforus Tyldesle appr*enticius* Hugonis Stanystret
It*em*, Robert*us* Aschwell*e* appr*enticius* Will*elm*i Gilb*er*t
It*em*, Will*elmu*s Bryskow appr*enticius* Joh*ann*is Welford
It*em*, Joh*ann*es Walssch*e* appr*enticius* Will*elm*i Downe
It*em*, Ric*ard*us Puys appr*enticius* Joh*ann*is Tewkysbury
It*em*, Joh*ann*es Veredygo appr*enticius* Ric*ard*i Mariot
It*em*, Will*elmu*s Wykwan appr*enticius* Will*elm*i Wykwan

col. 2 Lowys jur*ez*:[484]
Will*elmu*s Matthew appr*enticius* Georg*ii* Cressy – ii s.

[482] This entry is in a different hand.
[483] No sums of money are written beside these names, but one must assume the usual 20s. was paid for each.
[484] Although it is not stated, all these below must be *former* apprentices.

aforesaid mistery, for a certain sum of money – 5 marks. And upon this the aforesaid wardens gave permission to the aforesaid Henry to work well in honest places – 5 marks.

Nicholas Holonder was sworn on 10 July 1409 to keep and to serve well and faithfully all the ordinances written above – 2s. 4d. 1409 A + b p. 68 *cont.*

Memorandum that on 1 August Henry Mallyng was sworn before William Grantham, William Randolf, John Water and John Pake to keep and to serve well and faithfully the ordinances pertaining to the said mistery. 1409 A + a p. 105

Apprentices: 1409–10 col. 1
Firstly, Richard Cowlyng apprentice of William Grantham
Item, Ellis Harwood apprentice of William Randolf
Item, Thomas Swinscoe apprentice of John atte Water
Item, Peter Lawdy apprentice of John Pake
Item, Thomas Bamme apprentice of Robert Halle
Item, John Birling apprentice of John Wynne
Item, Nicholas Lovet apprentice of Henry Wortesburgh
Item, Richard Wynne apprentice of John Palyng
Item, Richard Mallyng apprentice of William atte Wood
Item, Richard Gybbe apprentice of Thomas Foxcote
Item, John Peraunt apprentice of William Hertwell
Item, Reynold Clypping apprentice of John Colney
Item, John Reep apprentice of John Botreux
Item, John Kyng apprentice of John Walshe
Item, William Smythe apprentice of Nicholas Woodhille
Item, Wiiliam Goolde apprentice of William Bismere
Item, John Wykes apprentice of John Broun
Item, John Bastard apprentice of John Allington
Item, Thomas Baarfoot apprentice of William Baldeswelle
Item, Christopher Tyldesley apprentice of Hugh Stanystreet
Item, Robert Ashwell apprentice of William Gilbert
Item, William Briscoe apprentice of John Welford
Item, John Walshe apprentice of William Downe
Item, Richard Puys apprentice of John Tewkesbury
Item, John Veredygo apprentice of Richard Mariot
Item, William Wykwan apprentice of William Wykwan

Serving-men sworn: col. 2
William Matthew apprentice of George Cressy – 2s.

Hugo Stanystret appr*enticius* Joh*ann*is atte Wat*er* – ii s.
Ric*ardus* Boorne appr*enticius* Georg*ii* Cressy – ii s.
Nich*ol*aus Ryecroft appr*enticius* Ric*ard*i Wethyall*e* – ii s.
Will*elmu*s Cowvele appr*enticius* Will*elm*i Granth*am* – ii s.
Joh*anne*s Eustace appr*enticius* Will*elm*i Louth*e* – ii s.
Will*elmu*s Markeby appr*enticius* Will*elm*i Pev*ere* – ii s.
Nich*ol*aus Hervestok*e* appr*enticius* Ph*ilipp*i Castill*e* – ii s.
Joh*anne*s Phelyp*pe* appr*enticius* Dederik Van Wett*er* – ii s.
Walt*er*us Walden*e* appr*enticius* Jacobi Buntyng – ii s.
Ric*ardus* Skot appr*enticius* Rob*er*ti Lemyng – ii s.
Ric*ardus* Stapilton*e* appr*enticius* Henr*ici* atte Felde, goldbet*er* – ii s.

1409–10 A + b p. 62[485] Tempore Will*elm*i Granth*am*, Will*elm*i Randolf, Joh*ann*is atte Wat*er et* Joh*ann*is Pake, custod*um* art*is* aur*ifabrie* anno r*egni regis* Henr*ici* quarti undecimo:

In p*rimis*, Thomas Oxenford p*ro* defectu op*eracion*is uni*us* bokyll *et* pendant – xii d.
It*em*, Wynt*er* de Southwerk*e* p*ro* defectu uni*us* cornu *et* reru*m* alior*um* – ii s.
It*em*, Simon Ferthyng p*ro* defectu op*eracion*is – xiiii d.
It*em*, Nich*ol*aus, ducheman, p*ro* defectu uni*us* bokill *et* pendant – ii s.
It*em*, Gerard Alfkyn p*ro* defectu op*eracion*is uni*us* cheyne – ii s.
It*em*, Jacob*us* Buk*e* p*ro* defectu op*eracion*is – ii s.
It*em*, Rob*er*tus Howys p*ro* defectu op*eracion*is – ii s.
It*em*, Joh*anne*s Cotton p*ro* rebellia – vi s. viii d.
It*em*, Will*elmu*s Gootle p*ro* defectu op*eracion*is – ii s.
It*em*, Kowvele p*ro* defectu op*eracion*is – ii s.
It*em*, Ric*hard* Wethiall*e* solvit p*ro* suo appr*enticio* p*ro* defectu suspecc*ion*is *et* t*re*spas – xx s.

1410–11 A + a p. 106[486] Ceux sount les nouns dez Gardeins eslutz al fest de Seint Dunston*e* l'an du regne le Roy Henr*i* quart puis le conquest xj^{me} tanq*e* al dit fest de Seint Dunston*e* l'an ensuaunt:

Joh*anne*s Bulstrode
Joh*anne*s Standelf
Joh*anne*s Lenam
Joh*anne*s Hill*es*

Appr*entic*e*s*:[487]
[488]It*em*, Joh*anne*s Boteler appr*enticius* Joh*ann*is Geoce
In p*rimis*, Walt*er*us Houghton*e* appr*enticius* Joh*ann*is Lutou*n*
It*em*, Will*elm*us Perot appr*enticius* Will*elm*i Mathew

485 A different hand starts here.
486 At the top of this page occurs the 'Jhc' monogram, apparently in the hand of the scribe.
487 No sums of money are written against these names, but we must assume the usual 20s. was paid for each.
488 This line must have been added after the others in this column, but this is not apparent from the ink or script, and it must have been done at the same time as the rest.

Hugh Stanystreet apprentice of John atte Water –	2s.
Richard Boorne apprentice of George Cressy –	2s.
Nicholas Ryecroft apprentice of Richard Withihale –	2s.
William Covele apprentice of William Grantham –	2s.
John Eustace apprentice of William Louth –	2s.
William Markeby apprentice of William Pevere –	2s.
Nicholas Hervestoke apprentice of Phillip Castille –	2s.
John Philipp apprentice of Dederik Van Wetter –	2s.
Walter Walden apprentice of James Buntyng –	2s.
Richard Skot apprentice of Robert Lemyng –	2s.
Richard Stapleton apprentice of Henry atte Field, goldbeater –	2s.

In the time of William Grantham, William Randolf, John atte Water and John Pake, wardens of the Goldsmiths' mistery in the year 11 Henry IV [1409–10]: 1409–10 A + b p. 62
Firstly, Thomas Oxenford for a defect in the workmanship of a buckle and pendant – 12d.
Item, [Richard] Wynter of Southwark for a defect in a horn and some other things – 2s.
Item, Simon Farthing for a defect in workmanship – 14d.
Item, Nicholas, 'Dutchman', for a defect in a buckle and pendant – 2s.
Item, Gerard Alfkyn for a defect in the workmanship of a chain – 2s.
Item, Jacob Bukke for a defect in workmanship – 2s.
Item, Robert Howes for a defect in workmanship – 2s.
Item, John Cotton for being rebellious – 6s. 8d.
Item, William Goteley for a defect in workmanship – 2s.
Item, Covele[200] for a defect in workmanship – 2s.
Item, Richard Withihale paid for his apprentice for a defect of suspicion[201] and an offence – 20s.

These are the names of the wardens elected at the feast of St Dunstan in the year 11 Henry IV [19 May 1410] until the said feastday of St Dunstan in the following year: 1410–11 A + a p. 106
John Bulstrode
John Standelf
John Lenham
John Hilles

Apprentices:
Item, John Boteler apprentice of John Joce
Firstly, Walter Houghton apprentice of John Luton
Item, William Perot apprentice of William Matthew

[200] This might be either William or Thomas Covele.
[201] Presumably of being suspected of some crime, the suspicion itself bringing the mistery into disrepute.

Item, Johannes Braghnam apprenticius Thome Braghnam
Item, Willelmus Sonyngle apprenticius Nicholai Woodhille
Item, Johannes Kemp apprenticius Willelmi Waltone
Item, Johannes Titgrove apprenticius Johannis Colney[489]
Item, Johannes Bevyngtone apprenticius Willelmi Belverge
Item, Adam Tyldysle apprenticius Johannis Cottoun
Item, Ricardus Yoolle apprenticius Willelmi Gartoun
Item, Thomas Bygwode apprenticius Willelmi Hope
Item, Johannes Oghgere apprenticius Johannis Clerk
Item, Matheus Phelyppe apprenticius Johannis Phelyppe
Item, Willelmus Keteryngham apprenticius Henrici Bamme
Item, Thomas Tunbrigge apprenticius Salamonis Oxney

Lowys jurez:

In primis, Johannes Manypeny, d'orbatour[490] –	ii s.
Item, Willelmus Holcroft –	ii s.
Item, Robertus Downe –	ii s.
Item, Willelmus Cheyne –	ii s.
Item, Johannes Carler –	ii s.
Item, Johannes Nortoun –	ii s.
Item, Robertus Baker –	ii s.
Item, Thomas Whatford –	ii s.
Item, Willelmus Steventoun –	ii s.
Item, Robertus Baker –	ii s.[491]
Item, Johannes Kebele –	ii s.

(Fait a remembrer qe Thomas Kyng, lumbard, ad lycense dez gardeyns avantditz d'overer bien et onestement pur un an, et sur ceo ad payé – xxvi s. viii d.)[492]

Norman – Bysmere:

Fait a remembrer qe come Johan Norman et William Bysmere sount obligez a Johan Bulstrode, Johan Standelf, Johan Lenam et Johan Hilles, gardiens, et a lours successours gardeins, en dieux obligacions chescun par soy mesmes en .x. li. appaiers al fest del Nativité de Seint Johan Baptiste proschein venant, l'an du regne le Roi Henri quart puis le conquest xiime, come par lez ditz obligacions pluis pleinement appert, sur le condicioun qu'ensuet, c'est assavoir qe si le dit Johan Norman desoreenavant disclaundra ou revila en ascun manere point parount il poet estre prové par vi foialx gentz l'avantdit William Bismere, q'adonqes le dit J. Norman paiera soun obligacion de .x. li. Et en mesme la manere qe si le dit William Bysmere desoreenavant disclaundra ou revyla en ascun manere point l'avantdit Johan Norman issint [qe poet][493] estre prové par

[489] A note in the LH margin: nihil quia fugetivus secunda septimana.
[490] The initial 'D' is very probably a scribal error, but could equally be correct and mean that he is the serving-man of a goldbeater.
[491] This appears to be a repeat but has not been scored out, whereas the line above has been firmly scored through since it contained a repeat of the entry for Thomas Whatford.
[492] This paragraph has been scored out.

Item, John Braghnam apprentice of Thomas Braghnam
Item, William Sonyngle apprentice of Nicholas Woodhille
Item, John Kemp apprentice of William Walton
Item, John Titgrove apprentice of John Colney[202]
Item, John Bevyngton apprentice of William Belverge
Item, Adam Tyldesley apprentice of John Cotton
Item, Richard Yoolle apprentice of William Gartoun
Item, Thomas Bigwood apprentice of William Hope
Item, John Oger apprentice of John Clerk[203]
Item, Matthew Philippe apprentice of John Philippe
Item, William Ketteringham apprentice of Henry Bamme
Item, Thomas Tunbridge apprentice of Solomon Oxney

Serving-men sworn:

Firstly, John Manypeny, goldbeater –	2s.
Item, William Holcroft –	2s.
Item, Robert Downe –	2s.
Item, William Cheyne –	2s.
Item, John Carler –	2s.
Item, John Norton –	2s.
Item, Robert Baker –	2s.
Item, Thomas Whatford –	2s.
Item, William Stevenson –	2s.
Item, Robert Baker –	2s.
Item, John Kebbell –	2s.

(Memorandum that Thomas Kyng, Lombard, has permission from the aforesaid wardens to work well and honestly for one year, and upon this he has paid – 26s. 8d.)

Norman – Bismere:
Memorandum that John Norman and William Bismere are bound by two obligatory bonds to John Bulstrode, John Standelf, John Lenham and John Hilles, wardens, and to their successors as wardens, each by himself in the sum of £10 to pay at the next feast of the Nativity of St John the Baptist in the year 12 Henry IV [24 June 1411], as more fully appears in the said letters of obligation, on the following condition, i.e. that if the said John Norman shall henceforth slander or insult in any way the aforesaid William Bismere thus that it may be proved by 6 loyal men, that then the said John Norman shall pay his bond of £10. And similarly that if the said William Bismere shall henceforth slander or insult in any way the aforesaid John Norman thus that it may be proved by

[202] LH margin note: 'Nil, because he ran away in his second week'.
[203] *alias* Mablean.

vi foialx gentz, q'adonq*e*s il paiera sou*n* oblig*acion* de .x. li., ou aut*re*ment l'av*a*ntditz oblig*acions* soient tenuz p*ur* null*es*.

1411 Huberd – Corbyn: Fait a remembr*er* q*e* come le vj^{me} jour d'aprill*e* l'an du regne le Roi Henr*i* quart xiime Joh*a*n Huberd *et* Joh*a*n Corbyn sount oblygez en dieux obligac*i*ons chescun p*ar* soy mesmes a Joh*a*n Bulstrode, Joh*a*n Standelf, Joh*a*n Lena*m* *et* Joh*a*n Hillys, gardeins, *et* a lour successo*ur*s gardeins, en .xl. s. appaiers al fest de Pent*ecoste,* come app*er*t p*ar* lez ditz oblig*acions*, s*ur* cest condic*i*ou*n* q*e* si le dit Joh*a*n Huberd disclaundra l'av*a*ntdit Joh*a*n Corbyn ou revyla issint [qe poet][494] estr*e* p*ro*vé p*ar* iiii foyalx gentz, q'adonq*e*s il payera sou*n* oblig*acion*. Et si l'av*a*ntdit Joh*a*n Corbyn desoreenav*a*nt revyla ou disclaundra l'av*a*ntdit Joh*a*n Huberd, q'adonq*e*s il payera sou*n* oblig*acion*.

p. 107 Fait a remembr*er* q*e* p*ur* ceo q*e* Joh*a*n Walsch*e* revyla dispytousement sez gardeyns av*a*ntdytz, s*ur* quell*e* enapr*é*s dev*a*nt lez hon*ur*ables gentz du dit mistier d'orfev*er*ie cria m*er*cy *et* [se][495] mist en g*ra*ce dez ditz gardeins *et* [se][496] offry d'estr*e* a lo*ur* ordinaunce p*ur* mesme trespas, les queux gardeins ové autres hon*ur*ables gentz de dit mistier ount ordeignez q*e* mesme Joh*a*n lesseroit sou*n* vestur*e* *et* payeroit al almoigne de Seint Dunston*e* – x li. s*ur* g*ra*ce.

Fait a remembr*er* q*e* p*ur* ceo q*e* Joh*a*n Martyn revyla dispetousement sez gardeins av*a*ntdytz, s*ur* quell*e* enapr*é*s dev*a*nt lez hon*ur*ables gentz de dit mistier d'orfev*er*ie cria m*er*cy *et* [se][497] mist en g*ra*ce dez ditz gardeins *et* [se][498] offry d'estr*e* a lo*ur* ordinaunce p*ur* mesme trespas, les queux gardeins ové autres hon*ur*ables gentz de dit mistier ount ordeignez q*e* mesme Joh*a*n lesseroit sou*n* vestur*e* *et* payeroit al almoigne de Seint Dunston*e* – C s.. s*ur* g*ra*ce.

1410–11 Fait a remembr*er* q*e* le xxviiie jo*ur* de Novembr*e* l'an du regne le Roi Henr*i* quart puis le conquest xiie, Thom*a*s de Roy de Pavye vient dev*a*nt lez gardeins p*ur* l'an esteantz *et* la ad jur*é* s*ur* le liv*er*e de bien *et* loyalment ov*er*er[499] d'or *et* d'arg*ent*; dount lez ditz gardeins ount doné licence au dit Thomas d'ov*er*er p*ur* un an, c'est assav*oir* del Feste de Toutz Seintz esteaunt l'an du Roy q'or est xiie tanq*e* al dit feste de Toutz Seintz l'an du Roi q'or est xiiie. Et s*ur* ceo l'av*a*nt[dit] Thomas ad payé – xxvi s. viii d.

1411–12 Ceux sount lez nouns dez gardeins eslutz al fest de Seint Dunston*e* l'an du
p. 108 regne le Roi Henr*i* quart puis le conquest xiime tanq*e* al dit feste de Seint Dunston*e* l'an ensuaunt:
Will*el*m*us* Fytzhugh*e*
Will*el*m*us* Downe
Joh*ann*es Tewkysbury
Rob*er*tus Browne

[493] MS: qest.
[494] MS: qestest.
[495] MS: ceo.
[496] MS: ceo.
[497] MS: ceo.
[498] MS: ceo.
[499] MS: dou*er*er.

6 loyal men, that then he shall pay his bond of £10, or otherwise the aforesaid bonds should be held null and void.

Huberd – Corbyn: 1411
Memorandum that on 6 April 1411 John Huberd and John Corbyn were bound by two bonds of obligation each by himself to John Bulstrode, John Standelf, John Lenham and John Hilles, wardens, and to their successors as wardens, in the sum of 40s. to be paid at the Feast of Whitsun, as appears in the two bonds of obligation, on this condition that if the said John Huberd shall slander or insult the aforesaid John Corbyn thus that it may be proved by 4 loyal men, that then he shall pay his bond. And if the aforesaid John Corbyn shall henceforth insult or slander the aforesaid John Huberd, that then he shall pay his bond.

Memorandum that whereas John Walsh contemptuously insulted his aforesaid p. 107 wardens, for the which he afterwards begged pardon before the honourable men of the said goldsmiths' mistery, and he placed himself within the jurisdiction of the said wardens and offered himself to be at their command for the same offence, the which wardens with other honourable men of the said mistery ordered that the same John should give up his livery clothing and should pay to the alms funds of St Dunstan – £10 subject to judgment.

Memorandum that whereas John Martyn contemptuously insulted his aforesaid wardens, for the which he afterwards begged pardon before the honourable men of the said goldsmiths' mistery, and he placed himself within the jurisdiction of the said wardens and offered himself to be at their command for the same offence, the which wardens with other honourable men of the said mistery ordered that the same John should give up his livery clothing and should pay to the alms funds of St Dunstan – 100s. subject to judgment.

Memorandum that on 28 November 1410, Thomas de Roy of Pavia came before 1410–11 the current year's wardens and there he swore on the book to work gold and silver well and faithfully, for which the said wardens gave permission to the said Thomas to work for one year, i.e. from the Feast of All Saints in the year 12 Henry IV until the said feast of All Saints in the year 13 Henry IV [1 November 1410 – 1 November 1411]. And upon this the aforesaid Thomas paid 26s. 8d.

These are the names of the wardens elected on the feastday of St Dunstan in 1411–12
the year 12 Henry IV until the said feastday of St Dunstan in the following p. 108
year [19 May 1411–19 May 1412]:

William FitzHugh
William Downe
John Tewkesbury
Robert Broun

1411 Johan Thomas apprentys J. Gale:
Fait a remembrer qe le xiii jour de Julet l'an du regne le Roi Henri quart puis le conquest xiime, Johan Thomas de Kyrtoun en Holand qe fuist apprentice de Johan Gale vient devant lez gardeins pur l'an esteantz et devant escriptz, et la ad juré sur le livere qe jammés ne overa nulle poynt d'orfeverie, a cause qe a present est obligé apprentice as Taillours, et q'il gardera en secreet lez pointz et privetees au dit mistier appurtenantz, et lez privetees au dit mistier appurtenantz a nully dirra ne discovera, ne jammés lez pointz avantditz usera privé ne appert, si Dieu soy eide et toutz seintz.[500]

1412 Fait a remembrer qe come William Gartoun, Johan Welford et Johan Newtoun, orfeours, sount obligez et cheschun par soy mesmes a William Fytzhughe, William Downe, Johan Tewkysbury et Robert Broune, gardeins d'orfeverie en Loundres, en .C. s. appaiers al fest de Pasche alors proschein ensuant come en lez ditz obligacions pluis pleinement appert, sur l[es][501] condiciouns q'ensuent:[502]

Walter Colney:
Fait a remembrer qe come Johan Colney et Stephen Colney sount obligez a William Fytzhughe, William Downe, Johan Tewkysbury et Robert Broune, gardeins, en xx li. appaiers al fest de Pentecoste alors proschein ensuant, come appert par la dit obligacion fait xix jour de Marcz l'an du regne le Roi Henri quart xiiie, sur le condicioun qu'e[n]suet, et e[s]t tiel qe si Walter Colney, frere as ditz Johan et Stephen et prentice au dit Johan Colney, le quelle Johan Colney ad relessé au dit Walter soun apprentice et frere sez termes de prenticialté d'un an et demi pur iiii marcz,[503] par assent dez gardeins pur l'an esteantz et lour compaignons Johan Blakedene, J. Bulstrode, J. Standelf, J. Norman, Richard Bartoun, R. Halle, J. Mapelisdene, J. Water, J. Pake, T. Popiltoun, J. Walsche, J. Martyn, R. Whethialle, qe si lez termes qe sount a dit Walter relessez par le dit Johan Colney ne soit fait par fraude ne collusioun parount la companye d'orfeverie ne nulle d'eux[504] ne soient empechez ne defamez ne par le dit Walter ne sez termes hendrez, q'adonqes le obligacion soit pur nulle ou autrement teigne sa force et vertue – iiii marcz.[505]

Johan Halle
Fait a remembrer qe le iiii. jour de maii l'an du regne le Roi Henri quart puis le conquest xiii^{e} Johan Halle, fytz au Johan Halle, grocer, et nadgairs prentice de Johan Huberd, orpheour, vient devant lez gardeins pur l'an esteantz et la ad

500 See also above, A + a, p. 96.
501 MS: la.
502 No condition follows.
503 The previous three words have been added interlinearly, probably just very slightly later, in the same hand.
504 The previous three words have been added interlinearly, but in the same hand and ink.
505 This sum of money is a slightly later addition in the same hand.

John Thomas, apprentice of John Gale: 1411
Memorandum that on 13 July 1411 John Thomas of Kirton in Holland [Lincs.], who had been the apprentice of John Gale, came before the current year's wardens named above, and there he swore on the book that he shall never do any goldsmith's work at all, for the reason that he is at present bound apprentice to the Tailors, and that he shall keep secret all the skills and the privities pertaining to the said mistery, and that he shall not tell or reveal any of the privities pertaining to the said mistery to anyone, nor shall he ever use any of the aforesaid skills either in private or publicly, so God may help him and all the saints.

Memorandum that William Gartoun, John Welford and John Newton, 1412
goldsmiths, are bound each for himself to William FitzHugh, William Downe, John Tewkesbury and Robert Broun, wardens of the Goldsmiths' Mistery of London, in the sum of 100s. to be paid at the next following feast of Easter, as in the said letters of obligation more fully appears, on the following conditions:

Walter Colney:
Memorandum that John Colney and Stephen Colney are bound to William FitzHugh, William Downe, John Tewkesbury and Robert Broun, wardens, in the sum of £20 to be paid at the next following feast of Whitsun, as appears by the said letters of obligation drawn up on 19 March 1412, on the following condition, and this is such that if Walter Colney, brother to the said John and Stephen and apprentice of the said John Colney, the which John Colney remitted to the said Walter, his apprentice and brother, one and half years of his apprenticeship terms for 4 marks, with the assent of the wardens of the current year and their companions John Blakedene, John Bulstrode, John Standelf, John Norman, Richard Barton, Robert Halle, John Maplesdene, John Water, John Pake, Thomas Poppleton, John Walsh, John Martyn, Richard Withihale, that if the remission of his terms to the said Walter by the said John Colney has not been done by any deceit or collusion by which the company of the goldsmiths or any one of them should be prosecuted or defamed, and that no harm is suffered through the said Walter or his terms, that then the bond should be declared void, and otherwise it shall hold its full strength and force – 4 marks.

John Halle:
Memorandum that on 4 May 1412 John Halle, son of John Halle, grocer, and formerly the apprentice of John Huberd, goldsmith, came before the current year's wardens and there he swore on the book that he shall never do any

juré *sur* le liv*er*e q*e* ja*m*més ne ov*er*a p*ri*vé ne app*er*t null*e* point d'orfev*er*ie, *et* lez pointz q*e* av*a*nt ad apris de dit mistier a nully dirra ne discov*er*a, ne ja*m*més usera en null*e* lieu ne dirra p*ri*vé ne app*er*t, si Dieu soy eyde *et* cez seintz.

1412 p. 109 Fait a remembr*er* q*e* a comou*n* assemblé del hon*ur*able cumpanye d'orfev*er*ie fait le xxiiime d'Aprill*e* l'an du regne n*ostr*e s*eignur* le Roi Henr*i* q'or est xiiie, en p*re*sence de Dru Barantyn*e*, Thomas Poll*e* *et* Will*ia*m Louth*e*, aldermans, *et* toutes autres comuners au dit mistier app*ur*tenantz, est g*ra*unté a Emmot Salesbury, wedew, a t*er*me de sa vie, p*ur* le bon*e* droyt *et* volunté p*ar* le dit Emmot fait au dit cu*m*panye et p*ur* le droit ez rentz *et* ten*ementz* q*e* la dit Emmot avoit en la cité de Loundr*es* *et* en lez subberdez d'icell*e*, le quell*e* droit l'av*a*nt[dite] Emmot ad au dit mistier relessé *et* de ce un relese ensealé, p*ar*ount la dit Emmot p*re*ndra chescun semayn*e* p*ar* t*er*me de vie av*a*ntdit – xiiii d. *et* un measou*n*, p*ri*s del an de xiii s. iiii d., et la vestur*e* de Seint Dunstou*n* quant le cumpanye est vestur*é*.

1411–12 App*ren*t*ices*:[506]
In p*rimis*, de Rob*er*to Schyrwode app*ren*t*icio* Roberti Botolf
It*em*, de Joh*ann*e Norma*n* app*ren*t*icio* Rog*er*i Barneston*e*
It*em*, de Will*el*mo Croyser app*ren*t*icio* Rob*er*ti Stanford
It*em*, de Salamanno Chervell*e* app*ren*t*icio* Will*el*mi Coup*er*
It*em*, de Ric*ard*o Brenlee app*ren*t*icio* Thome Oxenford
It*em*, de Joh*ann*e Russell*e* app*ren*t*icio* Henr*ici* Goldsmyth*e*
It*em*, de Egydeo Belyngdou*n* app*ren*t*icio* Raymundy Chaumbr*e*
It*em*, de Thoma Whytmore app*ren*t*icio* Johannis Cresbien
It*em*, de Ric*ard*o Raulyn app*ren*t*icio* Ric*ard*i Whethyall*e*
It*em*, de Will*el*mo Skot app*ren*t*icio* Henr*ici* Wortysburgh*e*
It*em*, de Will*el*mo Tunnvyle app*ren*t*icio* Joh*ann*is Colney
It*em*, de Rob*er*to Lowkyn*e* app*ren*t*icio* Joh*ann*is Byschop, jun*ioris*, goldbet*er*
It*em*, de Ric*ard*o Frytz app*ren*t*icio* Joh*ann*is Bulstrode
It*em*, de Ade Tildyslee app*ren*t*icio* Joh*ann*is Cottou*n*[507]

Lowys jurez:
In p*rimis*, de Joh*ann*e Newtou*n* quond*a*m app*ren*t*icio* Will*el*mi Gartou*n* – ii s.
It*em*, de Gwydo Akerman quond*a*m app*ren*t*icio* G*wydonis* Akerma*n* – ii s.
It*em*, de Ric*ard*o Robert [quond*a*m] app*ren*t*icio* Joh*ann*is Bischop, jun*ioris* – ii s.
It*em*, de Maykyn [quond*a*m app*ren*t*icio*] Joh*ann*is Flete, sen*ioris* – ii s.
It*em*, de Joh*ann*e Werk [quond*a*m] app*ren*t*icio* Will*el*mi Spark*e* – ii s.
It*em*, de Thoma Esex [quond*a*m] app*ren*t*icio* Barth*olome*i Belyngdon*e* – ii s.
It*em*, de Henrico Seburgh*e* [quond*a*m] app*ren*t*icio* Joh*ann*is Lena*m* – ii s.

506 No sums of money are listed against the following names, but one must assume the usual 20s. was paid for each.
507 He was listed the previous year also.

goldsmithry work either in private or in public, and that he will never tell nor reveal to anyone the skills of the said mistery which he has previously learnt, and that he will never practice them in any place nor will he tell of them in private or in public, so God may help him and His saints.

Memorandum that at the common assembly of the honourable company of the goldsmiths held on 23 April 1412, in the presence of Drew Barantyn, Thomas Polle and William Louth, aldermen, and all the other commoners belonging to the said mistery, a grant was made to Emmot Salisbury, widow, for her lifetime, [in return] for the legal rights and the will made in favour of the company by the said Emmot, and for the rights to the rents and tenements which the said Emmot had in the City of London and its suburbs, the which rights the aforesaid Emmot has transferred to the said mistery and has sealed a release and transfer document for this, by which the said Emmot will receive every week during her aforesaid lifetime – 14d. and housing,[204] yearly cost 13s. 4d., and the livery clothing of St Dunstan whenever clothing is issued to the company. 1412 p. 109

Apprentices: 1411–12
Firstly, from Robert Sherwood apprentice of Robert Botulf
Item, from John Norman apprentice of Roger Barnston
Item, from William Croyser apprentice of Robert Stanford
Item, from Solomon Chervelle apprentice of William Couper
Item, from Richard Brenlee apprentice of Thomas Oxenford
Item, from John Russell apprentice of Henry Goldsmith
Item, from Giles Billington apprentice of Raymund Chaumbre
Item, from Thomas Whitmore apprentice of John Cresbien
Item, from Richard Raulyn apprentice of Richard Withihale
Item, from William Skot apprentice of Henry Wortisburgh
Item, from William Tunnvyle apprentice of John Colney
Item, from Robert Lovekyn apprentice of John Bisshop, the younger, goldbeater
Item, from Richard Frytz apprentice of John Bulstrode
Item, from Adam Tyldesley apprentice of John Cotton

Serving-men sworn:
Firstly, from John Newton formerly apprentice of William Gartoun – 2s.
Item, from Guy Akerman formerly apprentice of Guy Akerman – 2s.
Item, from Richard Robert [formerly] apprentice of John Bisshop the younger – 2s.
Item, from Maykyn [formerly apprentice] of John Flete the elder – 2s.
Item, from John Werk [formerly] apprentice of William Spark – 2s.
Item, from Thomas Essex [formerly] apprentice of Bartholomew Billington – 2s.
Item, from Henry Seburghe [formerly] apprentice of John Lenham – 2s.

[204] The word '*measoun*' (or '*maison*') may at this date mean either a house, or a room in a house, or any residence or dwelling-place.

Item, de Johanne Horwelle [quondam] apprenticio Johannis Broune – ii s.
Item, de Johanne Poghelee [quondam] apprenticio Thome Senycle – ii s.
Item, de Johanne Pattysle [quondam] apprenticio Johannis Osborne – ii s.
Item, de Konne, Ducheman – ii s.
Item, de Thoma Lyncolne [quondam] apprenticio Henrici Bamme – ii s.
Item, de Willelmo Ramse [quondam] apprenticio Roberti Brenle – ii s.
Item, de Johanne Bury [quondam] apprenticio Johannis Wynne – ii s.

Guy Akerman:
Fait a remembrer qe pur taunt qe Guy Akerman qe fuist la prentyce de Guy Akerman fuist obligez apprentice a soun meistre et nient enrollez, ordeyné est qe l'avantdit Gwy servera come lowys par toutz jours et jammés ne tendra schoppe overt come meistre enfraunchisez, pur le quelle ordinance l'avantdit Guy ad payé as ditz gardeins – xx s. et a la dit ordinance d'estre tenuz et fermez est conducenduz. – xx s.

1412 Thomas Roy de Pavie:
Fait a remembrer qe le v jour de Marche l'an du regne le Roy Henri quart xiiie lez gardeins pur l'an esteantz ount grauntez a Thomas Roy de Pavye et luy lycence donez d'overer ez lieux covenables pur un an aprés la date d'iceste,[508] pur quelle graunt l'avantdit Thomas pur le suffraunce avantdit ad payé – xx s.

1412–13 Ceux sount lez nouns dez Gardeins eslutz al fest de Seint Dunstoun l'an du
p. 110 regne le Roi Henri quart puis le conquest xiiie tanqe al dit fest de Seint Dunstoun pur l'an ensuant:
Johannes Blakedene
Johannes Norman
Raymundus Chaumbre
Ricardus Whethialle

Apprentices:
In primis, de Thoma Reynere apprenticio Johannis Eylond – xx s.
Item, de Ricardo Herdene apprenticio Ricardi Litle – xx s.
Item, de Jacobo Tregustok apprenticio Johannis Mableaun – xx s.
Item, de Thoma Joly apprenticio Thome Southe – xx s.
Item, de Johanne Londoun apprenticio Roberti Lemyng – xx s.
Item, de Roberto Asscheby apprenticio Willelmi atte Wode – xx s.
Item, de Johanne Wellys apprenticio Stephani Colneye – xx s.
Item, de Johanne Hert apprenticio Johannis Halle, senioris – xx s.
Item, de Simone Horwode apprenticio Willelmi Fytzhughe – xx s.
Item, de Ricardo Geoce apprenticio Henrici Bamme – xx s.
Item, de Willelmo Suttone apprenticio Johannis Halle junioris – xx s.
Item, de Roberto Resby apprenticio Ricardi Bagnore – xx s.
Item, de Johanne Huberd juniore apprenticio Johannis Blakedene – xx s.

508 The previous four words have been inserted interlinearly, but at the same time of writing.

Item, from John Orwell [formerly] apprentice of John Broun – 2s.
Item, from John Poghelee [formerly] apprentice of Thomas Senycle – 2s.
Item, from John Pattesley [formerly] apprentice of John Osborne – 2s.
Item, from Konne, 'Dutchman' – 2s.
Item, from Thomas Lincoln [formerly] apprentice of Henry Bamme – 2s.
Item, from William Ramsey [formerly] apprentice of Robert Brenle – 2s.
Item, from John Bury [formerly] apprentice of John Wynne – 2s.

Guy Akerman:
Memorandum that whereas Guy Akerman who was the apprentice of Guy Akerman was bound apprentice to his master and not enrolled, it is ordered that the aforesaid Guy shall serve as a serving-man for ever and shall never keep an open shop as an enfranchised master, for the which order the aforesaid Guy has paid to the said wardens – 20s. and he has acquiesced in that the said order should be kept to as binding. – 20s.

Thomas Roy of Pavia: 1412
Memorandum that on 5 March 1412 the current wardens granted to Thomas Roy of Pavia and gave him permission to work in suitable places for one year following the date of this grant, for the which grant the aforesaid Thomas paid for the aforesaid permission – 20s.

These are the names of the wardens elected on the feastday of St Dunstan in the year 13 Henry IV [19 May 1412] until the said feastday of St Dunstan the following year: 1412–13 p. 110
John Blakedene
John Norman
Raymund Chambre
Richard Withihale

Apprentices:
Firstly, from Thomas Reyner apprentice of John Nayland – 20s.
Item, from Richard Herdene apprentice of Richard Litle – 20s.
Item, from James Tregewstek apprentice of John Mablean – 20s.
Item, from Thomas Joly apprentice of Thomas South – 20s.
Item, from John London apprentice of Robert Lemyng – 20s.
Item, from Robert Ashby apprentice of William atte Wood – 20s.
Item, from John Welles apprentice of Stephen Colney – 20s.
Item, from John Hert apprentice of John Halle the elder – 20s.
Item, from Simon Horwood apprentice of William FitzHugh – 20s.
Item, from Richard Joce apprentice of Henry Bamme – 20s.
Item, from William Sutton apprentice of John Halle the younger – 20s.
Item, from Robert Resby apprentice of Richard Bagnore – 20s.
Item, from John Huberd the younger apprentice of John Blakedene – 20s.

Lowys jurez:
In *primis*, de Ric*ardo* Wortilford quond*am* app*renticio* Thome Glade – ii s.
It*em*, de Thom*a* Wat*er* quond*am* app*renticio* Will*elm*i Fytzhugh*e* – ii s.
It*em*, de Joh*anne* Barde quo*nd*am app*renticio* Will*elm*i Barde – ii s.
It*em*, de Thom*a* Hunte quo*nd*am app*renticio* Joh*ann*is Hunte – ii s.
It*em*, de Joh*anne* Perou*n* quo*nd*am app*renticio* Rob*er*ti Hoos – ii s.
It*em*, de Drugon*e* Bethu*n* quo*nd*am app*renticio* Joh*ann*is Som*er*vyle – ii s.
It*em*, de Walt*er*o Colney quo*nd*am app*renticio* Joh*ann*is Colney – ii s.
It*em*, de Joh*anne* Draytou*n* quo*nd*am app*renticio* Joh*ann*is Standelf – ii s.
It*em*, de Ric*ardo* Chaumbr*e* quo*nd*am app*renticio* Raymundi[509] Chau*m*br*e* – ii s.
It*em*, de Thoma Stapilhi*r*st quo*nd*am app*renticio* Rob*er*ti Broun*e* – ii s.
It*em*, de Rog*er*o Gav*er*e quo*nd*am app*renticio* Joh*ann*is Gav*er*e – ii s.

Duchemen:
It*em*, de Joh*anne* Burryour*e* de Westvale c*er*v[o][510] Abbryght van Andirnak*e* – xx s.
It*em*, de Gerard s*er*vo Jacobi Bak*e* – xx s.

A + b p. 71 [511]M*emorandum* q*uo*d Will*elmu*s Bysmer*e* fuit invent*us* in defectu op*eracion*is div*er*sor*um* bokell' *et* pendant'.[512]

1412 (M*emorandum* q*uo*d die lune xi die Julii anno r*egni* r*egis* Henrici quarti xiii°
p. 72 tempore Joh*ann*is Blakeden*e et* Joh*ann*is Norma*n*, gardian[orum],[513] Rob*ertus* Hall, Raymund*us* Chaumbr*e et* Rob*ertus* Lemyng receperunt[514] in p*artem* soluc*ion*is reddit*us* in Frydaystrete – xxxvi li. xii.[515])[516]

M*emorandum* q*uo*d eod*em* die coram gardianis p*ro* anno existent*ibus et* Drugone Barantyne, Thoma Poll*e*, Will*elm*o Louth*e*, aldermannis, Will*elmo* Fytzhugh, Will*elm*o Downe, J. Tewkisbury, Rob*er*to Broon*e*, Will*elmo* Grantha*m*, Will*elm*o Randofe, Joh*anne* atte Wat*er*, J. Pake, J. Standelf, Ric*ardo* Barton, J. Bulstrode, Rob*er*to Hall*e*, Th*oma* Lamport, Joh*anne* Luton, Salamon Oxney, Th*oma* Popilton, J. Hill*es*, Rob*er*to Lemyng, Will*elm*o Hope, J. Martyn, J. Buntyng, ib*ide*m existent*ibus*, q*uo*d Pet[r]*us* Goldisburgh, cl*ericus*, recipiet p*ro* suo stupendio quolib*et* anno du*m* extat in officio – xl s. et suu*m* vest[it]u*m* quando ars vestit*ur*.

509 This name is written over an erased 'Radl'li'.
510 MS: 'C*ervus*', added above an erased 'app*renticio*'.
511 A new hand starts here. This entry is undated but is placed here since it is in the same hand as the following dated entries. It is however very possible, since it stands alone on a page, that it belongs to the previous year.
512 The rest of this page is blank.
513 MS: Gardianos.
514 A long 'j' is written between this word and the next, one presumes a stroke of the pen by mistake?
515 This figure is written at the far RH side and the insertion of the page into modern paper has obscured whether it was 12s. or 12d.
516 This whole paragraph has had diagonal lines scored through it to indicate deletion. See below, A + b, p. 75 for the full settlement being made.

Serving-men sworn:
Firstly, from Richard Wortilford formerly apprentice of Thomas Glade – 2s.
Item, from Thomas Water formerly apprentice of William FitzHugh – 2s.
Item, from John Barde formerly apprentice of Wililam Barde – 2s.
Item, from Thomas Hunt formerly apprentice of John Hunt – 2s.
Item, from John Peryn formerly apprentice of Robert Howes – 2s.
Item, from Drew Bethun formerly apprentice of John Somerville – 2s.
Item, from Walter Colney formerly apprentice of John Colney – 2s.
Item, from John Drayton formerly apprentice of John Standelf – 2s.
Item, from Richard Chaumbre formerly apprentice of Raymund Chaumbre – 2s.
Item, from Thomas Staplehurst formerly apprentice of Robert Broun – 2s.
Item, from Roger Gavere formerly apprentice of John Gavere – 2s.

'Dutchmen':
Item, from Johan Burryoure of Westphalia, the servant of Albright van Andirnak – 20s.
Item, from Gerard, servant of Jacob Bake – 20s.

Memorandum that William Bismere was found guilty of faulty workmanship of various buckles and pendants. A + b p. 71

(Memorandum that on Monday 11 July 1412 in the time of John Blakedene and John Norman, wardens, Robert Halle, Raymund Chaumbre and Robert Lemyng received in part payment for the tenement in Friday Street – £36 12.) 1412 p. 72

Memorandum that on the same day in the presence of the current year's wardens and Drew Barantyn, Thomas Polle, William Louth, aldermen, and William FitzHugh, William Downe, John Tewkesbury, Robert Broun, William Grantham, William Randolf, John atte Water, John Pake, John Standelf, Richard Barton, John Bulstrode, Robert Halle, Thomas Lamport, John Luton, Solomon Oxney, Thomas Poppleton, John Hilles, Robert Lemyng, William Hope, John Martyn, James Buntyng, [it was agreed] that Peter Goldsborough, clerk, should receive each year for his salary while he remains in office – 40s. and his livery clothing when clothing is issued to the mistery.

Fait a remembr*er* q*e* Will*ia*m Gootle fuist t*r*ové en defaut del ov*er*aigne d'arg*ent*, p*ur* quoy ad payé az gardeins – iii s. iiii d.[517]

A + a p. 111 Letherpole:

Fait a remembr*er* p*ur* ceo q*e* Will*ia*m Letherpole dispetousement revyla *et* disclaundra sez gardeins *et* eux disclaundra de robbery, et auxi revyla un Rog*er* Barneston*e* malousement a sou*n* schoppe en Chepe, et ap*rés* qu*a*nt le dit Will*ia*m fuist aresté *et* a p*ri*sou*n* del Countou*r* amesné, la le dit Will*ia*m defama sez avantditz gardeins dev*a*nt moultx div*erses* est*r*au*n*g*ers* de robberye, p*ur* la quell*e* trespas l'av*a*ntdit Will*ia*m p*ar* comaundem*en*t de Rob*er*t Chechely, adonq*e*s Mair*e* de Loundr*es,* fuist comaundé al p*ri*sou*n* de Newgate *et* la fuist p*ar* vi jo*ur*s. Et ap*rés* lez av*a*ntditz gardeins p*ar* assent dez ault*re*s gentz del dit cumpany, veyantz *et* eyantz consideraci*o*n q*e* l'av*a*ntdit Will*ia*m *et* ault*re*s hon*ur*ables gentz p*ur* luy ount requirez dez gardeins g*r*ace *et* compassiou*n*, lez quelx gardeins ount p*ar*doné au dit Will*ia*m s*ur* sou*n* bon*e* porte de payer al almoigne de Seint Dunstou*n* s*ur* g*ra*ce x li.

Le quell*e* g*ra*ce est tiell*e* q*e* si l'av*a*ntdit desore[en]av*a*nt revyla ou disclaundra ascuns dez cez gardeins ou ascun autr*e* del mistier*e* d'or[fe]v*er*ie, q'adonq*e*s paiera la so*m*me av*a*ntdit.

1412 Mablean:

Fait a remembr*er* p*ur* ceo q*e* Joh*a*n Mablean, orpheo*ur*, envoya hors de sou*n* pays p*ur* cez dieux frers, voillantz eux fair*e* app*ren*t*is* du dit mistier; lez queulx enfauntz p*ar* examinaci*o*n dez gardeins *et* aut*re*s div*er*ses gentz de ditz pays furent p*r*ovez q'ils furent en lo*ur* ditz pays l'un amenaunt un mendevant de pays en pays p*ur* mendyver sou*n* vyaunde, et l'autr*e* enfaunt fuist un miller*e* *et* ap*rés* un sout*er*; lez queux point*es* p*ar* assent de dit Joh*a*n Mablean lo*ur* frer*e* fuist rehercez dev*a*nt le gen*er*all*e* assemblé tenuz le lundy le xxix jo*ur* d'augst; et la, en p*re*sence de Dru Barantyn*e* *et* Will*ia*m Louthe, aldermans, *et* toutz ault*re*s de dit cumpanye, fuist ordeigné q*e* lez ditz enfantz *et* frers de dit Joh*a*n ja*m*més s*er*roient resceivez en dit mistier ne null*e* d'eux, mes p*ur* toutz jo*ur*s voydez. Et q*e* si desoreenav*a*nt ascuns gardeins [q'ils q'ils soient] resceivent p*ri*vé ou app*er*t ascuns d'ieux [des av*a*ntditz] enfantz, ou l'un d'ieux en lo*ur* temps resceiverent,[518] [qe] payent al almoigne de Seint Dunstou*n* – x li., et q*e* si l'av*a*ntdit Joh*a*n desore[en]avant p*r*oc[ur]ra[519] a ascun orpheo*ur* p*ur* cez ditz frers encountr*e* la forme av*a*nt rehercé, q'il pay[er]a[520] al almoigne de Seint Dunstou*n* – x li.

[517] This entry in French is in a different hand.

[518] MS: Et q*e* si desoreenav*a*nt ascuns gardeins resceivent p*ri*vé ou app*er*t ascuns d'ieux q'ils q*e* si le v*a*ntz enfantz ou l'un d'ieux en lo*ur* temps resceiverent.

[519] MS: p*r*ocra.

[520] MS: paya.

Memorandum that William Goteley was found at fault in the workmanship of silver, for which he paid to the wardens – 3s. 4d.

Liverpool: A + a p. 111
Memorandum that whereas William Liverpool contemptuously insulted and slandered his wardens and unjustly accused them of robbery, and also that he maliciously insulted one Roger Barnston in his shop in Cheap, and afterwards when the said William was arrested and taken to the Compter prison,[205] there the said William defamed his aforesaid wardens in front of a great number of strangers, falsely accusing them of robbery, for the which offence the aforesaid William, by the command of Robert Chichely, then Mayor of London, was ordered to be sent to Newgate prison and he was there for 6 days. And afterwards the aforesaid wardens with the assent of other men of the said company, seeing and having consideration that the aforesaid William had requested mercy and compassion of the wardens, as had other honourable people on his behalf, the which wardens pardoned the said William on condition of his good behaviour and to pay as to the alms funds of St Dunstan, subject to judgment – £10.

The which judgment is such that if the aforesaid shall henceforth insult or slander any one of his wardens or anyone else of the goldsmiths' mistery, that then he shall pay the aforesaid sum.

Mablean:
Memorandum that whereas John Mablean, goldsmith, sent out to his homeland for his two brothers, wishing to make them apprentices of the said mistery, about the which children by examination of the wardens and various other people from the said land it was proved that in their said land one of them had been leading a beggar from place to place to beg his food, and the other child had been a miller and afterwards a cobbler, the which facts by the assent of the said John Mablean their brother were recounted at length before the general assembly held on Monday 29 August, and there, in the presence of Drew Barantyn and William Louth, aldermen, and all others of the said company, it was ordered that the said children and brothers of the said John should neither one of them ever be admitted into the said mistery, but should be for ever excluded. And that if at any time from now on any wardens whoever they may be should during their term of office admit either secretly or openly the said children or one of them, they shall pay to the alms funds of St Dunstan – £10; and that if the aforesaid John shall from now on procure of any goldsmith on behalf of his said brothers against the ruling stated above, that he shall pay to the alms funds of St Dunstan – £10.

[205] The prison attached to the Mayor's court, of which the sheriffs were in charge.

1412 Mablean:

Fait a remembr*er* p*ur* ceo q*e* Joh*a*n Clerk al*ias* voc*atus*[521] Mablean revyla dispetousement sez gardeins p*ur* l'an esteantz, p*ur* quell*e* t*re*spas p*ar* comaundem*en*t de Will*ia*m Walderne adonq*e*s Mair*e* il fuist comaundé a Newgate *et* la dem*ur*ra p*ar* v jou*r*s. Apr*é*s quell*e* temps le xme jo*ur* de Novembr*e* l'an du Roi Henr*i* xiiiie en lo*ur* sale dev*a*nt Will*ia*m Louthe, alderm*an*, *et* toutz aut*re*s hon*ur*ables gentz del dit cumpany, l'av*a*ntdit Joh*a*n c*ri*a sez gardeins m*er*cy *et* p*ro*fra d'estr*e* a lo*ur* ordinanc*e*, p*ur* quell*e* t*re*spas il fuist juggé de paier al almoigne de Seint Dunstou*n* – x li. s*ur* lo*ur* g*ra*ce, le quell*e* g*ra*ce est tiell*e* q*u*'il payera chescun semaigne durant un an entier*e* a un povr*e* ho*m*me del dit cu*m*panie – viii d. s*ur* [soun][522] bon*e* porte. Et si en cas q'il trespasa as ascuns de cez gardeins et a sou*n* cumpany, q'adonq*e*s il payera la so*m*me de x li. av*a*ntesc*ri*pt, *et* a ceo ad trové plegg*e*s Will*ia*m Granth*a*m *et* Ric*hard* Bartou*n*.

p. 112[523] Barfore:

Fait a remembr*er* q*e* Nicholas Barforee, duchema*n* de Bruges, fuist t*ro*vé en defaut del ov*er*aigne d'un pier*e* voc*ata* un rubbie, le quell*e* rubbie fuist blank*e* et en le mye del dit pier*e* fuist un tente countr*e*fait au rubbie *et* mys s*ur* d'oor foyle et issint mys en un aungnell*e* et venduz p*ur* xx s., le quell*e* pier*e* ne vault iiii d. Et issint fuist t*ro*vé ové aultr*es* piers faulx countr*e*faitz, et ové d'or ov*er*aunt meyns q*e* l'assise ent ordeyné, p*ur* le quell*e* trespace il agrea ové lez gardeins p*ur* l'an esteantz p*ur* xx s., s*ur* condic*io*n q*e* si l'av*a*ntdit Nicholas desoreenav*a*nt soit t*ro*vé en tielx defautes av*a*ntesc*ri*ptz, q'adonq*e*s paiera – C s.

Hall*e* Petit:

1413 Fait a remembr*er* q*e* le iiie jo*ur* de marcz vient dev*a*nt lez gardeins p*ur* l'an esteantz Joh*a*n Hall*e* le Petyt p*ur* sclaundr*e* de dieux app*re*ntic*e*s lé quell*es* le dit Joh*a*n avoit av*a*nt cez heures, des queulx l'un duist avoir esté mort en p*re*sou*n* et fuist carié au le Spetill*e* de Seint Barth*olome*u *et* la moruist, et l'autr*e* app*re*ntice curra hors de cez t*e*rmes dev*a*nt le fyn de sou*n* app*re*nticialté, et auxint gentz diount q*e* la fe*m*me de dit Joh*a*n Hall*e* soluist bater*e* sez app*re*ntic*es*, p*ur* lez quelx t*re*spac*es* lez gardeins ount chargez *et* garnez l'av*a*ntdit Joh*a*n Hall*e* q*e* si soit t*ro*vé desoreenav*a*nt en tielx pointz, q'adonq*e*s voidera p*re*ntic*es* p*ur* toutz jou*r*s et ferra fyne ové lez gardeins.

[521] It was considered whether this should be expanded as the French 'al vocable', with the same meaning. The word 'vocable' is listed by e.g. Godefroy and the *OED*, but here 'al' has a suspension line through the 'l', and if in French one would have expected the whole word 'vocable'. One must therefore assume that the scribe is using the Latin phrase.

[522] MS: lo*ur*. See opposite page.

[523] This page and the previous one have been written by the same hand and apparently at the same time. Since the cases span a period of over a year, one may gather that these entries were made either from memory or, more probably, from notes.

Mablean: 1412
Memorandum that whereas John Clerk *alias* Mablean contemptuously insulted his current year's wardens, for the which offence by command of William Walderne then Mayor he was committed to Newgate [prison] and there he remained for 5 days. After which time on 10 November 1412 in their hall [Goldsmiths' Hall] before William Louth, alderman, and all the other honourable men of the said company, the aforesaid John begged pardon of his wardens and offered to put himself within their jurisdiction, for the which offence he was sentenced to pay to the alms funds of St Dunstan – £10 subject to their judgment, the which judgment is such that he shall pay each week for a whole year to a poor man of the said company – 8d., this on condition of [his][206] good behaviour. And if it should happen that he offend against any of his wardens or his company, that then he shall pay the sum of £10 as written above, and for this he found sureties – William Grantham and Richard Barton.

Barforee: p. 112
Memorandum that Nicholas Barforee, 'Dutchman' from Bruges, was found at fault in the workmanship of a stone called a ruby, the which ruby was a white [colourless] stone and in the middle of the said stone was an inserted 'tente'[207] counterfeiting a ruby and set on goldleaf and was thus set into a ring and sold for 20s., the which stone is not worth 4d. And he was also found with other false counterfeit stones, and with gold ready for working of a lower standard than the statutory quality, for the which offence he settled with the current year's wardens for 20s. on condition that if the aforesaid Nicholas should from henceforward be found guilty of such aforenamed offences then he shall pay – 100s.

Halle the younger:
Memorandum that on 3 March John Halle the younger came before the 1413
current year's wardens because of the disgrace of two apprentices whom the said John previously had, of the which one was said to have been killed in prison and was taken to St Bartholomew's Hospital and died there, and the other apprentice ran away and out of his terms before the end of his apprenticeship, and also people say that the said John Halle's wife used to beat his apprentices, for the which offences the wardens have charged and warned the aforesaid John Halle that if he should from henceforward be found guilty of such matters, that then he shall be excluded from having apprentices for all time and shall pay a penalty to the wardens.

206 The original has 'lour' = 'their', but this has been editorially changed to the more logical 'soun' = 'his', since it seems improbable that the poor man's good behaviour was intended to be an issue in this case.

207 This 'tente' might conceivably be some sort of paste (see *OED* sub TENT), but John Cherry is convinced that the better explanation is that the clear stone has been backed with red glass set on foil so that the redness shines through the clear glass. The use of the word 'tente' is therefore of note.

Gotlee:

1413 Fait a remembr*er* q*e* le iiie jo*ur* d'aprill*e* l'an du Roy Henr*i* quint puis le conquest p*rimer*, Will*iam* Gootlee fuist t*ro*vé faulx come de sou*n* argent ov*er*ant *et* issint ad sovent esté t*ro*vé, p*ur* quoy mesme le jo*ur* dev*a*nt lez gardeins p*ur* l'an esteantz *et* Joh*a*n Bulstrode, Joh*a*n Stande[l]f, Ric*hard* Bartou*n*, Perys Thorold, Joh*a*n Wat*er*, Joh*a*n Hall*e* le g*ra*unt, Joh*a*n Hall*e*, Joh*a*n Walsch*e*, Joh*a*n Parker *et* multx aut*re*s, l'av*a*ntdit Will*iam* se metta en g*ra*ce *et* d'estr*e* a lo*ur* ordynaunce, p*ur* le quell*e* trespace il paia a p*re*sent iii s. iiii d. *sur* la condic*iou*n q'ensuit: si q*e* l'av*a*ntdit Will*iam* desoreenav*a*nt soit t*ro*vé defectyf ez tielx pointz av*a*ntesc*rip*tz, q'adonq*e*s il payera al p*ri*mer foitz – xl. s. et al secounde temps – C. s. et al tierce foitz – x. li. *et* voyder la citee de Loundr*es* p*ur* toutes jo*ur*s.

Henr*i* Gosse:

Fait a remembr*er* q*e* le xxii jo*ur* d'aprill*e* l'an du regne le Roi Henr*i* quint p*rimer*, Henr*i* Gosse, goldsmyth de Wodstrete,[524] fuist t*ro*vé faulx en ov*er*aigne de xxii hanaps d'arg*ent* chacez, dez les queux ascuns sount lez p*ar*cell*es* endorez appell*ez* bolkuppys *et* ascuns pleynkuppys, p*ur* le quell*e* t*re*spas l'av*a*ntdit Henr*i* se metta en g*ra*ce dez gardeins p*ur* l'an esteantz et p*ur* le t*re*spas fait d'estr*e* a lo*ur* ordinance. Lez quelx gardeins p*ar* l'assent dez multx ault*re*s del dit cumpany luy p*ar*dona sur sou*n* bon*e* porte *et* bon*e* ov*er*aigne en temps a ven*ir*. Et p*ur* le t*re*spas av*a*ntfait l'av*a*ntdit Henr*i* paya as ditz gardeins – xx s. *sur* la condic*iou*n q'ensuit: c'est assavoir q*e* si l'av*a*ntdit Henr*i* soit t*ro*vé desoreenav*a*nt faulx ou defectyf en arg*ent* ou or ov*er*aunt, q'adonq*e*s il payera al p*rimer* foitz – C. s. et al secounde temps – x. li. et al tierce temps voidra la citee p*ur* toutz jo*ur*s.

1414–15 Les nouns dez Duchmen jurez el temps de Ric*hard* Georg*e*, Joh*a*n Hall*e*,
A + b Joh*a*n Fr*ere* *et* Rob*er*t Lemyng l'an du regne le roi Henr*i* Vte *secon*de:

p. 63[525] col. 1	Hans Ekhorn –	ii s.
	Gregory Craft –	ii s.
	It*em*, Herma*n* Spryg –	ii s.
	Nich*olas* Rycoltyssone –	ii s.
	Henr*y* Tyler –	ii s.
	Will*iam* Lasyng –	ii s.
	Deryk Van Wesyll*e* –	ii s.
	Lodewyk Craft –	ii s.
	Ph*ilipp*us Langvyle –	ii s.
	Lodewyk Moll*e* –	ii s.
	Gerard Van Braban –	ii s.
col. 2	Andrew –	scwor*e*
	Geyles –	iii s. iiii d.

[524] The previous three words are added above the line, but have been written at the same time as the rest.

[525] A new hand starts here and has written the heading and the first column; the second column is written in a different and very unformed hand.

Goteley:
Memorandum that on 3 April 1413 William Goteley was found defective in his silver prepared for working, and he has often been thus found defective, for the which reason on the same day before the current year's wardens and John Bulstrode, John Standelf, Richard Barton, Piers Thorold, John Water, John Halle the elder, John Halle, John Walsh, John Parker and many others, the aforesaid William submitted himself to judgment and agreed to abide by their orders, for the which offence he paid at the present time 3s. 4d. on the following condition: that if the aforesaid William should from henceforward be found defective in such aforenamed matters, that then he shall pay on the first occasion – 40s. and on the second occasion – 100s. and the third time £10 and expulsion for ever from the City of London. 1413

Henry Gosse:
Memorandum that on 22 April 1413 Henry Gosse, goldsmith of Wood Street, was found defective in the workmanship of 22 silver chased goblets, of the which some are parcel-gilt and are called 'bowl-cups' and some are plain cups, for the which offence the aforesaid Henry submitted himself to the judgment of the current year's wardens and agreed to abide by their orders for the offence committed. The which wardens with the assent of many others of the said company pardoned him on condition of his good behaviour and good workmanship in time to come. And for the previously committed offence the aforesaid Henry paid to the said wardens – 20s. on the following condition: i.e. that if the aforesaid Henry should from henceforward be found false or defective in silver or gold prepared for working, that then he shall pay on the first occasion – 100s. and on the second occasion – £10 and at the third occasion he shall be expelled for ever from the City.

The names of 'Dutchmen' sworn in the time of Richard George, John Halle, John Frere and Robert Lemyng in the year 2 Henry V [1414–15]: 1414–15 A + b p. 63 col. 1

Hans Ekhorn –	2s.
Gregory Craft –	2s.
Item, Hermann Spryck –	2s.
Nicholas Rycoltyssone –	2s.
Henry Tyler –	2s.
William Lasyng –	2s.
Deryk Van Wesylle –	2s.
Ludwig Craft –	2s.
Phillip Langvyle –	2s.
Ludwig Molle –	2s.
Gerard Van Brabant –	2s.

col. 2

Andrew –	sworn
Giles –	3s. 4d.

Geyles for*e* ii lowes us*er*er –	x s.
Rer*e* Leckton –	scwor*e*
Veyt Jhonson –	scwor*e*
Arnolde –	scwor*e*
Jhon Awfer –	scwor*e*
Bartlet Hereke –	scwor*e*
Heffrard Esplecoret –	scwor*e*

p. 64[526] The oth*e* of Duchmen

ȝe schul swer*e* ȝe schul be trewe & fey[th]ful lieges to our lord the kyng & to his heires kyng*es* of Ingelond, the pees of the Cite to kepe & buxom & obedient be to ȝour Wardeyns that be or schul be in tyme comynge, & redely come to ȝour Wardeyns what tyme ȝe be somoned or warned but ȝe have a resonable excusacion. Trewe gold & selver ȝe schul werke & do werke that is to wyten selver as good as the starlyng & the gold of the alay of the fifthe;[527] ȝe schul no desceyt wite be don in p*re*judice of the Craft; the privytes of the Craft ȝe schul hele & to no mon hem discov*ere*, ne noman the Craft[528] teche but he be take app*re*ntys bounde & arolled after the ordeignanc*es* in the Cite; ȝe schul non app*re*ntys take but he be Englissh & fre born & be schewed to the Wardeyns of the Craft that they mowe se that the p*er*sone be able to be in the same Craft; ȝe schul non alien ne foreyne resceyve ne sette in werke til ȝe bryng hym tofor*e* the Wardeyns that they mowe examyne hym of his conv*er*sacioun & that he fynde borwes wel & trewely to gov*er*ne hym & trewely to werke;[529] ȝe schul wyte ne knowe no foreyn, alien ne estraunger come to the Cite ne the suburbes to werke w*ith* hym self open no prively[530] ne with non other man aȝens the fo*ur*me aboveseyd, but ȝe anon warne ȝour Wardeyns; ȝe schul lette & withstonde to ȝo*ur* power that non alien ne est*ra*unger be resceyved in to the Crafte withoute the assent of the Wardeins,[531] & helpe to p*ur*sue in meyntenance of the gode gov*er*nayle of the C*ra*ft & the fraunchise of the Cite; & alle the ordeignanc*es* & poynt*es* in the Craft ordeyned or to be ordeyned to profyt & hono*ur* of the Craft ȝe schul kepe, meyntene & holde to ȝo*ur* power; ȝe schul no glas sette in gold.[532]

[526] A new hand starts here. This scribe uses yogh but not thorn. The last paragraph is in a different hand and ink, now very faded, and this hand has also written one interlinear addition to the text. This scribe uses both yogh and thorn.

[527] See below, p. 364, note 534.

[528] A cross has been placed against this word and another cross in the margin. The reason is unclear.

[529] As above, a cross has been placed against this word and another cross in the margin. The reason is unclear.

[530] MS: 'open no in musset', with the word 'musset' scored out and 'prively' written above it. One may wonder whether there was an earlier French version of this oath, as 'in musset' would seem perhaps a close translation from French?

[531] 'in to the Crafte . . . Wardeins' has been added between the lines after an omission mark by the hand that wrote the last section of this page.

[532] An omission mark is placed here between this word and the phrase 'So God ȝow helpe & holydam.'; the following section, down to 'fautyff – xx s.', has been written below as a separate paragraph but clearly intended to be inserted before the final words of the oath.

Giles – for [permission] to employ 2 serving-men –	10s.
Rere Leckton –	sworn
Veyt Johnson –	sworn
Arnold –	sworn
John Awfer –	sworn
Bartlet Hereke –	sworn
Geffrard Esplecoret –	sworn

The oath for 'Dutchmen' p. 64

You shall swear that you shall be true and faithful liegemen to our lord the King and to his heirs kings of England, and that you shall maintain the peace of the City and be compliant and obedient to your wardens whoever they be at the present time or in the future, and that you shall promptly attend upon your wardens whenever they summon or call you, unless you have a reasonable excuse. You shall work or have worked by others true gold and silver, that is silver of the standard of sterling and gold of the assay of the fifth. You shall not knowingly allow any deceit to be done to the prejudice of the mistery; you shall keep secret the privities of the mistery and shall reveal them to no one, nor shall you teach the craft to anyone unless he be bound apprentice and enrolled according to the City ordinances; you shall not take on any apprentice except one who is English and free born and who has been presented to the wardens of the mistery for them to see that he is a fit person to be in the same mistery; you shall not receive or set to work any alien or 'foreigner' before you have brought him before the wardens in order that they may examine him about his skill nor before he has found guarantors to exercise good and true authority over him and sureties that he will do true work; if you know of any foreigner, alien or outsider who has come to the City or its suburbs to work either on his own or with any other man either publicly or in private[208] in contravention of the above, then you shall at once let your wardens know about this; you shall as far as you are able hinder and prevent any alien or outsider being admitted to the mistery without the assent of the wardens, and you shall help to prosecute any action that shall maintain the good governance of the mistery and the liberties of the City; and you shall as far as you are able keep, maintain and hold to all the ordinances and articles ordained or that shall be ordained in the mistery for the profit and honour of the mistery; you shall set no glass gemstone in gold.

[208] 'musset' = 'hidden place'.

Ne ȝe ne schull*e* resceive ne take no noþ*er* mannys s*er*vant, p*re*ntys ne covenauntma*n* in to ȝour*e* hous ne in to ȝour*e* work*es* unto tyme þ*at* ȝe have leve of the Wardeyns of þe Craft. Ne ȝe ne schull*e* witdrawe nomannys custum*er* of þe forseyd Craft from hy*m* uppon peyne to paye to þe almesse of Seint Dunston at ev*er*y tyme so yfound fautyff – xx s. So God ȝow helpe & holydam.

p. 65 [blank]

p. 66[533] The oth*e* for Duchemen

Ȝe schull*e* swer*e* þ*at* ȝe schull*e* be feythfull*e* & trewe lieges to our*e* lord þe kyng and to his heirs kyng*es* of Ingelond; þe pees of þe Cite ȝe schull*e* kepe & buxum & obedient ȝe schull*e* be to ȝour Wardeyns þ*at* been for þe ȝeer. And redly ȝe schull*e* come to ȝour Wardeins what tyme þat ȝe been somonned or warned but ȝif ȝe have resonable excusac*io*n. Trewe gold & silv*er* ȝe schull*e* werke & do werke þ*at* is to wete silv*er* as gode as the starlyng & gold of þe allay of the forthe;[534] ȝe schull*e* no p*regi*dice ne deceyt wyte be doon*e* unto þe Craft, and þe p*ri*vetees of þe Craft ȝe schull*e* hele & hem unto no man descov*er*e ne telle. Ȝe schull*e* wete ne knowe no forein, alien ne est*ra*ung*er* come in to the Citee ne yn to þe subbarbys to werke w*ith* hym self ne with noþ*er* man openly ne p*ri*vely, aȝeins þe fo*ur*me aboveseyd, but ȝe anoon warne ȝour*e* Wardeins. Ne ȝe ne schull*e* no glas set in gold. Ne ȝe schull*e* no mannys s*er*vant, p*re*ntys ne covenauntman take in to ȝour*e* hous ne unto ȝour*e* work*es* wit oute leve of þe Wardeins or ellys of his maist*er* wich*e* he hath s*er*ved afore.[535] Ne ȝe schull*e* witdrawe nomannys custum*er* of þe Craft uppon payn to paye to þe almesse of Seint Dunston xl s.[536] at ev*er*y tyme þ*at* it may be p*ro*ved. And all*e* þe gode pointys and ordinances of þe Craft now maad or in tyme comyng to be made for hon*ur*e & furþering of þe Craft ȝe schull*e* maig[n]teigne, kepe & holde be all*e* ȝour*e* power*e*, so God ȝow helpe & holydom*e*.

1415–16 Ceux sount lez nouns dez gardeins eslutz al Fest de Seint Dunstou*n* l'an du
A + a p. 113 regne le Roi Henr*i* quint puis le Conquest tierce tanq*e* al dit feste de Seint Dunstou*n* l'an ensuant:[537]

Joh*ann*es Standelf
Joh*ann*es atte Wat*er*
Joh*ann*es Biernys
Joh*ann*es Geoos

533 A different hand has copied out this later version of the oath for Dutchmen. There are several omissions of passages in the earlier text, three significant differences noted below, and a number of minor changes in phraseology.

534 This is the most significant difference between the two versions. The word 'forthe' has been written between the lines; just before that on the line, something (presumably 'fif') has been fully erased, 'iiii' had been written over but then scored; this left the 'the' of 'fifthe', and 'forthe' has been added in. The assay or allay of the fourth was of 18 carats, whereas that of the fifth was of 19.2 carats, the touch of Paris. The standard was officially reduced in 1478: see Forbes, *Hallmark*, pp. 33–34; Reddaway and Walker, pp. 233, 317–21.

535 This difference is also significant.

536 The amount of the fine has doubled.

537 The monogram mark 'Jhc' has been written, apparently by the scribe, above the four names.

Nor shall you receive into your house nor take into your workshop the servant, apprentice or serving-man of another before you have permission from the wardens of the mistery. Nor shall you entice away the customer of any man of the aforesaid mistery, upon pain of having to pay to the alms funds of St Dunstan upon every occasion you might be found so guilty of offence – 20s. So may God and these relics be your helpers.

[blank] p. 65

The oath for 'Dutchmen' p. 66

You shall swear that you shall be true and faithful liegemen to our lord the King and to his heirs kings of England, and that you shall maintain the peace of the City and be compliant and obedient to your wardens for the current year. And you shall promptly attend upon your wardens whenever they summon or call you, unless you have a reasonable excuse. You shall work and have worked by others true gold and silver, that is silver of the standard of sterling and gold of the assay of the fourth. You shall not knowingly allow any harm or deceit to be done to the mistery; you shall keep secret the privities of the mistery and shall neither reveal nor tell them to anyone. If you know of any foreigner, alien or outsider who has come to the City or its suburbs to work either on his own or with any other man either publicly or in private in contravention of the above, then you shall at once let your wardens know about this. Nor shall you set any glass gemstone in gold. Nor shall you take into your house nor into your workshop anyone's servant, apprentice or serving-man without the permission of the wardens or else of the master whom he previously served. Nor shall you entice away the customer of any man of the mistery, upon pain of having to pay to the alms funds of St Dunstan – 40s. each time this might be proved. And you shall as far as you are able maintain, keep and hold to all the articles and ordinances now made or that shall be made in the future for the honour and advancement of the mistery; so may God and these relics be your helpers.

These are the names of the wardens elected on the feastday of St Dunstan in the year 3 Henry V [19 May 1415] until the said feastday of St Dunstan the following year: 1415–16 A + a p. 113

John Standelf
John atte Water
John Barnes
John Joce

1415 M*emorandum* qu*o*d vj[to] die Junii a*nn*o sup*radicto* Ric*ardus* Georg*e* *et* eius [socii][538] computaveru*n*t cora*m* Gardianis p*ro* a*nno* existent*ibus*. Unde om*n*ia computat*a* p*re*d*ictus* Ric*ardus* Georg*e* *et* eius socii sol*verun*t – iiii li. vi s. xi d.

1415–16 Et reddituarii eod*em* a*nn*o sol*verun*t om*n*ia allo*cata et* computat*a* – iiii li. x s. iii d.
Unde summ*a* to*talis* excedit ut p*atet* antea – viii li. xvii s. ii d.

1415 Joh*anne*s Bedeford:
M*emorandum* qu*o*d cu*m* Joh*ann*es Bedeford, quond*a*m app*renticius* Will*elm*i Gartou*n,* teneat*ur* p*er* suu*m* sc*ri*ptu*m* obligatoriu*m* Joh*ann*i Standelf, civi *et* aur*ifabro* London' ac illo anno un*i* gardianor*um*, in C. li. st*er*lingor*um* solvend*as* in festo S*anct*i Mich*ael*is Archangeli p*roximo* pr*o*ut in d*icto* sc*ri*pto oblig*atorio* plenius apparet, cui*us* dat*um* est xiiii° die Junii a*nno* r*egni* r*egis* Henr*ici* v[ti] iii°, cui*us* condici*o* tal*is* est q*uo*d si p*re*dict*us* Joh*anne*s Bedeford m*odo* app*renticii* uni*us* minstrall*i* in futur*o* nu*n*qu*a*m utit*ur* arte aur*ifabrie* in London' nec ex*tra* London' nec p*re*d*ict*am artem aurifabr*ie* in aliq*uo* m*odo* scandelizat nec secreta artis aur*ifabrie* alicui monstrat nec doceat, ut cora*m* p*re*d*ict*is gardianis p*ro* a*nn*o existent*ibus* p*re*dict*us* Joh*ann*es Bedeford sup*er* libru*m* juravit om*n*ia p*re*dict*a* artic*u*la custodir*e*, q*uo*d extunc p*re*sens oblig*acio* – C li. p*ro* null*a* h*a*beat*ur*, sin aute*m* in om*n*i suo robore p*er*maneat *et* virtute.

Barth*olome*us Seman:
M*emorandum* qu*o*d xii[mo] die Novembris anno regni regis Henrici quinti post conquestu*m* t*er*cio Barth*olome*us Seman, aurifaber *et* auribator, venit cora*m*[539] Joh*an*ne Standelf, Joh*anne* bethe Watyr, Joh*anne* Biernys *et* Joh*an*ne Geoce, ib*ide*m gardianos existent*es*, *et* eciam coram totam cometivam aurifabrie cu*m* d*ict*is gardianis ad eor*um* aulam existent*em*, *et* ib*ide*m juravit sup*er* librum d*ict*o die *et* anno ben*e* *et* fideli*ter* tener*e* [*et*] custodir*e* om*n*ia articula *et* statuta eidem cometive *et* mister*e* p*er*tinent*ia* ut juram[ine][540] d*ict*e mister*e* sc*ri*pt*o* plenius apparet.

1416 Thomas Newtou*n*:
M*emorandum* qu*o*d cu*m* Thom*a*s de Newtou*n*, quond*a*m app*renticius* Mathei Rudlee, civis *et* aurifabri London', teneat*ur* p*er* sc*ri*ptu*m* suu*m* oblig*atorium* Joh*ann*i Standelf, Joh*ann*i bythe Water, Joh*ann*i Biernys *et* Joh*ann*i Geoce, civib*us et* aur*ifabris* London', in x li. st*er*ling*orum* solvend*as* in festo Passche p*roximo* futur*o*, pr*o*ut in d*ict*o oblig*acione* plenius apparet, cui*us* dat*um* est xv die Februar*ii* a*nno* r*egni* r*egis* Henr*ici* quinti t*er*cio, cui*us* condici*o* est tal*is* q*uo*d si p*re*dict*us* Thom*a*s Newtou*n* in futur*o* nu*n*qu*a*m utit*ur* art*e*

538 MS: cucii.
539 This word can be used with either the accusative or ablative case, although the mingling of the two practised by this scribe is not generally recommended.
540 MS: jurameni.

Memorandum that on 6 June of the aforesaid year Richard George and his fellow wardens presented their account before the current year's wardens. From which, all things accounted for, the aforesaid Richard George and his fellow-wardens handed over – £4 6s. 11d. 1415

And the renters for the same year handed over, all things allowed for and accounted – £4 10s. 3d. 1415–16
Thus the sum total amounts as appears above to – £8 17s. 2d.

John Bedford: 1415
Memorandum that whereas John Bedford, formerly the apprentice of William Garton, is bound by his letters of obligation to John Standelf, citizen and goldsmith of London and that year one of the wardens, in the sum of £100 sterling to be paid at Michaelmas next [29 September] as more fully appears in the said letters of obligation, whose date is 14 June 1415, whose condition is such that if the aforesaid John Bedford should never in future as an apprentice of any craftsman practise the craft of goldsmithry in London or outside London, and if he does nothing to disgrace the aforesaid goldsmiths' mistery in any way, and if he does not reveal to another person nor teach them the secrets of the goldsmiths'mistery, as the aforesaid John Bedford swore on the book before the aforesaid current year's wardens to keep to all of the aforesaid points, that then the present bond in the sum of £100 should be held null and void, but otherwise it shall remain in all its strength and virtue.

Bartholomew Seman:
Memorandum that on 12 November 1415 Bartholomew Seman, goldsmith and goldbeater, came before John Standelf, John atte Water, John Barnes and John Joce, the present wardens, and also before the whole company of the Goldsmiths' Mistery present with the said wardens in their Hall, and there he swore on the book on that said date that he would keep and observe all the articles and statutes pertaining to the same company and mistery as appears more fully in the written form of the oath of the said mistery.

Thomas Newton: 1416
Memorandum that Thomas de Newton, formerly the apprentice of Matthew Rudlee, citizen and goldsmith of London, is bound by his letters of obligation to John Standelf, John atte Water, John Barnes and John Joce, citizens and goldsmiths of London, in the sum of £10 sterling to be paid at the next following Feast of Easter, as appears more fully in the said obligatory letters whose date is 15 February 1416 [n.s.] and whose condition is that if the aforesaid Thomas Newton shall never in the future practise the craft of

aur*ifabrie* in London' nec ex*tra* nec p*re*dic*t*am arte*m* in p*re*dic*t*o m*odo* sckandelizat nec secreta artis alicui monstrat nec doceat, ut cora*m* p*re*dic*t*is gardianis p*ro* a*nno* exeste*ntibus*[541] p*re*dic*tus* Thom*as* sup*er* libru*m* juravit om*n*ia p*re*dict*a* articu*l*a custodir*e*, q*uo*d extunc p*re*sens oblig*acio* – x li. p*ro* null*a* h*ab*eat*ur*, sin aute*m* in om*n*i suo robore p*er*maneat *et* virtute.

1416 Holcroft:

p. 114 Fait a remembr*er* p*ur* ceo q*e* Will*ia*m Holcroft dispetousement revyla sez gardeins p*ur* l'an esteantz encountr*e* lez estatutz d'orfev*er*ie au cont*ra*rie faitz, le quell*e* trespas fuist g*ra*unt ensaumple az altres juins ho*m*mes[542] du dit mistier de malfair*e* et dyre et le pluis,[543] si l'av*a*ntdit Will*ia*m ne fuist mye p*ur* sou*n* trespas chastysé. Le quell*e* Will*ia*m le secounde jo*ur* d'aprill*e* l'an du regne le Roi Henr*i* quint puis [le][544] conquest quarte, vient dev*a*nt lez ditz gardeins en lo*ur* co*mun*e sale, *et* la ové eux esteantz toutz lez hon*ur*ables gentz[545] de dit mistier dev*a*nt ces temps gardeins, *et* la dev*a*nt eux luy metta en lo*ur* g*ra*ce *et* p*ur* sou*n* trespas eux cria m*er*cy ov*er*tement s*ur* sez knees *et* outrement as eux paia .C. s. s*ur* lo*ur* g*ra*ce en condic*iou*n qu'ensuit, q*e* si l'av*a*ntdit Will*ia*m desoreenav*a*nt trespasa encountr*e* cez gardeins, q'adonq*e*s paiera la moite q*e* s*er*ra ordeigné p*ar* le hon*ur*able Cumpanye p*ur* sou*n* trespas issint fait.

1416 Ric*hard* Stacy:[546]

Fait a rem[em]b[r]*er*[547] q*e* le ii^{de} jour d'aprill*e* l'an du regne le Roi Henr*i* v^{te} puis [le][548] conquest quart, Richard[549] Stacy vient dev*a*nt lez gardeins p*ur* l'an esteantz p*ar* tout le co*mun*e assent del dit mistier, *et* la ad jur*é* b*ie*n *et* loialment ten*er*, s*er*ver *et* gard*er* toutes lez pointz *et* statutz au dit mistier app*ur*tenantz, come [par] le comune s*e*rem*en*t pluis pleinem*en*t app*er*t.

Ric*hard* Bradcok:

Fait a remembr*er* q*e* le viime jo*ur* d'aprill*e* l'an du regne le Roi Henr*i* v^{te} puis le conquest quarte, Richard Bradcoke vient dev*a*nt lez gardeins p*ur* l'an esteantz p*ar* tout le co*mun*e assent del dit mistier, *et* la ad jur*é* sur le liv*e*re b*ie*n *et* loialment ten*er*, s*er*ver *et* garder toutz les pointz *et* articles au dit mistier app*ur*ten*a*ntz, come p*ar* co*mun*e s*e*rement pluis pleinement app*er*t, *et* s*ur* ceo est

[541] *Sic.*

[542] The word 'altres' in this phrase presumably means that Holcroft himself was a 'yeoman' at this date.

[543] 'et le pluis' has been added by the scribe above the line.

[544] MS: sou*n.*

[545] Here the usage of 'hon*ur*ables gentz' is spelt out as referring to those who have previously held the office of warden. It may well be that one should interpret in this way on other occasions when the phrase is used.

[546] Neither Richard Stacy nor any of the three men who are listed next (Bradcok, Leget and Tyce) have appeared in the register previously, and there is no record of their having been apprentices. Their admission into the mistery and into the freedom of the City is therefore of note, as are the amounts paid. All four of these men played a large role hereafter in the mistery.

[547] MS: remb'e.

[548] MS: sou*n.*

[549] This name is written above an erased 'Thom*as*'.

goldsmithry in London or outside London, and if he never bring scandal upon the said craft in the aforesaid manner, and if he does not either reveal or teach the secrets of the craft to anyone, as the aforesaid Thomas has sworn on the book before the aforesaid current year's wardens to observe all the aforesaid points, that then the present bond in the sum of £10 – shall be held as null and void, but otherwise it shall remain in all its strength and virtue.

Holcroft: p. 114
Memorandum that whereas William Holcroft contemptuously insulted his current wardens in contravention of the statutes of the Goldsmiths' Mistery which expressly forbid this, the which offence would be a great example to the other yeomen[209] of the said mistery to do wrong and say wrong things and more, if the aforesaid William were not punished for his offence. The which William on 2 April 1416 came before the said wardens in their common hall, and there with them were all the honourable men of the said mistery who had previously been wardens, and there before them he submitted himself to their judgment and begged mercy for his offence openly upon his knees, and besides he paid to them 100s. subject to their judgment, on the condition that follows, that if the aforesaid William should from henceforward offend against his wardens, that then he shall pay the fine (mulct)[210] that shall be ordained by the honourable company for the offence he has thus committed.

Richard Stacy:
Memorandum that on 2 April 1416 Richard Stacy came before the current year's wardens with the common assent of all of the said mistery, and there he swore to hold, to serve and to keep well and faithfully all the articles and statutes pertaining to the said mistery, as appears more fully in the common oath.

Richard Bradcok:
Memorandum that on 7 April 1416 Richard Bradcok came before the current year's wardens with the common assent of all of the said mistery, and there he swore on the book to hold, to serve and to keep well and faithfully all the articles and ordinances pertaining to the said mistery, as appears more fully in the common oath, and upon this he was admitted to the said Company and

[209] The other 'juins hommes' might just be 'young men', but by this date the words carry the more technical sense of the 'yeomen' or 'bachelors', the junior members of the mistery who are of the freedom but not in the livery.

[210] The word 'moite' in the text would appear to be 'moité' = 'half', but it is difficult to understand in context here why the wardens would in advance agree to a fine being halved, unless this somehow refers to the 100s. William Holcroft has offered – but this will not fit with 'serra ordeigné'. The alternative explanation is that 'moite' is either a scribal copying error of 'molte' or a hitherto unattested form of 'multe' = 'mulct, fine', and this entirely fits the sense of the sentence.

resceyvé en dit cu*m*panye, *et* au dit f*ra*unchise en Gildehall*e* resseyvé, *et sur* ceo au Cumpanye ad payé – x. m*a*rcz.

Thom*a*s Leget:
Fait a remembr*er* q*e* le xme jo*ur* de Maii l'an du regne le Roi Henr*i* quint puis le conquest quarte, Thomas Leget vient dev*a*nt lez gardeins p*ur* l'an esteantz p*ar* tout le co*mun*e assent del dit mistier, *et* la ad jur*é sur* le liv*er*e de b*ie*n *et* loyalment teign*er*, garder *et* s*er*ver toutz lez pointz, statutz *et* articles au dit mistier app*ur*tenantz, come p*ar* le co*mun*e s*er*ement pleinement app*er*t, *et sur* ceo est resseyvé au dit Cumpanye *et* issint en le Guyldehall*e* come orphev*er* entr*é et* resseyvé, *et* p*ur* ceo l'av*a*ntdit Thomas au dit Cumpanye ad payé – C s.

Joh*anne*s Tyce:
Memorand*um* q*uo*d sexto die Apprill*is* anno r*egni* r*egis* Henrici quinti post conq*uestum*[550] quarto, ven[i]t[551] coram Nich*ola*o Wottou*n*, Maiore London' in domo habitac*i*onis sue, videli*ce*t in parochia S*anct*i Laurencii Pulteney London', tam custodes mistere aur*ifabrie* d*ict*e civitat*is* q*ua*m Joh*anne*s Tyce, civis *et* goldbeter London'. Qui quidem Joh*anne*s Tyce adtunc *et* ib*ide*m de pura *et* spontanea voluntate sua fidem dedit in man*ibus* dict*i* Maior*is* q*uo*d ip*s*e deinceps esse vellet de lib*er*ata sive vestu[r]*a*[552] mister*e* aur*ifabrie* p*re*d*ict*e, p*ro*mittend*um* se ult*er*ius p*ara*t*ur* esse quociens *et* qu*a* necesse fu*er*it *et* co*m*mode pot*er*it cu*m* cet*er*is ho*min*ib*us* eiusdem mister*e* in equitac*i*onib*us*, oblac*i*onib*us*, cont*ri*buc*i*onib*us et* soluc*i*onib*us* honorem *et* co*m*modu*m* civitatis v*e*l mistere p*re*dict*e* conc*er*nent*ibus*. Et eciam ad manutenend*um* juxta vires suas om*n*es ordinac*i*o*n*es *et* regulas mistere p*re*dict*e* etc.

Holcroft:
M*emorandum* q*uo*d cu*m* Will*el*m*u*s Holcroft teneat*ur et* obligat*ur* Joh*ann*i Standelf *et* suis sociis gardianis p*ro* a*nno* existent*ibus* in xx li. sterling*orum* solvend*as* in festo Nat*ivitatis* S*anct*i Joh*ann*is Bap*tis*te p*ro*ut in quad*a*m oblig*acione* inde fact*a* plenius apparet, cui*us* condic*i*o est tal*is* q*uo*d si inf*ra*sc*ri*ptus Will*el*m*u*s deinceps se b*ene et* honest*e* geret erg*a* suos gardianos p*ro* a*nno* existent*es* et sic de anno in annum d*ict*is gardianis *et* eor*um* succ*essoribus* gardianis, q*uo*d extunc p*re*sens oblig*acio* p*ro* null*a* h*ab*eat*ur*, sin aute*m* in om*n*i suo robore p*er*maneat *et* virtute.

1415–16 In p*rimis*, Rad*ulph*us Whytechirche app*renticius* Rog*er*i Barneston*e* – xx s.
p. 115[553] It*em*, Joh*anne*s Vook app*renticius* Joh*ann*is Chestyr – xx s.
It*em*, Ric*ardus* Hykkys app*renticius*[554] Thome Langtou*n* – xx s.
It*em*, Joh*anne*s Cowpland app*renticius* Will*el*mi Holcroft – xx s.
It*em*, Rog*er*us Lynacr*e* app*renticius* Will*elm*i Walton*e* – xx s.
It*em*, Rob*er*tus Clerk app*renticius* Joh*ann*is Paake – xx s.
It*em*, Thomas Samma app*renticius* Joh*ann*is Hill*es* – xx s.

550 The previous two words added above the line by the scribe.

551 MS: venet.

552 MS: vestut'. This form is otherwise unattested and the scribe may well have made an amalgam of 'vestitus' and 'vestura'.

553 This page has a large blank space at the top, which may well have been left for the usual heading to a year with a list of the year's wardens.

554 MS: app'n' app'n'.

admitted to the said franchise at the Guildhall, and upon this he paid to the Company – 10 marks.

Thomas Leget:
Memorandum that on 10 May 1416 Thomas Leget came before the current year's wardens with the common assent of all of the said mistery, and there he swore on the book to hold, to keep and to serve well and faithfully all the articles, statutes and ordinances pertaining to the said mistery, as appears more fully in the common oath, and upon this he was admitted to the said Company and thus was entered and admitted at the Guildhall as a goldsmith, and for this the aforesaid Thomas paid to the Company – 100s.

John Tyce:
Memorandum that on 6 April 1416 there came before Nicholas Wootton, Mayor of London, in his private house in the parish of St Lawrence Poultney, London, both the wardens of the Goldsmiths' Mistery of the said city and John Tyce, citizen and goldbeater of London. The which John Tyce then and there of his own free will pledged his faith while clasping hands with the said Mayor that he wished from thenceforward to be of the livery of the aforesaid Goldsmiths' Mistery, promising moreover that he would be prepared as often and wherever it should be necessary and that he was conveniently able to take part in and contribute to processions, offerings, contributions and payments that concern the honour and the advantage of either the City or the aforesaid mistery. And also that he will to the best of his ability maintain all the ordinances and rules of the aforesaid mistery, etc.

Holcroft:
Memorandum that whereas William Holcroft is bound to John Standelf and his fellow wardens for the current year in the sum of £20 sterling to be paid at the feast of St John the Baptist, as appears more fully in the bond drawn up concerning this, whose condition is such that if the undersigned William from henceforward shall behave himself well and honestly towards his current year's wardens and thus from year to year towards the said wardens and their successors, that then the bond shall be held to be void, but otherwise it shall remain in all its strength and virtue.

Firstly, Ralph Whitchurch apprentice of Roger Barnston –	20s.	1415–16
Item, John Vook apprentice of John Chester –	20s.	p. 115
Item, Richard Hykkys apprentice of Thomas Langton –	20s.	
Item, John Coupland apprentice of William Holcroft –	20s.	
Item, Roger Linacre apprentice of William Walton –	20s.	
Item, Robert Clerk apprentice of John Pake –	20s.	
Item, Thomas Samma apprentice of John Hilles –	20s.	

It*em*, Will*el*m*u*s Aleyn app*renticius* Joh*ann*is Pattyslee – xx s.
It*em*, Joh*anne*s Michellys app*renticius* Will*elm*i Fythhewe – xx s.
It*em*, Thomas Newtou*n* app*renticius* Maykyn*e* Rudlee – xx s.
It*em*, Will*el*mus Valaunce app*renticius* Rob*er*ti Lemyng – xx s.
It*em*, Joh*anne*s Hawerdyne app*renticius* Rob*er*ti Downe – xx s.
It*em*, Rob*er*tus Botiller app*renticius* Joh*ann*is Biernys – xx s.
It*em*, Joh*anne*s Groye app*renticius* Joh*ann*is Colneye – xx s.
It*em*, Laurencius Chyldemylle app*renticius* Ric*ard*i Georg*e* – xx s.
It*em*, Rob*ertus* Chaumb*er*leyn*e* app*renticius* Rob*er*ti Serle – xx s.
It*em*, Thom*as* Houghtou*n* app*renticius* Ric*ard*i Spenc*er* – xx s.
It*em*, Joh*anne*s Godfrey app*renticius* Joh*ann*is Tewkysbury – xx s.
It*em*,Thomas Blythe app*renticius* Joh*ann*is Tewkysbury – xx s.
It*em*, Joh*anne*s Cros app*renticius* Thome Lamport – xx s.
It*em*, Rob*ertus* Strykland app*renticius* Joh*ann*is Barde – xx s.

In p*rimis*, Thomas Wolf quond*a*m app*renticius* Joh*ann*is Chest*er* – ii s.
It*em*, de Joh*anne* Stalkeden*e* [quondam] app*renticius* Will*elm*i Louthe – ii s.
It*em*, Joh*anne*s Carbonell*e* [quondam] app*renticius* Ric*ard*i Georg*e* – ii s.
It*em*, Rob*er*tus M*er*lawe [quondam] app*renticius* Salamonis Oxney – ii s.
It*em*, Will*elmu*s Whyt [quondam] app*renticius* Wynaunt Wermys – ii s.
It*em*, Joh*anne*s Braunston*e* [quondam] app*renticius* Will*elm*i Louthe – ii s.

1416–17 Joh*anne*s Blakeden*e*
p. 116[555] Salamon Oxneye
Joh*anne*s Pake
Rob*ertus* Botolf

1416 Sol*ucio* – Rob*er*tus Hall*e*:
M*emorandum* q*uo*d xj° die Octob*ris* a*nno* r*egni* r*egis* Henrici quinti quarto Rob*er*tus Hall*e* recepit de Joh*ann*e Blakeden*e*, Salamone Oxney, Joh*a*nne Pake *et* Rob*er*to Botolf, gardianis p*ro* a*nno* existent*ibus* – xxxvi li. xiiii d. que p*re*d*ict*i gardiani receperunt de vet*er*is gardianis *et* redditu*ariis* ante illos existent*ibus*, ut p*atet per* eor*um* endent*ur*as compot*atas*, que quidem su*m*ma de xxxvi li. xiiii d. solut*a* est p*re*d*ict*o Rob*er*to Hall*e* in p*ar*te*m* soluc*io*nis de lxvi li. xiii s. iiii d. Et sic om*n*ia computat*a* ad diem p*re*d*ictu*m debent*um*[556] est p*re*d*ict*o Rob*er*to Hall*e* in claro – xxx li. xii s. ii d. ut p*atet* antea temp*o*re Ric*ard*i Georg*e*, Joh*ann*is Hall*e*, Joh*ann*is Frer*e et* Rob*er*ti Lemyng in sc*r*iptis.

M*emorandum* q*uo*d cu*m* Thomas Lagage de London', quond*a*m famul*us*[557] Joh*ann*is Lagage, civis *et* aurifab*ri* London', teneat*ur et* obligat*ur* Joh*ann*i Pake, civi *et* aur*ifabro* London', in centu*m* marc*as* sterlingor*um* solvend*as* in festo S*anct*i Mich*ael*is Archangeli p*ro*x*imo* futur*o*, cui*us* dat*um* est sexto die Septemb*ris* a*nno* r*egni* r*egis* Henrici v^{ti} quarto, cui*us* condic*i*o est tal*is* q*uo*d si

[555] The monograph mark 'Jhu' appears at the top of this page, apparently in the hand of the scribe.
[556] Here and below the form 'debent-' is used for 'debend-'.
[557] He is listed above as his apprentice.

Item, William Allone apprentice of John Pattesley –	20s.
Item, John Michellys apprentice of William FitzHugh –	20s.
Item, Thomas Newton apprentice of Matthew Rudlee –	20s.
Item, William Valaunce apprentice of Robert Lemyng –	20s.
Item, John Hawerdyne apprentice of Robert Downe –	20s.
Item, Robert Botiller apprentice of John Barnes –	20s.
Item, John Groye apprentice of John Colney –	20s.
Item, Lawrence Chyldemylle apprentice of Richard George –	20s.
Item, Robert Chamberlayne apprentice of Robert Serle –	20s.
Item, Thomas Houghton apprentice of Richard Spencer –	20s.
Item, John Godfrey apprentice of John Tewkesbury –	20s.
Item, Thomas Blythe apprentice of John Tewkesbury –	20s.
Item, John Cros apprentice of Thomas Lamport –	20s.
Item, Robert Strickland apprentice of John Barde –	20s.

Firstly, Thomas Wolf formerly apprentice of John Chester –	2s.
Item, from John Stalkendene [formerly] apprentice of William Louth –	2s.
Item, John Carbonelle [formerly] apprentice of Richard George –	2s.
Item, Robert Merlawe [formerly] apprentice of Solomon Oxney –	2s.
Item, William White [formerly] apprentice of Wynant van Worms –	2s.
Item, John Braunstone [formerly] apprentice of William Louth –	2s.

John Blakedene 1416–17
Solomon Oxney p. 116
John Pake
Robert Botulf

Payment – Robert Halle: 1416
Memorandum that on 11 October 1416 Robert Halle received from John Blakedene, Solomon Oxney, John Pake and Robert Botulf, wardens for the current year – £36 14d. which the aforesaid wardens had received from the previous year's wardens and renters present before them as appears in their indentured accounts, the which sum of £36 14d. was paid to the aforesaid Robert Halle in part payment of £66 13s. 4d. And thus all things accounted for on the aforesaid day Robert Halle is owed £30 12s. 2d. net, as appears previously in the records written in the time of Richard George, John Halle, John Frere and Robert Lemyng.[211]

Memorandum that whereas Thomas Lagage of London, formerly of the household of John Lagage, citizen and goldsmith of London, is bound to John Pake, citizen and goldsmith of London, in the sum of 100 marks sterling to be paid on the next following Michaelmas Day [29 September], the date of the bond being 6 September 1416, whose condition is such that if the aforesaid Thomas

[211] 1414–15.

predictus Thomas in tempore futuro numquam utitur arte aurifabrie in aliquo loco, nec secreta artis predicte alicui docuit vel docere faciat, ut predictus Thomas super dictas articulas voluntarie super librum juravit, quod extunc presens obligacio pro nulla habeatur, alioquin in omni suo robore permaneat et virtute. Et causa cuius juramenti quod idem Thomas inventus fuerat cum diversis defectis videlicet quod ipse sepe sicut latro spoliavit dictum Johannem Lagage magistrum suum.

Memorandum quod xiii° die Octobris anno supradicto in presencia Johannis Blakedene et sociorum suorum Gardianorum et aliorum dicte cometive, videlicet Johannis Standelf, Johannis bythe Water, Johannis Norman, Roberti Halle, Willelmi Hope, per comunem assensum die antedicto sigillum commune fuit fractum.[558]

1417 Halle:[559]
Memorandum quod die Jovis xxvii° die Februarii anno regni regis Henrici quinti quarto, tempore Johannis Blakedene, Salamonis Oxney, Johannis Pake et Roberti Botolf, custodum mistere aurifabrie, redditus in Fridaistrete quietus est et plene persolutus[560] Roberto Halle, Johanni Halle et Roberto Lemyng pro redditu predicto de omnibus solucionibus predictis aliquo modo debentis.

1416 Ricardus Stapilton:
A + b Memorandum quod Ricardus Stapilton, civis et auribator London', teneatur per
p. 72 *cont.* suum scriptum obligatorium Johanni Blakedene et Johanni Pake, civibus et aurifabris dicte civitatis, et Johanni Bisshop juniori et Henrico Wykwan, civibus et auribatoribus dicte civitatis, in x li. sterlingorum, cuius datum est xii° die Decembris anno regni regis Henrici V^ti^ iiii^to^, cuius condicio est talis quod si infrascriptus Ricardus ex parte sua teneat et custodiat bene et fideliter omnes articulos artis sue antedicte tam operacione quam gubernacione versus suam cometivam artis auribatorum sicut die predicto idem Ricardus super librum juravit bene et fideliter custodire, quod extunc presens obligacio pro nulla habeatur, alioquin in omni suo robore permaneat et virtute.

Memorandum quod die Jovis[561]

p. 73 [blank]

[558] On the common seal of the mistery see Reddaway and Walker, pp. 8 (n. 17), 110, 139. No reason is given here for the breaking of the seal, nor is it stated (although one must assume it) that a new one was made.

[559] This entry also appears on p. 75 of Book A + b.

[560] A + b: quietus est et solutus.

[561] The writing breaks off at this point. This is presumably the entry now in full on p. 75.

shall in the future never practise the craft of goldsmithry in any place, and if he does not teach to anyone the privities of the said mistery or have them taught by another, as the aforesaid Thomas has voluntarily sworn on the book to the aforesaid points, that then the present bond shall be held to be void, otherwise it shall remain in all its strength and virtue. And the cause of this oath was that the same Thomas was found guilty of a number of offences, i.e. that he had often like a thief stolen from the said John Lagage his master.

Memorandum that on 13 October of the aforesaid year in the presence of John Blakedene and his fellow wardens and others of the said company, i.e. John Standelf, John by the Water, John Norman, Robert Halle, William Hope, by common consent on the aforesaid day the common seal was broken.

Halle: 1417
Memorandum that on Thurday 27 February 1417 n.s. in the time of John Blakedene, Solomon Oxney, John Pake and Robert Botulf, wardens of the Goldsmiths' Mistery, the tenement in Friday Street was settled and payment made in full to Robert Halle, John Halle and Robert Lemyng for the aforesaid tenement, this settlement being for all aforesaid payments in any way owed.

Richard Stapleton: 1416
Memorandum that Richard Stapleton, citizen and goldbeater of London, is A + b
bound by his letters obligatory to John Blakedene and John Pake, citizens and p. 72 *cont.*
goldsmiths of the said City, and to John Bisshop the younger and Henry Wykwan, citizens and goldbeaters of the said City, in the sum of £10 sterling, the date of which bond is 12 December 1416, whose condition is such that if the undersigned Richard for his part holds to and keeps well and faithfully all the ordinances of his aforesaid mistery both those that concern workmanship and those relating to the governance of his company of the mistery of goldbeaters, as on the aforesaid day the said Richard swore on the book to keep them well and faithfully, that then the present bond shall be held to be void, otherwise it shall remain in all its strength and virtue.

Memorandum that on Thursday

[blank] p. 73

p. 74[562] The othe of the Wardeyns:[563]
Ȝe shull swer þat ȝe shull be feithfull & trewe to our*e* lord þe kyng & to hys heirs, & good & trewe assay make of gold & of selver, no man for favo*ur* ne love sparyng ne noman grevyng for hate. And all þe good ordenances of the craft ȝow shall kepe & mayntene to all ȝour poair. And wel & honestlych trete ȝour felawshyp. And just juges ȝe shull be upon þe causes of ȝour companye aft*er* ȝour concyence, & no singuler p*ro*fit to ȝour own p*er*sones do wherþorth þe comyn p*ro*fit of þe company shall be halmed, ne no man receyve to þe company w*ith* out þe sent of þe same compan[y].

[The othe of the renters][564]
Ȝe shul swer that ȝe shul wel & truly gadr*e* the rent app*er*tenant to the co*m*panye & wel & truly overse the same rente, & trewe accompte of the resceytes ȝelde to the co*m*panye wyth oute any theng*es* helyng, ne no renter ches wyth oute assent of your wardeyns, ne no preest remoove ne resceyve w*ith* oute assent of the same wardeyns, ne no rep*ar*aci*on* make w*ith* oute ov*er* sight & assent of twey cont*ra*rollers which be chose for the ȝer*e*.

1417 M*emorandum* q*uo*d cu*m* Will*elmus* Walton teneat*ur et* p*er* suu*m* sc*ri*ptu*m* oblig*atorium* obligat*ur* Will*elm*o Fitzhugh, Joh*ann*i Hill*es*, Ric*ard*o Wedyall*e et* Ph*ilipp*i Walsch*e*, civib*us et* aurifabr*is* London' ac gardianis d*ic*t*e* mister*e*, in x li. st*er*ling*orum* solvend*as* in festo Pasch*e* p*ro*x*imo* futur*o*, cui*us* dat*um* est v^{to} die Novemb*ris* a*nno* r*egni* r*egis* Henr*ici* V^{ti} quinto, cui*us* condic*i*o est tal*is* q*uo*d si Joh*ann*es Per*a*unt de London', aurifab*er* quond*a*m app*renticius* Will*el*mi Hertwell*e*, p*ro* quo id*em* Will*elmu*s Walton p*redic*t*i*s gardianis obligat*ur*, paret, ordinet seu parar*i* vel ordinar*i* faciet vinu*m* sufficient' ta*m* rubiu*m* q*ua*m albu*m et* s*er*viciam cu*m* uno q*ua*rt*er*io boni frument*i* p*ro* convivio mister*e* aurifabr*ie* ad eleccio*n*em d*ictorum* gardianor*um et* p*er* f*es*tu*m* Passche p*roximum* futur*um* et in celar*ium* reddit d*ictorum* aurifabr*ie* parat*um et* ordinatu*m* in Fasturlane, q*uo*d extunc p*re*sens oblig*acio* in q*uo* idem Will*elmu*s obligat*ur* p*ro* null*a* h*ab*eat*ur*, sin aute*m* in om*n*i suo robore p*er*maneat *et* virtute.

1417 Thom*as* Reyner:
p. 75[565] M*emorandum* q*uo*d xvii° die Novemb*ris* anno regni Regis Henrici quinti quinto Thomas Reyner, quond*a*m app*renticius* Joh*ann*is Neylond, venit die sup*radict*o coram gardianis p*ro* a*nno* existent*ibus et* aliis d*ic*t*e* cometive cu*m* ill*is*

[562] The first two paragraphs of this page are written in two separate hands; the third paragraph is in the same hand as that which wrote p. 72; this hand also writes p. 75. The scribes of the first two paragraphs have clearly been copying from an exemplar and it is to be noted that neither of them distinguishes 'y', thorn and yogh; the edition here has however done so following normal practice.

[563] One may compare the later oaths given in the *Book of Ordinances* and cited in Reddaway and Walker, pp. 212–21. That for the wardens is on p. 212.

[564] Cf. Reddaway and Walker, p. 213.

[565] The first entry on this page is omitted here since it has already appeared above (A + a, p. 116) and the wording is almost identical, the slight orthographic variants being of no significance and the only real difference being noted above.

The oath of the wardens p. 74
You shall swear that you shall be faithful and true to our lord the King and to his heirs, and that you shall make good and true assay of gold and of silver, that you shall spare no one out of favour or love and that you shall not cause harm to anyone out of hatred. And that you shall keep and maintain as far as lies in your power all the good ordinances of the mistery. And you shall treat all your fellows well and honestly. And you shall be just judges according to your conscience in all cases concerning your company, and that you shall do nothing to your own individual advantage whereby the common advantage of the company shall be harmed, and that you shall admit no one to the said company without the assent of the same company.

[The oath of the renters]
You shall swear that you shall well and truly collect the rent belonging to the company, and that you shall well and truly oversee the same rent[212] and render true account of the receipts to the company without concealing anything; that you shall not choose any renter without the assent of your wardens, nor shall you either write off or take receipt of any loans without the assent of the same wardens, nor shall you have any repairs done without this being supervised and consented to by two 'controllers'[213] elected for that year.

Memorandum that whereas William Walton is held and bound by his letters 1417
obligatory to William FitzHugh, John Hilles, Richard Withihale and Phillip Walsh, citizens and goldsmiths of London and wardens of the said mistery, in the sum of £10 sterling to be paid at the next following feast of Easter, the date of which bond is 5 November 1417, whose condition is such that if John Peraunt of London, goldsmith and formerly the apprentice of William Hertwell, on whose behalf the same William Walton is bound to the aforesaid wardens, provides and orders, or causes to be provided and ordered, sufficient wine, both red and white, and ale, and a quarter of good wheat for the feast of the Goldsmiths' Mistery held at the election of the said wardens and for the next feast of Easter, and delivers these, provided and ordered, to the cellar of the said Goldsmiths in Foster Lane, that then the present bond by which the same William is bound shall be held as void, otherwise it shall remain in all its strength and virtue.

Thomas Reyner: 1417
Memorandum that on 17 November 1417 Thomas Reyner, formerly apprentice p. 75
of John Nayland, came on the aforesaid day before the current year's wardens and others of the said company present with them, and there he swore on the

[212] The meaning of 'rent' has probably here shifted from that of 'rent-money' to that of 'property yielding rent; tenement'.

[213] It is uncertain whether one should translate this as the modern 'comptroller', and think that these men were elected to exercise control over financial expenditure, or whether they were rather experts in building works, whose job was to supervise the technical standard of repairs. Checking and control procedures for both may well have been organised.

existent*ibus*, *et* ib*ide*m juravit sup*er* libru*m* ben*e* *et* fideli*ter* co*m*morar*e* *et* s*er*vire Joh*ann*i Pake, mag*ist*ro suo, a die illo q*uo*d juravit usq*ue* ad f*estu*m S*anc*ti Petri q*uo*d d*icitu*r A Vincula p*roximum* futur*um* post dat*um* p*re*senciu*m* et ab illo festo S*anc*ti Petri usq*ue* ad finem et t*er*minu*m* triu*m* annor*um* extunc p*roxi*mor*um* sequen*tium* *et* plenar*ie* completor*um* m*odo* sui app*re*nticii absq*ue* aliq*u*a cont*ra*dicc*i*one.

1416–17 In p*rimis*, Rob*er*tus Broun*e* app*renticius* Joh*ann*is Blakeden*e* – xx s.
A + a p. 117 It*em*, Henr*icus* Barth*olome*u app*renticius* Salamonis Oxney – xx s.
It*em*, Will*el*mus Frederyk app*renticius* Joh*ann*is Pake – xx s.
It*em*, Michell*is* Lyghehee app*renticius* Joh*ann*is Mabelyan*e* – xx s.
It*em*, Joh*annes* Blekensop*e* app*renticius* Rob*er*ti Hall*e* – xx s.
It*em*, Nich*ola*us Kyrkham app*renticius* Ric*ard*i Skot – xx s.
It*em*, Henr*icus* Tann*er*er app*renticius* Joh*ann*is Northwell*e* – xx s.
It*em*, Joh*ann*es Swan app*renticius* Thome Rammy – xx s.
It*em*, Nich*ola*us Belyngdou*n* app*renticius* Ric*ard*i Chaumbr*e* – xx s.
It*em*, Will*el*mus Wytle app*renticius* Joh*ann*is Lagage – xx s.
It*em*, Joh*ann*es Croce app*renticius* Henr*ici* Raglee – xx s.
It*em*, Will*el*m*u*s Tann*er* app*renticius* Joh*ann*is Standelf – xx s.[566]

In p*rimis*, Roskyn*e* quond*am* app*renticius* Joh*ann*is Whyte – ii s.
It*em*, Thom*as* Rammy quond*am* app*renticius* Petri Meyr*e* – ii s.
It*em*, Petrus Brendewode quond*am* app*renticius* Joh*ann*is Pake – ii s.
It*em*, Joh*ann*es Godard quond*am* app*renticius* Barth*olome*i Seman – ii s.
It*em*, Henr*icus* Raglee quond*am* app*renticius* Georg*ii* Cressy – ii s.

1417–18 Ceux sount lez nouns dez Gardeins eslutz al fest de Seint Dunstou*n* l'an
p. 118 d[u][567] regne Henri quint puis [le][568] conquest quinte tanq*e* al dit fest de Seint Dunstou*n* l'an ensuant:[569]
(Will*el*mus Fithhewe)
(Rob*er*tus Hall*e*) – mortu*us*
(Joh*ann*es Hill*es*) Ric*ard*us Whethiall*e*
(Joh*ann*es Walsshe)

1417 Et quia Rob*er*tus Hall*e* fuit electus unnus[570] gardianor*um* cu*m* p*re*d*ic*tis Will*el*mo Fytzhugh*e*, Joh*ann*e Hill*es* *et* Joh*ann*e Walsch*e* et cito inf*ra* mensem S*anc*ti Dunstani p*re*dict*us* Rob*er*tus Hall*e* moriebat*ur*, Ricardus Whethiall*e* fuit electus unus gardianor*um* loco p*re*dicti Rob*er*ti Hall*e* ut p*atet* p*er* scr*i*ptu*m* prius.

1417–18 Will*el*mus Fytzhewe
Joh*ann*es Hill*es*
Ric*ard*us Whethiall*e*
Joh*ann*es Walsch*e*

566 This line has been added slightly later by the scribe in different ink.
567 MS: de.
568 MS: sou*n*.
569 The four names that follow have all been scored out, the notes about Robert Halle's death have been written to the RH side, and the new set of four names written underneath the first list.
570 *sic*.

book well and faithfully to live with and serve as his apprentice John Pake, his master, from that day on which he took the oath until the next feastday of St Peter ad Vincula [1 August] and from that feastday of St Peter for and until the end of three full years next following, without any dissension.

Firstly, Robert Broun apprentice of John Blakedene –	20s.	1416–17
Item, Henry Bartholomew apprentice of Solomon Oxney –	20s.	A + a p. 117
Item, William Frederyk apprentice of John Pake –	20s.	
Item, Michael Lyghehee apprentice of John Mablean –	20s.	
Item, John Blenkinsop apprentice of Robert Halle –	20s.	
Item, Nicholas Kirkham apprentice of Richard Skot –	20s.	
Item, Henry Tannerer aprentice of John Northwell –	20s.	
Item, John Swan apprentice of Thomas Remy –	20s.	
Item, Nicholas Billington apprentice of Richard Chaumbre –	20s.	
Item, William Wytle apprentice of John Lagage –	20s.	
Item, John Croce apprentice of Henry Ragley –	20s.	
Item, William Tanner apprentice of John Standelf –	20s.	

Firstly, Roskyne formerly apprentice of John White –	2s.
Item, Thomas Remy formerly apprentice of Peter Mayre –	2s.
Item, Peter Brentwood formerly apprentice of John Pake –	2s.
Item, John Godard formerly apprentice of Bartholomew Seman –	2s.
Item, Henry Ragley formerly apprentice of George Cressy –	2s.

These are the names of the wardens elected at the feast of St Dunstan in the 1417–18
year 5 Henry V [19 May 1417] until the same feastday of St Dunstan the next p. 118
year:
(William FitzHugh)
(Robert Halle) died
(John Hilles) Richard Withihale
(John Walsh)

And because Robert Halle was elected one of the wardens with the aforesaid William FitzHugh, John Hilles and John Walsh, and immediately within the month of St Dunstan the aforesaid Robert Halle died, therefore Richard Withihale was elected one of the wardens in the place of the aforesaid Robert Halle, as appears previously in the written record.[214]

William FitzHugh
John Hilles
Richard Withihale
John Walsh

[214] This might refer just to what is written above, but might refer to some other written record.

Appr*entys*:
In p*rimis*, de Ric*ardo* Offeld app*renticio* Joh*ann*is Luke – xx s.
It*em*, Barth*olome*us Bramsone app*renticius* Joh*ann*is Corby – xx s.
It*em*, Joh*ann*es Barbour app*renticius* Joh*ann*is Chest*er* – xx s.
It*em*, Joh*ann*es at Gate app*renticius* Joh*ann*is Horwell*e* – xx s.
It*em*, Galfr*idus* Newton*e* app*renticius* Thome Well*es* – xx s.
It*em*, Joh*ann*es Pumfreyt app*renticius* Joh*ann*is Martyn – xx s.
It*em*, Ric*ard*us d'Excetr*e* app*renticius* Will*elm*i Cheyne – xx s.
It*em*, Joh*ann*es Frensch*e* app*renticius* Will*elm*i Louth*e* – xx s.
It*em*, Walt*er*us Dene app*renticius* Will*elm*i Fithzhugh*e* – xx s.

1416–17 [571]It*em*, Thurstou*n* Furneys app*renticius* Will*elm*i Botoun – xx s.
It*em*, Joh*ann*es Craft app*renticius* Steph*an*i Colney – xx s.
It*em*, Joh*ann*es Biernys app*renticius* Henr*ici* Chaumb*er*leyn – xx s.
It*em*, Joh*ann*es Burtou*n* app*renticius* Joh*ann*is Draytou*n* – xx s.
It*em*, Thomas Reyner app*renticius* Joh*ann*is Pake – xx s.
It*em*, Will*el*mus Codyngtou*n* app*renticius* Joh*ann*is Ertou*n* – xx s.
It*em*, Joh*ann*es Fyssch*e*bourne app*renticius* Joh*ann*is Hall*e* – xx s.
It*em*, Joh*ann*es Grandou*n* app*renticius* [eius]dem[572] Joh*ann*is Hall*e* – xx s.
It*em*, Joh*ann*es Skynn*er* app*renticius* Rog*er*i Warburgh*e* – xx s.
It*em*, Joh*ann*es Prys app*renticius* Will*el*mi Markeby – xx s.
It*em*, Joh*ann*es Welford app*renticius* Thome Long – xx s.

– Lez quelx xi app*r*enticez av*a*ntescr*i*ptz furont resseyvez del an av*a*nt, del temps Joh*a*n Blakeden*e*, Salamon Oxney, Joh*a*n Pake *et* Rob*er*t Botolf, *et* lez aultr*es* ix app*rentices* del temps desuis escr*i*ptz en temps de Will*ia*m Fythzhugh*e*, Joh*a*n Hill*es*, Ric*hard* Wedyall*e* *et* Joh*a*n Walssch*e*.

1417–18 Lowez jurez:
In p*rimis*, Thom*as* Westle quo*n*d*am* app*renticius* Joh*ann*is Curraunt – ii s.
It*em*, Joh*ann*es Wat*er*le quo*n*d*am* app*renticius* Henr*ici* Wortisborow – ii s.
It*em*, Joh*ann*es Wethell*e* quo*n*d*am* app*renticius* Will*elm*i Adys – ii s.
It*em*, Henr*icus* Chaumb*er*leyn apud Algate – ii s.
It*em*, Joh*ann*es Laxam quo*n*d*am* app*renticius* Joh*ann*is Kanoun*e* – ii s.
It*em*, Joh*ann*es Sutton*e* quo*n*d*am* app*renticius* Rob*er*ti Lemyng – ii s.
It*em*, Matheus Phelyp [quo*n*d*am*] app*renticius* Joh*ann*is P[h]elyp[573] – ii s.
It*em*, Joh*ann*es Walsch*e* quo*n*d*am* [app*renticius*] Will*elm*i Downe – ii s.
It*em*, Rog*er*us Kendale quo*n*d*am* app*renticius* Ric*ardi* Bartou*n* – ii s.
It*em*, Thomas Bamme quo*n*d*am* app*renticius* Rob*er*ti Hall*e* – ii s.
It*em*, Will*elmus* Clynton*e* quo*n*d*am* app*renticius* Joh*ann*is Pake – ii s.
It*em*, Joh*ann*es Tewkysbury quo*n*d*am* app*renticius* Joh*ann*is Tewkisbury – ii s.

[571] The next eleven names are separated by a gap from those below, and this is explained at the foot of the list – see below.

[572] MS: idem.

[573] MS: Ppelyp.

Apprentices:

Firstly, from Richard Offield apprentice of John Luke –	20s.
Item, Bartholomew Bremsham apprentice of John Corby –	20s.
Item, John Barbour apprentice of John Chester –	20s.
Item, John atte Gate apprentice of John Orwell –	20s.
Item, Geoffrey Newton apprentice of Thomas Welles –	20s.
Item, John Pumfreyt apprentice of John Martyn –	20s.
Item, Richard de Exeter apprentice of William Cheyne –	20s.
Item, John Frenshe apprentice of William Louth –	20s.
Item, Walter Dene apprentice of William FitzHugh –	20s.

Item, Thurston Furneys apprentice of William Botoun –	20s.	1416–17
Item, John Craft apprentice of Stephen Colney –	20s.	
Item, John Barnes apprentice of Henry Chamberlayn –	20s.	
Item, John Burton apprentice of John Drayton –	20s.	
Item, Thomas Reyner apprentice of John Pake –	20s.	
Item, William Coddington apprentice of John Ireton –	20s.	
Item, John Fishbourne apprentice of John Halle –	20s.	
Item, John Grandon apprentice of the same John Halle –	20s.	
Item, John Skynner apprentice of Roger Warburgh –	20s.	
Item, John Pryce apprentice of William Markeby –	20s.	
Item, John Welford apprentice of Thomas Long –	20s.	

Of the apprentices written above, 11 were admitted in the previous year, in the time of John Blakedene, Solomon Oxney, John Pake and Robert Botulf, and the other 9 apprentices in the time as written above of William FitzHugh, John Hilles, Richard Withihale and John Walsh.

Sworn serving-men: 1417–18

Firstly, Thomas Westley formerly apprentice of John Coraunt –	2s.
Item, John Waterley formerly apprentice of Henry Wortesburgh –	2s.
Item, John Withihale formerly apprentice of William Adys –	2s.
Item, Henry Chamberlayn at Aldgate –	2s.
Item John Laxman formerly apprentice of John Canon –	2s.
Item, John Sutton formerly apprentice of Robert Lemyng –	2s.
Item, Matthew Philip [formerly] apprentice of John Philip –	2s.
Item, John Walsh formerly [apprentice] of William Downe –	2s.
Item, Roger Kendal formerly apprentice of Richard Barton –	2s.
Item, Thomas Bamme formerly apprentice of Robert Halle –	2s.
Item, William Clynton formerly apprentice of John Pake –	2s.
Item, John Tewkesbury formerly apprentice of John Tewkesbury –	2s.

Item, Johannes Oger quondam apprenticius Johannis Mablyane – ii s.
Item, Johannes Bulstrode quondam apprenticius Johannis Bulstrode – ii s.
Item, Walterus Chaddysley quondam apprenticius Johannis Halle, senioris – ii s.
Item, Johannes Hokere quondam apprenticius Willelmi Downe – ii s.
Item, Ricardus Wynne quondam apprenticius Johannis Palyng – ii s.
Item, Nicholaus Lovet quondam apprenticius Henrici Wortisburghe – ii s.

1417–18 Fayt a remembrer qe William Fytzhughe, Johan Hilles, Richard Wedyalle *et*
p. 119 Johan Walsche, lez gardeins avantescriptz pur l'an esteantz, ount ordeignez *et* faitz *et* en lour tresorye mys en garde un pyle de xvi marcz de Troye pur estre un standard pur governer toutes lez poysez au dit mistier appurtenantz en temps a venir.

1418 Fait a remembrer qe le xxiiii^e jour d'aprille l'an du regne le roi Henri quint vj^e, William Fytzhughe, Johan Hilles, Richard Wedyalle *et* Johan Walssche, gardeins pur l'an, ount faitez pleynal fyne et concord parentre Downe d'une part *et* Maykyn Rudle d'autre part. C'est assavoir: pur taunt qe le vantdit Robert Downe fait un playnt de trespas al Countre de Chepe envers l'avantdit Maykyn saunz le volunté *et* assent de cez gardeins *et* encountre soun cerement, lez avantditz gardeins ount juggez *et* par assent dez avantditz Robert Downe *et* Maykyn establiez qe si lez viscountz de Loundres pur lour profyt en temps a venir preig[n]drount en Chepe ou aillours ascun encerche pur ascun debat qe fuist cyavant p[ar][574]entre lez partiez avantdytz pendantz, qe al partie le fray fuist trové, l'avantdit Robert payera la moyté issint par le viscount recoveré, en quelle partie de eux fuist trové, et de ceo entavant qe l'avantdit Robert batust l'avantdit Maykyn malowsement cy come devant lez avantditz gardeins de record fust trové.

1418 Fait a remembrer qe el temps de William Fytzhughe, Johan Hilles, Richard
p. 120 Wedyalle *et* Johan Walsche est ordeigné *et* escript *et* en le tresorye mys un libre de velom contenant iiii^C foilles saunz lez custodyes, c'est assavoir iiii en primer comencement *et* iiii en le fyn;[575] le quelle libre fuist ordeigné al entent *et* profyt de tout la cumpanye; *et* pur ceo qe avant cez heures divercez evydencez ount esté embesylez *et* detraez, lez avantdytz gardeins ount lessé entrer toutz lez avantditz evydencez en l'avantdit libre pur le pluis record. Et lez avantditz evydencez chescun par soy mesmes come as ditz tenementz apparteignent en diverse kofyns *et* boxez mys, *et* issynt lez ditz boxez billez a dire qe de tielx tenementz specefyent, en chescun boxe quantz evydencez escriptz come en le libre est specefyé, auxi bien copiez come aultres chartres ensealez, les quelx copiez lez avantditz gardeins en defaut dez evydencez perduz et anientisez ount lez avantditz copiez hors de Guyldehalle retraez *et* portez. Que le kalender qe ysy est mys . . .[576]

574 MS: *pur*.

575 This book survives and is now bound in two volumes and known as the Register of Deeds (MSS 1642, 1643). The original parchment guard-leaves survive. On the prologue to this book and the languages in which it is written see Jefferson, 'The Language and Vocabulary . . .', pp. 176–77, 194, 197.

576 The writing breaks off at this point.

Item, John Oger formerly apprentice of John Mablean –	2s.
Item, John Bulstrode formerly apprentice of John Bulstrode –	2s.
Item, Walter Chaddesley formerly apprentice of John Halle the elder –	2s.
Item, John Hokere formerly apprentice of William Downe –	2s.
Item, Richard Wynne formerly apprentice of John Palyng –	2s.
Item, Nicholas Lovet formerly apprentice of Henry Wortesburgh –	2s.

Memorandum that William FitzHugh, John Hilles, Richard Withihale and 1417–18
John Walsh, the aforesaid current year's wardens, ordered and made and p. 119
placed in safe-keeping in their treasury a pile of 16 marks Troy weight that is to be a standard by which to control all weights belonging to the mistery in the future.

Memorandum that on 24 April 1418 William FitzHugh, John Hilles, Richard 1418
Withihale and John Walsh, wardens for the year, made plenary agreement and concord between Downe on the one side and Maykyn Rudle on the other, i.e. that whereas the aforesaid Robert Downe made a plaint of trespass against the aforesaid Maykyn at the Counter[215] in Cheap, without the will and consent of his wardens and in contravention of his oath, the aforesaid wardens judged and with the assent of the aforesaid Robert Downe and Maykyn established that if the sheriffs of London conduct in the future for their own benefit any enquiry in Cheap or elsewhere into the quarrel pending previously between the aforesaid parties, that the aforesaid Robert shall pay the half of any fine recovered by the sheriff to whoever may be found the guilty party for the affray, and this because the aforesaid Robert maliciously assaulted the aforesaid Maykyn as was proved and recorded before the aforesaid wardens.

Memorandum that in the time of William FitzHugh, John Hilles, Richard 1418
Withihale and John Walsh there was ordained and written up and placed in the p. 120
treasury a book of vellum containing 400 leaves plus the guardleaves, i.e. four at the beginning and four at the end, the which book was ordained for the use and the benefit of all the Company; and because in former times various documents have been embezzled[216] and taken away, the aforesaid wardens have had all the aforesaid documents copied up into the aforesaid book in order to have a better record. And the aforesaid documents have been placed in various chests and boxes each according to which tenement they belong, and the said boxes have been labelled to say that they refer to such tenements, and each box contains as many written documents as are specified in the book, both copies and in other cases sealed charters, the which copies were, in the absence of documents that had been lost and destroyed, retrieved and brought as copies from the Guildhall. That the list of contents which is thus placed . . .

[215] The Counter was the court or hall of justice of the Mayor.

[216] See *OED* for the now obsolete sense of this word: 'to make away with, fraudulently destroy (a charter, title-deed, etc.). In later use also, to mutilate, tamper with (a document or writing of any kind).'

1418–19 Ceux sount lez nouns dez gardeins eslutz al fest de Seint Dunstou*n* l'an du
p. 121 regne le Roy Henr*i* quint puis [le][577] conquest vj^e^ tanq*e* al dit feste de Seint Dunstou*n* l'an ensuant:

Ric*ard*us Georg*e*
Petrus Thorold
Barth*olome*us Sema*n*
Rob*er*tus Waltou*n*

Appr*en*t*ys*:

In p*rimis*, Thomas Orpher*e* appr*enticius* Joh*ann*is Peraunt – xx s.
It*em*, Joh*ann*es Castell appr*enticius* Thome Wilwez – xx s.
It*em*, Joh*ann*es Wodhous appr*enticius* Petri Brendewode – xx s.
It*em*, Joh*ann*es Kyrkh*a*m appr*enticius* Joh*ann*is Botou*n*[578] – xx s.
It*em*, Will*elmu*s Thakele appr*enticius* Joh*ann*is Tewkysbury – xx s.
It*em*, Ric*ardus* Londou*n* appr*enticius* Rob*er*ti Lemyng – xx s.
It*em*, Walt*er*us Lemyngtou*n* appr*enticius* Barth*olom*ei Seman – xx s.
It*em*, Andreas Lowthe appr*enticius* Salamonis Oxney – xx s.
It*em*, Thom*a*s Bevyngtou*n* appr*enticius* Joh*ann*is Cresbiene – n*ihi*l causa Maioris
It*em*, Will*elmu*s Fost*er* appr*enticius* Joh*ann*is Watirle – xx s.
It*em*, Henr*icus* Pole appr*enticius* Will*elm*i Gilb*er*t – xx s.

Lowez:[579]

In p*rimis*, de Joh*ann*e Kyng appr*enticius* Joh*ann*is Walsch*e* – ii s.
It*em*, Henr*icus* van Handernak appr*enticius* Albright Andirnak – xvi s.[580]
It*em*, Joh*ann*es Kemp appr*enticius* Will*elm*i Waltou*n* – ii s.
It*em*, Thomas Whitmore appr*enticius* Joh*ann*is Cresbiene – ii s.
It*em*, Joh*ann*es Be[v]yngtou*n* appr*enticius* Will*elm*i Belverge – ii s.
It*em*, Thomas Swynesco appr*enticius* Joh*ann*is Wat*er* – ii s.
It*em*, Rob*er*tus Goodg*r*ome appr*enticius* Will*elm*i Gilb*er*t – ii s.

1418–19 M*emorandum* de quad*a*m g*r*avamine *et* querela penden[te][581] int*er* Henricu*m* Whitbrede ex p*ar*te una *et* Joh*ann*em Eylond ex p*ar*te alt*er*a, videlic*et* de quad*a*m summa auri ponderis vii li. vendit*a* Thome Faukoner*e*, Aldermanne, p*er* p*re*dic*tu*m Joh*ann*em Eylond *et* p*er* adiuvamen p*re*dic*t*i Henrici Whitbred, et unde q*uo*d id*em* Henricus ad illud tempus deveniebat p*ro* p*re*dic*t*o Joh*ann*e plegiu*m et* manucaptore*m* d*ic*to Thome Faukon*er* p*ro* xxviii s. in vendic*ione* p*re*dic*t*i auri. Et p*os*tea p*re*dic*t*i Henricus *et* Joh*ann*es veniebant coram gardianis illo a*nno* existent*ibus* p*ro* g*r*avami*n*e p*re*dic*t*o *et* ib*id*em p*re*dic*t*i fecerun*t* securitate*m et* juramen esse *et* star*e* ad judiciu*m* p*re*dic*torum* gardianor*um* sup*er* recordu*m* p*re*dic*t*i Thome Faukon*er*. Quo

[577] MS: sou*n*.
[578] This latter name is written above an erased 'Rob*er*ti Lemyng'.
[579] Here, as in a number of other such lists, one might have expected 'quondam' or 'nuper' before the word 'apprenticius' against each name. These men are paying their 2s. on release from their terms of apprenticeship and whether they stay with their master or take work with another, they are now serving-men who must be paid, and are no longer apprentices.
[580] This sum is noteworthy.
[581] MS: pendens.

These are the names of the wardens elected at the feast of St Dunstan in the year 6 Henry V [19 May 1418] until the said feastday of St Dunstan the following year: 1418–19 p. 121
Richard George
Piers Thorold
Bartholomew Seman
Robert Walton

Apprentices:

Firstly, Thomas Orfeyre apprentice of John Peraunt –	20s.
Item, John Castell apprentice of Thomas Wylwes –	20s.
Item, John Woodhouse apprentice of Piers Brentwood –	20s.
Item, John Kirkham apprentice of John Boton –	20s.
Item, William Takeley apprentice of John Tewkesbury –	20s.
Item, Richard London apprentice of Robert Lemyng –	20s.
Item, Walter Leamington apprentice of Bartholomew Seman –	20s.
Item, Andrew Louth apprentice of Solomon Oxney –	20s.
Item, Thomas Bevington apprentice of John Cresbien – nothing, because of the Mayor[217]	
Item, William Foster apprentice of John Waterley –	20s.
Item, Henry Pole apprentice of William Gilbert –	20s.

Serving-men:

Firstly, from John Kyng [formerly] apprentice of John Walsh –	2s.
Item, Henry Van Andirnak [formerly] apprentice of Albright Andirnak –	16s.
Item, John Kemp [formerly] apprentice of William Walton –	2s.
Item, Thomas Whitmore [formerly] apprentice of John Cresbien –	2s.
Item, John Bevington [formerly] apprentice of William Belverge –	2s.
Item, Thomas Swinscoe [formerly] apprentice of John Water –	2s.
Item, Robert Goodgrome [formerly] apprentice of William Gilbert –	2s.

Memorandum about a certain accusation and plea pending between Henry Whitbread on the one side and John Nayland on the other, i.e. concerning a certain sum of gold weighing 7 pounds that was sold to Thomas Fauconer, alderman, by the aforesaid John Nayland and with the assistance of the aforesaid Henry Whitbread, and concerning which the same Henry at that time became the surety for the aforesaid John and mainpernor to the said Thomas Fauconer for 28s. in the sale of the aforesaid gold. And afterwards the aforesaid Henry and John came before the current year's wardens on account of the aforesaid accusation and there the aforesaid men gave surety and swore to be and to stand by the judgment of the aforesaid wardens on the report of the aforesaid 1418–19

[217] No further information seems to be available to explain this.

quid*a*m Thomas p*er* examinac*ion*em p*redictorum* gardianor*um* recordavit cu*m* p*redict*o Henrico contr*a* p*redictu*m Joh*ann*em Eylond, unde iid*em* gardiani sup*er* recordu*m* p*redictu*m judicaverunt q*uo*d p*redict*us Johannes Eylond solveret p*r*efat*o* Henrico xxviii s. p*r*edict*os*.

1419 Stalkynden*e*:

p. 122 M*emorandum* q*uo*d cu*m* Joh*ann*es Stalkynden*e* teneat*ur et* obligat*ur* Ric*ard*o Georg*e*, Petro Thorold, Barth*olome*o Seman *et* Rob*er*to Walto*u*n, gardianis, in xl li. sterlingor*um* solvend*as* in festo Nat*ivitatis* S*anct*i Joh*ann*is Bap*tis*te p*roxim*o futur*o*, cui*us* dat*um* xvj° die Maii a*nno* r*egni* r*egis* Henr*ici* V[ti] septi*mo*, cui*us* co*n*dici*o* tal*is* est, q*uo*d si Joh*ann*es infrasc*r*ipt*us* de cet*ero* n*e*c in futur*o* faciet n*e*c fieri p*r*ocurabit alico m*odo* p*ro* se vel aliq*uo* alio aliq*uas* petra[s][582] voc*atas* 'countrefaitz', videli*ce*t diamaundis, rubbees, baleys, zafyrs, p*er* quas aliquis defraudat*ur*, cu*m* id*em* Joh*ann*es sup*er* libru*m* juravit in aula aurifabrie cora*m* suis gardianis eo a*nno* existent*ibus et* tota cometiva eod*em* die p*ro* d*ict*a causa collogata, q*uo*d extunc p*re*sens obligac*i*o in q*ua* id*em* Joh*ann*es Stalkynden*e* obligat*ur* p*ro* null*a* h*ab*e[a]t*ur* sin autem in om*n*i suo robore p*er*maneat *et* effectu. Aut vendat v*e*l vender*e* faciat cecrete aut aperte, v*e*l aliqu*em* aliu*m* sciat v*e*l cognoscat vender*e et* facer*e* q*ua*m ip*s*e, p*r*edict*us* Joh*ann*es suos gardianos p*r*emuniat v*e*l p*r*emunir*e* faciat, v*e*l in p*r*edict*a* obligac*ion*e occurret in su*m*ma p*redict*a.[583]

1419 Henr*icus* Booste:

M*emorandum* q*uo*d cu*m* Henric*us* Booste de London', Ducheman *et* polisschou*r* pet*r*arum, teneat*ur et* obligat*ur* Ric*ard*o Georg*e*, Petro Thorold, Barth*olome*o Seman *et* Rob*er*to Walto*u*n, gardianis, in xl li. st*er*lingor*um* solvend*as* in festo Nat*ivitatis* S*anct*i Joh*ann*is Bap*tis*te p*roxim*o futur*o*, cui*us* dat*um* xvj° die Maii a*nno* r*egni* r*egis* Henr*ici* V[ti] septi*mo*, cui*us* co*n*dici*o* tal*is* est, q*uo*d si Henric*us* infrasc*r*ipt*us* de cet*ero* vel in futur*o* [non] faciet n*e*c fieri p*r*ocurabit aliq*uo* m*odo* p*ro* se vel p*ro* aliq*uo* alio aliq*uas* petra[s] voc*atas* 'countrefaitz', videli*ce*t diamaundis, rubbees, baleys, zafyrs, p*er* quas aliquis defraudat*ur*, cu*m* id*em* Henric*us* sup*er* libru*m* juravit in aula aurifabrie cora*m* suis gardianis eo a*nno* existent*ibus et* tota cometiva eod*em* die p*ro* d*ict*a causa collocata, v*e*l vendat v*e*l vender*e* faciat secrete aut aperte v*e*l aliqu*em* aliu*m* sciat v*e*l cognoscat vender*e* v*e*l facer*e* q*ua*m ip*s*e, p*r*edict*us* Henr*icus* suos gardianos[584] p*r*emuniat v*e*l p*r*emunir*e* faciat, q*uo*d extunc p*re*sens obligac*i*o in q*ua* id*em* Henr*icus* Booste obligat*ur* p*ro* null*a* h*ab*eat*ur* sin autem in om*n*i suo robore p*er*maneat *et* effectu.

1419 Peraunt:

M*emorandum* q*uo*d xviii° die Maii a*nno* r*egni* r*egis* Henrici V[ti] septi*mo* ordinatu*m* est cora*m* gardianis illo a*nno* existent*ibus et* Joh*ann*e Standelf,

[582] MS: 'petra', clearly written both here and below, the scribe apparently believing this to be a neuter plural?

[583] The last sentence has clearly been added as an afterthought but is in the same hand and ink.

[584] The word 'non' is added superscript at this point. The grammatical structure of the sentence makes it easy for a scribe to lose the logical thread, but the intended sense is clear.

Thomas Fauconer. And about this matter the said Thomas reported by examination of the aforesaid wardens in favour of the aforesaid Henry and against the aforesaid John Nayland, and therefore the the same wardens upon this aforesaid report judged that the aforesaid John Nayland should pay to the aforesaid Henry the aforesaid 28s.

Stalkendene: 1419
Memorandum that whereas John Stalkendene is held and bound to Richard p. 122
George, Piers Thorold, Bartholomew Seman and Robert Walton, wardens, in the sum of £40 sterling to be paid at the next following feastday of the Nativity of St John the Baptist [24 June], the date of which bond is 16 May 1419, and whose condition is such that if the undersigned John neither henceforth nor in the future shall make or cause to be made in any way either for himself or for anyone else any stones called 'imitation gemstones' i.e. diamonds, rubies, balas-rubies, sapphires, by which anyone might be deceived, as he has sworn on the book at Goldsmiths' Hall in the presence of his current year's wardens and the whole company assembled together on that day for that reason, that then the present bond by which the same John Stalkendene is bound shall be held to be void, but otherwise it shall remain in all its strength and effect. Or if he sell or causes to be sold either in private or in public, or if he should know of anyone other than himself either selling or making [such stones], the aforesaid John should inform his wardens or have them informed, or else he should be subject to the aforesaid bond in the aforesaid sum.

Henry Booste: 1419
Memorandum that whereas Henry Booste of London, 'Dutchman' and stone-polisher, is held and bound to Richard George, Piers Thorold, Bartholomew Seman and Robert Walton, wardens, in the sum of £40 sterling to be paid at the next following feastday of the Nativity of St John the Baptist [24 June], the date of which bond is 16 May 1419, and whose condition is such that if the undersigned Henry from henceforth and in future does not either make or cause to be made in any way for himself or for anyone else any stones called 'imitation gemstones' i.e. diamonds, rubies, balas-rubies, sapphires, by which anyone might be deceived, as the same Henry has sworn on the book at Goldsmiths' Hall in the presence of his current year's wardens and the whole Company assembled on that same day for that reason, and if he does not sell or cause to be sold either in private or in public, and if he knows of anyone other than himself either selling or making [such stones], if the said Henry informs his wardens or causes them to be informed, that then the present bond by which the same Henry Booste is bound shall be held to be void, but otherwise it shall remain in all its strength and effect.

Peraunt: 1419
Memorandum that on 18 May 1419 it was ordained in the presence of the current year's wardens and of John Standelf, John Water, John Tewkesbury,

Johanne Water, Johanne Tewkisbury, Ricardo Wedialle, Ricardo Spencer, Johanne Mabeleaun, Johanne Walsche, Johanne Pattisle *et* Galeas Taverne et multis aliis ibidem presentibus, quod Johannes Peraunt qui fuit inventus falsus in operacione de cupbondis unde libra argenti non valebat nisi – xxii s. viii d.,[585] et etiam in multis burcellis impletis cum lemaylle de plumbo *et* rosyne, per quas deceptiones *et* facta tota mistera aurifabrie fuerat defamata. Or[d]inatum est *et* constetutum quod predictus Johannes Peraunt in tempore futuro nunquam erit receptus in dictam cometivam videlicet nec operari, vendere, emere secrete vel apperte nec shopam vel cameram tenere, nec aliquis predicte mistere predicto Johanne adhererеat pro qua idem Johannes poterit adiuvari in aliquo, set in omnibus in futuro sicut vir *et* homo falsus *et* expulsus reprobari.

1419–20 Ceux sount lez nouns dez gardeins eslutz al feste de Seint Dunstoun l'an du
p. 123 regne le Roi Henri quinte puis [le][586] conquest viime tanqe al dit fest de Seint Dunstoun l'an ensuaunt:
Johannes Standelf
Johannes atte Water
Ricardus Spencer
Johannes Mablyan

Apprentys:

In primis, Edmundus Dunstalle apprenticius Willelmi Couper –	xx s.
Item, Willelmus Saays apprenticius Johannis Mabelyan –	xx s.
Item, Johannes Tibbes apprenticius Johannis Warde –	xx s.
Item, Johannes Elyys apprenticius Willelmi Belverge –	xx s.
Item, Walterus Gribbelle apprenticius Thome at Water –	xx s.
Item, Willelmus Porter apprenticius Willelmi Botoun –	xx s.
Item, Rogerus Roose apprenticius Willelmi Alkam –	xx s.
Item, Edwardus Dobbys apprenticius Thome Brynkle –	xx s.
Item, Henricus Gaddisby apprenticius Henrici Wykwane –	xx s.
Item, Robertus Baker apprenticius Johannis Paake –	xx s.
Item, Willelmus Leversegge apprenticius Roberti Kryngilford –	xx s.
Item, Willelmus Hotoft apprenticius Johannis Suttoun –	xx s.
Item, Johannes Harry apprenticius Rogeri Aleyn –	xx s.
Item, Petrus Silkstone apprenticius Stephani Colney –	xx s.
Item, Thomas Lenam apprenticius Johannis Lenam –	xx s.
Item, Ricardus Thurstone apprenticius Petri Thorold –	xx s.
Item, Johannes de Bethum apprenticius Johannis Horwelle –	xx s.
Item, Thomas Carsyntoun apprenticius Willelmi Gartoun –	xx s.

Lowez jurez:[587]

In primis, Ricardus Frytz apprenticius Johannis Bulstrode –	ii s.
Item, Willelmus Rus apprenticius Johann[i]s[588] Whitwelle –	ii s.
Item, Thomas Barde apprenticius Johannis Barde –	ii s.

585 See above, p. 290, note 399.
586 MS: soun.
587 All those listed below are once again *former* apprentices.
588 MS: Johannes.

Richard Withihale, Richard Spencer, John Mablean, John Walsh, John Pattesly and Galeas Taverne, and of many others there present, that John Peraunt who had been found guilty of deceit in the workmanship of decorative bands for cups of which the pound of silver was worth no more than 22s. 8d., and also in many bossells[218] which were filled with lead filings and rosin, because of which deceits and wrongful deeds the whole Goldsmiths' mistery had suffered defamation. It was ordained and decreed that the aforesaid John Peraunt should never in the future be received into the said company, i.e. neither to work nor to sell nor to buy, either in private or in public, nor to keep a shop nor a room, nor shall anyone of the aforesaid mistery support the aforesaid John in any way which could afford assistance to the same John in any manner, but he shall in all ways in future be condemned as a false man who has been expelled.

These are the names of the wardens elected at the feast of St Dunstan in the year 7 Henry V [19 May 1419], until the said feastday of St Dunstan the following year: 1419–20 p. 123

John Standelf
John atte Water
Richard Spencer
John Mablean

Apprentices:

Firstly, Edmund Dunstalle apprentice of William Couper –	20s.
Item, William Saays apprentice of John Mablean –	20s.
Item, John Tibbes apprentice of John Warde –	20s.
Item, John Elys apprentice of William Belverge –	20s.
Item, Walter Gribbelle apprentice of Thomas atte Water –	20s.
Item, William Porter apprentice of William Botoun –	20s.
Item, Roger Roose apprentice of William Alkam –	20s.
Item, Edward Dobbys apprentice of Thomas Brinkley –	20s.
Item, Henry Gaddisby apprentice of Henry Wykwan –	20s.
Item, Robert Baker apprentice of John Pake –	20s.
Item, William Leversegge apprentice of Robert Cringleford –	20s.
Item, William Hotoft apprentice of John Sutton –	20s.
Item, John Harry apprentice of Roger Aleyn –	20s.
Item, Peter Silkstone apprentice of Stephen Colney –	20s.
Item, Thomas Lenham apprentice of John Lenham –	20s.
Item, Richard Thurston apprentice of Piers Thorold –	20s.
Item, John de Bethum apprentice of John Orwell –	20s.
Item, Thomas Carsyntoun apprentice of William Gartoun –	20s.

Sworn serving-men:

Firstly, Richard Frytz [formerly] apprentice of John Bulstrode –	2s.
Item, William Russ [formerly] apprentice of John Whitwelle –	2s.
Item, Thomas Barde [formerly] apprentice of John Barde –	2s.

[218] *OED*: 'the "print" or ornamental medallion fixed in the bottom of a mazer or drinking bowl'.

It*em*, Will*elmus* Junyos app*renticius* Joh*ann*is Hall*e* – ii s.
It*em*, Rob*ertus* Asschby app*renticius* Will*elm*i atte Wode – ii s.

1420 Trompes & Clarions – the makyng & weight of them – A° viii H*enrici* V^{ti}[589]
Hit is to have in mynde that in the day of Seint Dunstou*n* the viii ȝer*e* of owr*e* kyng Henr*y* the V^{e}, John Standelf, John bithe Wat*er*, Ric*hard* Spenc*er* & John Mablian beying wardeins in that tyme of the craft of goldsmythrye maden a deliv*er*aunce to Salamon Oxney, John Paake, John Paddesle & John Martyn, wardeins for the ȝer*e* than next comyng & to her*e* successo*ur*s wardeins – iiii trumpys & iiii claryouns, the wych iiii trumpys & iiii claryouns John Standelf, John bithe Wat*er*, & her*e* felawes wardeins dede to make newe. And ther*e* longeth*e* to ev*er*y trump vii pieces & marked bi the lettres of a b c. And ther longeth*e* to ev*er*y claryoun viii pieces & marked be the lettres of a b c. And othir xi longettys not m*ar*ked. And xvi pomell*is* gylt. S*umma* of all the pieces of the forseyd tru*m*pys & claryounis amounten – iiii^{xx} vii weyyng bi the poys of Troie – xxii li. vii unc*is* di. un quart*er*un. . .

And al the alde pypes of silv*er* as thei wer*e* writen in the tyme of her*e* makyng as in the pap*er* moore openly declarys how many ther*e* be and of her*e* poys bi the poys of Troye.[590]

1420 Corbyn:
p. 124 Fait a remembr*er* q*e* le p*ri*m*er* jo*ur* de Fev*er*yll*e* l'an du regne le Roi Henr*i* quint q'or est viime, ordeiné est *et* establie p*ar* assent de Joh*a*n Standelf, alderma*n* del garde de Farendou*n* dedeins *et* gardein del hon*ur*able mistier *et* cumpanye d'orfav*er*ie en Loundr*es*, Joh*a*n Wat*er*, Joh*a*n Mabelyan *et* Richard Spenc*er* adonq*es* gardeins, ové l'assent, volunté *et* gr*a*unt del av*a*ndit hon*ur*able cumpanye, c'est assavoir Will*ia*m Fitzhugh*e*, Joh*a*n Blake[de]n*e*,[591] Salamon Oxney, Barth*olome*u Seman, Joh*a*n Palyng, Joh*a*n Wyssyngsete, Joh*a*n Tewkisbury, Joh*a*n Paake, Joh*a*n Hall*e*, Rob*er*t Broun*e*, Joh*a*n Walsch*e*, Joh*a*n Hill*es*, Ric*hard* Wedyall*e*, Ric*hard* Georg*e*, Piers Thorold, Joh*a*n Wynne, Rob*er*t Walton*e*, Will*ia*m Hope, Joh*a*n Emond, Will*ia*m Walton*e*, Joh*a*n Pattysle, Joh*a*n Martyn, Will*ia*m Botoun, Joh*a*n Hall*e* l'eisné, Rob*er*t Cryngilford, Joh*a*n Stalkenden*e*, Will*ia*m Gartou*n*, Joh*a*n Cresbien, Joh*a*n Orwell*e*, Joh*a*n Parker, Joh*a*n Colley, Joh*a*n Werk, Henr*i* Goldsmyth, Rog*er* Warburgh, Rob*er*t Downe, Rog*er* Aleyn, Thom*as* South*e*, Thom*as* Brynkele, Ric*hard* Sage, Thom*as* Leget, Will*ia*m Gilb*er*t, Thom*as* Hunte, Maykyn Rudlee, Rog*er* Barneston*e*, Joh*a*n Warde, Joh*a*n Wat*er*le, Thom*as* Remy, Will*ia*m Ketyll*e*, Will*ia*m Letherpole, Will*ia*m Coup*er*, Joh*a*n Biernys, Joh*a*n Martyn *et* toutes aultres al hon*ur*able cumpanye app*ur*ten*a*ntz, q*e* Joh*a*n Corbyn, jadys d'orfev*er*e en Chepe, s*er*ra voidé, houstee *et* removê hors del

[589] The main text of this item in English is in the same hand as the rest of the page (and preceding pages), but a somewhat later hand has written the title.
[590] See above, A + a, p. 74 (1391).
[591] MS: Blaken*e*.

Item, William Junyos [formerly] apprentice of John Halle – 2s.
Item, Robert Ashby [formerly] apprentice of William atte Wood – 2s.

Trumpets and Clarions – their making and weight – 8 Henry V 1420
Memorandum that on St Dunstan's Day in the year 8 Henry V [19 May 1420] John Standelf, John atte Water, Richard Spencer and John Mablean being at that time wardens of the Goldsmiths' Mistery handed over to Solomon Oxney, John Pake, John Pattesley and John Martyn, wardens of the following year, and to their successors as wardens: – 4 trumpets and 4 clarions, the which 4 trumpets and 4 clarions John Standelf, John atte Water and their fellow wardens had had newly made. And every trumpet consists of 7 pieces marked by the letters abc. And every clarion consists of 8 pieces marked by the letters abc. And there are also another 11 unmarked lengths. And 16 gilt pommels. The total of all the pieces of the aforesaid trumpets and clarions amounts to – 87, weighing 22lb. 7¾oz. Troy weight.

And all the old silver pipes [wind instruments] as written up at the time they were made and as appears more plainly in the register, how many there are and their weight in Troy weight.

Corby:[219] 1420
Memorandum that on 1 February 1420 n.s. it was ordained and established by p. 124
the assent of John Standelf, alderman of the Ward of Farringdon Within and Warden of the honourable Mistery and Company of Goldsmiths of London, John Water, John Mablean, Richard Spencer, wardens at that time, and with the assent, wish and approval of the aforesaid honourable company. i.e. William FitzHugh, John Blakedene, Solomon Oxney, Bartholomew Seman, John Palyng, John Wissyngsete, John Tewkesbury, John Pake, John Halle, Robert Broun, John Walsh, John Hilles, Richard Withihale, Richard George, Piers Thorold, John Wynne, Robert Walton, William Hope, John Edmund, William Walton, John Pattesley, John Martyn, William Botoun, John Halle the elder, Robert Cringleford, John Stalkendene, William Gartoun, John Cresbien, John Orwell, John Parker, John Colney, John Werk, Henry Goldsmyth, Roger Warburgh, Robert Downe, Roger Aleyn, Thomas South, Thomas Brinkley, Richard Sage, Thomas Leget, William Gilbert, Thomas Hunte, Maykyn Rudlee, Roger Barnston, John Warde, John Waterley, Thomas Remy, William Ketille, William Liverpool, William Couper, John Barnes, John Martyn and all others who belong to the honourable company, that John Corby,[220] formerly a goldsmith in Cheap, shall be expelled, ousted and removed from the aforesaid company for evermore, in such manner that the aforesaid

[219] I am greatly indebted to Dr Paul Brand in my translation and explication of the following case. Dr Brand has commented that the writer had clearly not quite mastered the legal jargon he was trying to use, and the language and phrasing are in places very odd. However, the general sense of the case is clear following the procedures of English civil litigation, and while no attempt has been made to amend the original, the translation here is modified slightly in places in order to read as correct legal sense.

[220] Although here as 'Corbyn', this man is generally known as 'Corby' and this has been adopted for the translation, but the name variant is worth noting.

av*a*ntdit cumpanye p*ur* toutes jo*ur*s, entaunt q*e* l'av*a*ntdit Joh*a*n Corbyn jammés n'av*er*a la vesture ne l'almoigne de Seint Dunstou*n* ne null*e* aultr*e* bienfait al av*a*ntdit cumpanye app*ur*tenaunt. Ne q*e* null*e* del av*a*ntdit hon*ur*able cumpanye ové l'av*a*ntdit Joh*a*n Corbyn vende ne compra, ne ové luy p*ri*vé ne app*er*t entremetta en null*e* man*er*e point. Ne lez brocours del av*a*ntdit cumpanye a luy moustr*e* ne vende null*e* man*er*e chose au dit mistier app*ur*ten*a*nt s*ur* peyne de perdr*e* lo*ur* offyce p*ur* toutz jo*ur*s. Et si ascun del av*a*ntdit cumpanye face le cont*ra*rie *et* de ceo soit p*ro*vé, q'il encource le peyne av*a*ntnomee. Et outr*e* please a toutes gentz sav*er* *et* entendr*e* la cause del ordin*a*nce av*a*ntesc*ri*pt. Enp*ri*mes l'av*a*ntdit Joh*a*n Corbyn ové l'assent de Will*ia*m Shirbo*ur*ne, Joh*a*n Carlell*e* *et* aultr*es* de lo*ur* compa*n*ye maliciousement *et* fauxeme*n*t p*ur*sua *et* empleda Ric*hard* Georg*e* *et* Pier*es* Thorold a Westm*oustier* *et* av*a*nt mon s*eignur* de Bedeford, adonq*e*s lieuten*a*nt d'Englet*er*e, p*ur* div*er*ses points *et* trespaces q*e* lez av*a*ntditz Ric*hard* *et* Piers duissent estr*e* fait env*er*s l'av*a*ntdit Joh*a*n Corbyn, del temps *et* an av*a*nt passé, en quell*e* aan lez av*a*ntditz Ric*hard* *et* Piers furent gardeins ové lo*ur* compaignons Barth*olome*u Seman *et* Rob*er*t Waltou*n* en mesme l'an gardeins, entaunt q*e* la matier*e* fuist pledé a un issue appellé 'Nisi prius' al esglise de Seint Martyn.[592] Et a quell*e* jo*ur* *et* lyeu lez p*ar*ties av*a*ntditz p*ar* lo*ur* conseill empleda *et* al p*ur*suite de av*a*ntdit Joh*a*n Corbyn dev*a*nt Will*ia*m Cheyne, Justice del Bank n*ost*re s*eignur* le Roi, la esteaunt p*re*sent Richard Whetyngdou*n*, adonq*e*s Mair de Loundr*es*, ové Bartou*n*, le Recordo*ur* de Loundr*es*, Will*ia*m Walder*ne*, Henr*i* Bartou*n*, Rob*er*t Chechely, Joh*a*n Standelf, aldermans de Loundr*es*, Will*ia*m Botiller, viscount de Loundr*es*, *et* multz aultrez; la enquest fuist appellé p*ur* passer p*ar*entr*e* lez p*ar*tiez, a quell*e* temps l'av*a*ntdit Joh*a*n Corbyn fuist nounsué de soun plé, *et* ne voet mye dem*ur*er la v*er*dite. Et av*a*nt ceo temps l'av*a*ntdit Joh*a*n Corbyn fuist t*ro*vé faux dev*a*nt Will*ia*m Sevenok*e* l'aan av*a*nt Mair*e* de Loundr*es*, come app*er*t en le Guyldehall*e* de Loundr*es* p*ar* un reconisaunce q*e* l'av*a*ntdit Joh*a*n Corbyn est obligez; le quell*e* Joh*a*n Corbyn come ho*m*me faux *et* atteint porta un brief hors de Westm*oustier* p*ur* voider le matier*e* hors del mayne del av*a*ntdit Mair*e* en g*ra*unt reproef *et* sklaundre del av*a*ntdit hon*ur*able cumpanye, p*ur* quelx trespacez, faulxtez *et* rep*ro*vez l'av*a*ntdit hon*ur*able cumpanye ount ordeinez *et* establiez les pointz av*a*ntesc*ri*ptz. Et les av*a*ntditz Mair*e* *et* cez aldermans p*ur* le fauxté q*e* l'av*a*ntdit Joh*a*n Corbyn ad faite *et* en est atteint ount forsbarrez *et* forsjuggez sou*n* fraunchyse.

p. 125[593] Chest*er*, p*ur* Corbyn:

Also a remembraunce maade that the same day & ȝeer*e* afore sayyd, that John Chest*er*, goldsmyth in Chepe, beeyng at the same assemble in Goldsmythys Hall with all the hon*ur*able cumpanye afore rehercyd, that ther*e* he sayde how that Corby & hys felawys weren falsly do unto & falsly & untruly they wer*e* p*er*soned. For wych wordys & seyyngs he maade menys unto the

[592] On this see Reddaway and Walker, p. 97: ' . . . an instance of that interesting constitutional expedient, an expedient already well-established and lasting until 1857, whereby matters within the jurisdiction of the city, but in which the king's courts at Westminster had been invoked, were fought out on the relatively neutral ground of the precinct of the collegiate church of St Martin le Grand . . .'. It was used as a venue for *nisi prius* sessions in the City.

[593] The monograph 'Jhu' appears in the scribe's hand at the top of this page.

John Corby shall never receive the livery nor the alms of St Dunstan nor any other benefit belonging to the aforesaid company. And that no one of the aforesaid honourable company shall either buy or sell with the aforesaid John Corby, nor shall anyone have any business with him at all either in private or in public. Nor shall the company's brokers display to him or sell anything whatsoever that pertains to the said mistery on pain of losing their job for ever. And if anyone of the aforesaid company should go against this and be found guilty of this, he shall incur the aforesaid penalty. And besides, let the reasons for the order written above be made known to all men: Firstly, the aforesaid John Corby with the assent of William Sherborne, John Carler and others of their group maliciously and falsely brought suit and impleaded Richard George and Piers Thorold at Westminster and before my Lord of Bedford, then Regent of England,[221] on various counts and offences which the aforesaid Richard and Piers were alleged to have committed against the aforesaid John Corby during the previous year, in which year the aforesaid Richard and Piers were wardens along with their fellow wardens Bartholomew Seman and Robert Walton, wardens in the same year, and the case went as far as to be pleaded to an issue and a *nisi prius* session called at the church of St Martin. And at that time and place the aforesaid parties through their counsel made their presentations to the jury and at the suit of the aforesaid John Corby the inquest was called before William Cheyne, justice of the King's Bench, in the presence of Richard Whittington, then Mayor of London, and Barton, the Recorder of London, William Waldern, Henry Barton, Robert Chichely, John Standelf, aldermen of London, William Botiller, sheriff of London, and many others; to consider its verdict between the parties, at which time the aforesaid John Corby was nonsuited in his plea and refused to abide by the verdict.[222] And before this time the aforesaid John Corby had been found guilty of deceit before William Sevenoke, Mayor of London in the previous year, as appears in [the records of] the Guildhall of London in a recognizance binding the aforesaid John Corby, the which John Corby, deceitfully and as a convicted man, brought a writ from Westminster in order to take the matter out of the hands of the aforesaid Mayor, to the great disgrace and discredit of the aforesaid honourable company, for the which offences, deceits and disgraces the aforesaid honourable company have ordained and established the aforesaid points. And the aforesaid Mayor and his aldermen, on account of the faithlessnesses of the aforesaid John Corby of which he has been convicted, have excluded him from and condemned him to lose his freedom [i.e. citizenship].

Chester, for Corby: p. 125
Item, memorandum that on the same day and in the same year aforesaid, John Chester, goldsmith in Cheap. who was present at the same assembly in Goldsmiths' Hall with all the honourable company named above, and there he said that Corby and his companions had been treated wrongly and that they had been falsely and untruly misrepresented. For the which words and sayings he

[221] i.e. at both the Common Bench (Common Pleas) and the King's Bench (or just possibly the council).

[222] Or alternatively 'to await the verdict', i.e. he left the court while the jury was considering its verdict and left before that verdict was given. This alternative translation has been suggested by Paul Brand. The interpretation above however seems in line with the character and behaviour of the man, see below, A + a, p. 128.

wardeins & unto the cumpany for to make amendys for his t*re*spas. The wych wardeins maden assemble for the same cause. And than the Monenday after the .v. day of Fev*er*yll in ȝer*e* aforesayd he cam unto the Hall afore the wardeins & afore all the worschipfull cumpany & ther*e* he put hym in awarde oppenly of the forseyd wardeins. The wych wardeins at that tyme be assent of all the cumpanye maden awarde that he sholde knele amydd*es* the Hall on booth his kneez & aske hem & all the cumpanye forȝevenes of that he had misseyde & doon*e*. The wych John Chest*er* p*ra*yed hem that he most so doon*e* & ther*e* openly he cryed hem m*er*cy & openly beknewe that he had mysseyde. For wych t*re*spas & misseyyng the wardeins be assent of all the cumpanye juggedent that the forseyd John Chest*er* scholde not wer*e* ne use ne have uppon he*m* in no wyse the last lyv*er*e of goldsmythes from that day unto that day a monenth next suyng. And ther*e* to he greed hym & thanked hem all. And than w*ith*in iii dayez suyng the same John Chest*er* as a rebell & an untrewma*n* dede the cont*ra*rie & brake her*e* award, with that he had agreed hym to & w*ith*in the same iii. or iiii. dayez went openly in Chepe in the same clothing, for wyche doyng he was openly rep*ro*ved & atteint. And tho he made newe menys unto the wardeins for to make amendys for hys t*re*spas, for wyche t*re*spas he his jugged to crye m*er*cy & to put hym in award. Wyche ward was that he shold not wer*e* his liv*er*e of the craft from that day unto Estyr Day next suyng. Where uppon he swore on a boke to kepe well & trewly. And also the same John Chest*er* took the wardeins be the hondys and aft*er* he*m* Ric*hard* Georg*e* & Piers Thorold, & swore on a boke openly afore all the companye that he from that day forth sholde nev*er* sue, avexe ne in no wyse greve the forseyd Ric*hard* & Piers ne noon of here felowes of thyng that had be doon*e* afore. Ne that he sholde nev*er* maynteyne ne helpe John Corbyn ne w*ith* hym in no wyse dele ne maynteyne.

1420 Shirbo*ur*ne p*ur* Corbyn:

Also Will*ia*m Shirbo*ur*ne the Fryday suyng the ix day of Fev*er*ill came unto the Hall afore hys wardeins & afore all the worschipfull cumpanye & ther*e* he put hym in award of the wardeins & of all the cumpanye of that that he had vexed Ric*hard* George & Piers Thorold. And also maynteyned John Corbyn aȝeins the cumpanye. The wich wardeins w*ith* assent of all the cumpanye ther*e* beeyng p*re*sent juggeden that he from that day forth shold nev*er* sue ne vexe the forsayd Ric*hard* ne Piers ne noon of her*e* felows wardeins openly ne prevely. Ne in no wyse maynteyne ne fav*er*e John Corbyn, wych that is forjugged of his f*ra*unchyse be the Mayr*e* & his aldirme*n*, and be assent of all the worschipfull cumpanye demissed & put owt of all gode feleschip & forjugged from all the beenfaitz of the craft. And ther*e* uppon the forseyd Will*iam* Shirbo*ur*ne hath be his owne gode wille swore on a booke in so fer forth that if the same Will*ia*m Shirbo*ur*ne be founde or p*ro*ved doyng the cont*ra*rie, that than the same Will*ia*m Shirbo*ur*ne schall nev*er* have no beenfait of the craft. But for ev*er* more be put owt of the cumpanye w*ith*oute any g*ra*ce. And ther*e* uppon he toke the forseyd Ric*hard* Georg*e* & Piers Thorold be the hondys & kyssed hem iii^{ez} in full record of pees.

requested the wardens and company that he might make amends for his offence. The which wardens gathered an assembly for this matter. And then on the Monday after 5 February in the aforesaid year [6 February 1420 n.s.] he came to the Hall and before the wardens and all the worshipful company, and there he openly submitted himself to the judgment of the wardens. The which wardens at that time with the assent of all the company judged that he should kneel on both his knees in the middle of the Hall and that he should beg them and all the company for forgiveness for all that he had wrongly said and done. The which John Chester asked to be allowed to do this and there in public he begged pardon of them and acknowledged that he had spoken wrongly. For the which offence and for his wrongful words the Wardens, by the assent of all the Company, judged that the aforesaid John Chester should not wear nor use nor have upon him in any way the last livery of the Goldsmiths from that day until the same day a month later. And he agreed to this and thanked them all. And then within the space of the next three days the same John Chester, as a rebel and a disloyal man, went against and broke the terms of this sentence to which he had agreed, and within the same three or four days he was going about openly in Cheap wearing the same livery clothing, for doing which he was in public found guilty again and convicted. And although he once more requested the wardens to be allowed to make amends for his offence, he was sentenced to beg mercy and to submit himself to judgment. And the judgment was that he should not wear his livery of the mistery from that day until the next following Easter Day. Whereupon he swore on a book to keep well and truly to this. And also the same John Chester held hands with the wardens and afterwards with Richard George and Piers Thorold and swore on a book in public before all the company that he from that day forth would never sue, cause trouble or in any way harm the aforesaid Richard and Piers or any of their companions on account of anything that had previously been done. And that he would never maintain nor help John Corby, nor would he have any dealings with him in any way, nor join with him in any maintenance.

Sherborne for Corby: 1420
Also William Sherborne on the Friday following 9 February [10 February 1420 n.s.] came to the Hall and before his wardens and before all the worshipful company, and there he submitted himself to the judgment of the wardens and all the company for the reason that he had caused trouble for Richard George and Piers Thorold, and also for having maintained John Corby against the company. The which wardens with the assent of all the company there present judged that he from that day forward should never sue nor cause trouble for the aforesaid Richard or Piers nor any of their fellow wardens either in public or in private. Nor should he in any way maintain or show any favour to John Corby who has been deprived of his citizenship by the Mayor and his aldermen, and who by the assent of all the worshipful company had been excluded and expelled from all good fellowship and had been excluded from all the benefits of the mistery. And thereupon the aforesaid William Sherborne of his own free will swore on a book to the effect that if the same William Sherborne shall be found guilty or proved to have gone against this, that then the same William Sherborne shall never receive any benefit of the mistery, but shall be expelled from the mistery without mercy. And at that he took the aforesaid Richard George and Piers Thorold by the hands and kissed them thrice in full sign of peace.

p. 127[594] Carler*e* p*ur* Corbyn:

Also the same day John Carler*e* come [afore][595] the wardeins unto the Hall afore all the worschipfull cumpanye & ther*e* he put [hym][596] in award of the forseyd wardeins. The wych wardeins be assent of all the cumpanye juggeden that he schold nev*er* maynteyne John Corby ne wit hym dele uppon peyne to lose all the beenfaitz of the craft. And furthermore that he schold nev*er* sue ne vexe in no wyse Ric*hard* Georg*e* ne Piers Thorold ne noon*e* of hir*e* felaws of thyng that had be doon*e* afore. The wich John Carler*e* took the forseyd Ric*hard* & Piers be the hondys & p*ra*yed hem of hir*e* maisterschip & of hir*e* gode will & oppon that he kyssed hem onys twyez thryez. And ther*e* uppon he swore on a book*e* to kepe his forward that he had behoten. And also to stonde & abyde the award that the wardeins wolde sey more ther*e* to in tyme to come.

Reginald Ernest:

1420 M*emorandum* q*uo*d septi*m*o die Januar*ii* a*nno* r*egni* r*egis* Henrici quinti post conq*uestu*m septi*m*o Reginaldus Ernest de London', aurifab*e*r, admissus est in lib*er*tatem civitat*is* London' et in lib*er*tate*m* mister*e* aur*ifabrie* tempore Joh*ann*is Standelf, aldermanni *et* gardiani, Joh*ann*is Wat*er*, Joh*ann*is Mabelyan *et* Ric*ard*i Spenc*er*, gardian*orum*, p*er* assensu*m* *et* voluntatem Will*elm*i Fitzhugh, Salamon Oxney, Joh*ann*is Blakeden*e*, Joh*ann*is Palyng, Ric*ard*i Georg*e*, Joh*ann*is Tewkysbury, Joh*ann*is Pake, Ric*ard*i Wedyall, Joh*ann*is Bernys, Will*elm*i Hope, Joh*ann*is Hill*es* *et* Joh*ann*is Walsch*e* *et* pluri*m*or*um* alior*um,* qui quid*e*m Reginaldus dedit p*redic*tis gardianis – x li.

Henr*icus* Clerk*e*:

M*emorandum* q*uo*d die *et* anno sup*ra*dict*is*, Henr*icus* Clerk*e* de London' admissus est in lib*er*tatem civitatis p*redic*te *et* in lib*er*tate*m* mister*e* aurifabrie sup*ra*dic*t*e, tempore p*redict*or*um* Joh*ann*is Standelf, aldermanni *et* gardiani, Joh*ann*is Wat*er*, Joh*ann*is Mabelyan *et* Ric*ard*i Spenc*er,* ad tunc existent*ium* gardian*orum*, pa*r*it*er* p*er* co*mun*em assensu*m* antesc*ri*ptor*um* *et* tociu*s* cometive, qui quidem Henricus Clerk*e* dedit p*redic*tis gardianis no*min*e tocius cometive – x m*ar*cz.

Benet Austyn:

M*emorandum* q*uo*d die *et* anno sup*ra*dict*is* Benet Augustyn, Ducheman, p*er* assensu*m* plu*ri*mor*um* totius cometive receptus est p*ro* uno for*inseco* brocour, qui quidem Benet dedit cometive – v li.

1420 Corby:

p. 128 Also a rememb*ra*unce made that the xv day of Maii in the ȝeer*e* afore sayd, at inst*a*unce & request of the Chauncceller*e* unto the Mair*e* of London at that tyme beyng hoos name is Richard Whetyngton, and aft*er*ward at inst*a*unce & request of the Mair*e* & his aldirmen unto the wardeins afore write for the ȝeer*e* beyng. How that John Corby wych was founden of record cont*ra*rie & rebell unto his

[594] p. 126 has been missed out of the pagination system.

[595] Missing in text and supplied by analogy with the previous entry.

[596] Missing in text and supplied by analogy with the previous entry.

Carler for Corby: p. 127
Also the same day John Carler came before the wardens at the Hall and before all the worshipful company, and there he submitted himself to the judgment of the aforesaid wardens. The which wardens with the assent of all the company judged that he should never support John Corby or have any dealings with him upon pain of losing all the benefits of the mistery. And further more that he should never sue nor cause any trouble in any way for Richard George or Piers Thorold or any of their fellows on account of anything that had been done before. The which John Carler took the aforesaid Richard and Piers by the hand and begged them as they were his masters and of their good will, and upon that he kissed them once, twice, thrice. And thereupon he swore on a book to keep henceforward to all that he had promised. And also to keep and abide by any future judgments that the wardens might further make about this matter.

Reginald Ernest: 1420
Memorandum that on 7 January 1420 n.s. Reginald Ernest of London, goldsmith, was admitted to the freedom of the City of London and into the freedom of the Goldsmiths' Mistery in the time of John Standelf, alderman and warden, John Water, John Mablean and Richard Spencer, wardens, with the assent and wish of William FitzHugh, Solomon Oxney, John Blakedene, John Palyng, Richard George, John Tewkesbury, John Pake, Richard Withihale, John Barnes, William Hope, John Hilles and John Walsh and many others, and the same Reginald gave the aforesaid wardens – £10.

Henry Clerk:
Memorandum that on the aforesaid date Henry Clerk of London was admitted to the freedom of the aforesaid city and into the freedom of the Goldsmiths' Mistery, in the time of the aforesaid John Standelf, alderman and warden, John Water, John Mablean and Richard Spencer, the current wardens, with also the communal assent of those written above and the whole company, and the same Henry Clerk gave to the aforesaid wardens in the name of the whole company – 10 marks.

Benet Augustyn:
Memorandum that on the aforesaid date Benet Augustyn, 'Dutchman', with the assent of many of the whole company was admitted as a foreign broker, and the same Benet gave to the company – £5.

Corby: 1420
Memorandum also that on 15 May of the aforesaid year, at the instance and p. 128
the request of the Chancellor to the then Mayor of London, whose name is Richard Whittington, and afterwards at the instance and request of the Mayor and his aldermen to the aforesaid current wardens: As John Corby was found guilty of going against and being rebellious to his wardens and all the company

wardeins and to all his cumpanye as in the pap*er* afoore write more openly specefyeth.. Wich John Corby at that day & tyme afore write come to the same wardeins & afore al the cumpanye at that tyme for the same caas assembled, and ther*e* swere on a booke be his owne fr*e* wille that he wolde stonde & abyde al the ordin*a*nces that the wardeins for that ȝeer*e* beyng and the wardeins for the next ȝeer*e* comyng and unto hem chosen, Will*ia*m Fitzhug*h*, Ric*hard* Wedyall, John Biernys, John Walsch*e*, to make amendys as hem thought be al heere wyttes of that that hem thought that the forsayd John Corby had trespased in hye and lowe in all man*er* pointys. And uppon that thei assingned the forsayd John Corby to come aȝein unto h*e*m the Friday next suyng to fulfille his p*ro*mys as he had behyght h*e*m & to her*e* what thei wolde ordeine to make pees & reste betwene hym & al the cumpanye for ev*er*, like as the Mair*e* & his aldermen had p*ra*yed the forsayd wardeins & al the cumpanye. At wych day beyng Fryday the morow aft*er* Assenc*i*on Day, the forsayd John Corby come afore the forsaid wardeins w*ith* othir unto he*m* chosen as forward was, and ther*e* he seyde openly that he wolde nev*er* abyde noon*e* award, but ȝif thei made hym p*re*ve unto the same award. And moreov*er* that what awarde so ev*er* they made that he the forsayd John Corby wolde shewe that award so maad unto his consaill to wete whethir that his consaill wolde assent therto or noon. And ther uppon he bad hem be avysed for he wolde do ne abyde nonothir wyse. Wich wardeins at that tyme be avise of hir*e* felawes unto hem chosen, as an untrewe man of his p*ro*mys and falsly forswore on a boke, lete hym passe & dede as ther*e* to no moore. And her*e* uppon in more record & testemonie for he*m* that been to come wardeins & gove*r*nours of this worschipful cumpanye as wel as for he*m* that have been, this ordin*a*nce of his fowle falsnesse & untrowthe is entred in this pap*er* of record for ev*er* to stonde in witnesse.

1420–21 Ceux sount lez nouns dez Gardeins eslutz al feste de Seint Dunstou*n* l'an du
p. 129[597] regne le Roi Henr*i* quint puis [le][598] conquest viii[e] tanq*e* al dit feste de Seint Dunstou*n* l'aan ensuaunt:

Salamon Oxneye
Joh*anne*s Paake
Joh*anne*s Pattisle
Joh*anne*s Martyn

No*mina* app*re*nticior*um*:[599]

In p*ri*mis, Walt*er*us Chaundeler app*re*nt*icius* Salamon*is* Oxneye –	xx s.[600]
Matheus Brayn app*re*nt*icius* Joh*anni*s Pake –	xx s.
Thomas Peryn app*re*nt*icius* Will*elm*i Cheyne –	xx s.
Thomas Gilimyn app*re*nt*icius* Joh*ann*is Edmund –	xx s.
Ric*ard*us Quyntyn app*re*nt*icius* Joh*ann*is Cresbien –	xx s.

597 The scribe has written the 'Jhc' monograph at the top of the page.
598 MS: sou*n*.
599 A new hand starts here, the title having been written in the old hand.
600 See also below, A + a, p. 130 where this entry occurs again two years later. A variety of reasons might account for this.

and this was recorded and is more fully explained as written out above in the register. The which John Corby on that day and at that time aforesaid came before the same wardens and before all the company then assembled for that same matter, and there he swore on a book of his own free will that he would keep to and abide by all the ordinances made by the current year's wardens and the wardens for the next following year, and by those elected to assist them: William FitzHugh, Richard Withihale, John Barnes, John Walsh, to make amends in the manner they all agreed to for all the offences great and small and in all ways that the aforesaid John Corby had committed. And upon that they told the aforesaid John Corby to come before them again on the next following Friday to fulfil his promise as he had given his word and to hear what they would ordain in order to make peace and concord between him and all the company for ever, as the Mayor and his aldermen had asked of the aforesaid wardens and all the company. On which day, the Friday after Ascencion Day [17 May 1420], the aforesaid John Corby came before the aforesaid wardens with others elected to sit with them as agreed previously, and there in public he said that he would never abide by any judgment unless they made him privy to it, and moreover that whatever judgment they made, he, John Corby, would show this to his counsel to find out whether his counsel would agree to it or not. And thereupon he declared to them that they should take note for he would abide by no judgment except in this manner. The which wardens at that time by the advice of those elected to sit with them, let him go as a man untrue to his promise and forsworn to his oath upon the book, and they did no more in this case. And in order to have a fuller record and witness to those that shall be in the future wardens and governors of this worshipful company as well as for those that have been in the past, this decree of his foul falsity and lack of faith is written up in this register that it may for ever stand in witness.

These are the names of the wardens elected at the feast of St Dunstan in the year 8 Henry V [19 May 1420] until the said feastday of St Dunstan in the following year: 1420–21 p. 129
Solomon Oxney
John Pake
John Pattesley
John Martyn

The names of apprentices:

Firstly, Walter Chaundeler apprentice of Solomon Oxney –	20s.
Matthew Brayn apprentice of John Pake –	20s.
Thomas Peryn apprentice of William Cheyne –	20s.
Thomas Gilmyn apprentice of John Edmund –	20s.
Richard Quyntyn apprentice of John Cresbien –	20s.

Joh*anne*s Holcroft app*renticius* Will*elm*i Waltone – xx s.
Thomas Sate app*renticius* Will*elm*i atte Welle – xx s.
Hugh Merskew app*renticius* Joh*ann*is Bulstrode – xx s.
Joh*anne*s London app*renticius* Thome Hunte – xx s.
Ric*ard*us Chapman app*renticius* Joh*ann*is fitz Rob*er*t – xx s.
(Thomas Peryn app*renticius* Will*elm*i Cheyne)[601] mortuus est *et igitur* vac*at*
Ric*ard*us Denyngton*e* app*renticius* Thome atte Watre – xx s.
Thomas Loghtburgh app*renticius* Petri Torald – xx s.
Will*elmu*s Jonesson app*renticius* Thome Brynkeley – xx s.
Ric*ard*us atte Water app*renticius* Ric*ard*i Withyhale – xx s.
Joh*anne*s Cook app*renticius* Joh*ann*is Baker – xx s.
Joh*anne*s Herry app*renticius* Rog*er*i Aleyn – xx s.
Will*elmu*s Berlyng app*renticius* Joh*ann*is Leget – xx s.
Hugh Fauset app*renticius* Joh*ann*is Norwell – xx s.
Joh*anne*s Swyst app*renticius* Will*elm*i Belverge. – xx s.

Allo*cati* jurat*i*:
Joh*anne*s Clerk nup*er* app*renticius* Will*elm*i Belverge – ii s. sol*utas*
Joh*anne*s Welles nup*er* app*renticius* Steph*an*i Colneye – ii s.[602]
Jacob*us* Tregeustek nup*er* app*renticius* Joh*ann*is Mabilyan – ii s. sol*utas*
Will*elmu*s Reygate nup*er* app*renticius* Rob*er*ti Broun*e* – ii s. sol*utas*
Petrus Tyse nup*er* app*renticius* Joh*ann*is Tyse – ii s. sol*utas*
John Gebou*n* aprent*icius* wyt Th*oma*s Wellys – ii s. – sol*utas*[603]

1420–21 A + b p. 58 (*cont.*) [604]N*omi*na jur*atorum* de Duchemen tempore Salamonis Oxney, Joh*annis* Pake, Joh*annis* Pattisley *et* Joh*annis* Martyn, gardianor*um* ann*o* r*egni* r*egis* H*enrici* qu*i*nti viii°, qui sunt jurati more ordinac*ionis* aur*ifabrie* etc.
Hans Ekorn
Herman Sprik
Coster, ducheman
Hans Holtous
Herman atte Welle
Janyn d'Eskevyn
Gyse Van Deste
Petre Van Duze
Reynald Erne
Dederyk Rokelond

601 This entry has been scored out and the attached note added later. It is very odd, since a Thomas Peryn, former apprentice of Wm Cheyne, is in 1425–26 listed as a serving-man. It does not seem possible either that it was Wm Cheyne who died, since he is listed in 1429–30 as the recent master of an apprentice.
602 Perhaps he did not pay up since no 'sol-' appears beside this figure – but perhaps it was paid but the record not brought up to date through an oversight.
603 This last entry has been added later in a different hand.
604 A different hand has written this whole entry on Dutchmen. About halfway down the list, upside down to the text, a different hand has scribbled a few indecipherable words.

John Holcroft apprentice of William Walton –	20s.
Thomas Sate apprentice of William atte Welle –	20s.
Hugh Merskew apprentice of John Bulstrode –	20s.
John London apprentice of Thomas Hunte –	20s.
Richard Chapman apprentice of John FitzRobert –	20s.
(Thomas Peryn apprentice of William Cheyne) – died and therefore void.	
Richard Dennington apprentice of Thomas atte Water –	20s.
Thomas Loughborough apprentice of Piers Thorold –	20s.
William Jonesson apprentice of Thomas Brinkley –	20s.
Richard atte Water apprentice of Richard Withihale –	20s.
John Cook apprentice of John Baker –	20s.
John Harry apprentice of Roger Aleyn –	20s.
William Birling apprentice of John Leget –	20s.
Hugh Fauset apprentice of John Norwell –	20s.
John Swyst apprentice of William Belverge – 20s.	

Serving-men sworn:

John Clerk former apprentice of William Belverge –	2s. – paid
John Welles former apprentice of Stephen Colney –	2s.
James Tregewstek former apprentice of John Mablean –	2s. – paid
William Reigate former apprentice of Robert Broun –	2s. – paid
Peter Tyce former apprentice of John Tyce –	2s. – paid
John Gybon apprentice with Thomas Welles –	2s. – paid

The names of 'Dutchmen' sworn in the time of Solomon Oxney, John Pake, John Pattesley and John Martyn, wardens in the year 8 Henry V [1420–21], who have been sworn according to the manner of the Goldsmiths' Mistery's ordinance: 1420–21 A + b p. 58 *cont.*

Hans Ekhorn
Hermann Spryck
Coster, 'Dutchman'
Hans Holthous
Hermann atte Welle
Janyn d'Eskevyn
Gyse van Deste
Peter van Duze
Reynald Erne
Dederik Rokelond

Gyse Panser
Joh*a*n de Gaver
Joh*a*n Shroykyn
Terry Teser
Lowys Pope
Hans Blythe
Swether Van Bremen
Gerard Bry[605]

1421–22 Memorand*um* de div*er*sis defectib*us* tempore Joh*ann*is Blakeden*e*, Joh*ann*is
p. 76[606] Palynge, Joh*ann*is Wynne *et* Will*elm*i Botun, custodum artis aurifabr*ie* anno r*egni* R*egis* Henr*ici* quinti nono:

In primis, Thomas Gabriell*e*[607] p*ro* def*ec*tu op*eracion*is – ii s.
It*em*, Rog*er*us Aleyn p*ro* def*ec*tu op*eracion*is – xx d.
It*em*, Tilmannus Cok p*ro* eodem – ii s.
It*em*, Petrus Brentwode p*ro* eodem – ii s.
It*em*, Will*elmu*s Litherpoll*e* p*ro* eodem – ii s.
It*em*, Joh*ann*es Bakere p*ro* eodem – ii s.
It*em*, Thomas Remy p*ro* eodem – iii s.
It*em*, Joh*ann*es Vngull*e* p*ro* eodem – ii s.
It*em*, Will*elmu*s Clynton*e* p*ro* div*ersis* defectib*us* – iii s. iiii d.
It*em*, Joh*ann*es Clerk p*ro* div*ersis* defectib*us* – iii s. iiii d.
It*em*, Thomas Gabriell*e*[608] p*ro* div*ersis* defectib*us* – vi s. viii d.
It*em*, Thomas Water p*ro* def*ec*tu – xviii d.
It*em*, Joh*ann*es Gebon app*re*ntic*ius* Isabell*e* Welles – ii s.
It*em*, Galfr*idus* Neuton app*re*ntic*ius* d*ic*te Isabell*e* – ii s.
It*em*, Joh*ann*es Vesseler p*ro* def*ec*tu op*eracion*is – ii s.
It*em*, Joh*ann*es Marwe p*ro* eodem – ii s.
It*em*, Henr*icus* Goldsmyth*e* p*ro* eodem – xxxiii s. iiii d.
It*em*,[609] Flemmyng p*ro* eodem – ii s.
It*em*, Ducheman de Westm*onasterio* p*ro* eodem – ii s.

[610]It*em*, ordinat*um* est p*er* p*re*d*ic*tos custodes p*ro* eo q*uo*d div*er*se debate *et* discensiones nup*er* suborte fu*er*unt int*er* Thomam Brynkeley *et* Joh*ann*em Sutton sen*iorem et* Thomam Swynesco, causa manutenencie cuiusdam mulieris de Hib*er*nia ac alior*um* Hib*er*nior*um* vocator*um* Huxt*er*s, ordinat*um* est q*uo*d si aliqua pars p*re*dict*orum* aliquo temp*or*e futur*o* manuteneat mulierem p*re*d*ic*tam aut alior*um* p*re*d*ic*t*orum* aliquem v*er*sus alium socior*um* suor*um* p*re*d*ic*tor*um*, q*uo*d ille qui ita fecit incurrat penam xx s. solvendam

[605] It is interesting to see that these 'Dutchmen' include some whose names make them sound more French than Dutch, and who most probably will have been Burgundians.

[606] A new hand starts here.

[607] The name 'Gabrielle' has been picked out and written again in the LH margin against this entry and the other below, probably to note his getting into trouble twice.

[608] See note above.

[609] A blank space has been left on this line and the next for the name to be filled in.

[610] This paragraph has for some reason been placed right at the bottom of the page, leaving a large blank space between the above list of fines and this; perhaps the space was left in case further 'everyday' fines needed to be noted that year.

Gyse Panser
Johan de Gaver
Johan Shroykyn
Terry Teser
Lewis Pope
Hans Blythe
Swether van Bremen
Gerard Bry

Memorandum about various offences in the time of John Blakedene, John Palyng, John Wynne and William Botoun, Wardens of the Goldsmiths' Mistery in the year 9 Henry V [1421–22]: 1421–22 p. 76

Firstly, Thomas Gabrielle for a defect in workmanship –	2s.
Item, Roger Aleyn for a defect in workmanship –	20d.
Item, Tilmann Cok for the same –	2s.
Item, Piers Brentwood for the same –	2s.
Item, William Liverpool for the same –	2s.
Item, John Baker for the same –	2s.
Item, Thomas Remy for the same –	3s.
Item, John Nongyl for the same –	2s.
Item, William Clynton for various defects –	3s. 4d.
Item, John Clerk for various defects –	3s. 4d.
Item, Thomas Gabrielle for various defects –	6s. 8d.
Item, Thomas Water for a defect –	18d.
Item, John Gybon, apprentice of Isabelle Welles –	2s.
Item, Geoffrey Newton, apprentice of the said Isabelle –	2s.
Item, John Vesseler for a defect in workmanship –	2s.
Item, John Marwe for the same –	2s.
Item, Henry Goldsmyth for the same –	33s. 4d.
Item, Fleming for the same –	2s.
Item, 'Dutchman' of Westminster for the same –	2s.

Item, it was ordained by the aforesaid wardens that whereas various quarrels and dissensions had recently arisen between Thomas Brinkley and John Sutton the elder and Thomas Swinscoe, on account of the maintenance of a certain Irishwoman and other Irishmen called 'Hucksters', it was ordained that if any one of the aforenamed at any time in the future should maintain the aforesaid woman or any of the other aforenamed people against any of his aforesaid companions [of the same mistery], that he who should act thus shall incur a

una*m* medietat*em* Guyhalde London' *et* alt*er*am medietatem elemosine S*anct*i Dunstani.

1422–23 Ceux sount les nouns des Gardeyns eslutz al fest de Seint Dunston l'an du
A + a regne le Roy H*enri* quint puis le conquest disme tanq*ue* al dit fest de Seint
p. 130[611] Dunston p*ro*schein avenir:

Joh*anne*s Hilles
Joh*anne*s Biernes
Joh*anne*s Walssh*e*
Will*elmu*s Walton[612]

No*min*a app*re*nticior*um*:

Thomas Standissh*e* app*re*nticius Johannis Donne –	xx s.
Will*elmu*s Burtou*n* app*re*ntic*ius* Joh*ann*is Kyng –	xx s.
Thomas Serle app*re*ntic*ius* Ric*ard*i Spenser –	xx s.
Joh*anne*s Donne app*re*ntic*ius* Rob*er*ti Donne –	xx s.
Joh*anne*s Buk app*re*ntic*ius* Joh*ann*is Wat*er*le –	xx s.
Will*elmu*s Mortymer app*re*ntic*ius* Will*elm*i Hertwell –	xx s.
Thomas Holdene app*re*nt*icius* Will*elm*i Moubray –	xx s.
Rob*er*tus Raulyn app*re*ntic*ius* Rog*er*i Aleyn –	xx s.
Will*elmu*s Forde app*re*ntic*ius* Henr*ici* Clerk –	xx s.
Ric*ard*us Style app*re*nt*icius* Will*elm*i Alum –	xx s.
Humfr*id*us Heyford app*re*nt*icius* Will*elm*i White –	xx s.
Will*elmu*s Jonessou*n* app*re*nt*icius* Will*elm*i Stevensou*n*[613] –	xvi s. viii d.
Rob*er*tus de Dyk app*re*ntic*ius* Ric*ard*i George –	xx s.
Hugo Cheynestone app*re*nt*icius* Joh*ann*is Gybou*n* –	xx s.
Joh*anne*s Pykard app*re*nt*icius* Will*elm*i Coup*ere* –	xx s.
Walt*er*us Chaundeler app*re*nt*icius* Salamon Oxney –	xx s.[614]
Joh*anne*s Davy app*re*nt*icius* Will*elm*i Reygate –	xx s.
Thomas Ledes app*re*nticius Nich*ola*i Lovet –	xx s.
Ph*ilipp*us Stafford app*re*nt*icius* Joh*ann*is Walssh*e*, jun*ioris* –	xx s.
Will*elmu*s Donvin app*re*nt*icius* Joh*ann*is Tewkesbury, jun*ioris* –	xx s.
Thom*a*s Pencher app*re*nt*icius* Joh*ann*is Sutton, jun*ioris* –	xx s.
Henr*icus* Bridsale app*re*nt*icius* Thome Swynesco –	xx s.
Joh*anne*s Du*n*stall*e* app*re*nt*icius* Will*elm*i Waryn –	xx s.
Thomas Henster app*re*nticius Joh*ann*is Sutton, sen*ioris* –	xx s.
Joh*anne*s Sutton app*re*ntic*ius* Joh*ann*is Halle –	xx s.

Alloc*ati* jur*ati*:

Will*elmu*s Alum nup*er* app*re*ntic*ius* Joh*ann*is Pattesley –	ii s.
Joh*anne*s Wynne [nuper] app*re*ntic*ius* Joh*ann*is Wynne –	ii s.[615]
Joh*anne*s Byrlyng [nuper] app*re*ntic*ius* Joh*ann*is Wynne –	ii s.

611 A new hand starts here.
612 The four names are bracketed and an abbreviated form of 'gardiani' written at the side.
613 A note here explains the unusual sum paid: xvi s. viii d. quia fugam fecit.
614 See the same entry above, A + a, p. 129 and note 600.
615 This entry and the next have been written in a different hand to the rest of the list.

penalty of 20s. one half of which shall be paid to the Guildhall of London and the other half to the alms funds of St Dunstan.

These are the names of the Wardens elected at the feast of St Dunstan in the year 10 Henry V [19 May 1422] until the said feastday of St Dunstan next following: 1422–23 A + a p. 130

John Hilles
John Barnes
John Walsh
William Walton

The names of apprentices:

Thomas Standish apprentice of John Donne –	20s.
William Burton apprentice of John Kyng –	20s.
Thomas Serle apprentice of Richard Spencer –	20s.
John Donne apprentice of Robert Donne –	20s.
John Buck apprentice of John Waterley –	20s.
William Mortimer apprentice of William Hertwell –	20s.
Thomas Holden apprentice of William Mowbray –	20s.
Robert Raulyn apprentice of Roger Aleyn –	20s.
William Forde apprentice of Henry Clerk –	20s.
Richard Style apprentice of William Allone –	20s.
Humphrey Heyford apprentice of William White –	20s.
William Jonessoun apprentice of William Stevenson –	16s. 8d.[223]
Robert de Dyk apprentice of Richard George –	20s.
Hugh Cheynestone apprentice of John Gybon –	20s.
John Picard apprentice of William Couper –	20s.
Walter Chaundeler apprentice of Solomon Oxney –	20s.
John Davy apprentice of William Reigate –	20s.
Thomas Leeds apprentice of Nicholas Lovet –	20s.
Phillip Stafford apprentice of John Walsh the younger –	20s.
William Donvin apprentice of John Tewkesbury the younger –	20s.
Thomas Pencher apprentice of John Sutton the younger –	20s.
Henry Bridsale apprentice of Thomas Swinscoe –	20s.
John Dunstalle apprentice of William Waryn –	20s.
Thomas Henster apprentice of John Sutton the elder –	20s.
John Sutton apprentice of John Halle –	20s.

Serving-men sworn:

William Allone formerly apprentice of John Pattesley –	2s.
John Wynne [formerly] apprentice of John Wynne –	2s.
John Birling [formerly] apprentice of John Wynne –	2s.

223 The unusual amount is 'because he ran away'.

(Thomas Standissh*e* app*renticius* Joh*ann*[is][616] Donne – ii s.
Will*elmus* Burtou*n* app*renticius* Joh*ann*is Kyng – ii s.
Thomas Serle app*renticius* Ric*ard*i Spenser – ii s.
Joh*ann*es Donne app*renticius* Rob*er*ti Donne – ii s.)[617]
Rob*er*tus Boteler nup*er* app*renticius* Joh*ann*is Biernes – ii s.
Ric*ard*us Raulyn nup*er* app*renticius* Ric*ard*i Widyhale – ii s.
Joh*ann*es Tumvyle nup*er* app*renticius* Joh*annis*[618] – ii s.
Joh*ann*es Huberd nup*er* app*renticius* Joh*ann*is Blakden*e* – ii s.
Drugo Waddesley nup*er* app*renticius* Th*ome* Lampord – ii s.
Simon Collessou*n* nup*er* app*renticius* Will*elm*i Fitzhugh*e* – ii s.
Joh*ann*es Normantou*n* nup*er* app*renticius* Rog*er*i Brenaston*e* – ii s.
Elias Harewod*e* nup*er* app*renticius* Will*elm*i Randolf – ii s.
Joh*ann*es Cary nup*er* app*renticius* Joh*ann*is Pattesley – ii s.
Rog*er*us Lynacre nup*er* app*renticius* Will*elm*i Waltou*n* – ii s.
Henr*icus* Toret nup*er* app*renticius* Thome Gabriell*e* – ii s.

Item, Joh*ann*es Couplond licenciatus fuit p*er* custodes p*redict*os q*uo*d ip*s*e lib*er*e op*er*ari possit in arte sua durante tempore app*re*nticialitatis sue *et* solvit ea de causa p*re*fatis custodib*us* – xl d.[619]

1423 Item, Gysebright de Deist, Ducheman, admissus fuit in lib*er*tatem mistere
p. 131 aurifabr*ie* xiiii° die May anno r*egni* r*egis* Henr*ici* sexti primo *et* solvit ea de causa gardianis tunc existen*tibus* – x li.

Melver:
Item, Fretheryk Melver, Ducheman, admissus fuit in lib*er*tatem d*ict*e mistere d*ict*is die *et* anno ad requisic*ion*em Ric*ard*i Whityngton, nup*er* civis *et* maioris London' *et* solvit ea de causa p*redict*is gardianis – iiii li.

1422–23 Hec sunt no*min*a illor*um* alienigen*arum* dimiss*orum* op*er*ari p*ro* tempore d*ict*or*um* custodu*m*:
In p*ri*mis, Gyse Paunser solvit ea de causa – xiii s. iiii d.
It*em*, Albright Leydon*e* p*ro* eodem – iiii s.
It*em*, Petrus Bomit – x s.
It*em*, Hans Croykyn – xiii s. iiii d.
It*em*, Hermanus – xiii s. iiii d.
It*em*, Gerardus Bry – x s.
It*em*, Janyn Eskevyn – vi s. viii d.
It*em*, Swether, Ducheman – x s.

616 MS: Johanne.

617 The previous four entries were written by the same scribe but in a different ink. All four lines have been scored out and the reason put in a note at the side: 'quia alibi'. The four entries all occur in this order above on this same page.

618 No surname is given.

619 This was possibly an older man already fully trained but needing to fulfil the requirements of apprenticeship in order to gain citizenship. However, a John Cowpland is listed as an apprentice in 1415–16 and by this date he might have been thought ready to come out of his apprenticeship terms. This however is not listed until 1429–30.

(Thomas Standish apprentice of John Donne – 2s.
William Burton apprentice of John Kyng – 2s.
Thomas Serle apprentice of Richard Spencer – 2s.
John Donne apprentice of Robert Donne – 2s.)
Robert Botiller formerly apprentice of John Barnes – 2s.
Richard Raulyn formerly appprentice of Richard Withihale – 2s.
John Tumvyle formerly apprentice of John – 2s.
John Huberd formerly apprentice of John Blakedene – 2s.
Drew Waddesley formerly apprentice of Thomas Lamport – 2s.
Simon Collissone formerly apprentice of William FitzHugh – 2s.
John Normantoun formerly apprentice of Roger Brenaston – 2s.
Elias Harwood formerly apprentice of William Randolf – 2s.
John Cary formerly apprentice of John Pattesley – 2s.
Roger Linacre formerly apprentice of William Walton – 2s.
Henry Toret formerly apprentice of Thomas Gabrielle – 2s.

Item, John Coupland was given permission by the aforesaid wardens that he might freely work at his craft during the time of his apprenticeship and for this he paid the aforesaid wardens – 40d.

Item, Gysebright de Deyste, 'Dutchman', was admitted to the freedom of the 1423
Goldsmiths' Mistery on 14 May of the year 1 Henry VI [1423] and for this p. 131
he paid to the current wardens – £10.

Melver:
Item, Frederick Melver, 'Dutchman', was admitted to the freedom of the said mistery on the same date at the request of Richard Whittington, lately citizen and Mayor of London, and for this he paid to the aforesaid wardens – £4.

These are the names of those aliens given permission to work in the time of 1422–23
the said Wardens:
Firstly, Gyse Paunser paid for this – 13s. 4d.
Item, Albright Leiden for the same – 4s.
Item, Peter Bomit – 10s.
Item, Hans Croykyn – 13s. 4d.
Item, Herman – 13s. 4d.
Item, Gerard Bry – 10s.
Item, Janyn Eskevyn – 6s. 8d.
Item, Swether, 'Dutchman' – 10s.

1422 Memorandum de defectibus etc tempore Johannis Hilles, Johannis Biernes,
A + b p. 77 Johannis Walsshe et Willelmi Walton, custodum etc, anno regni Regis Henrici quinti decimo:

In primis, Johannes Teukesbury junior pro defectu operacionis – ii s.
Item, Thomas Swynesco pro eodem – vi d.
Item, Johannes Walsshe junior – ii s.
Item, Robertus Donne – ii s.
Hermanus Fynk – ii s.
Willelmus Coupere – ii s.
Johannes Ungle – ii s.
Johannes Clerk – ii s.
Thomas Thomer – ii s.
Aurifaber Cantuariensis – ii s.
Johannes Paulyn – ii s.
Willelmus Lerpool – xx d.
Johannes Chestre – xii d.
Thomas Thomer – ii s.[620]
Johannes Normantoun – ii s.
Ricardus Chaumbre – ii s.
Johannes Teukesbury junior pro quadam transgressione – vi s. viii d.

1422–23 A + a p. 132[621] Fait a remembrer qe le mar.. jour . . . l'an le Roi H[enri] . . . Johan Hilles, Johan Biernes, Johan Walsshe et William Walton, adonqes gardeyns . . . . . . de.. a eux a lour comune . . . en la paroche de Seint Johan Zakarie . . . a luy q'ils feurent enfourmez q'il eust grandement trespassé pur ceo q'il eust diverses foitz estee . . . . . . aillours et cariez ovesque luy diverses choses d'orfevrie nient serchez n'assaiez ne touchez . . . . . . et deceit du poeple du roialme et esclaundre de tout la dicte mistere et encountre . . . . . . temps usez et faitz et demanderent de luy coment il luy vorroit excuser . . . . . . ensi fait il vorreit avower et ensi il vorroit faire en temps avenir . . . . . . non obstantz. Et les gardeyns demanderent de luy s'il voloit esteier . . . . . . il feust enfraunchizez en la dicte mistere en . . . et il disoit q'il ne vorroit . . . il disoit q'ils feurent . . . enemys et leur reprova vilenousement . . . nonobstaunt ils demanderent . . . . . . autres quatre prodeshommes de la dicte artifice a soun denomi.. propre . . . et eslist quatre hommes . . . Johan . . . , Salamon Oxney, Johan Palyng, et Johan Pake et ensura . . . a haut et bas al ordinance . . . aide d.. . . . hommes issint a eux associez et lesquelles quatre hommes issint esluz le pristrent . . . de faire bon fyn ovesque les ditz . . . et al jour par eux limité quaunt ils verr.. . . . lour agarde le dit Johan Teukesbury . . . et disoit expressément q'il ne vorroit attendre lour agarde et comaunda les ditz gardeins de faire lour mal.. . . . les ditz gardeins considerantz les grantz . . . rebellion, disobeisaunce et obstinacie qe le dit Johan Teukesbury

[620] One wonders whether this man was fined on two separate occasions or whether his name has been listed twice in error.

[621] This page is badly damaged. It would appear that the ink had faded badly (Prideaux, I, 18, comments that the page is mostly illegible), and that someone applied some chemical in an attempt to aid legibility. This has left the page a dull brown colour, leaves it still illegible, and has badly discoloured the verso of this leaf also.

Memorandum of offences etc in the time of John Hilles, John Barnes, John Walsh and William Walton, Wardens etc., in the year 10 Henry V [1422]: 1422 A + b p. 77
Firstly, John Tewkesbury the younger for a defect in workmanship – 2s.
Item, Thomas Swinscoe for the same – 6d.
Item, John Walsh the younger – 2s.
Item, Robert Donne – 2s.
Hermann Fynk – 2s.
William Couper – 2s.
John Nongyl – 2s.
John Clerk – 2s.
Thomas Thomer – 2s.
A goldsmith from Canterbury – 2s.
John Paulyn – 2s.
William Liverpool – 20d.
John Chester – 12d.
Thomas Thomer – 2s.
John Normantoun – 2s.
Richard Chaumbre – 2s.
John Tewkesbury the younger for a certain offence – 6s. 8d.

Memorandum that on Tuesday . . . in the year of King Henry . . . John Hilles, John Barnes, John Walsh and William Walton, then wardens . . . to them in their common . . . in the parish of St John Zachary . . . to him, that they had been informed that he had gravely offended in that he had several times been . . elsewhere and had taken with him various objects of goldsmithry that had not been examined nor assayed nor touched . . . and deceit of the people of the kingdom and the disgrace of the whole said mistery and in contravention of . . . practised in time . . . and they asked him how he proposed to exonerate himself . . . thus done he wished to avow and thus he wished to to do in future . . . notwithstanding. And the wardens asked him if he would stand by . . . he was admitted to the freedom of the said mistery . . . and he said that he did not wish . . . he said they were . . . enemies and he vilely insulted them . . . notwithstanding they asked . . . another four goodmen of the said mistery to be nominated by himself . . and elected four men . . . John . . ., Solomon Oxney, John Palyng and John Pake and he gave an assurance . . . entirely by the judgment . . . help of . . . the men thus associated with them, and the which four men thus elected took him . . . to make a good agreement with the said . . . and on the day set by them when they would see . . . their judgment the said John Tewkesbury . . . and he said outrightly that he did not wish to wait for their judgment and he bade them do their worst . . . the said wardens considering the great . . . rebellion, disobedience and obstinacy that the said John Tewkesbury 1422–23 A + a p. 132

ne vorroit . . . mesme . . . ovesq*e* plusou*rs* aut*res* p*ro*deshom*m*es de d*ict*e mistere alerent a Rob*er*t Chicheley adonqes Meire de [Loundres] . . . . . . de dit Joh*a*n Teukesbury *et* luy requirerent de sou*n* aide q*e* le dit Joh*a*n purreit estre . . . s'il . . . faitz as gentz de d*ict*e mistere p*ar* les nobles Rois d'Englet*er*re de . . . . la d*ict*e citee de tielx rebelles dev*a*nt ces heures faitz et . . . adonqes b.. . . . lour . . . un s*er*geaunt pur le dit Joh*a*n *et* luy co*m*mist a prison a dem*ur*er illoeqes jesques a celle temps q'il vorroit estre jus.. . . . solonc la custume de d*ict*e citee *et* illoeqes le dit Joh*a*n dem*ur*a tanqe le xii[e] jour d'octobre p*ro*schein . . . William Hankeford, Chief Justice du Bank le Roy, envoia un brief direct as viscontz de Londres pur le dit Joh*a*n en la fo*ur*me q'ensuit: Henricus dei gra*cia* Rex Angl*ie* *et* Francie *et* D*omin*us Hib*erni*e vicecomitib*us* London' sal*ut*em. Cum Joh*anne*s Teukesbury . . . n*ost*ri coram ip*s*o nup*er* rege appellasset Joh*anne*m Olyve de Lexlep' Com' Kildare in Hib[ernia] . . . . . . Glouc', in quo quidem appello partes p*redict*as placitaverunt ad ex.. sup*er* . . . . . . p*re*tato jur*a*.. int*er* partes p*redict*as posita fuit in respo*n*su coram ipso rege apud Westm*onasterium* usq*ue* in diem . . . Nisi Justic' ip*s*ius nup*er* Regis ad assisas in d*ict*o com*itatu* Gloucestr' capiend' assign' primo die l.. in festo S*anct*i Bartho*lomei* . . . in formam statutam in huiusmodi casu, p*ro*visi venissent. Ante quem quidem diem veni.. . . . nup*er* Regis pr.. n*ost*ri sine die remansit cicut nob*is* constat. At iam in cur*ia* n*ost*ra coram nob*is* . . . ip*s*ius Joh*anni*s Teukesbury . . . ip*s*e in prisona n*ost*ra in custodia v*est*ra sub apta custodia detinet*ur* quominus ip.. . . . . . . supplicatu*m* est sibi de remedio congruo in hac parte p*ro*videre. Et nos in hac parte fieri . . . . . . iniunge . . . exoneracione postposita q*uo*d corpus ip*s*ius Joh*anni*s Teukesbury in prisone . . . . . . securo conductu una cum causa detencionis sue h.. . . . apud . . . . . . nob*is* appellare . . . expedire . . . Angl' . . . Et h.. . . . W*illia*m Hankeford . . . brief feust r.. al dit Bank p*ar* les . . . . . . infra no*min*atus co*m*missus fuit prisone . . . . . . London' ad salvo custodiend' quousque pres.. . . . d*omi*no Rege ad diem et locum infra . . . . p*ro*schein ensuant . . . William Hankeford . . . brief . . . . . . p*re*dicte nup*er* . . . Joh*anni*s Teukesbury . . . et securo conductu una cum causa detencionis sue h*ab*er.. . . . apud . . . p*redict*o ad p*ro*sequend*um* quoddam appell.. . . . usu . . . Regis Angl*ie* . . . . . . q*uo*d idem Joh*anne*s co*m*missus fuit prisone . . . . . . quousq*ue* pref.. . . . Et
p. 133 . . . n*ost*ra . . . . . . nob*is* . . . | p*ro*cedere valeam*us* p*ro*ut de iure fore viderim*us* p*ro*cedend*um*. T*este* W Hankeford apud Westm*onasterium* xvi die Octobr*is* anno r*egni* n*ostri* primo. Et le quel brief feust auxint endosez *et* reto*ur*nez en la fourme q'ensuit:[622] Ego Rob*er*tus Chicheley, maior civitatis London', vob*is* significo q*uo*d int*er* cet*er*as lib*er*tates *et* consuetudines[623] in civitate London' a toto tempore cuius contrarii memoria ho*minu*m non existit usitat*as* *et* approbat*as* ac tam p*er* cartas p*ro*genitor*um* d*omi*ni Regis immo q*ua*m in Parliamento[624] eor*un*dem ratific[at]as[625] *et* confirmat*as* talis h*abetur* *et* a toto tempore p*redict*o h*ab*eat*ur* consuetudo in eadem civitate q*uo*d si quis civis vel

[622] The following document is found also in a copy at the Corporation of London Records Office, Plea and Memoranda Roll A 51, m. 5[b] (PM). Variant readings from this are noted here. See also *CPMR 1413–1437,* pp. 163–64. Unfortunately, no other copies of any other document referred to here have been traced at either the CLRO or the PRO.

[623] PM: consuetudines et libertates.

[624] PM: in diuersis parliamentis.

[625] MS: ratificas; PM: ratificatas.

did not wish . . . same . . . with several other goodmen of the said mistery went to Robert Chichely, then Mayor of London, . . . the said John Tewkesbury and requested his assistance that the said John might be . . if he . . . made to the people of the said mistery by the noble kings of England . . . the said City of such rebellious acts done in times past . . . then . . . their . . . a serjeant for the said John and committed him to prison to stay there until he accepted to submit himself to judgment . . . according to the custom of the said City, and there the said John stayed until 12 October following. . . . William Hankford, Chief Justice of the King's Bench, sent a writ addressed to the sheriffs of London concerning the said John, in manner following: Henry by the grace of God King of England and France and Lord of Ireland to the sheriffs of London: Greetings. Whereas John Tewkesbury . . . our before the late King himself accused John Olyve from Leixlip in County Kildare in Ireland . . . Gloucester, in which appeal the aforesaid parties pleaded . . . . . . having sworn an oath, between the aforesaid parties was made a respondent before the King himself at Westminster until the day . . . Unless the late King's Judge/Judges at the assizes in the said County of Gloucester took . . . assigned . . . on the first day . . . on the feastday of St Bartholomew [24 August] . . . in the statutory form that applies in such a case, they had come ?as appointed? Before which day came . . . the late King . . . our, remained *sine die* as we agreed. And now in our Court before us . . . of the same John Tewkesbury . . . himself in our prison in your custody under proper guard shall be detained until he . . . he was begged to provide a suitable remedy in this matter. And we in this matter . . to be done . . . enjoin . . exoneration postponed that the same John Tewkesbury in prison . . . under secure guard and with him the reasons for his detention . . . at . . . appeal to us . . . send . . . England . . . And . . . William Hankford . . . writ was . . . to the said bench by the . . . named below was sent to prison . . . London to be safely guarded until . . . the lord King on the day and in the place below . . . next following . . . William Hankford . . . writ . . . aforesaid late . . . of John Tewkesbury . . . and under safe conduct along with the reasons for his detention . . . at . . . aforesaid to prosecute a certain case . . . according to the custom . . . of the King of England . . . that the same John had been sent to prison . . . until the aforesaid . . . And . . . our . . . to us . . . | we are empowered to proceed as we p. 133
may see to do so according to the law. Witnessed by William Hankford at Westminster on 16 October in the first year of our reign [1422]. And this writ was thus endorsed and returned in the form that follows: I, Robert Chicheley, Mayor of the City of London, make known to you that among other liberties and customs used and approved since time immemorial in the City of London and ratified and confirmed both by charters of the ancestors of the lord King as also in Parliament,[224] there is one that has been held as a custom in the same city since time immemorial that if any citizen or freeman of the said City who

[224] PM: in various parliaments.

liber d*ict*e civitatis aliqua utens arte vel mistera rebelliose fregit, contravenit aut obstinacit*er* justificari renuerit p*er* bonas regulas *et* ordinac*ion*es p*er* mag*ist*ros jurat*os et* co*mun*itatem alicuius talis artis vel mistere p*ro* co*mun*i comodo p*opu*lari p*ro*vis*as*, ordinat*as et* usitat*as*, seu mag*ist*ros huiusmodi delinquentem *et* obstinatum corripientes redarguerit *et* despexerit *et* inde querela seu reportum ad maiorem d*ict*e civitatis p*ro* tempore existent*em* p*er* mag*ist*ros huiusmodi mistere deferebat*ur*,[626] tunc potest potuit, debet debuit *et* de toto tempore p*redict*o juxta consuetudinem sup*radict*am consuevit Maior d*ict*e civitatis qui p*ro* tempore fu*er*it committere queml*ibe*t taliter delinquentem *et* obstinatum prisone d*omi*ni Regis co*m*moraturi[627] in eadem quousq*ue* gr*a*tis justificari volu*er*it *et* emendacio competens fiat p*ro* delicto. Ac ubi p*ro* co*mun*i co*m*modo p*opu*lari p*er* mag*ist*ros *et* co*mun*itatem mistere aurifabr*ie* d*ict*e civitatis adiu fu*er*it p*ro*visum ordinat*um et* usitat*um* q*uo*d null*um* aurum vel argent*um* op*er*atum ad aliquas ferias vel nundinas ext*ra* d*ict*am civitatem p*er* aliquem lib*er*um seu civem d*ict*e mistere duceret*ur* quousq*ue* aurum vel argent*um* illud p*er* mag*ist*ros jurat*os* d*ict*e mistere p*ro* tempore existentes sup*er*inderet*ur* assaiaret*ur et* p*ro*baret*ur* si foret bon*um*, verum, congru*um et* p*er*fectum. Ibi viii[628] die Octobr*is* anno r*egni regis* Henr*ici* sexti post conquestum primo Joh*ann*es Hilles, Joh*ann*es Biernes, Joh*ann*es Walssh*e et* Will*elmu*s Walton*e*, nunc mag*ist*ri jurat*i* de mistera aurifabr*ie* d*ict*e civitatis, reportum *et* querelam ad me p*re*fat*um* Maiorem detulerunt[629] q*uo*d Joh*ann*es Teukesbury in br*evi* huic cedule consut*o* no*min*atus, civis *et* liber homo civitatis London' utens d*ict*a arte *et* mistera aurifabr*ie*, non t*antu*m rebelliose fregit contravenit *et* obstinacit*er* justificari renuit p*er* ordinac*io*nes sup*ra*dict*as* veru*m* eciam d*ict*os nunc mag*ist*ros ip*s*ud de p*re*missis *et* aliis defectib*us* in contemptu*m* bone regule d*ict*e mistere fact*is* corripientes violent*er* co*m*minando *et* falsos vocetando[630] despexit *et* irrep*ro*bavit[631] in p*re*sencia pl*ur*imor*um* ho*minu*m eiusdem mistere ad p*er*turbac*io*nem *et* co*m*moc*io*nem tocius mistere p*redict*e v*er*isimilem, petentes remedium consuetudini d*ict*e civitatis consonn*ans* adhiberi. Ob quod ego p*re*fatus maior adv*er*tens q*uo*d nisi mag*ist*ris misterar*um* d*ict*e civitatis in huiusmodi querelis favor debitus exhiberet*ur* ac p*er*v*er*sitati malignantis huismodi obviaret*ur* p*er*icula g*ra*viora int*er* co*mun*itates aliar*um* misterar*um* d*ict*e civitatis p*er* minores maiorib*us*[632] rebellantes de facili pot*er*int gen*er*ari, p*re*fatum Joh*ann*em Teukesbury quem multiplicit*er* obstinat*um et* delinquentem rep*er*i in hac parte juxta consuetudines sup*radict*as hacten*us* optent*as et* usitat*as* prisone d*omi*ni regis sub custodia Rob*er*ti Tatershale *et* Will*elm*i Estfeld, vic*ecomitum* d*ict*e civitatis co*m*misi salvo custodiend*um* in eadem quousq*ue* gr*a*tis justificari volu*er*it *et* emenda congrua fieret p*ro* delicto juxta consuetudines, lib*er*tates, bonas regulas *et* ordinac*io*nes sup*radict*as. Et aprés ceo, c'est assavoir a le quinszeine de Seint Hiller adonqes p*ro*schein ensuant, quant le dit Joh*a*n Olyve feust atteint a la sute de dit Joh*a*n Teukesbury de la robb*er*ie suisd*ict*e, mesme le Joh*a*n

[626] PM: deferatur.
[627] PM: moraturi.
[628] PM: xvj.
[629] PM: detulere.
[630] PM: vocitando.
[631] PM: reprobavit.
[632] PM: maioribus minores.

practises any craft or mistery should rebelliously break, contravene or obstinately refuse to be judged by the good rules and ordinances provided, ordained and practised for the common benefit of the people by the sworn masters and the commonalty of any such craft or mistery, or if he should rebuke and show contempt for the masters who thus chastise such a delinquent and obstinate man, and a plea or a report about this is taken by the masters of such a mistery to the current Mayor of the said City, then the current Mayor of the said City can and could, must and should, and he has been accustomed since time immemorial according to the aforesaid custom, to commit any such delinquent and obstinate man to the King's prison to stay there until he shall of his own free will consent to be judged and that proper amends be made for the offence. And whereas for a long time past it has been provided, ordained and practised by the masters and the commonalty of the Goldsmiths' Mistery of the said City for the common benefit of the people that no wrought gold or silver should be taken by any freeman or citizen of the said mistery to any market or fair outside the said City before that gold or silver shall have been inspected, assayed and tested by the current sworn masters of the said mistery to see that it be good, true, proper and perfect. Thus on 8 October[225] in the first year of the reign of King Henry VI [1422] John Hilles, John Barnes, John Walsh and William Walton, the present sworn masters of the Goldsmiths' Mistery of the said City, brought a report and a plea to me, aforesaid Mayor, that John Tewkesbury, named in the writ sewn to this schedule, citizen and freeman of the City of London who practises the said Goldsmiths' craft and mistery, had not only rebelliously broken and contravened the aforesaid ordinances and refused obstinately to be judged by them, but had also shown contempt for and had insulted those said present masters who were reproving him about the aforesaid and other offences committed in contempt of the good rules of the said mistery, violently threatening them and calling them false in the presence of many men of the same mistery, to the likely perturbance and disturbance of the whole of the aforesaid mistery, and they asked for a remedy to be brought in accordance with the custom of the said City. And about this matter I, aforesaid Mayor, observing that unless due favour were shown to the masters of the misteries of the said City in such-like pleas, and unless such malicious perversity be opposed, more serious troubles could easily be fomented among the communities of other misteries of the said City through the lesser men rebelling against the greater men, I committed the aforesaid John Tewkesbury, whom I found in this matter to be repeatedly delinquent and obstinate, to the King's prison in accordance with the aforesaid customs as they have obtained and been practised until now, and under the guard of Robert Tatershall and William Estfield, sheriffs of the said City, to be safely guarded in the same prison until he shall of his own free will consent to be judged and to make suitable amends for his offence according to the aforesaid customs, liberties, good rules and ordinances. And after this, a fortnight after the next following feastday of St Hilary [13 January] [27 January 1423 n.s.], when the said John Olyve was convicted of the aforesaid robbery on the suit of the said John Tewkesbury, the same John Tewkesbury was returned by the said

[225] PM: 16 October.

Teukesbury feust p*ar* le dit Mons*ire* Will*ia*m Hankeford remys a mesme la prisone en Loundres en quele il feust dev*a*nt pur illoeqes esteire al ordinance du Mair du d*ict*e citee. Et aprés ceo, c'est assavoir le xiie jour de Feverer adonqes p*ro*schein ensuant, Will*ia*m Walderne, donqes Meir de mesme la citee, co*m*myst le dit Joh*a*n Teukesbury as ditz gardeins pur esteier *et* obeier al ordinance des d*ict*es gardeyns *et* de toute la companie de d*ict*e artifice. Et issint mesme le Joh*a*n Teukesbury vient en la d*ict*e co*mun*e sale d'orfeou*r*s mesme le jour, *et* illoeqes engenulaunt sur ses genoles humblement luy surmyst *et* obeia d'esteier al ordinaunce des ditz gardeyns *et* de tout la companie *et* a ceo b*ie*n *et* loialment faire *et* perfourmir il le jura p*ar* le s*er*ement q'il eust fait devant a Dieu *et* Seint Dunston, et auxint p*ur* le greindre seureté il le ensura p*ar* sa mayn dextre en la main dextre de ch*es*cun des ditz gardeyns. Lesquelles gardeyns, ewe l'advys *et* advisement de tout la d*ict*e companye en cell*e* matire, mesmes les gardeyns p*ar* la co*mun*e assent de tout la companie suisdit illoeqes esteant agarderont q*e* le dit Joh*a*n Teukesbury pur les mesprisions *et* offences suisd*ict*es *et* auxint les ditz rebellion *et* disobeisaunce env*er*s ses gardeyns suisditz issint faitz paieroit al almoigne de Seint Dunston x li. Et lesquelles x li. feurent paiez illoeqes sanz autre delaie *et*c.

p. 134[633] [blank]

1423–24 Ceux sount les nouns des Gardeyns eslutz al fest de Seint Dunstoun l'an du
p. 135 regne le Roy Henry sisme prim*er* tanq*e* al fest de Seint Dunstoun av*a*ntdit adonqes p*ro*schein ensuant:

Rob*er*tus Walton*e*
Joh*anne*s Joce
Ric*ard*us Spenser
Joh*anne*s Edmond

1423 No*min*a ho*min*um receptor*um* ad elemosinam S*anct*i Dunstani in festo S*anct*i
A + b Dunstani anno regni Reg*is* Henr*ici* sexti primo:
p. 80[634] ad xviii d.: Thomas Cobe

ad xvi d.: Thomas Senycle
Thomas Dodesole

ad xiiii d.: Emma Salesbury

ad xii d.: Jacob*us* Buntyng
Will*elmu*s Maryner – moriebat*ur* – tunc p*roxim*o sequen*te*[635]
Joh*anne*s Hoghton
Joh*anne*s Halle – mortuus est xv° die Ap*ri*l*is* tunc p*roxim*o sequen*te*

[633] This page is blank.
[634] A new hand starts here.
[635] This, and the other notes about men who have died, has been added later in a very much more scribbled hand but by the same scribe. Here the 'tunc proxime sequente' is separated from the 'moriebatur' by a large gap, left no doubt for a more precise date.

Sir William Hankford to the same prison in London in which he had been before, to stay there at the disposition of the Mayor of the said City. And after that, i.e. on 12 February next following, William Walderne, then Mayor of the said City, handed over the said John Tewkesbury to the said Wardens, to remain by and to obey what was ordained by the said wardens and the whole company of the said mistery. And thus the said John Tewkesbury came to Goldsmiths' Hall on the same day and there kneeling on his knees he humbly submitted himself and obediently agreed to be at the ordinance of the said wardens and of all the company, and he swore that he would well and faithfully do and carry this out by the oath that he had previously made to God and St Dunstan, and for greater surety he promised this while holding by his right hand the right hand of each of the wardens. The which wardens, having taken the advice and counsel of all the said company about this matter, by the common assent of all the aforesaid company there present judged that the said John Tewkesbury should, for the aforesaid misdeeds and offences and also for the aforesaid rebellion and disobedience thus committed against his wardens, pay to the alms funds of St Dunstan £10. And the aforesaid £10 was paid there and then without any further delay etc.

[blank] p. 134

These are the names of the Wardens elected at the feast of St Dunstan in the 1423–24
year 1 Henry VI [19 May 1423] until the aforesaid feastday of St Dunstan p. 135
next following:
Robert Walton
John Joce
Richard Spencer
John Edmund

The names of men admitted to receive the alms of St Dunstan on the 1423
feastday of St Dunstan 1423: A + b p. 80

18d. – Thomas Cobe

16d. – Thomas Senycle
Thomas Dodesole

14d. – Emma Salisbury

12d. James Buntyng
William Mariner – died on the next following
John Houghtoun
John Halle – died on 15 April next following

Thomas Bokyll
Walt*er*us Sprynget
Thomas Mounde – qui moriebat*ur* quinto die Marcii tunc p*roximo* sequen*te*
Thom*as* Oxford[636]

ad viii d.: Will*elmu*s Waynflete
Thomas Gynge
Thomas Ufforde – et postea rec'[637]

ad vi d.: Joh*anne*s Peryn
Will*elmu*s Baldeswell*e*

A + a No*min*a app*re*nticior*um*
p. 135 *cont.*

Joh*anne*s Whisshe app*re*nticius Will*elm*i Goteley –	xx s.
Joh*anne*s Gannill*e* app*re*nticius Joh*ann*is Colney –	xx s.
Thomas Whitfeld app*re*nticius Thome Longe –	xx s.
Ric*ard*us Peye app*re*nticius Thome Welles –	xx s.
Laurencius Water app*re*nticius Joh*ann*is fitz Rob*er*t –	xx s.
Will*elmu*s Mundene app*re*nticius Will*elm*i Hope –	xx s.
Petrus Nangle app*re*nticius Joh*ann*is Nangle –	xx s.
Joh*anne*s Lilye app*re*nticius Joh*ann*is Huberd –	xx s.
Egidius Bremson*e* app*re*nticius Rob*er*ti Cryngelford –	xx s.
Henr*icus* Bedill*e* app*re*nticius Henr*ici* Rageley –	xx s.
Joh*anne*s Millyngton*e* app*re*nticius Rob*er*ti Bosoun –	xx s.
Joh*anne*s Permyter app*re*nticius Joh*ann*is Hilles –	xx s.
Rob*er*tus Batreaux app*re*nticius Joh*ann*is Teukesbury, jun*ioris* –	xx s.
Joh*anne*s Henryk app*re*nticius Thome Gabriell*e* –	xx s.

No*min*a allocator*um* jur*atorum*:

Will*elmu*s Tannere nup*er* app*re*nticius Joh*ann*is Standelf –	ii s.
Will*elmu*s Pertenale nup*er* app*re*nticius Joh*ann*is Wynne –	ii s.
Rob*er*tus Bosoun nup*er* app*re*nticius Thome Popultou*n* –	ii s.
Ric*ard*us Hustwayt nup*er* app*re*nticius Steph*an*i Colney –	ii s.
Will*elmu*s Shipwright nup*er* app*re*nticius Bartho*lome*i Seman –	ii s.
Joh*anne*s Frenssh*e* nup*er* app*re*nticius Will*elm*i Louthe –	ii s.
Joh*anne*s Sturdys nup*er* app*re*nticius Rob*er*ti Lemyng –	ii s.
Thomas Blythe nup*er* app*re*nticius Joh*ann*is Teukesbury sen*ioris* –	ii s.

[636] This name has been added later in a different hand.
[637] This incomplete note has been added later by the scribe. It may have been intended to mean that Ufford later received a higher amount?

Thomas Bokyl
Walter Sprynget
Thomas Mound – who died the next following 5 March
Thomas Oxford

8d. – William Waynflete
Thomas Genge
Thomas Ufford – and later he received

6d. – John Peryn
William Baldeswelle

Names of apprentices:		A + a
John Whisshe apprentice of William Goteley –	20s.	p. 135 *cont.*
John Gannille apprentice of John Colney –	20s.	
Thomas Whitfield apprentice of Thomas Longe –	20s.	
Richard Peye apprentice of Thomas Welles –	20s.	
Laurence Water apprentice of John FitzRobert –	20s.	
William Mundene apprentice of William Hope –	20s.	
Peter Nongyl apprentice of John Nongyl –	20s.	
John Lilye apprentice of John Huberd –	20s.	
Giles Bremson apprentice of Robert Cringleford –	20s.	
Henry Bedille apprentice of Henry Ragley –	20s.	
John Millington apprentice of Robert Bosoun –	20s.	
John Permyter apprentice of John Hilles –	20s.	
Robert Batreaux apprentice of John Tewkesbury the younger –	20s.	
John Henryk apprentice of Thomas Gabrielle –	20s.	

The names of serving-men sworn:	
William Tanner former apprentice of John Standelf –	2s.
William Pertenhall former apprentice of John Wynne –	2s.
Robert Bosoun former apprentice of Thomas Poppleton –	2s.
Richard Hustwayt former apprentice of Stephen Colney –	2s.
William Shipwright former apprentice of Bartholomew Seman –	2s.
John Frenshe former apprentice of William Louth –	2s.
John Sturdys former apprentice of Robert Lemyng –	2s.
Thomas Blithe former apprentice of John Tewkesbury the elder –	2s.

Memorand*um* q*uo*d Joh*anne*s Sturdys nup*er* app*re*nticius Rob*er*ti Lemyng admissus fuit isto anno in lib*er*tatem artis aurifabr*ie et* licenciatus op*er*ari infra tempus app*re*nticiatus sui *et* solvit ea de causa – xl s.

Item, eodem anno Joh*anne*s Waryn de com*itatu* Norff', jueler, admissus fuit in lib*er*tatem civitatis London' *et* misteram artis aurifabr*ie* p*er* assensum tam gardianor*um* q*ua*m totius co*mun*itatis d*ict*e mistere *et* solvit ea de causa *et* p*ro* introitu suo ad vesturam – xl li. vi s. viii d.
Et idem Joh*anne*s sacr*amentu*m p*re*stitit corporale ad se b*en*e *et* fidelit*er* ierend*um* s*ecun*d*u*m formam *et* consuet*udines* eiusdem mistere *etc.*[638]

p. 136 Item, eodem anno Hermanus van Pitte, Ducheman, admissus fuit in lib*er*tatem mistere aurifabr*ie* London' *et* solvit ea de causa – x li.
Janyn Eskeveyn for eo hoc – ii s.[639]

Item, eodem tempore Janyn Eskevyn admissus fuit simili modo *et* solvit ea de causa – x li.

Hic sunt no*mi*na alienigen*arum* dimiss*orum* op*er*ari tempore d*ict*or*um* custod*um*:
Postell, Ducheman – xiii s. iiii d.
Gerardus Bry – xiii s. iiii d.
Swether, Ducheman – xiii s. iiii d.
Albryght Laydon*e* de Holand – vi s. viii d.
Henr*icus* Holand – xvi s. viii d.
Walt*er*us Van Tuffen*e* – xx s.
Petrus Bunt – vi s. viii d.

(Item, Gyse Paunser, Ducheman, licenciatus est eodem anno op*er*ari in arte p*re*d*ict*a p*er* vi annos *et* dat – iiii li.)[640] Va*ca*t q*uia* relib*er*at*a* fuit p*re*d*ict*o Gyse d*ict*a s*umma* iiii li. tam de assensu tocius co*mun*itatis mistere p*re*d*ict*e q*ua*m p*re*d*ict*i Gyse.

Lev*er*pole:
Fait a remembr*er* q*e* pur taunt q*e* Will*ia*m Leverpole revyla dispitousement les gardeyns adonqes esteantz, il feust amesnez al prison *et* puis ap*rés* il se co*m*mist d'estere al ordenaunce des ditz gardeyns *et* sur ceo il feust obligez en une obligacion de x li. Et puis ap*rés* les ditz gardeyns p*ar* assent de tout la co*mun*e p*ar*donerent au dit Will*ia*m la d*ict*e somme de x li., sur condicion q'il se b*ie*n port*er*a env*er*s les ditz gardeyns q'ore sont *et* auxi env*er*s toutz aut*re*s gardeyns qi pur le temps s*er*ront; *et* aut*re*ment soit la d*ict*e so*m*me de x li. levez *et* recov*er*ez env*er*s luy, et la quele obligacion dem*our*et deinz la tresorie.

[638] This sentence has been added somewhat later in different ink but by the same scribe.
[639] This entry is in a different hand and has been added later. It is rather odd in the amounts paid stated here and below. One rather wonders if the 2s. is not a penalty fine and that the scribe here has misplaced this entry. Note also the odd mixture of languages.
[640] This entry has been scored out, 'va*cat*' has been written in the LH margin beside it, and the following note then added.

Memorandum that John Sturdys, former apprentice of Robert Lemyng, was admitted this year into the freedom of the Goldsmiths' Mistery and was given permission to work within the period of his apprenticeship, and for this he paid – 40s.

Item, the same year John Waryn of the County of Norfolk, jeweler, was admitted into the freedom of the City of London and of the Goldsmiths' Mistery, with the assent both of the Wardens and of the whole commonalty of the said mistery, and he paid for this and for his entry into the livery – £40 6s. 8d. And the same John took a corporal oath that he would well and faithfully conduct himself according to the form and customs of the same mistery etc.

Item, in the same year Hermann van Pitte, 'Dutchman', was admitted into the p. 136
freedom of the Goldsmiths' Mistery of London and for this he paid – £10.
Janyn Eskevyn for the same cause – 2s.

Item, at the same time Janyn Eskevyn was admitted in the same way and for this he paid – £10.

These are the names of aliens given permission to work during the time of the said Wardens:
Postell, 'Dutchman' – 13s. 4d.
Gerard Bry – 13s. 4d.
Swether, 'Dutchman' – 13s. 4d.
Albright Leiden from Holland – 6s. 8d.
Henry Holland – 16s. 8d.
Walter van Tuffene – 20s.
Peter Bunt – 6s. 8d.

(Item, Gyse Panser, 'Dutchman', was given permission that same year in work in the aforesaid mistery for 6 years and he gave – £4.) Annulled, because the said sum of £4 was repaid to the aforesaid Gyse with the assent both of the whole commonalty of the aforesaid mistery and of the aforesaid Gyse.

Liverpool:
Memorandum that whereas William Liverpool contemptuously insulted the current wardens, he was taken to prison and then afterwards he promised to stand by whatever was decreed by the said wardens, and he was then bound by letters obligatory in the sum of £10. And then afterwards the said wardens with the assent of the whole commonalty remitted the said sum of £10 to the said William, on condition that he shall behave well towards the said present wardens and also towards all future wardens, and otherwise the said sum of £10 shall be levied and recovered from him, and the said bond shall remain in the treasury.

Fait a remembr*er* q*e* Joh*an* Hilt, chapeleyn, feust p*re*senté mesme l'an a Sire Joh*an* Bernesley, p*ar*son*e* de l'esglise de Seynt Joh*an* Zacarie, pur illoeqes chaunter p*ur* l'alme de Drue Barayntyn *et* sa fe*mm*e *et* des aut*re*s p*ur* t*er*me de sa vie *et* a ceo il feust jurez le darreyn jo*ur* de marz mesme l'an.[641]

1423–24 A + b p. 78 Memorand*um* de defectib*us* op*er*acionu*m* *et*c tempore Rob*er*ti Walton, Joh*ann*is Joce, Ric*ard*i Spenser *et* Joh*ann*is Emond, custodu*m* *et*c anno regni Reg*is* Henr*ici* sexti primo:
In p*ri*mis, Joh*anne*s Kyngesden p*ro* def*ec*tu op*er*ac*io*nis – ii s.
It*em*, Petrus Brendwode p*ro* eodem – xii d.
It*em*, Will*elmu*s Hope p*ro* eodem – ii s.
It*em*, Joh*anne*s Coupeland p*ro* eodem – xx d.
It*em*, Hans Flemyng p*ro* eodem – xviii d.
It*em*, Lodowicus Pope p*ro* eodem – vi s. viii d.
It*em*, Dun Flemyng a Westm'[642] – xx d.

It*em*, Joh*anne*s Kyngesden*e* p*ro* quada*m* t*ra*nsgressione f*ac*ta cu*m* soc*io* suo in tab*er*na – xx d.
It*em*, Joh*anne*s Topclyf p*ro* eodem – iii s. iiii d.
It*em*, Clays, Ducheman, de fine q*uia* op*er*abat*ur* cu*m* Joh*ann*e Wat*er*ley sine licencia custodu*m* – vi s. viii d.

1424–25 A + a p. 137 Ceux sont les nouns des Gardeyns eslutz al feste de Seint Dunston l'an du regne le Roy Henry sisme secunde tanq*e* al feste de Seint Dunston av*a*ntdit adonqes p*ro*schein ensuant:
Joh*an* Pake
Joh*an* Pattisle
Thomas Leget
Rob*er*t Cryngelford

No*min*a app*re*nticior*um*:

Thomas Pitlesden*e* app*re*nticius Joh*ann*is Pauley –	xx s.
Will*elmu*s Gylmyn app*re*nticius Joh*ann*is Lagage –	xx s.
Joh*anne*s Bedford app*re*nt*icius* Joh*ann*is Stalkyngden*e* –	xx s.
Thomas Munden app*re*nt*icius* Ric*ard*i Frith*e* –	xx s.
Thomas Faukes app*re*nticius Will*elm*i Goteley –	xx s.
Ric*ard*us Neweman app*re*nticius Thome Codyngton –	xx s.
Will*elmu*s Coup*er*e app*re*nt*icius* Joh*ann*is Parker –	xx s.
Will*elmu*s Flour app*re*nt*icius* Ric*ard*i Withihale –	xx s.
Will*elmu*s Mariot app*re*nt*icius* Joh*ann*is Wynne –	xx s.
Henr*icus* Geyre app*re*nt*icius* Joh*ann*is Mabilian –	xx s.
Will*elmu*s Freke app*re*nt*icius* Joh*ann*is Hertwell*e* –	xx s.
Ric*ard*us Skarlet app*re*nt*icius* eiusdem Joh*ann*is –	xx s.

641 The note 'va*cat*' has been made in the LH margin against this entry, but it has not been scored out.

642 It is also very possible that the scribe has here gone into French, and that this should read 'd'un flemyng a Westm''.

Memorandum that John Hilt, chaplain, was presented in the same year to Sir John Barnsley, parson of the church of St John Zachary, to sing daily mass there during his lifetime for the soul of Drew Barantyn and his wife and others and he was sworn to this on the last day of March in the same year.

Memorandum about defects in workmanship etc in the time of Robert Walton, John Joce, Richard Spencer and John Edmund, Wardens etc, in the year 1 Henry VI [1423–24]: 1423–24 A + b p. 78

Firstly, John Kingsdon for a defect in workmanship – 2s.
Item, Piers Brentwood for the same – 12d.
Item, William Hope for the same – 2s.
Item, John Coupland for the same – 20d.
Item, Hans Flemyng for the same – 18d.
Item, Ludwig Pope for the same – 6s. 8d.
Item, Dun Flemyng[226] in Westminster – 20d.

Item, John Kingsdon for a certain offence committed with his companion in a tavern – 20d.
Item, John Topclyf for the same – 3s. 4d.
Item, Clays, 'Dutchman', from a fine because he was working with John Waterley without the permission of the Wardens – 6s. 8d.

These are the names of the Wardens elected at the feast of St Dunstan in the year 2 Henry VI [19 May 1424] until the next following feastday aforesaid of St Dunstan: 1424–25 A + a p. 137

John Pake
John Pattesley
Thomas Leget
Robert Cringleford

The names of apprentices:

Thomas Pitlesdene apprentice of John Pauley –	20s.
William Gilmyn apprentice of John Lagage –	20s.
John Bedford apprentice of John Stalkendene –	20s.
Thomas Munden apprentice of Richard Frithe –	20s.
Thomas Faukes apprentice of William Goteley –	20s.
Richard Newman apprentice of Thomas Coddington –	20s.
William Couper apprentice of John Parker –	20s.
William Flour apprentice of Richard Withihale –	20s.
William Mariot apprentice of John Wynne –	20s.
Henry Geyre apprentice of John Mablean –	20s.
William Freke apprentice of John Hertwell –	20s.
Richard Skarlet apprentice of the same John –	20s.

[226] Or: from a Fleming.

Martinus Peres app*rentic*i*us* Joh*ann*is Sturdys –	xx s.
Joh*ann*es Roberd app*rentic*i*us* Ric*ard*i Wynt*er* –	xx s.
Joh*ann*es Munton app*rentic*i*us* Joh*ann*is Teukesbury jun*ioris* –	xx s.
Will*elmus* Corbyn app*rentic*i*us* Joh*ann*is Topclyf –	xx s.
Rob*er*tus Toly app*rentic*i*us* Joh*ann*is Pattesley –	xx s.
Henr*icus* Cagge app*rentic*i*us* Galeas Taverne –	xx s.
(Will*iam*)[643] Hyle app*rentic*i*us* Thome Remy –	xx s.
Joh*ann*es Chille app*rentic*i*us* Joh*ann*is Philip –	xx s.
Nich*ol*aus Tomvyle app*rentic*i*us* Hermani Dagetes –	xx s.
Joh*ann*es Bertilmewessone app*rentic*i*us* Nich*ol*ai Lovet –	xx s.
Nich*ol*aus Maudesley app*rentic*i*us* Mathei Philip –	xx s.
Joh*ann*es Grene app*rentic*i*us* Joh*ann*is Cary –	xx s.

Alloc*ati* jur*ati*:

Will*elmus* Umvile nup*er* apprenticius Joh*ann*is Sutton*e* sen*ioris* –	ii s.
Joh*ann*es Cary nup*er* app*rentic*i*us* Joh*ann*is Pattesley –	ii s.
Thomas Elys nup*er* app*rentic*i*us* Joh*ann*is Biernes –	ii s.

Joh*ann*es Colney jun*ior* solvit p*re*fatis custodib*us* x s. p*ro* licencia h*ab*end*a* *oper*ari in arte sua durante tempore app*re*nticialitat*is* sue – x s.

It*em*, Nich*ol*aus Billyngdou*n* solvit p*re*fatis custodib*us* p*ro* eadem causa – v s.

Item, Rob*er*tus Assheby p*ro* eo q*uo*d ip*s*e rep*ro*bavit Rob*ert*em Cryngelford, unu*m* custodum artis p*re*d*ic*te, ordinatum fuit q*uo*d ip*s*e solv*er*et elemosine S*anc*ti Dunstani C s., unde p*er*donatu*m* fuit eidem lx s. *et* solvit xl s.

1425 Nota:

p. 138 Memorandu*m* q*uo*d quarto die Maii anno p*re*d*ic*to Swether Selvestre, Ducheman, venit coram p*re*fatis custodib*us* *et* ibidem juravit sup*er* librum bene, fidelit*er* *et* honeste op*er*ari infra cam*er*am suam auru*m* *et* argentu*m* ac om*n*ia secreta artis sue p*re*d*ic*te fidelit*er* custodire, et q*uo*d non recipiet in s*er*vient*em* suu*m* p*re*t*er* unu*m* s*er*vientem ad semel[644] *et* hoc erit p*er* spaciu*m* septem annor*um* *et* solvet p*ro* tali s*er*viente h*ab*endo custodib*us* p*ro* tempore introitus sui existentib*us* xx s. et juravit insup*er* q*uo*d non utet*ur* aliquib*us* feriis sive nundinis ext*ra* civitatem London', et p*ro* huiusmodi licencia sibi dat*a* solvit p*re*fatus Swether d*ic*tis custodib*us* – viii li.

1425 Nota:[645]

Memorandu*m* q*uo*d quartodec*imo* die Julii anno p*re*d*ic*to Hans Dubler ven*i*t coram p*re*fat*is* custodib*us* *et* ibid*e*m juravit sup*er* libru*m* q*uo*d nu*nqua*m

[643] This name has been erased but no replacement made.

[644] In 1427–28 he nevertheless obtained permission to take on two servants at the same time: see below, A + a, p. 145.

[645] This paragraph has been added in another hand, but at roughly the same time.

Martin Peres apprentice of John Sturdys –	20s.
John Robert apprentice of Richard Wynter –	20s.
John Munton apprentice of John Tewkesbury the younger –	20s.
William Corbyn apprentice of John Topclyf –	20s.
Robert Toly apprentice of John Pattesley –	20s.
Henry Cagge apprentice of Galeas Taverne –	20s.
(William) Hyle[227] apprentice of Thomas Remy –	20s.
John Chille apprentice of John Philip –	20s.
Nicholas Tomvyle apprentice of Hermann Dagetes –	20s.
John Bartholomewson apprentice of Nicholas Lovet –	20s.
Nicholas Maudesley apprentice of Matthew Philip –	20s.
John Grene apprentice of John Cary –	20s.

Serving-men sworn:

William Umvile former apprentice of John Sutton the elder –	2s.
John Cary former apprentice of John Pattesley –	2s.
Thomas Elys former apprentice of John Barnes –	2s.

John Colney the younger has paid the aforesaid wardens 10s. to have permission to work in his mistery [at his craft] during the time of his apprenticeship – 10s.

Item, Nicholas Billington has paid the aforesaid wardens for the same cause – 5s.

Item, Robert Ashby, whereas he spoke words against Robert Cringleford, one of the wardens of the aforesaid mistery, it was ordered that he should pay 100s. to the alms funds of St Dunstan, of which 60s. was remitted him and he paid 40s.

Note: 1425
Memorandum that on 4 May of the aforesaid year [1425] Swether Silvester, p. 138
'Dutchman', came before the aforesaid wardens and there he swore on the book to work gold and silver well, faithfully and honestly in his own room, and to keep faithfully all the secrets of his aforesaid mistery, and that he would not take on more than one serving-man at any one time and this for a period of seven years, and that he would pay 20s. to have such a serving-man to the wardens in office at the time of his admission, and he swore also that he would not frequent any markets or fairs outside the city of London, and to obtain such permission the aforesaid Swether paid to the said wardens – £8.

Note:
Memorandum that on 14 July of the aforesaid year Hans Dobler came before the aforesaid wardens and there he swore on the book that he would never

227 This is very probably William Hilles: see Name Index.

imposterum deliberaret aliqua jocalia de auro operata donec prius monstrarentur gardianis pro tempore existentibus sub pena . . .

1424–25 A + b p. 85[646] Memorandum de defectibus operacionum etc tempore Johannis Pake, Johannis Pattesley, Thome Leget et Roberti Cryngelford, custodum etc, anno regni Regis Henrici sexti secundo

In primis, Henricus Busshe pro defectu operacionis monilis auri pond' xv d. – xxxiii s. iiii d.

Item, Hans Unycorn pro defectu operacionis iii unc' anulorum auri en alay – xxxiii s. iiii d.

Item, Gyse Paunser pro defectu operacionis auri – xxxiii s. iiii d.

Item, Gyse Bryght a les frere[s] Austynes pro eodem – xxxiii s. iiii d.

Item, Ricardus Bradcok pro defectu operacionis unius anuli auri – xiii s. iiii d.

Item, Philippus, Ducheman, pro defectu etc i anuli auri pond' i d. – vi s. viii d.

Item, de Saundres Wyf pro defectu etc auri – x s.

Item, de Hermano Horn pro eodem etc – xl s.

Item, de Coster, Ducheman, etc pro eodem – vi s. viii d.

Item, de Roberto Walton pro eodem etc – vi s. viii d.

Item, de Saundres Wyf de defectu operacionis i bokel et i pendant argenti – ii s.

Item, de Dederyk en Suthwerk pro defectu operacionis ii poynt' argenti – ii s.

Item, de j[647] Ducheman a le Watergate en Suthwerk pro defectu operacionis argenti – ii s.

Item, de Johanne Norwelle pro defectu operacionis argenti etc – ii s.

Item, de Willelmo, Ducheman, pro defectu etc argenti – ii s.

1425–26 A + a p. 139 Ceux sont les nouns des Gardeins eslutz al feste de Seint Dunston l'an du regne le Roy Henry sisme tierce tanqe al feste de Seint Dunston avantdit adonqes proschein ensuaunt:

Johan Palynge
Richard Withihale
Willelmus Rus
Petrus Brendwode

Nomina apprenticiorum:

Simon Umfrey apprenticius Ricardi Bradcok –	xx s.
Thomas Prewe apprenticius Johannis Welles –	xx s.
Ricardus Sewale apprenticius Johannis Umvile –	xx s.
Thomas Shatkulle apprenticius Stephani Colney –	xx s.
Johannes Rothewelle apprenticius Johannis Colney –	xx s.
Johannes Hardyng apprenticius Johannis Lagage –	xx s.
Johannes Harsyk apprenticius Roberti Boteler –	xx s.

[646] A different hand starts here, the same as wrote pp. 76–78.
[647] This might possibly be 'J.' = Johan.

hereafter allow out of his workshop any decorative precious pieces worked in gold before they had been first inspected by the current wardens, upon penalty . . .

Memorandum about defects in workmanship etc. during the time of John Pake, John Pattesley, Thomas Leget and Robert Cringleford, wardens etc., in the year 2 Henry VI [1424–25]: 1424–25 A + b p. 85
Firstly, Henry Busshe for a defect in the workmanship of a gold collar[228] weighing 15dwt. – 33s. 4d.
Item, Hans Unycorn for a defect in the workmanship in 3 ounces of gold rings – in the alloy – 33s. 4d.
Item, Gyse Panser for a defect in the workmanship of gold – 33s. 4d.
Item, Gysebright at the Austin Friars for the same – 33s. 4d.
Item, Richard Bradcok for a defect in the workmanship of a gold ring – 13s. 4d.
Item, Philip, 'Dutchman', for a defect etc. in a gold ring weighing 1d. – 6s. 8d.
Item, from Saunders' wife for a defect etc. of gold – 10s.
Item, from Hermann Horn for the same etc. – 40s.
Item, from Coster, 'Dutchman', etc. for the same – 6s. 8d.
Item, from Robert Walton for the same etc. – 6s. 8d.
Item, from Saunders' wife for a defect in the workmanship of a silver buckle and pendant – 2s.
Item, from Dederyk in Southwark for a defect in the workmanship of 2 silver points[229] – 2s.
Item, from a 'Dutchman' at the Watergate in Southwark for a defect in the workmanship of silver – 2s.
Item, from John Norwell for a defect in the workmanship of silver etc. – 2s.
Item, from William, 'Dutchman', for a defect etc. of silver – 2s.

These are the names of the Wardens elected at the feast of St Dunstan in the year 3 Henry VI [19 May 1425] until the next following feastday of St Dunstan aforesaid: 1425–26 A + a p. 139
John Palyng
Richard Withihale
William Russ
Piers Brentwood

The names of apprentices:

Simon Umfrey apprentice of Richard Bradcok –	20s.
Thomas Prewe apprentice of John Welles –	20s.
Richard Sewale apprentice of John Umvile –	20s.
Thomas Shatkulle apprentice of Stephen Colney –	20s.
John Rothwell apprentice of John Colney –	20s.
John Harding apprentice of John Lagage –	20s.
John Harsyk apprentice of Robert Botiller –	20s.

228 The Latin 'monile' can be translated as 'necklace' or 'collar'. At this period it is likely that the reference is to a 'collar', an ornamental chain worn around the neck such as a livery collar.
229 'Points' are the ends of tags for dress. See G. Egan *et al.*, *Dress Accessories*, pp. 281–90: 'Lace Chapes'.

Ric*ard*us Morcok app*rent*icius Thome Whitmore –	xx s.
Will*elmu*s Hunte app*rent*icius Thome Remy –	xx s.
Will*elmu*s Eliot app*rent*icius Joh*ann*is Pake –	xx s.
Thomas Parker app*rent*icius Thurstani Furneys –	xx s.
Henr*icus* Hawe app*rent*icius Petri Torold –	xx s.
Joh*ann*es Hopkyn app*rent*icius Henr*ici* Wikwane –	xx s.
Joh*ann*es Frensshe app*rent*icius eiusdem Henr*ici* –	xx s.
Will*elmu*s Osmond app*rent*icius Will*elm*i Wikwane –	xx s.
Simon Benham app*rent*icius Joh*ann*is Waryn –	xx s.
Joh*ann*es Page app*rent*icius Joh*ann*is Teukesb*ur*y sen*ioris* –	xx s.
Ric*ard*us Arondell*e* app*rent*icius Rob*er*ti Assheby –	xx s.
Thomas Kayrus app*rent*icius Joh*ann*is Frenssh*e* –	xx s.
Thomas Whytbred app*rent*icius Will*elm*i Rus –	xx s.
Will*elmu*s Sexton*e* app*rent*icius Steph*an*i Colney –	xx s.
Joh*ann*es Jurdon*e* app*rent*icius Galfr*idi* Neweton*e* –	xx s.
Rob*er*tus Rose app*rent*icius Will*elm*i Rus –	xx s.
Henr*icus* Shordych*e* app*rent*icius Nich*ola*i atte Wode –	xx s.

Alloc*ati* jur*ati*:

Will*elmu*s Wikwane nup*er* app*rent*icius Henr*ici* Wikwane –	ii s.
Rob*er*tus Lovekyn nup*er* app*rent*icius Joh*ann*is Bisshop –	ii s.
Joh*ann*es Stok nup*er* app*rent*icius Ric*ardi* Stacy –	ii s.
Thurston Furneys nup*er* app*rent*icius Will*elm*i Botou*n* –	ii s.
Joh*ann*es Biernes nup*er* app*rent*icius Henr*ici* Chamb*er*leyn –	ii s.
Thomas Peryn nup*er* app*rent*icius Will*elm*i Cheyne –	ii s.
Joh*ann*es Colney jun*ior* nup*er* app*rent*icius Joh*ann*is Colney sen*ioris* –	ii s.
Thomas Herrysson*e* nup*er* app*rent*icius Joh*ann*is Joce –	ii s.
Galfr*idu*s Neweton*e* nup*er* app*rent*icius Thome Welles –	ii s.
Joh*ann*es Gate nup*er* app*rent*icius Joh*annis* Orewell*e* –	ii s.
Joh*ann*es Pryce nup*er* app*rent*icius Will*elm*i Markeby –	ii s.
Nich*ola*us Billyngdou*n* nup*er* app*rent*icius Elizabeth Fraunceys –	ii s.[648]
Laurencius Chylmylle nup*er* app*rent*icius Ric*ardi* George –	ii s.
Thomas Codyngton*e* nup*er* app*rent*icius Joh*ann*is Cheyham –	ii s.

It*em*, Matheus Philipp p*ro* eo q*uo*d ip*s*e rep*ro*bavit Henr*icum* Clerk nup*er* mag*istru*m suu*m* in p*re*sencia gardianor*um* – vi s. viii d.

1425 A*nno* 3° H. 6*i*:

p. 140 Hit is to remembr*e* how that in the begynnyng of Aprill*e* the third yeer of Kyng Harry the sixt, John Hilles, citezein & goldsmyth of London, had on John Richard to his app*re*ntis, the which app*re*ntis for div*er*s grete offences & trespaces that he had done to his mayst*er,* the same John Hilles wold have chastised hym as reson & the comune usage is of app*re*ntis to be chastised of her maystres whan they t*re*space, the which app*re*ntis, seyng that his maister wold have chastised hym & rewlid hym as reson wold, of v*er*rey malice & cursidnes as an obstinat app*re*ntis to his maist*er* went up forthwith on a staire

648 In 1416–17 he was listed as the apprentice of Richard Chaumbre. See above, A + a, p. 117, and Name Index.

Richard Morcok apprentice of Thomas Whitmore –	20s.
William Hunte apprentice of Thomas Remy –	20s.
William Eliot apprentice of John Pake –	20s.
Thomas Parker apprentice of Thurstan Furneys –	20s.
Henry Hawe apprentice of Piers Thorold –	20s.
John Hopkyn apprentice of Henry Wykwan –	20s.
John Frenshe apprentice of the same Henry –	20s.
William Osmond apprentice of William Wykwan –	20s.
Simon Benham apprentice of John Waryn –	20s.
John Page apprentice of John Tewkesbury the elder –	20s.
Richard Arundel apprentice of Robert Ashby –	20s.
Thomas Kayrus apprentice of John Frenshe –	20s.
Thomas Whitbread apprentice of William Russ –	20s.
William Sexton apprentice of Stephen Colney –	20s.
John Jurdone apprentice of Geoffrey Newton –	20s.
Robert Rose apprentice of William Russ –	20s.
Henry Shoreditch apprentice of Nicholas atte Wood –	20s.

Serving-men sworn:

William Wykwan former apprentice of Henry Wykwan –	2s.
Robert Lovekyn former apprentice of John Bisshop –	2s.
John Stok former apprentice of Richard Stacy –	2s.
Thurston Furneys former apprentice of William Botoun –	2s.
John Barnes former apprentice of Henry Chamberlayn –	2s.
Thomas Peryn former apprentice of William Cheyne –	2s.
John Colney the younger former apprentice of John Colney the elder –	2s.
Thomas Harryson former apprentice of John Joce –	2s.
Geoffrey Newton former apprentice of Thomas Welles –	2s.
John Gate former apprentice of John Orwell –	2s.
John Pryce former apprentice of William Markeby –	2s.
Nicholas Billington former apprentice of Elizabeth Fraunceys –	2s.
Laurence Chyldemylle former apprentice of Richard George –	2s.
Thomas Coddington former apprentice of John Cheyham –	2s.

Item, Matthew Philip, whereas he spoke words against Henry Clerk, his former master, in the presence of the Wardens – 6s. 8d.

The year 3 Henry VI: p. 140

Memorandum that at the beginning of April in the year 3 Henry VI [1425] John Hilles, citizen and goldsmith of London, took on John Richard as his apprentice, and for various great offences and misdeeds that he committed against his master the same John Hilles wished to chastise this apprentice as is reasonable and as is the common usage for apprentices to be chastised by their masters when they offend. The which apprentice, seeing that his master wished reasonably to chastise and restrain him, out of true malice and cursedness and as a refractory apprentice against his master, forthwith went up a staircase out of the shoppe beryng with hym a short spere the whiche he hid in the kychyn imagynyng to kille his maist*er,* the whiche spere s*er*vyd to open & to shette the wyndowys of the shoppe. And whan he had so do he come dou*ne* ayen & in the myddes of the stayre he reviled his maister ful dispitously & ungoodly & seid to hym: 'Come on now, for it is hy tyme & I have ordeyned for the, and as I mote be saved thou shalt nev*er* come in to thi chambre.' And his maist*er,* consideryng that tyme his cursidnesse & how he was p*ur*posid to kille hym, for to eschewe all*e* man*er* p*er*ill*e* of bothe sides, fair & wele went owt of his hous & ordeyned so that the same app*re*ntis was anone arested & broght in to the Countour. Wher as[649]h.. ... unto the tyme that the wardeyns of the craft of goldsmythes sent for hym to knowe this mat*ere* & rewle it to an ... ende as hit falleth for hem to do by her priveleges and custumes to correcte the t*re*spaces and defautes done with in the same craft, for the seyd John Hilles had playnyd unto hem on his app*re*ntis & told hem all*e* the mat*ere* aboveseid. And aft*er* about the last ende of May the seid app*re*ntis was sent fore to apere byfor John Palyng, Richard Whithihale, William Rus & Piers Brendewode,[650] the wardeyns of the same craft, in p*re*sence of his seid maist*er* & of John Pake, Piers Thorold, John Edmond, John Walssh*e*, William Walton*e*, John Cryngilford, John Botoun, John Teukesbury. Richard Spencer, John Wissyngsete & John Leget, goldsmythes, & there the seid John Hilles was examyned & he playned hym there openly on his app*re*ntis rehersyng his untrouth*e* & unbuxunesse & how he wold have killed hy*m* as hit is byfor rehersid. And the app*re*ntis was also examyned in the same mat*ere*, what he seid therto & how he wold excuse hym. And in p*re*sence of the seid wardeyns & all*e* the worshipfull*e* folke above seid, the app*re*ntis cowde not withsey that his mayst*er* put upon hym but openly knowlechid that he bere the seid wepyn in to the kychyn redy to defende hym with ayens his maist*er* as wele as he cowde. Upon which*e* knowlech*e* the seid wardeyns & felawship seydyn that the same app*re*ntis was foul defectif & askid hym how he wolde aquyte hym & make amendis to his mayster & he seid he had no good ne he wyst nev*er* how to make amendis but he desired to have s*er*vyd another man of the same craft. And the wardeyns cowde none fynde that hym wold have & so he was remytted ayen to the Countour at that tyme to be better avised ayens the next day that he were sent fore. And aft*er* the seid wardeyns examyned his maist*er* in p*re*sence of worshipfull*e* men of the same craft, askyng hym whethir he wold have his s*er*vice ayen or not. And he answerd: 'Nay'. And at the next day that the app*re*ntis come bifore the seid wardeins, thei asked hym how he was avised & what he wold do & if he had founde any wey how he myght make his pees with his maist*er* & he seid he wist not howe. And tho the seid wardeyns, consideryng the grete falsnesse, rebellyng & cursidnesse of the seid app*re*ntis, the whiche myght turne to undoyng & evill*e* ensample of many another app*re*ntis ayens her maistres in the same craft & in other also but if it had be dewly remedied, askid the seid app*re*ntis

[649] There is a small hole in the page here and on the next line.
[650] These four names have been underlined.

outside the shop carrying with him a short spear which he hid in the kitchen intending to kill his master (this 'spear' was used to open and shut the windows of the shop). And when he had done that he came down again and in the middle of the staircase he most contemptuously and wickedly insulted his master and said to him: 'Come on then, for it is high time and I am ready prepared for thee, and, God help me, thou shalt never enter thy chamber.' And his master, considering his wickedness at that time and that he was intending to kill him, in order to avoid any danger to either of them went straight out of his house and arranged for the same apprentice to be arrested forthwith and brought to the Counter.[230] And there he [remained] until the time that the Wardens of the Goldsmiths' Mistery sent for him to find out about this matter and pass judgment upon it, as it is incumbent upon them to do according to their privileges and customs in correcting the offences and defects committed within the same mistery, because the said John Hilles had lodged a complaint with them about his apprentice and had told them all the above. And at about the end of May the said apprentice was sent for to appear before John Palyng, Richard Withihale, William Rus and Piers Brentwood, the Wardens of the same mistery, in the presence of his said master and of John Pake, Piers Thorold, John Edmund, John Walsh, William Walton, John Cringleford, John Botoun, John Tewkesbury, Richard Spencer, John Wissyngsete[231] and John Leget, goldsmiths, and there the said John Hilles was examined and he made open complaint there about his apprentice, going through again all that is said above about his unfaithfulness, his disobedience and how he would have killed him. And the apprentice was also examined in the same matter, to see what he had to say about it and what excuses he might have. And in the presence of the said Wardens and all the worshipful men mentioned above, the apprentice could not deny what his master accused him of but openly acknowledged that he had taken the said weapon into the kitchen in order to defend himself against his master as well as he could. Upon which admission the said Wardens and fellowship said that the apprentice was basely at fault and they asked him how he wished to make atonement and to make amends to his master, and he said that he possessed nothing and knew not how to make amends, but he wished to serve another man of the same mistery. And the Wardens could find no one who would have him, and so he was sent back to the Counter to think carefully about what he would say on the next day when he was sent for. And afterwards the said Wardens examined his master in the presence of worshipful men of the same mistery, asking him whether he would take him back into service or not. And he answered 'No.' And on the next day when the apprentice came before the said Wardens, they asked him what conclusions he had come to, and what he wished to do, and if he had found any way that he might make his peace with his master, and he said that he knew not how. And then the said Wardens, considering the great falsity, rebellion and wickedness of the said apprentice, which might be an evil example against their masters and the cause of undoing to many other apprentices in the same mistery and in others unless it were duly remedied, asked the said apprentice upon the wish and the request

[230] The prison attached to the Mayor's court and of which the sheriffs were in charge.

[231] This man is a lawyer, elected into the Goldsmiths' Mistery in 1407–08 in order to be their 'counsel'. See A + a, p. 100 above.

by the desire & askynge of his maist*er* whethir he wold forswere the craft the toun but if it were a gest wyse, or abide stil in prison*e* til he had ordeyned such*e* wey & such*e* frenship that myght*e* fynde sufficiaunt seurtee & make sufficeant amendes to his maist*er* for the t*re*spas aboveseid, & bad hym chese which*e* he wold do of this at his own p*er*ill*e* & not another day to acuse ne defame the wardeyns ne the goodmen of the craft, whatev*er* fill*e* of hym, seying that thei constreyned hym therto, but that at his owne choys he shold chese & avise hym wele what he wold do. And at the last by his owne will*e* & p*ro*pre assent he chas to forswere the craft & the toun*e*. And moreov*er* John Walssh*e* & John Fynk the yong*er*, citezeins & goldsmythes of the same citee, recorded opynly with the maist*er* that it was trewe that the maist*er* seid ayens the app*re*ntis. And there the seid John Hilles delyverid to his app*re*ntis xx s. that he had in kepyng to his use & all*e* his (owne)[651] clothes & aray & also deliv*er*ed unto the seid wardeyns the endenture of his app*re*ntishood. And therupon the seid wardeyns by good delib*er*acion & assent of the worthi men afore nempned, & also the chois of the seid app*re*ntis, ordeyneden & awarded, & ȝaf for juggement that the seid app*re*ntis shold forswere the seid craft & the toun, not for to dwelle theryn, upon peyne that if ev*er* he used the seid craft & dwelled in London his endenture of app*re*ntisholde shold be deliv*er*ed ayen to his maist*er*, he for to take his axion & clayme ayens hym without eny allegance or condicion in all*e* man*er* wise as hole & effectuely as he had & myght have had the day that he did the t*re*spas to hym, notwithstondyng any thyng aft*er*ward done by the wardeyns.

1425–26 Item, p*ro* eo q*uo*d Hans Dropmond, Ducheman, s*er*viens Henr*ici* atte
p. 141[652] Busshe, pro eo q*uo*d inventus fuit defectivus in op*eracione* . . . div*er*sor*um* monili*um* auri in quodam giardino suspecto juxta les Crouched Freres . . . sup*er* sacr*amentu*m suum coram custodib*us* p*re*d*ict*is quod nunquam op*er*abit . . . in London' nec suburbiis eiusdem in cam*er*a sua nec alibi nisi erit cum uno mag*istr*o qui sit lib*er* homo civitatis p*re*dicte et . . . p*re*fatus Hans obligatus est p*er* quoddam script*um* suu*m* obligatori*um* in viginti libris quod . . . Thesaurar' . . . *et* solvit . . .

1425–26 Memorand*um* de defectib*us* op*er*acionu*m* tempore Joh*ann*is Palynge, Ric*ard*i
A + b p. 86 Withihale, Will*elm*i Rus *et* Petri Brendwode, custodum *etc*, anno r*egni* r*egis* Henr*ici* sexti t*er*cio:

In primis, Gyse Van Deyste p*ro* defectu op*eracion*is iiii anulor*um* et v monili*um* auri – xl s.
It*em*, Hans Cofman in Suthwerk p*ro* def*ect*u op*er*a*cion*is monili*um* auri – xiii s. iiiid.
It*em*, Jacobus Buk p*ro* def*ect*u op*eracion*is uni*us* anuli auri – vi s. viii d.

651 This word has been scored out.
652 This page has clearly been treated as scrap paper, and a number of scribbled sums, figures, and a few odd words are found, especially down the LH side. The short paragraph at the top is very faded, and, as on previous pages commented on, an attempt has been made to make these words more legible by applying some chemical solution, which has only resulted in bad discolouration of the paper.

of his master whether he would forswear the mistery and the City, and whether this would be a wise action, or whether he would stay in prison until he had devised a way and found such friends as might provide sufficient surety and make sufficient amends to his master for the aforesaid offence, and they asked him to choose which of these he would do, and this was to be at his own peril, and he must never at any other time, whatever might happen to him, accuse or defame the wardens nor the goodmen of the mistery, saying that they had forced him into this, but it should be his own choice, and he should consider and choose well what he wished to do. And in the end of his own free will and his own consent he chose to forswear the mistery and the City. And moreover John Walsh and John Fynk the younger, citizens and goldsmiths of the same City, put on public record with the master that what the master said against his apprentice was true. And at that time the said John Hilles handed over to his apprentice 20s. which he had in safe-keeping for him and all his (own) clothes and belongings, and he also handed over to the said Wardens his apprenticeship indenture. And then the said wardens with good consideration and with the assent of the worthy men aforenamed, and also by the choice of the said apprentice, ordained and judged and passed sentence that the said apprentice should forswear the said mistery and the City, that he should not live there, upon pain that if he ever practised the said craft and lived in London, his apprenticeship indenture would be handed over again to his master so that he might take action and claim against him, no alleviation or condition applying, and this to have as full effect and validity as it would have had on the day that he committed the offence against him, notwithstanding anything afterwards done by the wardens.

Item, whereas Hans Dropmond, 'Dutchman', servant of Henry atte Busshe, was found at fault in the workmanship . . . of various gold collars in a certain suspect garden next to the Crutched Friars . . . upon his oath in the presence of the aforesaid wardens that he shall never work . . . in London or in its suburbs, in his room or anywhere else unless it be with a master who is a freeman of the aforesaid City and . . . the aforesaid Hans is bound by certain letters obligatory in the sum of £20 which . . . Treasury . . . and he paid . . . 1425–26 p. 141

Memorandum about defects in workmanship during the time of John Palyng, Richard Withihale, William Rus and Piers Brentwood, Wardens etc., in the year 3 Henry VI [from 19 May 1425]: 1425–26 A + b p. 86

Firstly, Gyse van Deste for a defect in the workmanship of 4 gold rings and 5 gold collars – 40s.
Item, Hans Cofman in Southwark for a defect in the workmanship of gold collars – 13s. 4d.
Item, Jacob Bukke for a defect in the workmanship of a gold ring – 6s. 8d.

It*em*, Thomas South p*ro* def*ect*u op*er*aci*on*is argenti – vi s. viii d.

It*em*, Joh*anne*s Pope p*ro* eodem – ii s.

It*em*, Will*elmu*s Coup*ere* p*ro* eodem – ii s.

It*em*, Matheus Philipp*e* p*ro* eodem – iiii s.

It*em*, Will*elmu*s Stevenessone p*ro* eodem – ii s.

It*em*, Nich*ola*us Billyngdon p*ro* eodem – ii s.

It*em*, Ric*ardus* Bradcok quia recepit unu*m* app*r*enticiu*m* absq*ue* licencia gardianor*um* – vi s. viii d.

It*em*, Joh*anne*s Welles p*ro* eodem – vi s. viii d.

It*em*, Joh*anne*s Stok p*ro* eodem – vi s. viii d.

It*em*, Rob*er*tus Bosoun p*ro* div*er*sis defectib*us* – xx s.[653]

It*em*, recept*um* de executorib*us* Joh*ann*is de Gaunt, videl*ice*t Hans Holthous *et* Gerard Alfkyn – xl s.

1426–27 A+a p. 142[654] Ceux sont les nouns des Gardeyns eslutz al feste de Seint Dunston l'an du regne le Roi Henry sisme quart tanqe al [feste de Seint Dunston av*a*ntdit] adonqes p*ro*schein ensuant:

Joh*a*n Wynne
[William Boton]
[Joh*a*n Sutton, junior]
Joh*a*n [Orwell]

Nomina apprenticiorum

Joh*anne*s Marshalle apprenticius Joh*ann*is Wynne –	xx s.
Will*elmu*s . . .falle apprenticius Will*elm*i Soton –	xx s.
Thom*as* Message apprenticius Thome Codyngton –	xx s.
Thom*as* ?Hex?borogh apprenticius Will*elm*i Stevenson*e* –	xx s.
Joh*anne*s Res? . . . apprenticius Thome Reyner –	xx s.
Joh*anne*s Drayton apprenticius Isabelle Joce –	xx s.
Jacobus Gay apprenticius Joh*ann*is Emond –	xx s.
Joh*anne*s Goldford apprenticius Rob*er*ti Bosoun –	xx s.
Joh*anne*s Asshe[r]st apprenticius Will*elm*i Walton –	xx s.[655]
Joh*anne*s apprenticius Joh*ann*is Bustard –	xx s.
Will*elmu*s Fynyngham apprenticius Joh*ann*is Pake –	xx s.
Joh*anne*s Penne apprenticius Joh*ann*is Bowdon –	xx s.
Joh*anne*s Norman apprenticius Joh*ann*is Weterys –	xx s.
Rokewode apprenticius Joh*ann*is Bernes –	xx s.
Will*elmu*s Boston apprenticius Petri Brendewode –	xx s.
Joh*anne*s Wiltshire apprenticius Steph*an*i Colle –	xx s.
Joh*anne*s Chillwel(?) apprenticius Math*e*i Phillippe –	xx s.
Nich*ola*us Fissher apprenticius Joh*ann*is Fitzrobert –	xx s.

653 A LH margin note against this entry has been partially obscured by the insertion of the page into modern paper; it appears to say: [bo]sou*n*.

654 This page is also badly faded, and has also been used as scrap paper, but no chemical solutions have been applied to it, unless what appear to be inkspots in the lower RH part of the page are in fact spilt chemical drops. UV-light has been used but many readings are tentative.

655 The name 'Johannes Theke' has been written in above this line, and at the end of the line has been added 'Sanpayeers/Sanpayeynge'(?).

Item, Thomas South for a defect in the workmanship of silver – 6s. 8d.
Item, John Pope for the same – 2s.
Item, William Coupere for the same – 2s.
Item, Matthew Philip for the same – 4s.
Item, William Stevenson for the same – 2s.
Item, Nicholas Billington for the same – 2s.
Item, Richard Bradcok because he took on an apprentice without the permission of the wardens – 6s. 8d.
Item, John Welles for the same – 6s. 8d.
Item, John Stok for the same – 6s. 8d.
Item, Robert Bosoun for various defects – 20s.
Item, received from the executors of John de Ghent, i.e. Hans Holthous and Gerard Alfkyn – 40s.

These are the names of the wardens elected at the feast of St Dunstan in the year 4 Henry VI [19 May 1426] until the next following feastday of St Dunstan aforesaid: 1426–27 A + a p. 142
John Wynne
William Botoun
John Sutton the younger
John Orwell

The names of apprentices:

John Marshalle apprentice of John Wynne –	20s.
William . . falle apprentice of William Soton –	20s.
Thomas Message apprentice of Thomas Coddington –	20s.
Thomas Hexborogh (?) apprentice of William Stevenson –	20s.
John Res . . apprentice of Thomas Reyner –	20s.
John Drayton apprentice of Isabelle Joce –	20s.
James Gay apprentice of John Edmund –	20s.
John Goldford apprentice of Robert Bosoun –	20s.
John Ashurst apprentice of William Walton –	20s.[232]
John . . . apprentice of John Bustard –	20s.
William Finningham apprentice of John Pake –	20s.
John Penne apprentice of John Bowdon –	20s.
John Norman apprentice of John Weterys –	20s.
. . . Rockwood apprentice of John Barnes –	20s.
William Boston apprentice of Piers Brentwood –	20s.
John Wiltshire apprentice of Stephen Colney –	20s.
John Chillwel apprentice of Matthew Philip –	20s.
Nicholas Fisher apprentice of John FitzRobert –	20s.

[232] The note against the name of John Theke probably means ‘without paying’.

Tregenyk apprenticius Rog*er*i Warburgh*e* – xx s.
Joh*ann*es Burneille apprenticius Joh*ann*is Sutton, jun*ioris* – xx s.

Alloc*ati* jur*ati*:
Thomas Joly nup*er* apprenticius Thome S[outhe] – ii s.
Joh*ann*es Adys nup*er* apprenticius Steph*an*i Colle – ii s.
Rob*er*tus Brampton nup*er* apprent*icius* Joh*ann*is Pake – ii s.
Will*elmu*s Frederike nup*er* apprent*icius* Johannis Pake – ii s.
Ric*ard*us Water nup*er* apprent*icius* Joh*ann*is – ii s.

1426–27 A + b p. 87[656] Memorand*um* de defectib*us* op*er*acionu*m* temp*or*e Joh*ann*is Wynne, Will*elm*i Boton, Joh*ann*is Sutton jun*ioris et* Joh*ann*is Orwell, custodum *et*c, anno r*egni* R*egis* Henrici sexti quarto

In primis, de Will*elm*o Alkam – ii s.
De Tilmanno Gay – ii s.
De Galfr*id*o Newton – ii s.
De Joh*ann*e Clever p*ro* una defalt*a* cont*ra* ordinac*iones* – ii s.
De Joh*ann*e Stalkynden – ii s.
De Wynslowe Dobekyn – ii s.
De Thoma Elys – ii s.
De Will*elm*o Coup*er* – ii s.
De Swethir, Ducheman – ii s.[657]
De[658] Langlee – ii s.
De Joh*ann*e Luke op*er*acio*n*' domus in Bredstrete – vi s. viii d.
It*em*, Thomas Gabrielle[659] solvit q*uia* non p*re*sent*avit* app*re*ntic*ium* gardianis suis cont*ra* ordinac*ionem* – iii s. iiii d.
It*em*, de Henr*ico*, Ducheman, p*ro* licencia h*ab*enda ad op*er*and*um* – vi s. viii d.
It*em*, de Hans Blithe p*ro* eodem – vi s. viii d.
It*em*, de Blak Hans p*ro* defalt*a* cont*ra* ordinac*iones* – viii s. iiii d.
It*em*, de Magnus Awferdon p*ro* i defalt*a* – vi s. viii d.
It*em*, de Hans Holtehous p*ro* ven*ire* in lib*er*tatem – x li.

p. 88 [blank]

A + a p. 143 [blank]

[656] A new hand starts here.
[657] A LH margin note against this entry: S +.
[658] A space has been left to fill in the missing name.
[659] MS: Grabrielle. In the LH margin 'gabriell*e*' has been written, not in order to correct the spelling but, as with some others here, to pick out the name, probably because someone is counting the number of offences committed and the therefore appropriate penalty.

. . . Tregenyk apprentice of Roger Warburgh –	20s.
John Burneille apprentice of John Sutton the younger –	20s.

Serving-men sworn:

Thomas Joly formerly apprentice of Thomas South –	2s.
John Adys formerly apprentice of Stephen Colney –	2s.
Robert Brampton formerly apprentice of John Pake –	2s.
William Frederick formerly apprentice of John Pake –	2s.
Richard Water formerly apprentice of John –	2s.

Memorandum about defects in workmanship during the time of John Wynne, William Botoun, John Sutton the younger and John Orwell, Wardens etc., in the year 4 Henry VI [from 19 May 1426]: 1426–27 A + b p. 87

Firstly, from William Alkam – 2s.
from Tilmann Gay – 2s.
from Geoffrey Newton – 2s.
from John Clever for an offence against the ordinances – 2s.
from John Stalkendene – 2s.
from Winslow Dobekyn – 2s.
from Thomas Elys – 2s.
from William Coupere – 2s.
from Swethir, 'Dutchman' – 2s.
from Langley – 2s.
from John Luke for working at a house in Bread Street – 6s. 8d.
Item, Thomas Gabrielle paid for not having presented an apprentice to his Wardens against the ordinance – 3s. 4d.
Item, from Henry, 'Dutchman', to obtain permission to work – 6s. 8d.
Item, from Hans Blithe for the same – 6s. 8d.
Item, from Black Hans for an offence against the ordinances – 8s. 4d.
Item, from Magnus Afferdon for an offence – 6s. 8d.
Item, from Hans Holthous for entry into the freedom – £10.

[blank] p. 88

[blank] A + a p. 143

1427–28 p. 144[660] Ceux sount les nouns des Gardeyns eslutz al feste de Seint Dunston l'an du regne le Roy Henry sisme quint tanqe la dicte feste adonqes p*ro*schein ensuaunt:

Salamon Oxney
Petrus Thorold
Joh*ann*es Stalkenden
Joh*ann*es Werk

Nomina apprenticior*um*:[661]

Will*elmu*s Rotherh*a*m apprentic*ius* Will*elm*i Boton –	xx s.[662]
Joh*ann*es Sumpter apprenticius Rob*er*ti Walton –	xx s.
Joh*ann*es Burton apprenticius Ric*ard*i Bradcok –	xx s.
Thom*as* Tatele apprenticius Will*elm*i Tatele –	xx s.
Jhon Claud aprentice of Jhon Wynne –	xx s.[663]
. . .[664] apprenticius Rob*er*ti Boson –	xx s.
Joh*ann*es Fyler apprenticius Will*elm*i Waryn –	xx s.
Will*elmu*s Cambrey apprenticius Joh*ann*is Emond –	xx s.
Reinboldus Heryng apprentic*ius* Gise van Geste,[665] Ducheman –	xx s.
Ed*mund*us Seyntclowe apprentic*ius* Joh*ann*is Withyale –	xx s.
. . . apprenticius Rob*er*ti fitz Rob*er*t –	xx s.
Will*elmu*s Grobier apprenticius Will*elm*i Boton –	xx s.
Thomas Pomeray apprenticius Simonis Colson –	xx s.
Rad*ulph*us Thornage apprenticius Jacobi Tregewstek –	xx s.
Joh*ann*es Tregewstek apprenticius Jacobi Tregewstek –	xx s.
Nandewinus Tregare apprentic*ius* Thome Blythe –	xx s.
Rog*er*us Parker apprentic*ius* Johann[is][666] Downe –	xx s.[667]
James Goldsmyth apprenticius Steph*an*i Colle –	xx s.
. . . Von Vald apprenticius Joh*ann*is Crisbyn –	xx s.
Laur*encius* Lethyon apprenticius Joh*ann*is Waterley –	xx s.
Laurencius Bere apprenticius Joh*ann*is Werk –	xx s.
Thomas Erbery apprenticius Joh*ann*is Orwell –	xx s.
. . . apprenticius Joh*ann*is Bulstrode –	xx s.
Thom*as*[668] . . . apprenticius Joh*ann*is Bowdon –	xx s.
apprenticius Nich*ol*ai Lovet[669]	

Allocati jur*ati*:

Will*elmu*s Tatele nup*er* appr*enticius* Joh*annis* Tewkysbury sen*ioris* –	ii s.
Henr*icus* Horne nup*er* appr*enticius* Ric*ard*i Stacy –	ii s.
Joh*ann*es Weryng nup*er* appr*enticius* Th*om*e South –	ii s.
Thom*as* Penne nup*er* appr*enticius* Joh*ann*is Werk –	ii s.

660 A new hand starts here.
661 This list appears to have been written at various times, the scribe entering up the information as it was brought to him, and leaving spaces for further information, not all of which he obtained.
662 This line has been added later by the scribe.
663 This line has been added later by a different hand.
664 A blank space has been left for the name to be filled in later.
665 The name is clearly thus, but should perhaps read 'Deste': see Name Index.
666 MS: Johanne.
667 Another name has been added here but the ink has faded badly: '*et* Will' Aston'.
668 This is almost certainly Thomas Bowdon.
669 No figure of 20s. payment is added beside this name, which is very probably a scribal error.

These are the names of the Wardens elected at the feast of St Dunstan in the year 5 Henry VI [19 May 1427] until the next following feastday aforesaid: 1427–28 p. 144
Solomon Oxney
Piers Thorold
John Stalkendene
John Werk

The names of apprentices:

William Rotherham apprentice of William Botoun –	20s.
John Sumpter apprentice of Robert Walton –	20s.
John Burton apprentice of Richard Bradcok –	20s.
Thomas Takeley apprentice of William Takeley –	20s.
John Claud apprentice of John Wynne –	20s.
apprentice of Robert Bosoun –	20s.
John Fyler apprentice of William Waryn –	20s.
William Cambrey apprentice of John Edmund –	20s.
Reinbold Heryng apprentice of Gyse van Geste, 'Dutchman' –	20s.
Edmund Seyntclowe apprentice of John Withihale –	20s.
apprentice of Robert FitzRobert –	20s.
William Grobier apprentice of William Botoun –	20s.
Thomas Pomeray apprentice of Simon Colson –	20s.
Ralph Thornage apprentice of James Tregewstek –	20s.
John Tregewstek apprentice of James Tregewstek –	20s.
Nandewinus Tregaree apprentice of Thomas Blythe –	20s.
Roger Parker apprentice of John Downe –	20s.
James Goldsmith apprentice of Stephen Colney –	20s.
von Vald apprentice of John Cresbien –	20s.
Laurence Lethlyon apprentice of John Waterley –	20s.
Laurence Bere apprentice of John Werk –	20s.
Thomas Erbery apprentice of John Orwell –	20s.
apprentice of John Bulstrode –	20s.
Thomas apprentice of John Bowdon –	20s.
apprentice of Nicholas Lovet –	

Serving-men sworn:

William Takeley formerly apprentice of John Tewkesbury the elder –	2s.
Henry Horne formerly apprentice of Richard Stacy –	2s.
John Weryng formerly apprentice of Thomas South –	2s.
Thomas Penne formerly apprentice of John Werk –	2s.

1427 Memorand*um* q*uo*d xvii° die Octobr*is* anno regni regis Henrici sexti post conqu*estum* sexto, debates *et* discordie mote fuer*unt* inter Joh*ann*em Markeby *et* Joh*ann*em Chester, aur*ifabros*, p*ro* un*um* monile auri *et* un*um* annulu*m* auri,[670] qui quidem Joh*anne*s Markeby *et* Joh*anne*s Chester posuerunt se in arbitriu*m* Joh*anni*s Pake *et* Johannis Wynne, aur*ifabrorum*, p*er* mandatum Joh*anni*s Reynewell*e* abtunc Maioris civitatis London' *et* assensum d*ictorum* Joh*anni*s Markeby et Johannis [Chester] p*ro* omnib*us* causis int*er* d*ict*os Joh*ann*em Markeby *et* Joh*ann*em Chester adtunc mot*is*. Qui quidem Joh*anne*s Pake *et* Joh*anne*s Wynne nullum fecerunt arbitriu*m*. Et p*er* assensum d*ictorum* Joh*anni*s Markeby *et* Joh*anni*s Chester ven*erunt* hic dict*i* arbitratores *et* dict*i* Joh*annes et* Joh*anne*s d*ict*o xvii° die Octobr*is* [coram] Salmoni Oxney, Petro Torold, Joh*ann*i Stalkenden*e et* Johanni Werk adtunc gardian*is* mistere artis aur*ifabrorum* pre*dict*e *et* pecierunt[671] ob amorem dei q*uo*d ip*s*i voluer*unt* arbitrare p*ro* omnib*us* debat*is* anted*ict*is int*er* d*ict*os Joh*ann*em Markeby *et* Joh*ann*em Chester mot*is*. Qui quidem gardian*i et* Joh*anne*s Pake *et* Joh*anne*s Wynne eod*em* die[672] auditis eor*um* querelis arbitraver*unt* q*uo*d dict*us* Joh*anne*s Markeby sol*veret* p*re*fato Joh*ann*i Chester xvi s. *et* viii d. *et* q*uo*d dict*us* Joh*anne*s Chester relib*er*aret d*ict*o Joh*ann*i Markeby dict*um* monile auri *et* dict*um* annulum, is p*re*sent*ibus* Joh*ann*e Tewkisbury sen*iore*, Joh*ann*e Martyn, Will*elm*o Coup*er*, aur*ifabris*.

1427–28 Frenssh*e*:

p. 145 Item, Joh*anne*s Frenssh*e* p*ro* eo q*uo*d ip*s*e rebell*us* fuit v*er*sus gardianos suos *et* contra ordinac*ione*m, ordinatum fuit p*er* d*ict*os gardianos q*uo*d ip*s*e solv[er]et elemosine S*anct*i Dunstani – vi s. viii d.

Silvester:

Item, eod*em* anno Swether Silvester, Ducheman, admissus fuit in lib*er*tatem civitatis London' *et* in lib*er*tatem mistere aurifabror*um* p*er* assensum *et* voluntatem d*ictorum* gardianor*um et* tocius communitatis d*ict*e mistere *et* solvit eisdem gardian*is et* communitati eaq*ue* de causa – xii li.
Et q*uo*d h*ab*eret Thomam Arbury *et* Will*ia*m Arbury in s*er*vient*es* p*er* assenc*um* gardian*orum et* solvit ea de causa demi m*arcam*.[673]

Phillippe:

Item, Joh*anne*s Phillippe p*ro* eo q*uo*d ip*s*e rep*ro*bavit Joh*ann*em Stok, un*um* de vestur*a,* ordinat*um* fuit p*er* gardianos d*ict*e mistere q*uo*d ip*s*e solveret elemosine S*anct*i Dunstani vi s. *et* viii d., unde p*er*donat*us* fuit ad – xl d.

[670] The scribe appears to have his case endings wrong in the preceding phrase, but I have preferred not to amend.

[671] *Sic.*

[672] The word 'fecerunt' has been crossed out here.

[673] One may remember that in 1425 he had sworn 'q*uo*d non recipiet in s*ervient*em suu*m* p*reter* un*um* s*er*vientem ad semel', but for some reason he has now persuaded the wardens to grant permission for two servants.

Memorandum that on 17 October 1427 disputes and complaints arose between John Markeby and John Chester, goldsmiths, over a gold collar and a gold ring, and the said John Markeby and John Chester submitted themselves to the judgment of John Pake and John Wynne, goldsmiths, on the orders of John Reynwelle, then Mayor of the city of London, and with the assent of the said John Markeby and John Chester, for them to judge upon all matters that had at that time arisen between the said John Markeby and John Chester. The which John Pake and John Wynne made no judgment. And with the assent of the said John Markeby and John Chester the said judges came here and also the said John and John on the said 17 October before Solomon Oxney, Piers Thorold, John Stalkendene and John Werk, current wardens of the aforesaid Goldsmiths' Mistery and they asked for the love of God that they should consent to give judgment about all the aforesaid disputes between the said John Markeby and John Chester. The which wardens and John Pake and John Wynne on that same day, having heard their plaints, judged that the said John Markeby should pay to the aforesaid John Chester 16s. 8d. and that the said John Chester should hand over to the said John Markeby the said gold collar and the said ring, in the presence of John Tewkesbury the elder, John Martyn, William Couper, goldsmiths. 1427

Frenshe: 1427–28

Item, whereas John Frenshe rebelled against his wardens and against the ordinances, it was ordered by the said wardens that he should pay to the alms funds of St Dunstan – 6s. 8d. p. 145

Silvester:

Item, in the same year Swether Silvester, 'Dutchman', was admitted to the freedom of the city of London and the freedom of the Goldsmiths' Mistery with the assent and by the wish of the said wardens and of the whole commonalty of the said mistery and for this he paid to the same wardens and commonalty – £12.

And that he might have Thomas Arbury and William Arbury as his servants, with the assent of the wardens, for this he paid – ½ mark.

Philip:

Item, whereas John Philip spoke against John Stok, one of the livery, it was ordered by the wardens of the said mistery that he should pay to the alms funds of St Dunstan 6s. 8d., which was remitted to – 40d.

1427–28 A+b p. 89[674] Memorand*um* de defectib*us* oper*acio*nu*m* temp*or*e Salmonis Oxney, Petri Torold, Joh*ann*is Stalkenden [et Joh*ann*is][675] Werk, custodum mistere aur*ifabrorum* *etc*, *anno* *regni* R*egis* Henr*ici* sexti post conqu*estum* quinto:

In p*ri*mis de Perot Vinsile[676] p*ro* duob*us* defalt*is* cont*ra* ordina*ciones* – vi s.

It*em*, de Joh*ann*e Tewkisbury sen*iore*[677] p*ro* defalt*a* – xx d.

It*em*, de Remy p*ro* defalt*a* – ii s.

It*em*, de Thoma Gabriell*e* p*ro* defalt*a* – xvi d.[678]

It*em*, de Antonio Goldsmythe p*ro* una def*alta* – ii s.

It*em*, de Henrico Toret p*ro* una defalt*a* – xx d.

It*em*, de Joh*ann*e Van Hohne, Ducheman, p*ro* una defalt*a* – ii s.

It*em*, de p*ro* una defalt*a* – ii s.

It*em*, de Joh*ann*e Kynggesden p*ro* una defalt*a* – ii s.

It*em*, de Simone p*ro* una defalt*a* – ii s.

It*em*, de Joh*ann*e Colney p*ro* una defalt*a* – ii s.

It*em*, de Jurdan p*ro* una defalt*a* – ii s.

It*em*, de Patrik, Iryssheman, p*ro* licenc*ia* h*ab*end*a* ad op*er*and*um* – xiii s. iiii d.

It*em*, de Joh*ann*e Coster, Ducheman, pro se *et* famulo suo ad op*er*and*um* – xx s.

It*em*, de Henrico Bridd, Ducheman, p*ro* lic*encia* h*ab*end*a* – xiii s. iiii d.

It*em*, de Magnus Afferdon, Ducheman, p*ro* consili*o* – xx s.

It*em*, de Nich*ola*o Petirson, Ducheman, p*ro* defalt*a* – xii d.

It*em*, de Hans Blithe p*ro* una defalt*a* – ii s.

It*em*, de Thoma Swynesco p*ro* una defalt*a* – ii s.

It*em*, de Henri Van Coleyn p*ro* licenc*ia* h*ab*end*a* ad op*er*and*um* – xx s.

It*em*, p*ro* una defalt*a* – xx d.[679]

It*em*, p*ro* una alia defalt*a* – xx s. vii d. ob.[680]

It*em*, de Ducheman, famulo Joh*ann*is Paddysle, p*ro* defalt*a* – xxvi s. viii d.

It*em*, de Ducheman, p*ro* una defalt*a* – x s.

It*em*, de famulo Joh*ann*is Walden, operac' domus de Bredstrete – vi s. viii d.

It*em*, de Isabella Welles p*ro* una defalt*a* – ii s.

It*em*, de Arnoldo Hoveman, Duch*eman*, p*ro* una defalt*a* – vi s. viii d.

It*em*, de Will*elm*o Vandrungill*e* p*ro* lic*encia* h*ab*end*a* op*er*ar*i* cu*m* Joh*ann*e Phillippe – ii s.

It*em*, de Rob*er*to Downe p*ro* una defalt*a* – xx d.

674 A number of spaces have been left in the list below for an unknown name to be filled in in the gap. Three names also have crosses against them: the two for the Irishman Patrik, and that for Magnus Afferdon.

675 The page is slightly damaged in the RH corner here, but it rather looks as if the name added here had been missing anyway.

676 A gap was left before 'Perot' and the scribe has later learnt that this was the forename and he has inserted the surname above the line after an omission mark. See the last entry in this list for this man being fined twice.

677 The 'sen' has been added with an omission mark above the line, by the same scribe.

678 LH margin note: 'gabrielle'.

679 No gap is left for a name.

680 No space is left for a name here either, and since the amount of the fine is so odd it is a pity that no more information is given.

Memorandum about the defects in workmanship during the time of Solomon Oxney, Piers Thorold, John Stalkendene and John Werk, Wardens of the Goldsmiths' Mistery etc., in the year 5 Henry VI [from 19 May 1427]: 1427–28 A + b p. 89

Firstly from Perot Vinsile for two offences against the ordinances – 6s.
Item, from John Tewkesbury the elder for an offence – 20d.
Item, from Remy for an offence – 2s.
Item, from Thomas Gabrielle for an offence – 16d.
Item, from Anthony Goldsmith for an offence – 2s.
Item, from Henry Toret for an offence – 20d.
Item, from John Van Hohne, 'Dutchman', for an offence – 2s.
Item, from for an offence – 2s.
Item, from John Kingsdon for an offence – 2s.
Item, from Simon for an offence – 2s.
Item, from John Colney for an offence – 2s.
Item, from Jurdan for an offence – 2s.
Item, from Patrick, Irishman, to obtain permission to work – 13s. 4d.
Item, from John Coster, 'Dutchman', for himself and his servant to work – 20s.
Item, from Henry Bridd, 'Dutchman', to obtain permission – 13s. 4d.
Item, from Magnus Afferdon, for advice – 20s.
Item, from Nicholas Petirson, 'Dutchman', for an offence – 12d.
Item, from Hans Blithe for an offence – 2s.
Item, from Thomas Swinscoe for an offence – 2s.
Item, from Henry van Cologne to obtain permission to work – 20s.
Item, for an offence – 20d.
Item, for another offence – 20s. 7½d.
Item, from , 'Dutchman', servant of John Pattesley, for an offence – 26s. 8d.
Item, from , 'Dutchman', for an offence – 10s.
Item, from , servant of John Walden, for working at a house in Bread Street – 6s. 8d.
Item, from Isabella Welles for an offence – 2s.
Item, from Arnold Hoveman, 'Dutchman', for an offence – 6s. 8d.
Item, from William Vandrungille to obtain permission to work with John Philip – 2s.
Item, from Robert Downe for an offence – 20d.

It*em*, de Patrik , Iryssh*e*man, p*ro* lic*encia* h*abend*a op*erari* – vi s. viii d.
It*em*, de Perot Vinsile p*ro* una defalt*a* – vi s. viii d.

p. 90 D*e* Thoma Dodyngton p*ro* defalt*a* – ii s. sinis(?) lib' mister*e* p*redict*e
D*e* Alex*andro* Feryng appr*enticio* Joh*anni*s Gate – vi s. viii d. q*uod* pat*et*
D*e* Rob*er*to Wysbeche p*ro* licenc*ia* h*abend*a ad op*erandum* – v s.
D*e* Will*elm*o Hoke appr*enticio* Joh*anni*s Walden ad op*erandum* – vi s. viii d. q*uod* pat*et* lib'

1427 A debate betwene Goldsmythes & Bouchers for their stondyng in Chepe ut
A + a p. 146 patet tempor*e* Joh*anni*s Gedney, maior[is], a*nno* H*enrici* vj^{ti} vj^{to}:
Remembraunce made the thir[d] day of Novembr*e* the ȝere of oure Lorde God M^{l} CCCCx[x]vii and the sixte ȝere of the regne of Kyng Harry the sixte, that how of holde custume of the worshipfull cite of London the craftes of the saide citee hav used to ride with the maires of the same citee to the paleys of Westm*inster* atte othe takyng of the maires and fro thens to the citee ridyng ayen and the craftes ridyng afore the maire. Whan they come in Chepe every craft eche be other hovyng a hors bak abidyng tille the Mair*e* ride thurgh hem. And of olde tyme the goldsmythes of the saide citee whan of ther craft is no Mayr they have used to hove and to stonde above the Cros of Chepe afore the Goldsmytherowe witheoute eny forstallyng or stondyng afore of eny other craftes, tille nowe late hit fill that in the moneth*e* of the apostels Symond & Jude last past John Gedney, drap*er*, than beyng Mayer, as the saide goldsmythes rode afore hym comyng in to Chepe for to ha hoved and stonde in the place aforesaide as they have used tyme oute of mynde, kam the bochers of the same citee and hoved in the place there as the saide goldsmythes were wonyd to stonde and for no prayer of the wardeyns of the saide goldsmythes the saide bouchers wolde not voide were thurgh, hit happyd that ther fill*e* chauncemedle and stryfe amonge hem, for the whiche stryfe the saide bouchers compleynyd hem to the saide John Gedney, Mayr, and submytted hem high and lowe to stonde atte hys jugement and award. And the Mayr sente for the wardeyns of goldsmythes and tolde hem of the complaynt of the bouchers and how they had submytted hem to stonde to his award and axed the goldsmythes ȝyf they wolde do the same. And the wardeyns of the goldsmythes answerid the Mayr and seyd that they wolde be rewled hight and lowe atte hys award, knowyng welle hys discrec*io*n substanciall, wyse, and rightfulle. Where on the[681] saide Mayer the day of the the comemorac*io*n of all*e* sowles in hys parisshe cherche of Seynt Cristofores next the Stokkys, as well*e* the wardeyns of

[681] MS: the the.

Item, from Patrick , Irishman, to obtain permission to work – 6s. 8d.
Item, from Perot Vinsile for an offence – 6s. 8d.

From Thomas Doddington for an offence – 2s. – [?] paid(?) / in the book of(?) the aforesaid mistery[233] p. 90
- from Alexander Feryng, apprentice of John Gate – 6s. 8d. – as it appears
- from Robert Wisbech to obtain permission to work – 5s.
- from William Hoke, apprentice of John Walden, to work – 6s. 8d. as it appears (?)

A dispute between Goldsmiths and Butchers about their stand in Cheap as it appears in the time of John Gedney, Mayor, in the year 6 Henry VI: 1427 A + a p. 146
Memorandum recorded on 3 November 1427 that whereas by the old custom of the worshipful city of London the misteries of the said city have been accustomed to ride with the mayors of the same city to the Palace of Westminster at the time when they take their oath, and from thence to ride back to the city, the misteries riding before the Mayor. When they come into Cheap, they draw up, remaining on horseback, each mistery alongside the others, until the Mayor has ridden through past them. And from olden times the goldsmiths of the said city, when the Mayor is not of their mistery, have been accustomed to draw in and stand above the Cross in Cheap in front of Goldsmiths' Row, without there being any of any other mistery to get in there or stand there in front of them, until lately it happened that in the preceding month of the Apostles Simon and Jude [28 October], when the said goldsmiths rode in front of John Gedney, draper and at that time Mayor, as they came into Cheap and were to draw up and stand in the aforesaid place as they have been accustomed to do since time immemorial, the butchers of the same city came along and drew up in the place where the said goldsmiths were accustomed to stand, and the said butchers refused all requests of the wardens of the said goldsmiths and would not move out of the way, and so it happened that chance-medley[234] and fighting arose among them, on account of which strife the said butchers made a complaint to the said John Gedney, Mayor, and they submitted themselves entirely to abide by his judgment and sentence. And the Mayor sent for the wardens of the goldsmiths and told them about the butchers' complaint and that they had submitted themselves to abide by his judgment, and he asked the goldsmiths if they would do the same. And the wardens of the goldsmiths answered the Mayor and said that they would be entirely governed by his judgment, for they well knew that he was a man of great, wise and righteous discretion. And then the Mayor on All Souls Day [2 November] in his parish church of St Christopher near the Stocks Market, with the wardens of the goldsmiths as also the wardens of the butchers present

[233] The notes attached to these figures are very unclear and their sense uncertain, but they would seem to be references to another record kept elsewhere (in another book?).

[234] See *OED*: '[From the fact that medley is also a n., and chance medley a possible combination in the sense of 'fortuitous medley', the meaning has often been mistaken, and the expression misused.] 1. Law. Accident or casualty not purely accidental, but of a mixed character. Chiefly in manslaughter by chance-medley . . .'. Here however no death appears to have occurred, but only injuries.

goldsmythes as the wardeyns of the bouchers beyng *pre*sent afore hym, the mat*ers* of every p*ar*tye herde and cosideryd, the saide Mayer awardyd that the craft of goldsmythes fro hens forward shulde rejoyse here stondyng in the same place as they have usyd of olde tyme and chargyd the wardeyns of bothe craftes aforesaide to take eche other be the handys in signe of love and pees, and so they dede and charged hem that alle thyng afore doo shulde be no more spoked of, but every craft to love and cherisse other as they owyd to doo *etc*.

1428–29 Ceux sount lez nouns dez Gardeins eslutz al feste de Seint Dunstan l'an du p. 147 regne le Roy Henry sisme puis le conquest sisme tanqe al dit feste adonqes p*ro*schein ensuant:
Joh*anne*s Bernes
Joh*anne*s Emond
Steph*an*us Colney
Joh*anne*s Walssh*e* junior

Weston:
Be yt to remembre that grete discorde and debate were betwen Rob*er*t Bosoun, goldsmyth*e*, and Ric*hard* Weston, apprentic*e* of the same Rob*er*t, for wiche debate and discorde the forsaide Rob*er*t & Ric*hard* Weston they submyttyd hem to stonde to the awarde of her wardeyns that were for the tyme, that his for to saye John Bernes, John Emond, Steph*en* Colley & John Walsshe juni*or*, the wiche wardeyns ordynyd and det*er*mined that the same Ric*hard* Weston shulde ben enrolled to the same Rob*er*t hys master, and serve hym wele and trewly. And that alle maner thyng that weren betwen hem or may be duryng the apprenticialite, they shulde ben rewlyd ben the wardeyns that were for the tyme, hy and lowe as they wolde rewle hem.

Thornage:
For as moche as on*e* Thomas Thornage, the sonne of Laurence Thornage of the toune of Derby in the shire of Derby, the whiche shulde have ben the apprentice of on*e* John Kirkeby, goldsmyth, was founde fals in countrefetyng of a key of the tille[682] of his master, it is ordynyd and fully determynyd be the wardeyns that were for that tyme that the same Thom*a*s shulde ben utterly voyded and putte howt of the craft for evermore and never rejoyse no maner benefice of the craft.

1429 Coster: Memorand*um* q*uo*d xii° die Febr*uarii* anno p*re*d*ic*to Joh*anne*s Coster, Ducheman, venit coram p*re*fat*is* custodib*us et* ibid*e*m juravit sup*er* librum bene, fideliter *et* honeste op*er*ari infra cam*er*am suam aurum *et* argentum, ac omnia secreta artis sue p*re*d*ic*te fidelit*er* custodire, *et* licenc*iatus* fuit p*er* d*ic*tos custodes quantum in ill*is* est ad op*er*and*um* infra cam*er*am suam p*re*d*ic*tam durante vita sua, et solvit ea de causa x m*arc*as.

682 The use of this word here is interesting as the *OED*'s first citation for this is dated 1452, with the meaning: 'A small box, casket, or closed compartment, contained within or forming part of a larger box, chest, or cabinet; sometimes one that could be lifted out, sometimes a drawer in a cabinet or chest of drawers; used for keeping valuables, documents, etc., more safely.'

before him, heard and considered what each side had to say, and the said Mayor then judged that from henceforward the goldsmiths' mistery should enjoy the benefit of their site where they have from olden times been accustomed to stand, and he bade the wardens of both the aforesaid misteries to take each other by the hand in sign of love and peace, and this they did, and he enjoined them to speak no more about what had happened, but rather that each mistery should love and cherish each other as they ought to do etc.

These are the names of the Wardens elected at the feast of St Dunstan in the year 6 Henry VI [19 May 1428] until the same feastday next following: 1428–29 p. 147
John Barnes
John Edmund
Stephen Colney
John Walsh the younger

Weston:
Memorandum that there was great discord and debate between Robert Bosoun, goldsmith, and Richard Weston, apprentice of the same Robert, for the which debate and discord the aforesaid Robert and Richard Weston submitted themselves to stand by the judgment of their current wardens, i.e. John Barnes, John Edmund, Stephen Colney and John Walsh the younger, the which wardens ordered and determined that the same Richard Weston should be enrolled [as the apprentice of] the same Robert, his master, and should serve him well and faithfully. And that any matter that came up between them during the period of his apprenticeship should be ruled upon by the current wardens, entirely as they shall see fit to make any ruling.

Thornage:
Whereas one Thomas Thornage, the son of Laurence Thornage of Derby in Derbyshire, who should have been the apprentice of one John Kirkby, goldsmith, was found guilty of deceit in that he made a duplicate of the key of his master's till, it has been ordained and fully determined by the current wardens that the same Thomas should be totally expelled and ejected from the mistery for evermore, and should never enjoy any kind of benefit of the mistery.

Coster:
Memorandum that on 12 February of the aforesaid year [1429] John Coster, 'Dutchman', came before the aforesaid wardens and there he swore upon the book to work gold and silver well, faithfully and honestly within his own chamber, and faithfully to guard all the secrets of his aforesaid mistery, and he was given permission by the said wardens in as far as they are able to work within his aforesaid chamber for the period of his lifetime, and for this he paid 10 marks.

1429 [683]Mem*orandum* q*uo*d ix° die Maii anno r*egni* r*egis* Henr*ici* vj^ti post conqu*estum* vii°, Joh*ann*es Stafford recept*us* est in lib*eratam* eiusdem mister*e* ad eff*ectu*m de essend*o* de co*mun*i consilio mistere p*redict*e et ad hoc fecit fidem – sup*er* hoc concess*um* est ei p*er* assensum tam custodu*m* mistere p*redict*e q*ua*m totius co*mun*itatis eiusde*m* q*uo*d ip*s*e liberata*m* predic*t*am, (p*r*out ac Nich*ola*i Bepe p*r*out ho*min*es mister*e* *etc*.),[684] h*ab*ebit de dono absq*ue* aliquo p*ro* eadem lib*e*rata solvend*o, et* xl s annuati*m* etc quid*a*m etc

Item, eodem anno Joh*ann*es Kirkeby de Fourneys in com*itatu* Lancastr*ie* admissus est in lib*e*rtate*m* civitatis London' *et* in lib*e*rtate*m* mistere aurifabror*um* p*er* assensum *et* voluntate*m* d*icto*r*um* gardianor*um* *et* co*m*munitatis tocius d*ict*e mister*e* et solvit eisdem gardianis *et* co*mmun*itati causa p*re*d*ict*a – x li.

1428–29 Nomina apprenticior*um*:

p. 148[685] Joh*ann*es Ev*e*rton app*r*enticius Will*elm*i Belverge –	xx s.
Rich*ardu*s Weston app*r*enticius Rob*e*rti Bosoun –	xx s.
Will*elmu*s Bate app*r*enticius Thome Swynsco –	xx s.
Rob*e*rtus Hamelton app*r*enticius Joh*ann*is Tewkesbury jun*ioris* –	xx s.
Will*elmu*s Duke app*r*enticius Will*elm*i Moubray –	xx s.
Rob*e*rtus Russell app*r*enticius Nich*ol*ai Lovet –	xx s.
Ric*ard*us Baldeswell*e* app*r*entic*ius* Joh*ann*is Kebbell*e* –	xx s.
Thomas Bowdon app*r*entic*ius* Joh*ann*is Bowdon –	xx s.
Joh*ann*es Cowdray app*r*entic*ius* Thome Blyth –	xx s.
Nich*ola*us Stodeley app*r*entic*ius* Ric*ard*i Bradcok –	xx s.
Rob*e*rtus Croke app*r*ent*icius* Joh*ann*is Weryng –	xx s.
Thomas Sampson app*r*ent*icius* Tho*m*e Whitmore –	xx s.
Rob*e*rtus Irland app*r*ent*icius* Ric*ardi* Wat*er* – qu*i*a fug*it*[686] –	x s.
Thom*as* Burgh app*r*ent*icius* Joh*ann*is Cary –	xx s.
Henr*icus* Kent app*r*ent*icius* Drugonis Waddesley –	xx s.
Joh*ann*es Stokebrigge app*r*entic*ius* Rob*e*rti Asshby –	xx s.
Will*elmu*s Clayton app*r*ent*icius* Tho*m*e Herryson –	xx s.
Thomas Ekkreslee app*r*ent*icius* Thome Gabriell*e* –	xx s.
Joh*ann*es Feld app*r*ent*icius* Thurstan Fourneys –	xx s.
Will*elmu*s Kelk app*r*entic*ius* Mathei Philip –	xx s.

Alloc*ati* jur*ati*:

Matheus Brayn nup*er* app*r*ent*icius* Joh*ann*is Pake –	ii s.
Joh*ann*es Kirkeby[687]	ii s.
Joh*ann*es Bisshop nup*er* app*r*ent*icius* Will*elm*i Holmestede –	i s.
Ric*ard*us Chapman nup*er* app*r*ent*icius* Joh*annis* FitzRob*e*rt –	ii s.

683 A new hand starts here.

684 The words placed here in brackets have been added later between the lines.

685 The two tables of names on this page have been written in a different hand, the memo underneath in the same hand as the last two memos on the previous page, which then continues on the next page.

686 This note has been added later to explain why only half the due sum has been paid.

687 See the previous page and above for other information on this man.

Memorandum that on 9 May 1429 John Stafford was admitted to the livery of the same mistery with the purpose that he should be of common counsel to the aforesaid mistery, and he took his oath to this – after which with the assent both of the wardens of the aforesaid mistery and also of the whole commonalty it was granted to him that he should receive the said livery (just as Nicholas Bepe, just as the men of the mistery etc.) as a gift, without having to pay anything for the same livery, and that he should receive 40s. annually etc. who etc. 1429

Item, the said year John Kirkby of Furness in the county of Lancashire was admitted to the freedom of the city of London and the freedom of the Goldsmiths' Mistery with the assent and by the wish of the said wardens and commonalty of all the said mistery, and for this he paid to the same wardens and commonalty – £10.

The names of apprentices:		1428–29
John Everton apprentice of William Belverge –	20s.	p. 148
Richard Weston apprentice of Robert Bosoun –	20s.	
William Bate apprentice of Thomas Swinscoe –	20s.	
Robert Hamelton apprentice of John Tewkesbury the younger –	20s.	
William Duke apprentice of William Mowbray –	20s.	
Robert Russell apprentice of Nicholas Lovet –	20s.	
Richard Baldeswelle apprentice of John Kebbelle –	20s.	
Thomas Bowdon apprentice of John Bowdon –	20s.	
John Cowdray apprentice of Thomas Blithe –	20s.	
Nicholas Studley apprentice of Richard Bradcok –	20s.	
Robert Croke apprentice of John Weryng –	20s.	
Thomas Sampson apprentice of Thomas Whitmore –	20s.	
Robert Ireland apprentice of Richard Water – because he ran away –	10s.	
Thomas Burgh apprentice of John Cary –	20s.	
Henry Kent apprentice of Drew Waddesley –	20s.	
John Stockbridge apprentice of Robert Ashby –	20s.	
William Clayton apprentice of Thomas Harryson –	20s.	
Thomas Ekkreslee apprentice of Thomas Gabrielle –	20s.	
John Field apprentice of Thurstan Furneys –	20s.	
William Kelk apprentice of Matthew Philip –	20s.	

Serving-men sworn:	
Matthew Brayn formerly apprentice of John Pake –	2s.
John Kirkby –	2s.
John Bisshop formerly apprentice of William Holmstead –	2s.
Richard Chapman formerly apprentice of John FitzRobert –	2s.

Henr*icus* Pole nup*er* appr*en*t*icius* Will*elm*i Gilbert – ii s.
Joh*ann*es Wodehous nup*er* appr*en*t*icius* Petri Brendwode – ii s.
Thomas Gilmyn nup*er* appr*en*t*icius* Rob*er*ti Downe – ii s.
Simon[688] Crosse nup*er* appr*en*t*icius* Rob*er*ti Asshby – ii s.
Tho*ma*s Orfeyre nup*er* appr*en*t*icius* Joh*ann*is Walssh*e* juni*oris* – ii s.

Memorand*um* q*uo*d anno p*re*di*ct*o quidam Rob*er*tus Wysbech*e*, forincec*us* aur*ifaber*, p*er* gardian*os* mister*e* aur*ifabrorum* p*re*dict*e* licenciat*us* est ad s*er*viend*um* deinceps cuicu*mque* magi*st*ro aur*ifabro* lib*er*o d*ic*t*e* civit*atis* London' quamdiu sibi placu*er*it, et solvit ea de causa – xxvi s. viii d.

1428–29 A + b p. 90 *cont.* Memorand*um* de defectib*us* op*er*ac*i*onu*m* *et*c temp*or*e Joh*ann*is Biernes, Joh*ann*is Emond, Steph*an*i Colney *et* Joh*ann*is Walssh*e* juni*oris*, custod*um* mister*e* aur*ifabrorum* *et*c anno r*egni* R*egis* Henr*ici* vj^ti^ post conqu*estum* sexto:[689]

In primis, de Joh*ann*e Chestr*e* p*ro* una defalt*a* – ii s.
It*em*, de Thoma[690] Gabriell*e* p*ro* una defalt*a* – ii s.[691]
It*em*, de Ric*ard*o Wat*er* p*ro* i defalt*a* – ii s.
It*em*, de Joh*ann*e Frenssh*e* p*ro* i def*alta* – iiii s.
It*em*, de Thoma Codynton p*ro* i def*alta* – ii s.
It*em*, de Tho*ma* Thomer p*ro* i def*alta* – ii s.
It*em*, de Simone Kalson p*ro* i def*alta* – ii s.
It*em*, de Rob*er*to Bosoun p*ro* i def*alta* – ii s.[692]
It*em*, de Thoma Joce p*ro* i def*alta* – ii s.
It*em*, de Ric*ard*o Bradcok p*ro* i def*alta* – vi s. viii d.
It*em*, de Joh*ann*e Philip p*ro* i def*alta* – iii s.
It*em*, de Joh*ann*e Stok p*ro* i def*alta* – ii s.
It*em*, de Will*elm*o Waryn p*ro* i def*alta* – ii s.
It*em*, de Joh*ann*e Skynner p*ro* i def*alta* – ii s.
It*em*, de Will*elm*o Goteley p*ro* i def*alta* – ii s.
It*em*, de Joh*ann*e Weryng p*ro* i def*alta* – xvi d.
It*em*, de Thoma Gabriell*e* p*ro* i def*alta* – ii s.
It*em*, de Rumbald Rys p*ro* i def*alta* – iii s. iiii d.
It*em*, de Thoma Gabriell*e* p*ro* i def*alta* – xii d.

1429–30 A + a p. 149 Ceux sount les nouns des Gardeins eslutz en le fest de Seint Dunstan l'an du regne le Roy sisme puis le conquest septisme tanq*e* al fest de Seint Dunstan adonq*es* p*ro*schein ensuant:
Joh*ann*es Pake
Joh*ann*es Bernes
Joh*ann*es Sutton sen*ior*
Rob*er*tus Asshby

688 MS: 'Simonis', with the last two letters expuncted.
689 This regnal year corresponds to the date the wardens remitted office, in May of that year, the entry referring to fines during the previous year while they held office.
690 MS: 'Thomas', with the last letter perhaps expuncted.
691 The name 'gabrielle' has been picked out and written in the LH margin against this entry and the other two below for this man.
692 The name 'Bosoun' has been picked out and written in the LH margin.

Henry Pole formerly apprentice of William Gilbert – 2s.
John Woodhouse formerly apprentice of Piers Brentwood – 2s.
Thomas Gilmyn formerly apprentice of Robert Downe – 2s.
Simon Crosse formerly apprentice of Robert Ashby – 2s.
Thomas Orfeyre formerly apprentice of John Walsh the younger – 2s.

Memorandum that in the aforesaid year a certain Robert Wisbech, 'foreign'[235] goldsmith, was given permission by the wardens of the aforesaid Goldsmiths' Mistery to serve hereafter any master who is a goldsmith and a freeman of the said city of London for as long as he liked, and for this he paid – 26s. 8d.

Memorandum about defects in workmanship etc. during the time of John Barnes, John Edmund, Stephen Colney and John Walsh the younger, Wardens of the Goldsmiths' Mistery etc., in the year 6 Henry VI [from 19 May 1428]: 1428–29 A + b p. 90 *cont.*

Firstly, from John Chester for an offence –	2s.
Item, from Thomas Gabrielle for an offence –	2s.
Item, from Richard Water for an offence –	2s.
Item, from John Frenshe for an offence –	4s.
Item, from Thomas Coddington for an offence –	2s.
Item, from Thomas Thomer for an offence –	2s.
Item, from Simon Kalson for an offence –	2s.
Item, from Robert Bosoun for an offence –	2s.
Item, from Thomas Joce for an offence –	2s.
Item, from Richard Bradcok for an offence –	6s. 8d.
Item, from John Philip for an offence –	3s.
Item, from John Stok for an offence –	2s.
Item, from William Waryn for an offence –	2s.
Item, from John Skynner for an offence –	2s.
Item, from William Goteley for an offence –	2s.
Item from John Weryng for an offence –	16d.
Item, from Thomas Gabrielle for an offence –	2s.
Item, from Rumbold Rys for an offence –	3s. 4d.
Item, from Thomas Gabrielle for an offence –	12d.

These are the names of the Wardens elected at the feast of St Dunstan in the year 7 Henry VI [19 May 1429] until the next following feastday of St Dunstan: 1429–30 A + a p. 149

John Pake
John Barnes
John Sutton the elder
Robert Ashby

[235] i.e. not a citizen of London.

Reygate:
Memorandum quod cum Willelmus Reygate, civis et aurifaber London', teneatur et firmiter obligetur Johanni Pake et sociis suis gardianis pro isto anno existentibus in centum solidis sterlingorum solvendis in festo Natalis domini prout in quadam obligacione inde facta plenius apparet, cuius condicio est talis quod si infrascriptus Willelmus deinceps se bene et honeste geret et habebit erga suos gardianos pro anno existentes et societatem mistere predicte et sic de anno in annum dictis gardianis et societati mistere predicte et suis successoribus gardianis, quod extunc dicta obligacio pro nulla habeatur, alioquin in omni suo robore permaneat et virtute.

1429 Reygate: Fait a remembrer qe le ii^{de} jour de Novembre l'an du regne le Roy Henry vi viii^{e}, qe pur taunt qe William Reygate revyla et disoit maliciouses et faulx paroles de Johan Patteslee, un des audermans de Loundres qe adevant estoit gardein de la mistier des orfevres, come le le dit William conust luy mesmes, agardez feust par les gardeins qe le dit William paiera xx s. al almoigne de Seint Dunstan dount il paiera vi s. viii d. et les autres xiii s. iiii d. feurent pardonez. – vi s. viii d.

1429 Kyngesdene: Fait a remembrer qe le xx^{e} jour d'Ottobre l'an du regne le Roy Henry vj^{me} viii^{e} qe pur taunt qe Johan Kyngesdene fauxment et maliciousement desclaundra Piers Torold, nadgairs un des gardeins de la dicte mistier des orfevres, come mesme le Johan conust luy mesmes et dount il cria mercy du dicte Piers, agardee feust par les ditz gardeins et William Walton, Richard Spenser, Johan Walsshe, Piers Brendwode et Robert Bosoun qe le dit Johan Kyngesdene paiera xx s., dount il feust pardonez de vi s. viii d., et xiii s. iiii d. serront paiez, assavoir vi s. viii d. al almoigne de Seint Dunstan et autres vi s. viii d. a Piers Torold avantdit.

1429–30 Nomina apprenticiorum:

p. 150	Nicholaus Fyfhede apprenticius Thome Tounvyle –	xx s.
	Johannes Standyssh apprenticius Roberti Boteler –	xxs.
	Johannes Markes apprenticius Ricardi By theWater –	xx s.
	Thomas Coryngton apprenticius Salamonis Oxney –	xx s.
	Willelmus Welyngton apprenticius Thome Elys –	xx s.
	Willelmus Wylmot apprenticius de William Hert –	xx s.
	Willelmus Jay apprenticius de Johan Huberd –	xx s.
	Stephanus Sharp apprenticius Johannis Stalkendene –	xx s.
	Johannes de Bland apprenticius eiusdem Johannis Stalkendene –	xx s.
	Johannes Broune qui fuit apprenticius Johannis Corby –	xx s.
	Johannes Wyginche apprenticius Ricardi Spenser –	xx s.
	Johannes Hake apprenticius Roberti Asshby –	xx s.
	Thomas Cutson apprenticius Johannis Sutton, junioris –	xx s.
	Edmundus Capron apprenticius Johannis Sutton, senioris –	xx s.
	Johannes Holden apprenticius Nicholai Hervestok –	xx s.
	Robertus Burgh apprenticius Johannis Cary –	xx s.
	Thomas Smyth apprenticius Thome Leget –	xx s.
	Johannes Serle apprenticius Willelmi Moubray –	xx s.
	Johannes Gregory apprenticius Johannis Wynne junioris –	xx s.

Reigate:
Memorandum that whereas William Reigate, citizen and goldsmith of London, is firmly bound to John Pake and his fellow wardens for that year in the sum of 100s. sterling to be paid at Christmas, as in the letters obligatory drawn up concerning this more fully appears, whose condition is such that if the undersigned William from thenceforth shall behave and conduct himself well and honestly towards his current wardens and the society of the aforesaid mistery and thus from year to year towards the said wardens and society of the aforesaid mistery and their successors as wardens, that then the said bond shall be held as void, otherwise it shall remain in all its strength and effect.

Reigate: 1429
Memorandum that whereas on 2 November 1429 William Reigate insulted and spoke malicious and false words about John Pattesley, one of the aldermen of London who was previously a warden of the Goldsmiths' Mistery, as the said William himself admitted, it was judged by the wardens that the said William shall pay 20s. to the alms funds of St Dunstan, of which he shall pay 6s. 8d. and the other 13s. 4d. have been remitted – 6s. 8d.

Kingsdon: 1429
Memorandum that whereas on 20 October 1429 John Kingsdon falsely and maliciously slandered Piers Thorold, formerly one of the wardens of the Goldsmiths' Mistery, as the said John himself admitted and for which he begged forgiveness from the said Piers, it was judged by the said wardens and William Walton, Richard Spencer, John Walsh, Piers Brentwood and Robert Bosoun that the said John Kingsdon shall pay 20s., of which 6s. 8d. was remitted to him and 13s. 4d. shall be paid, i.e. 6s. 8d. to the alms funds of St Dunstan and the other 6s. 8d. to the aforesaid Piers Thorold.

The names of apprentices: 1429–30

Nicholas Fifehead apprentice of Thomas Tumvyle –	20s.	p. 150
John Standish apprentice of Robert Botiller –	20s.	
John Markes apprentice of Richard by the Water –	20s.	
Thomas Coryngton apprentice of Solomon Oxney –	20s.	
William Wellington apprentice of Thomas Elys –	20s.	
William Wilmot apprentice of William Hert –	20s.	
William Jay apprentice of John Huberd –	20s.	
Stephen Sharp apprentice of John Stalkendene –	20s.	
John de Bland apprentice of the same John Stalkendene –	20s.	
John Broun who was the apprentice of John Corby –	20s.	
John Wyginche apprentice of Richard Spencer –	20s.	
John Hake apprentice of Robert Ashby –	20s.	
Thomas Cutson apprentice of John Sutton the younger –	20s.	
Edmund Capron apprentice of John Sutton the elder –	20s.	
John Holden apprentice of Nicholas Hervestoke –	20s.	
Robert Burgh apprentice of John Cary –	20s.	
Thomas Smyth apprentice of Thomas Leget –	20s.	
John Serle apprentice of William Mowbray –	20s.	
John Gregory apprentice of John Wynne the younger –	20s.	

Nich*ola*us Alyngton app*ren*t*icius* Will*elm*i Alkam – xx s.
Will*elmus* Browne app*ren*tis de Nicol*e* at þe Wode – xx s.[693]

Alloc*ati* jur*ati*:
Joh*annes* Picard nup*er* app*ren*t*icius* Will*elm*i Coup*er* – ii s.
Thom*as* Tounvyle nup*er* app*ren*t*icius* Alis Blikden*e* – ii s.
Thom*as* Flete nup*er* app*ren*t*icius* Joh*annis* Flete – ii s.
Joh*annes* Coupelond nup*er* app*ren*t*icius* Joh*annis* Holcroft – ii s.
Will*elmus* Flo*ur* nup*er* app*ren*t*icius* Ric*ardi* Wethihale – ii s.
Thom*as* Lenh*a*m nup*er* app*ren*t*icius* Steph*ani* Colley – ii s.
Thom*as* Broun*e* nup*er* app*ren*t*icius* Joh*annis* Corby – ii s.
Joh*annes* Dunstall [nup*er*] app*ren*t*icius* Will*elm*i Waryn – ii s.
Joh*annes* Whyssh*e* nup*er* app*ren*t*icius* Will*elm*i Gotelee – ii s.
Will*elmus* Birlyng nup*er* app*ren*t*icius* Thom*e* Leget – ii s.
Joh*annes* Sutton nup*er* app*ren*t*icius* Joh*annis* Halle – ii s.
Will*elmus* Codyngton [nup*er*] app*ren*t*icius* Joh*annis* Irton*e* – ii s.
Ric*ard*us Dyster nup*er* app*ren*t*icius* Will*elmi* Cheyne – ii s.
Thom*as* Holden nup*er* app*ren*t*icius* Will*elmi* Moubray – ii s.

1429–30 Memorand*um* de defectib*us* op*er*acion*um* *et*c temp*or*e Joh*ann*is Pake,
A + b p. 91 Joh*ann*is Biernes, Joh*ann*is Sutton sen*ioris et* Rob*er*ti Asshby, custod*um*
mister*e* aur*ifabrorum et*c anno r*egni* R*egis* Henr*ici* vj^ti^ post conqu*estum* vii°.
In primis, de Joh*ann*e Ungell*e* p*ro* una defalt*a* – ii s.
It*em*, de Thoma Gabriell*e* p*ro* i defalt*a* – ii s.[694]
It*em*, de Joh*ann*e Corby p*ro* i defalt*a* – xx d.
It*em*, de Nich*ola*o Hervestok p*ro* i defalt*a* – ii s.
It*em*, de Joh*ann*e Ungell*e* p*ro* i defalt*a* – ii s.
It*em*, de Thoma Gabriell*e* p*ro* i defalt*a* – ii s.
It*em*, de Thoma Elys p*ro* i defalt*a* – ii s.
It*em*, de Joh*ann*e Ungell*e* p*ro* i defalt*a* – ii s.
It*em*, de Magno Verdon p*ro* i defalt*a* – vi s. viii d.
It*em*, de Nich*ola*o Wode p*ro* i defalt*a* – iii s. iiii d.
It*em*, de Thoma Gabriell*e* p*ro* div*ersis* defect*ibus* – ii s.
It*em*, de Thoma Lenh*a*m p*ro* i defalt*a* – ii s.
It*em*, de Gerardo Splynt p*ro* i def*alta* de xii anul*is et*c – x s.
It*em*, de Joh*ann*e Clynton p*ro* i defalt*a* – xvi d.
It*em*, de Will*elm*o Berwe, Ducheman, p*ro* i defalt*a* – xxii d.

15..? M.. Gilbert } leases
A + a M.. Mabbe } as
p. 151[695] Rob*er*t Chylde } Meryall

John Goodryche a draught
Mr Gardmor – .. Robert Ch..

[693] This line has been added slightly later in a different hand.
[694] The name 'gabrielle' has been picked out and written in the LH margin against all three entries for this man on this page. He has by now committed a very large number of offences and one might have expected some special sanctions against him, but this does not appear to have been done.
[695] This page is blank, apart from a sixteenth-century scribbled note at the top.

Nicholas Allington apprentice of William Alkam – 20s.
William Broun apprentice of Nicholas atte Wood – 20s.

Serving-men sworn:
John Picard formerly apprentice of William Couper – 2s.
Thomas Tumvyle formerly apprentice of Alice Blikdene – 2s.
Thomas Flete formerly apprentice of John Flete – 2s.
John Coupland formerly apprentice of John Holcroft – 2s.
William Flour formerly apprentice of Richard Withihale – 2s.
Thomas Lenham formerly apprentice of Stephen Colney – 2s.
Thomas Broun formerly apprentice of John Corby – 2s.
John Dunstalle [formerly] apprentice of William Waryn – 2s.
John Whisshe formerly apprentice of William Goteley – 2s.
William Birling formerly apprentice of Thomas Leget – 2s.
John Sutton formerly apprentice of John Halle – 2s.
William Coddington [formerly] apprentice of John Ireton – 2s.
Richard Dyster formerly apprentice of William Cheyne – 2s.
Thomas Holden formerly apprentice of William Mowbray – 2s.

Memorandum about defects in workmanship etc. during the time of John Pake, John Barnes, John Sutton the elder and Robert Ashby, Wardens of the Goldsmiths' Mistery etc. in the year 7 Henry VI [from 19 May 1429]: 1429–30 A + b p. 91
Firstly, from John Nongyl for an offence – 2s.
Item, from Thomas Gabrielle for an offence – 2s.
Item, from John Corby for an offence – 2s.
Item, from Nicholas Hervestoke for an offence – 2s.
Item, from John Nongyl for an offence – 2s.
Item, from Thomas Gabrielle for an offence – 2s.
Item, from Thomas Elys for an offence – 2s.
Item, from John Nongyl for an offence – 2s.
Item, from Magnus Verdon for an offence – 6s. 8d.
Item, from Nicholas Wood for an offence – 3s. 4d.
Item, from Thomas Gabrielle for various offences – 2s.
Item, from Thomas Lenham for an offence – 2s.
Item, from Gerard Splynt for an offence over 12 rings etc. – 10s.
Item, from John Clynton for an offence – 16d.
Item, from William Berwe, 'Dutchman', for an offence – 22d.

M.. Gilbert } leases 15..?
M.. Mabbe } as A + a p. 151
Robert Chylde } Meryall

John Goodryche a draught
Mr Gardmor – . . Robert Ch..

1430–31 A + b p. 92 Memorand*um* de defectib*us* op*er*acion*um* *et*c temp*or*e Will*elm*i Boton, Will*elm*i Walton, Joh*ann*is Wethyhale *et* Hen*ri*ci Ragley, custod*um* mister*e* aur*ifabrorum* *et*c anno r*egni* R*egis* Henr*ici* vj[ti] post conqu*estum* viii°.

In primis, de William Barrey, Duch*e*man, p*ro* i defalt*a* –	ii s.
It*em*, de Swether[696] *et*c p*ro* i defalt*a* –	xi s.
It*em*, de Arnold Benselord p*ro* i defalt*a* –	ii s.
It*em*, de Joh*ann*e Bysseford p*ro* i defalt*a* –	vi s. viii d.
It*em*, de Hans Cruyskyn p*ro* i defalt*a* –	ii s.
It*em*, de Gerard, Duch*e*man, p*ro* i defalt*a* –	ii s.
It*em*, de Joh*ann*e Powe, Duch*e*man, p*ro* i defalt*a* –	iii s. iiii d.
It*em*, de Joh*ann*e Sturdy p*ro* i defalt*a* –	ii s.
It*em*, de Nich*ola*o Wode p*ro* i defalt*a* –	ii s.
It*em*, de Joh*ann*e Stok p*ro* i defalt*a* –	ii s.
It*em*, de Ric*ard*o Water p*ro* i def*alta* –	ii s.

Ex*tra*nei jur*ati*:

In p*ri*mis de Will*elm*o Barrey –	ii s.
It*em*, de Hugon*e* de Lynne, Irissh*e*man –	ii s.
It*em*, de Patryk de Hib*ernia* –	ii s.
It*em*, de Will*elm*o Goldsmyth de Manchestr*e* –	ii s.

1431 p. 93 Also it is to be remembred that at the goyng out of William Boton, William Walton, John Wethehale and Henry Ragley, wardeins in the yer*e* of Kyng Harry the vj[te] the ix[e], of her wardeinship, they seyd wardeins left in the Hall*e* *et*c:

iii bordclothes of pleynecloth*e* & ii towailles of dyapr*e* werk longyng to the company *et*c.

It*em*, a pyle of laton of (v)[697] xvi m*a*rcz weght of Troy, left in the Hall*e* the same tyme & also a litell*e* touche and iiii nedeles therwith yn

It*em*, a steyned cloth*e* for the beme at Poules.

1431–32? A + a p. 152 Nomina app*re*nticior*um*:[698]

Joh*ann*es Aleyn app*re*ntic*ius* Thome Reyner –	xx s.
Will*elmus* Upnore app*re*ntic*ius* cum Joh*ann*e Orewell –	xx s.
Edwardus Vernay app*re*ntic*ius* cum Rob*er*to Bosh*a*m –	xx s.
Joh*ann*es Fyssher app*re*ntic*ius* cum Joh*ann*e Waryn –	xx s.
Joh*ann*es Louetoft app*re*ntic*ius* cum Joh*ann*e Mabilian –	xx s.
Ric*ard*us Palser*e* app*re*ntic*ius* cum Joh*ann*e Bisshop –	xx s.
Thom*a*s Bokenh*a*m app*re*ntic*ius* cum Barth*olome*o Bre*n*sam –	xx s.

696 A gap has been left before the name 'Swether' and a cross has been placed in the LH margin.

697 This figure has been scored out.

698 No date is given for these next two lists, but 1431–32 seems likely because of their position in the book. The wardens for that year are not known from either of the two record books but only from a document in the Register of Deeds, f. 135. One entry here, that of William Hilles, is repeated on p. 154 below in a list dated 1432–33, and it may well be that he came out of his terms at a date very close to that of the changeover of wardens, and somehow was placed on two separate lists.

Memorandum about defects in workmanship etc. during the time of William Botoun, William Walton, John Withihale and Henry Ragley, Wardens of the Goldsmiths' Mistery etc. in the year 8 Henry VI [from 19 May 1430]: 1430–31 A + b p. 92

Firstly, from William Barrey, 'Dutchman', for an offence –	2s.
Item, from Swether etc. for an offence –	11s.
Item, from Arnold Benselord for an offence –	2s.
Item, from John Bysseford for an offence –	6s. 8d.
Item, from Hans Cruyskyn for an offence –	2s.
Item, from Gerard, 'Dutchman', for an offence –	2s.
Item, from John Powe, 'Dutchman', for an offence –	3s. 4d.
Item, from John Sturdys for an offence –	2s.
Item, from Nicholas Wood for an offence –	2s.
Item, from John Stok for an offence –	2s.
Item, from Richard Water for an offence –	2s.

Aliens sworn:

Firstly, from William Barrey –	2s.
Item, from Hugh de Lynne, Irishman –	2s.
Item, from Patrick of Ireland –	2s.
Item, from William Goldsmyth[236] of Manchester –	2s.

Memorandum also that when William Botoun, William Walton, John Withihale and Henry Ragley, Wardens in the year 9 Henry VI [1430–31], demitted office [19 May 1431], the said Wardens left in the Hall etc.: 1431 p. 93

3 tablecloths of plain cloth and 2 cloths of diaper work belonging to the Company etc.

Item, a latten pile of 16 marks Troy weight, left in the Hall at the same time, and also a small touch and 4 needles with it.

Item, a stained cloth for the beam at St Paul's.[237]

The names of apprentices: 1431–32? A + a p. 152

John Aleyn apprentice of Thomas Reyner –	20s.
William Upnore apprentice with John Orwell –	20s.
Edward Verney apprentice with Robert Bosoun –	20s.
John Fisher apprentice with John Waryn –	20s.
John Louetoft apprentice with John Mablean –	20s.
Richard Palser apprentice with John Bisshop –	20s.
Thomas Bokenham apprentice with Bartholomew Bremsham –	20s.

[236] This might also be: William, goldsmith of Manchester.

[237] The stained cloth might have been either ornamental, possibly heraldic, or else figural, perhaps depicting a saint. The beam could have been the rood beam, or perhaps another beam, the one on which the Goldsmiths were accustomed to keep a light?

Rob*ertus* Kynton app*rentic*i*us* cum Joh*ann*e de Prys – xx s.
Joh*annes* Thomas app*rentic*i*us* cum Joh*ann*e Wethihale – xx s.
Thom*as* Ernest app*rentic*i*us* cum Joh*ann*e Berlyng – xx s.
Joh*annes* Bromley app*rentic*i*us* cum Thoma Weryng – xx s.
Ric*ard*us Piry app*rentic*i*us* cum Joh*ann*e Philipp*e* – xx s.

Allocat*i* jur*ati*:
Will*elmu*s Frekes nup*er* app*rentic*i*us* Will*elm*i Hertwell – ii s.
Will*elmu*s Hill*es* nup*er* app*rentic*i*us* Thom*e* Remy – ii s.[699]
Will*elmu*s Ford nup*er* app*rentic*i*us* Henr*ici* Clerk – ii s.
Will*elmu*s Bythewat*er* nup*er* app*rentic*i*us* Joh*annis* Bythewat*er* – vi s. viii d.[700]
Will*elmu*s Witfeld nup*er* app*rentic*i*us* Thom*e* Longe – ii s.
Will*elmu*s Wodeward nup*er* app*rentic*i*us* Joh*annis* Crisbien – ii s.
Humfrid*us* Hayford nup*er* app*rentic*i*us* Will*elm*i Allone – ii s.

1432–33 Ceux sount les nouns des Gardeins eslutz en le fest de Seint Dunstan l'an du
p. 153 regne le Roy Henry sisme puis le conquest disme tanq*e* au fest de Seint Dunstan adonq*es* p*ro*schein ensuant:
Thomas Leget
Joh*ann*es Walsh*e*
Thomas Rayner
Joh*ann*es Tewkesbury jun*ior*

p. 154 Nomina app*ren*ticior*um*:
Joh*annes* Broke app*renti*ci*us* Petri Brendwode – xx s.
Thom*as* Redyng app*renti*ci*us* Joh*annis* Sutton jun*ioris* – xx s.
Joh*ann*es Fayrehede app*renti*ci*us* Joh*annis* Wat*er*ley – xx s.
Henr*icus* Jacobson app*renti*ci*us* Joh*ann*is Estavyle – xx s.
Thom*as* Englond app*renti*ci*us* Thom*e* Blyth – xx s.
Will*elmu*s Copuldyk app*renti*ci*us* Joh*annis* Orewell*e* – xx s.
Will*elmu*s Steward app*renti*ci*us* Ric*ard*i Water – xx s.
Thom*as* Bele app*renti*ci*us* Joh*ann*is Swether – xx s.
Nicolas Fost*er* app*rentic*i*us* Joh*ann*[is][701] Wydyhale – xx s.[702]

Allocat*i* Jurat*i*:
Will*elmu*s Bagworth nup*er* app*renti*ci*us* Joh*ann*is P*ar*ker – ii s.
Joh*ann*es Sumpto*ur* nup*er* app*renti*ci*us* Rob*er*ti Walton – ii s.
Thom*as* Serle nup*er* app*renti*ci*us* Ric*ard*i Spenser – ii s.
Hugo Mirnskew nup*er* app*rentic*i*us* Will*elm*i Walton – ii s.
Will*elmu*s Hede (nup*er* app*renti*ci*us*)[703] fil*ius* Rob*er*ti Hede – ii s.
Joh*annes* Hopkyn nup*er* app*rentic*i*us* Henr*ici* Wykwan – ii s.
Rad*ulf*us Vernage nup*er* app*rentic*i*us* Rob*er*ti Walton – ii s.
Will*elmu*s de Hill*es* nup*er* app*renti*ci*us* Thom*e* Remy – ii s.[704]
Henr*icus* Geyre nup*er* app*rentic*i*us* Joh*ann*is Mabilyan – ii s.

[699] This entry appears again on p. 154 dated 1432–33.
[700] No explanation is given for this sum.
[701] MS: Joh*ann*e.
[702] This entry has been added later in a different hand.
[703] The words in brackets have been crossed through.
[704] See above, A + a, p. 152.

Robert Kynton apprentice with John de Pryce – 20s.
John Thomas apprentice with John Withihale – 20s.
Thomas Ernest apprentice with John Birling – 20s.
John Bromley apprentice with Thomas Weryng – 20s.
Richard Piry apprentice with John Philip – 20s.

Serving-men sworn:
William Frekes formerly apprentice of William Hertwell – 2s.
William Hilles formerly apprentice of Thomas Remy – 2s.
William Ford formerly apprentice of Henry Clerk – 2s.
William by the Water formerly apprentice of John by the Water – 6s. 8d.
William Whitfield formerly apprentice of Thomas Longe – 2s.
William Woodward formerly apprentice of John Cresbien – 2s.
Humphrey Hayford formerly apprentice of William Allone – 2s.

These are the names of the Wardens elected at the feast of St Dunstan in the year 10 Henry VI [19 May 1432] until the next following feastday of St Dunstan: 1432–33 p. 153
Thomas Leget
John Walsh
Thomas Reyner
John Tewkesbury the younger

The names of apprentices: p. 154
John Broke apprentice of Piers Brentwood – 20s.
Thomas Redyng apprentice of John Sutton the younger – 20s.
John Fayrehede apprentice of John Waterley – 20s.
Henry Jacobson apprentice of John Estavyle – 20s.
Thomas England apprentice of Thomas Blithe – 20s.
William Copuldyk apprentice of John Orwell – 20s.
William Steward apprentice of Richard Water – 20s.
Thomas Belle apprentice of John Swether – 20s.
Nicholas Foster apprentice of John Withihale – 20s.

Serving-men sworn:
William Bagworth formerly apprentice of John Parker – 2s.
John Sumpter formerly apprentice of Robert Walton – 2s.
Thomas Serle formerly apprentice of Richard Spencer – 2s.
Hugh Mirnskew formerly apprentice of William Walton – 2s.
William Hede (formerly apprentice) son of Robert Hede – 2s.
John Hopkyn formerly apprentice of Henry Wykwan – 2s.
Ralph Vernage formerly apprentice of Robert Walton – 2s.
William de Hilles formerly apprentice of Thomas Remy – 2s.
Henry Geyre formerly apprentice of John Mablean – 2s.

1432–33 A + b p. 79[705] A reme*m*brance that award mad upon Godard Sotte, Ducheman, hathe putte hym & sworn to upon a bok byfor John Walsche, Thom*as* Leget, John Tew[k]ysbery, Thom*as* Reyner, Gardeyns, John Pake, John Wethyale, John Sutton þe yunger, Ric*hard* Spencer, John Sutton þe elder, John Stalkenden, Wyl*ia*m Walton, to stonde award to al þ*e* men. And so þey award & mad by on asente þat þe forsayd Godard schal paye to be fre man i*n* þe company of goldsmythis L li. i*n* þ*at* forme: xx li. þat day that he wel desyr*e* þat þe wardeyns schal go wyt hym to þe Halle & aft*er*ward iii ȝer by ev*ery* ȝere x li. tyl þe xxx li. be com to þ*e* ende & to stonde to alle oþyr award*es* aftyr lyk as þe wardeins wyl entrete hym in goodly maner.

1433 [706]Godard*us* Sotte:

A + a p. 154 *cont.* Memor*andum* q*uo*d primo die April*is* anno r*egni* R*egis* Henr*ici* vj^ti post conqu*estum* xj°, Godardus Sotte, Ducheman, nup*er* s*er*viens Salamonis Oxney, admissus fuit in lib*er*tate*m* mister*e* aur*ifabrorum* p*re*dict*e et* in lib*ertatem* civit*atis et*c p*er* assensu*m et* voluntate*m* d*ictorum* gardianor*um et* tocius co*mun*itatis d*icte* mistere *et* solvit eisdem gardianis *et* co*mun*itati ea de causa in manib*us* – xx li.

Et etiam solvet dict*is* gardianis *et* co*mun*itati ex *et* p*ro* causa p*redic*ta – xx m*arcas*.

Videl*ice*t x m*arcas* inde in f*est*o Pasche p*roximo* futur*o et*c et x m*arcas* in f*est*o Pasche quod erit in anno d*omi*ni mill*esi*mo CCCC^mo xxxv^to.

1432 Wethihal, Hertwell*e*:

Memor*andum* q*uo*d xx° die Junii anno regni Regis Henr*ici* vj^ti post conqu*estum* x° Joh*anne*s Wethihale, civis *et* aurifaber London', venit coram Thoma Leget, Joh*ann*e Walsh*e*, Thoma Rayner *et* Joh*ann*e Tewkesbury jun*iore*, gardianis p*re*dict*is*, in aula aur*ifabrie et*c *et* secu*m* detulit *et* eis monstravit c*er*ta bona cuiusda*m* Joh*ann*is Hertwell*e,* nup*er* civis *et* aur*ifabri* London', invadiata eide*m* Joh*ann*i Wethihale p*ro* div*ersis* s*er*viciis dict*o* Joh*ann*i Hertwelle p*er* eunde*m* Joh*anne*m Wethihale prius nuncu[p]at*is*,[707] que quidem bona ponderat*a et* app*re*ciat*a* fuer*unt* ib*ide*m in p*re*senc*ia* dict*orum* gardian*orum*, videl*ice*t i goblet de argento pond' iiii unc*ias et* di*midiam*, p*recium* xi s. iiii d.. It*em*, i cheyne, i crosse, i nowche, v anul*os* de auro *et* ii p*arvos* diamaundes pond*erant*e*s* xxxvii d'weght – p*recium* xl s.

Summa – li s. iiii d.

1432–33 A + b p. 94 Memor*andum* de defectib*us* op*eraci*onu*m et*c temp*or*e Thome Leget, Joh*ann*is Walsh*e*, Tho*me* Rayner *et* Joh*ann*is Tewkesbury jun*ioris*, custod*um* mister*e* Aur*ifabrorum et*c a*nno* r*egni* R*egis* Henr*ici* vj^ti post conqu*estum* xj°.

In p*ri*mis, de Joh*ann*e Weryng p*ro* una defalt*a* –	ii s.
It*em*, de Rog*er*o Lenakr*e* p*ro* una defalt*a* –	xxi d.
It*em*, de Joh*ann*e Parker –	ii s.

[705] A new hand starts here. The whole entry has also had a cross put through it to indicate deletion.
[706] A new hand starts here.
[707] MS: nuncuat'.

Memorandum that a judgement was made for Godard Sotte, 'Dutchman', who took his oath on the book before John Walsh, Thomas Leget, John Tewkesbury, Thomas Reyner, wardens, John Pake, John Withihale, John Sutton the younger, Richard Spencer, John Sutton the elder, John Stalkendene, William Walton, that he would accept the judgment of all these men. And so they judged and by common consent decided that the aforesaid Godard shall pay £50 in order to be a freeman of the goldsmiths' company in this manner: £20 on the day that he wishes the wardens to go with him to the Hall, and then £10 each year for the next three years until the £30 is paid up, and also that he must abide by all other judgments made later which the wardens may properly make. 1432–33 A + b p. 79

Godard Sotte: 1433
Memorandum that on 1 April 1433 Godard Sotte, 'Dutchman', formerly the servant of Solomon Oxney, was admitted to the freedom of the aforesaid goldsmiths' mistery and into the freedom of the city etc., with the assent and by the wish of the said wardens and the whole commonalty of the said mister, and for this he paid into the hands of the same wardens and commonalty – £20. A + a p. 154 *cont.*
And he also was to pay for this to the said wardens and commonalty – 20 marks.
i.e. 10 marks at the next feast of Easter etc. and 10 marks at Easter in the year 1435.

Withihale, Hertwelle: 1432
Memorandum that on 20 June 1432 John Withihale, citizen and goldsmith of London, came before Thomas Leget, John Walsh, Thomas Reyner and John Tewkesbury the younger, the aforesaid wardens, at Goldsmiths' Hall etc. and he brought with him and showed them some goods of a certain John Hertwelle, formerly a citizen and goldsmith of London, previously given as pledges to the same John Withihale for various services, previously listed, done by the said John Withihale for the said John Hertwelle, the which goods were weighed and valued there in the presence of the said wardens, i.e. 1 silver goblet weighing 4½ oz. value – 11s. 4d. Item, 1 chain, 1 cross, 1 brooch, 5 gold rings and 2 small diamonds weighing 37 dwt. – value 40s.
Total 51s. 4d.

Memorandum about defects in workmanship etc. during the time of Thomas Leget, John Walsh, Thomas Reyner and John Tewkesbury the younger, Wardens of the Goldsmiths' Mistery etc. in the year 11 Henry VI [from 19 May 1432]: 1432–33 A + b p. 94

Firstly from John Weryng for an offence –	2s.
Item, from Roger Linacre for an offence –	21d.
Item, from John Parker –	2s.

It*em*, de Will*elm*o Alkham –	ii s.
It*em*, de Thoma Remy –	ii s.
It*em*, de Rob*er*to Asshby –	ii s.
It*em*, de Joh*anne*, Ducheman in le spitell*e* –	vi s. viii d.
It*em*, de Thoma Penne –	xvii d.
It*em*, de Swether, Ducheman –	vi s. viii d.
It*em*, de ii Duchemen a le Horn –	vi s. viii d.
It*em*, de Litel Hoggyn –	ii s.
It*em*, de Henr*ico* Polle –	xx d.
It*em*, de William Gotelye –	xx d.
It*em*, de Sutton, Halles man –	ii s.
It*em*, de Thoma Elys –	ii s.
It*em*, de une Frensshman in le Tour –	xxii s.
It*em*, de un Ducheman iux*ta* Swether –	xl d.
It*em*, de Thoma Gabriell*e* –	xii d.[708]
It*em*, de ux*or*e Hynkhorn –	v s.
It*em*, de Rob*er*to Bosoun –	ii s.[709]
It*em*, de uno Duch*e*man p*ro* q*ua*d*am* fine –	ii s.

1433 A + a p. 154 *cont.* Et etiam memor*andum* q*uo*d xix° die Maii in festo S*anct*i Dunstani anno r*egni* R*egis* Henr*ici* vj[ti] post conqu*estum* xj° in aula mister*e* aur*ifabrorum* London', Thomas Leget, Joh*annes* Walsh*e*, Thomas Rayner *et* Joh*ann*es Tewkesbury jun*ior*, custodes mister*e* p*re*dict*e*, delib*er*av*er*unt duo scripta obligator*ia* utrumq*ue* inde de dece*m* marc*is* st*er*lingor*um*. In quib*us* quidam Godardus Sotte, Ducheman, obligat*ur* Joh*ann*i Spenser, aur*ifabro*, ad usum mister*e* p*re*dict*e*. Solvend*is* ad c*er*tos dies ut sup*ra*, ad exitu*m* anni Joh*ann*i Wethyhale, Petro Brandewode, Joh*ann*i Werk *et* Joh*ann*i Frenssh*e*, qui erunt custodes p*ro* anno sequ*ente* *et*c ad salvo custod*ire* ad usu*m* mister*e* *et*c.

1433–34 p. 155[710] Ceux sount les nouns des Gardeins esluz en le fest de Seint Dunstan l'an du regne le Roy Henry sisme puis le conquest unzisme tanq*e* au fest de Seint Dunstan adonq*e*s p*ro*schein ensuant:
Joh*ann*es Wethyhale
Joh*ann*es Werk
Petrus Brendwode
Joh*ann*es Frenssh*e*

1434 Orden*a*nce of Duchemen made a*nno* H*enrici* vj[ti] xii°:
For as moche as þer be many werkers of Duchemen and oþer aliens in þe craft of goldsmythes within the lib*er*te of þe citee of London and oþer places, the whiche worken dayly falsly untrew gold and untrew silver, unto grete co*m*mune harme of all þe kynges peple, shame and desclaundre of all fremen goldsmythes of þe sayde citee, and woll noght obeye hem to the good rewles, gov*er*nance and correc*io*n of þe wardenis of the sayd crafte of

[708] The name 'gabriel*e*' has been picked out and written in the LH margin.
[709] The name 'bosoun' has been picked out and written in the LH margin.

Item, from William Alkam –	2s.
Item, from Thomas Remy –	2s.
Item, from Robert Ashby –	2s.
Item, from John, 'Dutchman' in St Mary Spital –	6s. 8d.
Item, from Thomas Penne –	17d.
Item, from Swether, 'Dutchman' –	6s. 8d.
Item, from 2 'Dutchmen' at the Horn –	6s. 8d.
Item, from Little Hoggyn –	2s.
Item, from Henry Polle –	20d.
Item, from William Goteley –	20d.
Item, from Sutton, the servant of Halle –	2s.
Item, from Thomas Elys –	2s.
Item, from a Frenchman in the Tower –	22s.
Item, from a 'Dutchman' with Swether –	40d.
Item, from Thomas Gabrielle –	12d.
Item, from Hynkhorn's wife –	5s.
Item, from Robert Bosoun –	2s.
Item, from a 'Dutchman' for a certain fee –	2s.

Memorandum also that on 19 May 1433 at the feast of St Dunstan at 1433
Goldsmiths' Hall in London, Thomas Leget, John Walsh, Thomas Reyner A + a
and John Tewkesbury the younger, wardens of the aforesaid mistery, handed p. 154 *cont.*
over two written bonds, both in the sum of 10 marks sterling, by each of which Godard Sotte, 'Dutchman', is bound to John Spenser, goldsmith, on behalf of the aforesaid mistery, the money to be paid on certain days specified as above, at the end of the year of office of John Withihale, Piers Brentwood, John Werk and John Frenshe who will be wardens for the following year, etc. to be kept safely on behalf of the mistery etc.

These are the names of the Wardens elected at the feast of St Dunstan in 1433–34
the year 11 Henry VI [19 May 1433] until the next following feastday of p. 155
St Dunstan:
John Withihale
John Werk
Piers Brentwood
John Frenshe

Ordinance *re* 'Dutchmen' made in the year 12 Henry VI: 1434
Whereas there are many 'Dutchmen' and other aliens working in the goldsmiths' mistery within the liberties of the city of London and elsewhere, who daily work dishonestly substandard gold and silver, to the great common harm of all the king's people, and to the shame and discredit of all freemen goldsmiths of the said city, and they refuse to obey the good rules and submit to the governance and correction of the current wardens of the said

goldsmythes for þe tyme beyng, the which be set on werk and have her levyng of goldsmythes that be fremen of þe sayde citee. Therefore, the xi day of Fev*er*er*e* in the xii ȝeer of Kyng Harry the sixt of his regne at þe Goldsmythes Hall of London at a gen*er*alle semblee for the goode rewles and gov*er*naunce of þe sayde crafte theer made, it was ordeyned, stablisshed and fully assented by John Wethyhale, John Werke, Piers Brendewode and John Frenssh*e*, wardeins of þe crafte aforeseyd, and many worthy and notable p*er*sones, þat is to sey John Pattesle and William Russe, aldermen, John Tewkesbury the elder, John Pake, John Tyce, Thomas Leget, William Walton, John Sutton the yonger, John Sutton the elder, William Moubray, Mathew Philippe, John Waryn, Thomas Longe and mony other good folk at þe sayd assemblee gadred, that after the xxi day of Fev*er*er*e* now next comyng, no man*er* man nor woman of þe sayd crafte shall set on werk nowther by himself nor be no mene p*er*sone ony suche ducheman or alien that usen to werk goldsmythrye in ony wyse, neyther by nor sell gold nor silver wrought nor unwrought by hemself nor be no mene p*er*sone in ony wyse of ony such ducheman or alien werker of goldsmythrye, except of c*er*tein p*er*sones duchemen, þat is to seyn Hans Laffert of Lymburgh, Reynald Lodynghous of Dortemone, Arnold Honover of Suthwerk, Denys Johnson of Suthwerk, Alard Petersone of Suthwerk, Couns Huke of the toun of Heldensem in Saxoyne, the which been under the rewle and gov*er*naunce of þe sayd wardeins, with mo þat after þis orden*a*nce shall be reherced, uppeyn of a C s. to be aveysed of him that doth þe cont*ra*rye of þis orden*a*nce. And so as ofte as ony man is found doyng þe contrarye of þis ordenaunce, þat he shall leese a C s. þat is to say vii marcs þ*er*of to þ'almowse of Seint Dunstan and þe remen*a*nt that is to sey vi s. viii d. to hym by whos relac*i*on ony such man that dothe ayeynst the sayd ordenaunce is aspyed and found fauty.

1434 No*ta* de soluc*ione* xx^{ti} m*arcarum* h*ab*ere licenc*iam* op*er*and*i*:
p. 156 Memorand*um* q*uo*d primo die Maii anno r*egni* R*egis* Henrici sexti post conq*uestu*m duodecimo, Reymundus de Wachter de Paris venit coram p*re*fatis custodib*us et* ib*id*em juravit sup*er* libru*m* ad bene, fideli*ter et* honeste op*er*and*um* infra cam*er*am suam aurum *et* argentu*m* ac omnia secreta artis aurifabror*um* London' fideli*ter* custodiend*um, et* licenciat*us* fuit p*er* d*ict*os Custodes quantu*m* in illis est ad op*er*and*um* infra cam*er*am suam p*redict*am cum iiii^{or} s*er*vientib*us* suis,[711] *et* solvit ea de causa – xx m*arcas*.

It*em*, eode*m* die Maii p*redic*ti Walt*er*us Gregory de Suthwerk, Ducheman, cora*m* dict*is* custodib*us* jurat*us* fuit ad op*er*and*um et* omnia alia faciend*um* p*r*out dict*us* Reymundus jurat*us* fuit et insup*er* idem Walt*er*us licenciat*us* fuit ad op*er*and*um et*c p*r*out dict*us* Reymund*us* lic*enciatus* fuit, exceptis servientib*us* eiusde*m* Walt*er*i, *et* solvit – iii li.

It*em*, sexto die Maii anno p*redict*o Joh*anne*s Luna de Holand coram dict*is* custodib*us* jurat*us* fuit ad op*er*and*um et* omnia alia faciend*um* p*r*out dict*us* Walt*er*us Gregory jurat*us* fuit et insup*er* idem Joh*anne*s Luna licenciat*us* fuit ad

710 A new hand starts here.

711 This phrase about servants, and the parallel ones in the next two entries have been added as an afterthought between the lines but in the scribe's own writing.

goldsmiths' mistery, and who work for and gain their livelihood from goldsmiths who are freemen of the said city. Therefore, on 11 February 1434 n.s. at Goldsmiths' Hall in London at a general assembly called for the good rule and governance of the said mistery, it was ordained, decided and fully agreed to by John Withihale, John Werk, Piers Brentwood and John Frenshe, wardens of the aforesaid mistery, and by many worthy and notable persons i.e. John Pattesly and William Russ, aldermen, John Tewkesbury the elder, John Pake, John Tyce, Thomas Leget, William Walton, John Sutton the younger, John Sutton the elder, William Mowbray, Matthew Philip, John Waryn, Thomas Longe and many other goodmen assembled together at the said meeting, that after 21 February next no man or woman of the said mistery shall engage for work, either by himself or through another, any such 'Dutchman' or alien who practises goldsmithry in any way, nor shall anyone either buy or sell gold or silver either wrought or unwrought, either by himself or through another, in any way of any such 'Dutchman' or alien worker in the craft of goldsmithry, excepting only certain 'Dutchmen' i.e. Hans Laffert of Limburg, Reynald Lodynghouse of Dortmund, Arnold Hanover of Southwark, Denis Johnson of Southwark, Alard Peterson of Southwark, Cowns Huke of the town of Hildesheim in Saxony, who are under the rule and governance of the said wardens, and others whose names will be listed after this ordinance, upon penalty of 100s. to be determined for any who infringe this ordinance. And as often as anyone is found guilty of infringement of this ordinance, he shall have to pay 100s., i.e. 7 marks of this to the alms funds of St Dunstan and the remainder i.e. 6s. 8d. to the one who has reported the case and by whose report any such man who has infringed the ordinance may be found guilty.

Note about the payment of 20 marks in order to have permission to work: p. 156
Memorandum that on 1 May 1434 Raymund de Wachter of Paris came before the aforesaid wardens and there he swore on the book that he would work gold and silver well, faithfully and honestly within his own chamber and that he would faithfully guard all the secrets of the goldsmiths' mistery of London, and he was given permission by the said wardens as far as in them lies to work within his said chamber with his four servants, and for this he paid – 20 marks.

Item, on the same day of May aforesaid Walter Gregory of Southwark, 'Dutchman', was sworn before the said wardens to work and to do all things in the same manner as the said Raymund was sworn, and upon this the same Walter was given permission to work etc. in the same manner as the said Raymund had been given permission, but excepting the servants of the same Walter, and he paid – £3.

Item, on 6 May of the aforesaid year John Luna from Holland was sworn before the said wardens to work and to do all things in the same manner as the said Walter Gregory was sworn, and upon this the same John Luna was given

op*erandum etc* p*r*out dict*us* Walt*er*us licenc*iatus* fuit, except*is* servientib*us* eiusde*m* Joh*ann*is, *et* solvit – v li.

It*em*, octavo die Maii anno p*redict*o Hans Cofman de Ulme in Sweven coram dict*is* custodib*us* jurat*us* fuit ad op*erandum et* om*n*ia alia faciend*um* p*r*out Reymundus de Wachter jurat*us* fuit et insup*er* idem Hans licenciat*us* fuit ad op*erandum etc* p*r*out dict*us* Reymund*us* licenciat*us* fuit ex*ceptis* s*er*vient*ibus* eiusdem Hans, *et* solvit – v m*arcas*.

It*em*, decimo die Maii anno p*redict*o Gerardus de Lownoyt de Henaude cora*m* dict*is* custodib*us* jurat*us* fuit ad op*erandum et* om*n*ia alia faciend*um* p*r*out Reymundus de Wachter jurat*us* fuit et insup*er* idem Gerardus licenciat*us* fuit ad op*erandum etc* p*r*out dict*us* Reymund*us* licenciat*us* fuit ex*ceptis* s*er*vient*ibus* eiusdem Gerardi, *et* solvit – viii m*arcas*.

It*em*, Hermannus Spryck de Suthwerk cora*m* dict*is* custodib*us* jurat*us* fuit ad op*erandum et* om*n*ia alia faciend*um* p*r*out Reymundus de Wachter jurat*us* fuit, et insup*er* idem Hermannus licenciat*us* fuit ad op*erandum etc* p*r*out dict*us* Reymundus licenciat*us* fuit, ex*ceptis* s*er*vient*ibus* eiusde*m* Hermanni, *et* solvit – xxvi s. viii d.

1433 p. 157 For as moche as be verray suggestion, notice and c*er*taine relac*io*n made by John Neylond and oþ*er* credible p*er*sones to John Wethihale, John Werk, Piers Brendwode and John Frenssh, wardeins of þe craft of goldsmythes of London, and to þe worshipfull bretheren of þe same crafte, how þe sayd John Neylond the which hath been a brother and of the clothyng of þe same craft mony yeres was, and is fallen into so grete pov*er*te and is indetted to div*er*ses p*er*sones of þe same craft þ*at* by liklyhode he shuld be imprisoned and nev*er* like to come oute þ*er*of but utterly ther to be destroyed. Therfor, the xii^e^ day of Juyn in the xi yeer of þe regne of Kyng Harry the sext, at þe Goldsmytheshall at a gen*er*all semblee for div*er*ses mat*er*es at that tyme theer made, considered þe pov*er*te and myschief that the sayde John Neylond was in, of pitee and vray almous it was graunted by the sayd wardeins and oþ*er* worthy and notable p*er*sones ther at þat tyme assembled, that is to say John Pattesle and William Russe, aldermen, John Pake, John Sutton þe yonger, John Walssh, William Walton, John Stalkenden*e*, Richard Spenser, Thomas Reyner, John Tewkesbury the yonger, John Sutton the elder, William Moubray, Mathew Philipp*e*, Robert Boteler, Thomas Long and William Allone, that þe sayd John Neylond shall have, take and receyve wekely fro þis day forwarde to þe terme of his lyfe xiiii d. by the handes of þe sayd William Allone of the renters þat now are and shall be for the tyme of þe almows of þe sayd craft, unto the tyme þe sayd William Allone be payed and satisfyed of xxii li. viii s. that þe sayd John Neylond duely owe him, ȝif so be the same John Neylond lyve so long, and yif he dye or þe sayd xxii li. viii s. be fully payed, that þan the paiement of the sayd wekely rent of xiiii d. cese and be voyde. And of the which xiiii d. so wekely to be receyved the sayd William Allone shall have viii d. by his owne graunt, and the sayd John Neylond vi d. to his levyng ward.

permission to work etc. in the same manner as the said Walter had been given permission, excepting the servants of the same John, and he paid – £5.

Item, on 8 May of the same year Hans Cofman of Ulm in Sweden was sworn before the said wardens to work and to do all things in the same manner as Raymund de Wachter was sworn, and upon this the same Hans was given permission to work etc. in the same manner as the said Raymund had been given permission, excepting the servants of the same Hans, and he paid – 5 marks.

Item, on 10 May of the aforesaid year Gerard de Lownoyt from Hainault was sworn before the said wardens to work and to do all things in the same manner as Raymund de Wachter was sworn, and upon this the same Gerard was given permission to work etc. in the same manner as the said Raymund had been given permission, excepting the servants of the same Gerard, and he paid – 8 marks.

Item, Hermann Spryck of Southwark was sworn before the said wardens to work and to do all things in the same manner as Raymund de Wachter was sworn, and upon this the same Hermann was given permission to work etc. in the same manner as the said Raymund had been given permission, excepting the servants of the same Hermann, and he paid – 26s. 8d.

Whereas by the truthful information, notice and sure report made by John 1433
Nayland and other trustworthy persons to John Withihale, John Werk, Piers p. 157
Brentwood and John Frenshe, wardens of the goldsmiths' mistery of London, and to the worshipful brethren of the same mistery, that the said John Nayland, who has for many years been a brother and of the livery of the same mistery, has fallen into such great poverty and is in debt to various people of the same mistery so that he is likely to be imprisoned and never be able to get out and it is likely that he would be entirely ruined there. Therefore on 12 June 1433 at Goldsmiths' Hall at a general assembly called at that time for various matters, having taken due account of the poverty and misfortune of the said John Nayland, of pity and true charity it was granted by the said wardens and other worthy and notable persons assembled there at that time, i.e. John Pattesley and William Russ, aldermen, John Pake, John Sutton the younger, John Walsh, William Walton, John Stalkendene, Richard Spencer, Thomas Reyner, John Tewkesbury the younger, John Sutton the elder, William Mowbray, Matthew Philip, Robert Botiller, Thomas Long and William Allone, that the said John Nayland shall have take and receive each week from this day forward until the end of his lifetime 14d. to be paid by the hand of the said William Allone from money supplied by the current and future renters from the alms funds of the said mistery until the time that the said William Allone shall have been fully paid the £22 8s. owed to him by the said John Nayland, if the same John Nayland shall live that long, and if he die or if the said £22 8s. be fully paid, then the payment of the said weekly rent of 14d. shall cease and be annulled. And of the 14d. thus received each week, the said William Allone shall have 8d. granted to himself, and the said John Nayland 6d. towards his livelihood.

1443 [712]For as moche as caryans of reknyng was betwene John Naylonde and Will*ia*m Allone of paymente of thys su*m*me above wretyn, John Sutton, alderman, John Walssh, Matthew Halle and Humfray Hayford, wardeins of the crafte of goldsmythes of London, Thomas Leget, John Whyn*e*, Thomas Reyner & John Werke hathe made an ende of alle maner of rekenyng betwen*e* them. And we have fownde that John Naylonde owythe to William Allone l s. the xix day of Auguste the ȝere of the regne of Kyng Harry the sext aft*er* quonqueste xxj^{ti} to be payde iiii d. wekely tyll the xxiii^{ti} day of May than to to be payde viii d. a weke tyll the su*m*me above wreten be full satysfyede.

1433–34 No*min*a app*re*nticior*um* temp*or*e Joh*ann*is Wethihale *et* soc*iorum* suo*rum* *etc*:

p. 158 Joh*ann*es Worlich app*re*ntic*ius* Will*elm*i Hert –	xx s.
Joh*ann*es Wyson app*re*ntic*ius* Will*elm*i Cros –	xx s.
Will*elmu*s Hull app*re*ntic*ius* Thome Whitfeld –	xx s.
Thom*as* Peretre app*re*ntic*ius* Mathei Philip*e* –	xx s.
Ric*ardus* Thwayt app*re*nt*icius* Henr*ici* Hewys –	xx s.
Ric*ardus* Sutton app*re*ntic*ius* Will*elm*i Waryn –	xx s.
Joh*ann*es Ayllebarn*e* app*re*nt*icius* Barth*olome*i Bremsa*m* –	xx s.
Will*elmu*s Pasmer*e* app*re*nt*icius* Tho*m*e Swynsco –	xx s.
Joh*annes* Dun app*re*nt*icius* Joh*annis* Sutton a le Sterr*e* –	xx s.
Will*elmu*s Gosse app*re*nt*icius* Joh*annis* Pris –	xx s.
Thom*as* Gerard app*re*nt*icius* Will*elm*i White –	xx s.
Joh*ann*es Amadas app*re*nt*icius* Joh*ann*is Bowdon*e* –	xx s.
Thom*as* Mordon*e* app*re*nt*icius* Joh*ann*is Kyrkeby –	xx s.
Ric*ardus* Asshhirst app*re*nt*icius* Will*elm*i Walton –	xx s.
Will*elmus* Brathenham app*re*nt*icius* Will*elmi* Port*er* –	xx s.
Joh*ann*es Brendwode app*re*nt*icius* Joh*ann*is Cary –	xx s.
Will*elmu*s Swetyng app*re*nt*icius* Joh*annis* Waryn –	xx s.
Joh*ann*es M*er*cer app*re*nt*icius* Tho*m*e Leget –	xx s.

Allocat*i* jurat*i*:

Joh*ann*es Grene nup*er* app*re*nt*icius* Joh*annis* Cary –	ii s.
Henr*icus* Saxby, Goldbet*er*, nup*er* app*re*nt*icius*[713] –	ii s.
Will*elmus* Osmond, Goldbet*er*, nup*er* app*re*nt*icius*[714] –	ii s.
Joh*ann*es Frenssh nup*er* app*re*nt*icius* Henr*ici* Wykwan –	ii s.
Joh*annes* Buk nup*er* app*re*nt*icius* [Johannis][715] Waterle –	ii s.
Ric*ardus* Messanger nup*er* app*re*nt*icius* Salam*onis* Oxney –	ii s.
Math*eus* Hall nup*er* app*re*nt*icius* Joh*annis* Pattesle –	ii s.
Will*elmu*s Cros nup*er* app*re*nt*icius* Joh*annis* Stok –	ii s.
Will*elmu*s Coup*er*e nup*er* app*re*nt*icius* Will*elmi* Coup*er* p*at*ris –	ii s.
Joh*annes* Offord nup*er* app*re*nt*icius* Joh*annis* Biernes –	ii s.

[712] A different hand has written this paragraph.
[713] Neither for this man nor the next are we given the master's name.
[714] In 1425–26 he was listed as the apprentice of William Wykwan.
[715] A blank space is left for the name, filled in here from information on A + a, p. 130.

Whereas there was a shortfall in the accounting between John Nayland and 1443 William Allone of payment of the sum written above, John Sutton, alderman, John Walsh, Matthew Halle and Humphrey Hayford, wardens of the goldsmiths' mistery of London, Thomas Leget, John Wynne, Thomas Reyner and John Werke have settled all matters relating to the accounting between them. And we have found that John Nayland owes 50s. to William Allone on 19 August 1443, this to be paid at 4d. per week until 23 May and then to be paid at 8d. per week until the above written sum shall have been fully paid off.

The names of apprentices in the time of John Wethihale and his fellow wardens etc.: 1433–34 p. 158

John Worlych apprentice of William Hert –	20s.
John Wyson apprentice of William Cros –	20s.
William Hull apprentice of Thomas Whitfield –	20s.
Thomas Peartree apprentice of Matthew Philip –	20s.
Richard Thwayt apprentice of Henry Hewys –	20s.
Richard Sutton apprentice of William Waryn –	20s.
John Ayllebarne apprentice of Bartholomew Bremsham –	20s.
William Pasmere apprentice of Thomas Swinscoe –	20s.
John Dun apprentice of John Sutton at the Star –	20s.
William Gosse apprentice of John Pryce –	20s.
Thomas Gerard apprentice of William White –	20s.
John Amadas apprentice of John Bowdon –	20s.
Thomas Mordone apprentice of John Kirkby –	20s.
Richard Ashurst apprentice of William Walton –	20s.
William Brathenham apprentice of William Porter –	20s.
John Brentwood apprentice of John Cary –	20s.
William Swetyng apprentice of John Waryn –	20s.
John Mercer apprentice of Thomas Leget –	20s.

Serving-men sworn:

John Grene formerly apprentice of John Cary –	2s.
Henry Saxby, goldbeater, formerly apprentice –	2s.
William Osmond, goldbeater, formerly apprentice –	2s.
John Frenshe formerly apprentice of Henry Wykwan –	2s.
John Buk formerly apprentice of John Waterley –	2s.
Richard Messynger formerly apprentice of Solomon Oxney –	2s.
Matthew Hall formerly apprentice of John Pattesley –	2s.
William Cros formerly apprentice of John Stok –	2s.
William Couper formerly apprentice of William Couper, his father –	2s.
John Offord formerly apprentice of John Barnes –	2s.

Ric*ardus* Thurston nup*er* appr*enticius* Pet*ri* Torold – ii s.
Joh*annes* Merssh nup*er* appr*enticius* Joh*annis* Wyn sen*ioris* – ii s.
Ric*ardus* Bevyngton nup*er* appr*enticius* Joh*annis* Biernes – ii s.
Joh*annes* Corbyn [nup*er*] appr*enticius* Joh*annis* Corbyn p*a*tris sen*ioris* – ii s.
Reymond*us* Wachter de Paris juratus est – ii s.

Memorand*um* q*uo*d quidam Joh*anne*s Goldsmyth de Coleyn licenc*iatus* fuit p*er* dict*os* custodes ad co*m*morand*um* cu*m* Will*elm*o Porter, aur*ifabro,* p*er* tres annos p*roximos* sequ*entes et* solvit – vi s. viii d.

Memor*andum* q*uo*d quia Will*elmu*s Porter v*er*ba scandalos*a et* opp*ro*brios*a* v*er*sus Barth*olomeu*m Bremsant locut*us* est cont*ra* ordinac*iones* etc, ideo idem Will*elmu*s solvit de fin*e* – vi s. viii d.

It*em*, Joh*anne*s Kebbell quia vend*idit* quenda*m* apprent*icium* sine licenc*ia* custod*um* sol*vit* – x s.

It*em*, Joh*anne*s Sumppter q*ui*a lic*enciatus* fuit p*er* custod*es* ad op*er*and*um et*c p*er* c*ertum* temp*us* sol*vit* – vi s. viii d.

It*em*, Walt*er*us nup*er* s*er*viens Salamonis Oxney q*ui*a v*er*ba scandalos*a et* opprobr*iosa* locut*us* fuit Joh*ann*i Stok de lib*er*ata con*tra* ordinac*iones et*c solvit – iii s. iiii d.

It*em*, quia Will*elmu*s Cros vend*idit* quenda*m* apprenticiu*m* suu*m* sine licencia cust*odum* con*tra* ordinac*iones* inde *et*c p*ro* x li., id*em* sol*vit* ex grac*ia* cust*odum* – xl s.

1434–35 p. 159 Ceux sount les nouns des gardeins esluz en le fest de Seint Dunstan l'an du regne le Roy Henry sisme puis le conquest duszisme tanq*e* au fest de Seint Dunstan adonq*e*s p*ro*schein ensuant:
Will*elmu*s Walton
Henr*icus* Ragley
Joh*anne*s Wynne
Matheus Philipp*e*

1434 Memor*andum* q*uo*d undecimo die Novembr*is* anno r*egni* R*egis* Henr*ici* vj^{ti} post conqu*estum* xiii^{o}, concessu*m* est p*er* Will*elmu*m Walton, Henr*icum* Ragley, Joh*ann*em Wynne *et* Matheu*m* Philipp*e*, custodes mister*e* aur*ifabrorum* London', ex assensu omniu*m* p*ro*boru*m* hominu*m* eiusdem mister*e* eiusdem civitatis, cuidam Reymundo de Wachter de Paris, q*uo*d idem Reymundus postq*ua*m ipse fiat ligens d*omi*ni n*ost*ri regis *et* concordav*er*it cu*m* cam*er*ario Guyhalde d*ic*t*e* civitatis p*ro*ut moris est p*ro* lib*er*tate sua h*ab*enda in d*ict*a civitate, admittat*ur* in lib*er*tate*m* d*ict*e mistere aur*ifabrorum* ad ita lib*er*e op*er*and*um* in d*ict*a mister*a* sicut aliquis eiusdem mistere d*ict*e civitatis, et solvit dict*is* custodib*us* ea de causa – xl li.

Richard Thurston formerly apprentice of Piers Thorold – 2s.
John Marsh formerly apprentice of John Wynne the elder – 2s.
Richard Bevyngton formerly apprentice of John Barnes – 2s.
John Corby [formerly] apprentice of John Corby the elder, his father – 2s.
Raymund Wachter of Paris has been sworn – 2s.

Memorandum that a certain John Goldsmyth from Cologne has been given permission by the said wardens to lodge for the next three years with William Porter, goldsmith, and he paid – 6s. 8d.

Memorandum that whereas William Porter spoke words of scandal and opprobrium against Bartholomew Bremsham, which is against the ordinances etc., for this cause the same William paid a fine of – 6s. 8d.

Item, whereas John Kebbell sold a certain apprentice without the permission of the wardens, he paid – 10s.

Item, whereas John Sumpter was given permission by the wardens to work etc. for a certain time, he paid – 6s. 8d.

Item, whereas Walter, formerly the servant of Solomon Oxney, spoke words of scandal and opprobrium to John Stok, who is of the livery, which is against the ordinances etc., he paid – 3s. 4d.

Item, whereas William Cros sold a certain apprentice of his for £10 without the permission of the wardens, which is against the ordinances made about this, he paid at the discretion of the wardens – 40s.

These are the names of the wardens elected at the feast of St Dunstan in the 1434–35
year 12 Henry VI [19 May 1434] until the next following feastday of St p. 159
Dunstan:
William Walton
Henry Ragley
John Wynne
Matthew Philip

Memorandum that on 11 November 1434 it was granted by William Walton, 1434
Henry Ragley, John Wynne and Matthew Philip, wardens of the goldsmiths' mistery of London, with the assent of all the goodmen of the same mistery of the same city, to one Raymund Wachter of Paris, that the same Raymund, after he has become a liegeman of our lord the King and once he has made an agreement with the Chamberlain of the Guildhall of the said city,[238] as is the custom, to obtain his freedom in the said city, shall be admitted to the freedom of the said goldsmiths' mistery to work freely thus in the said mistery in the same way as anyone of the same mistery of the said city, and for this he paid to the said wardens – £40.

[238] On the role of this officer see Betty R. Masters, *The Chamberlain of the City of London 1237–1987* (London, 1988).

1434–35 Nomina app*r*enticio*rum* temp*or*e Will*elm*i Walton *et* Henr*ici* Ragley *et*
p. 160 socio*rum* suo*rum*:

Will*elmu*s Percy app*r*entic*ius* Joh*an*nis Stalkenden*e* –	xx s.
Will*elmu*s Makelowe app*r*entic*ius* Will*elm*i Porter –	xx s.
Will*elmu*s Knyght app*r*entic*ius* Walt*er*i Chandeler –	xx s.
Rog*er*us Bernestone app*r*entic*ius* Jacobi Treygestok –	xx s.
Thom*as* Clerk app*r*entic*ius* Simonis Cros –	xx s.
Thom*as* Pynner app*r*entic*ius* Thome Reyner –	xx s.
Joh*ann*es Hopkyn app*r*entic*ius* Joh*ann*is Bowdon –	xx s.
Joh*ann*es[716] . . . app*r*entic*ius* Mathei Philipp*e* –	xx s.
Henr*icus* Gay app*r*entic*ius* Jacobi Gay –	xx s.

Allocat*i* jurat*i*:

Joh*ann*es Norman nup*er* app*r*entic*ius* Joh*ann*is Welles –	ii s.
Joh*ann*es Merston nup*er* app*r*entic*ius* Joh*annis* Wyn –	ii s.
Jacobus Gay nup*er* app*r*entic*ius* Joh*ann*is Emond –	ii s.
Ph*ilipp*us Stafford nup*er* app*r*entic*ius* Joh*ann*is Walssh –	ii s.
Joh*ann*es Asshurst nup*er* app*r*entic*ius* Will*elm*i Walton –	ii s.

1435–36 Theise ben the namys of the Wardeynys of the craft of goldsmythis chosyn
p. 161[717] in the feste of Seynt Dunston in the ȝere of Kyng Henry the vj^te^ aft*er* the conquest xiii thanne beinge:

Joh*ann*es Pattisle, alderman
Joh*ann*es Sutton, alderman
Joh*ann*es Waryn
Robert*us* Boteler

Nomina app*r*enticio*rum* eodem anno:

Tho*m*as Brygge app*r*ent*y*s with Rob*er*t Boteler –	xx s.
John Elys app*r*ent*icius* Joh*ann*is Norman –	xx s.
Henric*us* Grene app*r*entic*ius* Joh*ann*is Orwelle –	xx s.
John Holand app*r*ent*icius* Will*elm*i Prynce –	xx s.
Joh*ann*es Comb*es* app*r*entic*ius* Will*elm*i Hyllys –	xx s.
Salmon Petyt app*r*entic*ius* cu*m* Magnes de Ardrenak –	xx s.
Will*ia*m Denys app*r*entic*ius* Ricardi Bradcok –	xx s.
Edmund Manfeld app*r*entic*ius* Joh*ann*is Sturdyce –	xx s.
Will*elmu*s Beche app*r*entic*ius* Joh*ann*is Bowdon –	xx s.
Egidi*us* Schawe app*r*entic*ius* Tho*m*e Pynchard –	xx s.
Tho*m*as Sanfayle app*r*entic*ius* Will*elm*i Fynyngham –	xx s.
Robert*us* Elysmore app*r*entic*ius* Henrici Ragele –	xx s.
Will*elmu*s Salisbery app*r*entic*ius* Joh*ann*is Byschop –	xx s.
Joh*ann*es Coliere app*r*entic*ius* Joh*ann*is Werk –	xx s.
Joh*ann*es Herbard app*r*entic*ius* Will*elm*i Porter*e* –	xx s.
col. 2 John Wykwane app*r*ent*y*s w*ith* Will*ia*m Wykwane –	xx s.

[716] A blank space has been left for the surname.

[717] A new hand starts here. The layout of the table of names of apprentices and serving-men has also been changed, so that instead of an entry being all on one line, nearly all here are in two lines, bracketed together with the sum of money centrally to the RH side.

The names of apprentices in the time of William Walton and Henry Ragley and their fellow wardens: 1434–35 p. 160

William Percy apprentice of John Stalkendene – 20s.
William Makelowe apprentice of William Porter – 20s.
William Knyght apprentice of Walter Chaundeler – 20s.
Roger Barnston apprentice of James Tregewstek – 20s.
Thomas Clerk apprentice of Simon Cros – 20s.
Thomas Pynner apprentice of Thomas Reyner – 20s.
John Hopkyn apprentice of John Bowdon – 20s.
John apprentice of Matthew Philip – 20s.
Henry Gay apprentice of James Gay – 20s.

Serving-men sworn:
John Norman formerly apprentice of John Welles – 2s.
John Marston formerly apprentice of John Wynne – 2s.
James Gay formerly apprentice of John Edmund – 2s.
Phillip Stafford formerly apprentice of John Walsh – 2s.
John Ashurst formerly apprentice of Wiliam Walton – 2s.

These are the names of the Wardens of the Goldsmiths' Mistery elected at the feast of St Dunstan in the year 13 Henry VI [19 May 1435]: 1435–36 p. 161

John Pattesley, alderman
John Sutton, alderman
John Waryn
Robert Botiller

The names of apprentices in the same year:
Thomas Bridge apprentice with Robert Botiller – 20s.
John Elys apprentice of John Norman – 20s.
Henry Grene apprentice of John Orwell – 20s.
John Holland apprentice of William Prince – 20s.
John Combes apprentice of Wiliam Hilles – 20s.
Solomon Petyt apprentice with Magnus de Ardrenak – 20s.
William Denys apprentice of Richard Bradcok – 20s.
Edmund Manfield apprentice of John Sturdys – 20s.
William Beeche apprentice of John Bowdon – 20s.
Giles Shaw apprentice of Thomas Pynchard – 20s.
Thomas Sanfayle apprentice of William Finningham – 20s.
Robert Elysmore apprentice of Henry Ragley – 20s.
William Salisbury apprentice of John Bisshop – 20s.
John Coliere apprentice of John Werk – 20s.
John Herbard apprentice of William Porter – 20s.
John Wykwan apprentice with William Wykwan – 20s. col. 2

John Dalton app*r*ent*ys* w*ith* John Sutton, Ald*er*man – xx s.
John Bangore app*r*ent*ys* w*ith* John Pake – xx s.
Lambard de Wauyt*er* app*r*ent*ys* with Rumbold de Wauyt*er* – xx s.
George Manfeld app*r*ent*ys* w*ith* John Withiale – xx s.

No*min*a allocat*orum* jur*atorum*:[718]
John Lylye app*r*ent*ys* w*ith* John Heberd – ii s.
Richard Solander app*r*ent*ys* w*ith* Will*ia*m Alon*e* – ii s.
John Ev*er*tone app*r*ent*ys* w*ith* Will*iam* Belverge – ii s.
Tho*m*as White app*r*ent*ys* w*ith* Richard Robert – ii s.
Will*ia*m Fynyngham[719] app*r*ent*ys* with John Pake – ii s.
William Rothele app*r*ent*ys* w*ith* John Pake – ii s.
Tho*m*as Bowdon app*r*ent*ys* w*ith* John Bowdon – ii s.
John Cowdray app*r*ent*ys* w*ith* Tho*m*as Blythe – ii s.
Tho*m*as Whytbred app*r*ent*ys* w*ith* Will*ia*m Russ – ii s.
John Hakwelle app*r*ent*ys* w*ith* Will*ia*m Rus – ii s.
Roger Barber[720] app*r*ent*ys* w*ith* Will*ia*m Aston – ii s.
Richard Tregonoce app*r*ent*ys* w*ith* John Stok – ii s.

1435 Ordinau*n*sis of fyno*ur*is
A + b p. 81[721] Theise ben the ordinau*n*sis of the craft of fynouris of the cite of London for the goode governau*n*se of the same craft, by þe assent of Stevyn Bernard, John Whelere, Henry Bode and Tho*m*as Swayn, thanne fyno*ur*is of the seyd citee, þe xviii day August & þe xiii ȝeer of the regne of Kyng Henry þe vj^te aft*er* the conquest. To þe whiche ordinau*n*sis all*e* þe p*er*sonys afore seyd were sworn to kepe wel and trewly upon þe peynys undir writyn to paie and þey be fowdyn in defaute.

Fyrst, that no man of the same craft of fyno*ur*is afore seyd take none app*r*ent*is* unto þe tyme that he have schewid hym to þe wardeynys of goldsmythis of the said citee and to þe wardeynys of fynouris þ*at* schal be for þ*e* tyme that þay may have knowlache þ*at* he þat so schal be app*r*ent*is* be able of persone and þ*at* he be no boonde man born but fre born. And þ*at* þe same app*r*entis ouþ*er* his maist*er* schal paye to þe wardeynis of goldsmythis xx s., wheroffe vi s. viii d. schal be paid aȝen to þe wardeynis of fyno*ur*is. And what man of þe said craft of fyno*ur*is þ*at* doth the cont*r*arie of þ*i*s schal paye to þe alm*us* of Seynt Donstone – xl s.

Also, þ*at* no man of þe same craft of fyno*ur*is take no app*r*entic*e* but oon duryng the termis of hys app*r*entishode, exepte þ*e* laste ȝeer of þ*at* app*r*ent*is,* upon paine to paye to þe alm*us* of Seynt Dunstone – xl s.

[718] All those in the list below are of course *former* apprentices.
[719] The 'g' in this name has been added later by another hand, the same as changed the name 'Dore' to 'Barber' below.
[720] This surname has been inserted later by another hand above the name 'Dore' which is expuncted for deletion.
[721] A new hand starts here. One must also note that these pages are out of order chronologically, see Introduction, pp. xv–xvi.

John Dalton apprentice with John Sutton, alderman – 20s.
John Bangor apprentice with John Pake – 20s.
Lambard de Wauyter apprentice with Rumbold de Wauyter – 20s.
George Manfield apprentice with John Withihale – 20s.

The names of serving-men sworn:
John Lilye apprentice with John Huberd – 2s.
Richard Selander apprentice with William Allone – 2s.
John Everton apprentice with William Belverge – 2s.
Thomas White apprentice with Richard Robert – 2s.
William Finningham apprentice with John Pake – 2s.
William Rothley apprentice with John Pake – 2s.
Thomas Bowdon apprentice with John Bowdon – 2s.
John Cowdray apprentice with Thomas Blithe – 2s.
Thomas Whitbread apprentice with William Russ – 2s.
John Hakwell apprentice with William Russ – 2s.
Roger Barber apprentice with William Aston – 2s.
Richard Tregonoce apprentice with John Stok – 2s.

The ordinances of the finers 1435
These are the ordinances of the mistery of finers of the city of London, made for A + b p. 81
the good governance of the same mistery with the assent of Stephen Bernard, John Wheler, Henry Bode and Thomas Swayn, at that time finers of the said city, on 18 August 1435, and all the aforesaid persons were sworn to keep these ordinances well and faithfully upon pain of the fines written below if they be found guilty of any infringement.

Firstly, that no one of the aforesaid finers' mistery shall take on any apprentice until he has been presented to the current wardens of the goldsmiths of the said city and the current wardens of the finers, in order that they may know that he that is to be an apprentice is fit and capable and that he is not a bondman but free-born. And the same apprentice or his master shall pay 20s. to the wardens of the goldsmiths, of which 6s. 8d. shall be paid over to the wardens of the finers. And any man of the said finers' mistery who infringes this shall pay to the alms funds of St Dunstan – 40s.

Item, that no one of the finers' mistery shall take on more than one apprentice during the terms of his apprenticeship, except during the last year of that apprentice, upon pain of paying to the alms funds of St Dunstan – 40s.

Also, *þat* no foreyn man from *þis* tyme forþ be resseyvyd into þe craft of fyn*ou*ris to be made fre man w*it*owte assent & wille of þe wardeynis of þe craft
p. 82 of goldsmythis aforeseyd. And *þat* he make a fyn[722] as þay may acorde | wherof two partis schal go to þe use of þe craft of goldsmythis and þe þridde part schal go to þe use of þe craft of fyn*our*is.

Also, þat no man of þe craft of fynouris schal fyne eny selvir but *þat* it may bere [xviii][723] penyweyȝte of alay atte leste of Troye weyȝte for to be made *þer*of sterlyng, upon peyne for to paye atte fyrste tyme *þat* eny man is provid doynge þe contrarie of *þis* ordinau*n*se xviii d., and atte seconde tyme iii s., atte þrydde tyme vi s. viii d., and atte iiii tyme to be put owt of *þe* craft*is* as wel of goldsmythis as of fyn*our*is and lose alle *þe* benfet*is* *þat* he myȝte have had by þe same craft*is* for ev*er*more. And also þe fynys afore seyd, two part*is* schal go to þe craft of goldsmythis and þe þrydde part to þe craft of fyn*our*is afore said.

Also, *þat* ev*er*y man of þe same craft of fyn*our*is sette his marke to all*e* *þe* selvir þett he[724] fynyth upon þe peynys afore last rehersid for to paye in man*er* afore declarid.

Also, *þat* ev*er*y man of þe said craft of fyn*our*is come redily whan he is somonid byfore þe wardeynys of goldsmythis and þe wardeynys of fyn*our*is for þe good gov*er*nanse of þe same craft, for to be justified of her*e* t*re*spac*is* or wrongis yf eny þey doon (as God forbede), if þey have not a resonable excusacion, upon peyne to paye to þe alm*us* of Seynt Dunston xii d. at ech tyme *þat* he brekyth *þis* ordinanse.

p. 83 Also, þat þe wardeynys of þe craft of fyn*our*is ȝeerly ben sworn in þe Goldsmythis Halle in þe feste of Seynt Dunston as þe wardeynys of þe craft of goldbeteris be wont to be, to kepe alle þe goode rewlys & ordinau*n*sis as wel of her*e* owne craft as of þe craft of goldsmythis to here power*e* – to pay to the allm*us* of Sent Dunston vi s. viii d.[725]

p. 84 [blank]

A + a p. 162 Theyse ben the namis of the fynouris whiche ben resseyvyd in to the fraternite of þe craft of goldsmythes, and also þe fynys the wiche they hav payd for þe same cawse:
Steffan Bernard – vi s. viii d.
John Whelere – vi s. viii d.
Henry Bode – iiii li.
Tho*m*as Swayn – liii s. iiii d.

722 MS: affyn.
723 MS: xv. This must be a scribal error for 18 (xviii), the correct alloy quality for sterling at this date.
724 The word 'werkyþ' follows, but has been expuncted and a line drawn through it.
725 The last phrase has been added later in a different hand.

Item, that from henceforth no foreigner shall be admitted to the finers' mistery and made free of it without the assent and wish of the wardens of the aforesaid goldsmiths' mistery. And he shall pay a fee that they shall determine and agree, | of which two-thirds shall go to the use of the goldsmiths' mistery and one third p. 82
to the use of the finers' mistery.

Item, that no one of the finers' mistery shall refine any silver except that of a standard at least of [18] dwt. Troy weight alloy, so that sterling may be made of it, upon pain of paying at the first offence against this ordinance 18d., at the second 3s., at the third 6s. 8d. and at the fourth offence he shall be expelled from both the goldsmiths' and the finers' mistery and shall lose for evermore all the benefits that he might have had through the same misteries. And of the aforesaid fines, two-thirds shall go to the goldsmiths' mistery and one third to the aforesaid finers' mistery.

Item, that every man of the same mistery of finers shall put his mark upon all the silver that he refines, upon pain of the same penalties as listed above to be paid in the aforesaid manner.

Item, that every man of the said mistery of finers shall come promptly when summoned to the presence of the wardens of the goldsmiths and the wardens of the finers for the good governance of the mistery in order to be judged for any offences or wrongs they may have committed (which God forbid), unless they have a reasonable excuse, upon pain of paying to the alms funds of St Dunstan 12d. for each infringement of this ordinance.

Item, that the wardens of the finers' mistery shall be sworn each year at p. 83
Goldsmiths' Hall at the feast of St Dunstan, in the same manner as is accustomed for the wardens of the goldbeaters' mistery, and they shall swear to keep all the good rules and ordinances both of their own mistery and of the goldsmiths' mistery in as far as they are able – to pay to the alms funds of St Dunstan – 6s. 8d.

[blank] p. 84

These are the names of the finers who have been admitted to the fraternity A + a p. 162
of the goldsmiths' mistery, and also the fees which they have paid for this:
Stephen Bernard – 6s. 8d.
John Wheler – 6s. 8d.
Henry Bode – £4
Thomas Swayn – 53s. 4d.

1436 p. 163 Be it to remembre þat where Robert Boso[un],[726] citecein and goldsmyth of London, vilenously with malicious, sclandrous and heynous wurdis revylid and lyed John Pattyslee on off the wardeynis of þe craft of goldsmythis of London and also on of the ald*er*men of sayd cite, as it was enfourmyd to John Sutton, John Waryn, Rob*er*t Boteler, þre þe remnant of þe wardeynis of þe said craft, and to manye oþ*er*e worþy men of þe same craft there the xiii day of March þe xiiii ȝeer*e* of þe regne of Kyng Henry þe syxte aft*er* þe conquest, in the parysch of Seynt John Zakarye of London in þe Goldsmythis Halle, þere þe seyde wardeynys did do come afore hem þe seyde Rob*er*t Bosou*n*, and þere examinyd hym in p*re*sense of many worþy and goode men of þe same craft of þ*e* said malicious sclandrus & haynous wordis w*ith* revylyng and lying þe whiche þe said Rob*er*t aȝenseid not þe said wordis revylyng and lying, wher*e* upon þanne & þere it was axid by þe seyd þre wardeynys John Sutton, John Waryn & Rob*er*t Boteler & oþ*er* wurþi men of þe said craft, if he wolde submitte hi*m* and putte hym in awarde, ordinau*n*se & det*er*minacion & doom of þe saide John Sutton, John Waryn & Rob*er*t Boteler w*ith* þe assent & þe avyce of oþ*er* goode men of þe cumpani aforeseid for þe seide offense doon, þe same Rob*er*t Bosou*n* þanne & þere submyttid & putte hym to stonde & obeye to þe warde, ordinau*n*se, det*er*minacion & dome of þe said John Sutton, John Waryn, Rob*er*t Boteler w*ith* þe assent & good avyce of þe good men of þe said cumpanye for þe offense afforeseid. þanne afft*er*ward þe same day afforeseid atte said Goldsmythis Halle, first considerid þe said vilounous, malicious, sclandrus and haynous wordis w*ith* revyling & lyng afforesaid don to þe said John Pattisle, on of þe wardeynis aforesaid, souinge in to gret vilonye of þe said John Pattisle & of all þe said cu*m*panye, and moche þe more þ*at* he was stondynge ald*er*man at þ*at* same tyme & is ȝit and also for þe same Robert Boson nouþ*er* non oþ*er* of þe same craft scholde heraft*er* be so p*re*sou*n*tuous & so bold for to do such man*er* offense afforesaid. The said John Sutton, John Waryn, Rob*er*t Boteler, by assent and good avyce of many goode men of þe cu*m*panye aforesaid, warde, ordeyne, det*er*mine & deme þat þe saide Rob*er*t Bosou*n* from hens forward schal nouȝt have ne were the cloþyng of þe craft afforesaid nor were þe clothyng of þe same craft last passid, nor þat no brocour of þe said craft schal beie nor selle wiþ hym as w*ith* a fre man off þe same craft, nor he schal have þe benfaitis of þe same craft. And moreov*er* þ*at* þe same Rob*er*t Bosou*n* schal paie to þe alm*us* of Seynt Dunston in reffreschyng & relevyng of þe pore alm*us* men of þe broþ*er*hed of Seynt Dunston xx li., savynge grace of hys good amendyng & beryng.

1436 xix° die Appril*is* anno Henr*ici* sexti xiiii° p*er*donatus ad v li.[727]

[726] MS: Bosom.
[727] This note has been added later at the bottom of the page and is in the same scribe's hand.

Memorandum that whereas Robert Bosoun, citizen and goldsmith of London, churlishly with malicious, slanderous and hateful words insulted John Pattesley, one of the wardens of thegoldsmiths' mistery of London and also one of the aldermen of the said city, and accused him of lying, as it was reported to John Sutton, John Waryn and Robert Botiller, the other three wardens of the same mistery, and to many other worthy men of the same mistery present on 13 March 1436 n.s. in the parish of St John Zachary of London in the Goldsmiths' Hall, and the said wardens had the said Robert Bosoun summoned before them and there they examined him in the presence of many worthy and good men of the same mistery about the said malicious, slanderous and hateful words and the insults and accusations of lying, and the said Robert did not deny the words, the insults nor the accusation of lying, whereupon then and there the said three wardens: John Sutton, John Waryn and Robert Botiller, and other worthy men of the said mistery asked him if he would submit himself to the judgment, ordinance, decision and sentence of the said John Sutton, John Waryn and Robert Botiller with the assent and the advice of other goodmen of the aforesaid company for the said offence committed, and the same Robert Bosoun then and there submitted himself and agreed to abide by and obey the judgment, ordinance, decision and sentence of the said John Sutton, John Waryn and Robert Botiller with the assent and good advice of the goodmen of the said company for the aforesaid offence. And then later the same day aforesaid at the said Goldsmiths' Hall, having first considered the said churlish, malicious, slanderous and hateful words with the insults and the accusations of lying aforesaid against the said John Pattesley, one of the aforesaid wardens, that would lead to the great shame of the said John Pattesley and of all the said company, even more so since he was at that time and still is an alderman, and that neither the same Robert Bosoun nor anyone else of the same mistery should hereafter be so presumptuous nor so bold as to commit such an offence again, the said John Sutton, John Waryn and Robert Botiller with the assent and good advice of many goodmen of the aforesaid company, judge, ordain, decide and give sentence that the said Robert Bosoun shall from henceforward neither have nor wear the livery of the aforesaid mistery, nor shall he wear the previous livery of the same mistery, and that no broker of the said mistery shall either buy from or sell to him as they do with freemen of the said mistery, nor shall he have any of the benefits of the same mistery. And moreover that the same Robert Bosoun shall pay to the alms funds of St Dunstan for the relief and alleviation of the poor almsmen of the fraternity of St Dunstan – £20, this at discretion according to his making proper amends and his good behaviour. 1436 p. 163

On 19 April 1436 this was remitted down to £5.

1436–37 Theise be the namis of the Wardeynis chosin in the feste of Seint Dunston in
p.164 the ȝeer*e* of Kyng Henry the sixte aftir the conquest xiiii^{e} thanne beinge:

Joh*ann*es Pake
Ricardus Spenser
Tho*m*as Longe
Will*elmu*s Mowbray

col. 1 No*min*a app*re*nticior*um* eod*e*m anno:

Joh*ann*es Kelk app*re*nticius Math*e*i Philip – xx s.
Will*elmu*s Pottere app*re*nticius Thome Longe – xx s.
Joh*ann*es Brown app*re*nti*cius* Godardi Sotte – xx s.
Ricard*us* Chaundeler app*re*nti*cius* Joh*ann*is Orwelle – xx s.
Joh*ann*es Elinsale app*re*nti*cius* Joh*ann*is Grene – xx s.
Joh*ann*es Forster app*re*nti*cius* Will*elm*i Takele – xx s.
Tho*m*as Goland app*re*nti*cius* Joh*ann*is Sutton, Ald*er*man – xx s.
Henric*us* Belacis app*re*nti*cius* Joh*ann*is Tewkisbery – xx s.
Will*elmu*s of the Lowe app*re*nti*cius* Tho*m*e Herrissone – xx s.
Tho*m*as Bekkiswelle app*re*nti*cius* Will*elm*i Mowbray – xx s.

No*min*a app*re*nticior*um* de fyno*ur*is eode*m* anno:

Joh*ann*es Baylmont app*re*nti*cius* Henrici Bode[728] – xiii s. iiii d.
Joh*ann*es Hiatte app*re*nti*cius* Steffani Bernard:[729]
nichil solv*it* q*ui*a compactu*m* fuit antea sic p*ro* induccio*n*e socior*um* suor*um*.

col. 2 No*min*a allocator*um* eod*e*m anno:[730]

Will*elmu*s Schirborne app*re*nticius Joh*ann*is Walsche senior*is* – ii s.
Will*elmu*s Boston app*re*nti*cius* Petri Brendewode – ii s.
Steph*anu*s Scharp app*re*nti*cius* Joh*ann*is Stalkyndene – ii s.
Joh*ann*es Freman app*re*nti*cius* Joh*ann*is Tewkisbery – ii s.
Will*elmu*s Dewke app*re*nti*cius* Will*elm*i Mowbray – ii s.
Will*elmu*s Caumbrey app*re*nti*cius* Joh*ann*is Emond – ii s.
Laurensi*us* Lethlion app*re*nti*cius* Joh*ann*is Waterle – ii s.
Joh*ann*es Penne app*re*nti*cius* Joh*ann*is Bowdon – ii s.
Rob*ertus* Russell app*re*nti*cius* Nicho*la*i Lovet – ii s.
Joh*ann*es Rothewell*e* app*re*nti*cius* Joh*ann*is Colneye – ii s.
Tho*m*as Boteler app*re*nti*cius* Rob*er*ti Boson – ii s.
Nicho*las* Fyfede app*re*nti*cius* Joh*ann*is Townvyle – ii s.
Henric*us* Schingwell*e* app*re*nti*cius* Math*e*i Philip – ii s.
Will*elmu*s Wilmot app*re*nti*cius* Tho*m*e Elyce – ii s.
Tho*m*as Cotsou*n* app*re*nti*cius* Joh*ann*is Sutton, ald*er*man – ii s.
Will*elmu*s Clayton app*re*nti*cius* Tho*m*e Herrissone – ii s.
Will*elmu*s Bate app*re*nti*cius* Tho*m*ȩ Swynsco – ii s.

[728] There is a wormhole through the capital letter of this name.
[729] MS: Bernarard.
[730] All those in the list that follow are of course former apprentices, although the word 'nuper' has been omitted.

These are the names of the Wardens elected at the feast of St Dunstan in the year 14 Henry VI [19 May 1436]: 1436–37 p. 164
John Pake
Richard Spencer
Thomas Long
William Mowbray

The names of apprentices in the same year: col. 1

John Kelk apprentice of Matthew Philip –	20s.
William Pottere apprentice of Thomas Long –	20s.
John Brown apprentice of Godard Sotte –	20s.
Richard Chaundeler apprentice of John Orwell –	20s.
John Elinsale apprentice of John Grene –	20s.
John Forster apprentice of William Takeley –	20s.
Thomas Goland apprentice of John Sutton, alderman –	20s.
Henry Belacis apprentice of John Tewkesbury –	20s.
William of the Lowe apprentice of Thomas Harryson –	20s.
Thomas Bekkiswelle apprentice of William Mowbray –	20s.

The names of finers' apprentices in the same year:
John Baylmont apprentice of Henry Bode – 13s. 4d.
John Hiatte apprentice of Steffan Bernard –
he paid nothing since an agreement had been made previously for the admission of his associates.

The names of serving-men in the same year: col. 2

William Sherborne apprentice of John Walsh the elder –	2s.
William Boston apprentice of Piers Brentwood –	2s.
Stephen Sharp apprentice of John Stalkendene –	2s.
John Freman apprentice of John Tewkesbury –	2s.
William Duke apprentice of William Mowbray –	2s.
William Cambrey apprentice of John Edmund –	2s.
Laurence Lethlyon apprentice of John Waterley –	2s.
John Penne apprentice of John Bowdon –	2s.
Robert Russell apprentice of Nicholas Lovet –	2s.
John Rothwell apprentice of John Colney –	2s.
Thomas Botiller apprentice of Robert Bosoun –	2s.
Nicholas Fifehead apprentice of John Townvyle –	2s.
Henry Shyngwelle apprentice of Matthew Philip –	2s.
William Wilmot apprentice of Thomas Elys –	2s.
Thomas Cotsoun apprentice of John Sutton, alderman –	2s.
William Clayton apprentice of Thomas Harryson –	2s.
William Bate apprentice of Thomas Swinscoe –	2s.

1436 De executio*ne* p*er* Gardianos ap*ud* Westm*onasterium* *anno* xiiii^{o} H*enrici* vj^{ti}:
p. 165 Hit is to remembre þat þe xvj^{e} day off August the ȝeer*e* of Kyng Henry þe vj^{e} aft*er* þe conquest þ*e* xiiii^{e}, John Pake, Richard Spenser, Tho*mas* Longe and Will*iam* Mowbray beynge wardeynis for þe same ȝeer*e* wente to Westmynst*er* for to serche false workeris there, and þer*e* they fownde a fals boy þ*at* was sumtyme app*rentis* wiþ Richard Wynt*er* in Sowþwerk and þer*e* þey fownde hym workynge laton bondis & cop*ar* bondis for maseris, for notis & for hornis to þe nowmbre of ix ouþ*er* x at onys. And þey by the wille and assent of þe abbot hadde w*ith* hem þe erchedekin and þe serch*ere* to his schoppe & ther*e* þey clyppid hem on gobett*is* ev*er*ychone, and þer*e* þe party was put owt of his hows & his tool forfetid and born awey forþw*ith* to þe sercheris hows, and his dore lokkid & seelid in, and hymself jugid to sitte in þe stokkis by juggement of þe erchedekyn of þ*e* same place.

1437 De executio*ne* p*er* Gardianos ap*ud* S*anctu*m Barthel*omeu*m *anno* xv^{o} H*enrici* vj^{ti}:
Also hit is to remembre þ*at* þ*e* xx^{e} day of Aprill*e* þe xv^{e} ȝeer*e* of Kyng Henry above wrytyn, þe seide wardeynis wente to Seynt Bartholmewis, and þere þey spak w*ith* þe p*ri*our of þe same place of suche untrewe workeris þ*at* wer*e* enabitid in þe same place, þe whiche þe p*ri*our knew not, and whill*e* þe wardeynis & þe p*ri*our stod togedir cam on John Trivilias þ*at* was sum tyme a good workman of goldsmythis craft, and þer*e* þe p*ri*our comondid hym to come w*ith* hy*m* and w*ith* þe wardeynys for to brynge hem to his chau*n*br*e* & whan þey cam þer*e* he wold not lete hem in, & þe p*ri*our made hym to deliv*er* his keye to hym, and þane þey wente in and þere þey fownde div*er*ce bondis of laton þe whiche wer*e* kut in gobettis forþw*ith*, and also þ*er*e was fownde a pece in þe bedstraw þ*e* whiche was cop*ar* & ysylv*er*id above, the whiche was lykly for to have be sold for good selv*er*, and while þ*at* þ*i*s was avoynge þ*e* seide fals harlot stale awey owt of þe place & ellis he hadde be set in þe stokkis.

1436 De admission*e* div*er*c[*orum*] ho*min*[*um*][732] ap*ud* Calec*ium*:
(1448–49) p. 166[731] Be it remembred than in these wardeyns days, that is to sey the xiiiith ȝere of Kyng Herry the sexte, was sent by the citee of London to the segge of Calys certeyn sawdiou*rs*, that is to sey sper*es* & bowes, of the which sawdio*urs* this craft sonde ii speres & xii bowes which is entred in the grete boke of pap*er*[733] next the counte of Tho*mas* Leget, Barth*olomew* Bremsh*a*m, Humfrey Heyford & Herry Bode the xxvii ȝere of the said Kyng.

Book A, p. 32[734] Thes ben the p*a*rcell*es* of the expens*es* & costes spent & payd by the crafte of goldsmythes for div*ers* sper*es* & sowdiou*rs* sent by the cite of London to the sege of Calys the reigne of King Herry the sexte xiiiith that is to sey ii speres & xii bowes.
col. 1 My Mayster Paddisley Aldr*eman* – xl s.
My Mayster Sutton Aldr*eman* – xl s.

[731] This page has been written by a different hand.
[732] MS: div'c' ho̅ib'.
[733] i.e. the register now known as Book A = MS 1520.
[734] This entry in Book A is in the same hand as the entry on p. 166 of Book A + a. It is now no longer next to the account of Thomas Leget etc. (1448). It and the immediately preceding entries

An enforcement carried out at Westminster by the wardens in the year 14 Henry VI: 1436 p. 165
Memorandum that on 16 August 1436 John Pake, Richard Spencer, Thomas Long and William Mowbray, wardens for that year, went to Westminster in order to make a search for illicit workers there, and there they found an illicit boy who had formerly been an apprentice with Richard Wynter in Southwark, and they found him there working latten bands and copper bands for mazers, coconut cups and drinking-horns, making nine or ten at the same time. And at the wish and with the consent of the Abbot they took with them the archdeacon and the inspector[239] to his shop, and they cut each one of them into small pieces, and the boy was turned out of his house, his tool confiscated and taken away at once to the inspector's house, and his door was locked and sealed, and he himself was sentenced to sit in the stocks by judgment of the archdeacon of the same place.

An enforcement carried out by the wardens at St Bartholomew's in the year 15 Henry VI: 1437
Memorandum also that on 20 April 1437 the said wardens went to St Bartholomew's and spoke there with the Prior of the same place about some illicit workers who were living in the same place, about whom the Prior knew nothing, and while the wardens and the Prior were standing together, a certain John Trevilyas came along, who had previously been a good workman in the goldsmiths' mistery, and the Prior ordered him to come with him and the wardens and take them to his room, and when they got there he would not let them in, and the Prior made him hand over his key to him and then they went in, and there they found various latten bands which were at once cut up into small pieces, and there was also found there in the bedstraw a piece of copper silvered over which would very probably have been sold as good silver, and while all this was going on the false knave stole away out of the place, and otherwise he would have been put in the stocks.

The sending of various men to Calais: 1436 (1448–49) p. 166
Memorandum that during the term of these wardens, i.e. in the year 14 Henry VI [1435–36], certain soldiers were sent by the city of London to the siege of Calais, i.e. spearmen and bowmen, of which this mistery sent 2 spearmen and 12 bowmen, and this is recorded in the large paper register next to the accounts of Thomas Leget, Bartholomew Bremsham, Humphrey Heyford and Harry Bode, 27 Henry VI [1448–49].

These are the items of expenditures and costs paid out by the goldsmiths' mistery for various spears and soldiers sent by the city of London to the siege of Calais in the year 14 Henry VI [1436], i.e. 2 spearmen and 12 bowmen. Book A, p. 32

My Master Pattesley, alderman – 40s. col. 1
My Master Sutton, alderman – 40s.

[239] Inspectors or 'searchers' were regularly appointed by each of the City misteries, whose job was to inspect and test goods pertaining to that mistery in order to maintain standards.

My Maystres Rus – vi s. viii d.
John Whethale – x s.
Mathew Phelipp – x s.
Will*ia*m Walton – x s.
John Grene – x s.
John Pake – vi s. viii d.
John Waren – vi s. viii d.
John Wynn – vi s. viii d.
John Sturdys – vjs. viii d.
John Walssh – vi s. viii d.
Richard Spencer – vi s. viii d.
Herry Ragley – vi s. viii d.
Richard Bradcok – vi s. viii d.
Thom*as* Leget – vi s. viii d.
Will*ia*m Alone – vi s. viii d.
Rob*er*t Botiller – vi s. viii d.
Bartilmew Bramson – iii s. iiii d.
John Crewell – iii s. iiii d.
John Bowdon – iii s. iiii d.
John Toplyfe – iii s. iiii d.
John Werke – iii s. iiii d.
John Stok – iii s. iiii d.
Thom*as* Reyner – iii s. iiii d.
John Frenssh – iii s. iiii d.
Thom*as* Longe – iii s. iiii d.
John Byrlyng – iii s. iiii d.
Herry Pole – ii s.
Thom*as* Harryson – ii s.
John Huke – ii s.
Will*ia*m Mombrey – xx d.
Sutton the Elder – xx d.
John Heberd – xx d.
John Corby – xx d.
John Kebill*e* – xx d.
John Tewkysbury – xx d.
col. 2 John Adys – xx d.
John Stakenden – xx d.
Richard Heyward – xx d.
John Kyngesden – xx d.
Thom*as* Remye – xx d.
Mathew Halle – xx d.
Humfrey Heyford – xx d.
John Bisshop – xx d.
Nicholas At Wode – xx d.
Petyr Byrnwode – xx d.

relating to 1462 have clearly been written on separate sheets (but which have the same watermark as the rest forming the book) that have at some stage been bound into the book out of order (the succeeding entries relate to 1445 and should therefore have preceded as well). See Introduction, pp. xvii and xxii.

My Master Rus – 6s. 8d.
John Withihale – 10s.
Matthew Philip – 10s.
William Walton – 10s.
John Grene – 10s.
John Pake – 6s. 8d.
John Waryn – 6s. 8d.
John Wynne – 6s. 8d.
John Sturdys – 6s. 8d.
John Walsh – 6s. 8d.
Richard Spencer – 6s. 8d.
Harry Ragley – 6s. 8d.
Richard Bradcok – 6s. 8d.
Thomas Leget – 6s. 8d.
William Allone – 6s. 8d.
Robert Botiller – 6s. 8d.
Bartholomew Bremsham – 3s. 4d.
John Crewell – 3s. 4d.
John Bowdon – 3s. 4d.
John Topclyf – 3s. 4d.
John Werk – 3s. 4d.
John Stok – 3s. 4d.
Thomas Reyner – 3s. 4d.
John Frenshe – 3s. 4d.
Thomas Longe – 3s. 4d.
John Birling – 3s. 4d.
Harry Pole – 2s.
Thomas Harryson – 2s.
John Hook – 2s.
William Mowbray – 20d.
Sutton the elder – 20d.
John Huberd – 20d.
John Corby – 20d.
John Kebbell – 20d.
John Tewkesbury – 20d.
John Adys – 20d. col. 2
John Stalkendene – 20d.
Richard Heyward – 20d.
John Kingsdon – 20d.
Thomas Remy – 20d.
Matthew Halle – 20d.
Humphrey Heyford – 20d.
John Bisshop – 20d.
Nicholas atte Wood – 20d.
Peter Brentwood – 20d.

Rob*er*t Gyles – xx d.
Richard BytheWat*er* – xx d.
Thom*as* Berkman – xii d.
Nich*ol*as Lovette – xii d.
Rob*er*t Asshby – xii d.
Will*iam* Fenyngh*am* – xii d.
Robert Down – xii d.
Isabell*e* Joyce – viii d.
John Greton – vi d.

S*umma* to*talis* of the men in the lyvery is: xiii li. xv s. iiii d.

Nicholas Fyfeld – iii s. iiii d.
Horwode – iii s. iiii d.
Will*iam* Tanner – xx d.
Richard Crokelane – xx d.
Richard Fryth – xx d.
John Norman – xii d.
Will*iam* Hylle – xii d.
Thom*as* Cole – xii d.
Walter Ch*a*undeler – xii d.
John Childe – xii d.
John Kyrkeby – xii d.
Will*iam* Prynce – xii d.
Will*iam* Porter – xii d.
Thom*as* Tumvyle – xii d.
Hew Herrys – xii d.
John Weryng – viii d.
Rob*er*t Hede – viii d.
Will*iam* Hede – viii d.
p. 33, col. 1 John Gebon – viii d.
Jamys Gey – viii d.
John Benton – viii d.
Richard Messynger – vi d.
Herry Horn – vi d.
John Bastard – vi d.
Will*iam* Floure – vi d.
Richard Bawlyn – vi d.
Nich*olas* Hervestok – vi d.
John Hert – vi d.
Will*iam* Wodward – iiii d.
John A Werke – iiii d.

S*umma* of the younge not in the lyv*er*y – xxix s. x d.

Rombold Vant – liii s. iiii d.
Herry at Bussh – xxxiii s. iiii d.
Arnold Usman – xxvi s. viii d.
Jenyn Skeven – xx s.
Herman Vanpete – xx s.
Godard Sotte – xx s.

Robert Gyles – 20d.
Richard by the Water – 20d.
Thomas Berkman – 12d.
Nicholas Lovet – 12d.
Robert Ashby – 12d.
William Fenyngham – 12d.
Robert Down – 12d.
Isabelle Joyce – 8d.
John Greton – 6d.

Sum total from the men in the livery is £13 15s. 4d.

Nicholas Fyfield – 3s. 3d.
Horwood – 3s. 4d.
William Tanner – 20d.
Richard Crokelane – 20d.
Richard Fryth – 20d.
John Norman – 12d.
William Hilles – 12d.
Thomas Cole – 12d.
Walter Chaundeler – 12d.
John Childe – 12d.
John Kirkby – 12d.
William Prince – 12d.
William Porter – 12d.
Thomas Tumvyle – 12d.
Hugh Herrys – 12d.
John Weryng – 8d.
Robert Hede – 8d.
William Hede – 8d.
John Gybon – 8d. p. 33, col. 1
James Gay – 8d.
John Benton – 8d.
Richard Messynger – 6d.
Harry Horn – 6d.
John Bastard – 6d.
William Floure – 6d.
Richard Bawlyn – 6d.
Nicholas Hervestoke – 6d.
John Hert – 6d.
William Woodward – 4d.
John a Werke – 4d.

Sum from the yeomen not in the livery – 29s. 10d.

Rumbold Vant – 53s. 4d.
Henry atte Bushe – 33s. 4d.
Arnold Usman – 26s. 8d.
Janyn Eskevyn – 20s.
Hermann Vanpete – 20s.
Godard Sotte – 20s.

Swether Vanbrenen – xx s.
Hans Costard – xiiii s. iiii d.
Hans Blyth – xiii s. iiii d.
Walt*er* Tenefrous – xiii s. iiii d.
Herman Sprygge – xiii s. iiii d.
Gylis Panser – xiii s. iiii d.
Will*ia*m Garardson – xiii s. iiii d.
Magn*us* Vardon – x s.
Hans Dobler – vi s. viii d.
Hans Copeman – vi s. viii d.
Court Huke – vi s. viii d.
Petyr Browll – vi s. viii d.
Nich*olas* Moryng – vi s. viii d.
Arnold Bensrode – vi s. viii d.
Hans Kyrstian – vi s. viii d.
Herry Vandelyn – vi s. viii d.
Garlofe Spayne – vi s. viii d.
Lambert – v s.
Garard Hav*er*beke – iii s. iiii d.
John Pecok – iii s. iiii d.
col. 2 Fredryke Swert – iii s. iiii d.
Floure Clepyn – iii s. iiii d.
Olyver – iii s. iiii d.
John Duncard – iii s. iiii d.
Jacob Pemenet*er* – iii s. iiii d.
Hans Swan – iii s. iiii d.
Gylis Vanbrynen – iii s. iiii d.
Garard – iii s. iiii d.
Petyr Van Swethen – ii s. vi d.
Arnold Onofore – ii s.
Olyver Costard – xx d.
Deryke Van Wesill – xx d.
Arnold Smold – xx d.
Otte Van Touyn – xii d.
John Hawe – xii d.
Herry Lewten – viii d.

S*umma* of the Duchmen both in London, in Suthwerke & Westm' & in othir plac*es*: xix li. xiii s. x d.

S*umma* of all the hole crafte in gen*er*all is: xxxiiii li. xix s.

1436 A + a p. 167 Hit is to remembre that for as moche as þe xxvi day of Novembr*e* þe xv^e ȝeer*e* of Kyng Henri þe vj^e diverce debatis, dissensions & discordis wer*e* hangynge and movyd bytwene John Suttone, citteceyn and goldsmyth of London, þe sone of Lawrense Suttone, on þ*at* on partye and John Dun of London on þ*at* oþ*er* partye, goldsmyth þanne beynge app*re*ntis of þ*e* seyde John Sutton, John Pake, Richard Spenseer, Tho*m*as Longe, Will*ia*m Mowbray thanne beynge wardeynis of þe seid craft, stablisschidin and made a ful ende of all*e* man*er* materis and

Swether Vanbrenen – 20s.
Hans Costard – 14s. 4d.
Hans Blithe – 13s. 4d.
Walter Tenefrous – 13s. 4d.
Hermann Spryck – 13s. 4d.
Giles Panser – 13s. 4d.
William Garardson – 13s. 4d.
Magnus Vardon – 10s.
Hans Dobler – 6s. 8d.
Hans Copeman – 6s. 8d.
Court Huke – 6s. 8d.
Peter Browll – 6s. 8d.
Nicholas Moryng – 6s. 8d.
Arnold Bensebrod – 6s. 8d.
Hans Cristian – 6s. 8d.
Henry Vandelyn – 6s. 8d.
Gorlof Spayne – 6s. 8d.
Lambert – 5s.
Garard Haverbeke – 3s. 4d.
John Peacock – 3s. 4d.
Frederick Swert – 3s. 4d. col. 2
Floure Clepyn – 3s. 4d.
Olyver – 3s. 4d.
John Duncard – 3s. 4d.
Jacob Pemeneter – 3s. 4d.
Hans Swan – 3s. 4d.
Giles Vanbrynen – 3s. 4d.
Garard – 3s. 4d.
Peter Van Swethen – 2s. 6d.
Arnold Hanover – 2s.
Olyver Costard – 20d.
Deryk Van Wesill – 20d.
Arnold Smold – 20d.
Otte Van Touyn – 12d.
John Hawe – 12d.
Harry Luton – 8d.

Sum from the 'Dutchmen' both in London, in Southwark and Westminster and in other places – £19 13s. 10d.

Sum from the mistery as a whole – £34 19s.

Memorandum that whereas on 26 November 1436 various quarrels, dissensions and disagreements were pending and motions had been started between John Sutton, citizen and goldsmith of London, the son of Lawrence Sutton, on the one side and John Dun of London, goldsmith and at that time the apprentice of the said John Sutton, on the other side, the then wardens of the said mistery, John Pake, Richard Spencer, Thomas Long and William Mowbray, in their communal Hall on the aforesaid date ordained and settled finally all matters and 1436 A + a p. 167

causis byfore þ*at* tyme hangynge bytwene hem in her*e* gen*er*al halle þe day & ȝeer*e* above seyd in þe man*er* þ*at* folwyth: That is for to seye þ*at* þe seyde John Dun scholde fully be dischargid of his p*r*entyshood & servyse from þe seide John Sutton, and þe same John Dun to paye þ*er*fore and for alle oþ*er* materis gen*er*ally to his seyd maist*er* viii mark at certeyn dayes folwynge, þ*at* is for to seye at þe feste of þe Annunciacion of Owr Lady next folwynge þe date of þ*is* wrytyng vi s. viii d.; at þe feste of Seynt John Baptist þanne next seuynge vi s. viii d.; at Michelmasse þanne next folwynge vi s. viii d. and at Crystemasse þanne next folwynge vi s. viii d. and so forþ from feste to feste and from ȝeer to ȝeer ev*er*y ȝer*e* aft*er* oþ*er* continually suynge, in ev*er*y of þe seyde festis vi s. viii d. til þe forseid viii mark be fully peid, if þe seid John Dun lyve so longe, owt take þ*at* if þe seyd John Dun happe to deyȝe w*ith*ynne þe ful payment of þe seyde viii mark that þanne alle þe payment*is* that be to come aft*er* þe deces of þe seyd John Dun of þe foreseyd money schal cece and be holden for nouȝt and utt*er*ly for ev*er* be excludid, and for more seurte of þ*at* viii mark to be paid in þe maner*e* above wryten, on Henry Pool, citceyn and goldsmyth of London, stont bownde to þe seid John Sutton by his obligacion in þe forseid su*m*me. Furthermore it is acordid and awardid bi þe seyd wardeynis þat at þe fowr*e* ȝeris ende if þe seid John lyve so longe, whan þe seid viii mark is paid fulli, thanne þe seid John Dun schal paye or do paye to þe seid John Sutton, his executo*ur*is or his assygneis xl s., in þe whiche on Will*ia*m Redyng of Flamstede in Hertfordeschyr*e*, ȝeman, stont bounde inne by obligacion to þe seyde John Dun, but if it so be þ*at* þe seid John Sutton recov*er*e þe seid xl s. of þe seid William Redynge eny tyme raþ*er* w*ith*inne þ*e* forseid iiii ȝeer*es* of payment of þe seyd viii mark. And for more sewrte þ*er*offe þe seide John Sutton hath þ*e* seid obligacion of xl s. in his owne kepyng. Furþ*er*more, þe seyd wardeynis awardyn and ȝevyn for ful juggement by her*e* offyce & power*e* of her*e* wardeynschipe þ*at* whan þe seid John Sutton is paid & content of þe seid su*m*me of viii mark and þe seid xl s. þ*at* þanne þe seid John Sutton at þe ende of iiii ȝer*es* aforeseid schal make or do make þe seide John Dun in þe chau*n*bre of þ*e* ȝelde Halle as þ*e* man*er* is fre man on his owne cost w*ith*owtyn eny wiþseying or delay, up[on] peyne to paye to þ*e* wardeynys or her*e* successouris to þe uce of þe alm*us* of Seynt Dunston x li. of st*er*ling*es*; and for record and witnesse þ*at* þ*is* same award & juggement is don bi þe seid wardeynys and entrid of record in her*e* Halle, þe same wardeynis þe day, monethe & ȝeer*e* above writen to þis present writyng have set to her*e* selys.

1437–38 p. 168[735] Thise be the names of the Wardeyns chesin in the fest of Seint Dunstan in the ȝere of Kyng Henry the sext aftre the conquest xv^{ne} thanne beynge:
Thomas Leget
Thomas Reyner
Richard Bradcok[736]

[735] This page is written in the same hand as p. 166, which now continues forward.
[736] Only three Wardens are listed and this is confirmed by the entry on p. 169. The burdens of wardenship were not inconsiderable, and it would seem that there was this year a lack of suitable men for the post.

cases previously pending between them in the following manner: i.e. that the said John Dun should be fully discharged of his apprenticeship and service from the said John Sutton, and the same John Dun should pay for this and generally for all else to his said master: 8 marks, to be paid on specified days following, i.e. 6s. 8d. on the feastday of the Annunciation of Our Lady [25 March] that next follows after the date of the writing of this, 6s. 8d. at the next following feastday of St John the Baptist [24 June], 6s. 8d. at the next following Michaelmas Day [29 September], and 6s. 8d. at Christmas [25 December] next, and then henceforward from feast to feast and from year to year continuously following, 6s. 8d. on each of the said feastdays until the aforesaid 8 marks shall have been fully paid, if the said John Dun shall live as long as that, excepting that if the said John Dun should happen to die before the full payment of the said 8 marks has been made, then all payments of the said money due after the death of the said John Dun shall cease and be held invalid and entirely for ever excluded; and to have greater surety for the payment of the 8 marks in the above written manner, one Henry Pool, citizen and goldsmith of London, is bound by letters obligatory to the said John Sutton in the aforesaid sum. Furthermore, it is agreed and judgment given by the said wardens that at the end of the four years, if the said John Dun shall live till then, when the said 8 marks will have been fully paid, that then the said John Dun shall pay or get paid to the John Sutton, his executors or his assigns, 40s., in which sum one William Redyng of Flamstede in Hertfordshire, yeoman, is bound by letters obligatory to the said John Dun, unless the said John Sutton shall have recovered the said 40s. from the said William Redyng at any time before within the aforesaid 4 years of payment of the said 8 marks. And for greater surety of this, the said John Sutton has the said bond in the sum of 40s. in his own keeping. Furthermore, the said wardens give judgment in full by virtue of their office and the powers of their wardenship that when the said John Sutton has been paid and satisfied of the said sum of 8 marks and the said 40s., that then the said John Sutton at the end of the aforesaid 4 years shall make the said John Dun or see to it that he is made a freeman in the chamber of the Guildhall as the custom is, this to be at his own cost without any gainsaying or delay, upon pain of paying to the wardens or their successors £10 sterling for the use of the alms funds of St Dunstan. And as a record and witness that this same judgment and sentence have been made by the said wardens and entered in the records in their Hall, the same wardens on the day, month and year written above have set their seals to this present document.

These are the names of the wardens elected at the feast of St Dunstan in the year 15 Henry VI [19 May 1437]: 1437–38 p. 168

Thomas Leget
Thomas Reyner
Richard Bradcock

No*min*a app*r*enticior*um* eodem anno:
Joh*ann*es Goldsmyth app*r*ent*icius* cum Thoma Bretenh*am* – xx s.
Joh*ann*es Alcok app*r*ent*icius* cum Will*elm*o Rotheley – xx s.
Rob*er*tus Cok app*r*ent*icius* cum Laur*encio* Lethelyon – xx s.
Anton*ius* Faucet app*r*ent*icius* cum Matheo Phelipp*e* – xx s.
Simon Maufer [Manfer?] app*r*ent*icius* cum Barth*olom*eo Bremson – xx s.
Joh*ann*es Halward app*r*ent*icius* cum Joh*ann*e Wethyng – xx s.
Joh*ann*es Nicholl app*r*ent*icius* cum Thoma Whitebrede – xx s.
Thomas Lenger app*r*ent*icius* cum Joh*ann*e Coudray – xx s.
Thomas Hornby app*r*ent*icius* cum Joh*ann*e Hakwell – xx s.
Thomas Lambe app*r*ent*icius* cum Henr*ico* Shyn[g]well[737] – xx s.
Thomas Caprou*n* app*r*ent*icius* cum Jacobo Gay – xx s.
Joh*ann*es Abrah*am* app*r*ent*icius* cum Joh*ann*e Hopkyn – xx s.
Thomas Bretenh*am* app*r*ent*icius* cum Will*elm*o Hert – xx s.
Rog*er*us Willughson app*r*ent*icius* cum Thoma Harryson – xx s.
Joh*ann*es Bordet app*r*ent*icius* cum Thoma[738] Reyner – xx s.[739]
Will*elm*us Wenir app*r*ent*icius* cum Th[o]ma Reyner – xx s.

No*min*a allocat*orum* eodem anno:
Thomas Botiller app*r*ent*icius* cum Rob*er*to Bosou*n* – ii s.
Joh*ann*es Sutton filius Joh*ann*is Sutton sen*ioris* app*r*ent*icius* cum eodem Joh*ann*e – ii s.
Nich*ol*aus White app*r*ent*icius* cum Thoma Reyner – ii s.
Ric*ard*us Austyn app*r*ent*icius* cum Joh*ann*e Stok – ii s.
Joh*ann*es Hake app*r*ent*icius* cum Rob*er*to Assheby – ii s.

1438 No*ta* de fino[740] p*ro* op*er*ando de uno est*raneo*:
p. 169 Memorand*um* q*uo*d octavo die Maii anno sextodecimo Regis Henr*ici* sexti venit hic quidam Barth*olome*us Vanhusden, Ducheman, coram infrascriptis[741] Thoma Leget, Thoma Reyner et Ric*ardo* Bradcok, custodib*us* aur*ifabrorum*, et licenciatus fuit ad op*er*and*um et* exc*er*cend*um* mist*eram* aur*ifabrorum* in p*er*sona sua exceptis s*er*vient*ibus* durante t*er*mino quatuor anno*rum* tunc p*roxime* sequen*tium et* fecit finem cum eisdem custodib*us* ad – liii s. iiii d.

No*ta* de alio fino:
It*em*, eisdem die *et* anno, quidem Gerrardus *et* Walt*er*us, Duchemen manentes in Suth*e*werk in p*a*rochia S*anc*ti Olavi, venerunt coram p*re*fatis custodib*us et* licenciati fuerunt ad exc*er*cend*um et* occupand*um* mist*eram* aur*ifabrorum* in p*er*sonis suis, s*er*vient*ibus* except*is*, durante t*er*mino duo*rum* anno*rum* tunc p*roxime* sequen*tium et* fecit[742] finem cum eisdem custodib*us* ad – xl s.

737 A wormhole goes through and obscures the 'g'.
738 MS: Thomas.
739 This entry and the next have been entered up slightly later in different ink by the same scribe.
740 One would expect 'fine', but the form 'fino' is used several times in this part of the register.
741 This word indicates clearly that the entry here is a copy of another document, one to which the wardens have officially put their names. Other entries below similarly record that seals have been affixed.
742 *Sic*, which is possible although we do not know which of them paid; although it might have been intended to say that each paid this, or alternatively 'fecerunt' might have been intended.

The names of apprentices in the same year:

John Goldsmyth apprentice with Thomas Bretenham –	20s.
John Alcok apprentice with William Rothley –	20s.
Robert Cok apprentice with Laurence Lethlyon –	20s.
Anthony Faucet apprentice with Matthew Philip –	20s.
Simon Maufer/Manfer apprentice with Bartholomew Bremsham –	20s.
John Halward apprentice with John Wethyng –	20s.
John Nicholl apprentice with Thomas Whitbread –	20s.
Thomas Lenger apprentice with John Cowdray –	20s.
Thomas Hornby apprentice with John Hakwell –	20s.
Thomas Lambe apprentice with Henry Shyngwell –	20s.
Thomas Caproun apprentice with James Gay –	20s.
John Abraham apprentice with John Hopkyn –	20s.
Thomas Bretenham apprentice with William Hert –	20s.
Roger Willughson apprentice with Thomas Harryson –	20s.
John Bordet apprentice with Thomas Reyner –	20s.
William Wenir apprentice with Thomas Reyner –	20s.

The names of serving-men the same year:

Thomas Botiller apprentice with Robert Bosoun –	2s.
John Sutton, son of John Sutton the elder, apprentice with the same John –	2s.
Nicholas White apprentice with Thomas Reyner –	2s.
Richard Austyn apprentice with John Stok –	2s.
John Hake apprentice with Robert Ashby –	2s.

Memo about a fee paid by an alien for working: 1438
Memorandum that on 8 May 1438 a certain Bartholomew Van Husden p. 169
came before the undersigned Thomas Leget, Thomas Reyner and Richard Bradcok, wardens of the goldsmiths, and he was given permission to work and to practise the goldsmiths' craft, this permission being for himself only and excepting any servants, during a term of the next following four years, and he paid a fee to the same wardens of – 53s. 4d.

Memo about another fee:
Item, on the same date a certain Gerrard and Walter, 'Dutchmen' living in Southwark in the parish of St Olave's, came before the aforesaid wardens and were given permission to practise and engage in the goldsmiths' craft, this permission being for themselves alone and excepting any servants, during a term of the next following two years, and they paid a fee to the same wardens of – 40s.

1438–39 Thes been*e* þe names of þe Wardeins chosen*e* in feste of Sint Dunstane in
p. 170 þe[743] ȝere of Kyng Henry þe sexte aftre þe conquest xvj^{ne} þan beyng:

Joh*ann*es Wethyhale
Joh*ann*es Walsh*e*
Joh*ann*es Sutton, senior
Barth*olome*us Brempson

No*min*a app*ren*t*iciorum* eodem anno:

Thomas Gedney app*ren*tic*ius* cum Ric*ard*o Spenser –	xx s.
Will*elmu*s Sayles app*ren*tic*ius* cum Ric*ard*o Bradcok –	xx s.
Joh*ann*es Blagden app*ren*tic*ius* cum Thoma Pynchard –	xx s.
Joh*ann*es Sencler app*ren*t*icius* cum Matheo Philip*e* –	xx s.
Will*elmu*s Grene app*ren*t*icius* cum Thoma Thomvyle –	xx s.
Will*elmu*s Roger app*ren*t*icius* cum Joh*ann*e Kebbell*e* –	xx s.
Georgius of Geddyng app*ren*t*icius* cum Will*elm*o Wodewarde –	xx s.
Joh*ann*es Thelby app*ren*t*icius* cum Joh*ann*e Huberd –	x s.
– *et* non ult*ra* q*ui*a moderat*ur* p*er* discressio*n*em custod*um* eo q*uo*d pate*r* p*re*dic*t*i app*ren*t*i*c*ii* fuit aurifaber[744]	
Joh*ann*es Harper app*ren*t*icius* cum Joh*ann*e Benton –	xx s.
Alanus Neweman app*ren*t*icius* cum Rob*er*to Luskyn, Goldbeter –	xx s.
Joh*ann*es Prestman app*ren*t*icius* cum Will*elm*o Cam*er*ay –	xx s.
Thomas Hankys app*ren*t*icius* cum Thoma Randon –	xx s.
Alex'[745] Stokes app*ren*t*icius* cum Thoma Takele, jun*iore* –	xx s.
Adryan[746] app*ren*t*icius* cum Reymund*o* Wachter –	xx s.

No*min*a alloc*atorum* eodem anno:

Will*elmu*s Swynton app*ren*t*icius* cum Joh*ann*e Bowedon –	ii s.
Thomas Takeley app*ren*t*icius* cum Joh*ann*e Grene –	ii s.
Joh*ann*es Tebbys app*ren*t*icius* cum Joh*ann*e Warde –	ii s.
Joh*ann*es Tregustek app*ren*t*icius* cum Jacobo Tregustek –	ii s.

No*min*a app*ren*t*iciorum* de fyno*ur*s eodem anno:
Rob*er*tus Hille app*ren*t*icius* cum Henr*ico* Bode, fyno*ur* – xiii s. iiii d.

No*min*a capell*anor*u*m* p*re*sent*atorum et* jur*atorum* in tempore eor*unde*m custod*um*:

John Pomys, prest in þe chirche of Allhalown, singyng for Walpole	jur*ati*
Nicoll*e* Baunt, prest in þe chirche of Seint Mathewe, singyng fo[r] Thomas Polle	

Richard Wareyn, prest in þe chirche of Seint Fasters, singyng for John Mapulsden*e* and Will*ia*m Stamilden*e* & Alic*e* vx*or*e eor*unde*m – jur*atus*

[743] The date year 'xvj^{ne}' has been written in next and then scored out.

[744] This is presumably William Thelby – see Name Index.

[745] The -us abbreviation is used, suggesting the name was 'Alexus', 'Alexius' or 'Alexis', but the abbreviation might also have stood for 'Alexander', a name perhaps more commonly found (though still fairly unusual) in fifteenth-century England..

[746] A space follows, left blank for the surname.

These are the names of the wardens elected at the feast of St Dunstan in the year 16 Henry VI [19 May 1438]: 1438–39 p. 170
John Withihale
John Walsh
John Sutton the elder
Bartholomew Bremsham

The names of apprentices in the same year:

Thomas Gedney apprentice with Richard Spencer –	20s.
Wiliam Sayles apprentice with Richard Bradcok –	20s.
John Blagden apprentice with Thomas Pynchard –	20s.
John Sencler apprentice with Matthew Philip –	20s.
William Grene apprentice with Thomas Tumvyle –	20s.
William Roger apprentice with John Kebbel –	20s.
George of Gedding apprentice with William Woodward –	20s.
John Thelby apprentice with John Huberd –	10s.
– and no more because it was reduced at the discretion of the wardens since the father of the said apprentice was a goldsmith	
John Harper apprentice with John Benton –	20s.
Alan Newman apprentice with Robert Luskyn, goldbeater –	20s.
John Prestman apprentice with William Cameray –	20s.
Thomas Hankys apprentice with Thomas Randon –	20s.
Alex[ander?] Stokes apprentice with Thomas Takeley the younger –	20s.
Adrian apprentice with Raymund Wachter –	20s.

The names of serving-men in the same year:

William Swynton apprentice with John Bowdon –	2s.
Thomas Takeley apprentice with John Grene –	2s.
John Tebbys apprentice with John Ward –	2s.
John Tregewstek apprentice with James Tregewstek –	2s.

The names of finers' apprentices in the same year:
Robert Hille apprentice with Henry Bode, finer – 13s. 4d.

The names of chaplains presented and sworn during the term of the same wardens:
John Pomys, priest in the church of All Hallows, singing mass for Walpole
Nichol Baunt, priest in St Matthew's church, singing mass for Thomas Polle
} sworn
Richard Wareyn, priest at St Vedast's church, singing mass for John Maplesdene and William Stameldene and Alice, wife of these same men – sworn

Thomas Randolf, prest in þe chirche of Seint John Zacarie, singyng for Drwe Barantyne – jur*atus*
Henri Emplyngh*a*m, prest in þe chirche of Seint Petre, singing for John Walpole & Alica ux*or*e eius – jur*atus* – xvi die Maii a*nno* xviii°.[747]

1438–39 In tempore John Wydyhale et soci[orum] su[orum][748]
p. 171 Be it hadde in mynde þat where John Wethihale, John Walsh*e*, John Sutton and Bartholomewe Bremson, wardeins of þe craft of goldsmyth*e*s in þe ȝere of Kyng Henry þe vj^te aftre þe conquest xvj^ne, have resceyved of Reymond Wachter for a prentys of his called[749] Adryan xx s. for þe entre of þe same prentys. Nev*er*thelesse, þe seid wardeins woll for hem and hur successours þat if þe frendes of þe seid child and þe seid Reymond can nought accorde so þat þe seid child abide not with þe seid Reymond, þat þan þei seid xx s. shall stande hym in discharge of a nother app*re*ntys what tyme þe seid Reymond woll take a nother be þe sight of þe wardeins for þe tyme beyng, whereto þe seid wardeins sette hur seall.

1438 No*ta* de feodo Thome Thorp, Su*m*monitor*is* de S*caccar*io d*omi*ni Regis: Me*morandum* q*uo*d in festo S*anct*i Dunstani anno regni Regis Henr*ici* sexti post conquestum Angli*e* xvj^mo, Thomas Thorp, su*m*monitor de s*caccar*io d*omi*ni regis, ex assensu *et* concensu custodum *et* co*mun*itatis mistere[750] aur*ifabrorum* London' receptus est in lib*er*atam eiusdem mistere *et* retentus est ad essend*um* de consilio mistere p*re*d*ict*e et ad hoc fecit fidem. Et sup*er* hoc concessum est eo p*er* assensum *et* concenssum tam custodum qu*a*m tocius co*mun*itatis mistere p*re*d*ict*e q*uo*d ip*s*e liberat*am* p*re*d*ict*am cont*inentem* .v. virg*as* p*ro* toga *et* capuc*io* tociens quociens ho*min*es eiusdem mistere h*ab*ebit de dono absq*ue* aliquo p*ro* eadem lib*er*at*a* solvend*o*, et eciam concess*um* [est] eidem Thome q*uo*d ip*s*e annuatim h*ab*ebit p*ro* feod*o* suo xl s. p*er* manus cust*odum* mistere p*re*d*ict*e p*ro* tempore existent*ium*.[751]

1438 Me*morandum* q*uo*d primo die Octobr*is* anno xvii^mo Regis Henr*ici* sexti,
A + b Will*elmu*s Porter p*ro* contemptu facto cont*ra* p*re*ceptum custodum in[753]
p. 95[752] capiendo bona *et* catalla a possessione Thome Brynkeley, s*er*vientis ip*sorum* custodum, p*ro* quo contemptu p*re*d*ict*us Will*elmu*s posuit seip*sum* in gr*aci*am ip*sorum* custodum *et* co*mun*itatis artis p*re*d*ict*e *et* genuflectendo petiebat de p*re*fatis custodib*us* mi*sericord*iam, pro quo[754] contemptu consideratum fuit q*uo*d p*re*d*ict*us Will*elmu*s fac*er*et finem cum eisdem,

[747] This date is written very faintly, in the same scribe's hand.
[748] MS: sociis suis.
[749] A blank space has been left for the missing name.
[750] The word 'p*re*d*ict*e' follows but is expuncted.
[751] See also below, A + a, p. 176 where it is recorded that in 1441 Thorp is made free of the mistery. It would appear that here in 1438 his admission to the livery is dependent upon his post as legal advisor, whereas in 1441 he is granted a lifetime privilege.
[752] A different hand has written this page; the previous hand then returns on p. 96.
[753] MS: 'de in capiendo', the word 'de' being underlined for deletion.
[754] The first letter 'q' of this word appears to have been altered from an 's'.

Thomas Randolf, priest at the church of St John Zachary, singing mass for Drew Barantyn – sworn
Henry Emplyngham, priest at St Peter's church. singing mass for John Walpole and Alice, his wife – sworn – 16 May 1440.

During the term of office of John Withihale and his fellow wardens: p. 171
Memorandum that whereas John Withihale, John Walsh, John Sutton and Bartholomew Bremsham, wardens of the goldsmiths' mistery in the year 16 Henry VI [1438–39], have received from Raymund Wachter 20s. for an apprentice of his called Adrian, for the entry of the same apprentice, nevertheless, the said wardens state their wish for themselves and for their successors that if the said child's 'friends' and the said Raymund cannot agree with the result that the said child does not stay with the said Raymund, that then the said 20s. shall stand to his credit for another apprentice at whatever time the said Raymund shall take another, who shall be inspected by the current wardens, and to this the said wardens set their seals.

Memo about the fee of Thomas Thorp, Summoner[240] of the King's Exchequer:
Memorandum that at the feast of St Dunstan in the year 16 Henry VI [19 May 1438] Thomas Thorp, Summoner of the King's Exchequer, with the assent and consent of the wardens and commonalty of the goldsmiths' mistery of London, was admitted to the livery of the same mistery and was retained as counsel to the aforesaid mistery and he pledged his faith to this. And besides with the assent and consent of both the wardens and the whole commonalty of the aforesaid mistery it was granted to him that whenever it is issued to the men of the same mistery he shall have the aforesaid livery, of 5 yards for a gown and hood, as a gift without having to pay anything for the same livery cloth, and it is also granted to the same Thomas that he shall receive 40s. annually as his fee by the hands of the current wardens of the aforesaid mistery.

Memorandum that on 1 October 1438 William Porter for the contempt he had shown for the instructions of the wardens relating to the seizing of goods and chattels from the possession of Thomas Brinkley, servant of those wardens,[241] for the which contempt the aforesaid William submitted himself to the judgment of the same wardens and commonalty of the aforesaid mistery, and on bended knee he asked the aforesaid wardens for mercy, and for this contempt it was considered that the aforesaid William should pay a penalty A + b p. 95

[240] The officer of a secular court responsible for citing persons to appear or for calling jurors (*MED*).

[241] i.e. the beadle.

taxat*um* p*er* eosdem custodes *et* co*mun*itatem ad – xl s., de quib*us* custodes p*re*dic*t*i relaxarunt eidem Will*elm*o xxxvi s. viii d. de p*re*dic*t*is xl s. et sic remanet de p*re*dic*t*is xl s. eisdem custod*ibus* *et* co*mun*itati debit*um* – xl d.

1439–40 In tempore Will*elm*i Walton *et* soc*iorum* suor*um*

A + a p. 172[755] These ben þe names of þe Wardeins chosyn in þe feste of Seint Dunstan in þe ȝere of Kyng Henr*y* sexte aftre þe conquest xvii^ne^ þan beyng:

Will*elmu*s Walton
Joh*anne*s Orwell
Thomas Herryson
Joh*anne*s Grene

col. 1 No*mina* app*re*nticior*um* eodem anno:

Rob*er*tus Popley app*renticius* cum Joh*ann*e Grene – xx s.
Ric*ard*us Preston app*renticius* cum Jacobo Gey – xx s.
Tristan Philpot app*renticius* cum Rob*er*to Bosou*n* – xx s.
Jacobus Framsh*a*m app*renticius* cum Will*elm*o Prynce – xx s.
Joh*anne*s Loldon app*renticius* cum Will*elm*o Rothley – xx s.
Joh*anne*s Pegeon app*renticius* cum Joh*ann*e Sturdys – xx s.
Olyverus Berker app*renticius* cum Rog*er*o Berker – xx s.
Henr*icus* Corbes app*renticius* cum Ric*ard*o Bradcok – xx s.
Joh*anne*s of Trente app*renticius* cum Nich*ola*o Wode – xx s.
Henr*icus* Padyngton app*renticius* cum Henr*ico* Chilwell – xx s.
Joh*anne*s Highsette app*renticius* cum Thomas Leget – xx s.
Will*elmu*s Ogle app*renticius* cum Will*elm*o Porter – xiii s. iiii d.
non plus quia p*er* eor*um* discressionem p*er*donat'[756] –
Ric*ard*us Bon app*renticius* cum Barth*olome*o Bremson – xx s.
Joh*anne*s Broun app*renticius* cum Will*elm*o Alon – xx s.
col. 2 Thomas Vandernak app*renticius* cum Ric*ard*o Messanger – xx s.
Thomas Withehale app*renticius* cum Joh*ann*e Orwell – xiii s. iiii d.[757]
Salmon Cary app*renticius* cum Thoma Tumvyle – xiii s. iiii d.
John Charlton app*renticius* cum Roberto Botiller – xx s.[758]

No*mina* jur*atorum* voc*atorum* alloc*atorum*:

Will*elmu*s Broun app*renticius* cum Nich*ola*o atte Wode – ii s.
Rob*er*tus Kynton app*renticius* cum Joh*ann*e Sturdys – ii s.
Joh*anne*s Bastard, jun*ior*, app*renticius* cum Joh*ann*e Bastard sen*iore* – ii s.
Joh*anne*s Gregory app*renticius* cum Joh*ann*e Wyn*ne* – ii s.
Joh*anne*s Worlych app*renticius* cum Will*elm*o Hert – ii s.
Henr*icus* Hav*er*yng app*renticius* cum Thoma Remy – ii s.
Thomas Sampson app*renticius* cum Joh*ann*e Parker – ii s.
Will*elmu*s Essex app*renticius* cum Joh*ann*e Corby sen*iore* – ii s.
Ric*ard*us Carmarthyn app*renticius* cum Joh*ann*e Topclyff – ii s.
Will*elmu*s Upnore app*renticius* cum Joh*ann*e Orwell – ii s.

755 A new hand starts here.
756 The scribe has made a doodle that seems to indicate that an amount should be filled in.
757 No reason is given for the lower amounts paid by this man and the next.
758 This entry has been written in slightly later by the same scribe.

fine which was assessed by the same wardens and commonalty at 40s., of which the aforesaid wardens remitted 36s. 8d. to the same William of the aforesaid 40s., and thus there remained to the same wardens and commonalty of the aforesaid 40s. the sum owed of – 40d.

During the term of William Walton and his fellow-wardens 1439–40
These are the names of the Wardens elected at the feast of St Dunstan in the year 17 Henry VI [19 May 1439]: A + a p. 172
William Walton
John Orwell
Thomas Harryson
John Grene

The names of apprentices in the same year: col. 1

Robert Popley apprentice with John Grene –	20s.
Richard Preston apprentice with James Gay –	20s.
Tristan Philpot apprentice with Robert Bosoun –	20s.
James Framsham apprentice with William Prynce –	20s.
John Loldon apprentice with William Rothley –	20s.
John Pigeon apprentice with John Sturdys –	20s.
Oliver Barker apprentice with Roger Barker –	20s.
Henry Corbes apprentice with Richard Bradcok –	20s.
John of Trent apprentice with Nicholas Wood –	20s.
Henry Paddington apprentice with Henry Chilwell –	20s.
John Highsette apprentice with Thomas Leget –	20s.
William Ogle apprentice with William Porter –	13s. 4d.
– no more because it was remitted at their discretion	
Richard Bon apprentice with Bartholomew Bremsham –	20s.
John Broun apprentice with William Allone –	20s.
Thomas Vandernak apprentice with Richard Messynger –	20s. col. 2
Thomas Withihale apprentice with John Orwell –	13s. 4d.
Solomon Cary apprentice with Thomas Tumvyle –	13s. 4d.
John Charlton apprentice with Robert Botiller –	20s.

The names of those sworn who are called serving-men:

William Broun apprentice with Nicholas atte Wood –	2s.
Robert Kynton apprentice with John Sturdys –	2s.
John Bastard the younger, apprentice with John Bastard the elder –	2s.
John Gregory apprentice with John Wynne –	2s.
John Worlych apprentice with William Hert –	2s.
Henry Havering apprentice with Thomas Remy –	2s.
Thomas Sampson apprentice with John Parker –	2s.
William Essex apprentice with John Corby the elder –	2s.
Richard Carmarthyn apprentice with John Topclyff –	2s.
William Upnore apprentice with John Orwell –	2s.

1439 p. 173 Be it hadde in myende þat where as div*er*ses stryves and debates er and have ben betwyx John Adys, goldsmyth of London, on one partie, and Will*ia*m Pryence of London, goldsmyth, on þat other pa[r]tie, have putte hem*e* and auther of hem*e* in þe awarde, reule and ordinaunce of Will*ia*m Walton, John Orwell, Thomas Harryson and J*o*hn Grene, wardeins of þe crafte of þe goldsmythes of London in þe ȝere, withinne deret*io*n of all matiers, quarelles, trespases and debates done and graune frome þe begynnyng of þe warlde unto þe xviii day of July in þe ȝere of Kyng Henry þe vj^te^ aftre þe conquest xvii^ne^, whech wardeins awarde, ordeyne and deme þe same xviii day þat outher of þe seide John Adys and William Pryence shall giffe to other a diner*e* atte þer leser, and þat nauther shall take ne withdrawe other custumers frome other, nor call chapman frome one shoppe to a nother, and þat nouther shall sturre nor labour ne durre sturre ne labour to hire auther other oute of house or shoppe, and þat nauther shall giffe to other wordes of evasion nor of debate frome hense forwarde uppon payn of forfait*ur*e of C s. to be disposed be þe wardeins of þe seid craft for þe tyme beyng in þe almous of Seint Dunstan also ofte as auther offende to other in þe pointes above seide, to þe which reule, ordinaunce and arbitrement þise seid parties have agreed hem*e* for ev*er* – *et*c.

1440 Be it hadde in mynde þat þe xi day of May þe xviii^ne^ ȝere of Kyng Harry þe sext aftre þe conquest, where diverse debates, discordes and variance were betwyx John Boudon, goldsmyth, on þat on*e* part and Roger Hogkyns, late hys app*re*ntys, on þat other parte, þe seid parties have putte hem in þe awarde of Will*ia*m Walton, John Orewell, Thomas Harryson and John Grene, þan wardeins of þe craft of goldsmythes, whech wardeins warde and ordein*e* þat þe seid Roger Hogkyns shall be clerely discharged frome þe seid John Boudon and frome hym shall be quyte for all man*er* accions for div*er*se causes examined and p*ro*ved afore þe seid wardeins, and þat þe seid John Boudon shall make fre þe seid Roger atte þe ende of þe t*er*mes contened in his endenture in also much as in hym is aftre þe custume of þe citee of London, and þat auther shall make to other an acquitance of all man*er* accions *et*c. whech be made and don*e* forthwith.

1440 Me*morandum* qu*o*d xvj^mo^ die Maii anno xviii^mo^[759] Regis Henr*ici* sexti, concessum est p*er* Joh*ann*em Paddesley,[760] Joh*ann*em Sutton, alderm*an*, *et* Will*ia*m Walton, Joh*ann*em Orwell, Thomam Harryson *et* Joh*ann*em Grene, adtunc custodes mistere aur*ifabrorum* London', ex assensu *et* concensu tocius co*mun*itatis eiusdem mistere, cuidam Joh*anni* Birlyng, nup*er* app*renticio* cum Joh*ann*e Wynne, nup*er* cive *et* aur*ifabro* London', licet idem Joh*ann*es Birlyng irrotulat*us* fuit ad artem pannar*iorum* in Guihalda London' *et* de eadem arte lib*er*tatem civitat*is*[761] London' h*ab*uit, idemq*ue* Joh*ann*es renuncians artem illam petens ip*su*m in artem aur*ifabrorum* admitti *et*c., p*re*dic*t*i alderman, custodes *et* co*mun*itates p*er* assensum p*re*dic*to*rum *et* p*ro* bono *et* gratuito gub*er*nac*io*ne ac fidelitate *et* industria eiusd*em* Joh*anni*s Birlyng concesserunt ip*su*m in p*re*dic*t*am artem aur*ifabrorum* admitti *et*c. et

[759] MS: xviii^no^.
[760] The Mayor of London.
[761] MS: ciuitat*is* ciuitat*is*.

Memorandum that whereas there are and have been various quarrels and contentions between John Adys, goldsmith of London, on the one side and William Prince of London, goldsmith, on the other side, they have submitted themselves each one of them to the judgment, ruling and ordinance of William Walton, John Orwell, Thomas Harryson and John Grene, wardens that year of the goldsmiths' mistery of London, within [their] direction concerning all matters, quarrels, trespasses and contentions that have been and have arisen between them since the beginning of the world until 18 July 1439, the which wardens judge, ordain and pass sentence on the same 18 July that each of the said men, John Adys and William Prince, shall at a time chosen by them give a dinner to the other, and that neither of them shall take or draw away the other's customers from him, nor shall they call a chapman from one shop to another, and that neither of them, either themselves or through another, shall work at getting the other evicted from his house or shop, and that neither shall speak words of prevarication or of contention to the other from henceforward, upon pain of a penalty of 100s. to the alms funds of St Dunstan to be used as directed by the current wardens of the said mistery, this penalty for each time that one of them may offend against the other in any of the aforesaid ways, and to this ruling, ordinance and judgment the said parties have agreed for ever – etc. 1439 p. 173

Memorandum that on 11 May 1440, whereas there were various quarrels, contentions and disagreements between John Bowdon, goldsmith, on the one side and Roger Hogkyns, formerly his apprentice, on the other side, the said parties have submitted themselves to the judgment of William Walton, John Orwell, Thomas Harryson and John Grene, then wardens of the goldsmiths' mistery, the which wardens judge and ordain that the said Roger Hogkyns shall be entirely discharged from the said John Bowdon and shall be quit from him for all manner of actions for various matters examined before the said wardens and of which proofs were given, and that the said John Bowdon shall as far as in him lies make the said Roger a freeman according to the custom of the city of London at the end of the terms stated in his indentures, and that each shall give an acquittance to the other of all manner of actions, etc. and this is to be made and done forthwith. 1440

Memorandum that on 16 May 1440 it was granted by John Pattesley, [Mayor], John Sutton, alderman, and William Walton, John Orwell, Thomas Harryson and John Grene, then wardens of the goldsmiths' mistery of London, with the assent and consent of the whole commonalty of the same mistery, to one John Birling, formerly an apprentice with John Wynne, formerly citizen and goldsmith of London, that although the same John Birling had been enrolled at the Guildhall of London in the drapers' mistery and from that mistery had obtained the freedom of the city of London, the same John was now making a renunciation of that mistery and seeking to be admitted into the goldsmiths' mistery etc., the said alderman, wardens and commonalties with the assent of the aforesaid and on account of the good and willing behaviour, faithfulness and industriousness of the same John Birling have granted that he may be admitted

p*redic*t*us* Joh*anne*s Birlyng juratus est ad b*ene et* fideli*ter* se gub*er*nand*um* *secundum* consuet*udines et* ordina*ciones* eiusdem mistere, *et*c.

1439–40 Me*morandum* de defectib*us* op*er*acion*um et*c tempore Will*elm*i Walton,
A + b p. 96 Joh*ann*is Orwell, Thome Harryson *et* Joh*ann*is Grene, custodum mistere aur*ifabrorum* London' *et*c a*nno* xvii^{mo} R*egis* H*enrici* vj^{ti}.
In primis, recept' de Wylli*am* Ro[th]ley[762] p*ro* def*ect*u in op*er*a*ci*one – p*ro* insufficient*ibus* girdelbokelles invent*is* in custod*ia* sua apud Stirbrigge – ii s.
It*em*, recept' de Joh*anne* Pake p*ro* una zona invent*a* apud Stirbrigge – xii d.
It*em*, recept' de Hans Sowe, Ducheman, p*ro* i defectu – xvi d.
It*em*, recept' de Laur*encio* Leth*e* Lyon p*ur* i defaute – v s.
It*em*, recept' de Joh*anne* Fenyngh*am* p*ur* une defaute – vi s. viii d.
It*em*, recept' de Thoma Sampson p*ur* i defaute – ii s.
It*em*, recept' de Henr*ico* Chikwell*e*[763] de fine quia h*ab*uit quemdam s*er*vientem non monstrat*um* custod*ibus* *secund*um consuetud*ines* eiusdem mistere – xl d.
It*em*, recept' de Henr*ico* Chikwell*e* quia fecit pactu*m* de op*er*a*ci*one cuiusd*am* nutte deaurat*i* cont*ra* ordinac*ion*em eo q*uo*d voluit compon*er*e unam unc*am* deaurat*ionis* ad xviii d. – iii s. iiii d.
It*em*, de Thoma Tumvyle p*ur* i defalta – ii s.

1440–41 Thise ben þe names of þe wardeins of goldsmythes chosen in þe feste of
A + a p. 174 Seint Dunstan in þe ȝere of Kyng Henry þe vj^{te} aftre þe conquest xviii^{ne} and þan beyng:
Matheus Phelip
Joh*anne*s Waryn
Joh*anne*s Adys
Joh*anne*s Birlyng

col. 1 No*min*a app*r*ent*iciorum* eodem anno viz:

Thom*a*s Corbet app*r*ent*icius* cum Ric*ardo* Bradcok –	xx s.
St*e*ph*anu*s Juell*e* app*r*ent*icius* cum John Byschop –	xx s.
Edward*us* Baudon app*r*ent*icius* cum Will*iam* Hede –	xx s.
Will*iam* Hatfeld app*r*ent*icius* cum John Wareyn –	xx s.
John Wodehyll*e* app*r*ent*icius* cum Henr*y* Poole –	xx s.
Will*iam* Leicestr*e* app*r*ent*icius* cum Will*el*mo Cam*er*ay –	xx s.
Henr*icus* Horne app*r*ent*icius* cum Thom*a*s Swynisco –	xx s.
Matheo Dyves app*r*ent*icius* cum Will*elm*o Flour*e* –	xx s.
Ric*ardus* Wryght app*r*ent*icius* cum Will*elm*o Flour*e* –	xx s.
Roger*us* Wolf app*r*ent*icius* cum Hu*m*frey Hayford –	xx s.
John Scuse app*r*ent*icius* cum Laurenc*io* Lethlyon –	xx s.

762 The two words of this name have been written over another that has been completely erased, the result being very unclear but recognisable as almost certainly this man.
763 Following this the words 'p*ur* i defaute' have been scored out.

into the aforesaid goldsmiths' mistery etc., and the aforesaid John Birling has been sworn to conduct himself well and faithfully according to the customs and ordinances of the same mistery etc.

Memorandum about defects in workmanship etc. during the term of office of William Walton, John Orwell, Thomas Harryson and John Grene, wardens of the goldsmiths' mistery of London etc. in the year 17 Henry VI [from 19 May 1439]: 1439–40 A + b p. 96

Firstly, received from William Rothley for a defect in workmanship – for sub-standard girdle buckles found in his possession at Stourbridge – 2s.
Item, received from John Pake for a girdle found at Stourbridge – 12d.
Item, received from Hans Sowe, 'Dutchman', for a defect – 16d.
Item, received from Laurence Lethlyon for a defect – 5s.
Item, received from John Fenyngham for a defect – 6s. 8d.
Item, received from Thomas Sampson for a defect – 2s.
Item, received from Henry Chigwell for a fine because he had a certain serving-man who had not been shown to the wardens according to the customs of the same mistery – 40d.
Item, received from Henry Chigwell because he made an agreement about the workmanship of a certain gilded coconut-cup that was against the ordinance in that he intended to make one ounce of gilding for 18d. – 3s. 4d.
Item, from Thomas Tumvyle for a defect – 2s.

These are the names of the goldsmiths' wardens elected at the feast of St Dunstan in the year 18 Henry VI [19 May 1440]: 1440–41 A + a p. 174

Matthew Philip
John Waryn
John Adys
John Birling

The names of apprentices in the same year, i.e.: col. 1

Thomas Corbet apprentice with Richard Bradcok –	20s.
Stephen Juelle apprentice with John Bisshop –	20s.
Edward Baudon apprentice with William Hede –	20s.
William Hatfield apprentice with John Waryn –	20s.
John Woodhill apprentice with Henry Poole –	20s.
William Leicester apprentice with William Cameray –	20s.
Henry Horne apprentice with Thomas Swinscoe –	20s.
Matthew Dyves apprentice with William Flour –	20s.
Richard Wryght apprentice with William Flour –	20s.
Roger Wolf apprentice with Humphrey Hayford –	20s.
John Scuse apprentice with Laurence Lethlyon –	20s.

Ric*ardus* Bedell app*renticius* cum John Hatwell*e* – xx s.
Will*iam* [Di]este[764] app*renticius* cum Jenyn Skevyn – xx s.
Oliver Stryng*er* app*renticius* cum Will*el*mo Jor[d?]er[765] – xx s.
Simone Margery app*renticius* cum Will*el*mo Schypwryght – xx s.
Henr*icus* Crowmyng app*renticius* cum Magn*us*[766] – xx s.
App*rentice* with Thomas Swayn*e*, fyno*ur*, afore þ*e* composic*io*n – vi s. viii d.[767]
col. 2 Thom*as* Dallyng app*renticius* cum Will*iam* Boston – xx s.
Aleyn Newma*n* app*renticius* cum Logan, goldbetyr – xx s.
Thom*as* Altam app*renticius* cum John Wynne – xiii s. iiii d.[768]
Ric*hard* Horne app*renticius* cum Henr*y* Horne, hys fadyr – xiii s. iiii d.
Will*iam* Waldyngton app*renticius* cum John Kebyll*e* – xx s.
Lowes – Joh*ann*es Dorman app*renticius* cum Joh*ann*e French – xii d.[769]

These ben the names of þe swory*n* men of y*n*glessh men:[770]
Will*iam* Hoke app*renticius* cum Wakkyn Walden – ii s.
Tom*as*[771] Belle app*renticius* cum Swethy*r* – ii s.
John Clenveld app*renticius* cum John Tyse – ii s.
Thom*as* Canne app*renticius* cum John Tyse – ii s.
Ric*hard* Typuppe app*renticius* cum John Tyse – ii s.
John Dun app*renticius* cum John Sutton – ii s.
Thom*as* Prany[772] app*renticius* cum Rob*ert* Boteler – ii s.
Edward Verney app*renticius* cum Rob*ert* Bosun – ii s.
John Elys app*renticius* cum John Sutton, Alderma*n* – ii s.
Will*iam* Radderam app*renticius* cum Will*iam* Botown – ii s.
Will*iam* Kelke app*renticius* cum Matheo Phelyp – ii s.
Thom*as* Ernest app*renticius* cum John Byrlyng – ii s.
John Eyland app*renticius* cum John Wynne – ii s.
John Broke[773] app*renticius* cum Petro Brundewode – ii s.
Thom*as* Smyth*e* app*renticius* w*ith* Thom*as* Leget – ii s.
John Seyncler*e* app*renticius* cum Rob*ert* Downe – ii s.
Henr*y* Aur*e* app*renticius* cum Will*el*mo Coke of Glowcestr*e* – ii s.
Nich*ol*aus Allyngton app*renticius* cum Thoma Elys – ii s.
Thom*as* Stevnys[774] – ii s.
Will*el*mus Canstede app*renticius* cum Will*el*mo Botun – ii s.

764 A wormhole through this name makes it uncertain.
765 A wormhole through this name makes it uncertain.
766 A gap is left for the surname to be filled in.
767 This appears to be a separate entry (rather than extra information about the preceding entry), the apprentice's name being unknown. The ordinances for the finers of 1435 (see A + b, pp. 81–83 above) laid down that the Goldsmiths' Mistery should receive 13s. 4d. for each apprentice, and it would appear that this record is regulating the position of an apprentice who was taken on before 1435 and for whom thus this lower fee has been agreed.
768 No reason is given for the lesser amount paid for this man and the next.
769 This entry is clearly in the wrong place, and the word 'Lowes' is added in the LH margin, in the same hand and ink but obviously after the scribe realised the error. The half fee paid is not explained.
770 All those listed below are again former apprentices.
771 This name is written to the LH side of an erased 'Will*iam*'.
772 This name is written over a scored out 'Bremy'.
773 This name is writen over the scored out 'Brundewode'.
774 No information is given about his master.

Richard Bedell apprentice with John Hatwelle –	20s.
William Dieste apprentice with Janyn Eskevyn –	20s.
Oliver Strynger apprentice with William Jorder –	20s.
Simon Margery apprentice with William Shipwright –	20s.
Henry Crowmyng apprentice with Magnus –	20s.
Apprentice with Thomas Swayne, finer, before the settlement –	6s. 8d.
Thomas Dallyng apprentice with William Boston –	20s. col. 2
Alan Newman apprentice with Logan, goldbeater –	20s.
Thomas Altam apprentice with John Wynne –	13s. 4d.
Richard Horne apprentice with Henry Horne, his father –	13s. 4d.
William Waldyngton apprentice with John Kebbell –	20s.
Serving-man – John Dorman apprentice with John Frenshe –	12d.

These are the names of Englishmen sworn:

William Hoke apprentice with Watkyn Walden –	2s.
Thomas Belle apprentice with Swethyr –	2s.
John Clenvyle apprentice with John Tyse –	2s.
Thomas Canne apprentice with John Tyse –	2s.
Richard Typuppe apprentice with John Tyse –	2s.
John Dun apprentice with John Sutton –	2s.
Thomas Prany apprentice with Robert Botiller –	2s.
Edward Verney apprentice with Robert Bosoun –	2s.
John Elys apprentice with John Sutton, alderman –	2s.
William Radderam apprentice with William Botoun –	2s.
William Kelke apprentice with Matthew Philip –	2s.
Thomas Ernest apprentice with John Birling –	2s.
John Eyland apprentice with John Wynne –	2s.
John Broke apprentice with Piers Brentwood –	2s.
Thomas Smythe apprentice with Thomas Leget –	2s.
John Seynclere apprentice with Robert Downe –	2s.
Henry Aure apprentice with William Coke of Gloucester –	2s.
Nicholas Allington apprentice with Thomas Elys –	2s.
Thomas Stevens –	2s.
William Canstede apprentice with William Botoun –	2s.

1440–41 A + b p. 97[775] M*emorandum* de defectibus op*eracionum etc* temp*o*re Mathe[i][776] Phelip, John Wareyn, John Adys, John Byrlyng, custodum mistere aur*ifabrorum* London' *etc* a*nno* xix^{o} r*egis* H*enrici* vj^{ti}.

The val*or* of þe lb. of the sylv*er* of John Clenvile xxiiii s., wher of ye iii q^{a} hang' be a bill*e*.[777]

In prim*is*, recept' of John Clenvile for defawte in werkyng – xl s.
It*em*, of the same John Clenvile for evens werkyng – iii li.
It*em*, of Will*ia*m Flowr*e* and Copelond for a gyrdill – ii s.
It*em*, Will*ia*m Flowr*e* for defaute y*n* werkyng of a cuppe and restyng of a ma*n* of the crafte w*ith* owte leve. And for goyng to May*d*ston feyr*e* w*ith* owte leve – xviii s.
It*em*, of Will*ia*m P*ri*nce for sale of gylt won*e* under the p*ri*ce – iii s. iiii d.
It*em*, of John Werk w*ith* owte Temple Barr*e* for a defawte y*n* werky*ng* – xii d.
It*em*, of John Ufford for a defawte in werkyng – ii s.
It*em*, of Ric*hard* Selander for restyng of a ma*n* w*ith* owte leve – iii s. iiii d.
It*em*, of Wakkyn Chawdeler for a defaute – ii s.
It*em*, of Walt*er* Rocandell*e* for a defaute y*n* werkyng of goold – vi s. viii d.
It*em*, of Andrew Swan for a defaute y*n* werkyng of goold – iii s. iiii d.
It*em*, of Arnold Smole agens the Wadyngate for a defaute yn werkyng of goold – iii s. iiii d.
It*em*, of Hans Dobeler for a defaute yn werkyng – ii s.
It*em*, of John Hawe for a defawte and dysobeysans and vexyng of þe wardeynys – xx s.
It*em*, of Mo*n*ke for a defawte in werkyng – ii s.
[778]It*em*, of Thom*as* Bragnam for a defaute of ii bokelles & wheche remayn in þer handes of þe wardeins for þe mony – xxii d.
p. 98 It*em*, of Swether, Duchman, for a defaute in workyng and all*e* thynges afore þe xx day of May – xxvi s. viii d.
It*em*, take of Thom*as* Broun a spone beyng in þe Tresore for evydence of div*er*se spones take of hym for þe wheche he is banyshed .
It*em*, take of Cawode, clerk, xii spones wheche were fyned and deliv*er*ed to þe party and a part is in þe Tresore.
It*em*, take of Greneley, upholder in Suthwerk, vii spones not gode wheche remayne in þe Tresorye – p*er* s*er*vientem Thome Leget.
It*em*, take of Pope Wyse, burnesher, wheche were made in Newgate be Thornton son, chapman, remaign in þe Tresorie wheche bene ii peces countrefete silver.
It*em*, iii bondes were take of Gridley Wyse, burnysher, wheche ben false boundes and remaigne in þe Tresorye.
It*em*, ii bondes in þe same forme of other div*er*se people, and remaigne in þe same forme.

[775] A new hand starts here.
[776] MS: Math*eo*.
[777] This line is written by the same scribe and in the same ink, but must have been inserted by him in a gap left between the heading and the 'In primis . . .' line.
[778] A new hand starts here.

Memorandum about defects in workmanship etc. during the term of Matthew Philip, John Waryn, John Adys, John Birling, wardens of the Goldsmiths' Mistery of London etc. in the year 19 Henry VI [from 19 May 1440]: 1440–41 A + b p. 97

The value of the lb. of the silver of John Clenvyle – 24s., three-quarters of which are still under consideration – a certificate has been made out.

Firstly, received from John Clenvyle for a defect in workmanship – 40s.
Item, from the same John Clenvyle for working in the evening[242] – £3.
Item, from William Flour and [John] Coupland for a girdle – 2s.
Item, William Flour for a defect in the workmanship of a cup, and for the arresting of a man of the mistery without leave. And for going to Maidstone Fair without leave – 18s.
Item, from William Prince for the sale of gilt wares[243] below the price[244] – 3s. 4d.
Item, from John Werk outside Temple Bar for a defect in workmanship – 12d.
Item, from John Ufford for a defect in workmanship – 2s.
Item, from Richard Selander for the arresting of a man without leave – 3s. 4d.
Item, from Watkyn Chaundeler for a defect – 2s.
Item, from Walter Rocandelle for a defect in the workmanship of gold – 6s. 8d.
Item, from Andrew Swan for a defect in the workmanship of gold – 3s. 4d.
Item, from Arnold Smole at the Wading Gate for a defect in the workmanship of gold – 3s. 4d.
Item, from Hans Dobler for a defect in workmanship – 2s.
Item, from John Hawe for a defect and for disobedience and trouble to the wardens – 20s.
Item, from Monke for a defect in workmanship – 2s.
Item, from Thomas Braghnam for a defect over 2 buckles, which remain in the wardens' hands for the money – 22d.
Item, from Swether, 'Dutchman', for a defect in workmanship and everything before 20 May – 26s. 8d. p. 98
Item, taken from Thomas Broun a spoon, which is in the treasury as evidence of various spoons taken from him, for which he is expelled.
Item, taken from [Robert] Cawood, clerk, 12 spoons which had been refined and delivered to the party and a part of this is in the treasury.
Item, taken from Greneley, upholder in Southwark, 7 sub-standard spoons which remain in the treasury – by Thomas Leget's servant.
Item, taken from Pope Wyse, burnisher, 2 pieces of counterfeit silver which were made in Newgate by Thornton's son, chapman, and which remain in the treasury.
Item, 3 bands were taken from Gridley Wyse, burnisher, which were fake bands and they remain in the treasury.
Item, 2 bands of similar form were taken from various other people, and they remain in the same manner.

242 This was forbidden by ordinance (because of bad light); see above, p. 135.
243 See *OED* sub WONE n.3, of which this present example would seem to be an unusual usage.
244 This must refer to an officially set price, cf. above, A + b, p. 96, A + a, p. 49, A + b, p. 19; and see Forbes, *Hallmark*, p. 31.

It*e*m, þe fote and þe bonde of an horn countrefete wheche*e* be false and untrewe, take of Wauter Roucandell*e*.
It*e*m, of a fesicyan called Chipstede, wheche*e* was forsworn to þe craft,[779] div*er*se nuttes garnyshed, and atte þe instance of Rob*er*t Cawode þei were fyned and deliv*er*ed to hym for he claymed þe same, where of remaigneth a p*ar*cell*e* in þe Tresorye.

p. 99 Thise ben þe forfaites resceyved of Will*ia*m Walton and his felowes, oure predecessours *etc*:
Furst, ii cuppes countrefete silver, ii cheyns countrefete gold, þe harnesyng of a nutte countrefete gilte, and a maser bonde, wheche*e* remaigne in þe Tresorye.

1441 Be it remembred þat where div*er*se debates and stryves bene betwen*e* Will*ia*m
A + a p. 175 Rotheley & Will*ia*m Hoke, goldsmythes, have putte hem in awarde of Mathewe Phelip, John Waryn, John Adys, John Birlyng, wardeins of þe same craft, of all man*er* debates and stryves betwene hem afore þe viii day of Marche þe xix ȝere of Kyng Henry sext, wheche*e* award and arbitre þat if auther of þe said parties disclaundre or noise auther other of ony defaute don*e* be auther of hem*e* but onely say þat he fyndes hym*e* greved of to þe wardeins for þe tyme beyng, uppon payn*e* of forfaiture to þe almus of Seint Dunstane atte ev*er*y tyme – xl s., so þat it may be resonably proved be iiii of þer*e* neightbours of trewe p*er*sones.

1440–41 Me*morandum:* where þat George Malefeld, sun of Richard Malefeld, late þe app*re*ntice of John Wethyhale nowe dede, was be Elizabeth, late þe wyfe of þe said John and executrice of his testement, relesed and surrended þe t*er*mes of þe said app*re*ntice a fore þe Chaumberleyn*e* unto þe fulfillyng of his endenture frome þe date þerof þe vii^{ne} ȝere þan next folowyng, where he was bound be his endent*ur*e to s*er*ve as app*re*ntice be ix^{ne} ȝere. And þan be þe avyse of þe said Chaumberleyn*e* and also of þe said Elizabeth and other executo*urs* of þe said John Wethehale, þe said app*re*ntice was co*m*mitted be his awn assent to Thomas Harryson, goldsmyth, to s*er*ve with hym as app*re*ntice duryng þe t*er*me of vii^{ne} ȝere aftre þe date and cowen*a*nt of his endent*ur*e beyng relesed and p*ar*dond as it appereth uppon þe said endent*ur*e. Nev*er*thelesse þe said Thom*as* hath sold to þe said George his t*er*mes wheche*e* were to come aftre þe viii day of Decembr*e* þe xix^{ne} yere of Kyng Henry þe vj^{te} for a su*m*me betwyx hem accorded. Wheche*e* doyng and sale is cont*ra*rie to þe ordin*a*nce of þis craft. Where fore þe said Mathew Phelip, John Waryn, John Adys & John Birlyng, wardeins, be þe autorite to hem co*m*mitte and also be þe assent of þe said Thom*as* Harryson, it is ordeined þat þe said Thomas Harryson shall paye to þe almus of Seint Dunstan xxxiii s. iiii d.,[780] and doo þat in hym is as may be atte þe ende of þe t*er*mes of þe said George with þe p*ar*don, to make þe said George freman accordyng to þe custume of London, uppon payne to forfaite to þe almus of Seint Dunstan – x m*ar*c*s* &c. And also if it so be that þe said George auther in worde or dede misgov*er*ne hym aȝenst þe said Thomas Harryson or his wyfe or elles if he or his wyfe disclaundre þe said Thomas or his wyfe, he

[779] See above, A + a, p. 98.
[780] This sum has been written also in the LH margin beside this line.

Item, the base and the band for a drinking-horn, counterfeit, fake and fraudulent, taken from Walter Rocandelle.
Item, from a physician called Chipstead, who had forsworn the mistery, various decorated coconut-cups, which at the instigation of Robert Cawood had been refined and delivered to him, for he laid claim to the same, and of which a part remains in the treasury.

These are the forfeited goods received by William Walton and his fellow p. 99
wardens, our predecessors, etc.
Firstly, 2 cups of counterfeit silver, 2 chains of counterfeit gold, the ornamental pieces for a coconut-cup of counterfeit gilt, and a band for a mazer, which remain in the treasury.

Memorandum that whereas there are various contentions and quarrels between 1441
William Rothley and William Hoke, goldsmiths, they have submitted themselves A + a p. 175
to the judgment of Matthew Philip, John Waryn, John Adys and John Birling, wardens of the same mistery, on all manner of contentions and quarrels between them before 8 March 1441, and they judge and arbitrate that if either of the said parties should slander or defame the other or if either of them tell the current wardens of any offence committed by either of them and says that he finds himself harmed by it, this shall be upon pain of a penalty for each occasion of 40s. to the alms funds of St Dunstan, if it may be reasonably proved by 4 of their neighbours of good character.

Memorandum: whereas George Malefeld, son of Richard Malefeld, formerly 1440–41
the apprentice of John Withihale who is now dead, had the terms of his apprenticeship released and surrendered to him before the Chamberlain by Elizabeth, the late wife of the said John and the executrix of his will, until the fulfilment of his indenture from its date to one seven years later, whereas he was bound by his indenture to serve 9 years as an apprentice. And then by the advice of the said Chamberlain and also of the said Elizabeth and other executors of the said John Withihale, the said apprentice was with his own assent committed to Thomas Harryson, goldsmith, to serve with him as an apprentice during the term of the 7 years, after the date and the agreement made for the release and remission of his indenture, as appears in the said indenture. Nevertheless, the said Thomas has sold to the said George his terms after 8 December 1440 for a sum agreed between them. This act and sale are in contravention of the mistery's ordinance, and therefore the said Matthew Philip, John Waryn, John Adys and John Birling, wardens, by the authority entrusted to them and also with the assent of the said Thomas Harryson, have ordained that the said Thomas Harryson shall pay to the alms funds of St Dunstan 33s. 4d. and that he shall as far as in him lies, at the end of the terms of the said George as remitted to him, make the said George a freeman according to the custom of London, upon pain of a penalty to the alms of St Dunstan of – 10 marks etc. And also that if it should happen that the said George should either in word or deed misbehave against the said Thomas Harryson or his wife, or if either he or his wife should slander the said Thomas

shall paie atte ev*er*y tyme to þe almus of Seint Dunstan – C s., so þat it may be proved be iiii neghburs laufully. And also þat þe said George shall deliv*ere* to þe said Thom*as* Harryson atte þe ende of ii ȝere a child which is with þe said George conable taght and araied as a p*re*ntice of his degre in þe same craft, if he lyffe &c. And also þe said Thomas Harryson or his wyfe shall not disclaundre ne myssay of þe same George and his wyfe uppon above said. And in þe same forme above said.

p. 176 Me*morandum* þat where accorde was hadde betwene Rob*er*t Boteler and Will*ia*m Alone of John Broun*e*, sonne of Will*ia*m Broune of Dereh*a*m, late þe app*re*ntice of þe saide Will*ia*m Alone, be þe avyse and assent of Mathewe Phelip, John Waryn, John Adys and John Birlyng, wardeins of þis craft, that þe saide Rob*er*t Boteller shuld have þe said late app*re*ntice of þe said Will*ia*m Alone be a lettre of sale þerof be þe said Will*ia*m Alone to þe forsaid Rob*er*t Boteller, made be þe assent of þe said app*re*ntice, payng to þe said Will*ia*m Alone for þe said app*re*ntice t*er*mes &c – xl s. in money. Whiche was don*e* and paied. And where as þe said app*re*ntice aftre made an newe endent*ure* to John Sutton, alderman, to be with hym and leveyng þe furst cowenant, all þat notwithstandyng, be þe avyse of þe saide wardeins, also be þassent of þe said John Sutton and other div*er*se þat haade ben*e* wardeins, it is accorded þat þe said Rob*er*t Boteller shall have þe said app*re*ntice accordyng to þe lettre of sale þerof made be þe said Will*ia*m Alone late his maistre, and also liv*ere* of þe said app*re*ntice. Wheche was done. And þat þe said Rob*er*t Boteller and Will*ia*m Alone accordyng to þe custume of þe citee of London shall doo þat in hem*e* is atte þe ende of þe t*er*mes of þe said app*re*ntice, so þat he reule hym as app*re*ntice and be well*e* gov*er*ned, to make hym freman atte þe cost of þe said app*re*ntice &c.

Me*morandum* þat where it was so þat div*er*ses noises and wordes of disclaunder were said be Will*ia*m Prynce uppon Will*ia*m Walton, wherefore it is ordeined be þe same wardeins that if þe said Will*ia*m Prynce frome hense forward say ony wordes of disclaundre or noyse þe said Will*ia*m, so þat it may be deuly p*ro*ved be dewe examinac*io*n of trewe men and resonable witnesse of neyghburs, þat þan þe said Will*ia*m Prynce shall paye atte ev*er*y tyme to þe almus of Seint Dunstan xl s. And for þe which*e* wordes þat þe said Will*ia*m hath said þe said Will*ia*m shall crye þe said Will*ia*m Walton mercy, wheche is done. And also þe said Will*ia*m Walton shall not giffe non occasion to þe said Will*ia*m uppon þe said payne &c.

1441 Ordinaunce for spanges

A + b p. 52 Be it hadde in mynde where as div*er*se ordinaunce were made and ordeined for workyng and makyng of spanges afore þis day, wheche be nowe confermed and forthermore ordined and establyshed þe xxviii day of March*e* þe xix^{ne} ȝere of

or his wife, then he shall for each occasion pay 100s. to the alms funds of St Dunstan, provided this can be lawfully proved by 4 neighbours. And also that the said George shall at the end of 2 years hand over to the said Thomas Harryson a child who is with the same George, and he shall be properly taught and clothed as an apprentice of his standing in the same mistery, this provided he live etc. And also that the said Thomas Harryson and his wife shall neither slander nor speak against the same George and his wife, upon pain of the aforesaid penalty and in the same aforesaid manner.

Memorandum that whereas an agreement was made between Robert Botiller and p. 176
William Allone regarding John Broun, son of William Broun of Dereham, formerly the apprentice of the said William Allone, and by the advice and with the assent of Matthew Philip, John Waryn, John Adys and John Birling, wardens of this mistery, it was agreed that the said Robert Botiller should obtain the said former apprentice of the said William Allone by a letter of sale by the said William Allone to the aforesaid Robert Botiller, made with the assent of the said apprentice, paying for the said apprentice's terms etc. to the said William Allone – 40s. cash. Which was done and paid. And whereas the said apprentice afterwards made a new indenture to John Sutton, alderman, to be with him and to abandon the first agreement. Notwithstanding all this, by the advice of the said wardens and also with the assent of the said John Sutton and of various other previous wardens, it is agreed that the said Robert Botiller shall obtain the said apprentice in accordance with the letter of sale relating to him made by the said William Allone, his former master, and also that the said apprentice shall be handed over to him. Which was done. And that at the end of the said apprentice's terms, the said Robert Botiller and William Allone according to the custom of the City of London shall as far as in them lies, provided that he conducts himself as an apprentice and has been well-behaved, make him a freeman at the costs of the said apprentice, etc.

Memorandum that whereas various rumours and slanderous words were spoken by William Prince about William Walton, for this reason it is ordained by the same wardens that if from henceforward the said William Prince shall speak any words of slander or shall spread rumours about the said William, provided this may be duly proved by proper examination of worthy men and the reasonable witness of neighbours, that then the said William Prince shall pay at each occasion to the alms funds of St Dunstan – 40s. And for the words which the said William has said, the said William shall beg forgiveness of the said William Walton, and this has been done. And also that the said William Walton shall occasion no cause to the said William, upon pain of the said penalty etc.

Ordinance for spangles[245] 1441

Memorandum that whereas various ordinances have been previously made and A + b p. 52
ordained for the working and the making of spangles, these are now confirmed and it is furthermore ordained and established on 28 March 1441 by Matthew

[245] Spangles are small, round, thin pieces of silver (or other metal) used as dress decorations. Many were sold to embroiderers.

Kyng Henry þe vj[te] be Mathewe Phelip, John Waryn, John Adys and John Birlyng, þan wardeins of the craft of goldsmythes, be þe auttorite to hem co*m*mitte and be all*e* þe feliship of þe said craft and also be þe assent and agrement of John Godard, Thomas Canne, John Clenvyle and Richard Typuppe, wirkers and makers of spanges, in þe name of all*e* workers and makers of spanges, in maner and forme þat folou*e*th: þat is to sey, þat no man frome þis day forward usyng to make spanges selle non unse of spanges white beneth*e* þe su*m*me of iii s. viii d. nor non unse gilte undre þe su*m*me of v. s. iiii d. nor non unse duble gilte undre þe su*m*me of vi s. to no foreyn, uppon payn to paye atte ev*er*y tyme þat he that so selleth or ony of hem so sellyng contrarie to þis ordinaunce or ony man usyng þe same frome hense forward to þe almus of Seint Dunstan – xl s. of sterlynges,[781] whereof the wardeins of goldsmythes shall have to hur almus xxvi s. viii d. and þe wardeins of goldbeters xiii s. iiii d.

1441 Thorp fact*us* est lib*er*at*us*:
A + a It*em*, in festo S*anc*ti Georgii anno xix[no] Regis Henr*ici* sexti Thomas Thorp de
p. 176 *cont.* sc*acca*rio d*omi*ni regis was amitted into þe fredom of goldsmythes and brotherhode of Seint Dunstan be John Pattesle, þan Mair of London, John Sutton, þan shireve, Mathewe Philip, John Waryn, John Adys and John Berlyng, þan wardeins of þe craft of goldsmythes, be a gen*er*all assemble of all þe craft, be all þer assentes and will*es*, to occupie and enjoye þe same craft and fredom for ev*er*more as on of þe same craft and brotherhode, and so he is made freman here and in Ʒeldhalle both, and þer uppon he is sworn to be goode, faithfull*e* and trewe accordyng to þe othe of þe same craft. And þer uppon he gaff to þe almus of Seint Dunstan atte his begynnyng – xxvi s. viii d.[782]

1441 Be it remembred þ*at* on Seint Dunstanes day þe xix[th] ȝeer of Kyng Henry þe vj[te]
p. 177[783] it was gr*a*unted and full assentid be John Paddesle, Mair*e*, John Sutton, alderman, Mathew Philip, John Waren, John Adys & John Birlyng and all oþ*er* of þe felawship of þe said craft of goldsmythes, þ*at* Rob*er*t Langford, citezein of London, shall be a broþ*er* of þe said craft, for which gr*a*unt þe said Rob*er*t hath relesed þee xx s. which was allowed to John Stafford, late of counsell w*ith* þe said craft. And þe said Rob*er*t hath paide for his entre – vi s. viii d.

No*ta* de fino iiii[or] li. xiii[s] et iiii[d]. p*ro* amissione lib*er*tat':
Be it hadde in mynde þat Hans Costard, Ducheman, is amitted into þe fredom of goldsmythes of London to use þe same craft as a freman of þe same craft be þe assent of all þe cumpany, and so he is made freman, for wheche cause he hath paied to þe almus of Seint Dunstan – iiii li. xiii s. iiii d. And þereppon he is sworn accordyng to þe oth*e* of þe same craft.

[781] The amount of the fine has been picked out by writing 'xl s.' in the LH margin.
[782] See also above, A + a, p. 171 and note 751.
[783] The first paragraph at the top of this page is in a similar but different hand.

Philip, John Waryn, John Adys and John Birling, then wardens of the Goldsmiths' Mistery, by the authority entrusted to them and by all the fellowship of the said mistery, and also with the assent and agreement of John Godard, Thomas Canne, John Clenvyle and Richard Typuppe, spangle-workers and spangle-makers, in the name of all spangle-workers and spangle-makers, in the manner and form that follows, i.e. that no one from this day forward who practises the making of spangles shall sell any ounce of white silver spangles at less than 3s. 8d., nor any ounce of gilded spangles at less than 5s. 4d., nor any ounce of double-gilt spangles at less than 6s. to anyone outside the mistery, upon pain from henceforward of paying at each occasion that he so sells or anyone so sells in contravention of this ordinance or anyone practising the same – 40s. sterling to the alms funds of St Dunstan, of which the Goldsmiths' wardens shall have for their alms funds 26s. 8d. and the Goldbeaters' wardens shall have 13s. 4d.

Thorp is made free: 1441
Item, on the feastday of St George in the year 19 Henry VI [23 April 1441] A + a
Thomas Thorp of the King's Exchequer was admitted to the freedom of the p. 176 *cont.*
goldsmiths' mistery and the fraternity of St Dunstan by John Pattesley, then Mayor of London, John Sutton, then sheriff, Matthew Philip, John Waryn, John Adys and John Birling, then wardens of the goldsmiths' mistery, by a general assembly of the whole mistery and at the wishes and with the assent of all, to enjoy all the benefits of the same mistery and freedom for evermore as one of the same mistery and fraternity, and so he is made a freeman both here and in the Guildhall, and thereupon he has been sworn to be good, faithful and true according to the oath of the same mistery. And thereupon he gave to the alms of St Dunstan at his entry – 26s. 8d.

Memorandum that on St Dunstan's Day in the year 19 Henry VI [19 May 1441] p. 177
it was granted and fully assented to by John Pattesley, Mayor, John Sutton, alderman, Matthew Philip, John Waryn, John Adys and John Birling and all others of the fellowship of the said goldsmiths' mistery, that Robert Langford, citizen of London, shall be a brother of the said mistery, for the which grant the said Robert has paid over the 20s. authorised to John Stafford, late legal counsel to the said mistery. And the said Robert has paid for his entry – 6s. 8d.

Memo about a fee of £4 13s. 4d. for admission to the freedom:
Memorandum that Hans Costard, 'Dutchman', has been admitted into the freedom of the goldsmiths of London, to practise the same craft as a freeman of the same mistery, with the assent of all the company, and thus he has been made a freeman, for which cause he has paid to the alms funds of St Dunstan – £4 13s. 4d. And thereupon he has been sworn according to the oath of the same mistery.

No*ta* de fino xx li. p*ro* amission*e* lib*er*tat' mister*e*:
Be it hadde in myende þat Frederyk Swart, Ducheman of Saxon*e*, is amitted into þe fredom of goldsmythes of London, to use þe same craft as a freman of þe same craft, be þe assent of all þe cumpany, and so he is made freman, for which*e* cause he hath paied to þe almus of Seint Dunstan – xx li.
An þer uppon he is sworn accordyng to þe oth*e* of þe same craft.

Be it hadde in mynde þat John Dungmanson, alowes with Will*ia*m Floure, hath paied to þe craft – vi s. viii d.

Item, of Richard of Bristowe, alowes with Thomas Takeley – v s. viii d.

Be it hadde in mynde þat Giles in Seint Clement Lane is licensed, hym*e* self with ii s*er*v*a*ntz wheche bene with hym nowe, to worke in his chaumbre be þe space of iii ȝere next folowyng. Where uppon he is sworn to work good gold and silver, for which*e* cause he shall paye – x s.

Me*morandum* þat Reymond Vaughter hath made a fyne with þe wardeins to be spared of þe office of rentership as for on ȝer*e* – xx s.

1440–41 The names of Dewchemen swory*n*:
p. 178, col. 1[784] Jeny*n* Archer*e* (oþ*er* wyse calld Blak Jenyn)[785] – ii s.
John Wyslet – ii s.
Andrew Swan – ii s.
John Hawe – ii s.
Garlowe Spayne – ii s.
Thom*as* Atys – ii s.
Gerard Rewe – ii s.
John Gerwar*e* – ii s.
Jacob*us* Bernacale – ii s.
Gylis y*n* Clem*entes* Lane – ii s.
Walt*er* Rocandell*e* – ii s.
Cowns Huke – ii s.
John Vansyth – ii s.
Dyryk Cowsma*n* – ii s.
John Chestyr of Lyncolne
nate y*n* Seland – ii s.
Will*ia*m atte þe brygge fote – ii s.
Nic*o*las Tunne – ii s.
Jacob*us* Butte – ii s.
Bartelotte Duchema*n* – ii s.
Ev*er*ard Esplyngworth – ii s.
Swethyr*e* Duchema*n* – ii s.
Henri hys man – ii s.
Thom*as* Gaitter*e* – ii s.

784 This page is written in the same hand as that of the first paragraph of p. 177.
785 The phrase in brackets has been added later as an afterthought.

Memo about a fee of £20 for admission to the freedom of the mistery:
Memorandum that Frederick Swart, 'Dutchman' from Saxony, has been admitted to the freedom of the goldsmiths of London, to practise the same craft as a freeman of the same mistery, with the assent of all the company, and thus he has been made a freeman, for the which cause he has paid to the alms funds of St Dunstan – £20.
And thereupon he has been sworn according to the oath of the same mistery.

Memorandum that John Dungmanson, serving-man with William Flour, has paid to the mistery – 6s. 8d.

Item, from Richard of Bristol, serving-man with Thomas Takeley – 5s. 8d.

Memorandum that Giles in St Clement's Lane has been given permission, for himself with 2 servants who are at present with him, to work in his chamber for the next 3 years following. Whereupon he has been sworn to work true gold and silver, and for this cause he shall pay – 10s.

Memorandum that Raymund Wachter has agreed a fine with the wardens to be spared the office of renter for one year – 20s.

The names of 'Dutchmen' sworn: 1440–41 p. 178 col. 1

Janyn Archer (otherwise known as Black Janyn) – 2s.	
John Wyslet –	2s.
Andrew Swan –	2s.
John Hawe –	2s.
Garlowe Spayne –	2s.
Thomas Atys –	2s.
Gerard Rowe –	2s.
John Gerware –	2s.
Jacob Bernacale –	2s.
Giles in St Clement's Lane –	2s.
Walter Rocandelle –	2s.
Cowns Huke –	2s.
John Vansyth –	2s.
Derek Cowsman –	2s.
John Chester of Lincoln born in Zeeland –	2s.
William at the bridge foot –	2s.
Nicholas Tunne –	2s.
Jacob Butte –	2s.
Bartelotte, 'Dutchman' –	2s.
Everard Esplyngworth –	2s.
Swether, 'Dutchman' –	2s.
Henry, his man –	2s.
Thomas Gaittere –	2s.

John Smyth –	ii s.
Maynard Donet –	ii s.
Gylys Bloyard –	ii s.
Gerard Hav*er*beke –	ii s.
Barth*olome*us Alman –	ii s.
Henri Staunton –	ii s.
Petrus Swalantyn –	ii s.
Barth*olmeu*s Lambspryng –	ii s.
Welford Ducheman*n* –	ii s.
Ad*a*m Adrian –	ii s.
Harma*n* Van Huse –	ii s.
Steph*an*[786] Cotyl –	ii s.
Otte Ev*er*ardson –	ii s.
col. 2 Henr*y* Fans –	ii s.
John Bemund –	ii s.
Fretheryk Swart –	ii s.
Martyn of Lothewyk –	ii s.
Arnolde Osenbregh –	ii s.[787]
Henr*y* Van Deynson –	ii s.
Gyyssebryht Van Meghen –	ii s.
Albryght of Ledoun –	xii d.[788]
John Vangute –	ii s.
Henr*y* Vanandirnak –	ii s.
Dyryk Campe –	ii s.[789]
Rog*er* Walle –	ii s.
Cornelius Tristram –	ii s.
Lener*e* Myleward –	ii s.
Hans Cristian –	ii s.
Arnold Smole –	ii s.
John Dankard –	ii s.
John Costard –	ii s.
Jacob Rygvenson –	ii s.
Gerard Bolle –	ii s.
Arnold Onover*e* –	ii s.
Henr*y* Luton –	ii s.
Brylys Lev*er*man w*ith* Fredryk –	ii s.
John Ecorn –	ii s.
Magnus Wode –	ii s.[790]

1441 M*emorandum* þat St*eph*ene Barnard, fynere, & John Wheler*e*, fyner, anno xix[791]
p. 179 þe xix day of Agust put him*e* in award of þe wardeins of þe craft, Mathie Phelip, John Wareyn, John Adys, John Byrlyng, of div*er*se stryves & disclaundris wordis. As for þat we award þat ȝif þer be any of them þat

786 MS: Stheph*an*.
787 The next name in the list has been erased: 'Arnolde Anneide – ii s.'
788 No information is given as to why this man paid only half the amount.
789 The next name is also erased: 'Henr*y* Wale of Hanburgh – ii s.'
790 This last entry has been added slightly later.
791 The two words giving the year have been added slightly later above the line.

John Smyth –	2s.
Maynard Donet –	2s.
Giles Bloyard –	2s.
Gerard Haverbeke –	2s.
Bartholomew Alman –	2s.
Henry Staunton –	2s.
Peter Swalantyn –	2s.
Bartholomew Lambspryng –	2s.
Welford, 'Dutchman' –	2s.
Adam Adrian –	2s.
Hermann Van Huse –	2s.
Stephen Cotyl –	2s.
Otto Everardson –	2s.
Henry Fans –	2s. col. 2
John Bemund –	2s.
Frederick Swart –	2s.
Martin of Lothewyk –	2s.
Arnold Osnabruck –	2s.
Henry Van Deynson –	2s.
Gysebright Van Meghen –	2s.
Albrecht of Leiden –	12d.
John Vangute –	2s.
Henry Van Andernak –	2s.
Derek Campe –	2s.
Roger Walle –	2s.
Cornelius Tristram –	2s.
Lenere Myleward –	2s.
Hans Cristian –	2s.
Arnold Smole –	2s.
John Tankard –	2s.
John Costard –	2s.
Jacob Rygvenson –	2s.
Gerard Bolle –	2s.
Arnold Hanover –	2s.
Henry Luton –	2s.
Brylys Leverman, with Frederick –	2s.
John Ecorn –	2s.
Magnus Wood –	2s.

Memorandum that Stephen Barnard, finer, and John Wheler, finer, on 19 August 1441
1441 submitted themselves to the judgment of the wardens of the mistery, p. 179
Matthew Philip, John Waryn, John Adys and John Birling, for various contentions and slanderous words. For this case we judge that if either of them

slaunderit other from þis day forward þat he shall pay to þe almes of Sen[t] Dunston C s., were of þe crafte of fynoris shall have xxxiii s. iiii d. w*ith* þat that þei bryng sufficient rekorde, þe [whech][792] ward was mad*e* in Goldsmythis Halle þe xxii day of Septemb*re*.

1440–41 Adhuc no*min*a de allowes jur*atorum*:

George Malefeld app*renticius* cum Joh*ann*e Wythihale –	ii s.
Joh*annes* Mapysden*e* app*renticius* cum patre suo –	ii s.
Walt*er*us Mapysden*e* app*renticius* cum patre suo –	ii s.
It*em*, a Goldsmyth of Wycombe –	ii s.
Nich*ola*us Studley app*renticius* cum Ric*ard*o Bradcok –	ii s.

1441 Be yt in mend that we, Math*ew* Phelyp, John Waryn, John Adys and John
p. 180[793] Byrlyng, now wardeynys of the crafte of goldsmythys of þe cyte of London, doon for to ben knowyn þat þe v^e^ day of May the ȝer*e* of þe regne of Kyng Henr*y* þe vj^e^ aft*re* the *con*quest þe xix^e^, Auncell, P*riour* of Lewes, sent y*n* to London and deliv*er*yd unto us þe forseyd wardeynys a schyp of sylv*er* for an almosse dysch, p*a*rcell*e* þ*er*of gylt, p*ra*yng us be þe auteryte and power*e* that we have of owr sov*er*ayn lord þe kyng for to make serche & assaye yf yt wer*e* true stuff and wrowht as yt owȝht for to be, aftre as þe rewle & ordina*n*ce of owr crafte. Wher*e*upon we be þe autorite & power*e* aboveseyd serchyng & assayng þe forseyd schyp of sylv*er*, we fynde þe same schyp not clenly wrowȝht ne truly as yt ought to be. Wheche because of dyv*ers* dysceytys and untrue stuff that bin funde we have brokyn þe forseyd schyp, that ys to say fyndyng yn ix toret*es* that stood þ*er*upon stuffyd w*ith* tynne & ledd amountyng þe weighte of x unc*es* & i q*uarter* of T*ro*y, wheche schyp of silv*er* w*ith* stuff above sayd so brokyn, we have delyv*er*yd aȝen to þe sayd P*riour* þe day and ȝer*e* above wretyn, wheche thyng so be us don we have entryd in owr regestre yn þe Halle of owr crafte[794] for mor*e* evydence, recordyng þe untrewthe of John Blemell*e,* other*e*wyse cald Radle or Goldsmyth of Lewes, wheche made þe forseide schyp as we ben enformyd. Into wetenesse wher*e*of we have put our*e* sealles to þat oon p*a*rte of þys endent*ure* þe day & ȝer*e* above sayd.

1441 Me*morandum* that where as div*er*se spones were take of Thomas Broun, goldsmyth, wheche spones be not of þe value of xvi s vi d. þe pounde. Wherefore þe said Thomas was take and sent to Ludgate.[795] Whe[re]uppon dewe examinac*io*n was made and þe said Thomas couth not withsay bot þe said spones were of his makyng. Wherefore it is ordeined the xviii day of August be a gen*er*all semble, þer bei*n*g John Paddesley þan Mair and John Sutton þan Shiriff, þe wardeins for þis ȝere and all*e* other of þe same craft, þat þe said Thomas is banyshed þe citee of London and þe suburbes, and þat he shall not work within þe said citee, þe suburbes, ne with non man of þe said craft be sette

[792] MS: gwech*e*.
[793] The first paragraph on this page is written in the same hand as the first paragraph of p. 177 and p. 178.
[794] This being here this record in the register, the text clearly being copied from the indenture.
[795] 'Ludgate' is written above 'Newgate' which has been expuncted.

from this day forward slanders the other, that he shall pay to the alms funds of St Dunstan 100s., of which the finers' mistery shall have 33s. 4d. provided they bring a sufficient record, and this judgment was given in Goldsmiths' Hall on 22 September.

The names until now of serving-men sworn: 1440–41

George Malefeld apprentice with John Withihale –	2s.
John Mapesdene apprentice with his father –	2s.
Walter Mapesdene apprentice with his father –	2s.
Item, a goldsmith from Wycombe –	2s.
Nicholas Studley apprentice with Richard Bradcok –	2s.

Memorandum that we, Matthew Philip, John Waryn, John Adys and John 1441
Birling, the present wardens of the goldsmiths' mistery of the city of London, p. 180
make it known that on 5 May 1441 Auncell, Prior of Lewes, sent to London and delivered to us the aforesaid wardens a nef[246] of silver made as an alms dish, which was parcel gilt, asking us by the authority and power that we have from our sovereign lord the King to inspect and assay it to find out if it was of true material and wrought as it should be according to the rules and ordinances of our mistery. Whereupon we, having made inspection and assay of the aforesaid silver nef by the aforesaid authority and power, find that the same nef is not properly nor honestly wrought as it should be. And on account of various deceitfulnesses and dishonest material that have been found, we have broken up the aforesaid nef, i.e. the finding of 9 turrets[247] standing upon it which were stuffed with tin and lead amounting to a weight of 10¼ ounces Troy. The aforesaid silver nef broken up and with its material we have sent back to the said Prior on the date written above, and we have recorded these our acts in our register in our mistery's Hall so that fuller evidence is kept, recording the dishonesty of John Blemelle, otherwise called Radle or Goldsmith of Lewes, who made the aforesaid nef as we have been informed. To witness of which we have put our seals to one part of this indenture on the aforesaid date.

Memorandum that whereas various spoons were taken from Thomas Broun, 1441
goldsmith, which were not of the value of 16s. 6d. per lb., for which the said Thomas was taken and sent to Ludgate. Whereupon due examination was made and the said Thomas could not deny that the said spoons were of his making. Wherefore it is ordained on 18 August by a general assembly, at which were present John Pattesley, then Mayor, John Sutton, then sheriff, this year's wardens and all others of the same mistery, that the said Thomas be banished from the city of London and the suburbs, and that he shall not work within the said city or its suburbs, nor be given work by anyone of the said mistery, this to

[246] See C.C. Oman, *Medieval Silver Nefs* (London: HMSO, 1963). These vessels formed in the shape of a ship could be used as incense boats, smaller ones might be used as salts, and the largest were 'status symbols'. Their use as alms dishes is documented: William of Wykeham, for instance, bequeathed one such in his will of 1404.

[247] These were almost certainly turrets = small towers, but one should perhaps not entirely discard the alternative turret = torret = 'a ring, or the like, often moving on a swivel, whereby an object can be attached to a chain' (*OED*). Either of these would seem possible accoutrements for this alms dish, but small decorative towers would more easily be stuffed with tin and lead.

on werk, for ev*er*more to endure withoute[796] ende, and if he don þe contrarie þan to be co*m*mitte to prison p*er*petuell*e*.

1441 M*emorandum* þat þe xv day of May in þe ȝer*e* of Kyng Henry þe vj^te^ xix ȝer*e*, Swether, Duchman, put hi*m* in award of þe hold wardeynis and þe nuue, þat is to say Math*eu* Phelip, John Wareyn, John Adys & John Birlyng, Richard Spenc*er*, John Wynne, Robard Boteller, John Sturdeys. And we have warded for div*er*se trespas & defauttis & rebelions & [offencys][797] afore þis day, And he xal aske foreȝevenesse and pay to þe seyd craft xxvi s. viii d. Also we awarde yif he be take w*ith* any fautis or trespasis aft*re* þe day of þis award, þat he shall pay to þe almesse of Seynt Dunston C s. w*ith*out any redemsion.

1441–42 Thise ben þe names of þe wardeins of goldsmythes in þe fest of Seint
p. 181 Dunstan in ȝere of Kyng Henry þe sext xix^ne^ aftre þe conquest and þan beyng:

Ric*ard*us Spenser
Joh*ann*es Wynne
Rob*er*tus Boteller
Joh*ann*es Sturdys

col. 1 No*m*i*n*a app*ren*t*iciorum* eodem anno:
Hugo Filcok app*ren*t*icius* cum Joh*ann*e Sturdys – xx s.
Joh*ann*es Atkyn app*ren*t*icius* cum Joh*ann*e Asshurst – xx s.
Will*elmu*s Bisshop app*ren*t*icius* cum Thoma Rymer – xx s.
Will*elmu*s Padyngton app*ren*t*icius* cum Will*elm*o Bate – xx s.
Will*elmu*s Grisby app*ren*t*icius* cum Petro Brundewode – xx s.
Joh*ann*es Catell*e* app*ren*t*icius* cum Joh*ann*e Sutton, Alderman – xx s.
(Will*elmu*s Crosby app*ren*t*icius* cum Petro Brundewode – xx s.)[798]
Oliverus Davy app*ren*t*icius* cum Joh*ann*e Birlyng – xx s.
Joh*ann*es Autell*e* app*ren*t*icius* cum Joh*ann*e Pake – xx s.
Joh*ann*es Thorn*e* app*ren*t*icius* cum Henr*ico* Shyngwell*e* – xx s.
Thomas Webbe[799] app*ren*t*icius* cum Henr*ico* Shyngwell*e* – xx s.
Joh*ann*es Hamerton app*ren*t*icius* cum Joh*ann*e Bernes – xx s.
Joh*ann*es Harryes app*ren*t*icius* cum Jacobo Tregustok – xx s.
Will*elmu*s Lelom app*ren*t*icius* cum Will*elm*o Floure – xx s.
Joh*ann*es Frythe app*ren*t*icius* cum Will*elm*o Hoke – xiii s. iiii d.[800]
col. 2 Rog*er*us Spenser app*ren*t*icius* cum Thoma Sampson – xx s.
Will*elmu*s Russelle app*ren*t*icius* cum Joh*ann*e Sturdys – xx s.
Joh*ann*es Blowre app*ren*t*icius* cum Thoma Prany – xx s.

No*m*i*n*a app*ren*t*iciorum* de lez fynou*r*s:
Thomas Godehewe app*ren*t*icius* cum Thoma Swayn – xiii s. iiii d.

796 The words 'the grace of alle asemble' follow, but 'the' appears to be scored through, the other words are underlined, and it would seem that they were intended for deletion.
797 MS: of prentys.
798 This sum of money has been scored out and the entry has a note against it in the LH margin: 'Vacat quia supra.' One may presume Grisby to be the correct form of his name.
799 A different hand has added above the line here: 'otherwise Atkyns.'
800 No explanation is given for this lower figure.

endure for evermore without end, and if he goes against this, then he shall be committed to perpetual imprisonment.

Memorandum that on 15 May 1441 Swether, 'Dutchman', submitted himself to the judgment of the old and the new wardens, i.e. Matthew Philip, John Waryn, John Adys and John Birling, Richard Spencer, John Wynne, Robert Botiller, John Sturdys. And we have judged that for various offences, defects, rebelliousness and offences before this day he shall ask forgiveness and pay to the said mistery 26s. 8d. And we also judge that if he be caught in any defect or offence after the day of this judgment, that he shall then pay to the alms funds of St Dunstan – 100s. without any remission. 1441

These are the names of the wardens of the goldsmiths [elected] at the feast of St Dunstan in the year 19 Henry VI [19 May 1441]: 1441–42 p. 181

Richard Spencer
John Wynne
Robert Botiller
John Sturdys

The names of apprentices in the same year: col. 1

Hugh Filcok apprentice with John Sturdys –	20s.	
John Atkyn apprentice with John Ashurst –	20s.	
William Bisshop apprentice with Thomas Rymer –	20s.	
William Paddington apprentice with William Bate –	20s.	
William Grisby apprentice with Piers Brentwood –	20s.	
John Catelle apprentice with John Sutton, alderman –	20s.	
(William Crosby apprentice with Piers Brentwood –	20s.)[248]	
Oliver Davy apprentice with John Birling –	20s.	
John Autelle apprentice with John Pake –	20s.	
John Thorne apprentice with Henry Shyngwelle –	20s.	
Thomas Webbe, *alias* Atkyns, apprentice with Henry Shyngwelle –	20s.	
John Hamerton apprentice with John Barnes –	20s.	
John Harryes apprentice with James Tregewstek –	20s.	
William Lelom apprentice with William Flour –	20s.	
John Frythe apprentice with William Hoke –	13s. 4d.	
Roger Spenser apprentice with Thomas Sampson –	20s.	col. 2
William Russell apprentice with John Sturdys –	20s.	
John Blowre apprentice with Thomas Prany –	20s.	

The names of finers' apprentices:
Thomas Godehewe apprentice with Thomas Swayn – 13s. 4d.

[248] The note says: 'Annulled because above.'

1441–42 M*emorandum* qu*o*d hic sunt defectus tempore Ric*ard*i Spenser *etc*, anno xix^{no}
A + b p. 100 regis Henry sexti:

In primis, recept' de Will*elm*o Duke for a defaute in workyng – ii s.
It*em*, recept' de Gisebryght Vansant cum Ric*ard*o Bradcok for a defaute – xii d.[801]
It*em*, recept' de Arnold Annore for a defaute in workyng – ii s.
It*em*, recept' de Will*elm*o Wilmote for a defaute in workyng – ii s.
It*em*, recept' de Rog*er*o Vansith for a defaute in workyng – ii s.
It*em*, recept' de Will*elm*o Venryth for a defaute in workyng – ii s.
It*em*, recept' de Henr*ico* Luton, Ducheman, for a defaute in workyng of div*er*se colers of my lord of Gloucestre – ii s.
It*em*, recept' de Petro Hansheld for a defaute in workyng }
It*em*, de eodem for he sold a warre in stede of masur } xx d.
It*em*, recept' de Hanse of Coleyn for a defaute in workyng[802]
It*em*, recept' de Thoma Fluchard,[803] Dowcheman, for a defaute in workyng – iii s. iiii d.
It*em*, recept' de Joh*ann*e Dunstall for a defaute in workyng – ii s.
It*em*, recept' de Will*elm*o Hoke p*ro* quadam t*ra*vstre[804] et defectus – ii s.
It*em*, recept' de Will*elm*o Gate for a defaute in workyng – ii s.
It*em*, recept' de Will*elm*o Percy for a defaute in workyng – ii s.
It*em*, recept' de Joh*ann*e Rotherh*a*m for a defaute in workyng – ii s.
It*em*, recept' de Will*elm*o Tumvyld for a defaute in workyng – iii s. iiii d.
It*em*,[805]

1441 Be it hadde in mynde þat where div*er*se debates were betwene John Sutton,
A + a p. 182 alderman, on þat on part, and John Tankard on þat other part, for makyng of an hede of xj^{Ml} virgenys whech*e* þe Duke of Gloucestre com*m*aunded þe said John Sutton to doo make. Nev*er*thelesse þe said parties have putte hem in awarde of John Wynne, Rob*er*t Boteller and John Sturdys, wardeins of þe same craft,[806] & Rumbold Waghter & Will*ia*m Moubrey in þis case to hem assined be þe assent of þe parties above said, þe which*e* wardeins and arbit*our*s awarde and ordeine þe xx day of Juyn þat þe said John Sutton

801 This sum has been written in after scoring out the sum of ii s. previously entered.
802 No figure has been given for this man's fine.
803 This name has been composed in a separate hand by changing the letters of the previously written 'Pynchar'. The same hand has also added the word 'Dowcheman' above the line.
804 Or 'transtre': the fourth letter might be either 'n' or 'u'.
805 The scribe has clearly prepared the page with a line down of 'It*em*'s, but has miscalculated the number needed.
806 No reason is given why Richard Spencer, prime warden that year, is not sitting in judgment on this case, which would be usual. It is possible that the scribe has omitted his name in error, since one might otherwise have expected to find 'three of the wardens . . .' rather than just 'wardens . . .'.

Memorandum that these are the defects during the term of Richard Spencer etc. in the year 19 Henry VI [from 19 May 1441]: 1441–42 A + b p. 100
Firstly, received from William Duke for a defect in workmanship – 2s.
Item, received from Gisebright Vansant [working with] Richard Bradcok for a defect – 12d.
Item, received from Arnold Annore for a defect in workmanship – 2s.
Item, received from William Wilmot for a defect in workmanship – 2s.
Item, received from Roger Vansith for a defect in workmanship – 2s.
Item, received from William Venryth for a defect in workmanship – 2s.
Item, received from Henry Luton, 'Dutchman', for a defect in the workmanship of various collars for my lord of Gloucester[249] – 2s.
Item, received from Peter Hansheld for a defect in workmanship } 20d.
Item, from the same man for selling a 'warre' as a mazer[250]
Item, received from Hans of Cologne for a defect in workmanship –
Item, received from Thomas Fluchard, 'Dutchman', for a defect in workmanship – 3s. 4d.
Item, received from John Dunstall for a defect in workmanship – 2s.
Item, received from William Hoke for a certain [female] tranter[251] and for a defect – 2s.
Item, received from William Gate for a defect in workmanship – 2s.
Item, received from William Percy for a defect in workmanship – 2s.
Item, received from John Rotherham for a defect in workmanship – 2s.
Item, received from William Tunnvyle for a defect in workmanship – 3s. 4d.
Item

Memorandum that whereas there were various quarrels between John Sutton, alderman, on the one side and John Tankard on the other side, about the making of a head of the 11,000 virgins[252] which the Duke of Gloucester had ordered the said John Sutton to have made. Nevertheless, the said parties have submitted themselves to the judgment of John Wynne, Robert Botiller and John Sturdys, wardens of the same mistery, and Reymund Wachter and William Mowbray, assigned to act with them in this case with the consent of the aforesaid parties, the which wardens and arbiters judge and ordain on 1441 A + a p. 182

[249] Humphrey, Duke of Gloucester.

[250] The *OED* and the *MED* both give 'warre' as a knot in wood, and the *MED* (with quotes from 1371–1500) gives it as a type of wood from which cups or bowls are made and suggests that it might have been 'highly figured or knotty wood', perhaps burlwood or boxwood. From the entry here we see that the word must also have been used for objects made of this wood. A mazer was so called because it was made of maplewood, characterised by its variegated, dappled appearance. Peter Hansheld had sold a cup made of inferior wood with knots in it that he passed off as being a maplewood cup, a mazer. These cups were often decorated with silver bands and mountings, and thus came under the jurisdiction of the Goldsmiths.

[251] The meaning of 'travstre' (or 'transtre') is unclear but 'tranter' seems a very possible one here. A tranter (in Latin 'traventarius', 'tranvetarius' etc., fem.'traventrix'; in French 'traventer') was an itinerant vendor, 'a man who does jobs with his horse and cart; a carrier; a hawker . . . a huckster; also one who buys up things to sell them elsewhere; a tapster' (see *OED*). The ordinances of the Goldsmiths strictly forbade dealings with such persons. Cf. the case above, A + b, p. 76, concerning a female huckster.

[252] This was presumably a reliquary in the shape of a head, made to contain a relic (a head) of one of the 11,000 virgin martyrs, companions of St Ursula. See for instance D.H. Farmer, *The Oxford Dictionary of Saints* (Oxford, 1978 and later editions).

shall paie for all*e* thyng þat þe said John Tankard can aske auther for makyng or stuffe of þe said hede and all*e* other thynges þat he þe said J. Tankard can clayme of þe said John Sutton, þe said John Sutton shall paie to þe said John Tankard – iiii li. of sterlynges and of hym to be quite for ev*er*more &c.

1442–43 Thise ben the names of the Wardeyns of Goldsmythes chosen in the fest of
p. 183[807] Seynt Dunstan the xx^{te} ȝere of Kyng Henry the vj^{te} aftre the conquest and þan beyng:

Thomas Leget
Thomas Reyner
Joh*anne*s Wark
Barth*olome*us Bremsh*am*

No*min*a appr*en*ti*ciorum* eodem anno:	
Thomas Tatum app*rentice* with Thomas Leget –	xx s.
Georgius Willughby app*rentice* with John Wordlych –	xx s.
John Bifeld apprentice with Thomas White, Goldbeter –	xiii s. iiii d.
Thomas Sely app*rentice* with Will*ia*m Prynse –	xx s.
Will*elmu*s Proude app*rentice* with Will*ia*m Prynse –	xx s.
Salman Chest*er* app*rentice* with John Wynne –	xx s.
Rob*er*tus Hardyng app*rentice* with Will*ia*m White –	xx s.
John Rowe app*rentice* with Will*ia*m Hilles –	xx s.
Thomas Weyner app*rentice* with Mathewe Hall*e* –	xx s.
Henry Gate app*rentice* with Will*ia*m Kelke –	xiii s. iiii d.[808]
John Elyot app*rentice* with Will*ia*m Boston –	xx s.
Will*ia*m Preston app*rentice* with Sutton atte Sterre –	xx s.
col. 2 Petrus Trent app*rentice* with Mangnus –	xx s.
Thomas Blyth app*rentice* with John Teukesbury –	xiii s. iiii d.[809]
Cormok app*rentice* with John Corby –	xx s.[810]

(There is)[811]

No*min*a p*er*sonar*um* de novo jur*atorum*:	
In primis, de Joh*ann*e Thomas nup*er* app*ren*ti*cio* cum Joh*ann*e Withehale –	ii s.
Item, de Joh*ann*e Aleyn nup*er* app*ren*ti*cio* cum Thoma Reyner –	ii s.
Item, de Rob*er*to Elsmer nup*er* app*ren*ti*cio* cum Henr*ico* Ragley –	ii s.
Item, de Joh*ann*e Hopkyn nup*er* app*ren*ti*cio* cum Joh*ann*e Boudon –	ii s.
Item, de Joh*ann*e Amadas nup*er* app*ren*ti*cio* cum eodem Boudon –	ii s.
Item, de Will*el*mo Lincoln nup*er* app*ren*ti*cio* cum Will*elm*o Aston –	ii s.
Item, de Henr*ico* Benet nup*er* app*ren*ti*cio* cum Joh*ann*e Pake –	ii s.

Duchemen:	
Gerrard Will*ia*m, Ducheman with Garrard –	ii s.

807 A new hand starts here.
808 No reason is given for this lower figure.
809 No reason is given for this lower figure.
810 This entry has been added later in a different hand and ink.
811 These two words are written here in a tidy sixteenth-century hand.

20 June that the said John Sutton shall pay for everything that the said John Tankard can ask for, either for material or for workmanship of the said head, and for everything else that the said John Tankard can claim of the said John Sutton, the said John Sutton shall pay to the said John Tankard – £4 sterling, and he shall be quit of him for evermore etc.

These are the names of the Goldsmiths' Wardens elected at the feast of St Dunstan in the year 20 Henry VI [19 May 1442]: 1442–43 p. 183

Thomas Leget
Thomas Reyner
John Werk
Bartholomew Bremsham

The names of apprentices in the same year:

Thomas Tatum apprentice with Thomas Leget –	20s.
George Willughby apprentice with John Worlych –	20s.
John Byfield apprentice with Thomas White, goldbeater –	13s. 4d.
Thomas Sely apprentice with William Prince –	20s.
William Proude apprentice with William Prince –	20s.
Solomon Chester apprentice with John Wynne –	20s.
Robert Hardyng apprentice with William White –	20s.
John Rowe apprentice with William Hilles –	20s.
Thomas Weyner apprentice with Matthew Halle –	20s.
Henry Gate apprentice with William Kelke –	13s. 4d.
John Elyot apprentice with William Boston –	20s.
William Preston apprentice with Sutton at the Star –	20s.
Peter Trent apprentice with Magnus –	20s. col. 2
Thomas Blithe apprentice with John Tewkesbury –	13s. 4d.
Cormok apprentice with John Corby –	20s.

(There is)

The names of persons newly sworn:

Firstly, from John Thomas, formerly apprentice with John Withihale –	2s.
Item, from John Aleyn formerly apprentice with Thomas Reyner –	2s.
Item, from Robert Elsmer formerly apprentice with Henry Ragley –	2s.
Item, from John Hopkyn formerly apprentice with John Bowdon –	2s.
Item, from John Amadas formerly apprentice with the same Bowdon –	2s.
Item, from William Lincoln formerly apprentice with William Aston –	2s.
Item, from Henry Benet formerly apprentice with John Pake –	2s.

'Dutchmen':

Gerrard William, 'Dutchman' with Garrard –	2s.

Will*elmus* Newark cum Hans Sw[eth]er[812] – ii s.
Hans Ducheman cum Matheo Phelip – ii s.

1442–43 M*emorandum* qu*o*d hic sunt defectus temp*ore* Thome Leget *etc* a*nno* r*egni*
A + b R*egis* Henr*ici* vj[ti] xxp[o]:
p. 101[813] In primis, recept' de Will*ia*m Rothley[814] p*ro* i defalt*a* – ii s.
It*em*, rec' de Joh*anne* Rothewell p*ro* i defalt*a* – ii s.
It*em*, rec' de W*illelmo* Floure p*ro* i defalt*a* – ii s.
It*em*, rec' de Laur*encio* Lelyon p*ro* quodam fine – iii s. iiii d.
It*em*, rec' de Will*elm*o Wymot – iii s.
It*em*, rec' de Joh*anne* Plentfeld p*ro* quoda*m* fine – vi s. viii d.
It*em*, rec' de Joh*anne* Norman – ii s.
It*em*, rec' de Joh*anne* Bowdon p*ro* vendic*io*ne app*re*nticii sui *et* p*ro* fine – xl s.
It*em*, rec' de Walt*er*o ap*ud* Stokkes p*ro* fine – xx d.
It*em*, rec' de[815] Duk p*ro* fine – xx d.
It*em*, rec' de Joh*anne* Worldlich p*ro* fine – ii s.
It*em*, rec' de[816] Mapelden p*ro* fine – xx d.
It*em*, rec' de Will*elmo* Upnore p*ro* revilyng uni*us* socii – vi s. viii d.
It*em*, rec' de Will*elm*o Kelk p*ro* eadem causa – iii s. iiii d.
It*em*, rec' de Joh*anne* Elys p*ro* eadem causa – vi s. viii d.
It*em*, rec' de Henr*ico* Haveryng p*ro* fine – xx d.
It*em*, rec' de Henr*ico* Pole quia no*n* equitavit cu*m* Maiore – ii s.

1443–44 M*emorandum* þ*at* these ben þ*e* namys of þeme þ*at* were fund defectyfe in þ*e*
p. 102[817] tyme of John Sutton, alderman, John Walsche, Mathew Hall*e* & Humfray Hayford:
Ferst, resceyvid of John Topklyf – ii s.
It*em*, John Bornam – ii s.
It*em*, resceyvid of Will*ia*m Browne – ii s.
It*em*, resceyvid of Nicolas Stodeley – ii s.
It*em*, resceyvid of Arnold Annon*e* – ii s.
It*em*, resceyvid of John Thomas – ii s.
It*em*, resceyvid of Mangn*us*, Dowcheman – ii s.
It*em*, resceyvid of Will*ia*m Hoke – ii s.
It*em*, resceyvid of Thomas Prany – ii s.
It*em*, resceyvid of Harry Luton – ii s.
It*em*, resceyvid of Pakys men – ii s.
It*em*, Swether, Dowcheman – ii s.
It*em*, John Buck, resceyvid – ii s.
It*em*, resceyvid of Cownce Couvyle, Dowcheman – ii s.
It*em*, resceyvid of Will*ia*m Prence – ii s.

812 A hole goes right through the centre of this name.
813 A new hand starts here.
814 This man's name has been substituted in different ink by another scribe for another name now too far erased to be legible.
815 A gap has been left for the first name of this man. William?
816 A gap has been left for the first name of this man.
817 A new hand starts here.

William Newark with Hans Swether –	2s.
Hans, 'Dutchman' with Matthew Philip –	2s.

Memorandum that these are the defects during the term of Thomas Leget etc. in the year 21 Henry VI [from 19 May 1442]: 1442–43 A + b p. 101
Firstly, received from William Rothley for a defect – 2s.
Item, received from John Rothwell for a defect – 2s.
Item, received from William Flour for a defect – 2s.
Item, received from Laurence Lethlyon for a certain fine – 3s. 4d.
Item, received from William Wilmot – 3s.
Item, received from John Plentfield for a certain fine – 6s. 8d.
Item, received from John Norman – 2s.
Item, received from John Bowdon for the sale of his apprentice and for a fine – 40s.
Item, received from Walter at the Stocks Market for a fine – 20d.
Item, received from [William] Duke for a fine – 20d.
Item, received from John Worlych for a fine – 2s.
Item, received from Mapelden[253] for a fine – 20d.
Item, received from William Upnore for insulting a companion – 6s. 8d.
Item, received from William Kelk for the same reason – 3s. 4d.
Item, received from John Elys for the same reason – 6s. 8d.
Item, received from Henry Havering for a fine – 20d.
Item, received from Henry Pole because he did not ride with the Mayor – 2s.

Memorandum that these are the names of those found at fault during the term of John Sutton, alderman, John Walsh, Matthew Halle and Humphrey Hayford [from 19 May 1443]: 1443–44 p. 102

Firstly, received from John Topclyff –	2s.
Item, John Bornam –	2s.
Item, received from William Browne –	2s.
Item, received from Nicholas Studley –	2s.
Item, received from Arnold Annore –	2s.
Item, received from John Thomas –	2s.
Item, received from Magnus, 'Dutchman' –	2s.
Item, received from William Hoke –	2s.
Item, received from Thomas Prany –	2s.
Item, received from Harry Luton –	2s.
Item, received from Pake's men –	2s.
Item, Swether, 'Dutchman' –	2s.
Item, John Buck, received –	2s.
Item, received from Cownce Couvyle, 'Dutchman' –	2s.
Item, received from William Prince –	2s.

253 This is probably one of the Mapesdene family, possibly the father since his first name does not seem to have been used? See Name Index.

Item, resceyvid of Bradcokys wyfe –	ii s.
Item, resceyvid of John Gregory –	ii s.
Item, resceyvid of Bartelet, Dowcheman –	v s.

Item, in þe tyme of þe wardens afor wryten þey take of forfettis ii masere bondys of latyn & gylt the t'one was taken of Nicolas Arteys & þe tothere of Marke þat weddyd Dirlyngley wyfe.
Item, in cownterfetys nedels of silver CCCC iiii^{xx} & viii nedels. Item, iii toretys for haucys.[818]
Item, xvi erbekes[819] cownterfet silver, all þis taken of diverse alyantes & strangers.

1444–45 Thes ben þe names of þeme þat were fownd defectyfe yn þe tyme of Wylliam
p. 103[820] Walton, Wylliam Bysmere, Wylliam Porter & Wylliam Rotheley:

	Fyrst of Edwarde Verney –	ii s.
	Item, of Wylliam Hylles –	iii s.
	Item, of John Bolton –	iii s. iiii d.
	Item, of John Gwyne –	iii s. iiii d.
	Item, of Laurence Lethelyon –	xii d.
	Item, of Wylliam Whyte –	x d.
	Item, of Wylliam Prynce & of Wylliam Codynton –	ii s.
	Item, of Rychard Austen –	iii s.
	Item, of John Benton –	ii s.
	Item, of Bame, the sergaunt[821] –	ii s.
	Item, of Watkyn Longes man[822] –	ii s.
	Item, of Thomas Tomvylle –	ii s.
	Item, of Wylliam Wylmot –	ii s.
	Item, of Watkyn[823] Mapysden –	ii s.
	Item, of John Hopkyn –	ii s.
	Item, of Wylliam Batte –	ii s.
	Item, of Rychard Austen –	ii s.
	Item, of Thomas Tomvylle –	iii s. iiii d.
	Item, of Edwarde Verneye –	ii s.
	Item, of Thomas Joly –	xii d.
Book A,	of William Wodeward –	vi s. viii d.
p. 9[824]	of William Wodewarde for sellyng of untrewe gold –	vi s. viii d.

818 Or 'hautys'. It certainly looks more like hautys than haucys in this scribe's writing, but see note 255 on opposite page.
819 This word is unclear and might also be read as 'erbekeres', 'ervekes', 'ervekeres' or 'errekes'. None of these unfortunately is recognisable as an attested word which could make sense in context, and this remains therefore as problematical.
820 A new hand starts here. Book A, p. 9 also contains this list of fines, written out in a different hand; the few variants are given below.
821 Book A gives his name as John Bamme, sergeant.
822 Book A: Walter Longesman.
823 Book A: Walter.
824 The first two entries here occur at the end of the list which is that of Book A + b, p. 103. The following and fuller entries follow.

Item, received from Bradcok's wife –	2s.
Item, received from John Gregory –	2s.
Item, received from Bartelet, 'Dutchman' –	5s.

Item, during the term of the above written wardens they have confiscated 2 mazer bands of latten and gilt, one taken from Nicholas Arteys and the other from Mark who married Dirlyngley's wife.[254]
Item, of counterfeit silver needles – 488 needles. Item, 3 torets for hose?[255]
Item, 16 drinking-vessels (?)[256] of counterfeit silver, all this taken from various aliens and 'strangers'[257].

These are the names of those who were found at fault during the term of William Walton, William Bismere, William Porter and William Rothley [from 19 May 1444]: 1444–45 p. 103

Firstly, from Edward Verney –	2s.
Item, from William Hilles –	2s.
Item, from John Bolton –	3s. 4d.
Item, from John Gwyne –	3s. 4d.
Item, from Laurence Lethlyon –	12d.
Item, from William White –	10d.
Item, from William Prince and William Coddington –	2s.
Item, from Richard Austen –	3s.
Item, from John Benton –	2s.
Item, from Bamme, the bedel –	2s.
Item, from Watkyn Longesman[258] –	2s.
Item, from Thomas Tumvyle –	2s.
Item, from William Wilmot –	2s.
Item, from Watkyn Mapesdene –	2s.
Item, from John Hopkyn –	2s.
Item, from William Bate –	2s.
Item, from Richard Austen –	2s.
Item, from Thomas Tumvyle –	3s. 4d.
Item, from Edward Verney –	2s.
Item, from Thomas Joly –	12d.
from William Woodward –	6s. 8d. Book A, p.
from William Woodward for selling sub-standard gold –	6s. 8d.

254 i.e. widow.

255 The Old French word 'toret', modern English 'terret', 'turret' or 'torret' is defined by the *OED* as: 'A round or circular loop or ring, esp. one turning on a swivel, by which a string, ribbon, or chain is attached to anything; each of the two rings by which the leash is attached to the jesses of a hawk; in horse-harness, one of the two (brass) rings fixed upright on the pad, or saddle, and on the harness, through which the driving reins pass. Also, any ring attached elsewhere to the harness for a similar purpose.' John Cherry has given me the additional information that 'a toret is a linking piece, often composed of three rings or a trefoil, that can be used for dress or dress ornament.' The 'haucys' are therefore probably 'hose' and the torrets are for dress-wear, but since the word could be read as 'hautys' one should perhaps consider other possible meanings.

256 See opposite page. A 'beker' was a precious or ornate drinking-vessel and this is suggested here only as a possible guess as to the meaning.

257 i.e. men from the provinces, non-citizens.

258 It is possible that this is not a surname, and that this should read: Watkyn, Long's man (i.e. of Thomas Long).

Also of – iii li. xvi s. vi d. resceyved of diverse persones for certein defautes done ayenst the wardeins and other of the said craft in the said tyme:
of Bartholomeu Bremson for an after accompt – x s.[825]
of Thomas Goore, scowrer, for i trespas don in Juyn Gardeyn[826] – vi s. viii d.
of John Wordlyche for sellyng of his apprentice withoute leve – vi s. viii d.
of Bartholomeu Bremson for withstondyng the wardeins in takyng of assaie – vi s. viii d.
of William Wodeward for i trespas done ayenst German Bostones man – vi s. viii d.
of John Ireton for settyng a straunger a work withoute leve – iii s. iiii d.
of William Hylle – vi s. viii d.
of John Ireton for licence of a Ducheman to worke with him for iiii yeer – xiii s. iiii d.
of John of Bolton for i trespas doon ayenst Crisbyn mayde in the Halle – iii s. ii d.
of Harry Pole for disobeisaunce to his wardeins – xiii s. iiii d.

Summa – iii li. xvi s. vi d.

p. 10 Also they accompten of – xxiii li. xix s. iiii d. resceyved of certein persones that payd to the costes of the ministrals ayenst the comyng of the Quene,[827] whos names folowyn in forme underwriten:
col. 1 of John Aleyn – vi s. viii d.
of Thomas Pynchard – xvi d.
of Richard Brome – ii s.
of Thomas Cottesson – v s.
of William Elsonby – vi s. viii d.
of Edward Verney viii s. iiii d.

[825] Bartholomew Bremsham had been warden in 1438–39 and 1442–43 and would thus have been responsible for monies at those times. He might also have served as renter at some point, although no record of this exists (few of the renters for this period are known to us, but it was common for a man to serve as renter before being elected as a warden). As both renter and warden, he would have been responsible for a proper rendering of account at the end of his period of office, and it would seem that he is here being fined for a delay in such rendering of account.

[826] A long series of documents, dating from the years of the mayoralty of Ralph Hardell (1254–57) to 26 March 1391, relating to the land known as Jewyn Garden are in the Register of Deeds, ff. 17r–28v.

[827] The arrival of Margaret of Anjou, Henry VI's queen, in 1445. A proxy marriage had taken place in France before Margaret's departure for England in February 1445. See R.A. Griffiths, *The Reign of King Henry VI*, 2nd edn (Stroud, 1998), pp. 315–16. On her entry into London see in particular: *The Great Chronicle of London*, ed. A.H. Thomas and I.D. Thornley (London, 1938 and facsimile reprint 1983), pp. 177–78; John Stow, *Annales, or a Generall Chronicle of England* . . . (London, 1631), pp. 384–85; C. Brown, 'Lydgate's Verses on Queen Margaret's Entry into London', *Modern Language Review* VII (1912), 225–34; R. Withington, 'Queen Margaret's Entry into London 1445', *Modern Philology* XIII (1915–16), 53–57.

Also: £3 16s. 6d. received from various persons for certain offences committed against the wardens and others of the said mistery during the said period:
from Bartholomew Bremsham for an account rendered late – 10s.
from Thomas Goore, scourer, for an offence committed in Jewyn Garden – 6s. 8d.
from John Worlych for selling his apprentice without leave – 6s. 8d.
from Bartholomew Bremsham for opposing the wardens from making an assay – 6s. 8d.
from William Woodward for an offence committed against German Boston's man – 6s. 8d.
from John Ireton for putting a foreigner to work without leave – 3s. 4d.
from William Hilles – 6s. 8d.
from John Ireton for permission for a 'Dutchman' to work with him for 4 years – 13s. 4d.
from John of Bolton for an offence committed against Cresbien in the Hall – 3s. 4d.
from Harry Pole for disobedience to his wardens – 13s. 4d.

Total – £3 16s. 6d.

Item, they account for – £23 19s. 4d. received from certain persons who paid towards the expenses of the minstrels at the arrival of the Queen, and their names are written below: p. 10
from John Aleyn – 6s. 8d. col. 1
from Thomas Pynchard – 16d.
from Richard Brome – 2s.
from Thomas Cotsoun – 5s.
from William Elsonby – 6s. 8d.
from Edward Verney – 8s. 4d.

of John Donne – iii s. iiii d.
of William Wilmot – x s.
of William Lyncoln – xvi d.
of John Hopkyn – xx d.
of Laurence Chyldmylle – vi s. viii d.
of William Broun – vi s. viii d.
of Nichol Fyfehide – iii s.
of Thomas Sampson – xiii s. iiii d.
of William Essex – ii s.
of John Ireton – ii s.
of Thomas Serle – ii s.
of Nicholas Tonvylle – vi s. viii d.
of John Mapesdene – vi s. viii d.
of Herry Tyfret – iii s. iiii d.
of John Wordhohe – v s.
of John Ufford – xx d.
of William Tanner – ii s. viii d.
of Robert Russell – xii d.
of Richard Massynger – iii s. iiii d.
of Thomas Wolf – xii d.
of Watkyn Longisman – xx d.
of William Hulle – iii s. iiii d.
of John Buk – x s.
of Harvy Haveryng – xx d.
of William Gosse – xii d.
of William Stuwardy – vi s. viii d.
of John Topclyf – vi s. viii d.
of Pakes Wyf – vi s. viii d.
of John Martyn – ii s.
of Thomas Longe – v s.
of Thomas Preyne – iii s. iiii d.
of William May, turnour – iii s.
of Bartholomeu Boorne xii d.
of John Norman – vi s. viii d.
of Thomas Joly – xiii s. iiii d.
of John Swether – iii s. iiii d.
of Arnold Osynbrig – v s.
of Bartholomeu Lambspryng – xiii s. iiii d.
of Giles Baynam – xiii s. iiii d.
col. 2 of John Sutton at Sterre – x s.
of John Lylye – vi s. viii d.
of Harry Horne – iii s. iiii d.
of John Clenvyle – xx s.
of Thomas Leget – xx s.
of Elys Horwode – iii s. iiii d.
of Laurence Lethlyon – viii s. viii d.
of Watkyn Chaundeler – iii s. iiii d.

from John Donne – 3s. 4d.
from William Wilmot – 10s.
from William Lincoln – 16d.
from John Hopkyn – 20d.
from Laurence Chyldemylle – 6s. 8d.
from William Broun – 6s. 8d.
from Nicholas Fifehead – 3s.
from Thomas Sampson – 13s. 4d.
from William Essex – 2s.
from John Ireton – 2s.
from Thomas Serle – 2s.
from Nicholas Tonvylle – 6s. 8d.
from John Mapesdene – 6s. 8d.
from Harry Tyfret – 3s. 4d.
from John Wordhohe – 5s.
from John Ufford – 20d.
from William Tanner – 2s. 8d.
from Robert Russell – 12d.
from Richard Messynger – 3s. 4d.
from Thomas Wolf – 12d.
from Watkyn Longisman[259] – 20d.
from William Hulle – 3s. 4d.
from John Buk – 10s.
from Harvey Havering – 20d.
from William Gosse – 12d.
from William Stuwardy – 6s. 8d.
from John Topclyff – 6s. 8d.
from Pake's wife – 6s. 8d.
from John Martyn – 2s.
from Thomas Long – 5s.
from Thomas Prany – 3s. 4d.
from William May, turner – 3s.
from Bartholomew Boorne – 12d.
from John Norman – 6s. 8d.
from Thomas Joly – 13s. 4d.
from John Swether – 3s. 4d.
from Arnold Osnabrück – 5s.
from Bartholomew Lambsspryng – 13s. 4d.
from Giles Baynam – 13s. 4d.
from John Sutton at the Star – 10s. col. 2
from John Lilye – 6s. 8d.
from Harry Horne – 3s. 4d.
from John Clenvyle – 20s.
from Thomas Leget – 20s.
from Elys Horwood – 3s. 4d.
from Laurence Lethlyon – 8s. 8d.
from Watkyn Chaundeler – 3s. 4d.

[259] Or perhaps: 'Watkyn, Long's man'.

of Robert Lovekyn, goldbeter – viii s. iiii d.
of Thomas Peryn – xiii s. iiii d.
of John Hook – ii s.
of Thomas Stapilherst – xx d.
of Janyn Skyveyn – xiii s. iiii d.
of Thomas Swayn – xiii s. iiii d.
of Blak Petre – xiii s. iiii d.
of Richard Stapylton, goldbeter – iii s. iiii d.
of William Bate – v s.
of John Wheler, fynour – vi s. viii d.
of Robert Kympton – vi s. viii d.
of John Philip & Will Danyell – vi s. viii d.
of Jacob Richardson – iii s. iiii d.
of Arnold an Over[828] – iii s. iiii d.
of Herman at the Blak Egle – vi s. viii d.
of Albright Goldsmith – xx d.
of Deryk Harrystvyke – ii s.
of Derryk in the spitell – ii s. iiii d.
of Hans Garlof – iii s.
of Hans Cristian – iii s. iiii d.
of Gisbright – xx d.
of Bartelot in Lovettes Aley – xvi d.
of Harry Luton – xii d.
of Swan Andrewe – ii s.
of Couns Gaysmere – xviii d.
of Lambert Goldsmyth – xviii d.
of Walter Rulecandell – v s. iiii d.
of Gerard Haverbek – xx s.
of Magnus of Ardern – xiii s. iiii d.
of Hans Doubelers man – ii s.
of Arnold Bensebrod – x s.
of Robert Baker – iii s. iiii d.
of William Allone – xvi d.

Summa: xxiii li. xix s. iiii d.[829]

p. 12 Also the same yeer the xxx day of Novembre it liked oure souverain lordis highnesse to directe his gracious lettres under his prive signet to the said wardeins, the tenour wherof folowith in forme underwriten:

To oure welbeloved William Walton, William Bismere, William Porter and William Rotheley, wardeins of the craft of goldsmythes withynne our citee of London:

By the kynge:

Welbeloved. We grete you wel. And suppose that ye have understondyng howe we have nowe late sent oure right entirely welbeloved cosyn the Marcheys of

[828] *sic.*

[829] As so often in these and other medieval records, this sum given here is not in fact the sum of the above individual amounts.

from Robert Lovekyn, goldbeater – 8s. 4d.
from Thomas Peryn – 13s. 4d.
from John Hook – 2s.
from Thomas Staplehurst – 20d.
from Janyn Eskevyn – 13s. 4d.
from Thomas Swayn – 13s. 4d.
from Black Peter – 13s. 4d.
from Richard Stapleton, goldbeater – 3s. 4d.
from William Bate – 5s.
from John Wheler, finer – 6s. 8d.
from Robert Kynton – 6s. 8d.
from John Philip and Will Danyell – 6s. 8d.
from Jacob Richardson – 3s. 4d.
from Arnold Hanover – 3s. 4d.
from Hermann at the Black Eagle – 6s. 8d.
from Albright Goldsmith – 20d.
from Derek Harrystvyke – 2s.
from Derek in St Mary Spital – 2s. 4d.
from Hans Garlof – 3s.
from Hans Cristian – 3s. 4d.
from Gisebright – 20d.
from Bartelot in Lovett's Alley – 16d.
from Harry Luton – 12d.
from Andrew Swan – 2s.
from Couns Gaysmere – 18d.
from Lambert Goldsmyth – 18d.
from Walter Rocandelle – 5s. 4d.
from Gerard Haverbek – 20s.
from Magnus of Ardern – 13s. 4d.
from Hans Dobler's man – 2s.
from Arnold Bensebrod – 10s.
from Robert Baker – 3s. 4d.
from William Allone – 16d.

Total: £23 19s. 4d.

Item, the same year on 30 November it pleased our sovereign lord's highness p. 12
to send his gracious letters under his privy signet to the said wardens, the tenour of which follows in the underwritten manner:

To our well-beloved William Walton, William Bismere, William Porter and William Rothley, Wardens of the Goldsmiths' Mistery within our City of London:

From the King:

Well-beloved, we greet you well, and we suppose that you know that we have recently sent our right entirely well-beloved cousin the Marquis of

Suffolk to conveye unto our presence our moost entierly welbeloved wif the quene, whom thorgh goddes mercy we trust to have withynne right brief tyme. And for as moche as it hath ben accustumed for our honneur & the worship of this our reaulme that at such time as the quenes have comyn toward our citee of London, the Mair, aldremen and all the craftes of oure said citee have resceived theim on the wey in the moost honest fourme that they best couthe devise, amonges the whiche as we ben enfourmed your craft have at all times notably acquited theim, and in especial at our comyng home from oure coronacion at Parys. Wherof we can you right singuler & special thankes. And pray you that ayenst the comyng of our said wyf ye wolle prepare you to mete hir in the moost goodly wise that shall now be thought unto you moost for our honneur & worship of this our reaulme. Wherynne ye shall do unto us right good pleasir & cause us to shewe un to you the favour of our good grace in time to come. Yeven under our signet at our Castell of Wyndesore the xxix day of Novembre.

Whiche lettres resceived, the said wardeins dide do make a semble of alle the hoole livere, and ther declared un to them the tenour of the said lettres and there dide it to be radde opynly. Wheruppon the said wardeins be the advise of John Pattesle & John Sutton, aldremen, & other of the said feleship there being present, it was ordeined & appointed in the forme that foloweth: That is to sey that every man ayenst the comyng of the Quene that were in the livere shold have bawdrykkes of silver abowte their nekkes with ii hangers behinde or iii as theim liked, and with short hoodes of scarlet jagged. And every man that had be wardein or renter shold have his folower clothed in white bustian with a blak jagge be neth of i quarter breed and a blak hood abowte his nek beeten with goldsmythes werke, with blak felt hattes upon their heedes; the whiche thinges so done diverse persones of the said feleship that might not for sikenesse nor age and other persones that were not likly to ride aggreed with the said wardeins to paye to the costes of minstrals at the day of the ridyng, the names of whom with the sommes that they payd be writen before in the resceitz of the said wardeins accompte.[830]

1445 M*emorandum* þ*e* viii day of Apryll þe ȝere of the reyne of Kyng Henri þ*e* sext
A + b p. 104 after þe conquest xxiii^{ti}, that Wyll*ia*m Walton, Wyll*ia*m Bysmer, Wyll*ia*m Porter & Wyll*ia*m Rotheley theyne beyng wardens, was ordeynyd by þe felyschype at asemble, þere beyng John Sutton, aldreman, Mathew Philippe, John Walche, Thom*as* Rayn*er*, John Adys, John Wynne, John Waryn, Thom*as* Legget, John Worke, Robert Boteler, John Sturdis, Thom*as* Harison, John Grene, Bartylmew Bremson, John Byrlyng, Mathew Hall, John Orwell, Umfrey Hayforde, Harri Polle, Wyll*ia*m Boston, Wyll*ia*m Hyll*es*, Rog*er* Barker, Wyll*ia*m Prince & John Byschoppe w*ith* odere dyv*er*ce of þe same felyschype, aȝeynst þe comyng of Qwene Margret that ev*er*y man þ*at* schulde

[830] i.e. Book A, p. 10 above.

Suffolk to convey to our presence our most entirely well-beloved wife, the Queen, whom through God's mercy we trust to have within a very short time. And whereas it has been the custom for the honour of ourselves and the reverence of this our kingdom that whenever Queens have arrived in our city of London the Mayor, aldermen and all the misteries of our said city have received them along their route in the best manner they could devise, amongst whom, as we have been informed, your mistery has always most notably acquitted itself, especially at the time of our arrival home from our coronation in Paris, for which we know that you should have most especial and singular thanks. And we pray you that at the arrival of our said wife you shall prepare yourselves to meet her in the best manner that you shall think fit for the honour and reverence of this our kingdom. And in this you will bring us the greatest pleasure and will cause us in time to come to show you the favour of our good grace. Given under our signet at our Castle of Windsor on 29 November.

When they had received this letter, the said wardens convened an assembly of the whole livery, and there they declared to them the tenour of the said letter and had it read out openly to them. Whereupon the said wardens with the advice of John Pattesley and John Sutton, aldermen, and others of the said fellowship then present, ordained and appointed in the manner that follows: i.e. that at the arrival of the Queen every man who was in the livery should have baldrics of silver about his neck with two hangers behind, or three if they liked, and short hoods of scarlet with an indented edge. And every man who had been a warden or a renter should have his follower clothed in white bustian with a black jack [tunic] beneath made of one quarter length of broad[260] and a black hood about his neck embroidered with goldsmiths' work,[261] with black felt hats upon their heads. When this had been decided, various people of the said fellowship who were not able to ride because of sickness or old age, and others who were not qualified to ride, made an agreement with the said wardens to make a payment towards the cost of the minstrels on the day of the procession, and their names with the sums that they paid are written above in the receipts section of the said wardens' accounts.

Memorandum that on 8 April 1445 while William Walton, William Bismere, 1445
William Porter and William Rothley were wardens, it was ordained by the A + b
fellowship at an assembly at which were present John Sutton, alderman, p. 104[262]
Matthew Philip, John Walsh, Thomas Reyner, John Adys, John Wynne, John Waryn, Thomas Leget, John Werk, Robert Botiller, John Sturdys, Thomas Harryson, John Grene, Bartholomew Bremsham, John Birling, Matthew Hall, John Orwell, Humphrey Hayford, Harry Pole, William Boston, William Hilles, Roger Barker, William Prince and John Bisshop with various others of the same fellowship, that at the arrival of Queen Margaret every man who was to ride in procession, this to be at the discretion of

[260] This might have been broadcloth, but was here very probably broad-silk. See *OED*.
[261] i.e. with spangles: see below.
[262] It is interesting to note that some changes have taken place between November and April in the ceremonial attire prescribed. One may also compare the above with the account given in the *Great Chronicle of London* and in John Stow's *Annales*: see p. 528, note 827 above.

ryde be þe dyscressyons of ix p*er*sonys amytted unto þ*e* same wardenys schulde have baudrykes w*ith* too hangerys behynde & rede hodys gagyd w*ith* owȝte tepettys & all tho þ*at* haven beyn wardens & renterys schulde have foloerys arayed yn gownes of wyght bustian gagyd w*ith* blake & blake hodys gaged & set w*ith* spang*es* of sylver.

Book A, p. 12 *cont.* And the names of theim that aggreed with the said wardeins to pay to the said costes and paid not folowen in the fourme underwriten:

Richard Hayward – xvi d.
Willelmus Codyngton – xx d.
William Hart – xx d.
John Wordeliche – v s.
(John Thomas – xx d.)[831]
John Bastard – xii d.
Walter Mapesdene – iii s.
John Patryk – xx d.
German Bostons man – ii s.
John Broyne – xx d.
p. 13 John Tewkesbury – vi s. viii d.
John Broun – iii s. iiii d.
William Beeche – iii s. iiii d.
John Norwell – ii s.
John Morys – iii s. iiii d.
Hugh Fawsyde – ii s.
Thomas Broun – iii s. iiii d.
Thomas Pomerey – xii d.
Richard Selander – xiii s. iiii d.
John Kebell – vi s. viii d.
William Takele – xx d.
Hans Blithe – iii s. iiii d.
Thomas Ernest – xx s.
Thomas Steven – xii d.
John Olyf – iii s. iiii d.
(William Mounbray – ii s.)[832]
Gerard Rowe – xx d.
Hans Dowbeleres wyf – vi s. viii d.
Joce Style – ii s.
Herman Selkhove – ii s. vi d.
Janyn Archer – iii s. iiii d.
John Wyflete – xx s.
Hans Cristian – xvi s. viii d.
William Gerard – xx s.
John Tankard – xiii s. iiii d.

Summa – ix li. iii s. ii d.

[831] This entry has been scored out, perhaps because he later paid up.
[832] This entry has also been scored out.

9 persons appointed to assist the same wardens, should wear a baldric with two hangers behind and red hoods gauged[263] and without tippets, and all those who have been wardens and renters should have their followers clothed in gowns of white bustian gauged with black thread and black hoods gauged and decorated with silver spangles.

And the names of those who made an agreement with the said wardens to make a payment towards the said costs and who did not pay follow below: Book A, p. 12 *cont.*

Richard Hayward – 16d.
William Coddington – 20d.
William Hart – 20d.
John Worlych – 5s.
(John Thomas – 20d.)
John Bastard – 12d.
Walter Mapesdene – 3s.
John Patrick – 20d.
German Boston's man – 2s.
John Broyne – 20d.
John Tewkesbury – 6s. 8d. p. 13
John Broun – 3s. 4d.
William Beeche – 3s. 4d.
John Norwell – 2s.
John Morys – 3s. 4d.
Hugh Fauset – 2s.
Thomas Broun – 3s. 4d.
Thomas Pomeray – 12d.
Richard Selander – 13s. 4d.
John Kebbell – 6s. 8d.
William Takeley – 20d.
Hans Blithe – 3s. 4d.
Thomas Ernest – 20s.
Thomas Steven – 12d.
John Olyve – 3s. 4d.
(William Mowbray – 2s.)
Gerard Rowe – 20d.
Hans Dobler's wife – 6s. 8d.
Joyce[264] Style – 2s.
Hermann Selkhove – 2s. 6d.
Janyn Archer – 3s. 4d.
John Wyflete – 20s.
Hans Cristian – 16s. 8d.
William Gerard – 20s.
John Tankard – 13s. 4d.

Total: £9 3s. 2d.

[263] To gauge = 'to draw up in a series of parallel gatherings' (*OED*).
[264] This name was used for both men and women in the Middle Ages.

p. 11 Expenses necessarie . . .

. . .

Also for diverse costes & expensis ayenst the comyng of the quene, that is to wite for gownes, hoodes & other thinges necessarie – v li.

non allocata

Of the whiche v li. the wardeins and the companie for diverse thinges that meve them disalowe the olde wardeins & charge them ther with.

1446–47 Joh*ann*es Adys
A + b Joh*ann*es Grene
p. 105[833] Will*elm*us Boston
Will*elm*us Hylles

} wardeins of goldsmythes the xxiiii^{ti} ȝeer of Kyng H*enry* the vj^{te}

1446 [834]Be it remembred that the xiii day of Juyn the ȝer of regne of Kyng Henr*y* the vj^{te} aft*er* the conquest xxiiii^{ti}, for as moche as diverse matiers of controv*er*sie were moved & had be certein of the feleship of Seint Fasters P*ar*ysshe on the oo p*ar*tye & Will*iam* Porter on the other p*ar*te, as for the lyvere of a portows[835] which that the said William Porter had delyvered to oon S*ir* Roger Bredde[836] aȝens the wylle of the ȝever of the said portows, it is ordeined & awarded by John Adys, John Grene, William Boston & William Hylles, wardeins of the said craft, by the advyse of Matheu Philip, John Walssh*e*, Thomas Leget, John Waryn, Thom*as* Reyner, Joh*ann*es Orewell, Rob*ert* Botiller, Matheu Halle, Humfrey Hayford & John Byrlyng, that the said William Porter shall delyvere the said booke to S*ir* Thomas Baby the morne after by none at the ferthest w*ith* owte any cont*ra*diccion or elles the said S*ir* Roger to be utterly discharged of his s*er*vice be the said tyme. Forthermore, where as certein debate & contraversie were moved & had betwene the said Will*iam* Porter, Robert Langford & Harry Poole, it was ordeined & awarded by the said wardeins & feleship for the good ende of pees & love to be had betwene them heraft*er* that the said Will*iam* Porter shal make at his owne cost*es* to the said Rob*ert* Langford & Henry Poole & to the said wardeins a competent dyner at suche tyme as the said wardeins wol assigne, & in like wise the said Robert & Henry shall make to the said Will*iam* Porter a dyner when they be required. And ȝef it can be duely p*ro*ved hereafter that the said Will*iam* Porter move or stere any mater as for the Sadillers p*ar*tye aȝenst any of his feleship of the said p*ar*yssh wherof any debate or rancour myght growe, that then the said Will*iam* Porter shall pay unto the almesse of Seint Dunston xl s. And in like wyse ȝef the said Will*iam* Porter renounce or disobbey any of these p*re*misses that then he pay to the almesse xl s.[837]

p. 106 [blank]

[833] A new hand starts here.

[834] Book A, p. 37 also has a copy of this that contains no notable variants, only a few small orthographic differences and changes in word order.

[835] Spelt 'portoos' in Book A.

[836] A: 'Brodde' – the letter in A + b is unclear and this might be its reading too.

[837] A sixteenth-century hand has written 'Fine' below this, and also some other note, now faded away, possibly the date.

Expenses necessary: p. 11

. . .

Item, for various costs and expenses at the arrival of the Queen, i.e. for gowns, hoods and other necessary things – £5.

not authorised

Of the which £5, the wardens and the company for various reasons that they take into consideration will not authorise this, and they set it in the receipts section of the previous wardens' accounts.[265]

John Adys
John Grene
William Boston
William Hilles } wardens of the goldsmiths in the year 24 Henry VI [from 19 May 1446] 1446–47 A + b p. 105

Memorandum that on 13 June 1446, whereas various matters of controversy 1446 had been raised by certain members of the fellowship of St Vedast's parish on the one hand and William Porter on the other, concerning the handing over of a portable breviary which the said William Porter had handed over to a certain Sir Roger Bredde, against the wishes of the giver of the said breviary, it is ordained and judged by John Adys, John Grene, William Boston and William Hilles, wardens of the said mistery, by the advice of Matthew Philip, John Walsh, Thomas Leget, John Waryn, Thomas Reyner, John Orwell, Robert Botiller, Matthew Halle, Humphrey Hayford and John Birling, that the said William Porter shall hand over the said book to Sir Thomas Baby tomorrow morning by noon at the latest and without any dispute, or else the said Sir Roger shall be entirely discharged of his service by the said time. Furthermore, whereas there had been various quarrels and controversy raised between the said William Porter, Robert Langford and Harry Poole, it was ordained and judged by the said wardens and fellowship, in order to ensure the good result of peace and goodwill between them hereafter, that the said William Porter shall at his own expense offer a suitable dinner to the said Robert Langford and Henry Poole and the wardens, at a time to be assigned by the said wardens, and similarly the said Robert and Henry shall when requested offer a dinner to the said William Porter. And if it can hereafter be properly proved that the said William Porter is stirring up anything with the Saddlers' party against any of the fellowship of the said parish as a result of which any quarrel or rancour might arise, that then the said William Porter shall pay to the alms funds of St Dunstan – 40s. And likewise if the said William Porter shall deny or disobey any of the foregoing, then he shall pay to the alms funds – 40s.

[blank] p. 106

[265] This is interesting as an insight into the auditing procedure, which was clearly at this date still done before an assembly, the new wardens acting as auditors for those demitting office. The exchequer-board system of accounting used must be remembered, and when this £5 was disallowed, the wardens have directed that the tokens or counters for this amount should be returned to the 'Charge' or 'Income and Receipts' section.

Select Bibliography

1. MANUSCRIPTS

London

The Worshipful Company of Goldsmiths:
MS 1518 (Wardens' Accounts and Court Minute Book A + a)
MS 1519 (Wardens' Accounts and Court Minute Book A + b)
MS 1520 (Wardens' Accounts and Court Minute Book A)
MSS 1642, 1643 (Register of Deeds)
MS 2524 (Book of Ordinances, vol. I: 1478–83)
MS 1744 (Book of Charters).[1]
MS E III, 4 (1), *olim* Guildhall MS 8749.

Public Record Office, Kew:
PRO C66/166

Corporation of London Records Office:
Plea and Memoranda Roll A 1 b

2. PRINTED WORKS

Agricola, *De Re Metallica* (Halle, 1556); trans. H.C. and L.H. Hoover (London, 1912).

Alexander, J. and P. Binski, eds, *Age of Chivalry: Art in Plantagenet England 1200–1400* (London, 1987).

Anglo-Norman Dictionary, ed. W. Rothwell *et al.* (London: MHRA, 1977–92). (*AND*)

Badcock, W., *A New Touchstone for Gold and Silver Wares* (London, 1677; reprinted Shannon, Ireland, 1970).

Beaven, A.B., *The Aldermen of the City of London*, 2 vols (London, 1908–13).

Bimbenet-Privat, Michèle, *Les Orfèvres parisiens de la Renaissance, 1506–1620* (Paris: Commission des travaux historiques de la Ville de Paris, 1992).

Bimbenet-Privat, M., *L'Orfèvrerie parisienne de la Renaissance: trésors dispersés* (Paris: Centre culturel du Panthéon, 1995).

Boileau, Etienne, *Le Livre des Métiers*, ed. René de Lespinasse and François Bonnardot, *Histoire générale de Paris: Les métiers et corporations de la ville de Paris – XIIIe siècle* (Paris: Imprimerie Nationale, 1879); also ed. G.-B. Depping,

[1] These are nineteenth-century copies of documents at the PRO.

Reglemens sur les arts et métiers de Paris, rédigés au XIIIe siècle et connus sous le nom du Livre des Métiers d'Etienne Boileau (Paris, 1837).

Bonefant-Feytmans, A.-M., 'La corporation des orfèvres de Bruxelles au Moyen Age', Académie Royale de Belgique, *Bulletin de la Commission Royale d'Histoire*, no. CXV (1950), 85–171.

Brault-Lerch, S., *Les Orfèvres de Franche-Comté et de la Principauté de Montbéliard du Moyen Age au XIXe siècle,* Dictionnaire des poinçons de l'orfèvrerie provinciale française, 1 (Geneva: Droz, 1976).

Brown, C., 'Lydgate's Verses on Queen Margaret's Entry into London', *Modern Language Review* 7 (1912), 225–34.

Calendar of the Charter Rolls, 5 vols (London, 1903–16).

Calendar of the Close Rolls preserved in the Public Record Office: . . . 1237–42 (London, 1911).

Calendar of the Close Rolls preserved in the Public Record Office: Henry IV, vol. III: 1405–1409 (London, 1931).

Calendar of Early Mayor's Court Rolls preserved among the Archives of the Corporation of the City of London at the Guildhall, A.D. 1298–1307, ed. A.H. Thomas (Cambridge, 1924).

Calendar of Inquisitions post mortem, ed. J.L. Kirby, vol. XVIII (London, 1987).

Calendar of Letter-Books preserved among the Archives of the Corporation of the City of London, A-H, ed. R.R. Sharpe (London, 1899–1907).

Calendar of Plea and Memoranda Rolls preserved among the Archives of the Corporation of the City of London at the Guildhall. I: *1323–1364*; II: *1364–81*; III: *1381–1412*; IV: *1413–37*, ed. A.H. Thomas (London, 1926–43); V: *1437–57*; VI: *1458–82*, ed. P.E. Jones (London, 1954–61).

Calendar of Wills proved and enrolled in the Court of Husting, London, 1258–1688, ed. R.R. Sharpe, 2 vols (London, 1889–90).

Campbell, M., 'English Goldsmiths in the Fifteenth Century' in *England in the Fifteenth Century*, ed. D. Williams (London, 1987), pp. 43–52.

Campbell, M., 'Gold, Silver and Precious Stones' in *English Medieval Industries*, ed. J. Blair and N. Ramsay (London, 1991), pp. 107–66.

Carlin, M., *Medieval Southwark* (London, 1996).

Chaffers, W., *Gilda Aurifabrorum* (London, 1883).

Chaffers, W., *Hall Marks on Gold and Silver Plate*, 6th edn (London, 1883).

Cherry, John, *Goldsmiths*, Medieval Craftsmen (London: British Museum, 1992).

Clode, C.M., *Memorials of the Guild of Merchant Taylors of the Fraternity of St John the Baptist in the City of London and of its Associated Charities and Institutions* (London, printed for private circulation, 1874).

Clode, C.M., *The Early History of the Guild of Merchant Taylors of the Fraternity of St John the Baptist, London, with Notices of the Lives of Some of its Eminent Members,* 2 vols (London, printed for private circulation, 1888).

Colvin, H.M., *The History of the King's Works*, vols I and II (London, 1963).

Cook, W.T., *The Bells of St Paul's* (London, 1981).

Coulet, N., 'Les confréries de métier à Aix au bas moyen âge', Lambrechts and Sosson, pp. 55–73.

Dictionary of Medieval Latin from British Sources, ed. R.E. Latham *et al.* (Oxford, 1975–). (*DMLBS)*

Dictionnaire des poinçons de l'orfèvrerie provinciale française (Geneva: Droz, 1976–).

Dictionnaire étymologique de l'ancien français, ed. Kurt Baldinger *et al.* (Tübingen, 1971–). (*DEAF*)

Douet-d'Arcq, L., *Comptes de l'argenterie des rois de France au XIVe siècle*, Société de l'histoire de France (Paris, 1851), pp. 345–408: 'Table des mots techniques'.

Douet-d'Arcq, L., *Nouveau recueil de comptes de l'argenterie des rois de France* (Paris, 1874).

Dugdale, W., *The History of St Paul's Cathedral* (London, 1658); Id., edited with additions (London, 1818).

Egan, G. and F. Pritchard *et al.*, *Dress Accessories c. 1150 – c . 1450*, Museum of London, Medieval Finds from Excavations in London, 3 (London: HMSO, 1991).

Ekwall, E., *The Concise Oxford Dictionary of English Place-Names*, 4th edn (Oxford, 1960).

Evans, Joan, *A History of Jewellery 1100–1870* (London, 1953).

Feys, J.M.E., 'Documents concernant le métier des orfèvres à Bruges', *Annales de la Société d'Emulation de Bruges* 31 (1880), 119–24.

Fisher, John H., 'A Language Policy for Lancastrian England', *PMLA* (October 1992), 1168–80.

Forbes, J.S., *Hallmark: A History of the London Assay Office* (London: Unicorn Press, 1999).

Galbraith, V.H., ed., *The Anonimalle Chronicle 1333–1381*, Publications of the University of Manchester, no. 175, Historical Series no. 45 (Manchester, 1927).

Gay, V., *Glossaire archéologique du moyen âge et de la Renaissance*, 2 vols (Paris, 1887–1928).

Genard, P., 'Notice sur la corporation des orfèvres d'Anvers', *Annales de l'Académie d'archéologie de Belgique*, 4e série, 45 (1889), 291–334.

Girtin, T., *The Mark of the Sword: A Narrative History of the Cutlers' Company 1189–1975* (London, 1975).

Glanville, P., *Silver in England* (London, 1987).

Godefroy, F., *Dictionnaire de l'ancienne langue française* (Paris, 1880–1902).

Griffiths, R.A., *The Reign of King Henry VI*, 2nd edn (Stroud, 1998), pp. 315–16.

Hare, Susan M., 'The History of the Goldsmiths' Company from their Records', *Proceedings of the Society of Silver Collectors*, II (Pring, 1982), pp. 174–79.

Hare, S.M., 'The Records of the Goldsmiths' Company', *Archives*, 16 (1984), 376–84.

Heal, Ambrose, *The London Goldsmiths 1200–1800* (London, 1935).

Hector, L.C. and B.F. Harvey, *The Westminster Chronicle 1381–1394*, Oxford Medieval Texts (Oxford, 1982).

Herbert, W., *The History of the Twelve Great Livery Companies of London*, 2 vols (London, 1834–36).

Hook, D., Susan La Niece and John Cherry, 'A Fifteenth-Century Mercury-Silvered Buckle from Hillington, Norfolk', *The Antiquaries Journal* 68 (1988), 301–05.

Hope, Valerie, *My Lord Mayor: Eight Hundred Years of London's Mayoralty* (London, 1989).

Hovland, S.R., 'Apprenticeship in the Records of the Goldsmiths' Company of London, 1444–1500', *Medieval Prosopography* 22 (2001) 89–114.

Jackson, C.J., *An Illustrated History of English Plate*, 2 vols (London, 1911).

Jefferson, Lisa, 'The Language and Vocabulary of the Fourteenth- and early

Fifteenth-Century Records of the Goldsmiths' Company', *Multilingualism in Later Medieval Britain* (Proceedings of the conference held at the University of Wales, Aberystwyth, 10–13 September 1997), ed. D.A. Trotter (Cambridge, 2000), pp. 175–211.

Jefferson, L. and W. Rothwell, 'Society and Lexis: A Study of the Anglo-French Vocabulary in the Fifteenth-Century Accounts of the Merchant Taylors' Company', *Zeitschrift für französische Sprache und Literatur* 107 (1997), 273–301.

Jenkins, Peter, *Unravelling the Mystery: The Story of the Goldsmiths' Company in the Twentieth Century*, 2 vols (London, 2000).

John of Gaunt's Register (1371–75), ed. S. Armitage-Smith, Camden Society, 3rd series, 20 and 21 (1911); *John of Gaunt's Register (1379–83)*, ed. E.C. Lodge and R. Somerville, Camden Society, 3rd series, 56 and 57 (1937).

Johnson, R.P., 'Notes on Some Manuscripts of the *Mappae Clavicula*', *Speculum* 10 (1935), 72–81.

Kingdon, J.A., ed., *Facsimile of the First Volume of MS Archives of the . . . Company of Grocers . . . A.D. 1345–1463* (London, 1883–86).

Lambrechts, P. and J.-P. Sosson, *Les Métiers au Moyen Âge: aspects économiques et sociaux. Actes du colloque internationale de Louvain-la-Neuve 7–9 octobre 1993*, Publications de l'Institut d'Etudes Médiévales: Textes, Etudes, Congrès, vol. 15 (Louvain-la-Neuve, 1994).

Lang, Jennifer, *Pride without Prejudice: The Story of London's Guilds and Livery Companies* (London, 1975).

La Niece, Susan, 'Silver Plating on Copper, Bronze and Brass', *The Antiquaries Journal* 70 (1990), 102–14.

Larousse, *Grand Dictionnaire universel du XIXe siècle* (Slatkine reprint, 1982), VII.936–44: 'Essai des monnaies et des matières d'or et d'argent'.

Latham, R.E., ed., *Revised Medieval Latin Word-List* (Oxford, 1965).

Lightbown, R.W., *Secular Goldsmiths' Work in Medieval France: A History*, Reports of the Research Committee of the Society of Antiquaries of London, 36 (London, 1978).

Lightbown, R.W., *French Silver* (London, 1978).

Lightbown, R.W., *Mediaeval European Jewellery* (London, 1992).

Littré, E., *Dictionnaire de la langue française* (Paris, 1863–72; suppl. 1877; new edn: Paris, 1970–71).

Masters, Betty R., *The Chamberlain of the City of London 1237–1987* (London, 1988).

Matthews, W.R. and W.M. Atkins, *A History of St Paul's Cathedral and the Men Associated with it* (London, 1957).

Melling, J.K., *Discovering London's Guilds and Liveries*, 5th edn. (Princes Risborough, 1995).

Middle English Dictionary, ed. H. Kurath *et al.* (Ann Arbor: University of Michigan Press, 1956–). (*MED*)

Nightingale, P., *A Medieval Mercantile Community: The Grocers' Company and the Politics and Trade of London 1000–1485* (New Haven and London, 1995).

Oman, C., *English Silversmiths' Work, Civil and Domestic* (London, 1965).

Oman, C., *English Domestic Silver* (London, 1934; 7th edn 1968).

Oman, C., *British Rings 800–1914* (London, 1974).

Oman, C., *Victoria and Albert Museum Catalogue of Rings 1930* (Ipswich, 1993).

Osberg, Richard H., 'The Goldsmiths' "Chastell" of 1377', *Theatre Survey* 27 (1986), 1–15.

Oxford English Dictionary, 2nd edn, ed. J.A. Simpson and E.S.C. Weiner (Oxford, 1989). (*OED*)

Pearl, Morris and Valerie, 'A Revolt in 1529 by Yeomen against the Wardens of the Goldsmiths' Company', *The Review of the Worshipful Company of Goldsmiths*, 1979–80 (London: The Goldsmiths' Company, 1980), 23–27.

Phillipps, Sir Thomas, '*Mappae Clavicula*: A Treatise on the Preparation of Pigments during the Middle Ages', *Archaeologia* 32 (1847), 183–244.

Pridcaux, W.S., *Memorials of the Goldsmiths' Company, being gleanings from their records between the years 1335 and 1815*, 2 vols (London, printed for private circulation, 1896).

Purey-Cust, A.P., *The Collar of SS: A History and a Conjecture* (Leeds: Richard Jackson, 1910).

Reddaway, T.F. and L.E.M. Walker, *The Early History of the Goldsmiths' Company, 1327–1509* (London, 1975).

Reddaway, T.F., 'The London Goldsmiths c. 1500', *Transactions of the Royal Historical Society*, 5th series, 12 (1962), 49–62.

Reddaway, T.F., 'The King's Mint and Exchange in London 1343–1543', *EHR* 82 (1967), 10–23.

Rey, Alain, ed., *Dictionnaire historique de la langue française*, 2 vols (Paris, 1992).

Reynolds, C., 'The Shrewsbury Book, British Library, Royal MS 15E.VI', *Medieval Art, Architecture and Archaeology at Rouen*, ed. Jenny Stratford, The British Archaeological Association, Conference Transactions for the year 1986 (London, 1993), 109–116.

Rosser, G., 'Workers' Associations in English Medieval Towns', in Lambrechts and Sosson, pp. 283–305.

Rotuli Parliamentorum, ed. J. Strachey *et al.*, vols i–iii (Record Commission, London, 1767–77).

Simpson, W. Sparrow, ed., *Documents Illustrating the History of St Paul's Cathedral* (London: Camden Society, 1880).

Smith, Cyril Stanley and John G. Hawthorne, *Mappae Clavicula: A Little Key to the World of Medieval Techniques*, Transactions of the American Philosophical Society, n.s. 64, pt. 4 (Philadelphia, 1974).

Statutes of the Realm, ed. T.E. Tomlins *et al.*, 9 vols (London, 1810–22).

Stow, John, *Annales, or a Generall Chronicle of England . . .* (London, 1631).

Stow, John, *A Survey of London Written in the Year 1598*, ed. H. Morley (Sutton paperback edn, 1994).

Stratford, Jenny, *The Bedford Inventories: The Worldly Goods of John, Duke of Bedford, Regent of France (1389–1435)*, Reports of the Research Committee of the Society of Antiquaries of London, no. 49 (London, 1993).

Theophilus, *On Divers Arts*, ed. and trans. C.R. Dodwell (London, 1961); also trans. J.G. Hawthorne and C.S. Smith (Chicago, 1963).

Thomas, A.H. and I.D. Thornley, eds, *The Great Chronicle of London* (London, 1938 and facsimile reprint, 1983).

Thouvenin, A., 'La soudure dans la construction des oeuvres d'orfèvrerie antique et ancienne', *Revue archéologique de l'Est et du Centre-Est* 24 (1973), 11–68.

Tobler-Lommatzsch, *Altfranzösisches Wörterbuch* (Berlin, 1925–). (TL)

Touching Gold and Silver: 500 Years of Hallmarks (Catalogue of an exhibition of 7–30 November 1978).

Unwin, G., *The Guilds and Companies of London*, with a new introduction by W.F. Kahl (London, 1963).

Veale, E.M., *The English Fur Trade in the Later Middle Ages* (Oxford, 1966).

Veale, E.M., 'The "Great Twelve": Mistery and Fraternity in Thirteenth-Century London', *BIHR* 64 (1991), 237–63.

von Wartburg, W. *Französisches Etymologisches Wörterbuch* (Bonn, Leipzig: Klopp, 1928–).

Walsingham, Thomas, *Historia Anglicana*, ed. H.T. Riley, 2 vols, Rolls Series 28.1 (London, 1863–64).

Wilson, Christopher, *The Honour and Glory of London: The Architecture of St Paul's Cathedral 1087–1547* (forthcoming).

Withington, R., 'Queen Margaret's Entry into London, 1445', *Modern Philology* 13 (1915–16), 53–57.

Name Index

All variant spellings of a surname found in the texts are listed here. The choice of headword under which to list a person has been determined by either the most commonly known form (e.g. Whittington, rather than Whetyngdoun, for the Mayor of London of that name); or by the modern version of the placename (e.g. Canterbury, rather than Cauntirbery), except that where doubt subsists as to the place, no change has been made; or by choosing among variants the one most commonly used by members of a family (e.g. Barantyn for all those who may be found with either that spelling or Barantyne, Barentyn, or Barrantyn); or, occasionally only, by use of a modern form of a word denoting a trade or profession (e.g. Goldbeater, rather than Goldbetere). Names in square brackets denote spellings that never in fact occur in the text, and these are always immediately followed by the spelling(s) actually found (e.g. [Newark] Newerk).

It can at times be difficult to determine whether entries refer to two separate people or to the same person. Cross-references in the index below indicate some of these queries. When in doubt, I have usually preferred to make two entries rather than one, and those using this index should check all variant spellings of a name with care against the relevant entries in the texts.

The dates given are the dates at which mention is found of a person; for apprentices in particular, one should note that these are not by any means always the date on which the apprentice was taken on, and not always that on which he was registered, since many are only named at the time they come out of terms, or at other times.

The information given for each person is that to be found in these texts alone, no reference being made, except in a very few rare cases, to other sources.

Abbreviations: app. = apprentice; ent. = entry to the freedom of the Goldsmiths' Mistery; f. = fined; iss. = issue from terms of apprenticeship; test. = testified (witness); W. = warden.

Subject Index